A

N(

The Complete Encyclopedia

of

Television Programs

1947-1979

SECOND EDITION, REVISED

Volume 2

M - Z

Vincent Terrace

South Brunswick and New York:

A. S. Barnes and Company

London: Thomas Yoseloff Ltd

The Complete Encyclopedia
of
Television Programs

m

McCLOUD

See title: "Four-In-One," *McCloud* segment.

McCOY

See title: "NBC Sunday Mystery Movie," *McCoy* segment.

MAC DAVIS

Listed: The television programs of singer-composer Mac Davis.

The Mac Davis Show—Musical Variety—60 minutes—NBC—July 11, 1974 - August 29, 1974.

Host: Mac Davis.

Orchestra: George Wyle.

Additional Orchestration: Sid Feller.

The Mac Davis Show—Musical Variety—60 minutes—NBC—December 19, 1974 - May 22, 1975.

Host: Mac Davis.

Regulars: Kay Dingle, Bo Koprel, The Tony Modente Dancers.

Orchestra: Mike Post.

Special Musical Material: Billy Barnes, Earl Brown.

The Mac Davis Show—Musical Variety—60 minutes—NBC—March 18, 1976 - June 17, 1976.

Host: Mac Davis.

Regulars: Shields and Yarnell, The Strutts, Ron Silver.

Orchestra: Tom Bahler, Mike Post.

Choreographer: Jim Bates.

Executive Producer: Gary Smith, Dwight Hemion.

Producer: Mike Post, Steve Binder, Nancy Henson.

Director: Steve Binder, Jim Cox.

McDUFF, THE TALKING DOG

Comedy. Background: The town of Peach Blossom. The comic misadventures of Calvin Campbell, a young, trouble-prone veterinarian. His escapades are helped and hindered by McDuff, the ghost of a sheep dog who appears and speaks only to him.

CAST

Dr. Calvin Campbell	Walter Willson
Amos Ferguson, his neighbor	Gordon Jump
Squeaky, Amos's nephew	Johnnie Collins III
Mrs. Osgood, Calvin's housekeeper	Monty Margetts
Kimmy Campbell, Calvin's sister	Michelle Stacy
McDuff's Voice	Jack Lester

Music: Richard LaSalle.

Executive Producer: William P. D'Angelo, Ray Allen, Harvey Bullock.

Producer: Victor Paul.

Director: Gordon Wiles, James Sheldon, William P. D'Angelo.

McDUFF, THE TALKING DOG—30 minutes—NBC—September 11, 1976 - November 20, 1976.

McHALE'S NAVY

Comedy. Distinguished by two formats.

Format One: September 11, 1962 - September 7, 1965.

Background: The South Pacific; the island of Taratupa during World War II. The bickering relationship between Lieutenant Quinton McHale, the commander of Squadron 19 and P.T. Boat 73; and Captain Wallace B. Binghamton, the commanding officer who feels that his life is plagued by McHale and his crew of pirates who have turned the island into "the Las Vegas of the Pacific."

Determined to enjoy the serenity the war provides from his nagging wife, Binghamton endlessly—but fruitlessly—schemes to expose McHale's illegal gambling activities, which he hopes will lead to a court-martial and transfer.

Format Two: September 14, 1965 - August 30, 1966.

Background: Voltafiore, a small town in Southern Italy, 1944, where McHale, his Squadron 19, and Captain Binghamton are transferred to assist in the European theatre of war. Stories follow the previous format: Binghamton's determined efforts to rid his life of McHale.

CAST

Lt. Cdr. Quinton McHale	Ernest Borgnine
Captain Wallace B. Binghamton ("Old Lead Bottom")	Joe Flynn

McHale's Crew (8):

Ensign Charles Parker	Tim Conway
Seaman Lester Gruber	Carl Ballantine
Seaman Harrison "Tinker" Bell	Billy Sands
Seaman Willy Moss	John Wright
Seaman Happy Haines	Gavin MacLeod
Seaman Virgil Farrell	Edson Stroll
Quarter Master Christopher	Gary Vinson
Fuji Kobiaji, an unreported prisoner of war captured by McHale; now their chief cook and bottle washer	Yoshio Yoda
Lt. Elroy Carpenter, Binghamton's aide	Bob Hastings
Molly Turner, the chief nurse (format 1)	Jane Dulo
Admiral Bruce Rogers (format 1)	Roy Roberts
Admiral Benson (format 1)	Bill Quinn
Chief Tali Urulu, the native chief, a witch doctor and con-artist (format 1)	Jacques Aubuchon
Colonel Harrington (format 2)	Henry Beckman
General Bronson (format 2)	Simon Scott
Mario Lugatto, the mayor of Voltafiore (format 2)	Jay Novello
Dino, the mayor's aide (format 2)	Dick Wilson
Mama Rosa Giovanni, the restaurant owner (format 2)	Peggy Mondo
Lt. Gloria Winters, Christopher's girlfriend, then wife (format 2)	Cindy Robbins

Music: Axel Stordahl.

Producer: Edward J. Montagne.

Note: Seaman Virgil Farrell is also known as Virgil Edwards; and Col. Harrington is also known as Col. Harrigan.

McHALE'S NAVY—30 minutes—ABC—September 11, 1962 - August

30, 1966. 138 episodes. Syndicated.

MACK AND MYER FOR HIRE

Comedy. The misadventures of Mack and Myer, bumbling craftsmen struggling to succeed in the business world.

CAST

Mack	Mickey Deems
Myer	Joey Faye

MACK AND MYER FOR HIRE—15 minutes—Syndicated 1963. 200 episodes.

McKEEVER AND THE COLONEL

Comedy. Background: The Westfield Military Academy for boys. Stories depict the antics of Gary McKeever, a mischievous cadet; and the attempts of Harvey Blackwell, the school's commander, to discipline the boy.

CAST

Colonel Harvey Blackwell	Allyn Joslyn
Cadet Gary McKeever	Scott Lane
Sergeant Barnes, the Colonel's aide	Jackie Coogan
Miss Warner, the school dietician	Elizabeth Fraser
Tubby, a cadet	Keith Taylor
Monk, a cadet	Johnny Eimen

McKEEVER AND THE COLONEL—30 minutes—ABC—September 23, 1962—September 1963. 26 episodes. Syndicated.

MacKENZIE'S RAIDERS

Western. Background: Texas, 1870s. Organizing a small group of raiders, Colonel Ranald S. MacKenzie, an undercover agent with the U.S. Fourth Cavalry, attempts to end the reign of terror begun by marauding Mexican renegades.

CAST

Col. Ranald S. MacKenzie	Richard Carlson

The Raiders: Louis Jean Heydt, Morris Ankrum, Brett King, Jim Bridges, Charles Boax, Kenneth Alton.

MacKENZIE'S RAIDERS—30 minutes—Syndicated 1958. 39 episodes.

THE McLEAN STEVENSON SHOW

Comedy. Background: Evanston, Illinois. The misadventures of Mac Ferguson, a hardware store owner, as he struggles to cope with life, both at work and at home.

CAST

Mac Ferguson	McLean Stevenson
Peggy Ferguson, his wife	Barbara Stuart
Janet, their divorced daughter	Ayn Ruymen
Chris Ferguson, their son	Steve Nevil
Muriel, Peggy's mother	Madge West
David, Janet's son	David Hollander
Jason, Janet's son	Jason Whitney

Music: Paul Williams.

Executive Producer: Monty Hall.

Producer: Arnold Margolin, Don Van Atta.

Director: Alan Myerson, Bill Hobin.

THE McLEAN STEVENSON SHOW —30 minutes—NBC—December 1, 1976 - March 9, 1977.

McMILLAN

See title: "NBC Sunday Mystery Movie," *McMillan* segment.

McMILLAN AND WIFE

See title: "NBC Mystery Movie," *McMillan and Wife* segment.

McNAUGHTON'S DAUGHTER

Crime Drama. Background: Los Angeles, California. The cases and courtroom prosecutions of Laurie McNaughton, trial lawyer and Deputy District Attorney.

CAST
Laurie McNaughton	Susan Clark
Lou Farragut, her investigator	James Callahan
Charles Quintero, the D.A.	Ricardo Montalban

Music: George Romanis.

Music Supervision: Hal Mooney.

Executive Producer: David Victor.

Producer: Harold Gast.

Director: Daniel Haller, Gene Nelson, Jack Arnold.

McNAUGHTON'S DAUGHTER—60 minutes—NBC—March 24, 1976 - April 7, 1976. 3 episodes.

MADE IN AMERICA

Game. Involved: A celebrity panel of three, and self-made millionaire guests. Through a series of question-and-answer probe rounds with guests, panelists have to establish their identities.

Host: Bob Maxwell.

Panelists: Jan Sterling, Don Murray, Walter Slezak.

MADE IN AMERICA—30 minutes—CBS—April 5, 1964 - September 6, 1965.

MADIGAN

See title: "NBC Wednesday Mystery Movie," *Madigan* segment.

MAGGIE AND THE BEAUTIFUL MACHINE

Health-Exercise. Exercises and health tips designed to improve the body machine.

Hostess: Maggie Lettvin.

Assistants: Five noncelebrity guests.

Music: Recorded.

MAGGIE AND THE BEAUTIFUL MACHINE—30 minutes—PBS—1972-1974.

THE MAGGIE McNELLIS SHOW

Women. Celebrity interviews, human interest accounts, nightclub reviews, fashion previews, and gossip.

Hostess: Maggi McNellis.

THE MAGGI McNELLIS SHOW—30 minutes—ABC—July 3, 1952 - September 1952.

THE MAGIC CLOWN

Children. Games, songs, and magic performed against a circus background.

Host: Zovella, the Magic Clown (conducting the entire show by himself).

THE MAGIC CLOWN—15 minutes NBC—1949-1954.

THE MAGIC COTTAGE

Children. Stories, songs, fairy tales, games, and art instruction set against the background of a school classroom.

Hostess: Pat Meikle.

Substitute Host: Hal Cooper.

Assistant: Robert Wilkinson.

THE MAGIC COTTAGE—30 minutes —DuMont—1949-1953.

THE MAGIC GARDEN

Children. Background: The Magic Garden, a small, forestlike area where the make believe becomes real. With hostesses Carole and Paula, and through the antics of puppets Sherlock Squirrel and Flap the bird, stories, songs and related entertainment, geared for children, is charmingly and amusingly presented.

CAST

Carole	Carole Demas
Paula	Paula Janis
Sherlock	Cary Antebi
Flap	Cary Antebi

Music: Alton Alexander, George Kayatta, Alexander Demas.

Producer-Director: Irv Jarvis, Joseph L. Hall.

THE MAGIC GARDEN—30 minutes —Syndicated 1974. Originally produced as a local program by WPIX-TV in New York.

THE MAGICIAN

Adventure. Background: Hollywood, California. The story of Anthony Blake, the world's greatest magician. Incorporating the wizardry of his craft, he attempts to assist people in distress—people who are seeking escape, but who are unable to turn to police for help.

CAST

Anthony Blake (referred to as Anthony Dorian in the pilot film)	Bill Bixby
Max Pomeroy, a newspaper columnist, his contact	Keene Curtis
Jerry Anderson, the pilot of Blake's Boeing 737, the *Spirit*	Jim Watkins
Dennis Pomeroy, Max's son	Tod Crespi
Dominick, the owner of the Magic Castle Club	Joseph Sirola

Announcer: Bill Baldwin.

Music: Pat Williams.

THE MAGICIAN—60 minutes—NBC —October 2, 1973 - May 20, 1974. 24 episodes.

THE MAGIC LADY

Children. Songs, fairy tales, guests, and magic performances.

CAST

The Magic Queen	Geraldine Larsen

Boko, her pixie
helper   Jerry Maren

THE MAGIC LADY–30 minutes–
Syndicated 1951. 13 episodes.

THE MAGIC LAND OF ALLAKAZAM

Children. Background: The magical kingdom of Allakazam. Mythical adventures detailing illusionist Mark Wilson's battle against evil.

CAST
Mark Wilson   Himself
Nani Darnell, his
  wife   Herself
Mike Wilson, their
  son   Himself
Rebo the Clown   Bev Bergerson
The King of Allakazam   Bob Towner
Perriwinkle   Chuck Barnes

Puppets: Basil the Bunny; Doris the Dove; Bernard the Rabbit.

Producer: Jack Wipper, Mark Wilson, Dan Whitman.

THE MAGIC LAND OF ALLAKA-ZAM–30 minutes. CBS–October 1, 1960 - September 1962; ABC–September 29, 1962 - September 28, 1963; ABC–April 25, 1964 - September 1964. 39 episodes.

MAGIC MIDWAY

Circus Variety Acts.
Ringmaster: Claude Kirchener.
Regulars: Bonnie Lee, a baton twirling champion; Bill "Boom Boom"

Bailey; Phil "Coo Coo" Kiley; Douglas "Mr. Pocus" Anderson.
Music: The Jazz Band of Lou Stern and the Circus Seven.

MAGIC MIDWAY–30 minutes–NBC –September 22, 1962 - March 16, 1963. 26 episodes.

MAGIC MONGO

See title: "The Krofft Supershow II," *Magic Mongo* segment.

THE MAGIC OF MARK WILSON

Variety. A half-hour series that spotlights the talents of magician Mark Wilson.
Host: Mark Wilson.
Regulars: Nani Darnell, Greg Wilson.
Music: Frank Ortega.
Producer-Director: Herb Waterson.

THE MAGIC OF MARK WILSON–30 minutes–Syndicated 1977.

THE MAGIC RANCH

Children. Performances by guest magicians.
Host: Don Alan.
Producer: George Anderson.

THE MAGIC RANCH–30 minutes– ABC–September 30, 1961 - December 17, 1961. Syndicated.

THE MAGIC VAULT

Anthology. Dramatizations depicting

the plight of people suddenly caught in unusual happenings.

THE MAGIC VAULT—30 minutes—Syndicated 1952. 104 episodes.

THE MAGILLA GORILLA SHOW

Animated Cartoon. Background: Los Angeles, California. The misadventures of Magilla, a mischievous, fun-loving gorilla, the permanent resident at Mr. Peebles Pet Shop. A Hanna-Barbera production.

Additional characters: Mr. Peebles, the pet shop owner; and Ogee, the little girl who longs to have Magilla as her own pet.

Additional segment: "Ricochet Rabbit." Plagued by the antics of his three fumbling deputies, Punkin' Puss, Mush Mouse, and Droop-a-Long, Sheriff Ricochet Rabbit attempts to maintain law and order.

Characters' Voices

Magilla Gorilla	Allan Melvin
Mr. Peebles	Howard Morris
Ogee	Jean VanderPyl
Punkin' Puss	Allan Melvin
Mush Mouse	Howard Morris
Ricochet Rabbit	Don Messick
Droop-a-Long	Mel Blanc

Music Supervision: Hoyt Curtin.

THE MAGILLA GORILLA SHOW—30 minutes—Syndicated 1964. 58 episodes.

MAGNAVOX THEATRE

Anthology. Dramatic presentations.
Producer: Garth Montgomery.
Director: Carl Beier.

Sponsor: Magnavox.

MAGNAVOX THEATRE—60 minutes—CBS 1950.

THE MAGNIFICENT MARBLE MACHINE

Game. Two teams, each composed of one celebrity and one noncelebrity contestant, compete. A question is read and, via electronics, the clue word appears on a board with a line of dashes to indicate the amount of letters contained in the answer. Contestants are first to play and the one who first sounds a buzzer signal receives a chance to answer. If correct, one point is scored; if not, the opponent receives a chance to answer. The celebrities next receive a chance at play. The team that is first to score four points is the winner and receives the opportunity to play the Magnificent Marble Machine, a huge, electronic pinball machine. The team receives two minutes at play and each time a bumper is hit five hundred points is scored and a prize is won. If the player reaches a goal of 15,000 points he receives the opportunity to play the gold money ball wherein, within one minute of play, each bumper that is hit earns $500. Players compete until defeated.

Host: Art James.

Announcer: Johnny Gilbert.

Music: Mort Garson; Score Productions.

Executive Producer: Merrill Heatter, Bob Quigley.

Producer: Robert Noah.

THE MAGNIFICENT MARBLE MACHINE—30 minutes—NBC—July 7, 1975 - June 11, 1976.

THE MAGNIFICENT SIX AND A HALF

Comedy. Background: England. The misadventures of seven children, six boys (the Magnificent Six) and a young girl (the Half). Produced in England.

CAST

Steve	Len Jones
Whizz	Michael Auderson
Dumbo	Ian Ellis
Toby	Brinsley Forde
Stodger	Lionel Hawkes
Pee Wee	Kim Tallmadge
Liz	Suzanne Togni

THE MAGNIFICENT SIX AND A HALF—18 minutes (approx.)—Syndicated 1970. 12 episodes.

THE MAIL STORY

See title: "Handle with Care."

MAIN CHANCE

Drama. Background: London, England. The cases and courtroom defenses of David Main, Barrister. Produced in England.

Starring: John Stride as David Main.

MAIN CHANCE—60 minutes—Syndicated 1970. 13 episodes.

MAJOR ADAMS, TRAILMASTER

See title: "Wagon Train."

MAJOR DELL CONWAY OF THE FLYING TIGERS

Adventure. Background: Los Angeles, California. The exploits of Major Dell Conway, the chief pilot of the Flying Tigers Airline. Stories depict his investigations into cases on behalf of G-2, American Military Intelligence.

Starring: Ed Peck as Major Dell Conway.

Producer: General Genovese.

Sponsor: Johnson Candy.

MAJOR DELL CONWAY OF THE FLYING TIGERS—30 minutes—DuMont 1951.

MAKE A FACE

Game. Three competing players. Each player sits before three revolving wheels that contain pictures of celebrities cut into puzzle parts. Within specified time limits, players have to assemble and identify the personalities. Each correct identification awards points. Winners, the highest scorers, receive merchandise prizes.

Host: Bob Clayton.

Assistant: Rita Mueller.

Producer: Art Baer, Herbert Gottlieb.

Director: Lloyd Gross.

MAKE A FACE—30 minutes—ABC—October 2, 1961 - March 30, 1962. Also: ABC—September 29, 1962 - December 22, 1962.

MAKE A WISH

Educational. Children six to eleven years of age. Through animation, films, songs, and sketches, the differences between fantasy and the real world are explained.

Host: Tom Chapin.

Orchestra: Bernie Green.

MAKE A WISH—30 minutes—ABC—
Premiered: September 12, 1971.

MAKE THE CONNECTION

Game. Involved: Two specially
selected contestants and a celebrity
panel of four. Through question-and-
answer rounds with the contestants,
celebrities have to determine when,
where, why, and how their paths have
crossed with the laymen players.
Prizes are awarded to the contestants
if the panel fails to uncover the
relationship.

Host: Jim McKay.

Panelists: Gloria DeHaven, Betty
   White, Eddie Bracken, Gene
   Klavan.

MAKE THE CONNECTION—30 minutes—NBC—July 7, 1955 - September
29, 1955.

MAKE ME LAUGH

Game. Contestants, one at a time,
stand opposite three guest comics.
The comics then provoke and attempt
to make the contestants laugh.
Object: For the contestant to remain
straight-faced. Rounds are divided
into one minute segments with the
contestant receiving one dollar per
second until he laughs.

Host: Robert Q. Lewis.

Assistant: Renny Peterson.

MAKE ME LAUGH—30 minutes—
ABC—March 20, 1958 - June 12,
1958.

MAKE MINE MUSIC

Musical Variety.

Hostess: Carole Coleman.

Regulars: Larry Douglas, Bill Skipper.

Music: The Tony Mottola Trio.

MAKE MINE MUSIC—30 minutes—
CBS 1948.

MAKE ROOM FOR DADDY

Comedy. Distinguished by two formats.

Format One: 1953-1957.
   Background: 505 East 50th Street,
New York, Apartment 542, the residence of the Williams family: Danny,
a nightclub entertainer at the Copa
Club; his wife, Margaret; and their
children, Terry and Rusty. Stories
depict the home and working life of
Danny Williams, a man whose career
often leaves him with little time to
spend with his beloved family.

CAST

Danny Williams	Danny Thomas
Margaret Williams	Jean Hagen
Teresa Williams (Terry)	Sherry Jackson
Russell Williams (Rusty)	Rusty Hamer
Louise, their maid	Amanda Randolph
Jesse Leeds, Danny's agent	Jesse White
Elizabeth Margaret O'Neal (Liz), Danny's press agent	Mary Wickes
Ben Lessy, Danny's piano player	Himself
Frank Jenks, Danny's taylor	Himself
Phil Arnold, Danny's agent (later epi-	

sodes)   Horace McMahon
Charlie Helper, the
     owner of the Copa
     Club   Sid Melton

Williams family dog, a terrier: Laddie.

Music: Herbert Spencer, Earle Hagen.

Format Two: 1957-1964.
     Background: Same. Shortly after
Margaret's death (the cause is not
stated), Rusty contracts the measles.
Hiring Kathleen O'Hara, a beautiful
registered nurse, widow, and mother
of a young daughter,* to care for
Rusty, Danny and she fall in love and
marry one year following. Stories relate the trials and tribulations of the
Williams family.

CAST
Danny Williams   Danny Thomas
Kathy Williams (also
     referred to by the
     maiden name, Kathleen
     Daly)   Marjorie Lord
Terry Williams   Sherry Jackson
                              Penny Parker
Rusty Williams   Rusty Hamer
Patty Williams
     (O'Hara)   Lelani Sorenson
Linda Williams   Angela Cartwright
Louise, their
     maid   Amanda Randolph
Elizabeth Margaret
     O'Neal   Mary Wickes
Charlie Helper   Sid Melton
Bunny Helper, Charlie's
     wife   Pat Carroll
Phil Arnold, Danny's
     agent   Sheldon Leonard
Uncle Tonoose, the
     head of the Williams
     family   Hans Conried

*When first introduced in 1957, her name was
Patty. When the series switched to another network, the original actress was replaced and the
character name changed to Linda.

Pat Hannegan, a night
     club comedian, Terry's
     boyfriend; later her hus-
     band (1960)   Pat Harrington, Jr.
Harry Ruby, Danny's song
     writer   Himself
Gina Minelli, an
     Italian exchange student
     residing with the
     Williamses   Annette Funicello
Piccola Pupa, a
     young Italian singer
     discovered by
     Danny   Herself
Buck, Gina's boy-
     friend   Richard Tyler
José Jiménez, the
     elevator operator   Bill Dana
Alfie, a Copa Club
     waiter   Bernard Fox
Mr. Heckendorn, the
     building superin-
     tendant   Gale Gordon
Mr. Svenson, the building
     janitor   John Qualen
Mr. Daly, Kathy's
     father   William Demarest

Music: Herbert Spencer, Earle Hagen.

MAKE ROOM FOR DADDY—30
minutes—ABC—September 29, 1953 -
July 17, 1957. CBS (as "The Danny
Thomas Show")—30 minutes—
October 7, 1957 - September 14,
1964. 336 episodes. Spin-off series:
"Make Room for Granddaddy," See
title.

MAKE ROOM FOR GRANDDADDY

Comedy. To bridge the six-year gap
between "Make Room for Daddy"
and "Make Room for Granddaddy,"
two specials were aired:

"Make More Room for Daddy," NBC,

1967. Completing his college education, Rusty enlists in the army, where he meets, falls in love with, and marries Susan MacAdams, a colonel's daughter.

And, "Make Room for Granddaddy," CBS, 9/14/69. Discharged from the service, Rusty enrolls in medical school. Expecting their first child, he and Susan set up housekeeping away from the family nest.

The following background information provides the basis for the finished product: "Make Room for Granddaddy," ABC, 9/23/70.

Danny and Kathy are in Europe on a show-business engagement; Linda is residing at a boarding school in Connecticut to prevent any interference to her education; Rusty and Susan are struggling newlyweds; and Terry, the mother of a six-year-old son, Michael, is preparing to join her husband, Bill Johnson, a serviceman who is stationed in Japan. Michael is to stay with Bill's parents until he and Terry settle and find a house.

For reasons which are not explained, Terry is now married to Bill Johnson, not Pat Hannegan, as in the original series.

The Series:

Background: 505 East 50th Street, Manhattan, Apartment 781. Returning home after their European engagement, and welcomed by the family, Danny and Kathy discover Terry's plans. Wanting Michael to remain with them, Danny persuades Terry to let him stay with them for several days and let him decide where he'll be the happiest. Danny and Kathy cater to his every whim, and Michael chooses to remain with them. Stories relate the trials and tribulations of the individual members of the Williams family.

CAST

Danny Williams	Danny Thomas
Kathy Williams	Marjorie Lord
Linda Williams	Angela Cartwright
Rusty Williams	Rusty Hamer
Charlie Helper	Sid Melton
Michael Johnson	Michael Hughes
Rosey Robbins, Danny's accompanist	Rosey Grier
Uncle Tonoose	Hans Conried
Susan Williams	Jana Taylor
Terry Johnson	Penny Parker
Henry, the elevator operator	Stanley Myron Handleman

Music: Earle Hagen.

MAKE ROOM FOR GRANDDADDY—30 minutes—ABC—September 23, 1970 - September 2, 1971. 24 episodes.

MAKE YOUR OWN KIND OF MUSIC

Variety. Musical numbers interspersed with comedy sketches.

Hosts: Karen and Richard Carpenter (brother and sister).

Regulars: Al Hirt, Mark Lindsay, The New Doodletown Pipers, Patchett and Tarses (comics).

Orchestra: Allyn Ferguson, Jack Elliott.

MAKE YOUR OWN KIND OF MUSIC—60 minutes—NBC—July 20, 1971 - September 7, 1971. 8 tapes.

MALIBU RUN

Adventure. A spin-off from "The Aquanauts." Background: Malibu Beach in Southern California. The cases of diving instructors and part-time private investigators Larry Lahr and Mike Madison.

CAST

Larry Lahr	Jeremy Slate
Mike Madison	Ron Ely
Chaplan	Charles Thompson

Music: Andre Previn.

MALIBU RUN—60 minutes—CBS—May 21, 1961 - September 27, 1961.

MALIBU U.

Musical Variety. Background: Malibu U., a mythical college based on the beach of Southern California. Performances by the sixties' top music personalities.

Host (the Dean): Ricky Nelson.

President of the Student Body: Robbie Porter.

Featured: The Bob Banas Dancers, The Malibuties (bikini clad girls).

Music: Recorded and/or provided by guests.

MALIBU U.—30 minutes—ABC—July 2, 1967 - September 1, 1967.

MAMA

See title: "I Remember Mama."

MAMA ROSA

A serial drama that depicts the trials and tribulations of an Italian-American family. Broadcast on ABC from April 23, 1950 to June 15, 1950. The series, which was broadcast live in California and seen on kinescope in other areas of the country, was the

first series to originate on the West Coast, where it began as a local show on KFI-TV in 1948.

THE MAN AGAINST CRIME

Crime Drama. Background: New York City. The investigations of Mike Barnett, an unarmed private detective.

CAST

Mike Barnett	Ralph Bellamy
	Frank Lovejoy
Pat Barnett, his brother	Robert Preston

Ralph Bellamy's stand-in: Art Fleming.

Producer: Edward J. Montagne, Paul Nickell.

Director: Paul Nickell.

Sponsor: Camel Cigarettes.

THE MAN AGAINST CRIME—30 minutes—CBS—October 4, 1949 - October 2, 1953. 82 episodes. Syndicated title: "Follow That Man."

THE MAN AND THE CHALLENGE

Adventure. The story of Glenn Barton, a United States government research scientist assigned to test the limits of human endurance.

Starring: George Nader as Glenn Barton.

THE MAN AND THE CHALLENGE—30 minutes—NBC—September 12, 1959 - September 3, 1960. Syndicated. 36 episodes.

THE MAN AND THE CITY

Drama. Background: A turbulent

Southwestern metropolis, the unidentified fictional equivalent of Albuquerque, New Mexico. The story of Thomas Jefferson Alcala, its mayor, a man who strays from the offices of city hall, mixes with the people, and struggles to solve their problems.

CAST

Thomas Alcala	Anthony Quinn
Andy Hays, his assistant	Mike Farrell
Marian Crane, his secretary	Mala Powers
Josefina, his housekeeper	Carmen Zapata

THE MAN AND THE CITY—60 minutes—ABC—September 15, 1971 - January 5, 1972. 13 episodes.

MAN BEHIND THE BADGE

Anthology. Crime dramatizations based on official law-enforcement records.

Host-Narrator: Charles Bickford.

Producer: Jerry Robertson, Bernard Prockter.

Sponsor: Bristol-Myers.

MAN BEHIND THE BADGE—30 minutes—Syndicated 1954.

A MAN CALLED SHENANDOAH

Western. Era: The 1860s. A man, for unknown reasons, is shot and left to die on the Prairie. He is later found by two bounty hunters who bring him back to town where they hope to collect a reward in the event that he's wanted. Kate, a saloon girl, cares for him and nurses him back to health.

A Man Called Shenandoah. Robert Horton and guest star Beverly Garland.

Regaining consciousness, he finds himself a man without a memory—unaware of whom or what he was. Through Kate's assistance, he escapes his captors' bounds. The series follows the trail of an amnesiac—A Man Called Shenandoah—seeking an identity and a home.

CAST

Shenandoah	Robert Horton
Kate (first episode)	Beverly Garland

Music: George Stroll, Robert Van Eps.

A MAN CALLED SHENANDOAH— 30 minutes—ABC—September 13, 1965 - September 5, 1966. 34 episodes.

THE MAN CALLED X

Spy Drama. The investigations of Ken

Thurston; an American intelligence agent who operates under the code name X.

Starring: Barry Sullivan as Ken Thurston.

THE MAN CALLED X—30 minutes—Syndicated 1956. 39 episodes.

THE MANCINI GENERATION

Musical Variety.

Host: Henry Mancini.

Music: The forty-piece Mancini Orchestra.

Additional Orchestrations: Alan Copeland.

Featured segment: "The Film Spot." Original celluloid sequences for Mancini compositions.

THE MANCINI GENERATION—30 minutes—Syndicated 1972.

THE M AND M CANDY CARNIVAL

Variety. Background: A carnival. Performances by undiscovered professional talent. Winners, determined by a judge, receive a twenty-five-dollar savings bond and a week's pro-booking at the Hamid Steel Pier in Atlantic City, New Jersey.

Ringmaster: Barry Cossell.

Judge: George Hammond.

Clowns: Don Lenox, Bill Bailey.

Orchestra: Gene Crane.

THE M AND M CANDY CARNIVAL —30 minutes—CBS 1952.

MANDRAKE THE MAGICIAN

Adventure. Early history: During the twelfth century, wizards carried on the secrets of ancient Egypt and the magic of ancient China. Sweeping the western world, the hordes of Genghis Khan destroyed the wizards and their lore. The few who managed to escape established the College of Magic in a Tibetan valley wherein the lore was preserved. Once a decade, one youth is selected from thousands of applicants and taught the ancient secrets.

The twentieth century. Brought to the college by his father, a former graduate who has only a few months to live, Mandrake is taught the ancient secrets by Theron, the Master of Magic.

Ten years later, Mandrake becomes greater than his masters, and, upon his release from the college, he teams with his servant, Lothar. Stories depict their crusade against evil. Based on the stories by Lee Falk and Phil Davis.

CAST
Mandrake the Magician   Coe Norton
Lothar   Woody Strode

MANDRAKE THE MAGICIAN—30 minutes—Syndicated 1954. Withdrawn.

THE MAN FROM ATLANTIS

Science Fiction Adventure. Background: California. A storm, deep in the Pacific Ocean, unearths the sole survivor of the fabled lost kingdom of Atlantis and brings it to shore. As it nears death from a malody that science cannot cure, Elizabeth Merrill, a naval doctor with the foundation for oceanic research, returns it to the sea and saves its life. Though the government permits the Atlantian, named Mark Harris by Elizabeth, to return to his former existence, Mark decides to remain with the foundation—to help us further our knowledge of the sea—and to gain his own knowledge about us. Stories detail Mark's work on behalf of the foundation.

CAST

Mark Harris	Patrick Duffy
Dr. Elizabeth Merrill	Belinda Montgomery
Dr. Miller Simon, Elizabeth's associate	Kenneth Tigar
Ginny Mendoza, the secretary-receptionist at the foundation	Annette Cardona
C.W. Crawford, the head of the foundation	Alan Fudge

Executive Producer: Herbert F. Solow.

Producer: Robert Lewin.

Director: Marc Daniels, Reza S. Badiyi, Lee H. Katzin, Charles S. Dubin.

Music: Fred Karlin.

THE MAN FROM ATLANTIS—60 minutes—NBC—Premiered: September 1977. Previously seen as a series of specials on 3/4/77, 4/22/77; and 5/17/77.

THE MAN FROM BLACKHAWK

Western. Era: the 1870s. The cases of Sam Logan, a special investigator for the Blackhawk Insurance Company.

Starring: Robert Rockwell as Sam Logan.

THE MAN FROM BLACKHAWK—30 minutes—ABC—October 9, 1959 - September 24, 1960. 37 episodes. Syndicated.

THE MAN FROM INTERPOL

Crime Drama. The investigations of Tony Smith, a New Scotland Yard inspector assigned to active duty with the International Police Force (Interpol).

CAST

Tony Smith	Richard Wyler
The Superintendant	John Longden

Music: Tony Crombie.

THE MAN FROM INTERPOL—30 minutes—NBC—January 23, 1960-October 22, 1960. 39 episodes.

THE MAN FROM U.N.C.L.E.

Adventure. Background: New York City. A dry cleaning establishment, Del Florias Taylor Shop, is the secret headquarters of U.N.C.L.E., the United Network Command for Law

The Man From U.N.C.L.E. Left to right: Robert Vaughn, David McCallum, Leo G. Carroll.

Enforcement, an international organization responsible for the welfare of peoples and nations against the evils of THRUSH, a secret international organization bent on world domain.

Stories relate the investigations of Napoleon Solo and his partner, Illya Kuryakin, U.N.C.L.E. agents battling the forces of global crime and corruption as influenced by THRUSH.

CAST

Napoleon Solo	Robert Vaughn
Illya Kuryakin	David McCallum
Alexander Waverly, the head of	
U.N.C.L.E.	Leo G. Carroll
Del Floria, the owner	
of the taylor	
shop	Mario Siletti
Heather, an U.N.C.L.E.	
agent	May Heatherly
U.N.C.L.E. Girls	Julie Ann Johnson
	Sharon Hillyer

Music: Jerry Goldsmith; Lalo Schifrin; Leith Stevens.

Additional Music: Gerald Fried, Morton Stevens.

Executive Producer: Norman Felton.

Producer: Sam Rolfe, Anthony Spinner, Boris Ingster.

Director: Daniel Hallenback, Boris Sagal, John Newland, Don Medford.

Creator: Norman Felton, Sam Rolfe.

THE MAN FROM U.N.C.L.E.—60 minutes—NBC—September 22, 1964 - January 15, 1968. 104 episodes. Syndicated. Spin-off series: "The Girl from U.N.C.L.E." (see title).

MANHATTAN HONEYMOON

Interview-Quiz. Three engaged or married couples are first interviewed, then, after relating experiences, they compete in a series of general-knowledge question-and-answer rounds. Each correct answer scores one point. Winners, the highest scorers, receive an all-expense-paid honeymoon in New York.

Hostess: Neva Patterson.

MANHATTAN HONEYMOON—30 minutes—ABC—February 22, 1954 - April 21, 1954.

MANHATTAN SHOWCASE

Variety. Performances by undiscovered professional talent.

Host: Johnny Downs.

Assistant: Helen Gallagher.

Music: The Tony Mottola Trio.

MANHATTAN SHOWCASE—15 minutes—CBS 1949.

THE MANHATTAN TRANSFER

Variety. A nostalgic series that recalls the music, song, and dance of the 1930s and 40s.

Hosts: The Manhattan Transfer, a flashy vocal quartet comprised of Laurel Masse, Janis Seigel, Alan Paul, and Tim Hauser.

Orchestra: Ira Newborn.

Executive Producer: Aaron Russo.

Producer: Bernard Rothman, Jack Wohl.

Director: Ron Field.

THE MANHATTAN TRANSFER—60 minutes—CBS—August 10, 1975 - August 31, 1975.

MANHUNT

Crime Drama. Background: San Diego, California. The investigations of Lieutenant Howard Finucane and his partner, police reporter Ben Andrews, into gangland-associated crimes.

CAST
Lt. Howard Finucane   Victor Jory
Ben Andrews   Patrick McVey

MANHUNT—30 minutes—Syndicated 1959. 78 episodes.

THE MANHUNTER

Crime Drama. Background: Cleary County, Idaho, during the Public Enemy days of the Depression era (1934). The cases of Dave Barrett, farmer, an amateur crimefighter who assists law-enforcement officials by tracking down wanted criminals for their offered rewards.

CAST
Dave Barrett   Ken Howard
Lizabeth Barrett, his
  sister   Hilary Thompson
James Barrett, his
  father   Ford Rainey
Mary Barrett, his
  mother   Claudia Bryar
Sheriff Paul Tate   Robert Hogan
Music: Duante Tatro.

THE MANHUNTER—60 minutes—CBS—September 11, 1974 - April 10, 1975. 24 episodes.

MAN IN A SUITCASE

Adventure. Background: London, England. The investigations of John McGill, a former American intelligence agent turned private detective. Produced in England.

Starring: Richard Bradford as John McGill.

Music: Albert Elms.

MAN IN A SUITCASE—60 minutes—ABC—May 3, 1968 - September 20, 1968. 28 episodes. Syndicated.

MANNIX

Crime Drama. Distinguished by two formats.

Format One:

Background: Los Angeles, California. The cases of Joe Mannix, an investigator for Intertect, a computerized private detective organization. Stories depict the conflict that exists between Mannix, a loner who constantly defies rules and regulations and is opposed to computerized detection; and Lou Wickersham, his superior, who believes in the scientific approach to solving crimes and is opposed to Joe's continual use of unorthodox methods of handling cases.

CAST
Joe Mannix   Michael Connors
Lou Wickersham   Joseph Campanella
Music: Lalo Schifrin.

MANNIX—60 minutes—CBS—September 7, 1967 - August 31, 1968.

Format Two:

The investigations of Joe Mannix, a private detective operating independently from his home in Los Angeles.

CAST
Joe Mannix   Michael Connors

Peggy Fair, his
  secretary   Gail Fisher
Lt. Arthur Malcolm,
  L.A.P.D.   Ward Wood
Lt. George Kramer   Lawrence Linville
Lt. Adams Tobias   Robert Reed
Lt. Daniel Ives   Jack Ging
Toby Fair, Peggy's
  son   Mark Stewart

Music: Lalo Schifrin; Kenyon
  Hopkins.

Producer: Ivan Goff, Ben Roberts.

Director: Sutton Roley, Fernando
  Lamas, Barry Crane, Don Taylor,
  Harry Harvey, Jr., Gerald Mayer,
  Allen Reisner, Seymour Robbie,
  Lee H. Katzin, Murray Golden,
  Arnold Laven, Paul Krasny.

Mannix's Address: 17 Paseo Verde.

MANNIX—60 minutes—CBS—September 21, 1968 - August 27, 1975. 194 episodes.

MAN OF THE WEST

See title: "Frontier Doctor."

MAN OF THE WORLD

Mystery. The assignments of Michael Strait, an international photojournalist.

Starring: Craig Stevens as Michael Strait.

MAN OF THE WORLD—60 minutes—Syndicated 1962. 20 episodes.

A MAN'S WORLD

See title: "Henry Morgan."

MANTRAP

Discussion. One male guest, representing a topic of current interest, appears and sits opposite a panel of three women. Both sides first state their opinions, then debate the issue.

Host: Al Hamel.

Regular Panelists: Meredith MacRae, Phyllis Kirk, Jaye P. Morgan, Carol Wayne, Selma Diamond.

Music: Recorded.

MANTRAP—30 minutes—Syndicated 1971.

THE MAN WHO NEVER WAS

Spy Drama. Background: Europe. Pursued by East German police, who uncovered his identity, Peter Murphy, American espionage agent, wanders onto the grounds of an estate, the scene of a society party. Straying from the house, multimillionaire Mark Wainwright—Murphy's exact double—is mistaken for Peter by the police and killed. Walking toward Wainwright, Murphy is mistaken for Mark by the Wainwright chauffeur and told of an impending meeting. Following through with the charade, he is driven to the Wainwright residence.

First meeting Peter, Eva, Marks's beautiful wife, is unaware that he is an imposter. Attending a meeting wherein Roger Berry, Mark's ambitious half-brother, is to assume control of Eva's family corporation, she becomes aware of a difference when Peter refuses to sign the transfer papers. Leaving the Berry residence, Eva questions the stranger posing as her husband. Unable to reveal his true identity, he tells her about Mark and asks her to continue posing as his wife. Mystified, but needing Mark Wainwright alive to save her family corporation, she agrees.

The body of Mark Wainwright is prepared as Peter Murphy, convincing East German officials that Peter Murphy is dead.

Posing as Mark Wainwright, agent Peter Murphy continues in his capacity as a spy and, assisted by Eva Wainwright, undertakes hazardous missions for the U.S. Government.

CAST

Peter Murphy/Mark Wainwright	Robert Lansing
Eva Wainwright	Dana Wynter
Jack Forbes, Murphy's superior	Murray Hamilton
Roger Berry	Alex Devion

Music: Lionel Newman.

THE MAN WHO NEVER WAS—30 minutes—ABC—September 7, 1966 - December 29, 1966. 18 episodes.

MAN WITH A CAMERA

Crime Drama. Background: New York City. The investigations of Mike Kovac, a free-lance photo-journalist who acquires material by assisting police and solving crimes perpetrated against insurance companies.

CAST

Mike Kovac	Charles Bronson
Lt. Donovan	James Flavin

Producer: Don Sharpe, Warren Lewis, A.E. Houghton.

MAN WITH A CAMERA—30 minutes —ABC—October 10, 1958 - January 29, 1960. 29 episodes. Syndicated.

MAN WITHOUT A GUN

Western. Background: Yellowstone, Dakota, during the 1870s. The story of newspaper editor Adam MacLean and his attempts to establish peace through the power of the press.

CAST

Adam MacLean	Rex Reason
Marshal Frank Tallman	Mort Mills

MAN WITHOUT A GUN—30 minutes —Syndicated 1958.

MANY HAPPY RETURNS

Comedy. Background: Los Angeles, California. The misadventures of widower Walter Burnley, the manager of the complaint department of Krockmeyer's Department Store. Plagued by a misplaced staff and a boss who refuses to hear of the word *return,* Burnley struggles to resolve complaints in a way that will please both the customer and his employer.

CAST

Walter Burnley	John McGiver
Joan Randall, his married daughter	Elinor Donahue
Bob Randall, her husband	Mark Goddard
Laurie Randal, their daughter	Andrea Sacino
Lynn Hall, a staff member	Elena Verdugo
Joe Foley, a staff member	Richard Collier
Wilma Fritter, a staff member	Jesslyn Fax
J. L. Fox, the store manager, Burnley's employer	Jerome Cowan
Owen Sharp, the store owner	Russell Collins

Many Happy Returns. Elena Verdugo and John McGiver.

MANY HAPPY RETURNS—30 minutes—CBS—September 21, 1964 - April 12, 1965. 26 episodes

THE MANY LOVES OF DOBIE GILLIS

Comedy. The saga of a young man's indecision about life.

Formats:

September 29, 1959 - September 12, 1961:

Background: Central City, 285 Norwood Street, the business location of the Gillis Grocery Store, and the residence of the Gillis family: Herbert, the owner; his wife, Winnie; and their son, Dobie. Stories relate: Dobie's continual thoughts about the future; his running battle with his father over the prospect of acquiring work; his relationship with his Beatnick friend, his "good buddy," Maynard G. Krebs; and his endless romantic heartaches, most of which center around Thalia Menninger, a beautiful, greedy, self-centered young woman who struggles to improve Dobie and find him the job that will enable him to make "oodles and oodles of money" though not for her, the last hope her family has, but for her family—a sixty-year-old father with a kidney condition, a mother who isn't getting any younger, a sister who married a loafer, and a brother who is becoming a public charge.

September 26, 1961 - September 18, 1962:
Dobie and Maynard's experiences as army privates.

September 26, 1962 - September 18, 1963:

Completing their military service, and still undecided about life, Dobie and Maynard enroll in college. Stories depict, in addition to Dobie's romantic misadventures, his and Maynard's struggles to find their place in life.

CAST

Dobie Gillis	Dwayne Hickman
Maynard G. Krebs	Bob Denver
Thalia Menninger	Tuesday Weld
Herbert T. Gillis	Frank Faylen
Winifred Gillis (Winnie)	Florida Friebus
Zelda Gilroy, the girl who schemes to win Dobie's love	Sheila James
Chatsworth Osborne, Jr., a rich, spoiled friend	Steve Franken
Clarissa Osborne, Chatsworth's mother	Doris Packer
Leander Pomfritt*	Herbert Anderson William Schallert
Ruth Adams**	Jean Byron
Imogene Burkhart***	Jean Byron

*In format one, the high school English teacher; in format 3, a college instructor.
**In format one, the math teacher.
***In format three, the college anthropology instructor.

The Many Loves of Dobie Gillis. Left to right: Frank Faylen, Dwayne Hickman, Bob Denver.

Davey Gillis, Dobie's
    brother   Darryl Hickman
Duncan Gillis, Dobie's
    cousin   Bob Diamond
Virgil T. Gillis, Dobie's
    cousin   Roy Hemphill
Jerome Krebs, Maynard's
    cousin   Michael J. Pollard
Charlie Wong, the owner of the
    ice cream parlor, the
    after school
    hangout   James Yagi
                           John Lee
Milton Armitage, Dobie's rival
    for Thalia   Warren Beatty
Clarice Armitage, Milton's
    mother
    (early format 1)   Doris Packer
Riff Ryan, a friend, the
    record shop
    owner   Tommy Farrell
Maude Pomfritt, Leander's
    wife   Joyce Van Patten

Trembly, the Osborne
    butler   David Bond
The Osborne
    Chauffeur   Angelo DeMeo
Dean Magruder, the head of
    S. Peter Pryor Jr. College,
    the university attended
    by Dobie and
    Maynard   Raymond Bailey
Lt. Meriwether, Dobie's
    commanding
    officer   Richard Claire
Blossom Kenny, a member
    of the school
    board   Marjorie Bennett

Also: Diana Millay, Ronny Howard, Jack Albertson, Jo Anne Worley.

Music: Lionel Newman.

Executive Producer: Martin Manulis.

Producer: Joel Kane, Guy Scarpitta.

Director: David Davis, Thomas Montgomery, Ralph Murphy, Stanley

Z. Cherry, Guy Scarpitta, Rod Amateau.

Creator: Max Shulman.

Note: On May 10, 1977, CBS presented an unsold pilot entitled, "Whatever Happened To Dobie Gillis?" which reunited the original cast after 14 years. Dobie, now forty years old and married to Zelda, is a partner with his father in an expanded Gillis Grocery Store, and the father of his own teenage son, Georgie (played by Stephen Paul). Maynard, now an entrepreneur, returned to help Dobie celebrate his 40th birthday.

Credits: Music: Randy Newman.

Executive Producer: George Komack.

Producer: Michael Manheim.

Director: James Komack.

THE MANY LOVES OF DOBIE GILLIS—30 minutes—CBS—September 29, 1959 - September 18, 1963. 147 episodes. Syndicated. Also known as "Dobie Gillis."

MARCH OF TIME THROUGH THE YEARS

History. Background: A projection room. Screenings of old March of Time newsreels with the added commentary of guests.

Host: John Daly.

MARCH OF TIME THROUGH THE YEARS—30 minutes—ABC—October 1, 1952 - December 11, 1952.

MARCUS WELBY, M.D.

Medical Drama. Background: Santa Monica, California. The story of doctors Marcus Welby, a general practitioner, and his young assistant, Steven Kiley, who attempt to treat people as individuals in an age of specialized medicine and uncaring doctors.

CAST

Marcus Welby	Robert Young
Steven Kiley	James Brolin
Consuelo Lopez, their nurse	Elena Verdugo
Myra Sherwood, widow, Welby's romantic interest	Anne Baxter
Nurse Kathleen Faverty	Sharon Gless
Janet Blake, Kiley's romantic interest (married on 10/21/75)	Pamela Hensley

Music: Leonard Rosenman.

Executive Producer: David Victor.

Producer: David J. O'Connell.

Director: Leo Penn, Jon Epstein, Hollingsworth Morse, Arnold Laven, Jerry London, David Alexander, Nicholas Cosalano, Bruce Kessler.

MARCUS WELBY, M.D.—60 minutes—ABC—September 23, 1969 - May 11, 1976. Syndicated. 172 episodes. Also known as "Robert Young, Family Doctor."

THE MARGE AND GOWER CHAMPION SHOW

Comedy. The misadventures of Marge and Gower Champion, husband and wife professional dancers, as they attempt to establish and live a life apart from the hectic demands of show business.

CAST

Marge Champion	Herself
Gower Champion	Himself
Marge's father, their agent and business manager	Jack Whiting
Cozy, a friend of theirs, a drummer	Buddy Rich
Amanda	Peg La Centra
Miss Weatherly	Barbara Perry

Music: Alan Bergman.

THE MARGE AND GOWER CHAMPION SHOW—30 minutes—CBS—March 31, 1957 - June 9, 1957.

MARGE AND JEFF

Comedy. Background: New York City. The misadventures of Marge and Jeff Green, newlyweds struggling to survive the difficult first years of marriage.

CAST

Marge Green	Marge Green
Jeff Green	Jeff Cain

Family dog: Paisley, a cocker spaniel.

MARGE AND JEFF—15 minutes—DuMont—1953 - 1954.

MARGIE

Comedy. Background: the small New England town of Madison during the 1920s. The experiences of Margie Clayton, a pretty, delightful, and resourceful high-school girl; a carbonated teenager with an unquenchable thirst for life and an uncontrollable penchant for trouble.

CAST

Margie Clayton	Cynthia Pepper
Harvey Clayton, her father, a bank vice president	Dave Willock
Nora Clayton, her mother	Wesley Thackitt
Cornell Clayton, her brother	Johnny Bangert
Phoebe Clayton, her sophisticated aunt	Hollis Irving
Heywood Botts, Margie's boyfriend	Tommy Ivo
Maybell Jackson, Margie's girlfriend	Penny Parker
Johnny Green, a friend	Richard Gering
Mr. Jackson, Maybell's father	Herb Ellis
Mrs. Jackson, his wife	Marine Stuart

MARGIE—30 minutes—ABC—October 12, 1961 - August 31, 1962. 26 episodes. Syndicated.

THE MARILYN McCOO AND BILLY DAVIS, JR. SHOW

Variety. Music, songs, and comedy sketches.

Hosts: Marilyn McCoo and Billy Davis, Jr.

Regulars: Lewis Arquette, Tim Reid, Jay Leno.

Orchestra: John Myles.

Special Musical Material: Phil Moore.

Executive Producer: Dick Broder.

Producer: Ann Elder, Ed Scharlach.

Director: Gerren Keith.

Choreographer: Ron Poindexter.

THE MARILYN McCOO AND BILLY DAVIS, JR. SHOW—30 minutes—CBS—June 15, 1977 - July 20, 1977. 6 tapes.

MARINE BOY

Animated Cartoon. Era: Twenty-first-century Earth. The investigations of Marine Boy, an agent for the Ocean Patrol, an international defense organization established beneath the sea. Produced in Japan.

Characters:
Marine Boy
Splasher, his pet dolphin
Professor Fumble
Mr. Beacon
Dr. Mariner, Marine Boy's father, the head of the Ocean Patrol
Corrie, a member of the Ocean Patrol
Piper, a member of the Ocean Patrol
Voltan, a member of the Ocean Patrol

Voices: Jack Grimes, Caroline Owens, Jack Cortes.

Music: Norman Gould.

Theme: Ernest Gold.

Executive Producer: Stanley Jaffee.

MARINE BOY—30 minutes—Syndicated. 1966. 78 episodes.

MARKHAM

Crime Drama. Background: Los Angeles, California. The investigations and courtroom defenses of Roy Markham, a wealthy attorney.

CAST
Roy Markham	Ray Milland
John Riggs, his employer	Simon Scott

Music: Stanley Wilson.

Narrator: Ray Milland.

Producer: Joe Sistiam, Warren Duff.

MARKHAM—30 minutes—CBS—May 2, 1959 - September 29, 1960. 60 episodes.

MARK SABER

Crime Drama. Distinguished by two formats.

Format One, American:

The Mark Saber Mystery Theatre—30 minutes—ABC—September 1951 - September 1954. Syndicated title: "Homicide Squad."
Background: New York City. The invesitgations of Mark Saber, a plainclothes detective with the Homicide Division of the New York Police Department.

CAST
Mark Saber	Tom Conway
Sgt. Tim Maloney, his assistant	James Burke

Producer: J. Donald Wilson, Roland Reed.

Director: Eugene Forde.

Sponsor: Sterling Drug Company.

Format Two, British:

Saber Of London—30 minutes—NBC—October 13, 1957 - September 1959. Syndicated title: "Uncovered."
Background: London, England. The investigations of Mark Saber, the one-armed Chief Inspector of Scotland Yard.

CAST
Mark Saber	Donald Gray
His Assistants:	
Barney O'Keefe	Michael Balfour
Stephanie Ames	Diane Decker
Peter Paulson	Neil McCallum
Bob Page	Robert Arden
Eddie Wells	Garry Thorne
Inspector Parker	Colin Tapley

Producer: Edward Donziger, Harry Donziger, Harry Lee.

MARLO AND THE MAGIC MOVIE MACHINE

Children. Background: The sub-sub basement of the L. Dullo Computer Company in New York City. The series revolves around Marlo Higgins, a struggling computer operator who was banished to the basement by his employer, Leo Dullo. Here, by day, he continues working, making his dull job exciting by secretly perfecting the L. Dullo Computer. After working hours, he opens a secret doorway and activates his invention—the Magic Movie Machine, a computer that can display a wide variety of historic films and video-tape material, and can also talk, tell jokes, and relate funny stories. Acting as a disc jockey, Marlo and his Magic Movie Machine present films, stories, jokes, and other related entertainment for children.

Starring: Laurie Faso as Marlo Higgins.

Voice of the Movie Machine: Mert Hoplin.

Music: Pete Dino; Score Productions.

Executive Producer: Sanford H. Fisher.

Producer: Ted Field.

Director: George Jason, Lynwood King.

MARLO AND THE MAGIC MOVIE MACHINE—60 minutes—CBS Owned and Operated Stations—Premiered: April 3, 1977.

THE MARRIAGE

Comedy-Drama. Background: New York City. The life of the close-knit Marriott family: Ben, an attorney; his wife, Liz; and their children, Emily and Peter.

CAST

Ben Marriott	Hume Cronyn
Liz Marriott	Jessica Tandy
Emily Marriott	Susan Strasberg
Peter Marriott	Malcolm Brodrick
Bobby Logan, Emily's boy friend	William Redfield

THE MARRIAGE—30 minutes—NBC —July 1, 1954 - August 19, 1954.

MARSHAL DILLON

See title: "Gunsmoke."

THE MARTHA RAYE SHOW

Variety. Music, songs, dances, and slapstick comedy sketches.

Hostess: Martha Raye.

Her Comedy Foil: Rocky Graziano.

Featured: The Martha Raye Dancers.

Orchestra: Carl Hoff.

THE MARTHA RAYE SHOW—60 minutes—NBC—December 26, 1953 - May 29, 1956.

THE MARTHA WRIGHT SHOW

Musical Variety.

Hostess: Martha Wright.

Vocalists: The Norman Paris Chorus.

Orchestra: Bobby Hackett.

THE MARTHA WRIGHT SHOW—15 minutes—ABC 1954.

MARTIN KANE

Crime Drama. Distinguished by two

formats.

Format One:

Martin Kane, Private Eye—30 minutes —NBC—September 11, 1949 - September 1953.

Background: New York City. The investigations of Martin Kane, a private detective who achieves his desired results through determination and force of character.

CAST

Martin Kane William Gargan
  (1949-1951)
Martin Kane (1951-1952) Lloyd Nolan
Martin Kane (1952-1953) Lee Tracy

Happy McMann, his
  aide Walter Kinsella
Sergeant Ross,
  N.Y.P.D. Nicholas Saunders
The Police Captain Frank M. Thomas
Lt. Gray King Calder

Music: Charles Paul.

Announcer: Fred Uttal.

Producer: Frank Burns, Edward C. Kahan, Ed Sutherland.

Sponsor: U.S. Tobacco.

Format Two:

The New Adventures Of Martin Kane —30 minutes—NBC—September 1953 - June 17, 1954. Syndicated title: "Assignment: Danger."

Background: Europe. The cases of Martin Kane, an American private detective who assists various international police departments.

Starring: Mark Stevens as Martin Kane.

Music: Charles Paul.

Announcer: Fred Uttal.

Producer: Frank Burns.

Sponsor: U.S. Tobacco.

THE MARTY FELDMAN COMEDY MACHINE

Comedy. A blend of contemporary humor with that of the Max Sennett era type of slapstick comedy.

Starring: Marty Feldman, British comedian.

Regulars: Barbara Feldon, Orson Welles, Spike Milligan, Fred Smoot, Leonard Schultz, Thelma Houston, Fred Roman.

Music: Recorded.

THE MARTY FELDMAN COMEDY MACHINE—30 minutes—ABC—April 12, 1972 - August 23, 1972. Taped in London. American audiences were first introduced to Marty Feldman via "Dean Martin Presents the Golddiggers." Marty's previous series (British; BBC-1; BBC-2): "Marty"; "Marty on the Telly in England"; and "The Frost Report."

THE MARVEL SUPER HEROES

Animated adaptations of five *Marvel* comic book characters: "Captain America," "The Incredible Hulk," "Iron Man," "Mighty Thor," and "Sub Mariner." 195 six minute, 30 second films. Syndicated 1965.

THE MARY HARTLINE SHOW

Children. Music, songs, and games.

Hostess: Mary Hartline ("Queen of the Super Circus.")

Music: Chet Robel.

THE MARY HARTLINE SHOW—30 minutes—ABC—February 12, 1951 - June 15, 1951.

MARY HARTMAN, MARY HARTMAN

Serial. Background: 343 Bratner Avenue in the Woodland Hills section of mythical Fernwood, Ohio. The series, which satirizes life, focuses on the endless frustrations of Mary Hartman, a typical middle-aged housewife and mother.

CAST

Mary Hartman	Louise Lasser
Tom Hartman, her husband	Greg Mullavey
Cathy Schumway, Mary's sister	Debralee Scott
Loretta Haggers, Mary's neighbor	Mary Kay Place

Mary Hartman, Mary Hartman. Front row left to right: Claudia Lamb, Philip Bruns, Debralee Scott. Back row left to right: Greg Mullavey, Dody Goodman, Louise Lasser, and Victor Kilian.

Charlie Haggers, Loretta's husband	Graham Jarvis
George Schumway, Mary's father	Philip Bruns
Martha Schumway, Mary's mother	Dody Goodman
Raymond Larkin, Mary's grandfather	Victor Kilian
Police Sgt. Dennis Foley	Bruce Solomon
Heather Hartman, Mary's daughter	Claudia Lamb
Mae Olinski, the bookkeeper at the auto plant	Salome Jens
Roberta Walashak, the social worker	Samantha Harper
Clete Meizenheimer, the TV reporter	Michael Lembeck
Dr. Ferman	Oliver Clark
Mona McKenzie, the sexy sex therapist	Sallie Janes
Tiny, an employee at the auto plant	Hugh Gilian
Merle Jeeter, the mayor	Dabney Coleman
Wanda Jeeter, his wife	Marian Mercer
Jimmy Joe Jeeter, Merle's son	Sparky Marcus
Mac Slattery, the truck driver	Dennis Burkley
Lila, the Jeeter's sexy maid	Marjorie Battles
Tex, an auto plant employee	Sid Haig
Vernon Bales, the plant manager	David Byrd
Dewey Johnson, the janitor	Richard Ward
Garth Gimble, the Hartman's neighbor	Martin Mull
Pat Gimble, his wife	Susan Browning
Barth Gimble, Garth's	

twin brother | Martin Mull
Annie "Tippytoes" Wylie,
the lesbian | Gloria DeHaven
Garth Gimble, Jr.,
Garth's son | Eric Shea
Muriel Haggers,
Charlie's evil
ex-wife | L. C. Downey
Detective Johnson | Ron Feinberg
Steve Fletcher, the
deaf-mute, Cathy's
boyfriend | Ed Begley, Jr.
Howie Freeze, Cathy's
boyfriend | Sid Weisman
The Capri Lounge
Bartender | Robert Stoneman
Betty McCullogh,
the Hartman's
neighbor | Vivian Blaine
Voice in the opening
calling "Mary
Hartman, Mary
Hartman" | Dody Goodman

Also: Reva Rose (as Blanche Fedders), Norman Alden (Leroy Fedders), Sudi Bond (Fannie); Billy Beck (Lt. Trask), Larry Haddon (Ed), Beeson Carroll (Howard), John Fink (Brian Adams) Andra Akers (Christine Adams), Matthew La Borteaux (Big Foot's child).

Guests: Dr. Joyce Brothers, Dinah Shore, Gore Vidal, David Susskind, Merv Griffin.

Music: Earle Hagen.

Music Supervision: Bobby Knight.

Executive Producer: Norman Lear.

Producer: Lew Gallo, Vivi Knight, Perry Krauss, Eugenie Ross-Leming, Brad Buckner.

Director: Joan Darling, Jim Drake, Mack Bing, Art Wolff, Bob Lally, Nessa Hyams, Giovanni Nigro, Harlene Kim Friedman, Jack Heller, Dennis Klein, Hal Alexander.

Creator: Gail Parent, Ann Marcus, Jerry Adelman, Daniel Gregory Browne.

MARY HARTMAN, MARY HARTMAN—30 minutes—Syndicated 1976.

MARY KAY AND JOHNNY

Comedy. Background: Greenwich Village, New York. The marital misadventures of Mary Kay and Johnny Stearns, television's first domestic couple. Based on their actual experiences.

CAST
Mary Kay Stearns | Herself
Johnny Stearns | Himself

Announcer: Jim Stevenson.

Producer: Ernest Walling.

Director: Garry Simpson, Joe Cavalier.

Sponsor: Whiteball.

MARY KAY AND JOHNNY—30 minutes—NBC—1947 - 1950.

THE MARY MARGARET McBRIDE SHOW

Celebrity Interview.

Hostess: Mary Margaret McBride.

Announcer-Assistant: Vincent Connolly.

Producer: Stella Karn, George Foley.

Director: Garry Simpson.

THE MARY MARGARET McBRIDE SHOW—30 minutes—NBC 1948.

The Mary Tyler Moore Show. Mary Tyler Moore.

THE MARY TYLER MOORE SHOW

Comedy. Background: Minneapolis-St. Paul, Minnesota. The misadventures, joys, sorrows, and romantic heartaches of Mary Richards, a beautiful young bachelorette.

Stories depict: her home life at 119 North Weatherly, Apartment D, with her friends, Rhoda Morganstern, the upstairs tenant, an interior decorator at Hempel's Department Store; and Phyllis Lindstrom, a busybody, the owner of the building; and her working life in the newsroom at WJM-TV Channel 12, where, as the associate producer of "The Six O'Clock News" program, she struggles to function in the man's world of an irascible producer, Lou Grant; a soft-hearted newswriter, Murray Slaughter; and a naricissistic anchorman, Ted Baxter.

CAST

Mary Richards	Mary Tyler Moore
Rhoda Morganstern	Valerie Harper
Lou Grant	Edward Asner
Ted Baxter	Ted Knight
Murray Slaughter	Gavin MacLeod
Phyllis Lindstrom	Cloris Leachman
Bess Lindstrom, Phyllis's daughter	Lisa Gerritsen
Gordon Howard (Gordie), the station weatherman	John Amos
Ida Morganstern, Rhoda's mother	Nancy Walker
Martin Morganstern, Rhoda's father	Harold Gould
Georgette Franklin, Ted's romantic interest	Georgia Engel
Sue Anne Nevins, the host of Channel 12's "Happy Homemaker Show"	Betty White
Dotty Richards, Mary's mother	Nanette Fabray
Walter Reed Richards, Mary's father, a retired doctor	Bill Quinn
Marie Slaughter, Murray's wife	Joyce Bulifant
Pete, a newsteam staff member	Benjamin Chuley
Edie Grant, Lou's ex-wife	Priscilla Morrill
Andy Rivers, Mary's occasional date	John Gabriel
Charlene McGuire, Lou's girlfriend	Sheree North
David Baxter, Ted and Georgette's adopted son	Robbie Rist
The Bartender at the Happy Hour Bar	Peter Hobbs Chuck Bergansky
Howard Gordon, Edie's second husband	Brad Trumbull
Janey, Lou and Edie's daughter	Nora Heflin

Music: Pat Williams.

Theme vocal: "Love Is All Around," Sonny Curtis.

Executive Producer: James L. Brooks, Allan Burns.

Producer: Stan Daniels, Ed Weinberger.

Director: Jay Sandrich, Marjorie Mullen, James Burrows, Harry Mastrogeorge, Mel Ferber, Doug Rogers.

Creator: James L. Brooks, Allan Burns.

Note: In later episodes Mary is promoted to producer of the news show; Ted and Georgette married on November 8, 1975.

THE MARY TYLER MOORE SHOW

—30 minutes—CBS—Premiered: September 19, 1970. Spin-off series: "Rhoda" (see title).

M*A*S*H

Comedy. Background: The 4077th M*A*S*H (Mobile Army Surgical Hospital) in Korea, 1950. The story of how medical men retain their sanity amid the insanity of war and their humanity in the face of dehumanization. Episodes focus on the antics of two skilled surgeons: Captain Benjamin Franklin "Hawkeye" Pierce, and Captain "Trapper" John McIntyre, reluctant draftees determined to make the best of the miserable conditions that exist. Though constantly breaking rules and regulations, defying their superior officers, pursuing nurses, and plaguing the life of Major Frank Burns, the saving of human life is uppermost in their thoughts—thoughts coupled with the realization that the war and the killing will all one day end. Situations are played to the limits of television permissiveness. Based on the movie of the same title.

CAST

Captain Benjamin Franklin Pierce (Hawkeye)	Alan Alda
Captain John McIntyre (Trapper John)	Wayne Rogers
Lt. Col. Henry Blake, the soft-hearted commanding officer	McLean Stevenson
Major Margaret Houlihan (Hot Lips), the head nurse	Loretta Swit
Corporal Radar O'Reilly, Henry's aide, possesses E.S.P.	Gary Burghoff
Major Frank Burns, Margaret's romantic interest	Larry Linville
Father John Mulcahy, the company priest	George Morgan
	William Christopher
Lieutenant Maggie Dish, a nurse	Karen Philipp
Spearchucker Jones, a doctor	Timothy Brown
Lieutenant Ginger Ballis, a nurse	Odessa Cleveland
Corporal Maxwell Klinger the man who, dressing as a woman, seeks a psycho discharge	Jamie Farr
Ho-John, Hawkeye's Korean houseboy	Patrick Adiarte
Ugly John, the anesthetist	John Orchard
General Hamilton Hammond, the chief medical officer	G. Wood
Lieutenant Leslie Scorch, a nurse	Linda Meiklejohn
Lieutenant Jones, a nurse	Barbara Brownell
Nurse Louise Anderson	Kelly Jean Peters

Nurse Baker	Jean Powell
Nurse Maggie Cutler	Marcia Strassman
	Lynette Mettey
General Brandon	
Clayton	Herbert Voland
The cook	Joseph Perry
Mr. Kwang, the bartender in the officers club	Leland Sung
Colonel Sherman Potter, replaced Col. Blake	Harry Morgan
Captain B. J. Hunnicutt, replaced Trapper John	Mike Farrell
Colonel Flagg, the hard-nosed CIA Agent	Edward Winter
Major Sidney Freedman, the compassionate psychiatrist	Allan Arbus
Nurse Bigelow	Enid Kent
Nurse Abel	Judy Farrell
Major Donald Penobscott, Margaret's romantic interest (married 3/15/77)	Beeson Carroll

Music: Johnny Mandell; Lionel Newman; Duante Tatro.

Executive Producer: Larry Gelbart, Gene Reynolds.

Producer: Alan Katz, Don Reo.

Director: Alan Alda, Hy Averback, Jackie Cooper, Gene Reynolds, Harry Morgan, Burt Metcalfe, Joan Darling, William Jurgenson, George Tyne.

M*A*S*H—30 minutes—CBS—Premiered: September 17, 1972.

THE MASK

Mystery. Background: New York City. The investigations and courtroom defenses of Walter and Peter Guilfoyle, brothers, attorneys.

CAST

Walter Guilfoyle	Gary Merrill
Peter Guilfoyle	William Prince

THE MASK—60 minutes—ABC—January 10, 1954 - April 28, 1954. Television's first hour-long mystery series. Broadcast live on Sunday evenings, and rebroadcast (kinescope) on Tuesday and Wednesday evenings.

MASLAND AT HOME

Musical Variety.

Host: Earl Wrightson.

Music: The Norman Paris Trio.

Producer: Franklin Heller.

Sponsor: Masland Carpets.

MASLAND AT HOME—15 minutes—ABC—March 30, 1951 - May 22, 1951.

MASQUERADE

Anthology. Improvisational adaptations of folk tales.

CAST

Avery Schreiber, Barbara Sharma, Alice Playten, Bill Hinnant, Barbara Minkus, Seth Allen, Jacques Lynn Colton, Louise Lasser, J. J. Barry, Abraham Sobaloff, Phil Burns, Sudie Bond, Barbara Tracy.

Included: "The Emperor's New Clothes"; "The Legend of Sleepy Hallow"; "The Pied Piper of Hamelin"; "The Man Who Stole His Beard"; "Czar of the Sea"; "The Man With the Secret Smile"; "The Elephant's Child"; "The Green Fairy"; "Jack and the Beanstalk."

MASQUERADE–30 minutes–PBS– October 5, 1971 - December 28, 1971.

MASQUERADE PARTY

Game. Distinguished by two formats.

Format One:
Masquerade Party–30 minutes. NBC–July 14, 1952 - August 25, 1952; CBS–June 22, 1953 - September 13, 1954; ABC– September 29, 1954 - December 15, 1956; CBS– August 4, 1958 - September 15, 1958. CBS–November 2, 1959 - January 18, 1960.

Object: For five celebrity panelists to identify elaborately disguised guest personalities. Each panelist is permitted to ask five questions of the guest. Each second of questioning scores one dollar to a maximum of three hundred dollars. At the end of five minute segments, or at any time in between, panelists may hazard to guess the identity of the guest. Whether correct or incorrect, the money that is established is donated to charity.

Hosts: Bud Collyer; Eddie Bracken; Peter Donald; Bert Parks; Robert Q. Lewis; Douglas Edwards.

Panelists: Phil Silvers, Ilka Chase, Adele Jergens, Peter Donald, Madge Evans, Buff Cobb, John Young, Ogden Nash, Johnny Johnston, Betsy Palmer, Frank Palmer, Jonathan Winters, Jinx Falkenberg, Pat Carroll, Faye Emerson, Gloria DeHaven, Audrey Meadows, Sam Levinson, Lee Bowman.

Announcer: Don Morrow, William T. Lazar.

Format Two:

Masquerade Party–30 minutes–Syndicated 1974.

Follows the basis of the first format with the following changes: Three celebrity panelists who are permitted to ask only three questions of guests; and a studio audience participation segment that replaces the money segment of the first version. After the panel's questioning, two selected studio-audience members appear on stage and state who they believe the mystery guest is. The disguise is removed, and the player who is correct, if any, receives a merchandise prize.

Host: Richard Dawson.

Panelists: Bill Bixby, Lee Meriwether, Nipsey Russell.

Announcer: Jay Stewart.

Music: Sheldon Allman.

MASTERPIECE PLAYHOUSE

Anthology. Dramatizations based on the plays of William Shakespeare, Oscar Wilde, Richard Sheridan, and Anton Chekov.

Producer: Curtis Canfield, Albert McCleery.

Director: William Corrigan, Albert McCleery.

MASTERPIECE PLAYHOUSE–60 minutes–NBC 1950.

MASTERPIECE THEATRE

Anthology. A series of British produced serials.

Host: Alistair Cooke.

Included:

Clouds of Witness. Background: London, England. The investigations of Lord Peter Wimsey, a British sleuth, into the murder of his sister's fiancé. A five-part adaptation of the Dorothy Sayers story.

CAST

Lord Peter Wimsey	Ian Carmichael
Lady Mary Wimsey	Rachel Herbert
Bunter	Glyn Houston
Parker	Mark Eden
The Duke of Denver	David Langton
Denis Cathcart	Anthony Ainley
Cynthia	Kate O'Mara
Rachel	Petronella Ford

Cousin Bette. Background: Paris, 19th century. Bette Fisher, a spinster "embittered by her poor relation status in the influential Hulot family," amuses herself by housing an artist protégé, Steinbeck. Suddenly, bitterness and resentment is triggered when he is stolen from her and married by her cousin. The story relates her demand for and attempts to achieve revenge. A five-part adaptation of the Honore de Balzac novel.

CAST

Bette Fisher	Margaret Tyzack
Valerie Marneffe	Helen Mirren
Steinbeck	Colin Baker
Hector	Thorley Walters
Hortense	Harriett Harper
Adeline	Ursula Howells
Johann Fischer	Robert Speight
Marie	Sally James
Marneffe	Oscar Quitak
Crevel	John Bryans
Henri Montes	Edward De Souza

Elizabeth R. Background: Sixteenth-century England. A six-part chronicling of the reign of Elizabeth, the daughter of Henry VIII, as the Queen of England (1558-1603).

CAST

Elizabeth	Glenda Jackson
Cecil	Ronald Hines
Mary, Queen of Scots	Vivian Pickles
The Bishop	Esmond Knight
Dudley Leicester	Robert Hardy
Kat	Rachel Kempson
Alencon	Michael Williams
King Philip	Peter Jeffrey
Sir Francis Drake	John Woodvine
The Duke of Medina	Gordon Gostelow
Sir Walter Raleigh	Nicholas Selby
Elizabeth Vernon	Sonia Fraser
Lady Leicester	Angela Thorne
Earl of Essex	Robin Ellis

The First Churchills. Background: England during the Restoration period. The life and times of John Churchill, the first Duke of Malborough. A twelve-part dramatization.

CAST

John Churchill	John Neville
Sarah Jennings	Susan Hampshire
Charles II	James Villiers
Duke of York	John Westbrook
Duchess of Cleveland	Morra Redmond
Manmouth	James Kerry
Sidney Godolphin	John Standing
Lawrence Hyde	John Ringham
Rochester	Graham Armitage
Princess	Lisa Daniely
Margaret Godolphin	Holly Wilson
Princess Anne	Margaret Tyzack
Prince of Orange	Alan Rowe
Bishop Compton	George Merritt

Poldark. Background: Europe during the 1700s. A sixteen-part romantic adventure, based on four novels by Winston Graham, that focuses on the life of Ross Poldark, a dashing war veteran, in the period immediately following the Revolution.

CAST

Ross Poldark	Robin Ellis
Elizabeth	Jill Townsend
Demelza	Angharad Rees
Verity	Norma Streader
Zacky	Forbes Collins

Upstairs, Downstairs. Background: Edwardian England. A depiction of life in a fashionable London townhouse; the interactions of a family, the Bellamys, living upstairs; and, forming their own family, their servants, who live downstairs. A fifteen-part dramatization.

CAST

Richard Bellamy	David Langton
James Bellamy	Simon Williams
Hazel Bellamy	Meg-Wynn Owen
Virginia Bellamy	Hannah Gordon
Rose, the maid	Jean Marsh
Hudson, the butler	Gordon Jackson
Mrs. Bridges	Angela Baddeley
Alfred the footman	George Innes
Edward the footman	Christopher Beeny
Daisy, the maid	Jacqueline Tong
Sarah	Pauline Collins
Watkins	John Alderton
Emily	Evin Crowley
Lady Marjorie	Rachel Gurney
Lil	Angela Brown
Georgina Worsley	Leslie-Anne Down

Music: Alexander Faris.

Producer: John Hawkesworth.

Creator: Jean Marsh, Eileen Atkens.

The Bellamy's Address: 165 Eaton Place.

Vanity Fair. Depicted: The life of an amoral adventuress, Becky Sharp, "a female Napoleon determined to claw her way up in the world by fair means or foul." Charted: Her progress through the nineteenth century. A five-part adaptation of the William Thackeray novel.

CAST

Becky Sharp	Susan Hampshire
Amelia Sedley	Marilyn Taylerson
Joseph Sedley	John Moffatt
Sir Pitt Crawley	Michael Rothwell
Fawdon Crawley	Dyson Lovell
Miss Crawley	Barbara Couper
George Osborne	Roy Marsden
Dobbin	Bryan Marshall
Pauline	Consuela Burke

MASTERPIECE THEATRE—60 minutes—PBS—Premiered: January 10, 1971.

THE MATCH GAME

Game. Distinguished by two formats.

Format One:

THE MATCH GAME—30 minutes—NBC—December 31, 1962 - September 20, 1969.

Two teams compete, each composed of three members—one celebrity captain and two noncelebrity contestants. The host reads an incomplete sentence (e.g., "Tarzan said to Jane, why don't you BLANK your hair"). Players than fill in the blank with the word or words each feels will best complete the thought. Answers are revealed and if two players match by using the same word, twenty-five points is scored. If the celebrity matches the two players, fifty points is scored. The team first to score one hundred points is the winner. Points are transferred to cash and the team receives a chance to earn additional money via "The Studio Audience Match."

Questions, asked of one hundred members of a studio audience weeks ago, are restated. After players verbally state their answers, the studio-audience responses are revealed. Each match awards the team fifty dollars.

Host: Gene Rayburn.

Announcer: Johnny Olsen.

Music: Recorded.

Format Two:

MATCH GAME '73/'74—30 minutes —CBS—Premiered: June 25, 1973.

Two competing contestants, the champion and the challenger. The challenger selects one of two questions, A or B, which the host than reads to a panel of six celebrity guests (e.g. "George didn't like his first BLANK"). Panelists than fill in the blank with the word or words that each feels will best complete the thought. The players verbally reveal their responses. Panelists, one at a time, reveal their answers, and each match awards the player one point. The champion receives the remaining question and the game is played in the same manner. Two such rounds are played and the highest scoring player is the winner and receives one hundred dollars and a chance to play "The Super Match."

First half of "The Super Match." One word (e.g., "Fat BLANK") is revealed on a game board. Below it are three cash amount responses: $100, $250, and $500. The player chooses three celebrities who each state a word with which to fill in the blank. The player is permitted to choose any of their answers or use his own. If the answer he uses matches one of the cash amounts, he receives the chance to win ten times that amount in the second half.

Second half. The player selects one celebrity to whom the host reads a question that requires a blank to be filled in. The player verbally states his answer; if he matches the celebrity's written answer, he receives ten times the amount he won in the first half.

Players compete until defeated.

Host: Gene Rayburn.

Announcer: Johnny Olsen.

Regular Panelists: Brett Somers, Richard Dawson.

Music: Score Productions.

Syndicated Version: "Match Game P.M." Basically the same as version two with the only difference being that contestants can win up to $10,000 in the Super Match. All credits are the same. 30 minutes— Syndicated 1975.

MATCHES 'N' MATES

Married couples compete in a game wherein they have to match hidden answers with concealed questions.
Host: Art James.

30 minutes—Syndicated 1967.

MATINEE IN NEW YORK

Variety. Music, songs, and celebrity interviews.
Game portion: Selected studio-audience members compete in question-and-answer rounds. Winners, the highest scorers, receive a merchandise prize.

Game Emcees: Bill Cullen, Bill Goodwin.

Interview Host: Ted Collins.

Announcer: Andre Baruch.

Orchestra: Jack Miller.

MATINEE IN NEW YORK—60 min-utes—NBC—June 9, 1952 - August 1952.

MATINEE THEATRE

Anthology. Dramatic presentations broadcast live from Burbank each weekday afternoon.

Host: John Conte.

Producer: Albert McCleery.

Included:

Beyond A Reasonable Doubt. The story concerns a school teacher and his efforts to clear himself of a false murder charge.

CAST
Cara Williams, De Forest Kelley, Charlie Evans.

Springfield Incident. The story concerns Abraham Lincoln's efforts to clear two brothers accused of murder

CAST
Tom Tryon, Ann Harding, Marshall Thompson, Alan Hale.

Fortune's Child. A café owner attempts to solve a custody battle over a girl.

Starring: Charles McGraw.

Mail Order Bride. A doctor attempts to assist a man who discovers his mail-order bride is quite older than he expected.

Starring: Jack Kelly.

MATINEE THEATRE—60 minutes—NBC—October 31, 1955 - June 27, 1958.

THE MATT DENNIS SHOW

Musical Variety.

Host: Matt Dennis, pianist.

Musical Backing: Trigger Albert (bass), Mundell Lowell (guitar), Jimmy Campbell (drums).

THE MATT DENNIS SHOW—15 minutes—NBC—June 27, 1955 - August 29, 1955.

MATT HELM

Crime Drama. Background: California. The investigations of Matt Helm, a dashing government intelligence agent turned private detective.

CAST
Matt Helm	Tony Franciosa
Miss Kronski, his lawyer and romantic interest	Laraine Stephens
Lt. Hanrahan	Gene Evans
Ethel, Matt's telephone answering service girl	Jeff Donnell

Music: Morton Stevens; Jerrold Emil; John Parker.

Producer: Ken Pettus, Charles B. Fitzsimmons.

Director: Earl Bellamy, Richard Benedict, Don Weis, John Newland.

MATT HELM—60 minutes—ABC—September 20, 1975 - November 3, 1975.

MATT LINCOLN

Drama. Background: Los Angeles, California. The cases of Matt Lincoln, a psychiatrist who practices preventive psychiatry and struggles to assist people in early stages of emotional distress to prevent the need for further, more complicated treatment.

CAST

Matt Lincoln	Vince Edwards

His Assistants:

Tag	Chelsea Brown
Jimmy	Felton Perry
Kevin	Michael Larrain
Ann	June Harding

Music: Oliver Nelson.

MATT LINCOLN–60 minutes–ABC –September 24, 1970 - January 14, 1971. 13 episodes.

MATTY'S FUNDAY FUNNIES

Animated Cartoon. The overall title for a series of Harvey Films theatrical cartoons: "Casper, the Friendly Ghost," about a ghost who seeks only to make friends; "Baby Huey," the story of a mischievous, overgrown baby duck; and "Little Audrey," a mischievous little girl.

Series Animated Hosts: Matty and Sisterbelle.

MATTY'S FUNDAY FUNNIES–30 minutes–ABC–October 11, 1959 - December 31, 1961. From January 6, 1962 to September 22, 1962, the series featured the adventures of "Beany and Cecil," about a boy and his pet sea serpent.

MAUDE

Comedy. Background: 39 Crenshaw Street, Tuckahoe, New York, the residence of the Findlays: Walter, the owner of "Findlay's Friendly Appliances" store; his wife, Maude; her

Maude. Left to right: Adrienne Barbeau, Beatrice Arthur, Bill Macy, Esther Rolle.

divorced daughter, Carol; and Carol's eight-year-old son, Philip. The story of Maude Findlay, out-spoken and liberal, a woman who, married for the fourth time, struggles to solve the incidents that creep in, disrupt, and threaten to destroy her attempts to achieve a lasting relationship with Walter. A spin-off from "All in the Family," wherein the character of Maude, Edith's cousin, appeared several times.

CAST

Maude Findlay	Beatrice Arthur
Walter Findlay	Bill Macy
Carol Trener	Adrienne Barbeau
Philip Trener	Brian Morris
Arthur Harmon, their neighbor, a doctor	Conrad Bain
Vivian Harmon, Arthur's wife	Rue McClanahan
Florida Evans, the Findlay maid (early episodes)	Esther Rolle
Mrs. Naugatuck, the Findlay maid (later episodes)	Hermione Baddeley
Chris, Carol's fiancé, a pediatrician	Fred Grandy
Henry Evans, Florida's husband	John Amos

Sam, the bartender   Jan Arvan
Fred, the bar-
    tender   Fred Zuckert
Bert Beasley, Mrs. Nell
    Naugatuck's husband (married
    11/22/76)   J. Pat O'Malley
Victoria Butterfield, the
    Findlay's housekeeper
    (after Nell
    Naugatuck)   Marlene Warfield

Music: Alan Bergman, Marilyn
    Bergman, Dave Grusin.

Executive Producer: Norman Lear,
    Rod Parker.

Producer: Bob Weiskopf, Bob Schiller.

Creator: Norman Lear.

Director: Hal Cooper.

MAUDE—30 minutes—CBS—Pre-
miered: September 12, 1972. Spin-off
series: "Good Times" (see title).

MAURICE WOODRUFF PREDICTS

Variety. Predictions coupled with
celebrity interviews.

Host: Maurice Woodruff.

Co-Hosts-Announcers: Robert Q.
    Lewis; Vidal Sasson.

MAURICE WOODRUFF PREDICTS
—60 minutes—Syndicated 1969.

MAVERICK

Western. Background: The Frontier,
1880s. The exploits of Bret and Bart

Maverick. The original logo appearing on the
Warner Brothers series.

Maverick, brothers, self-centered, unconventional, and untrustworthy gentlemen gamblers. Seeking rich prey, they roam throughout the West, and more often than not, assist people they find in distress.

Though considered a western adventure, "Maverick" is actually a spoof of westerns, wherein the less-than-honorable intentions of the Mavericks are meant to satirize the square Western Code and the square-headed lawmen.

CAST
Bret Maverick	James Garner
Bart Maverick	Jack Kelly
Beau Maverick, their British cousin	Roger Moore
Samantha Crawford, a friend, a con-artist	Diane Brewster
Dandy Jim Buckley, a con artist friend	Efrem Zimbalist, Jr.
Beauregard "Pappy" Maverick, their father	James Garner
Gentleman Jack Darby	Richard Long

Music: David Buttolph.

MAVERICK—60 minutes—ABC—September 22, 1957 - July 8, 1962. Syndicated. 124 episodes.

MAX LIEBMAN PRESENTS

Variety. A series of lavish monthly specials.

Regulars: Gale Sherwood, Bambi Linn, Rod Alexander, David Atkinson, The Bil and Cora Baird Marionettes.

Orchestra: Charles Sanford.

Producer: Max Liebman, Bill Hobin.

Sponsor: Oldsmobile.

Included:

Satins and Spurs. A romantic comedy about a rodeo queen who falls in love with a magazine reporter.

CAST
Cindy: Betty Hutton; Tex: Guy Raymond; Dirk: John Wheeler; Tony: Kevin McCarthy; Ursula: Neva Patterson.

A Connecticut Yankee. The story of a modern day groom-to-be who is sent back in time to the days of King Arthur. Based on the Rodgers and Hart musical.

CAST
Martin Barrett: Eddie Albert; Sandy: Janet Blair; King Arthur: Boris Karloff; Sir Kay: John Conte.

Heidi. A musical adaptation of Johanna Spyri's classic story about a lovable Swiss orphan named Heidi.

CAST
Heidi: Jeannie Carson; Peter: Wally Cox; Grandfather: Richard Eastham; Frau Rottenmeier: Elsa Lanchester; Karla Sesseman: Natalie Wood.

MAX LIEBMAN PRESENTS—90 minutes—NBC. September 12, 1954 - June 4, 1955 (11 shows); October 1, 1955 - June 9, 1956 (11 shows).

MAYA

Adventure. Background: India. Terry Bowen, an American boy from Montana, arrives in Bombay to join his father, great white hunter Hugh Bowen. At the American Counsel, he discovers that his father is missing and is believed to have been killed by the man eating tiger of Karkata while on a safari. Believing that no animal can kill his father, he escapes from the local authorities who want to send him back to America, and begins a search to find him.

Journeying to Karkata, he meets Raji, an Indian boy who was left alone in the world when a flood destroyed his village, and his pet elephant, Maya. When it was claimed that Maya did not legally belong to Raji, and that she was to be shipped to the desert for a lifetime of labor, he and Maya ran away, and now, a fugitive, he is wanted by police for stealing the elephant.

Fourteen and homeless, the two boys join forces: Raji to help Terry find his father; and Terry to help Raji return Maya to the land of her birth and freedom.

Resourceful and determined, the two boys struggle to maintain their independence and complete their self imposed missions.

CAST

Terry Bowen	Jay North
Raji	Sajid Khan

Narrator: Marvin Miller.

Music: Hans Salter.

MAYA—60 minutes—NBC—September 16, 1967 - February 11, 1968. 18 episodcs.

MAYBERRY R.F.D.

Comedy. Background: Mayberry, North Carolina. The simple pleasures and trying times of Sam Jones, a full-time farmer and a part-time city councilman. A spin-off from "The Andy Griffith Show."

CAST

Sam Jones, a

widower	Ken Berry
Mike Jones, his son	Buddy Foster
Millie Swanson, Sam's romantic interest	Arlene Golonka
Goober Pyle, the gas-station attendant	George Lindsey
Bee Taylor, Sam's housekeeper	Frances Bavier
Howard Sprague, the county clerk	Jack Dodson
Emmet Clark, the fix-it-shop owner	Paul Hartman
Ralph, Mike's friend	Richard Steele
Aunt Alice, Sam's housekeeper (later episodes)	Alice Ghostley
Arnold, Mike's friend	Sheldon Collins
Martha Clark, Emmet's wife	Mary Lansing

Music: Earle Hagen.

Executive Producer: Andy Griffith, Richard O. Linke.

Producer: Bob Ross.

MAYBERRY R.F.D.—30 minutes—CBS—September 23, 1968 - September 6, 1971. 78 episodes. Syndicated.

MAYOR OF HOLLYWOOD

Variety. Interviews with and performances by celebrity guests.

Host: Walter O'Keefe.

Announcer: Lou Crosby.

Orchestra: Irvine Orton.

MAYOR OF HOLLYWOOD—30 minutes—NBC—July 9, 1952 - September 18, 1952.

MAYOR OF THE TOWN

Comedy. Background: The town of Springdale. The home and working life of Thomas Russell, the first citizen, now mayor.

CAST

Mayor Thomas Russell	Thomas Mitchell
Minnie, his secretary	Jean Byron
Butch Russell, his nephew	David Saber
Marilly, his house-keeper	Kathleen Freeman
Joe Ainsley, his nemesis	Tudor Owen
Also	Eve Miller

Music: Albert Glasser.

MAYOR OF THE TOWN—30 minutes—Syndicated 1954. 39 episodes.

ME AND THE CHIMP

Comedy. Background: San Pascal, California. Escaping from an Air Force research center, a chimpanzee takes refuge in a drainpipe near a playground, where he is found by two children, Scott and Kitty Reynolds.

Bringing the chimp home, the children encounter the objections of their father, Dr. Mike Reynolds, a dentist who feels that the chimp (named Buttons after his continual habit of pressing buttons) dislikes him. Demanding that Buttons must go, Mike is approached by his wife, Liz, who persuades him to devote time to Buttons—to get to know and love him as she and the children do.

Stories concern Mike's struggles to adjust to the prospect of having a chimpanzee around the house.

CAST

Mike Reynolds	Ted Bessell
Liz Reynolds	Anita Gillette
Kitty Reynolds	Kami Cotler
Scott Reynolds	Scott Kolden
Buttons	Jackie

ME AND THE CHIMP—30 minutes—CBS—January 13, 1972 - May 18, 1972. 13 episodes.

MEDALLION THEATRE

A series of thirty-minute anthology dramas first broadcast by CBS in 1953.

Producer: Leonard Valenta, Mort Abrams.

MEDIC

Medical Dramatizations. Authentic and sophisticated approaches to medical problems and practices. Filmed at various Los Angeles hospitals. Varying casts and stories.

Host-Narrator: Richard Boone, appearing as Dr. Konrad Styner.

Theme: Blue Star.

Music: Victor Young.

Executive Producer: Worthington Miner.

Producer: Frank LaTourette.

Director: Ted Post, George Cahan.

Creator: James Mosher.

Program Open:

Dr. Styner: "My name is Konrad Styner. I'm a doctor of medicine. Tonight's story has the title [name of episode]. Guardian of birth, healer of the sick, comforter of the aged. To the profession of medicine, to the men and women who labor in its cause, this story is dedicated."

Included:

Someday We'll Laugh. The trials and tribulations of a general practitioner.

CAST

Eddie Firestone, Whitney Blake, Jack Tesler.

To The Great A Most Seldom Gift. The story of a successful businessman who struggles to hide the fact of an ulcer.

CAST

Harry Townes, June Vincent, Pat Knudson.

The Good Samaritan. When a woman is injured in an automobile accident and suffers partial paralysis, her husband believes it is Dr. Styner's fault and brings a malpractice suit against him. The story depicts the hospital board hearing.

CAST

Richard Boone, Helen Mack, Paul Newland, Andrew Duggan.

MEDIC–30 minutes–NBC–September 13, 1954 - August 27, 1956. Syndicated. 59 episodes.

MEDICAL CENTER

Medical Drama. Background: The University Medical Center in Los Angeles, California. The story of two doctors: Paul Lochner, the administrative surgeon, the wiser and older, established in his ways; and Joe Gannon, the professor of surgery, the younger, gifted, and progressive. Adult and technically accurate, episodes depict the problems that face doctors in a large city hospital.

CAST

Dr. Paul Lochner	James Daly
Dr. Joe Gannon	Chad Everett
Nurse Chambers	Jayne Meadows
Dr. Bartlett	Corinne Comacho
Nurse Holmby	Barbara Baldavin
Nurse Courtland	Chris Huston
Nurse Higby	Catherine Ferrar
Nurse Murphy	Jane Dulo
Nurse Wilcox	Audrey Totter

Music: George Romanis; Lalo Schifrin; John Parker.

MEDICAL CENTER–60 minutes– CBS–September 24, 1969 - September 6, 1976. Syndicated. 144 episodes.

MEDICAL STORY

Anthology. Dramatizations stressing an open, human approach to the problems of medicine as seen through the eyes of the doctor rather than the patient.

Creators: David Gerber, Abby Mann.

Music: Richard Shores; Jerry Goldsmith.

Executive Producer: David Gerber, Abby Mann.

Producer: Christopher Morgan.

Director: Paul Wendkos, Garry Nelson.

Included:

Million Dollar Baby. The story of Alma Geary, a blind woman who brings a malpractice suit against the doctor who delivered her prematurely twenty-two years before, claiming that his improper use of pure oxygen caused her loss of sight.

CAST

Dr. Amos Winkler: John Forsythe; Liz Winkler: Geraldine Brooks; Alma

Geary: Catherine Burns.

Us Against the World. The story focuses on the problems faced by three female surgeons in a busy hospital.

CAST

Sunny: Meredith Baxter Birney; Audrey: Donna Mills; Hope: Christine Belford; Kim: Linda Purl.

MEDICAL STORY—60 minutes—NBC—Premiered: September 4, 1975.

MEET BETTY FURNESS

Women. Guests, interviews, and topics of special interest to housewives.

Hostess: Betty Furness.

Regulars: Don Cherry, Hank Ford, Bill Stern, David Ross.

Music: The Buddy Weed Trio.

MEET BETTY FURNESS—15 minutes—NBC 1953.

MEET CORLISS ARCHER

Comedy. The misadventures of Corliss Archer, a pretty, unpredictable teenage girl. Based on the radio program of the same title.

Versions:

Meet Corliss Archer—30 minutes—CBS—1951 - 1952 (Live.)

CAST

Corliss Archer	Lugene Sanders
Harry Archer, her father, an insurance salesman	Fred Sheldon
Janet Archer, his wife	Frieda Inescort
Dexter Franklin, Corliss's boyfriend	Bobby Ellis

Announcer: John Heistand.

Producer: Helen Mack.

Director: Alan Dinehard.

Meet Corliss Archer—30 minutes—CBS—1954 - 1955. (Filmed.)

CAST

Corliss Archer	Ann Baker
Harry Archer	John Eldridge
Janet Archer	Mary Bain
Dexter Franklin	Bobby Ellis

Music: Felix Mills.

Narrator-Producer: Hy Averback.

MEETING OF THE MINDS

See title: "Steve Allen."

MEET McGRAW

Crime Drama. The investigations of McGraw, a roving private detective, "a professional busy-body who wanders from state to state minding other people's business."

Starring: Frank Lovejoy as McGraw (unidentified by a first name).

MEET McGRAW—30 minutes—NBC—July 2, 1957 - June 24, 1958; ABC—November 23, 1958 - October 9, 1959. Syndicated.

MEET ME AT THE ZOO

Educational. Background: The Philadelphia Zoo. Curators discuss and relate aspects of various exhibits.

Host: Freeman Shelly.

MEET ME AT THE ZOO—30 minutes—CBS 1953.

MEET MILLIE

Comedy. Background: New York City. The trials and tribulations of Millie Bronson, a secretary who is secretly in love with her employer's son, Johnny Boone. Stories depict her mother's attempts to spark a romance between the two.

CAST

Millie Bronson	Elena Verdugo
Mrs. Bronson, her mother, a widow	Florence Halop
Johnny Boone	Ross Ford
Alfred Prinzmetal, a friend	Marvin Kaplan
J.R. Boone Sr., her employer	Earl Ross

Meet Millie. Florence Halop and Elena Verdugo.

Mrs. Boone, his wife	Isabel Randloph
Mr. Weems, a friend, the owner of a ranch in Texas	Harry Cheshire

Announcer: Bob Lemond.

Music: Irving Miller.

Producer: Frank Galen.

MEET MILLIE—30 minutes—CBS—October 25, 1952 - February 28, 1956.

MEET MR. McNUTLEY

See title: "The Ray Milland Show."

MEET THE PRESS

In-depth News Interview.

Hosts: Martha Rountree, Ned Brooks, Lawrence E. Spivak.

Press Representatives: Four guests.

MEET THE PRESS—30 minutes—NBC—Premiered: November 20, 1947.

MEET YOUR COVER GIRL

Interview. Fashion models appear and discuss various aspects of their careers, including background and home life.

Hostess: Robin Chandler.
Producer: Stanley Poss.
Director: Herbert Sussan.

MEET YOUR COVER GIRL—30 minutes—CBS 1949.

MEET YOUR MATCH

Game. One preselected contestant

chooses one person from the studio audience as his opponent. A general-knowledge question-and-answer session is conducted wherein each correct response awards cash. If one player fails to correctly answer a question, he is defeated, and the opponent, the winner, receives the money he has accumulated and the privilege to choose another player with whom to match wits.

Host: Jan Murray.

MEET YOUR MATCH—30 minutes—NBC—August 25, 1952 - September 1, 1952.

THE MELBA MOORE-CLIFTON DAVIS SHOW

Variety. Music, song, dance, and comedy set against the background of a Manhattan brownstone.

Hosts: Melba Moore, Clifton Davis.

Regulars: Ron Carey, Timmie Rogers, Dick Libertini, Liz Torres.

Announcer: Johnny Olsen.

Orchestra: Charles H. Coleman.

THE MELBA MOORE-CLIFTON DAVIS SHOW—60 minutes—CBS—June 7, 1972 - July 5, 1972.

MELODY, HARMONY, RHYTHM

Musical Variety.

Host: Lynne Barrett.

Dancers: Dula & Lorenski.

Music: The Tony DiSimone Trio.

MELODY, HARMONY, RHYTHM—30 minutes—NBC 1948. CBS—15 minutes—1950.

MELODY STREET

Musical Variety. An informal stroll down Tin Pan Alley.

Host: Elliott Lawrence.

Music: The Tony Mottola Trio.

MELODY STREET—30 minutes—DuMont—1953 - 1954.

MELODY TOUR

Musical Variety. Staged tours of the world via music.

Host: Stan Freeman.

Regulars: Norman Scott, Nancy Kenyon, Jane Remes, Peter Gladhe, Nellie Fisher, Robert Rounsville, Jonathan Lucas.

Orchestra: Harry Sosnick.

MELODY TOUR—30 minutes—ABC —July 8, 1954 - September 30, 1954.

THE MEL TORMÉ SHOW

Musical Variety.

Host: Mel Tormé, "The Velvet Fog."

Regulars: Peggy King, Ellen Martin, Kaye Ballard, The Mello-Larks.

Music: The Red Norvo Trio; The Terry Gibbs Quintet.

Producer: Bob Bach.

Director: Lloyd Gross.

THE MEL TORMÉ SHOW—30 minutes—CBS—1951 - 1952.

THE MEMORY GAME

Game. Five competing female contestants, each of whom begin with fifty dollars. Each is presented with a packet of five questions and given twenty-five seconds to study them. At the end of the time, the questions are taken back and the host asks one player a question. If she cannot answer it, she is permitted to pass it to any other player by calling her number (1,2,3,4, or 5). The player who correctly answers the question receives five dollars; if a player cannot correctly answer it, five dollars is deducted. The player last to correctly answer a question becomes the player to receive the next question.

Round Two: Questions are marked by a one- to ten-second time limit. The game follows in the same manner, but if a player is caught by a buzzer when asked or passing a question, she has to answer it. Question values and deductions are ten dollars.

Final Round: Involves the champion, the highest scoring player. After she wages any amount of her accumulated earnings, the host asks her one question. If she correctly answers it, she receives the wagered amount; if she is unable, the amount is deducted.

Host: Joe Garagiola.

Announcer: Johnny Olsen.

THE MEMORY GAME—30 minutes—NBC—February 15, 1971 - July 30, 1971.

THE MEN

Mystery-Adventure. The overall title for three rotating series: "Assignment: Vienna," "The Delphi Bureau," and "Jigsaw."

Assignment: Vienna. Background: Vienna, Austria. The cases of Jake Webster, a United States government undercover agent who poses as the bartender-owner of Jake's Bar and Grill.

CAST

Jake Webster	Robert Conrad
Major Bernard Caldwell, his contact	Charles Cioffi
Inspector Hoffman	Anton Diffring

Music: Dave Grusin; John Parker.

The Delphi Bureau. Background: Washington, D.C. The Delphi Bureau is a top-secret intelligence agency responsible only to the President of the United States. Offices and staff are nonexistent and its purpose is to protect national security. Glenn Garth Gregory, a research specialist with a photographic memory, is its chief operative; and Sybil Van Loween, a beautiful but mysterious Washington society hostess, is his contact. Stories depict Gregory's investigations.

CAST

Glenn Garth Gregory	Laurence Luckinbill
Sybil Van Loween	Celeste Holm Anne Jeffreys

Music: Frank DeVol; Harper McKay.

Jigsaw. Background: The State Missing Persons Bureau in Sacramento, California. The investigations of Lieutenant Detective Frank Dain, its one-man operative who possesses a genius for solving complicated, clueless mysteries.

Starring: James Wainwright as Lt. Frank Dain.

Music: Harper McKay.

THE MEN—60 minutes—ABC—September 21, 1972 - September 1, 1973. 24 episodes.

MEN AT LAW

Crime Drama. Background: The Neighborhood Legal Services offices in Century City, downtown Los Angeles, California. The cases of David Hansen, Deborah Sullivan, and Gabriel Kay, lawyers who defend indigent clients. Emphasis is placed on courtroom proceedings. A spin-off from "The Storefront Lawyers."

CAST

David Hansen — Robert Foxworth
Deborah Sullivan — Sheila Larken
Gabriel Kay — David Arken
Attorney Devlin
  McNeil — Gerald S. O'Loughlin
Kathy, their
  secretary — Nancy Jeris

MEN AT LAW—60 minutes—CBS—January 20, 1971 - September 1, 1971. 13 episodes.

MEN IN CRISES

Documentary. Films recalling the vital decisions of men whose leadership has shaped twentieth-century history.

Narrator: Edmond O'Brien.

MEN IN CRISES—30 minutes—Syndicated 1954. 32 episodes.

THE MEN FROM SHILOH

See title: "The Virginian."

MEN INTO SPACE

Adventure. The story of the U.S. government's attempts to further its space program.

CAST

Col. Edward
  McCauley — William Lundigan
Mary McCauley, his
  wife — Joyce Taylor
Lt. Johnny Baker — Corey Allen
Capt. Harvey Sparkman — Kem Dibbs
Music: David Rose.

MEN INTO SPACE—30 minutes—CBS—September 30, 1959 - September 7, 1960. 38 episodes. Syndicated.

MEN OF ANNAPOLIS

Anthology. Dramatizations based on incidents in the training of men attending Annapolis, the U.S. Naval Academy. Filmed with the technical assistance of the U.S. Naval Academy and the Department of Defense. The midshipmen of Annapolis perform in all stories.

Included:

The Crucial Moment. Constantly rejected by the Navy football team, Paul Towner is suddenly given a chance when the coach sees him play. The story depicts his attempts to prove his worthiness in an important game.

Starring: Jack Diamond, Robert J. Stevenson, Mason Alan Dinehart, Keith Vincent.

Sink Or Swim. A sensitive nineteen-year-old midshipman decides to assert himself against his father's domination and try out for the Academy's water-polo team.

Starring: Mark Damon.

The Blue And Grey. Shortly before the Army-Navy football game, three midshipman conspire to perform a long-coveted feat.

Starring: Darryl Hickman.

MEN OF ANNAPOLIS–30 minutes–
Syndicated 1957. 39 episodes.

MENSHA THE MAGNIFICENT

Comedy. The misadventures of
Mensha Shrunk, the manager of a
decrepit restaurant.

CAST
Mensha Shrunk	Himself
His employer, the owner of the restaurant	Jean Cleveland
Also	Vinton Hayworth
	Danny Leane

Producer: Martin Goodman.

Director: Alan Newman.

MENSHA THE MAGNIFICENT–30
minutes–NBC 1950.

THE MEREDITH WILSON SHOW

Musical Variety.

Host: Meredith Wilson.

Orchestra: Meredith Wilson.

THE MEREDITH WILSON SHOW–
30 minutes–NBC–July 31, 1949 -
September 1949.

MESSING PRIZE PARTY

A game show, hosted by Bill Slater,
and featuring couples performing
stunts for prizes.

30 minutes–CBS 1949.

MERV GRIFFIN

Listed: The television programs of
singer-actor Merv Griffin.

**Song Snapshots On A Summer Holi-
day**–Musical Variety–15 minutes–
CBS 1954.

Host: Merv Griffin.

Hostess: Betty Ann Grove.

Featured: The Peter Birch Dancers.

Orchestra: Unidentified.

Play Your Hunch–Game–NBC–
1958. (See title.)

Keep Talking–Game–ABC–1959.
(See title.)

The Merv Griffin Show–Talk/Variety
–55 minutes (Daily)–NBC–
1962-1963.

Host: Merv Griffin.

Orchestra: Under direction of guest
   leaders.

NBC–October 1, 1962 - March 29,
1963.

Word For Word–Game–NBC–1963.
(See title.)

Hollywood Talent Scouts–Variety–
CBS–1963. (See title.)

The Merv Griffin Show–Talk/Variety
–90 minutes–Syndicated 1965.

Host: Merv Griffin.

Announcer: Arthur Treacher.

Orchestra: Mort Lindsey.

The Merv Griffin Show–Talk/Variety
(11:30 p.m.–1:00 a.m., EST)–CBS–
August 18, 1969 - February 11, 1972.

Host: Merv Griffin.

Announcer: Arthur Treacher.

Orchestra: Mort Lindsey.

The Merv Griffin Show—Talk/Variety—90 minutes—Syndicated 1972.

Host: Merv Griffin.

Orchestra: Mort Lindsey.

M—G—M PARADE

Documentary. Metro—Goldwyn—Mayer's first television venture. A behind-the-scenes look at Hollywood, its past and present (1955). Features: Tours, interviews and guests from the M—G—M Culver City lot sound stages, and film sequences highlighting various Metro features.

Host: George Murphy.

Co-Host: Pete Smith.

Premiere guest: Dore Schary, the studio head.

M—G—M PARADE—30 minutes—ABC—September 14, 1955 - May 2, 1956.

MIAMI UNDERCOVER

Crime Drama. Background: Miami Beach, Florida. Posing as a sophisticated man-about-town, Jeff Thompson, a troubleshooter hired by the Miami Hotel Owners Association, attempts to eliminate the sources of trouble that invade Florida.

CAST
Jeff Thompson   Lee Bowman
Rocky, his partner   Rocky Graziano

MIAMI UNDERCOVER—30 minutes—Syndicated 1961. 38 episodes.

MICHAEL SHAYNE, PRIVATE DETECTIVE

Crime Drama. Background: Miami Beach, Florida. The investigations of private detective Michael Shayne. Based on the character created by Brett Halliday.

CAST
Michael Shayne   Richard Denning
Lucy Hamilton, his
  secretary   Patricia Donahue
                       Margie Regan
Tim Rourke,
  a photographer-re-
  porter   Jerry Paris
Lieutenant Gentry,
  Florida Sheriff's
  Office   Herbert Rudley
Dick Hamilton, Lucy's
  kid brother   Gary Clark
Joe Demarest   Meade Martin
Richard Banke-McCord   Will Gentry

Music: Leslie Stevens.

MICHAEL SHAYNE, PRIVATE DETECTIVE—60 minutes—NBC—September 1960 - September 1961. Syndicated. 32 episodes.

THE MICHAELS IN AFRICA

Documentary. Various aspects of the people and animals of South Africa.

Hosts—Narrators: George and Marjorie Michaels (Mr. & Mrs.).

THE MICHAELS IN AFRICA—30 minutes—Syndicated 1958.

MICKEY

Comedy. Background: The Newport Arms Hotel in Newport Beach, California. The trials and tribulations of its owner-operators, the Gradys: Mickey, a retired businessman; his wife, Nora; and their children, Timmy and Buddy.

CAST

Mickey Grady	Mickey Rooney
Nora Grady	Emmaline Henry
Timmy Grady	Timmy Rooney
Buddy Grady	Brian Nash
Sammy Ling, the hotel's Chinese manager	Sammee Tong

MICKEY—30 minutes—ABC—September 16, 1964 - January 13, 1965. 17 episodes.

THE MICKEY MOUSE CLUB

Children. Background: The Mickey Mouse Club House. Music, songs dances, cartoons, guests, news features, and adventure serials.

Host: Jimmie Dodd.

The Mickey Mouse Club. The Mouseketeers. © *Walt Disney Productions.*

Co-Host: Roy Williams ("The Big Mooseketeer").

Assistant: Bob Amsberry.

The Mouseketeers: Annette Funicello, Darlene Gillespie, Carl "Cubby" O'Brien, Karen Pendleton, Bobby Burgess, Tommy Cole, Cheryl Holdridge, Lynn Ready, Doreen Tracy, Linda Hughes, Lonnie Burr, Bonni Lynn Fields, Sharon Baird, Ronnie Young, Jay Jay Solari, Margene Storey, Nancy Abbate, Billie Jean Beanblossom, Mary Espinosa, Bonnie Lou Kern, Mary Lou Sartori, Bronson Scott, Dennis Day, Dickie Dodd, Michael Smith, Ronald Steiner, Mark Sutherland, Don Underhill, Sherry Allen, Paul Peterson, Judy Harriett, John Lee Johnson, Eileen Diamond, Charley Laney, Larry Larsen, Don Agrati (a.k.a. Don Grady).

Professor Wonderful: Julius Sumner Miller.

Music: The Disneyland Band, Joseph Dubin, Buddy Baker, William Lava, Joseph Mullendore, Franklin Marks.

Voice of the Animated Jiminy Cricket: Cliff Edwards.

Voice of Mickey Mouse: Jim Macdonald (for the TV series; Walt Disney's voice is heard as Mickey prior to 1949).

Narrator of the Mickey Mouse Newsreel: Hal Gibney.

Special News Correspondent: Dick Metzzi.

Director of the Mouseketeers: Sid Miller, Clyde Geronimi.

Executive Producer: Walt Disney.

Producer: Bill Walsh, Dick Darley.

Director: Jonathan Lucas, William Beaudine, Charles Haas, Lee

Clark.

Choreography: Tom Mahoney.

Serials:

Adventures In Dairyland. Background: The McCandless Sunny Acres Dairy Farm in Wisconsin. Its operation as seen through the eyes of guests Annette Funicello and Sammy Ogg. Their efforts are complicated by Moochie, the McCandlesses' mischievous young son.

CAST

Annette Funicello: Herself; Sammy Ogg: Himself; Moochie McCandless: Kevin Corcoran; Mr. McCandless: Herb Newcombe; Mrs. McCandless: Mary Lu Delmonte; Jimmy McCandless, their son: Glen Garber; Pauli, the ranch hand: Fern Parsons.

The Adventures of Clint and Mac. Background: London, England. The story of two boys, Clint Rogers, an American, and his friend, Alastair "Mac" MacIntosh, as they attempt to solve a crime—the theft of the original manuscript of *Treasure Island.*

CAST:

Clint Rogers: Neil Wolfe; Alastair MacIntosh: Jonathan Bailey; Inspector MacIntosh, Mac's father: John Warwick; Mac's mother: Dorothy Smith; Clinton Rogers, Clint's father: Bill Nagy; Clint's mother: Mary Barclay; Pamela Stuart, Clint and Mac's friend: Sandra Michaels; John Stuart, Pam's father: Gordon Harris; Toby Jug, the criminal: George Woodbridge.

Annette. Background: The town of Ashford. The story of Annette McCleod, a country girl who comes to live with her relatives in the big city. The serial focuses on her attempts to adjust to a life she finds new and confusing and her efforts to win the

The Mickey Mouse Club. *Adventures in Dairyland.* Kevin Corcoran. © *Walt Disney Productions.*

The Mickey Mouse Club. *Annette.* Left to right: Sylvia Fields, Annette Funicello, Richard Deacon. © *Walt Disney Productions.*

friendship of Laura Rogan, a girl who takes an instant dislike to her.

CAST

Annette McCleod: Annette Funicello; Dr. Archie McCleod, her uncle: Richard Deacon; Lila McCleod, Archie's sister: Sylvia Fields; Katie, their housekeeper: Mary Wickes; Laura Rogan: Jymme Shore; Stephen Abernathy, Annette's friend: Tim Considine; Annette's friends: Val Abernathy: Doreen Tracy; Mike Martin: David Stollery; Jet Maypen: Judy Nugent; Moselle Corey: Shelley Fabares; Olmstead Ware: Ruby Lee; Kitty: Sharon Baird; Madge: Cheryl Holdridge.

Border Collie. Background: Hamilton County in Southern Illinois. The story of Rod Brown, a young boy and his attempts to train a Scottish Border Collie named Scamp for competition in a local dog show.

Starring: Bobby Evans as Rod Brown.

Also: Arthur Allen.

Narrator: Alvy Moore.

The Boys of the Western Sea. Background: Russia. The story of a teenage boy named Paul and his struggles to support his brother and sister, as a fisherman, after his father's untimely death. Filmed in Russia; dubbed in English. Credits are not given.

Corky and White Shadow. Background: The small Midwestern town of Beaumont. Assisted by her German Shepherd dog, White Shadow, a young girl, Corky Brady, attempts to capture the Durango Dude, an outlaw sought by her father, Sheriff Matt Brady.

CAST

Corky Brady: Darlene Gillespie; Matt Brady: Buddy Ebsen; Uncle Dan:

The Mickey Mouse Club. *Corky and White Shadow.* Darlene Gillespie and her dog Chinook. © *Walt Disney Productions.*

Lloyd Corrigan; White Shadow: Chinook.

The Hardy Boys and the Mystery of the Applegate Treasure. Background: The town of Bayport. Amateur detectives, brothers Joe and Frank Hardy, attempt to solve the baffling theft of pirate treasure from the estate of Silas Applegate.

CAST

Joe Hardy: Tim Considine; Frank Hardy: Tommy Kirk; Iola Morton, Joe's girlfriend: Carole Ann Campbell; Fenton Hardy, the boys' father: Russ Conway; Gertrude Hardy, Fenton's sister: Sarah Selby; Silas Applegate: Florenz Ames.

The Hardy Boys and the Mystery of Ghost Farm. Amateur sleuths Joe and Frank Hardy attempt to solve the baffling mystery of a farm supposedly haunted by a ghost. Cast listing is exactly the same as the above "Hardy Boys" mystery (which see).

The Mickey Mouse Club. *The Hardy Boys and the Mystery of Ghost Farm.* Left to right: Tim Considine, and Tommy Kirk. © *Walt Disney Productions.*

Moochie of the Little League. Background: The Town of Winston. The comic escapades of Montgomery "Moochie" Morgan, Jr., as he struggles to succeed as a Little Leaguer with the Bobcats baseball team.

CAST
Moochie: Kevin Corcoran; Montgomery Morgan, Sr., Moochie's father: Russ Conway; Louise Morgan, Moochie's mother: Frances Rafferty; Marion Morgan, Moochie's sister: Dorothy Green; Bee Bee Preston, Moochie's friend: Annette Gorman; Fred Preston, Bee Bee's father: Alan Hale, Jr.; Andy Clinton, the manager: James L. Brown; Lou Rosen, the team owner: Stu Erwin; Cecil Bennett, a friend: Reginald Owen.

Moochie of Pop Warner Football. Sequel to the above serial. Moochie's experiences—and misadventures—as a member of the Pop Warner Football team, Pee Wee division. Cast is exactly the same as the above "Moochie" serial with the addition of Dennis Joel as Moochie's friend.

The Secret of Mystery Lake. Background: Real Foot Lake in Tennessee. The story concerns naturalist Bill Richards as he attempts to uncover the wonders of Nature as it abounds in and around the lake.

CAST
Bill Richards: George Fenneman; Lanie Thorne, his pretty guide: Gloria Marshall.

Spin and Marty. Background: The Triple R Ranch in North Fork, a Summer boys camp. The experiences of two boys, Spin Evans and Marty Markham. The story itself concerns their efforts to train for competition in a local rodeo.

CAST
Spin Evans: Tim Considine; Marty Markham: David Stollery; Jim Logan, the ranch head: Roy Barcroft; Bill Burnett, the counselor: Harry Carey, Jr.; Perkins, Marty's guardian: J. Pat O'Malley; Sam, the cook: Sammee Tong. Campers: Ambitious: B.G. Norman; Joe: Sammy Ogg; George: Joe Wong; Speckle: Tim Hartnagel.

The Further Adventures of Spin and Marty. Continued events in the lives of Spin Evans and Marty Markham. The story concerns itself with the rivalry that ensues between Spin and Marty for the affections of Annette, a pretty young lady attending the Circle H Girls Camp.

CAST
Exactly the same as in "Spin and Marty" with these additions: Annette:

The Mickey Mouse Club. *The New Adventures of Spin and Marty.* Darlene Gillespie and Annette Funicello. © *Walt Disney Productions.*

Annette Funicello; Ollie, the wrangler: Dennis Moore; Moochie O'Hara, a camper: Kevin Corcoran.

The New Adventures of Spin and Marty. The story concerns Spin and Marty's attempts to stage a variety show to pay for damages caused by Marty's jalopy when it ran into the ranch house.

CAST
Exactly the same as in "Spin and Marty" with these additions: Annette: Annette Funicello; Darlene, Annette's friend: Darlene Gillespie; Moochie, a camper: Kevin Corcoran; Hank, the wrangler: Dennis Moore.

What I Want To Be. Background: Kansas City, Missouri. The training and study periods of two young hopefuls: Patricia Morrow, airline stewardess; and Duncan Richardson, pilot.

Starring: Patricia Morrow, Duncan Richardson, and, as the reporter: Alvy Moore.

THE MICKEY MOUSE CLUB—60 and 30 minute versions—ABC—October 3, 1955 - September 25, 1959. Syndicated. See also: "The New Mickey Mouse Club."

THE MICKEY ROONEY SHOW

See title: "Hey, Mulligan."

MICKEY ROONEY'S SMALL WORLD

Discussion. Eight children, aged four to eight, who vary from program to program, appear and are first questioned about themselves, then ask questions and discuss various matters with a guest celebrity.

Host: Mickey Rooney.

Music: Recorded open and close (theme: "It's A Small World").

Executive Producer: Mickey Rooney.

MICKEY ROONEY'S SMALL WORLD—30 minutes—Syndicated 1975.

MICKIE FINN'S

Musical Variety. Background: The Mickie Finn Nightclub, "America's number one speakeasy," in San Diego, California. The music, song, and dance of yesteryear—from the Gay Nineties to the Sensational Sixties.

Host: Fred Finn.

Hostess: Mickie Finn (Mrs.)

Regulars: Alex, the headwaiter; Hoot, the doorman; The Mickie Finn Waitresses.

Mickie Finn's. Fred Finn and Mickie Finn.

Vocals: Mickie Finn and guests.

Choreographer: Alex Plasschaert.

Music: The Mickie Finn Band. Comprising: Fred Finn (piano); Mickie Finn (banjo); Spider Marillo (drums); Bobby Jensen (trumpet); Story Gormley (tuba); Owen Leinhard (trombone); Don Van Paulta, the Flying Dutchman (banjo).

MICKIE FINN'S—30 minutes—NBC—April 21, 1966 - September 1, 1966.

THE MIDNIGHT SPECIAL

Variety. Performances by Rock, Pop, and Soul personalities.

Hosting: Weekly guests.

Premiere Hostess: Helen Reddy.

Announcer: Wolfman Jack.

Music: Provided by guests.

Premiere Guests: Curtis Mayfield, Don McLean, Rare Earth, Sam Neely, Ike and Tina Turner. The Byrds, The Impressions.

THE MIDNIGHT SPECIAL—90 minutes—NBC (1:00 a.m. - 2:30 a.m., EST)—Premiered: February 2, 1973.

MIDWESTERN HAYRIDE

Musical Variety. Performances by Country and Western personalities.

Hosts: Paul Dixon, Dean Richards, Willie Thall, Bill Thall.

Regulars: Phyllis Brown, Bonnie Lou, Helen Scott, Billy Scott, Paul Arnold, Mary Jane Johnson, Clay Eager, Phyllis Holmes, Bill Holmes, Freddy Langdon, Tommy Watson, Zeeke Turner, Wally Praetor, Martha Hendricks, Barney Sefton, Jim Philpot, Ernie Lee, Judy Perkins, Kenny Roberts, Bob Shredi, The Pleasant Valley Boys, The Country Briar Hoppers, The Hometowners, The Kentucky Boys, The Midwesterners, The Lucky Pennies, The Trail Blazers, The Girls Of The Golden West, The Brown Ferry Four.

Announcer: Hal Woodward.

Music: The Pleasant Valley Rangers.

MIDWESTERN HAYRIDE—30 and 60 minutes versions—Syndicated—1947-1967. Also appeared on ABC: June 29, 1957 - September 22, 1958.

THE MIGHTY HERCULES

Animated Cartoon. Background: The Learien Valley in Ancient Greece. The exploits of Hercules, the legendary hero of mythology.

Characters:
Hercules. Positioned on Mount Olymus, he receives his power by exposing his magic ring to lightning
Wilamene, the evil sea witch
Deadalius, the villainous wizard
Helena, the beautiful maiden
Newton, half human and half horse, a friend of Hercules
Tweet, half human and half horse, a friend of Hercules

THE MIGHTY HERCULES—05 minutes—Syndicated 1960. 130 episodes.

THE MIGHTY HEROES

An animated cartoon that details the exploits of Diaper Man, a daring avenger who, working out of a crib and with the aide of an incredible baby bottle, battles evil. 26 eight minute films; Syndicated 1966.

THE MIGHTY MOUSE PLAYHOUSE

Animated Cartoon. The exploits of Mighty Mouse, the courageous and daring defender of the weak and oppressed.

Voice of Mighty Mouse: Tom Morrison.

Narrator: Tom Morrison.

Music: Philip Scheib.

Producer: Bill Weiss.

Director: Eddie Donnelly, Manning Davis, Connie Rosinski.

THE MIGHTY MOUSE PLAYHOUSE—30 minutes (four six minute segments)—CBS—December 10, 1955 - September 2, 1967. 150 episodes. Syndicated.

MIKE AND BUFF

Celebrity Interview.

Host: Mike Wallace.

Hostess: Buff Cobb (Mrs.)

MIKE AND BUFF—45 minutes—CBS 1951.

THE MIKE DOUGLAS SHOW

Discussion-Variety.

Host: Mike Douglas.

Music: The Ellie Frankel Quartet; The Joe Harnell Sextet; The Frank Hunter Band. The Joe Massimino Band.

THE MIKE DOUGLAS SHOW—90 minutes—Syndicated 1966.

MIKE HAMMER, DETECTIVE

Crime Drama. Background: New York City. The investigations of Mike Hammer, a suave, sophisticated, quick-tempered, and rugged private detective. Based on the character created by Mickey Spillane.

Starring: Darren McGavin as Mike Hammer.

Narrator: Darren McGavin.

Music: David Kahn, Melvyn Lenard.

MIKE HAMMER, DETECTIVE—30 minutes—NBC—1958 - 1959. Syndicated.

THE MIKE WALLACE INTERVIEW

Interview. Probing discussions on topical issues.

Host: Mike Wallace.

THE MIKE WALLACE INTERVIEW —30 minutes—Syndicated 1957. ABC run: April 28, 1957 - September 14, 1958.

THE MILLIONAIRE

Drama. Of the two billion four hundred million people populating the world in 1955, only nineteen of these were worth five hundred million dollars or more. One such man was John Beresford Tipton, manufacturer, bachelor, multibillionaire.

Residing at Silverstone, his sixty-thousand-acre estate, Tipton conducted his business activities and lived his life of treasured seclusion. Upon doctor's orders that he find a means of relaxation, he undertook a most unusual hobby.

Seated in the study, toying with one of his ivory chess figures, Tipton sends for his executive secretary and confidant, Michael Anthony.

Mike: "You sent for me sir?"

Tipton: "You know Mike, these chessmen were the first luxury I ever allowed myself. . . .I. . .decided to make my hobby a chess game with human beings."

Mike: "Human beings sir?"

Tipton: "I'm going to choose a number of people for my chessmen and give them each a million dollars. . . .The bank [Gotham City Trust and Savings] will issue the check. . . .No one is ever to know that I'm the donor. . . . I want a complete report on what happens to each person's life in writing. . . ."

After his death, the will instructed Michael Anthony to reveal the files of people, selected by a means known only to Tipton, who were mysteriously presented with a tax-free cashier's check for one million dollars. In flashback sequences, John Beresford Tipton's intrusion on fate is revealed as stories disclose whether the money helped or hindered lives.

CAST

Michael Anthony	Marvin Miller
John Beresford Tipton (never fully seen), voiced by	Paul Frees
Andrew V. McMahon, the president of the	

bank   Roy Gordon

Announcer: Ed Herlihy.

Music: Stanley Wilson; George Sharder.

Included:

The Susan Birchard Story. Receiving the check, a young woman attempts to recapture her past and returns to the home town of her youth to find the childhood sweetheart she never stopped loving.

CAST

Susan Birchard: Luana Patten; Tony Cassella: Brett Halsey; Susan as a girl: Reba Waters; Harvey: Leon Tyler; Nancy: Eve Brent.

The Peter Bartley Story. Separated from his two brothers many years ago after his parents were killed in an automobile accident, Peter Bartley, the recipient of the check, returns to the orphanage and begins a search to find them.

CAST

Peter Bartley: John Ericson; Sister Mary: Jeanette Nolan; Dora McKenna: Kay Elhardt; James Bartley: Roland Green; Peter as a boy: John Washbrook; James as a boy: Rene Karper; John as a boy: Mickey Morgan.

The Jerry Bell Story. Considering himeslf unattractive, writer Jerry Bell meets and falls in love with a blind girl named Myra. Suddenly wealthy, he arranges for her sight-restoring operation. Realizing that she may never love him after she sees him, he walks out on her. Returning to a favorite spot of theirs on the beach, he and Myra meet—and find their love unchanged.

CAST

Jerry Bell: Charles Bronson; Myra: Georgianna Johnson.

THE MILLIONAIRE—30 minutes—CBS—January 19, 1955 - September 1960. 188 episodes. Syndicated. Also known as "If You Had a Million."

MILTON BERLE

Listed: The television programs of comedian Milton Berle.

The Texaco Star Theatre—Variety (outlandish, slapstick comedy)—60 minutes—NBC—September 21, 1948 - June 9, 1953.

Host: Milton Berle, "Mr. Televison."

Regulars: Dolores Gray, Sid Stone (Milton's pitchman), Arnold Stang (as Francis, his stagehand), Bobby Clark, Ruth Gilbert (as Berle's secretary), Willie Field, the Merry Texaco Repairmen, The Balicana Ivanko Troupe, The Dunhills.

Commercial Spokesman: Jimmy Nelson, ventriloquist; his dummy: Danny O'Day.

Orchestra: Allen Roth.

The Milton Berle Show—Variety—60 minutes—NBC—September 29, 1953 - June 14, 1955.

Host: Milton Berle.

Regulars: Arnold Stang, Ruth Gilbert, Nancy Walker, Connie Russell, Charlie Applegate, Fred Clark, The Herb Rose Dancers.

Announcer: Jack Lescoulie.

Orchestra: Allen Roth.

The Milton Berle Show—Variety—60 minutes—NBC—September 27, 1955 -

June 5, 1956.

Format: Varying, tailored to the talents of guests.

Host: Milton Berle.

Orchestra: Victor Young.

The Kraft Music Hall—Variety—30 minutes—NBC—October 8, 1958 - May 13, 1959. (See title.)

Jackpot Bowling—Contest—30 minutes—NBC—September 19, 1960 - March 13, 1961.

Host: Milton Berle.

Play-by-play call: Chick Hearn.

Format: Two competing players. Object: To score six strikes during a nine-frame game. If one bowler achieves it, he is awarded five thousand dollars; if neither player achieves it, the bowler with the most strikes receives one thousand dollars.

The Milton Berle Show—Variety—60 minutes—ABC—September 9, 1966 - January 6, 1967.

Host: Milton Berle.

Regulars: Irving Benson (as Shpritzer, the studio audience heckler), Bobby Rydell, Donna Loren, The Berle Girls, The Louis Da Pron Dancers.

Announcer: Dick Tufeld.

Orchestra: Mitchell Ayres.

MILTON THE MONSTER

Animated Cartoon. Background: Horrible Hill in Transylvania. The misadventures of Milton, "the world's most lovable monster." A Hal Seeger production.

Additional characters: Professor Wierdo, Kool, Flukey Luke, Foxy, Muggy Doo, Penny Penguin, Stuffy Derma.

Additional segment: "The Adventures of Fearless Fly." An insect's lone battle against evil.

Voices: Bob McFadden, Beverly Arnold.

Music: Winston Sharples.

MILTON THE MONSTER—30 minutes—ABC—October 9, 1965 - September 2, 1967. 26 episodes.

MIND YOUR MANNERS

Panel Discussion. Teenagers relate their feelings on various topical issues.

Moderator: Allen Ludden.

MIND YOUR MANNERS—30 minutes—NBC 1952.

MINDY CARSON SINGS

Musical Variety.

Hostess: Mindy Carson.

Announcer: Don Pardo.

Regulars: Florian ZaBach, Danny Horton.

Orchestra: Earl Sheldon; Norman Cloutier.

MINDY CARSON SINGS—30 minutes—NBC—1949 - 1951.

THE MISCHIEF MAKERS

Comedy. Original Hal Roach "Our Gang" theatrical silent films. See title: "The Little Rascals."

MISS SUSAN

Serial. Background: Ohio. The cases of Susan Peters, a lawyer handicapped through a spinal injury.

CAST

Susan Peters   Herself
Her nurse   Katherine Grill
Her housekeeper   Natalie Priest
Also: Robert McQueeny, John Lormer.

Producer: Ted Ashley.

Sponsor: The Colgate-Palmolive Company.

MISS SUSAN—15 minutes—NBC 1951.

MISSING LINKS

Game. First reading a story that contains specific blanks, a contestant then chooses one guest from a panel of three celebrities and bets points on his ability to fill in the missing words within a specified time limit. Winners, the highest scorers, receive merchandise prizes.

Host (NBC): Ed McMahon.

Host (ABC): Dick Clark.

MISSING LINKS—30 minutes. NBC—September 9, 1963 - March 27, 1964; ABC—March 30, 1964 - December 25, 1964.

MISSION: IMPOSSIBLE

Adventure. The cases of the I.M.F. (Impossible Missions Force), a top secret U.S. government organization that handles dangerous and highly sensitive international assignments. Stories depict the step-by-step planning and final execution of highly tense and complicated missions.

Mission: Impossible. Bottom, left: Peter Lupus, Greg Morris, Peter Graves. Top, left: Barbara Bain. Top right: Martin Landau.

CAST

Jim Phelps, the head of the I.M.F.   Peter Graves
Dan Briggs, the original head of the I.M.F. (1966-1967)   Steven Hill
Cinnamon Carter, an I.M.F. agent whose specialty is distraction   Barbara Bain
Rollin Hand, an I.M.F. agent, a master of disguises   Martin Landau
Barney Collier, an I.M.F. agent, an electronics expert   Greg Morris
Willy Armitage, an I.M.F. agent, the strongman   Peter Lupus
Paris (replaced Rollin Hand)   Leonard Nimoy
Dana (replaced Cinnamon)   Lesley Ann Warren

Casey (replaced
  Dana)   Lynda Day George
Mimi Davis, an
  occasional I.M.F.
  agent   Barbara Anderson
Doug, an occasional
  I.M.F. agent   Sam Elliot
The recorded voice
  which gives Jim his
  assignment   Bob Johnson

Girls used in the interim between
Barbara Bain and Lesley Ann Warren:

Tracey   Lee Meriwether
Beth   Ann Howes
Lisa   Michele Carey
Monique   Julie Gregg
Nora   Antoinette Bower
Valerie   Jessica Walter

Also, various villanious roles: Sid
  Haig.

Music: Lalo Schifrin.

Additional Music: Richard Markowitz,
  Gerald Fried, Richard Haig,
  Robert Dransin, Jerry Fielding,
  Kenyon Hopkins, Benny Golson,
  Harry Geller, Robert Prince,
  Leith Stevens.

Executive Producer-Creator: Bruce
  Geller.

Producer: Stanley Kallis, Lee H. Kat-
  zin, Richard Benedict, Robert
  Thompson, John W. Rogers,
  Joseph Gantman, Robert F.
  O'Neil, Laurence Heath, Bruce
  Lansbury.

Director: Richard Benedict, Leonard
  J. Horn, Lee H. Katzin, Michael
  O'Herlihy, Alexander Singer,
  Stuart Hagmann, Bruce Kessler,
  Reza S. Badiyi, Marvin Chomsky,
  Barry Crane, Murray Golden,
  George Fenady, Robert Butler,
  Robert Gist, John Moxey, Paul
  Stanley, Alf Kjellin, Lewis Allen,
Marc Daniels, Robert Totten,
Don Richardson, Sutton Roley,
John Florea, Virgil W. Vogel, Da-
vid Rich, Paul Krasny, Seymour
Robbie, Gerald Mayer, Terry
Becker, Allan Greedy.

MISSION: IMPOSSIBLE—60 minutes
—CBS—September 17, 1966 - September 8, 1973. 171 episodes. Syndicated.

MISSION MAGIC

Animated Cartoon. Background: A
classroom. The story of six students,
Carol, Vinnie, Kim, Socks, Harvey,
and Franklin; their teacher, Miss
Tickle, and troubleshooter Rick
Springfield, who comprise the Adven-
turers Club.

Pinpointing trouble in a magic
fantasy land, Rick contacts Miss
Tickle through the magic gramaphone.
Miss Tickle then approaches the statue
of Tut Tut the cat, and speaks the
magic words: "Tut Tut, cat of ancient
lore, it's time to draw the magic
door." The cat comes to life and Miss
Tickle draws a door on a blackboard.
The door becomes real, opens and,
engulfing them all, transports them to
wherever Rick is. Incorporating her
magic powers, Miss Tickle attempts to
resolve difficulties. Completing their
mission they are automatically transported back to the classroom.

Additional characters: Tolamy, Rick's
  pet owl; and Mr. Samuels, the
  principal.

Voices: Rick Springfield, Erica
  Scheimer, Howard Morris, Lane
  Scheimer, Lola Fisher.

Music: Yvette Blais, Jeff Michael.

MISSION MAGIC—30 minutes—ABC
—September 8, 1973 - August 31,
1974. 13 episodes.

THE MISSUS GOES A SHOPPING

With host John Reed King and assistant Jimmy Brown, the show features women shoppers competing in stunt contests for prizes. 30 minutes—CBS 1946.

MIXED DOUBLES

Comedy Serial. Background: New York City. The trials and tribulations of young marrieds, two newlywed couples who live side by side in one-room apartments. The men are both underpaid copyrighters in the same ad agency, and the wives struggle to make ends meet on scanty paychecks.

CAST

The hypochondriac, aggressive husband	Billy Idelson
His serious wife	Ada Friedman
Their neighbor, the healthy go-getter	Eddy Firestone
His glamorous, frivolous wife	Rhoda Williams

Also: Calvin Thomas.

Producer-Director: Carleton E. Morse.

MIXED DOUBLES—30 minutes—NBC 1949.

MOBILE ONE

Drama. Background: California. The daily adventures of reporter Pete Campbell and his cameraman, Doug McKnight, newsmen employed by television station KONE, Channel 1. (Mobile One is the code name for their car.)

CAST

Pete Campbell	Jackie Cooper
Doug McKnight	Mark Wheeler
Maggie Spencer, their assignment editor	Julie Gregg
Bruce Daniels, a station employee	Gary Crosby

Music: Nelson Riddle.

Executive Producer: Jack Webb.

Producer: William Bowers.

Director: Don Taylor, Joseph Pevney, George Sherman.

MOBILE ONE—60 minutes—ABC—September 12, 1975 - December 29, 1975.

MOBY DICK AND THE MIGHTY MIGHTOR

Animated Cartoon. Background: The Prehistoric Era.

Moby Dick. The exploits of Moby Dick, the legendary white whale. Utilizing his tremendous speed, he struggles to protect his human foundlings, shipwrecked youngsters Tom and Tub, from danger.

The Mighty Mightor. The story of Tor, a young boy who possesses the power to change his meek self into the Mighty Mightor, a hero of unparalleled power. Episodes depict his battle against the evils of a savage era.

Characters' Voices

Tom	Bobby Resnick
Tub	Barry Balkin
Scooby, the seal	Don Messick
Mightor	Paul Stewart
Tor	Bobby Diamond
Sheera	Patsy Garrett
Pondo	John Stephenson
L'il Rock	Norma McMillan
Ork	John Stephenson
Tog	John Stephenson

Moby Dick. Scooby the seal (left), Moby Dick, and Tom and Tubb. *Courtesy Hanna-Barbera Productions.*

Music: Hoyt Curtin.

MOBY DICK AND THE MIGHTY MIGHTOR— 30 minutes —CBS—September 9, 1967 - September 6, 1969. A Hanna-Barbera Production. 26 episodes.

MODERN ROMANCES

Serial. Dramatizations based on modern romance stories. Five chapters comprise each story; casts and authors change weekly.

Hostess-Narrator: Martha Scott.

Host-Narrator: Mel Brandt.

Producer: William Stark, Jerry Layton.

Sponsor: The Colgate-Palmolive Company.

MODERN ROMANCES—15 minutes NBC—October 4, 1954 - September 19, 1958.

THE MOD SQUAD

Crime Drama. Background: Los Angeles, California. Arrested on minor charges, three young adults, Pete Cochran (a joy ride in a stolen car), antiestablishment, the troubled reject of a wealthy family; Julie Barnes (no visible means of support), a poor white girl who wants no part of her mother's existence as a prostitute; and Linc Hayes (during a Watts raid), a tough ghetto Negro, are recruited by Adam Greer, the captain of the L.A.P.D. to form the Mod Squad, a special youth detail of undercover agents designed to infiltrate the organizations that are impenetratable by police. Stories focus on their investigations and their attempts to seek their own identities.

CAST

Pete Cochran	Michael Cole
Julie Barnes	Peggy Lipton
Linc Hayes	Clarence Williams III
Adam Greer	Tige Andrews

Music: Earle Hagen; Shorty Rogers; Billy May.

Executive Producer: Aaron Spelling, Danny Thomas.

Producer: Harve Bennett, Tony Barrett.

Director: Gary Nelson, Robert M. Lewis, Earl Bellamy, Terry Becker, Don Taylor, Lee H. Katzin, Gene Nelson, Michael Caffrey.

THE MOD SQUAD—60 minutes—ABC—September 24, 1968 - August 23, 1973. 124 episodes. Syndicated.

THE MOHAWK SHOWROOM

Musical Variety.

Hostess: Roberta Quinlan.

Host: Morton Downey.

Regulars: Carmen Mastren, The Chieftains.

Announcer: Bob Slanton.

Music: The Harry Clark Trio.

Producer: George R. Nelson, Roger Muir.

Director: Dick Schneider, Clark Jones.

Sponsor: Mohawk Carpets.

THE MOHAWK SHOWROOM—15 minutes—NBC—1949.

MOMENT OF DECISION

Anthology. Retitled episodes of "Ford Theatre."

Included:

Sudden Silence. A small-town sheriff arrests a young man for murder. When he is sentenced to death, the man's father vows to get even. The story concerns the sheriff's efforts to safeguard himself and his family.

CAST
Barbara Stanwyck, Jeff Morrow, Trevor Bardette.

Stand By To Dive. The story concerns a young naval officer who is assigned to the command of his father—a man he has not seen since his parent's divorce.

CAST
Farley Granger, Onslow Stevens, William Leslie, Roger Smith.

Fear Has Many Faces. During the Korean War, a sergeant is forced to kill a soldier who makes a break for the rear. The story concerns the torment that ensues as a result of the act.

CAST
James Whitmore, June Lockhart, Don Haggerty.

MOMENT OF DECISION—30 minutes—ABC—July 3, 1957 - September 1957.

MOMENT OF FEAR

Anthology. Dramatizations depicting the plight of people suddenly confronted with unexpected, perilous situations.

Included:

Farewell Performance. A psychological tale of a ventriloquist who finds confidence in his dummy after his wife leaves him.

CAST
Nimbo: John Hoyt; Julie: Joan Shawlee; Inspector: Alan Napier; George: Leslie Bradley.

A Little White Lye. Moving into a house, the scene of a brutal murder, a young couple attempt to uncover the sources of ghostly sounds in the night.

CAST
Ellen Rogers: Dorothy Malone; Dick Rogers: Michael Pate.

The Earring. A man attempts to blackmail his former fiancée, now the wife of a successful attorney.

CAST
Lydia: Greer Garson; David: Edward Franz; Phil: Philip Reed; Johnny: Norman Lloyd.

MOMENT OF FEAR—30 minutes—NBC—July 1, 1960 - September 1960; July 1961 - September 1961; June 1962 - September 1962; July 1963 - September 1963; May 19, 1964 - September 15, 1964; June 1965 - September 1965.

MOMENT OF TRUTH

Serial. Background: A small college town in Canada. The dramatic story of Dr. Wallace Bennett, professor and practicing psychologist. Episodes relate the conflicts and tensions that arise from the interactions of the characters—his family, friends, and colleagues.

CAST
Dr. Wallace Bennett	Douglas Watson
Nancy Bennett	Louise King
Helen Gould	Lucy Warner
Jack	Steven Levy
Professor Hamilton	Bob Christie
Wilma Leeds	Lynne Gorman
Carol	Toby Tarnow
Barbara Wallace	Mira Pawluk
Vince Conway	Peter Donat
Shelia	Barbara Pierce
Dr. Russell Wingate	Ivor Barry
Lila	Sandra Scott
Steve	Tom Fielding
Monique	Fernande Giroux
Dexter	Chris Wiggins
Eric	John Horton
Mr. Leeds	Robert Goodier
Johnny Wallace	Michael Dodds
Diane	Anne Campbell
Linda	Anna Hagan
Gil Bennett	John Bethune

MOMENT OF TRUTH—30 minutes—NBC—January 4, 1965 - November 5, 1965.

MONA McCLUSKEY

Comedy. Background: Hollywood, California. The trials and tribulations of Mona McCluskey, a beautiful film actress who, earning five thousand dollars per week, lives in a moderately furnished two-room apartment away from the Affluent Society to please

Mona McClusky. Juliet Prowse and Denny Miller.

her husband, U.S. Air Force sergeant Mike McCluskey, who earns and insists they subside on his salary of five hundred dollars per month.

Incorporating methods that are a bit deceiving, Mona struggles to supplement the strained family budget without arousing Mike's suspicions.

CAST

Mona McCluskey (stage name: Mona Jackson)	Juliet Prowse
Mike McCluskey	Denny Miller
General Crone, Mike's commanding officer	Herbert Rudley
Sgt. Stan Gruzewsky, Mike's friend	Robert Strauss
Alice, Stan's romantic interest	Elena Verdugo
General Somers	Frank Wilcox
Mr. Caldwell, the studio producer	Bartlett Robinson

Music: Sonny Burke.

Theme: "Yes Sir, That's My Baby."

MONA McCLUSKEY—30 minutes—NBC—September 16, 1965 - April 14, 1966. 26 episodes.

THE MONEYCHANGERS

Drama. A four-part miniseries based on the novel by Arthur Hailey. A behind-the-scenes look at the world of banking—a world dominated by greed, corruption, sex, and power.

CAST

Alex Vandervoort	Kirk Douglas
Roscoe Heyward	Christopher Plummer
Miles Eastin	Timothy Bottoms
Margot Bracken	Susan Flannery
Edwina Dorsey	Anne Baxter
Avril Devereaux	Joan Collins
Nolan Wainwright	Percy Rodrigues
Jerome Patterson	Ralph Bellamy
Tony Bear	Robert Loggia
Beatrice Heyward	Jean Peters
Celia Vandervoort	Marisa Pavan
Lewis Dorsey	Hayden Rorke
Wizard Wong	James Shigeta
Harold Austin	Patrick O'Neal
George Quartermain	Lorne Greene
Dr. McCartney	Helen Hayes

Music: Henry Mancini.

Producer: Ross Hunter, Jacque Mapes.

Director: Boris Sagal.

THE MONEYCHANGERS—6 hrs., 30 minutes—NBC—December 4, 1976 - December 19, 1976.

THE MONEY MAZE

Game. Two married couples compete. One member of each team stands before a large maze that is constructed on stage level one. The other member of each team is situated on stage level two, where they compete for points. A category topic is revealed (e.g., "Girls in Movies") with two clues ("My Friend (Irma)" and "Hello (Dolly)"). One player (through a flip-of-coin decision) chooses one clue and challenges his opponent to answer it. If he can, he receives one point. A new clue appears and he now challenges his opponent to answer one. Eight clues are played per category. A miss ends the round and awards points to the player with the last correct response.

The player with the highest score at the end of several rounds receives a chance to play the money maze. Five large boxes, which are constructed in the maze are lit. Each contains one figure of ten thousand dollars. The player on stage level two directs his partner who has to run through the maze, enter each of the five boxes, press a button to activate a light, and return to his or her point of destination to press a red button—all within a one-minute time limit. Cash awards are determined by the number of boxes that are activated and whether or not the player made it back to the starting point before time expired.

Host: Nick Clooney.

Announcer: Alan Caulfield.

Music: Score Productions.

THE MONEY MAZE—30 minutes—ABC—December 23, 1974 - July 4, 1975.

THE MONKEES

Comedy. The misadventures of The Monkees, a Rock and Roll quartet as they romp through various comic escapades. Slapstick situations are played within nonrealistic frameworks and encompass speed photography and photographic nonsense.

CAST

Davy Jones	Himself
Mike Nesmith (Wool Hat)	Himself
Mickey Dolenz	Himself
Peter Tork	Himself

Music: The Monkees.

Background Score: Stu Phillips.

Music Supervision: Don Kirshner.

Producer: Robert Rafelson, Ward Sylvester.

Director: Robert Rafelson, Bruce Kessler, Gerald Shepard, David Winters, Peter H. Torkleson, James Frawley.

THE MONKEES—30 minutes—NBC—September 12, 1966 - August 19, 1968. CBS—September 13, 1969 - September 2, 1972. ABC—September 9, 1972 - September 1, 1973. 58 episodes.

THE MONROES

Western. Background: Wyoming, 1875. Arriving in the Teton Mountain region, a family of pioneers, the Monroes (parents: Albert and Mary; and their children: Clayt, eighteen; Kathleen, sixteen; twins Fennimore and Jefferson, twelve; and Amy, six) seek an unknown valley wherein Albert laid claim to land ten years ago.

Crossing the treacherous Snake River, Albert and Mary are caught in its turbulent current and drowned. In a tragic moment, the children are orphaned. (Clayt, narrating:) "I was ...the oldest...I kept wondering what Pa would do. We couldn't stay here, and we didn't have a farm

The Monkees. Left to right: Mike Nesmith, Davy Jones, Mickey Dolenz, Peter Tork. © *Screen Gems.*

anymore to go back to. And up ahead there was nothing but wilderness—and one valley Pa had marked with a pile of rocks. But I was the Pa now, and I had no choice, I had to find that valley for him. We moved out into cold, strange country. All I had to guide me was a map Pa made for me ten years before."

After several days, landmarks begin to appear and the countryside begins to fit the map. Entering the valley, Clayt finds the pile of rocks—and his father's belt buckle—placed there ten years before (Clayt:) "Now it was ours, to root down, to hold—if we could."

The struggles of the Monroe children as they attempt to establish their parent's dream—a homeland.

"It's just as Pa said, if it were easy, it wouldn't be worth having."

CAST

Clayt Monroe	Michael Anderson, Jr.
Kathleen Monroe	Barbara Hershey
Amy Monroe	Tammy Locke
Jefferson Monroe (Big Twin)	Keith Schultz
Fennimore Monroe (Little Twin)	Kevin Schultz
Jim, a renegade Indian befriended by the Monroes	Ron Soble
Major Mapoy, the land baron opposed to the Monroes' settling	Liam Sullivan
Ruel Jaxon, the Major's aide	James Westmoreland

Mr. Buttermore, the Major's aide	John Doucette
Albert Monroe (first episode)	Russ Conway
Mary Monroe (first episode)	Marilyn Moe
Sleeve, an employee of Mapoy	Ben Johnson
John Bradford, Mapoy's trail scout	Buck Taylor

Music Supervision: Lionel Newman.

THE MONROES—60 minutes—ABC—September 7, 1966 - August 30, 1967. Syndicated. 26 episodes.

THE MONSTER SQUAD

Comedy. While working as a night watchman at Fred's Wax Museum, Walt, a young student attending a criminology college, activates his invention, a crime computer, and, through its oscillating vibrations, it brings to life three legendary monsters—Dracula, Frankenstein, and the Werewolf. Hoping to make up for their past misgivings (creatures feared for centuries), they join Walt, and working independently of police, attempt to solve crimes.

CAST

Walt	Fred Grandy
Dracula	Henry Polic II
Bruce W. Wolf (the werewolf)	Buck Kartalian
Frank N. Stein	Michael Lane
Officer McMac Mac	Paul Smith

Music: Richard LaSalle.

Executive Producer: William P. D'Angelo, Ray Allen, Harvey Bullock.

Producer: Michael McClean.

Director: Herman Hoffman, James Sheldon.

THE MONSTER SQUAD—30 minutes—NBC—Premiered: September 11, 1976.

THE MONTEFUSCOS

Comedy. Background: New Canaan, Connecticut. The trials and tribulations of three generations of a large Italian-American family, the Montefuscos. Created by Bill Persky and Sam Denoff.

CAST

Tony Montefusco, the father, a painter	Joe Sirola
Rose Montefusco, his wife	Naomi Stevens
Frankie Montefusco, their son, a dentist	Ron Carey
Joseph Montefusco, their son, a priest	John Aprea
Nunzio Montefusco, their son, an unemployed actor	Sal Viscuso
Angelina Cooney, their married daughter	Linda Dano
Jim Cooney, Angelina's husband	Bill Cort
Theresa Montefusco, Frankie's wife	Phoebe Dorin
Antonio Cooney, Angelina and Jim's son	Damon Raskin
Gina Montefusco, Frankie and Theresa's daughter	Dominique Pinassi
Jerome Montefusco, Frankie and Theresa's son	Jeff Palladini

Music: Jack Elliott, Allyn Ferguson.

Executive Producer: Bill Persky, Sam Denoff.

Producer: Tom VanAtta, Bill Idelson.

Director: Bill Persky, Don Richardson.

Creator: Bill Persky, Sam Denoff.

THE MONTEFUSCOS—30 minutes—NBC—September 4, 1975 - October 23, 1975.

MONTGOMERY'S SUMMER STOCK

Anthology. Original dramatic productions aired as a summer replacement for "Robert Montgomery Presents."

Stock Performers: Elizabeth Montgomery, Vaughn Taylor, John Newland, Judy Parrish, Margaret Hayes.

MONTGOMERY'S SUMMER STOCK—30 minutes—NBC—June 1953 - September 1953.

MONTY NASH

Spy Drama. The cases of Monty Nash, a U.S. government special investigator who handles top-secret White House affairs. Based on the spy yarns by Richard Jessup.

Starring: Harry Guardino as Monty Nash.

MONTY NASH—30 minutes—Syndicated 1971. 31 episodes.

MONTY PYTHON'S FLYING CIRCUS

Satire. An absolutely meaningless title; tasteless, uneven, and insane material; men in female drag; glamorous women in various stages of undress; language not normally heard in American television programs (e.g., "filthy bastard"); and sexually provocative animation—all of which is ingeniously interwoven into a highly intellectual and entertaining program.

Produced by the British Broadcasting Corporation, which first began airing it in 1969 as an answer to America's "Laugh-In," it is created by five men, all graduates of Oxford or Cambridge, who use live action and animation to achieve their comedic results. An American artist provides the extremely lifelike animation. Whether enjoyable or not rests solely with the individual.

Starring: Graham Chapman, John Cleese, Eric Idle, Terry Gilliam, Terry Jones, Michael Palin.

Regulars: Donna Reading, Carol Cleveland, Katy Wayech, Dick Vosburgh.

Animation: Terry Gilliam.

Music: Recorded.

MONTY PYTHON'S FLYING CIRCUS—30 minutes. Imported by the member stations of the Eastern Educational Network in 1974.

MOREY AMSTERDAM

Listed: The television programs of comedian Morey Amsterdam.

Stop Me If You've Heard This One—Comedy Game—30 minutes—NBC 1948. Originally aired locally in Los Angeles in 1945 before switching to a network. The first television series to be broadcast with a live studio audience.

Emcee: Ted Brown.

Panelists: Morey Amsterdam, Lew Lehr, Cal Tinney.

Format: The Emcee reads an incomplete joke that has been submitted by a home viewer. A panel of three than have to complete it with an original, funny punch line. The sender receives five dollars for submitting the joke, and an additional five dollars if the panel fails to complete it.

The Morey Amsterdam Show—Variety—30 minutes—CBS 1948. The humor is set against the background of the Silver Swan Cafe, wherein Morey developed his "shtick" (gimmick)—his ability to provide an appropriate joke for any topic asked of him.

Host: Morey Amsterdam.

Regulars: Art Carney (Newton, the Waiter), Rosemary Clooney, Francey Lane, Jacqueline Susann.

Orchestra: Ray McKinley.

The Morey Amsterdam Show—Variety—30 minutes—DuMont 1949.

Host: Morey Amsterdam.

Regulars: Vic Damone, Art Carney, Mary Raye and Naldi.

Announcer: Don Russell.

Orchestra: Johnny Guarnieri.

Broadway Open House—Variety—NBC—1950. (See title.)

Battle Of The Ages—Game—DuMont—1951. (See title.)

The Morey Amsterdam Show—Variety—Local New York, WNBT-TV (now WNBC)—45 minutes (11:15 p.m.-Midnight)—1953.

Host: Morey Amsterdam.

Regulars: Connie Russell, Jean Martin.

Orchestra: Milton DeLugg.

The Morey Amsterdam Show—Variety—Local New York, WABC-TV—60 minutes—1954.

Host: Morey Amsterdam.

Vocalist: Francey Lane.

Orchestra: Milton DeLugg.

Can You Top This?—Game—30 minutes—Syndicated 1970. (See title.)

MORNING COURT

Courtroom Drama. Reenactments based on actual metropolitan courtroom cases. Actors portray all of the involved.

Judges: William Gwinn, Georgiana Hardy.

MORNING COURT—30 minutes—ABC—October 10, 1960 - May 12, 1961.

THE MORNING SHOW

Information-Entertainment. The CBS competition for NBC's "Today Show."

Hosts: Walter Cronkite, Jack Paar, Will Rogers, Jr.

News Reporters: Walter Cronkite, Charles Collingwood.

Regulars: Edie Adams, Dick Van Dyke, The Bill and Cora Baird Puppets.

Music: Jose Melis.

Producer: Avarm Westin, James Calligan, John Cosgrove, Robert Northsheld, James Fleming.

THE MORNING SHOW—2 hours
(7:00 a.m.-9:00 a.m., EST)
—CBS—January 20, 1956 - April 5,
1957. Also known as "Good Morning." Premiered earlier, in some markets on March 15, 1954.

THE MORNING SHOW

Talk-Variety.

Host: Ed Nelson.

Semiregulars: Rona Barrett, Mr.
  Blackwell, Dr. Julius Sumner
  Miller.
THE MORNING SHOW—90 minutes
Syndicated 1969. 130 tapes. Also
known as: "The Ed Nelson Show."

MORNING STAR

Serial. "No matter how dark the night
there is always a new dawn to come,
the sun is but a Morning Star...."
Background: New York City. The
dramatic story of Kathy Elliot, a
model caught in the intrigue and the
excitement of high fashion. Episodes
relate her struggles, "facing today and
looking forward to tomorrow's bright
promise."

CAST
Kathy Elliot	Elizabeth Perry
Jan	Adrienne Ellis
Ed Elliot	Ed Prentiss
Ann Burton	Olive Dunbar
Aunt Milly	Sheila Bromley
George Ross	Burt Douglas
Joan Mitchell	Betty Lou Gerson
Bill Riley	Edward Mallory
Joan Mitchell	Betty Lou Gerson
Eve Blake	Floy Dean
Stan Manning	John Stephenson
Dr. Blake	William Arvin
Jerry	Michael Bell
Joe Bernie	Norman Burton

Marcus Stein	Michael Fox
Eric Manning	Ron Jackson
The Man	Vic Tayback
Mrs. Allison	Phyllis Hill

Creator: Ted Corday.

MORNING STAR—30 minutes—NBC—
September 27, 1965 - July 1, 1966.
188 episodes.

THE MORTON DOWNEY SHOW

Musical Variety.

Host: Morton Downey.

Announcer: Bob Stanton.

Orchestra: Carmen Mastren.

THE MORTON DOWNEY SHOW—15
minutes—NBC 1949. Also known as
"The Mohawk Showroom."

MOSES THE LAWGIVER

Drama. Background: Egypt during the
thirteenth century b.c. A six-part
series, drawn from the book of
Exodus, that follows Moses as he
defies the Egyptian empire to deliver
the Jews from their enslavement and
lead them to the promised land. Produced by England's Independent Television Corporation and Italy's
RAI-TV.

CAST
Moses	Burt Lancaster
Moses, as a young man	Will Lancaster
Aaron	Anthony Quayle
Zipporah	Irene Papas
Miriam	Ingrid Thulin
Pharaoh	Laurent Teizieff
Dathan	Yousef Shiloah
Joshua	Aharon Ipale

Eliseba	Marina Berti	
Pharaoh's wife	Melba Englander	
Caleb	Michele Placido	
Koreh	Antonio Piovonelli	
Jethro	Shmuel Rodensky	

Narrator: Richard Johnson.

Music: Ennio Morricone.

Additional Music and Songs: Dov Seltzer.

MOSES THE LAWGIVER—60 minutes—CBS—June 21, 1975 - August 7, 1975.

THE MOST DEADLY GAME

Crime Drama. Background: Los Angeles, California. The cases of master criminologist Ethan Arcane, and his protégés, Vanessa Smith, and Jonathan Croft. Stories relate their attempts to solve crimes of the most deadly nature—murder.

The Most Deadly Game. Left to right: George Maharis, Ralph Bellamy, and Yvette Mimieux.

CAST

Ethan Arcane	Ralph Bellamy
Vanessa Smith	Yvette Mimieux
Jonathan Croft	George Maharis

Music Supervision: Lionel Newman.

THE MOST DEADLY GAME—60 minutes—ABC—October 10, 1970 - January 16, 1971. 13 episodes.

THE MOST IMPORTANT PEOPLE

Musical Variety.

Host: Jimmy Carroll (accompanying himself on the piano).

Hostess: Rita Carroll (Mrs.)

THE MOST IMPORTANT PEOPLE— 15 minutes—DuMont 1950.

THE MOST IN MUSIC

Musical Variety. Programs are tailored to the talents of guests. Produced in England.

Hosts: Weekly guests, including Barbara McNair, Vikki Carr, Johnny Mathis.

Featured: The Irving Davies Dancers, The Michael Sammes Singers.

Orchestra: Jack Parnell.

THE MOST IN MUSIC—60 minutes— Syndicated 1966.

M.V.P. (MOST VALUABLE PLAYER)

Interview. Interviews with sports figures and show-business personalities.

Host: Johnny Bench, Cincinnati Reds catcher.

Music: Recorded.

M.V.P.—30 minutes—Syndicated 1971.

MOST WANTED

Crime Drama. Background: Los Angeles, California. The investigations of the Most Wanted Unit, an elite law enforcement division of the L.A.P.D. designed to specialize in cases involving the most wanted criminals.

CAST
Captain Lincoln Evers   Robert Stack
Sgt. Charlie Nelson   Shelly Novack
Officer Kate Manners   Jo Ann Harris
The Mayor   Harry Rhodes

Music: Lalo Schifrin, Richard Markowitz.

Executive Producer: Quinn Martin, John Wilder, Paul King.

Producer: Harold Gast.

Director: Don Medford, Virgil W. Vogel, William Wiard, Corey Allen.

MOST WANTED—60 minutes—ABC —October 16, 1976 - April 4, 1977.

MOTHERS DAY

Game. Three mothers compete in various contests based on the operation of a household. Winners, those who successfully complete all tasks, are crowned. "Mother for a Day," and receive merchandise prizes.

Host: Dick Van Dyke.

Assistants: Betty Anders, Dotty Mack.

`MOTHERS DAY—30 minutes—ABC —October 3, 1958 - January 2, 1959.

THE MOTHERS-IN-LAW

Comedy. Background: Hollywood, California. Residing at 1805 Ridgewood Drive are the Hubbards: Herb, an attorney; his wife, Eve; and their daughter Suzie. Living next door, at 1803 Ridgewood Drive are the Buells: Roger, a television script writer; his wife, Kaye; and their son, Jerry.

Raised and growing up together, Suzie and Jerry fall in love, and, after completing high school, marry and establish housekeeping in the converted Hubbard garage.

Stories depict: the struggles of young marrieds; and the trials and tribulations of their bickering mothers-in-law, who, wanting only the best for their children, continually meddle in their lives.

CAST
Eve Hubbard   Eve Arden
Herb Hubbard   Herbert Rudley
Kaye Buell   Kaye Ballard
Roger Buell   Roger C. Carmel
    Richard Deacon
Suzie Hubbard
   (Buell)   Deborah Walley
Jerry Buell   Jerry Fogel
Dr. Butler, Suzie's
   pediatrician   Herb Voland
Raphael del Gado,
   a friend, a Mexican
   Bull Fighter   Desi Arnaz

Music: Wilbur Hatch.

THE MOTHERS-IN-LAW—30 minutes—NBC—September 10, 1967 - September 7, 1969. 56 episodes. Syndicated.

THE MOTOROLA TV HOUR

An early anthology series of sixty-minute dramas sponsored by the

Magnavox Corporation. Produced by Herbert Brodkin.

MOTOR MOUSE

Animated Cartoon. A spin-off from "The Cattanooga Cats." A Hanna-Barbera production.

Segments:

Motor Mouse And Auto Cat. The story of Auto Cat's endless attempts to outrace Motor Mouse.

It's The Wolf. Mildew the wolf's pursuit of the poor defenseless lamb, Lambsy. Savior of the lamb is Bristol Hound—"Bristol Hound's my name, saving sheep's my game."

Segment Hosts: The Cattanooga Cats: Country Kitty Jo, Groovey, Chessie, Scoots.

Characters' Voices

Motor Mouse	Dick Curtis
Auto Cat	Marty Ingels
Mildew Wolf	Paul Lynde
Lambsy	Marty Ingels
Bristol Hound	Allan Melvin
Country	Bill Galloway
Groovey	Casey Kaseem
Scoots	Jim Begg
Kitty Jo	Julie Bennett
Chessie	Julie Bennett

Music: Hoyt Curtin.

MOTOR MOUSE—30 minutes—ABC —September 12, 1970 - September 4, 1971. 26 episodes. Syndicated.

THE MOUSE FACTORY

Children's Variety. Guest celebrities appear and relate various aspects of the world assisted by film clips from Walt Disney features.

Appearing: Annette Funicello, discussing the career of Mickey Mouse; Jonathan Winters, interplanetary travel; Joe Flynn, water sports; Wally Cox, dancing; Pat Paulsen, sports; Johnny Brown, aviation; Pat Buttram, bull fighting; Jo Anne Worley, women's lib; John Astin, the story of Pluto, the klutz canine.

Music Supervision: George Bruns.

THE MOUSE FACTORY—30 minutes—Syndicated 1972. 17 episodes.

THE MOVIE CLASSICS OF DAVID O. SELZNICK

Movies. A film tribute to director David O. Selznick.

THE MOVIE CLASSICS OF DAVID O. SELZNICK—90 minutes—ABC— June 22, 1972 - July 13, 1972.

THE MOVIE GAME

Game. Basis: Movie trivia—who did what and who played whom. Rounds are divided into "Screentests," worth twenty points; and "Closeups," which are played after each "Screentest" and worth five points each. Distinguished by two formats:

Format One:

Two competing teams, each composed of three members (two celebrities and one noncelebrity contestant). The Screentest Round: The contestant competes. The host asks a question and the first player to identify himself through a buzzer signal receives a chance to answer. If correct, points are awarded. The

Closeup segment: two questions are directed to that contestant's celebrity partners. Correct answers award five points. The contestant scoring the highest is the winner and receives two hundred and fifty dollars.

Host: Sonny Fox.
Assistant: Army Archid.
Announcer: Johnny Gilbert.
Music: Recorded.

Format Two:
Six celebrity guests who comprise two three-member teams. The Screentest Round: the host states a question. The team first to identify themselves through a buzzer signal receives a chance to answer. If correct, the points are scored. The closeup Round, containing three questions, is directed to that team. Winners are the highest-scoring teams. Their preselected home viewer (via post card) receives two hundred and fifty dollars.

Host: Larry Blyden.
Assistant: Army Archid.
Announcer: Johnny Gilbert.
Music: Recorded.

Additional segments (both versions):
The Film Clip Round. Questions are based on the observation of film clips. Worth twenty points.
The Action Round. Specially prepared scenes are performed by the losing team. One member of the winning team has to identify its concealed name or title. Additional cash is awarded if successful.
Army Archid's Portrait of a Star. A specially prepared biography is read. The team who correctly identifies the personality receives fifty points.

THE MOVIE GAME—30 minutes—Syndicated 1969.

MOVIELAND QUIZ

Game. Set: A theatre front. Object: For a contestant to identify celluloid personalities, cast roles, or film titles. Cameras dolly up to and hold still shots of selected frames; questions are then asked regarding these. Cash is awarded with each correct response.

Host: Arthur Q. Bryan.
Assistant-Cashier: Patricia Bright.
Producer: Lester Lewis.
Director: Ralph Warren.

MOVIELAND QUIZ—30 minutes—ABC—August 12, 1948 - September 1948.

MOVIN' ON

Drama. Background: Various areas between Oregon, Utah, and Nevada. The experiences of two gypsy truck drivers: Sonny Pruitt, a tough, uneducated veteran; and his partner, Will Chandler, a rebellious, college-educated youth, who is seeking to discover how the other half lives.

CAST

Sonny Pruitt	Claude Akins
Will Chandler	Frank Converse
Myrna, Sonny's girl-friend	Janis Hansen
Betty, Will's girl-friend	Ann Coleman
Benjy, a gypsy truck driver	Rosey Grier
Moose, his partner	Art Metrano

Music: George Romanis.
Additional Music: Earle Hagen.

Theme: Merle Haggard.

Executive Producer: Barry Whitz, Philip D'Antoni.

Producer: Ernie Frankel.

Director: Bob Helljan, Lawrence Dobkin, Corey Allen, Michael Schultz, Leo Penn.

MOVIN' ON—60 minutes—NBC—September 12, 1974 - April 20, 1976; June 1, 1976 - September 14, 1976.

MR. ADAMS AND EVE

Comedy. Background: Hollywood, California. The home and working lives of Eve and Howard Adams, a husband-and-wife show business couple.

CAST

Howard Adams	Howard Duff
Eve Adams (stage name: Eve Drake)	Ida Lupino
J.B. Hafter, the studio producer	Alan Reed
Steve, the Adam's agent	Hayden Rorke
Elsie, the Adams's housekeeper	Olive Carey
The director	Larry Dobkin
The slate boy	Alan Wood
The assistant director	Paul Grant

Producer: William Webb, Warner Toub, Jr., Frederick de Cordova.

Director: Frederick de Cordova.

MR. ADAMS AND EVE—30 minutes —CBS—January 4, 1956 - September 23, 1958. 66 episodes. Syndicated.

MR. AND MRS. MYSTERY

Mystery. Background: New York City, 46 Perry Street, Apartment 3-C. The cases of criminologist John Gay and his wife, his self-proclaimed assistant, Barbara.

CAST

John Gay	Himself
Barbara Gay	Herself

MR. AND MRS. MYSTERY—15 minutes—CBS—1949 - 1950.

MR. AND MRS. NORTH

Mystery. Background: Greenwich Village in New York City, the residence of the Norths: Jerry, a former private detective turned publisher, and his attractive, level-headed wife, Pamela. Stories depict their investigations when Pam accidentally stumbles upon and involves Jerry in crimes. Based on the stories by Frances and Richard Lockridge.

CAST

Jerry North	Joseph Allen (1949)
	Richard Denning (1952-54)
Pamela North	Mary Lou Taylor (1949)
	Barbara Britton (1952-54)
Lieutenant Bill Weingand	Francis DeSales

Music: Charles Paul

Producer: John W. Loveton.

Director: Marc Daniels.

Sponsor: Colgate; Revlon.

MR. AND MRS. NORTH—30 minutes—NBC 1949; CBS—October 3, 1952 - September 25, 1953; NBC—January 26, 1954 - July 20, 1954. 57 episodes. Syndicated

MR. ARSENIC

Drama. True crime exposés.

Host: Burton Turkus, the author of *Murder Inc.*

MR. ARSENIC—30 minutes—ABC—May 8, 1952 - June 26, 1952.

MR. BLACK

Anthology. Mystery presentations.

Host: Anthony Christopher, as Mr. Black (situated in a cobweb, flickering light atmosphere).

MR. BLACK—30 minutes—ABC—September 19, 1949 - November 7, 1949.

MR. BROADWAY

Drama. Background: New York City. The exploits of Mike Bell, a sophisticated Broadway press agent.

CAST
Mike Bell   Craig Stevens
Hank McClure, his contact
    man   Horace McMahon
Toki, his girl
    friday   Lani Miyazaki

MR. BROADWAY—60 minutes—CBS —September 26, 1964 - December 26, 1964. 13 episodes.

MR. CITIZEN

Anthology. Dramatizations that detail the unselfish acts of heroism of ordinary people. The person whose story is selected receives the "Mister Citizen Award."

Host: Allyn Edwards.

Award Presenter: Senator Clifford Chase.

Organist: John Gart.

MR. CITIZEN—30 minutes—ABC—April 20, 1955 - July 20, 1955.

MR. DEEDS GOES TO TOWN

Comedy. Background: New York City. The misadventures of Longfellow Deeds, a philosophical country gentleman who inherits the multimillion-dollar Deeds Enterprises after the death of his uncle Alonzo. Stories depict his attempts to adjust to life in the big city; and his efforts to run a corporation that he feels can easily take advantage of people.

CAST
Longfellow Deeds   Monte Markham
Tony Lawrence, Deeds's
    assistant   Pat Harrington, Jr.
Henry Masterson, the
    chairman of the
    board   Herbert Voland

Mr. Deeds Goes To Town. Monte Markham (seated), and Pat Harrington. © *Screen Gems.*

George, Deeds's
Butler   Ivor Barry

Deeds's dog: Sam.

Music: Warren Barker.

MR. DEEDS GOES TO TOWN—30
minutes—ABC—September 26, 1969 -
January 16, 1970. 17 episodes.

MR. DISTRICT ATTORNEY

Crime Drama. Dramatizations based
on the facts of crime from the files of
the District Attorney's office.

CAST
Paul Garrett, Mr. District
Attorney   Jay Jostyn
                                David Brian
Edith Miller, his
secretary   Vicki Vola
                                Jackie Loughery
Harrington, his Irish
investigator   Len Doyle

Voice of the Law: Jay Jostyn; David
Brian.

Announcer: Fred Uttal.

Music: Peter Van Steeden.

Producer-Director: Edward Byron.

Sponsor: Bristol-Myers.

Program Open:

Announcer: Mr. District Attorney,
champion of the people, defender of truth, guardian of our
fundamental rights to life,
liberty, and the pursuit of happiness.

D.A.: And it shall be my duty as
District Attorney not only to
prosecute to the limit of the law
all persons accused of crimes
perpetrated within the country
but to defend with equal vigor

the rights and privileges of all
citizens.

MR. DISTRICT ATTORNEY—30
minutes—Syndicated 1951. 78 episodes. Based on the radio program of
the same title.

MR. ED

Comedy. Background: Los Angeles,
California. Settling into their first
home, newlyweds Wilbur Post, architect, and his wife, Carol, discover a
horse in the barn. Meeting Roger
Addison, a neighbor, they discover
that the horse is theirs, left to them
by the previous owner. Unable to part
with the animal, Wilbur persuades
Carol to let him keep it.

Shortly after, while brushing the
horse (named Mr. Ed), Wilbur discovers that he possesses the ability to
talk and, because Wilbur is the only
person he likes well enough to talk to,
will speak only to him.

Stories depict the misadventures
that befall Wilbur as he struggles to
conceal the fact of his possession of a
talking horse—"the playboy horse of
Los Angeles."

CAST
Wilbur Post   Alan Young
Carol Post   Connie Hines
Roger Addison, their
neighbor   Larry Keating
Kay Addison, his
wife   Edna Skinner
Gordon Kirkwood, their
neighbor   Leon Ames
Winnie Kirkwood, his
wife   Florence MacMichael
Mr. Carlisle, Carol's
father   Barry Kelly
Voice of Mr.
Ed   Allan "Rocky" Lane
Paul Fenton, Kay's

brother   Jack Albertson
Dr. Bruce Gordon, the
   psychiatrist   Richard Deacon

Music: Jay Livingston, Ray Evans; Raoul Kraushaar; Dave Kahn.

Executive Producer: Al Simon, Arthur Lubin.

Producer: Herbert W. Browar.

Director: Arthur Lubin.

The Posts Address: 1720 Valley Road.

MR. ED–30 minutes. Syndicated 1960-1961; CBS–October 1, 1961 - September 4, 1966. 143 episodes. Syndicated.

MR. GARLUND

Drama. The story of Frank Garlund, a youthful tycoon (thirty years of age), financial wizard, and mysterious industrial head, a key figure in national and international affairs. Raised by a wealthy Chinese gentleman, Po Chang, his ancestry remains a mystery. In flashback sequences, the lives of people who had come in contact with him during his struggle to reach the top of the financial ladder are dramatized.

CAST
Frank Garlund   Charles Quinlivan
Po Chang   Philip Ahn
Kam Chang, his foster
   brother, the owner of
   a pawn shop in San Francisco's
   China Town   Kam Tong

MR. GARLUND–30 minutes–CBS– October 7, 1960 - January 13, 1961. Also known as: "The Garlund Touch."

MR. I MAGINATION

Children. Background: The mythical kingdom of Imagination Town, a place where children's dreams come true. Fantasy is coupled with education as vignettes dramatize legendary figures and events of past history.

Host: Paul Tripp, as Mr. I Magination.

Regulars: Johnny Stewart, Michael Petrie, Ruth Enders, Butch Cavell, Ted Tiller, Joe Silvan, David McKay, Donald Devlin, Don Harris, Clifford Sales, Robin Morgan, Richard Trask.

Orchestra: Ray Carter.

Producer: Norman and Irving Pincus, Worthington Miner.

Director: Don Richardson.

Sponsor: Nestle.

MR. I MAGINATION–30 minutes– CBS–April 24, 1949 - June 28, 1952.

MR. LUCKY

Adventure. Background: Los Angeles, California. The story of Joe Adams, alias Mr. Lucky, gambler, the owner of the *Fortuna,* a fancy supper club and gambling yacht. Episodes depict his struggles to maintain an honest operation.

CAST
Mr. Lucky   John Vivyan
Andamo, his partner   Ross Martin
Maggie Shank, his girl-
   friend   Pippa Scott
Lieutenant Rovacs,
   L.A.P.D.   Tom Brown
The *Fortuna*
   Maitre'd   Jed Scott

Music: Henry Mancini.
Producer: Blake Edwards, Gordon Oliver, Jack Arnold.

MR. LUCKY—30 minutes—CBS—October 24, 1959 - September 10, 1960. 34 episodes. Syndicated.

MR. MAGOO

Animated Cartoon. The misadventures of Quincy Magoo, a near-sighted gentleman.

Additional characters: Charlie, his Japanese houseboy; Waldo and Presley, his nephews.

Voice of Mr. Magoo: Jim Backus.

Music: Shorty Rogers.

MR. MAGOO—05 minutes—Syndicated 1963. 130 episodes.

MR. MAYOR

See title: "Captain Kangaroo."

MR. NOVAK

Drama. Background: Jefferson High School in Los Angeles, California. Stories depict the life of John Novak, English professor, a tough-minded idealist; student-teacher relationships; and the struggles of beginners as they learn the ropes of the teaching profession.

CAST

John Novak	James Franciscus
Albert Vane, the principal	Dean Jagger
Martin Woodridge, an English instructor, the principal in the last thirteen episodes	Burgess Meredith
Miss Wilkinson	Phyllis Avery
Paul Webb	David Sheiner
Mr. Peeples	Stephen Brooks
Miss Scott	Marian Collier
Mr. Butler	Vince Howard
Miss Dorsey	Marjorie Corley
Mr. Parkson	Peter Hansen
Mrs. Vreeland	Anne Seymour
Miss Pagano	Jeanne Bal

Music: Lyn Murray.

Producer: William Froug, John T. Dugan, Jack E. Neuman.

MR. NOVAK—60 minutes—NBC—September 24, 1963 - August 31, 1965. 60 episodes. Syndicated.

MR. PEEPERS

Comedy. Background: Jefferson Junior High School in Jefferson City. The simple pleasures and trying times of Robinson J. Peepers, a timid and mild-mannered Biology instructor.

CAST

Robinson J. Peepers	Wally Cox
Harvey Weskitt, his friend, the English teacher	Joseph Foley
	Tony Randall
Nancy Remington, the school nurse, Robinson's girlfriend; married on May 23, 1954	Norma Crane
	Patricia Benoit
Marge Weskitt, Harvey's wife	Georgianna Johnson
Mrs. Gurney, a friend	Marion Lorne
Mr. Remington, Nancy's father	Ernest Truex
Mrs. Remington, Nancy's mother	Sylvia Field
Mr. Bascomb, the principal	George Clark

Also   David Tyrell

Orchestra: Bernie Green.

Producer: Fred Coe, Hal Keith.

Sponsor: Reynolds Metals.

MR. PEEPERS—30 minutes—NBC—
July 3, 1952 - June 12, 1955.

MR. ROBERTS

Comedy-Drama. Background: The
South Pacific during World War II.
The story of Lieutenant Douglas
Roberts, cargo officer of the *Reluctant*, a U.S. Navy cargo ship nicknamed "The Bucket" by its reluc-
tant-to-serve crew. Feeling he is dis-
placed, and longing to serve aboard a
fighting vessel, he seeks to acquire a
transfer, but, by shouldering the
antics of his men, he encounters the
hostility of the ship's commander,
Captain John Morton, who, feeling
that the morale of his men precedes
Roberts's wants, refuses to forward
his letters to the proper authorities.
Through his continual efforts, a sentimental version of the war is seen.

CAST

Lt. J.G. Douglas Roberts	Roger Smith
Captain John Morton	Richard X. Slattery
Ensign Frank Pulver, the lazy, disorganized morale officer	Steve Harmon
Doc, the surgeon	George Ives
Seaman D'Angelo	Richard Sinatra
Seaman Mannion	Ronald Starr
Seaman Reber	Roy Reese

MR. ROBERTS—30 minutes—NBC—
September 17, 1965 - September 2,
1966. 30 episodes.

MR. ROGERS' NEIGHBORHOOD

Educational. The program concerns
the emotional development of
children from three to eight years of
age. Through actual demonstrations
and guests who discuss topics, an
attempt is made to help children cope
with or overcome their problems.

Host: Fred Rogers.

Music: John Costa.

Neighbors: Betty Aberlin, Jewel Walker, Francois Clemmons, Joe
Negri (as the handyman).

Executive Producer: Fred Rogers.

Producer: Bill Moates, Bob Walsh.

Director: David Fu-Yung Chen, Bill
Moates, Bob Walsh.

MR. ROGERS' NEIGHBOR-
HOOD—30 minutes. NET—October
1967 - October 1970. PBS—October
1970 - June 1975. Syndicated to PBS
stations.

MR. SMITH GOES TO WASHINGTON

Comedy. Background: Washington,
D.C. After the death of a senator,
Eugene Smith, a country politician, is
elected to replace him. Encompassing
mature wisdom, boyish charm,
warmth, and dignity, he struggles to
adjust to the norms of Capitol life.
Based on the movie.

CAST

Eugene Smith	Fess Parker
Patricia Smith, his wife	Sandra Warner
Cooter Smith, his uncle, a guitar-playing rural philosopher	Red Foley
Miss Kelly, his secretary	Rita Lynn

Arnie, his butler　　　　　Stan Irwin

MR. SMITH GOES TO WASHINGTON—30 minutes—ABC—September 29, 1963 - March 30, 1964.

MR. T AND TINA

Comedy. Background: Chicago. The trials and tribulations of Taro Takahashi, a widowed Japanese businessman who moves from Tokyo to Chicago with his family: his children, Sachi and Aki, his uncle Matsu, and his live-in sister-in-law, Michi. Stories focus on the complications that ensue following his hiring Tina Kelly, a dizzy young American woman, as governess for his children.

CAST

Taro Takahashi, executive
　　v.p. of Moyati
　　Industries　　　　　Pat Morita
Tina Kelly　　　　　Susan Blanchard
Sachi Takahashi　　　　　June Angela
Aki Tahahashi　　　　Gene Profanata
Uncle Matsu　　Jerry Hatsuo Fujikawa
Michi　　　　　　　　　Pat Suzuki
Miss Llewellyn, the manager of
　　the apartment
　　building　　Miriam Byrd-Nethery
Harvard, the maintenance
　　engineer　　　　　　Ted Lange

Music: George Tipton.

Executive Producer-Creator: James Komak.

Producer: Madelyn Davis, Bob Carroll, Jr.

Director: James Sheldon, Rick Edlestein, James Komack, Dennis Steinmetz.

MR. T AND TINA—30 minutes—ABC —September 26, 1976 - October 30, 1976. 5 episodes.

MR. TERRIFIC

Comedy. Background: Washington, D.C. Experimenting with methods to cure the common cold, a U.S government research scientist discovers a power pill. Tested, it produces incredible strength in animals, but makes the strongest of men quite ill. Faced with a problem, Barton J. Reed, the Bureau of Special Projects subchief, begins the secret search—"to find the one and only man."

After many months, their search ends at Hal and Stanley's Gasoline Station. Approached, Stanley Beemish, the proprietor, "a weak and droopy daffodil," is persuaded to test the pill. Seconds after taking it, he is transformed into the invincible Mr. Terrific. Sworn in as an agent, Stanley Beemish adopts a dual life: as a private citizen; and as the U.S. government's secret weapon against crime.

Stories depict Stanley's investigations and the problems that befall the costumed avenger: his inability to locate assigned targets when airborne; his struggles to adjust to a secret alias; and his attempts to cope with the predicaments that occur when the pill, lasting only one hour in effectiveness, wears off at crucial moments.

CAST

Stanley Beemish/Mr.
　　Terrific　　　　　Stephen Strimpell
Hal, Stanley's
　　partner　　　　　　Dick Gautier
Barton J. Reed　　　　John McGiver
Hanley Trent, Reed's
　　assistant　　　　　　Paul Smith

Music: Gerald Fried.

MR. TERRIFIC—30 minutes—CBS— January 9, 1967 - August 28, 1967.

MR. WIZARD

Educational. The basics of various scientific experiments.

Host-Instructor: Don Herbert (Mr. Wizard).

Assistants, including: Bruce Lindgren (as Willie Watson), Rita MacLaughlin, Alan Howard, Buzzy Podwell, Betty Sue Albert.

MR. WIZARD—30 minutes—NBC—March 5, 1951 - September 5, 1965: also: NBC—September 11, 1971 - September 2, 1972.

MRS. G GOES TO COLLEGE

Comedy. Background: An unidentified college that resembles the University of Southern California. The trials and tribulations of Sarah Green, a middle-aged widow who enrolls in the school to reach a long-sought dream—her college education.

CAST
Sarah Green	Gertrude Berg
Professor Crayton, her advisor; a visiting instructor from England	Sir Cedric Hardwicke
Maxfield, her boarding-house landlady	Mary Wickes
Joe Caldwell, a freshman	Skip Ward
Susan, Sarah's daughter	Marion Ross
Jerry Green, Sarah's son	Leo Penn
George Howell	Paul Smith
Irma Howell	Aneta Corsaut
Carol	Karyn Kubcinet

Music: Herschel Burke Gilbert.

MRS. G GOES TO COLLEGE—30 minutes—CBS—October 4, 1961 - April 5, 1962. 26 episodes.

M SQUAD

Crime Drama. Background: Chicago. The story of Lieutenant Frank Ballinger, a special plainclothes detective with the M Squad division of the Chicago Police Department. Episodes depict his investigations into cases that surpass the requirements of systematic law-enforcement procedure.

CAST
Lt. Frank Ballinger	Lee Marvin
Captain Grey	Paul Newlan

Narrator: Lee Marvin.

Music: Stanley Wilson.

M SQUAD—30 minutes—NBC—September 20, 1957 - January 29, 1960. Syndicated. 117 episodes.

MUGGSY

Drama. Background: An unidentified city that is representative of any city where situations depicted on the program actually happen. The series explores life in the inner city as seen through the eyes of Margaret "Muggsy" Malloy, a thirteen-year-old orphan, and her older half-brother, her guardian, Nick Malloy, a taxicab driver. The program, though aimed at children, is realistic and penetrating. Taped in Bridgeport, Connecticut.

CAST
Margaret "Muggsy" Malloy	Sarah MacDonnell
Nick Malloy	Ben Masters
Gus, their friend	Paul Michael

Clytmnestra, Muggsy's
friend　　　　　　Star-Shemah
T.P., Clytmnestra's
brother　　　　　Danny Cooper

Music Performed By: Blood, Sweat, and Tears.

Musical Coordinator: Robert Gessinger, Phebe Haas.

Executive Producer: George Heineman.

Director: Bert Saltzman, J. Philip Miller, Sidney Smith.

MUGGSY—30 minutes—NBC—September 11, 1976 - April 9, 1977.

MULLIGAN'S STEW

Drama. Background: Birchfield, California. The story of the Mulligan family—Michael, a high school athletic coach, his wife, Jane, the school nurse, their three children, Mark, Melinda, and Jimmy, and their four adopted children, Stevie, Adam, Polly, and Kimmy—who became a part of the family after Mike's sister and husband perished in a plane crash. The series focuses on the attempts of the family members to accept and understand each other's differences.

CAST
Michael Mulligan　Lawrence Pressman
Jane Mulligan　　　Elinor Donahue
Mark Mulligan　　　Johnny Whitaker
　　　　　　　　　　Johnny Doran
Melinda Mulligan　　Julie Haddock
Jimmy Mulligan　　　K.C. Martel
Stevie Mulligan　　Suzanne Crough
Adam "Moose"
　Mulligan　Christopher Ciampa
Polly Mulligan　　Lory Kochheim
Kimmy Mulligan, an adopted
　　Vietnamese orphan Sunshine Lee

Music: George Tipton.

Producer: Joanna Lee.

MULLIGAN'S STEW—60 minutes—NBC—Premiered: October 25, 1977.

THE MUNSTERS

Comedy. Background: Mockingbird Heights, 1313 Mockingbird Lane, the creepy, spider-web-covered residence of the Munsters, a family who resemble celluloid fiends of the 1930s: Herman (a Frankenstein-like creature), a funeral director at Gateman, Goodbury, and Graves; his wife, Lily (a female vampire); their ten-year-old son, Edward Wolfgang (a werewolf); Lily's father, Count Dracula (Grandpa), a 378-year-old mad scientist; and their "poor unfortunate" niece, Marilyn, young and beautiful, the black sheep of the family.

The Munsters. Fred Gwynne (top), Yvonne DeCarlo (left), Beverly Owen, Al Lewis, and Butch Patrick (bottom).

Living in their own world, and believing themselves to be normal, the family struggles to cope with the situations that foster their rejection by the outside world.

CAST

Herman Munster	Fred Gwynne
Lily Munster	Yvonne DeCarlo
Grandpa	Al Lewis
Marilyn Munster	Beverly Owen
	Pat Priest
Marilyn Munster (feature version, "Munster Go Home")	Debbie Watson
Edward Wolfgang Munster (Eddie)	Butch Patrick
Mr. Gateman, Herman's employer	John Carradine
Clyde Thornton, Herman's co-worker	Chet Stratton
Dr. Edward Dudley, the Munster family physician	Paul Lynde

Munster family pets: Spot, a prehistoric creature found by Grandpa while digging in the backyard; Igor the bat; and an unnamed raven who constantly speaks the immortal words of Edgar Alan Poe— "Nevermore."

Music: Jack Marshall.

Music Supervision: Stanley Wilson.

Producer: Joe Connelly, Bob Mosher.

Director: Seymour Burns, Joseph Pevney, Lawrence Dobkin, Earl Bellamy, David Alexander, Jerry Paris, Charles R. Rondeau, Gene Reynolds, Ezra Stone, Norman Abbott, Charles Barton.

Eddie's doll: Woff Woff (a werewolf).

THE MUNSTERS—30 minutes—CBS —September 24, 1964 - September 8, 1966. 70 episodes. Syndicated.

THE MUPPET SHOW

Variety. A adult oriented series wherein the Muppets (fanciful puppets created by Jim Henson) perform in sketches (with guests), sing, and dance.

Host: Kermit the Frog (manipulated and voiced by Jim Henson).

Voices: Frank Oz, Jim Henson, Jerry Nelson, Richard Hunt, Peter Friedman, John Loveday, Jane Henson.

Puppet Operators: Carolyn Wilcox, Mari Kaestyle, Dave Goelz, Larry Jameson, Richard Hunt, Frank Oz, Jim Henson.

Orchestra: Jack Parnell.

Music Conductor: Derek Scott.

Executive Producer: Jim Henson.

Producer: Jack Burns.

Director: Peter Harris.

THE MUPPET SHOW—30 minutes— Syndicated 1976.

MUSIC BINGO

Game. A musical adaptation of bingo. Two competing contestants. An instrumental selection is played by the orchestra. The player first to sound his buzzer receives a chance to identify the song title. If correct, a square is marked on a large electronic game board. Object: To complete the bingo board through the identification of song titles. Winners receive merchandise prizes.

Host: Johnny Gilbert.

Orchestra: Harry Salter.

MUSIC BINGO—30 minutes. NBC—June 5, 1958 - December 5,

1958; ABC—December 8, 1958 - January 1, 1960.

MUSICAL CHAIRS

Game. Three celebrity panelists who play for home viewers. A vocal group presents a musically oriented question. Panelists then have to answer it by impersonating its recording artist. One point is awarded for each correct impersonation and answer. Winners are the highest point scorers. Home viewers receive cash prizes.

Host: Bill Leyden.

Panelists: Bobby Troup, Johnny Mercer, Mel Blanc.

Vocalists: The Cheerleaders.

Orchestra: Bobby Troup.

MUSICAL CHAIRS—30 minutes—NBC—July 9, 1955 - September 17, 1955.

MUSICAL CHAIRS

Game. Four contestants compete. A song, either sung by the host or a guest, is stopped one line before its conclusion. Three possible last lines to the song appear on a board. Players then press a button and lock in their choice. The player who was first to press in receives a chance to select a line. If he is correct, he receives money. If not, the player who was second to press in receives a chance. In round one, three songs are played and each is worth fifty dollars. In round two, each of the three songs played is worth seventy-five dollars. Round three is the elimination round and at the end of each song, the player with the lowest score is defeated. Each song is worth one hundred dollars. The winner is the highest-scoring player.

Host: Adam Wade.

Announcer: Pat Hernan.

Music: The Musical Chairs Orchestra directed by Derek Smith.

MUSICAL CHAIRS—30 minutes—CBS—June 16, 1975 - October 31, 1975.

MUSICAL COMEDY TIME

Variety. Guest performers recreate great moments from hit Broadway plays.

Producer: Richard Berger, Bernard L. Schubert.

Director: William Corrigan, Richard Berger.

MUSICAL COMEDY TIME—30 minutes—NBC 1950.

MUSIC BOWL

A fifteen minute variety series, broadcast on CBS in 1950, and starring Danny O'Neil and Carolyn Gilbert.

MUSIC CITY U.S.A.

Musical Variety. Performances by Country and Western artists.

Hosts: Jerry Naylor; Teddy Bart.

MUSIC CITY U.S.A.—60 minutes—Syndicated 1968. 13 tapes.

MUSIC COUNTRY

See title: "Dean Martin Presents Music Country."

MUSIC '55

Musical Variety. An intimate party flavor is emphasized as all fields of music are explored.

Host: Stan Kenton.

Guests, representing selected fields: Jaye P. Morgan, Peggy Lee, Duke Ellington, Louis Armstrong, Ella Fitzgerald, Woody Herman, Lena Horne, Frankie Laine.

Announcer: Stu Metz.

Orchestra: Stan Kenton.

MUSIC '55—30 minutes—CBS—July 12, 1955 - September 1955.

MUSIC FOR A SPRING NIGHT

Musical Variety.

Host: Glenn Osser.

Vocalists: The Glenn Osser Chorus.

Orchestra: Glenn Osser.

MUSIC FOR A SPRING NIGHT—60 minutes—ABC—March 20, 1960 - May 11, 1960.

MUSIC FOR A SUMMER NIGHT

Musical Variety.

Host: Glenn Osser

Vocalists: The Glenn Osser Chorus.

Orchestra: Glenn Osser.

MUSIC FOR A SUMMER NIGHT—60 minutes—ABC—June 3, 1959 - September 21, 1959.

MUSIC FROM MEADOWBROOK

Musical Variety. Background: Frank Dailey's Meadowbrook in Cedar Grove, New Jersey.

Host: Jimmy Blaine.

Music: King Guron's Rhythm Orchestra; Ray McKinley's Band.

MUSIC FROM MEADOWBROOK—60 minutes—ABC—May 23, 1953 - September 26, 1953.

MUSIC HALL AMERICA

Musical Variety.

Hosts: Guests.

Regulars: Dean Rutherford, Sadi Burnett, The Even Dozen.

Orchestra: Bill Walker.

Choreography: Jean Sloan.

Vocal Backgrounds: L'Adidas.

Executive Producer: Lee Miller.

Director: Lee Bernhardi.

MUSIC HALL AMERICA—60 minutes—Syndicated 1976.

MUSIC ON ICE

Musical Variety. Background: An "ice capade."

Host: Johnny Desmond.

Regulars (skating personalities): Jacqueline du Bief; Skip Jacks, The Dancing Blades.

Orchestra: Bob Boucher.

MUSIC ON ICE—60 minutes—NBC— May 8, 1960 - September 1960.

THE MUSIC PLACE

Variety. Performances by Country

and Western entertainers.

Host: Stu Phillips.

Regulars: Bob and Pat Geary.

Producer: Gary Brockhurst.

THE MUSIC PLACE—30 minutes—Syndicated 1975.

THE MUSIC SCENE

Musical Variety. A modern version of "Your Hit Parade." Performances by the top artists in various fields of music (Country and Western, Ballad, Rock, Folk, and Blues). Musical numbers are interwoven with comedy sketches.

Host: David Steinberg.

The Music Scene Troupe: Paul Reid Roman, Lilly Tomlin, Larry Hankin, Christopher Ross, Pat Williams.

Orchestra: Pat Williams.

THE MUSIC SCENE—45 minutes—ABC—September 22, 1969 - January 12, 1970. 13 episodes.

THE MUSIC SHOP

Musical Variety. Performances by the recording industry's top personalities.

Host: Buddy Bergman.

Orchestra: Buddy Bergman.

THE MUSIC SHOP—30 minutes—NBC—January 11, 1959 - March 8, 1959.

THE MUSIC SHOW

Musical Variety.
Host: Robert Trendler.

Regulars: Mike Douglas, Elena Warner, Jackie Van, Henri Noel.

Orchestra: Robert Trendler.

THE MUSIC SHOW—30 minutes—DuMont 1953.

MY FAVORITE HUSBAND

Comedy. Background: New York City. The trials and tribulations of the Coopers: George, a young bank executive, and his beautiful but scatter-brained wife, Liz.

CAST

Liz Cooper	Joan Caulfield
	Vanessa Brown
George Cooper	Barry Nelson
Gilmore Cobb, their neighbor, a peanut manufacturer	Bob Sweeney
Myra Cobb, his wife	Alexandra Talton

Orchestra: Lud Gluskin.

Producer: Norman Tokar.

Sponsor: International Silver

MY FAVORITE HUSBAND—30 minutes—CBS—September 12, 1953 - December 27, 1955.

MY FAVORITE MARTIAN

Comedy. Background: Los Angeles, California. Enroute to the office, *Los Angeles Sun* newspaper reporter Tim O'Hara, witnesses the crash landing of a damaged U.F.O. Investigating, he discovers and befriends its passenger, a professor of anthropology from Mars whose specialty is the primitive planet Earth. Tim takes the marooned professor back to his apartment where the Martian adopts the guise of Martin O'Hara, an uncle staying with Tim after a long journey.

Hindered by a lack of scarce items—which are presently unknown on Earth—Martin struggles to repair his crippled craft, conceal his identity, and adjust to the discomforts of a primitive, backward planet.

CAST

Martin O'Hara (Uncle Martin)	Ray Walston
Tim O'Hara	Bill Bixby
Lorelei Brown, Tim's landlady	Pamela Britton
Detective Bill Brennan, L.A.P.D., Martin's rival for Lorelei's affections	Alan Hewitt
Mr. Burns. Tim's employer	J. Pat O'Malley
The police captain	Roy Engle

Music: George Greeley.

MY FAVORITE MARTIAN—30 minutes—CBS—September 15, 1963 - September 4, 1966. 107 episodes. Syndicated. Spin-off series: "My Favorite Martians" (see title).

MY FAVORITE MARTIANS

Animated Cartoon. A spin-off from "My Favorite Martian." Background: Los Angeles, California. A damaged alien spacecraft lands on Earth. Its occupants, Uncle Martin, his nephew Andy, and their dog, Oakie Doakie, are befriended by the sole witnesses, newspaper reporter Tim O'Hara and his niece Katy.

Sheltering the stranded Martians, Tim arouses the suspicions of freelance security officer Bill Brennan, who sets his goal to uncover Martin's true identity.

Plagued by the discomforts of primitive Earth, Martin struggles to conceal his and Andy's true identities and to make the repairs needed to return home to Mars.

Additional Characters: Lorelei Brown, Tim's landlady; Brad Brennan, Bill's son; and Chump, Brad's pet chimpanzee.

Voices: Jonathan Harris, Edward Morris, Jane Webb, Lane Scheimer.

Music: The Horta-Mahana Corporation.

MY FAVORITE MARTIANS—25 minutes—CBS—September 8, 1973 - August 30, 1975. 16 episodes.

MY FRIEND FLICKA

Adventure. Background: The Goose Bar Ranch in Coulee Springs, Wyoming during the early 1900s. The series, which details the experiences of the McLaughlins, a horse-ranching family, focuses on the adventures shared by their young son, Ken, and his horse, Flicka (Swedish for Little Girl), a once wild stallion given to him by his father in an attempt to help teach him responsibility. Based on the stories by Mary O'Hara.

CAST

Rob McLaughlin, the father	Gene Evans
Nell McLaughlin, his wife	Anita Louise
Ken McLaughlin	Johnny Washbrook
Gus Broeberg, their ranchhand	Frank Ferguson
Hildy Broeberg, Gus's niece	Pamela Beaird
Sheriff Walt Downey	Hugh Sanders
	Sydney Mason
The U.S. Marshal	Craig Duncan

Sgt. Tim O'Gara, Rob's
   friend   Tudor Owen
Flicka   Wahama

Music Supervision: Alec Compinsky.

Producer: Alan A. Armor, Peter Packer, Sam White, Herman Schlom.

Director: Robert Gordon, James Clark, Frederick Stephani, Nathan Juran, Albert S. Rogell.

MY FRIEND FLICKA—30 minutes. CBS—February 10, 1956 - September 1959; ABC—September 30, 1959 - December 31, 1963; CBS—September 30, 1961 - September 26, 1964. 39 episodes. Syndicated.

MY FRIEND IRMA

Comedy. Distinguished by two formats.

Format One: (1952-1953)
   Background: New York City; Mrs. O'Reilly's Boarding House, 185 West 73rd Street, Manhattan, Apartment 3-B, the residence of secretaries Irma Peterson, a beautiful but dumb blonde, and Jane Stacey, a level-headed girl who is constantly plagued by Irma's scatterbrained antics.

Stories depict their romantic heartaches: Irma and her boyfriend, the impoverished and jobless Al, a con artist who sees her, his "Chicken," as only a means by which to further his harebrained money-making ventures; and Jane and her boyfriend, her multi-millionaire employer, Richard Rhinelander III, an investment counselor whom she struggles to impress and hopefully one day marry.

Jane, aware of a studio and home audience, speaks directly to the camera and establishes scenes.

Format Two: (1953-1954)
   Background: Same. In an opening curtain speech, Irma informs viewers of Jane's transfer to Panama; and of her acquiring a new roommate, newspaperwoman Kay Foster, by placing an ad in the classified section of the newspaper.

Stories continue to relate the life of a beautiful proverbially dumb blonde; and the trials and tribulations of her roommate, who becomes the recipient of her harebrained attempts to assist others.

My Friend Irma. Marie Wilson.

CAST

Irma Peterson	Marie Wilson
Jane Stacey	Cathy Lewis
Kay Foster	Mary Shipp
Al	Sid Tomack
Richard Rhinelander III	Brooks West
Joe Vance, Irma's romantic interest (later episodes)	Hal March
Mrs. O'Reilly, Irma's landlady	Gloria Gordon
Mrs. Rhinelander, Richard's socialite	

mother   Margaret DuMont
Professor Kropotkin,
    the girl's downstairs
    neighbor, a violinist at
    The Paradise Burlesque
    Cafe   Sig Arno
Mr. Clyde, Irma's
    employer   Donald MacBride
Bobby Peterson, Irma's
    ten-year-old
    nephew   Richard Eyer
The neighbor   John Carradine
Also: Frances Mercer, Aileen Carlyle.

Orchestra: Lud Gluskin.

Announcer: Frank Bingham.

Producer: Richard Whorf, Cy Howard.

Creator: Cy Howard.

Sponsor: Camel Cigarettes.

MY FRIEND IRMA—30 minutes—
CBS—January 8, 1952 - June 25,
1954.

MY FRIEND TONY

Crime Drama. Background: Los
Angeles, California. The investigations
of John Woodruff, private detective
and criminologist professor at
U.C.L.A.; and his Italian partner,
Tony Novello, whom he befriended
while in service during World War II.

CAST
John Woodruff   James Whitmore
Tony Novello   Enzo Cerusico

MY FRIEND TONY—60 minutes—
NBC—January 5, 1969 - August 31,
1969. 16 episodes.

MY HERO

Comedy. Background: The Thackery
Realty Company in Los Angeles, California. The trials and tribulations of
Robert S. Beanblossom, a carefree and
easygoing salesman.

CAST
Robert S. Beanblossom Bob Cummings
Julie Marshall, the office
    secretary   Julie Bishop
Mr. Thackery, their
    employer   John Litel

Producer: Mort Green.

Sponsor: Dunhill Products.

MY HERO—30 minutes—NBC—
November 8, 1952 - September 12,
1953. Syndicated. Also known as
"The Robert Cummings Show."

MY LITTLE MARGIE

Comedy. Background: New York
City; The Carlton Arms Hotel, Apartment 10-A, the residence of the

My Little Margie. Gale Storm and Charles
Farrell.

Albrights: Vernon, widower, vice-president of the investment firm of Honeywell and Todd; and his beautiful twenty-one-year old daughter, Margie.

Stories depict the problem that each has, and their individual attempts to solve it:

Vern's problem: Margie—"I've been both mother and father to her since she was born. She's grownup now....When she was a little I could spank her and make her mind me. I had control over her....When she disobeyed I took her roller skates away for a week. What can you do when a girl reaches this age? She's completely out of hand. I've got a problem, believe me, I've got a problem."

Margie's problem: Vern—"I've raised him from...my childhood. He's nearly fifty now and you'd think he'd settle down, wouldn't you?....Today, he looks better in shorts on a tennis court than fellows twenty-five. Girls wink at him and what's worse he winks back at them. I want a nice old comfortable father. I try to look after him, but he just won't settle down. I've got a problem, believe me, I've got a problem."

Intervening in Vern's romantic life, Margie attempts to achieve her goal; and Vern, by threatening to deprive Margie of her desires, struggles to acquire an obedient, nonmeddling daughter.

CAST

Margie Albright	Gale Storm
Vern Albright	Charles Farrell
Freddy Wilson, Margie's impoverished boy-friend	Don Hayden
George Honeywell, Vern's employer	Clarence Kolb
Roberta Townsend, Vern's romantic interest	Hillary Brooke
Mrs. Odettes, the Albrights' eighty-three-year-old neighbor	Gertrude Hoffman
Charlie, the elevator operator	Willie Best

Music: Lud Gluskin.

Producer: Hal Roach, Jr.

Director: Walter Strenge.

Sponsor: Philip Morris; Scott Paper.

MY LITTLE MARGIE—30 minutes—CBS—June 16, 1952 - September 8, 1952; June 1, 1953 - July 30, 1953; NBC—September 9, 1953 - August 24, 1955. 126 episodes. Syndicated.

MY LIVING DOLL

Comedy. Background: Los Angeles, California. Completing United States Space Project AF 709, a delicate, intricate, and beautifully constructed female robot, the ultimate in feminine composition, Dr. Carl Miller assigns her (Rhoda) to psychiatrist Dr. Bob McDonald to mold her character.

Living with his sister, Irene, he introduces Rhoda as a patient who requires constant care and attention. Encountering Irene's interference, and the smooth techniques of his bachelor-playboy friend, Dr. Peter Robinson, who has fallen in love with her, Bob struggles to develop her mind and character for the benefit of science.

CAST

Rhoda	Julie Newmar
Bob McDonald	Bob Cummings
Irene McDonald	Doris Dowling

My Living Doll. Julie Newmar and Bob Cummings.

Peter Robinson   Jack Mullaney
Carl Miller   Henry Beckman

MY LIVING DOLL—30 minutes—CBS—September 27, 1964 - September 8, 1965. 26 episodes.

MY MOTHER THE CAR

Comedy. Background: Los Angeles, California. Planning to purchase a station wagon, lawyer Dave Crabtree is distracted when he becomes fascinated with a decrepit 1928 Porter. Inspecting it, he hears a feminine voice call his name. Finding that the voice emerges from the radio, he discovers that the car is his mother, the late Abigail Crabtree, reincarnated.

Purchasing her, he returns home and encounters the objections of his family, who want a station wagon. Hoping to change their minds, the car is overhauled in a custom body shop, and the exquisite Touring Mobile, license plate PZR 317, is still rejected by his family.

Concealing the fact of reincarnation, Dave struggles to defend his mother against a family who eagerly await a station wagon; and, from the devious attempts of Captain Bernard Mancini, an antique car collector who is determined to add the Porter to his collection.

CAST

Dave Crabtree	Jerry Van Dyke
Barbara Crabtree, his wife	Maggie Pierce
Mother's voice	Ann Sothern
Captain Bernard Mancini	Avery Schreiber
Cindy Crabtree, Dave and Barbara's daughter	Cindy Eilbacher
Randy Crabtree, Dave and Barbara's son	Randy Whipple

Music: Paul Hampton.

MY MOTHER THE CAR—30 minutes—NBC—September 14, 1965 - September 6, 1966. 30 episodes. Syndicated.

MY NAME'S McGOOLEY, WHAT'S YOURS?

Comedy. The bickering relationship between a scheming father and his obnoxious, beer-swilling son-in-law.

CAST

The father	Gordon Chates
His daughter	Judi Farr
The son-in-law	John Meillon

MY NAME'S McGOOLEY, WHAT'S

YOURS?–30 minutes–Syndicated 1966.

MY PARTNER THE GHOST

Crime Drama. Background: London, England. While investigating a case, private detective Marty Hopkirk is killed. Returning as a ghost, he appears only to his former partner, Jeff Randall. Assisted by Jeff, he solves his murder, but violates an ancient rhyme ("Before the sun shall rise on you, each ghost unto his grave must go. Cursed the ghost who dares to stay and face the awful light of day") and is cursed to remain on Earth for one hundred years.

Spiritually assisting his wife, Jean, Marty assumes his former position as a private detective. Stories depict his and Jeff's case investigations.

CAST

Marty Hopkirk	Kenneth Cope
Jeff Randall	Mike Pratt
Jean Hopkirk, working as Jeff's secretary	Annette Andre
Police Inspector Large	Ivor Dean

Music: Edwin Astley.

Producer: Monty Berman.

Director: Cyril Frankel, Jeremy Summers.

Creator: Dennis Spooner.

MY PARTNER THE GHOST–60 minutes–Syndicated (U.S.) 1973. 26 episodes. An ITC Presentation.

MY SISTER EILEEN

Comedy. Background: Greenwich Village in New York City. The trials and

My Partner the Ghost. Left to right: Mike Pratt, Kenneth Cope, and Annette Andre. *Courtesy Independent Television Corp.; an ATV Company.*

tribulations of sisters Ruth and Eileen Sherwood: Ruth, a writer for *Manhattan* magazine; and Eileen, an actress. Based on the movie.

CAST

Ruth Sherwood	Elaine Stritch
Eileen Sherwood	Shirley Boone
Mr. Appopolous, the owner of the Appopolous Arms, an apartment house where the girls reside	Leon Belasco
Marty, Eileen's agent	Stubby Kaye
Robert Beaumont, Ruth's publisher	Raymond Bailey
Chick Adams, a newspaper reporter on the *Daily News*	Jack Weston
	Linden Charles
Bertha Bronsky, a friend	Rose Marie
Galavan	Richard Deacon
Walters	Henry Hunter

MY SISTER EILEEN—30 minutes—CBS—October 5, 1960 - April 12, 1961. 26 episodes.

MY SON JEEP

Comedy. The story of Doc Allison and his attempts to reconstruct his life after the death of his wife. Episodes focus on the antics of Jeep, his mischievous young son.

CAST

Doc Allison	Jeffrey Lynn
Jeep Allison	Martin Houston
Peggy Allison, Jeep's sister	Betty Lou Keim
Barbara, Doc's receptionist	Anne Sargent
Mrs. Birby, the Allison housekeeper	Leona Powers

MY SON JEEP—30 minutes—ABC—June 1954 - September 1954.

MYSTERIES OF CHINATOWN

Crime Drama. Background: San Francisco's Chinatown. The investigations of Dr. Yat Fu, owner of a curio shop and amateur crime sleuth.

CAST

Dr. Yat Fu	Marvin Miller
Ah Toy, his niece	Gloria Saunders
Police Lieutenant Hargrove	Bill Eythe
Police Lieutenant Cummings	Richard Crane

Also: Robert Bice, Marya, Wong Artarno, Ed MacDonald.

MYSTERIES OF CHINATOWN—30 minutes—ABC—December 4, 1949 - October 2, 1950.

MYSTERY CHEF

Cooking. Step-by-step methods in the preparation of meals.

Host: John McPherson (when first televised the chef was not identified).

MYSTERY CHEF—30 minutes—NBC—1949. Based on the radio program.

MYSTERY FILE

See title: "Q.E.D."

MYSTERY IS MY BUSINESS

See title: "Ellery Queen."

My Three Sons. Left to right: Tim Considine, Stanley Livingston, Fred MacMurray, William Frawley, Don Grady.

MY THREE SONS

Comedy. Background: The town of Bryant Park. The trials and tribulations of the Douglas family—Steve, widower, aeronautical engineer; his sons, Mike, Robbie, and Chip; and their grandfather, Michael Francis O'Casey, "Bub."

Changes:

1965: Charlie O'Casey, a retired sailor, replaces Bub. Mike, the elder son, marries Sally Ann Morrison. Leaving the family nest, they move east where Mike acquires a job as a psychology instructor. Shortly after, Chip, the youngest, befriends an orphaned boy, Ernie Thompson, whom Steve later adopts.

1967-1970: Transferred to North Hollywood, Steve and the family relocate. Attending college,

Robbie, the middle child, meets, falls in love with, and marries Kathleen Miller; later, they are the parents of triplets: Steve Douglas, Jr., Charley Douglas, and Robbie Douglas II.

1970-1971: Attending high school, Ernie encounters difficulty with a new teacher, Barbara Harper, widow, and mother of a young daughter, Dodie. Attempting to resolve the difficulty, Steve meets, falls in love with, and marries Barbara. Shortly after, Chip, who is attending college, meets, falls in love with and marries Polly Thompson, a coed.

1972: Arriving from Scotland seeking a first lady, Laird (Lord) Fergus McBain Douglas betrothes Terri Dowling, a cocktail waitress working at the Blue Berry Bowling Alley as Lady Douglas.

Stories from 1967 - 1972 mirror the lives of the individual members of the Douglas family

CAST

Steve Douglas	Fred MacMurray
Michael Francis "Bub" O'Casey	William Frawley
Charley O'Casey (Uncle Charley)	William Demarest
Mike Douglas	Tim Considine
Robbie Douglas	Don Grady
Chip (Richard) Douglas	Stanley Livingston
Sally Ann Douglas (Morrison)	Meredith MacRae
Barbara Douglas (Harper)	Beverly Garland
Katie Douglas (Miller)	Tina Cole
Ernie Douglas (Thompson)	Barry Livingston
Polly Douglas	

(Thompson, unrelated to Ernie)	Ronnie Troup
Dodie Douglas (Harper)	Dawn Lyn
Steve Douglas, Jr.	Joseph Todd
Charley Douglas	Michael Todd
Robbie Douglas II	Daniel Todd
Terri Dowling	Anne Francis
Fergus McBain Douglas (enacted by)	Fred MacMurray
Fergus McBain Douglas (voiced by)	Alan Caillou
Bob Walters, Steve's employer	Russ Conway John Gallaudet
Sylvia Walters, his wife	Irene Hervey
Tom Williams, Polly's father*	Norman Alden
Margaret Williams, Polly's mother	Doris Singleton
Also	Jodie Foster

The Douglas Family Dog: Tramp.

Music: Frank DeVol.

Executive Producer: Don Fedderson.

Producer: Fred Henry, Edmund Hartmann, George Tibbles.

Director: Gene Reynolds, Frederick de Cordova, James V. Kern.

*For unknown reasons, Polly's last name was changed with the introduction of her parents.

MY THREE SONS—30 minutes—ABC—September 29, 1960 - September 9, 1965; CBS—September 16, 1965 - August 24, 1972. CBS Daytime rebroadcasts: December 20, 1971 - September 1, 1972. 369 episodes.

MY TRUE STORY

Anthology. Dramatic adaptations of stories appearing in *My True Story* magazine.

Announcer: Herbert Duncan.

Producer-Director: Charles Powers.

MY TRUE STORY—30 minutes—ABC—May 5, 1950 - September 22, 1950.

MY WORLD . . . AND WELCOME TO IT

Comedy. Background: Westport, Connecticut. The real life and dream world of John Monroe, a cartoonist for *Manhattanite* magazine. Discontented with his job; uneased over the smartness of children and the hostility of animals; intimidated by his loving wife, Ellen, and his precocious daughter, Lydia; and scared to death of life, he retreats to his secret world of imagination, wherein his cartoons become real, life becomes tolerable, and he is a king—irresistible to women and a tower of strength in the eyes of men. Animation is combined with live action to present life as seen through the eyes of John Monroe. Based on "drawings, stories, inspirational pieces, and things that go bump in the night" by James Thurber.

CAST

John Monroe	William Windom
Ellen Monroe	Joan Hotchkis
Lydia Monroe	Lisa Gerritsen
Hamilton Greeley, John's employer	Harold J. Stone
Phil Jensen, a magazine writer	Henry Morgan
Ruth Jenson, Phil's wife	Olive Dunbar

Monroe family dogs: Irving and Christabel.

Music: Warren Barker; Danny Arnold.

MY WORLD . . . AND WELCOME TO IT—30 minutes—NBC—September 15,

1969 - September 7, 1970. Rebroadcasts: CBS—May 25, 1972 - September 7, 1972. 26 episodes.

n

NAKED CITY

Crime Drama. Background: New York City. The grueling day-to-day activities of the police detectives assigned to Manhattan's 65th precinct. Realistic police drama; filmed in the streets, on the sidewalks, and in the buildings of New York, The Naked City.

CAST—1958-1960

Detective Lieutenant Dan Muldoon	John McIntire
Detective Jim Halloran	James Franciscus
Janet Halloran, his wife	Suzanne Storrs

Music: Billy May, George Duning.

CAST—1960-1963

Detective Adam Flint	Paul Burke
Sergeant Frank Arcaro	Harry Bellaver
Detective Mike Parker	Horace McMahon
Libby, Adam's girl-friend	Nancy Malone

Also: Hal Gaetano, Max Klevin, stuntmen appearing in roles requiring daredevil action.

Music: Nelson Riddle.

NAKED CITY—30 minutes—ABC—September 30, 1958 - October 5, 1960; 60 minutes—ABC—October 12, 1960 - September 11, 1963. Syndicated. 39 half-hour, and 99 one hour episodes.

NAKIA

Crime Drama. Background: Davis County, New Mexico. The investigations of Deputy Nakia Parker, a Navajo Indian who sometimes finds his heritage and beliefs clashing with the law he has sworn to uphold.

CAST

Deputy Nakia Parker	Robert Forster
Sheriff Sam Jericho	Arthur Kennedy
Deputy Irene James	Gloria DeHaven
Deputy Hubbel Martin	Taylor Lacher
Half Cub	John Tenorio, Jr.
Ben Redearth	Victor Jory

Music: Leonard Rosenman.

NAKIA—60 minutes—ABC—September 21, 1974 - December 28, 1974. 15 episodes.

THE NAMEDROPPERS

Game. Involved: Three guest celebrities who comprise the panel; twenty selected studio audience contestants; and two Namedroppers (per show), people who are in some way related to the celebrities. One Namedropper appears and briefly tells how he is related to one of the celebrities, but not to which one. Each of the celebrities then relates a story concerning their relationship, but only one story is true. Two of the twenty studio audience members compete at a time. The eighteen remaining players each press a button and select the celebrity each believes is related to the Namedropper. The stage players then verbally divulge their choice. The celebrity identifies the Namedropper; and the studio audience votes are revealed. Each incorrect vote awards the correct player ten dollars; if neither is correct, the Namedropper receives the money. Two such rounds are played per game, enabling all twenty contestants to compete during a five-day period.

Hosts: Al Loman and Roger Barkley.

Announcer: Kenny Williams.

Music: Recorded.

THE NAMEDROPPERS—30 minutes —NBC—October 2, 1969 - March 27, 1970.

THE NAME OF THE GAME

Crime Drama. Background: Los Angeles, California; the offices of *Crime* magazine. The investigations of three men: Glenn Howard, its publisher, a man who built the defunct *People* magazine into a multi-million dollar empire; Dan Farrell, the senior editor, a former F.B.I. agent conducting a personal battle against the underworld (his wife and child were a victim of their bullets); and Jeff Dillon, the editor of the *People* segment of *Crime.* Their individual attempts to uncover story material are depicted on a rotational basis.

CAST

Glenn Howard	Gene Barry
Jeff Dillon	Tony Franciosa
Dan Farrell	Robert Stack
Peggy Maxwell, their girl friday	Susan Saint James
Joe Sample, a reporter	Ben Murphy
Andy Hill, a reporter	Cliff Potter
Ross Craig, a reporter	Mark Miller

Music: Dave Grusin; Stanley Wilson.

THE NAME OF THE GAME—90 minutes—NBC—September 20, 1968 - September 10, 1972. Syndicated.

THE NAME'S THE SAME

Game. Through question-and-answer probe rounds with John and/or Jane Does—people who possess famous names—a celebrity panel has to identify their famous birth names. Players receive cash prizes based on the number of probing questions asked of them by the panel. Ten questions is the limit; and twenty-five dollars is the amount that is awarded if the panel fails to identify the name.

Hosts: Robert Q. Lewis; Dennis James; Bob Elliott and Ray Goulding.

Panelists: Joan Alexander, Bess Myerson, Gene Rayburn, Arnold Stang, Abe Burrows, Meredith Wilson, Audrey Meadows, Laraine Day, Walter Slezak, Roger Price.

Announcers: John Reed King; Lee Vines.

Producer: Mark Goodson, Bill Todman.

Director: Jerome Schnur.

Sponsor: Swanson Foods; Ralston Purina Company.

THE NAME'S THE SAME—30 minutes—ABC—December 12, 1951 - October 7, 1955.

NAME THAT TUNE

Musical game. Distinguished by six formats.

Format One:

Name That Tune—30 minutes—NBC—1953-1957; CBS—1957-1960.

Two contestants stand approximately twenty feet from hung bells. A musical selection is played. Recognizing it, players run up to and ring the bell. The first player to sound his bell is permitted to identify the song title. If correct, he receives the tune and cash. Three such wins and he receives the opportunity to double his earnings via a mystery melody round, wherein he must idenitfy as many song titles as possible within a specified time limit.

Hosts: Red Benson; Bill Cullen; George de Witt.

Songstress: Vicki Mills.

Announcers: Johnny Olsen; Wayne Howell.

Orchestra: Harry Salter; Ted Rapf.

Format Two:

Name That Tune—30 minutes—NBC—Syndicated 1970.

Same as Format One.

Host: Richard Hayes.

Format Three:

Name That Tune—30 minutes—NBC—July 29, 1974 - January 3, 1975.

Two competing contestants.
Round One: A musical selection is played. Recognizing the tune, players run up to and ring a bell that is hung approximately ten feet away. The first player to sound his bell receives the chance to identify the song. If correct, he receives the tune. Five songs are played, and the contestant who identifies three receives ten points.

Round Two: Varies greatly in presentation; but the basic format is to identify three out of five tunes for ten points.

Round Three: The host relates clues to the identity of a song title. Players then bet as to the amount of notes (from seven down to one) it will take them to identify the tune. The lowest bidder receives the opportunity. The player who acquires three out of five tunes is the winner and receives twenty points.

The winner, the highest point scorer, receives a chance to earn money via "The Golden Melody." Object: To identify six song titles in one minute. Each correct response awards two hundred dollars.

Host: Dennis James.

Announcer: John Harlan.

Orchestra: Bob Alberti.

Format Four:

Name That Tune—30 minutes—Syndicated 1974.

Same as Format Three.

Host: Tom Kennedy.

Announcer: John Harlan.

Orchestra: Bob Alberti.

Format Five:

The $100,000 Name That Tune—30 minutes—Syndicated 1976. The game is played the same as format three, with the added bonus of allowing a player to win $100,000 by correctly identifying a very difficult mystery tune.

Host: Tom Kennedy.

Model: Geri Fiala.

Announcer: John Harlan.

Orchestra: Tommy Oliver.

$100,000 Pianist: Joe Harnell.

Executive Producer: Ralph Edwards.

Director: John Dorsey.

Format Six:

Name That Tune—30 minutes—NBC—January 3, 1977 - June 10, 1977. Played the same as format three. Credits are the same as format five with the exclusion of the $100,000 pianist.

The Nancy Drew Mysteries. Jean Rasey (left), and Pamela Sue Martin. *Courtesy of the Call-Chronicle Newspapers, Allentown, Pa.*

NANCY

Comedy. Background: Center City, Iowa. Meeting and falling in love, Adam Hudson, veterinarian, and Nancy Smith, the daughter of the President of the United States, marry. Stories depict their romantic misadventures; and their struggles to adjust to a marriage wherein their lives are more public than private.

CAST

Nancy Hudson (Smith)	Renne Jarrett
Adam Hudson	John Fink
Abby Townsend, Nancy's guardian	Celeste Holm
Everett Hudson, Adam's uncle	Robert F. Simon
Willie Wilson, a newspaper reporter	Eddie Applegate
Secret Serviceman Turner	William H. Bassett
Secret Serviceman Rodriquez	Ernesto Macias

Music: Sid Ramin.

NANCY—30 minutes—NBC—September 17, 1970 - January 7, 1971. 13 episodes.

THE NANCY DREW MYSTERIES

Mystery. Background: The town of River Heights, New England. The adventures of Nancy Drew, the pretty, proficient teenage daughter of criminal attorney Carson Drew. Stories concern her investigations as she attempts to help her father solve baffling crimes. Based on the stories by Carolyn Keene. Alternates with "The Hardy Boys Mysteries."

CAST

Nancy Drew	Pamela Sue Martin
Carson Drew	William Schallert
George Fayne, Nancy's girlfriend	Jean Rasey
Ned Nickerson, Carson's assistant	George O'Hanlon, Jr.
The Sheriff	Robert Karnes

Music: Stu Phillips, Glen A. Larson.

Executive Producer: Glén A. Larson.

Producer: Arlene Sidaris, B.W. Sandefur.

Director: E.W. Swackhamer, Noel Black, Michael Caffrey, Alvin Ganzer, Jack Arnold, Andy Sidaris.

THE NANCY DREW MYSTERIES—

60 minutes—ABC—Premiered: February 6, 1977.

Nanny and the Professor. Juliet Mills.

THE NANCY WALKER SHOW

Comedy. Background: Hollywood, California. The misadventures of Nancy Kitteridge, theatrical agent and mother whose troubles stem not only from her difficulties in handling clients, but in her inability to cope with her family: her husband, Kenneth, a retired Naval officer, and her neurotic daughter, Lorraine.

CAST

Nancy Kitteridge	Nancy Walker
Kenneth Kitteridge	William Daniels
Lorraine	Beverly Archer
Terry Folsom, Nancy's assistant	Ken Olfson
Glen, Lorraine's husband	James Cromwell

Music: Marilyn Bergman, Alan Bergman, Nancy Hamlisch.

Theme Vocal: Nancy Walker.

Executive Producer: Norman Lear.

Producer: Rod Parker.

Director: Hal Cooper, Alan Rafkin.

Creator: Norman Lear, Rod Parker.

THE NANCY WALKER SHOW—30 minutes—ABC—September 30, 1976 - December 23, 1976. Returned with a final first run episode on July 11, 1977.

THE NANETTE FABRAY SHOW

See title: "Yes Yes Nanette."

NANNY AND THE PROFESSOR

Comedy. Background: 10327 Oak Street, Los Angeles, California, the residence of Professor Harold Everett, widower, mathematics instructor at Clinton College; his children, Hal, Butch, and Prudence; and their beautiful, but mysterious housekeeper, Phoebe Figalilly, "Nanny," a woman who, when the professor needed assistance, mysteriously appeared and acquired the position.

Stories depict the events that befall the Everett family—unexplainable, but favorable situations that are seemingly caused by Nanny, who is neither magic nor a witch, but possesses the ability to spread love and joy.

CAST

Phoebe Figalilly (Nanny)	Juliet Mills
Professor Harold Everett	Richard Long
Hal Everett	David Doremus
Bentley (Butch) Everett	Trent Lehman
Prudence Everett	Kim Richards
Francine Fowler, Hal's	

girlfriend   Eileen Baral
Florence Fowler, her
   mother   Patsy Garrett
Aunt Henrietta, Nanny's
   relative   Elsa Lanchester
Everett Family Pets: Waldo, a dog;
   Mertyl and Mike, guinea pigs;
   Sebastian, a rooster; Jerome and
   Geraldene, kids (baby goats).

Music: George Greeley; Charles Fox.

Executive Producer: David Gerber.

Producer: Wes McAfee, Charles B. Fitzsimmons.

NANNY AND THE PROFESSOR–30 minutes–ABC–January 21, 1970 - December 27, 1971. 65 episodes. Syndicated.

NASH AIRFLYTE THEATRE

Anthology. Dramatic presentations.

Host: William Gaxton.

Producer-Director: Marc Daniels.

Sponsor: Nash.

NASH AIRFLYTE THEATRE–30 minutes–CBS–1950 - 1951.

NASHVILLE 99

Crime Drama. Background: Nashville, Tennessee. The cases of Stonewall "Stoney" Huff, and Trace Mayne, his partner, police detectives attached to the Nashville Metropolitan Police Department. (Nashville 99: Stoney's badge number.)

CAST
Det. Lt. Stoney
   Huff   Claude Akins
Det. Trace Mayne   Jerry Reed

Birdie Huff, Stoney's
   mother   Lucille Benson
R.B., a deputy   Charlie Pride

Music: Earle Hagen.

Music Supervision: Lionel Newman.

Executive Producer: Ernie Frankel.

Director: Don McDougall, Lawrence Dobkin, George Sherman.

NASHVILLE 99–60 minutes–CBS–April 1, 1977 - April 22, 1977. 3 episodes.

NASHVILLE NOW

See title: "The Ian Tyson Show."

NATIONAL GEOGRAPHIC

Documentary. Films exploring various aspects of man's world.

Host-Narrator: Joseph Campanella.

Music: Walter Scharf.

NATIONAL GEOGRAPHIC–60 minutes–Syndicated 1971. Compiled from a CBS network series of specials.

NATIONAL VELVET

Drama. The story of a young girl, Velvet Brown, and her attempts to train her horse, King, for competition in the Grand National Steeplechase. Based on the motion picture.

CAST
Velvet Brown   Lori Martin
Herbert Brown, her
   father, the owner of
   a farm   Arthur Space
Martha Brown, her
   mother   Ann Doran

Edwina Brown, her older
sister   Carole Wells
Donald Brown,
her younger
brother   Joey Scott
Mi Taylor, their
handyman   James McCallion

Music: Robert Armbruster.

NATIONAL VELVET—30 minutes—NBC—September 18, 1960 - September 10, 1962. 58 episodes. Syndicated.

NATION AT WAR

Documentary. Films highlighting the major events of World War II from 1936 to 1946.

Host-Narrator: Budd Knapp.

NATION AT WAR—30 minutes—Syndicated 1961. 13 episodes.

THE NAT KING COLE SHOW

Musical Variety.

Host: Nat King Cole.

Regulars: The Randy Van Horne Singers, The Boataneers.

Orchestra: Gordon Jenkins; Nelson Riddle.

THE NAT KING COLE SHOW—30 minutes—NBC—November 5, 1956 - December 17, 1957.

NAVY LOG

Anthology. Dramatizations based on incidents in the lives of the men in service of the U.S. Navy.

Included:

Storm Within. A Navy psychiatrist attempts to cure a depressed chief quartermaster after an act of heroism.

CAST
Harry Bellaver, John Zaremba.

One If By Sea. Braving the hazards of a raging sea, a captain struggles to attend a meeting in North Africa.

CAST
Reed Hadley, John Hoyt, Leonard Penn.

Survive. After their ship is attacked by enemy fire, three men, adrift in the Atlantic, struggle for survival.

CAST
Scotty Beckett.

Phantom Of The Blue Angels. The story of a jet pilot's involvement with secretive, off-duty activities.

CAST
Paul Picerni, William Phipps, Edward Binns, Tony Rock, Morgan Jones.

NAVY LOG—30 minutes—CBS—September 20, 1955 - September 1956; CBS—October 17, 1956 - September 25, 1958. 102 episodes. Syndicated.

NBC ACTION PLAYHOUSE

Anthology. Rebroadcasts of dramas that were originally aired via "The Bob Hope Chrysler Theatre."

Host: Peter Marshall.

Included:

Verdict For Truth. Believing his brother was wrongly sentenced to the gas chamber, a lawyer attempts to uncover the truth.

CAST

Reynolds: Cliff Robertson; Cooper: Michael Sarrazin; Emily: Jo Ann Fleet.

Nightmare. Assisted by her sister's husband, a girl seeks to kill her crippled twin.

CAST

Isobel/Vicky: Julie Harris; Morgan: Farley Granger; Detective Ryan: Thomas Gomez.

The Crime. A vengeful prosecuting attorney attempts to pin a murder on the girl who jilted him.

CAST

Abe Perez: Jack Lord; Sarah Rodman: Dana Wynter; DA Hightower: Pat O'Brien.

NBC ACTION PLAYHOUSE—60 minutes—NBC—June 24, 1971 - September 7, 1971; May 23, 1972 - September 5, 1972.

NBC ADVENTURE THEATRE

Anthology. Rebroadcasts of dramas that were originally aired via "The Bob Hope Chrysler Theatre."
Hosts: Art Fleming; Ed McMahon.

Included:

Echoes Of Evil. Through the testimony of a reformed gangster, a D.A. attempts to apprehend an underworld dope-ring leader.

CAST

Oscar Teckla: Barry Sullivan; Sara: Jane Wyatt; Martin Vesper: Nehemiah Persoff; Florence: Joan Hackett.

Corridor 400. A nightclub entertainer attempts to apprehend a narcotics kingpin for the F.B.I.

CAST

Anita King: Suzanne Pleshette; Ralph Travin: Theodore Bikel; Donald Guthrie: Andrew Duggan.

Deadlock. A woman's efforts to achieve revenge by planting a bomb in a police station.

CAST

Virginia: Lee Grant, Detective Baker: Jack Kelly; Detective Owens: Tige Andrews; Stacy Carter: Brooke Bundy.

NBC ADVENTURE THEATRE—60 minutes—NBC—July 24, 1971 - September 4, 1971; June 15, 1972 - August 31, 1972.

NBC BANDSTAND

See title: "Bandstand."

NBC BEST SELLERS

See title: "Best Sellers."

NBC COMEDY THEATRE

Anthology. Rebroadcasts of comedy episodes that were originally aired via "The Bob Hope Chrysler Theatre."
Host: Jack Kelly.

Included:

Dear Deductible. A songwriter and a socialite attempt to solve their tax problems by marrying and filing a joint return.

CAST
Mike Galway: Peter Falk; Virginia Ballard: Janet Leigh; Eddie: Norman Fell.

Holloway's Daughters. Unofficially assisted by his two teenage daughters, a detective attempts to solve a jewel theft.

CAST
George Holloway: David Wayne; Nick Holloway: Robert Young; Fleming Holloway: Brooke Bundy; Casey Holloway: Barbara Hershey; Martha Holloway: Marion Ross.

The Reason Nobody Hardly Ever Seen A Fat Outlaw In The Old West Is As Follows:. An outlaw, The Curly Kid, attempts to make a name for himself.

CAST
Curly: Don Knotts; Sheriff: Arthur Godfrey; Pauline: Mary-Robin Reed.

NBC COMEDY THEATRE—60 minutes—NBC—July 7, 1971 - August 30, 1971; July 8, 1972 - September 4, 1972.

NBC COMICS

See title: "The Telecomics."

THE NBC FOLLIES

Variety. A revue based on the music, song, dance, and comedy of vaudeville.

Host: Sammy Davis, Jr.

Regulars: Mickey Rooney, The Carl Jablonski Dancers.

Announcers: Colin Mayer, John Harlan.

Orchestra: Harper MacKay.

THE NBC FOLLIES—60 minutes—NBC—September 13, 1973 - December 27, 1973. 7 tapes.

THE NBC MOVIE OF THE WEEK

Movies. Theatrical features produced especially for television.

Announcer: Peggy Taylor, Donald Rickles.

Included:

How To Breakup a Happy Divorce. The story concerns a woman's attempts to win back her ex-husband from the woman who caused their marital breakup.

Cast: Ellen Dowling: Barbara Eden; Carter Dowling: Peter Bonerz; Jennifer: Liberty Williams; Tony: Hal Linden.

Flood. A disaster film wherein a small town is threatened by the imminent collapse of an earthen dam.

Cast: Steve Brannigan: Robert Culp; Paul Blake: Martin Milner; Abbie Adams: Carol Lynley; Mary: Barbara Hershey.

Night Terror. The story concerns a woman who, after witnessing a murder on a desert highway, suddenly finds her own life in jeopardy when she is stalked by the killer.

Cast: Carol Turney: Valerie Harper; Killer: Richard Romanus.

THE NBC MOVIE OF THE WEEK—90 minutes—NBC—Premiered: October 13, 1976.

NBC MOVIES

Movies. Theatrical releases.

Announcers: Don Rickles, Don Stanley, Frank Barton, Peggy Taylor, Eddie King.

Titles:

NBC SATURDAY NIGHT AT THE MOVIES—2 hours—NBC—Premiered: September 23, 1961.

NBC MONDAY NIGHT AT THE MOVIES—2 hours—NBC—Premiered: September 16, 1968.

NBC TUESDAY NIGHT AT THE MOVIES—2 hours—NBC—September 14, 1965 - September 7, 1971; January 1973 - September 1973; Returned: Premiered: September 9, 1974.

NBC WEDNESDAY NIGHT AT THE MOVIES—2 hours—NBC—1964-1965; January 1974 - September 3, 1974.

NBC MYSTERY MOVIE
NBC SUNDAY MYSTERY MOVIE

Crime Drama. The overall title for a series of nine rotating crime dramas.

The Series:

Amy Prentiss. Background: San Francisco, California. The story of Amy Prentiss, widow, the chief of detectives, a woman with style and intelligence who often finds her investigations compounded by resentment from her male colleagues.

CAST

Amy Prentiss	Jessica Walter
Sgt. Tony Russell	Steve Sandor
Detective Roy Pena	Art Metrano
Joan Carter, Amy's secretary	Gwenn Mitchell
Chief Demsey	M. Emmet Walsh
Jill Prentiss, Amy's daughter	Helen Hunt

Music: John Cacavas; Don Costa.

Columbo. Background: Los Angeles, California. The investigations of Lieutenant Columbo, an underpaid and untidy L.A.P.D. homicide detective. Slurred in speech and fumbling in exterior, his forceful nature and razor-sharp mind enable him to solve baffling acts of criminal injustice.

CAST

Lieutenant Columbo	Peter Falk
Captain Sampson	Bill Zuckert

Music: Bernard Segal, Jeff Alexander, Oliver Nelson, Dick De Benedictis, Billy Goldenberg.

Producer: Everett Chambers.

Director: Patrick McGoohan, Bernard Kowalski, Robert Douglas, Harvey Hart.

Hec Ramsey. Background: New Prospect, Oklahoma, 1901. The investigations of Deputy Hector (Hec) Ramsey, an ex-gunfighter turned law enforcer who attempts to solve crimes by means of scientific evaluation and deduction.

CAST

Deputy Hec Ramsey	Richard Boone
Sheriff Oliver B. Stamp	Rick Lenz
Amos B. Coogan, the town barber and doctor	Harry Morgan
Norma Muldoon, a widow, Hec's romantic interest	Sharon Acker
Andy Muldoon, her	

son   Brian Dewey

Narrator: Harry Morgan.

Music: Fred Steiner; Lee Holdridge.

Lanigan's Rabbi. Background: Cameron, California. The cases of Paul Lanigan, the police chief, and his friend and sometimes assistant, David Small, a Rabbi who preaches at the Temple Beth Halell Synagogue.

CAST

Paul Lanigan	Art Carney
Rabbi David Small	Stuart Margolin (pilot)
	Bruce Solomon
Kate Lanigan, Paul's wife	Janis Paige
Miriam Small, David's wife	Janet Margolin
Lieutenant Osgood	Robert Doyle
Bobbi, the reporter	Barbara Carney
Hannah Prince, one of the Rabbi's perishoners	Reva Rose

Music: Don Costa.

Executive Producer: Leonard B. Stern.

Producer: David J. Connell.

Director: Leonard B. Stern, Joseph Pevney, Noel Black.

McCloud. Background: New York City. The investigations of Sam McCloud, a deputy marshall from Taos, New Mexico assigned to the Manhattan 27th precinct to study metropolitan crime-detection methods.

CAST

Deputy Sam McCloud	Dennis Weaver
Police Chief Peter B. Clifford	J.D. Cannon
Sergeant Joe Broadhurst	Terry Carter
Chris Coughlin,	

Sam's romantic interest   Diana Muldaur

Music: Richard Clements.

Additional Music: Stu Phillips.

Executive Producer: Glen A. Larson.

Director: E.W. Swackhamer, Lou Antonio, Noel Black, Bruce Kessler.

McCoy. Background: Los Angeles, California. The exploits of McCoy, an engaging con artist who, to pay off his gambling debts, first undertakes a criminal case, then, by incorporating his unique skills, seeks to solve the crime.

CAST

McCoy	Tony Curtis
Gideon Gibbs, his assistant	Roscoe Lee Browne

Music: Billy Goldenberg, Dick De Benedictis.

Producer: Roland Kibbee.

McMillan And Wife. Background: San Francisco, California. The saga of Sally McMillan, the pretty, but trouble-prone wife of police commissioner Stewart "Mac" McMillan. Stories depict their investigations into crimes Sally accidentally stumbles upon and in which she involves Mac.

CAST

Stewart McMillan	Rock Hudson
Sally McMillan	Susan Saint James
Sergeant Charles Enright	John Schuck
Mildred, the McMillan's housekeeper	Nancy Walker
Maggie, Mac's secretary	Gloria Stroock
Chief Paulson	Bill Quinn

Music: Jerry Fielding.

Executive Producer: Leonard B. Stern.

Producer: Jon Epstein.

NBC Sunday Mystery Movie: McMillan and Wife. Susan Saint James and Rock Hudson.

Director: Lou Antonio, Harry Falk, Bob Finkel, James Sheldon, Lee H. Katzin.

McMillan. Revised title after the departure of Susan Saint James (her character, Sally, was killed in a plane crash) and Nancy Walker. Background: San Francisco, California. The cases of Stewart McMillan, the police commissioner.

CAST

Stewart McMillan	Rock Hudson
Agatha Thornton, his housekeeper	Martha Raye
Lt. Charles Enright	John Schuck
Sgt. Di'Maggio	Richard Gilliland
Maggie, Mac's secretary	Gloria Stroock
Chief Paulson	Bill Quinn

Music: Jerry Fielding.

Executive Producer: Leonard B. Stern.

Producer: Jon Epstein.

Director: Jackie Cooper, James Sheldon.

Quincy, M.E. See title.

NBC MYSTERY MOVIE—90 minutes —NBC—September 15, 1971 - September 12, 1972; as "NBC Sunday Mystery Movie:" Premiered: September 17, 1972.

NBC's SATURDAY NIGHT

Variety. Musical acts coupled with topical comedy. Broadcast live from New York City (11:30 p.m.-1:00 a.m., E.S.T.)

Hosts: Guests, including George Carlin, Rob Reiner, Lily Tomlin, Robert Klein.

Regulars (billed as "The Not Ready For Prime Time Players"): Chevy Chase, Jim Henson and the Muppets, Danny Ackroyd, John Belushi, Jane Curtin, Garrett Morris, Laraine Newman, Gilda Radner.

Announcer: Don Pardo.

Orchestra: Howard Jones, Howard Shore.

Musical Director: Paul Shaffer.

Producer: Lorne Michaels.

Director: Dave Wilson.

NBC's SATURDAY NIGHT—90 minutes—NBC—Premiered: October 11, 1975.

NBC THURSDAY NIGHT AT THE MOVIES

Theatrical and made for television films. Listed are examples of the films produced especially for television. See "NBC Movies" for the additional network film series.

Who Is the Black Dahlia? (1975). A haunting film that details veteran police inspector Harry Hanson's investigation into the mysterious, bizarre death of Elizabeth Short, whose body, drained of blood and bisected at the waist, was found in a Los Angeles field on January 15, 1947. The case concerning Miss Short, who had a penchant for black clothing and a tattoo of a black dahlia, is still unsolved.

CAST
Elizabeth Short: Lucie Arnaz; Insp. Harry Hanson: Efrem Zimbalist, Jr.; Also: Gloria DeHaven, June Lockhart, Ronny Cox, Macdonald Carey.

Ransom for Alice (1977). Background: Seattle during the 1890s. The story of two law officers— one male, the other female—as they attempt to find a girl kidnapped by a white slavery ring.

CAST
Deputy Jeannie Cullen: Yvette Mimieux; Deputy Kirk: Gil Gerrard; Marshal Pete Phelan: Charles Napier; Yankee Sullivan: Gavin MacLeod.

Snowbeast (1977). A thriller that centers on a Rocky Mountain resort that is terrorized by a killer beast similar to Bigfoot.

CAST
Ellen Seberg: Yvette Mimieux; Gar Seberg: Bo Svenson; Carrie Bill: Sylvia Sidney; Sheriff Paraday: Clint Walker.

NBC THURSDAY NIGHT AT THE MOVIES–2 hours–NBC–May 22, 1975 - August 28, 1975; Returned–January 15, 1976 - September 8, 1977.

NBC WEDNESDAY MYSTERY MOVIE

Crime Drama. The overall title for six rotating series: "Banacek"; "Cool Million"; "Faraday and Company"; "Madigan"; "The Snoop Sisters"; and "Tenafly."

Banacek. Background: Boston. The investigations of Thomas Banacek (pronounced: Ban-a-check), a self-employed insurance-company detective who recovers stolen merchandise for ten percent of its value.

CAST
Thomas Banacek	George Peppard
Felix Mulholland, his information man, the owner of a rare-book store	Murray Matheson
Jay Drury, his chauffeur	Ralph Manza
Carlie Kirkland, an agent for the Boston Insurance Company	Christine Belford

Music: Billy Goldenberg; Jack Elliot and Allyn Ferguson.

Cool Million. The investigations of Jefferson Keyes, a former U.S. government agent turned confidential private detective who charges one million dollars and guarantees results or refunds the money. Unable to afford a busy signal, he establishes a base in Lincoln, Nebraska (where telephone lines are always open), in the home of a woman named Elena. When his special telephone number, 30-30100, is dialed, Elena, the only person able to contact him, relays the message to him.

CAST
Jefferson Keyes	James Farentino
Tony Baylor, the pilot of his	

private jet	Ed Bernard
Elena	Adele Mara

Music: Billy Goldenberg.

Faraday And Company. Background: Los Angeles, California. Escaping from a Caribbean prison after twenty-eight years of internment on false charges, Frank Faraday returns to the States and, after exposing and apprehending the man responsible for his plight, assumes his former position as private detective with his son, Steve, a security consultant for industry. Stories relate the investigations of a 1940s-style private detective and the dated techniques he uses to apprehend the seventies generation of criminal.

CAST

Frank Faraday	Dan Dailey
Steve Faraday	James Naughton
Louise "Lou" Carson, Frank's former Secretary—and Steve's mother	Geraldine Brooks
Holly Barrett, their secretary	Sharon Gless

Music: Jerry Fielding.

Madigan. Background: New York City. The investigations of Sergeant Dan Madigan, an embittered plainclothes detective attached to the Manhattan tenth precinct.

Starring: Richard Widmark as Sgt. Dan Madigan.

Music: Jerry Fielding.

The Snoop Sisters. Background: New York City. The investigations of Ernesta and Gwen Snoop, sisters, eccentric fictitious mystery story writers who become involved with and solve crimes while seeking story material.

CAST

Ernesta Snoop	Helen Hayes
Gwen Snoop	Mildred Natwick
Lt. Steve Ostrowski, N.Y.P.D., their nephew	Bert Convy
Barney, an ex-con hired by Steve to watch over his mischievous aunts	Lou Antonio

Music: Jerry Fielding.

Tenafly. Background: Los Angeles, California. The investigations of Harry Tenafly, a private detective employed by Hightower Investigations, Incorporated.

CAST

Harry Tenafly	James McEachin
Ruth Tenafly, his wife	Lillian Lehman
Lorrie, his secretary	Rosanna Huffman
Lt. Sam Church, L.A.P.D.	David Huddleston
Herb Tenafly, Harry and Ruth's son	Paul Jackson

Their other son, an infant, is not given credit.

Music: Gil Mellé.

NBC WEDNESDAY MYSTERY MOVIE—90 minutes—NBC—September 13, 1972 - January 9, 1974. As "NBC Tuesday Mystery Movie:" 90 minutes—NBC—January 15, 1974 - September 4, 1974.

NBC WORLD PREMIERE MOVIE

Movies. Feature films produced especially for television.

Included:

Once Upon A Dead Man. Through the efforts of his scatterbrained wife, a police commissioner becomes involved in a charity auction theft and murder. The pilot film for "McMillan and Wife."

CAST

Stewart McMillan: Rock Hudson; Sally McMillan: Susan Saint James.

Emergency. The exploits of Squad 51 of the Los Angeles County Fire Department. The pilot film for "Emergency."

CAST

Dr. Brackett: Robert Fuller; Nurse McCall: Julie London; Dr. Early: Bobby Troup; John Gage: Randolph Mantooth; Roy DeSoto: Kevin Tighe.

Ellery Queen: Don't Look Behind You. The famed gentleman detective attempts to apprehend a strangler.

CAST

Ellery Queen: Peter Lawford; Insp. Richard Queen: Harry Morgan; Celeste: Stefanie Powers.

NBC WORLD PREMIERE MOVIE–2 hours–NBC–September 17, 1971 - September 8, 1972.

NEEDLES AND PINS

Comedy. Background: New York City; 463 7th Avenue, Manhattan, the business address of Lorelei Fashions. Life in the aggravating world of the garment industry as seen through the experiences of Wendy Nelson, a struggling young apprentice fashion designer.

Needles and Pins. Deirdre Lenihan and Norman Fell.

CAST

Wendy Nelson	Deirdre Lenihan
Nathan Davidson, the manufacturing head	Norman Fell
Harry Karp, Nathan's brother-in-law and partner	Louis Nye
Charlie Miller, the firm salesman	Bernie Kopell
Sonia Baker, the firm bookkeeper	Sandra Deel
Max, the material cutter	Larry Gelman
Myron Russo, the pattern maker	Alex Henteloff
Julius Singer, the competitor, the owner of Singer Sophisticates	Milton Selzer
Elliott, the waiter at the local restaruant	Joshua Shelley

Music: Mike Post and Pete Carpenter.

NEEDLES AND PINS–30 minutes–NBC–September 21, 1973 - December 28, 1973. 14 episodes.

THE NEIGHBORS

Game. Five actual neighbors, all of whom are female, are involved. Two are selected as the players; the remaining three comprise the panel. A question, that refers to one of the two players, is read. Each player has to predict to whom the question refers—herself or her neighbor. The answers are based on a survey of the panel, and if the player's choice agrees with the panel's, she receives $25. Four such questions are played. Round two concerns the players' abilities to pinpoint which neighbor said something about her. A statement, made by one of the panelists, about one of the players, is read. Each panelist relates a story telling why she made the statement. Having heard all three stories, the player picks the one she feels actually made the statement. One hundred dollars is scored if she is correct. Four such situations are played. In round three, the host reads a statement about one of the two players that all three panelists agree with. Players have to determine to whom the statement refers. Four such questions are played, worth $50, $100, $200, and $500. The player with the highest cash score is the winner.

Host: Regis Philbin.

Model: Jane Nelson.

Announcer: Joe Sinan.

Music: Stan Worth.

Producer-Director: Bill Carruthers.

THE NEIGHBORS—30 minutes—ABC—December 29, 1975 - April 9, 1976.

NEVER TOO YOUNG

Serial. Background: Malibu Beach, California. The overall behavior and problems of eight young people: Alfie, the owner of "Alfie's Cafe," the local beach hangout; his girlfriend, Barbara; and teenagers: Joy, Susan, Jo Jo, Tad, Chet, and Tim.

CAST

Alfie	David Watson
Tad	Michael Blodgett
Joy	Robin Grace
Jo Jo	Tommy Rettig
Chet	Tony Dow
Susan	Cindy Carol
Barbara	Pat Connolly
Tim	Dack Rambo
Rhoda, Joy's mother	Patrice Wymore
Frank, Susan's father	John Lupton
Rhoda's sister	Merry Anders

Announcer: Roger Christian.

Music: Ray Martin.

NEVER TOO YOUNG—25 minutes—ABC—September 27, 1965 - June 24, 1966.

THE NEW ADVENTURES OF BATMAN

Animated Cartoon. The further crime fighting adventures of Batman, Robin, and Batgirl. See title "Batman" for storyline information.

Characters' Voices:

Batman	Adam West
Robin	Burt Ward
Batgirl	Melendy Britt
Batmite, the mouse	Lennie Weinrib

Music: Yvette Blais, Jeff Michael.

Executive Producer: Lou Scheimer, Norm Prescott.

Producer: Don Christensen.

THE NEW ADVENTURES OF BAT-MAN—25 minutes—CBS—Premiered: February 12, 1977.

THE NEW ADVENTURES OF CHARLIE CHAN

Mystery. Background: Europe. The investigations of Charlie Chan, a courteous, shrewd, and philosophical Chinese detective. Based on the character created by Earl Derr Biggers.

CAST
Charlie Chan	J. Carrol Naish
Barry Chan, his Number One Son	James Hong
Inspector Duff	Rupert Davies
Inspector Carl Marlowe	Hugh Williams

Executive Producer: Leon Fromkess.

Producer: Rudolph Flothow, Sidney Marshall.

Director: Leslie Arliss, Charles Bennett, Jack Gage, Charles Haas, Don Chaffey, Leslie Goodwins, Alvin Rakoff.

THE NEW ADVENTURES OF CHARLIE CHAN—30 minutes—Syndicated 1957. 39 episodes.

THE NEW ADVENTURES OF GILLIGAN

Animated Cartoon. A spin-off from "Gilligan's Island." Background: A small uncharted island in the South Pacific. Shipwrecked after their charter ship, the S.S. *Minnow*, is damaged in a tropical storm at sea, the five passengers and two crew members establish a community when all attempts to acquire help fail. Stories relate their struggle for survival; their attempt to understand nature; and compatibility with one's fellow human.

Characters' Voices
Jonas Grumby, the skipper	Alan Hale
Gilligan, his bumbling first mate	Bob Denver
Ginger Grant, a beautiful movie actress	Jane Webb
Thurston Howell III, a multimillionaire	Jim Backus
Lovey Howell III, his wife	Natalie Schafer
Roy Hinkly, a brilliant research scientist, the professor	Russell Johnson
Mary Ann Summers, a clerk from Kansas	Jane Edwards

Music: Yvette Blais, Jeff Michael.

THE NEW ADVENTURES OF GILLIGAN—30 minutes—ABC—Premiered: September 7, 1974.

THE NEW ADVENTURES OF HUCKLEBERRY FINN

Adventure. Adapted from the novel, *The Adventures of Huckleberry Finn*, by Mark Twain. Pursued by the vengeful Injun Joe, Huckleberry Finn, Becky Thatcher, and Tom Sawyer run into a cave where they are engulfed by a fierce, raging sea and transported to strange fantasy lands that are populated by cartoon characters. Assisting where needed, they seek to escape from Injun Joe and find the secret of the way back to their homes in Hannibal, Missouri, 1845. Live action is played against superimposed animated backgrounds.

CAST

Huckleberry Finn   Michael Shea
Becky Thatcher   Lu Ann Haslam
Tom Sawyer   Kevin Schultz
Injun Joe   Ted Cassidy

Voices: Hal Smith, Ted de Corsia, Peggy Webber, Jack Krusacher, Paul Stewart, Mike Road, Vic Perrin, Charles Lane, Julie Bennett, Paul Frees, Marvin Miller.

Music: Hoyt Curtin.

THE NEW ADVENTURES OF HUCKLEBERRY FINN—30 minutes —NBC—September 15, 1968 - September 7, 1969. 20 episodes.

THE NEW ADVENTURES OF MARTIN KANE

See title: "Martin Kane."

THE NEW ADVENTURES OF PERRY MASON

See title: "Perry Mason."

THE NEW ADVENTURES OF PINOCCHIO

Marionettes. The adventures of Pinocchio, the wooden boy who was brought to life to please the lonely old man Gipetto, and his friend, Jiminy Crickett. Filmed in Animagic (giving life to marionettes).

Music: Jules Bass.

THE NEW ADVENTURES OF PINOCCHIO—05 minutes—Syndicated 1961. 130 episodes.

THE NEW ADVENTURES OF SUPERMAN

See title: "The Adventures of Superman."

THE NEW ADVENTURES OF WONDER WOMAN

Adventure. A spin-off from "Wonder Woman," which see for background information. (Storyline begins where the original leaves off.) Having successfully aided America in its fight against the Nazis, Diana Prince, alias Wonder Woman, returns to Paradise Island following World War II in 1945.

Now, thirty-two years later (1977), as a plane carrying U.S. Government agents to a special meeting in Latin America passes through the Bermuda Triangle, an enemy saboteur, who is later caught, releases a gas that renders the crew and passengers unconscious. Caught in the magnetic field of the Triangle, the jet comes under the control of the inhabitants of the uncharted Paradise Island—a race of

The New Adventures of Wonder Woman. Lynda Carter and Lyle Waggoner. *Courtesy of the Call-Chronicle Newspapers, Allentown, Pa.*

super women called Amazons. Entering the downed aircraft, the Princess Diana is startled to see whom she believes is Major Steve Trevor, a mortal she aided during the 1940s. When brought to the medical center and treated, Diana learns that her Steve is now U.S. Government Security Agent Steve Trevor, Jr., son of the late Major General Steve Trevor.

Realizing that the world is still threatened by evil, Diana requests permission from her Queen Mother to become an emissary and assist the outside world in its battle for truth and justice. A special council meeting is held and Diana's request is granted. To protect her true identity as Wonder Woman, the Princess again adopts the guise of Diana Prince. Steve is then hypnotized and led to believe that Diana is his replacement assistant, whom he is to meet in Latin America.

From her Queen Mother, Diana receives the special wrist bracelets, made of feminum, to reflect bullets; the magic belt to maintain her strength and cunning away from Paradise Island; the magic lariat, which compels people to tell the truth; and the magic tiara, which contains a special ruby that enables Diana to contact her mother whenever the need arises. Diana then chooses a revealing red, white, and blue costume to signify her allegiance to freedom and democracy.

The passengers and crew, still unconscious, are placed back aboard the plane. Diana pilots it to twelve thousand feet, sets it on automatic, then plays a special musical tune to awaken those aboard. As they begin to regain consciousness, Diana leaves through an escape hatch and boards her invisible plane, which she uses to ensure the jet's safe arrival in Latin America.

At the scheduled meeting, Diana introduces herself to Steve—who, upon seeing her—accepts her as his assistant. (Later, when returning to Washington, D.C., Diana gains access to the government's computerized personnel files and programs her own employment record—the final step to again create Diana Prince—now assistant to Steve Trevor of the I.A.D.C. [Inter Agency Defense Command], and protect her true identity as Wonder Woman.)

Stories depict Diana's exploits as she battles for freedom and democracy throughout the world as the mysterious Wonder Woman. (By performing a twirling striptease, the attractive Diana Prince emerges into the gorgeous Wonder Woman.) Based on the characters created by Charles Moulton.

CAST

Diana Prince/	
Wonder Woman	Lynda Carter
Steve Trevor, Jr.	Lyle Waggoner
Joe Atkinson, Steve's	
superior	Normann Burton
The Queen	
Mother	Beatrice Straight

Music: Artie Kane.

Theme: Charles Fox, Norman Gimbel.

Executive Producer: Douglas S. Cramer, Wilfred Baumes.

Producer: Charles B. Fitzsimons, Mark Rodgers.

Animation: Phill Norman.

THE NEW ADVENTURES OF WONDER WOMAN—60 minutes—CBS—Premiered: September 16, 1977.

THE NEW ANDY GRIFFITH SHOW

Comedy. Background: Greenwood, North Carolina. The trials and tribulations of Andy Sawyer, former sheriff and justice of the peace turned mayor.

The New Andy Griffith Show. Top: Andy Griffith, Marty McCall; bottom: Lori Ann Rutherford, Lee Ann Meriwether.

CAST

Andy Sawyer	Andy Griffith
Lee Sawyer, his wife	Lee Ann Meriwether
Lori Sawyer, their daughter	Lori Ann Rutherford
T.J. Sawyer, their son	Marty McCall
Nora, Lee's sister	Ann Morgan Guilbert
Buff MacKnight, the senior town councilman	Glen Ash

Music: Earle Hagen.

THE NEW ANDY GRIFFITH SHOW –30 minutes–CBS–January 8, 1972 - June 4, 1972. 13 episodes.

THE NEW ARCHIE/SABRINA HOUR

Animated Cartoon. Newly animated adventures of the Archie Gang— Archie, Veronica, Jughead, Valerie, Reggie, and Hot Dog; and Sabrina, the teenage witch. See also: "The Archie Show," and "Sabrina, the Teenage Witch."

Voices: Dallas McKennon, Jane Webb, Don Messick, John Erwin, Jose Flores, Howard Morris.

Music: Yvette Blais, Jeff Michael.

Executive Producer: Norm Prescott, Lou Scheimer.

Producer: Don Christensen.

THE NEW ARCHIE/SABRINA HOUR–60 minutes–NBC–Premiered: September 10, 1977.

THE NEW BILL COSBY SHOW

Variety. Various songs, dances, and comedy sketches that depict the world as seen through the eyes of comedian Bill Cosby.

Host: Bill Cosby.

Regulars: Susan Tolsky, Lola Falana, Foster Brooks, Oscar De Grury, Erin Fleming, The Donald McKayle Dancers.

Announcer: Lola Falana.

Orchestra: Quincy Jones; Bobby Bryant.

Featured Sketch: "The Wife of the Week." A domestic sketch wherein a guest actress portrays Bill's constantly nagging wife.

THE NEW BILL COSBY SHOW–60 minutes–CBS–September 11, 1972 - May 17, 1973.

THE NEW BREED

Crime Drama. Background: Los Angeles, California. The investigations of the Metropolitan Squad, a special L.A.P.D. detective force designed to disrupt the workings of organized crime.

CAST

Lieutenant Price Adams	Leslie Nielsen
Sergeant Vince Cavelli	John Beradino
Captain Keith Gregory	Byron Morrow
Officer Joe Huddleston	John Clark
Officer Pete Garcia	Greg Roman

THE NEW BREED—60 minutes—ABC—October 3, 1961 — September 15, 1962. 36 episodes. Syndicated.

THE NEW CANDID CAMERA

See title: "Candid Camera."

THE NEW CASPER CARTOON SHOW

See title: "Casper, the Friendly Ghost."

THE NEW CBS FRIDAY NIGHT MOVIE
THE NEW CBS TUESDAY NIGHT MOVIE

Movies. Feature-length suspense thrillers produced especially for television.

Included:

The Cable Car Murder. A detective attempts to solve a contract murder committed in broad daylight.

CAST

Van Alsdale: Robert Hooks; Sgt. Cassidy: Jeremy Slate; Kathie Cooper: Carol Lynley; McBride: Robert Wagner.

Death Of Innocence. The ordeal of a mother as she witnesses her daughter's murder trial.

CAST

Elizabeth Cameron: Shelley Winters; Buffie Cameron: Tisha Sterling.

Black Noon. A minister's battle against an unseen power that is gripping a desert town in a strange hold of misfortune.

CAST

The Rev. Mr. Keyes: Roy Thinnes; Lorna Keyes: Lynn Loring; Deliverance: Yvette Mimieux.

She Waits. The story of a young bride stalked by the spirit of her husband's first wife.

CAST

Laura Wilson: Patty Duke; Mark Wilson: David McCallum; Sarah Wilson: Dorothy McGuire; Dr. Carpenter: Lew Ayres; Dave Brody: James Callahan.

THE NEW CBS FRIDAY NIGHT MOVIE—90 minutes—CBS—September 17, 1971 - September 8, 1972.

THE NEW CBS TUESDAY NIGHT MOVIE—90 minutes—CBS—September 12, 1972 - September 3, 1974.

THE NEW CHRISTY MINSTRELS SHOW

Musical Variety.

Starring: The New Christy Minstrels: Ann White, Paul Potash, Art

Podell, Barry Kane, Karen Gunderson, Barry McGuire, Nick Woods, Clarence Treat, Larry Romos.

Regulars: Rowlf, the hound-dog muppet; The Chuck Casey Singers, The Doerr-Hutchinson Dancers.

Orchestra: Peter Matz.

THE NEW CHRISTY MINSTRELS SHOW—30 minutes—NBC—August 5, 1964 - September 2, 1964.

NEW COMEDY SHOWCASE

Pilot Films. Proposed comedy series for the 1960-1961 season.

Included:

Johnny Come Lately. The misadventures of television newscaster Johnny Martin.

CAST
Johnny Martin: Johnny Carson; Eddie: Dick Reeves; Miss Talbot: Marie Windsor.

They Went Thataway. Fancying himself as the meanest man in the West, Black Ace Burton begins his quest to acquire the title.

CAST
Black Ace Burton: James Westerfield; Poison Pete: Ron Haggerthy; Sam Cloggett: Wayne Morris.

The Trouble With Richard. The misadventures of a good-natured bank teller.

CAST
Richard: Dick Van Dyke; Gramps: Parker Fennelly.

You're Only Young Once. After their children are married, a middle-aged couple attempt to rediscover life.

CAST
Charles Tyler: George Murphy; Kit Tyler: Martha Scott; Lois: Sué Randall; Arthur: Roger Perry.

NEW COMEDY SHOWCASE—30 minutes—CBS—August 1, 1960 - September 19, 1960.

THE NEW DICK VAN DYKE SHOW

Comedy. Distinguished by two formats.

Format One:

The New Dick Van Dyke Show—30 minutes—CBS—September 18, 1971 - September 3, 1973.

Background: Carefree, Arizona. The trials and tribulations of Dick Preston, the host of "The Dick Preston Show," a ninety-minute talk-variety program produced by KXIU-TV, Channel 2, in Phoenix.

CAST
Dick Preston	Dick Van Dyke
Jenny Preston, his wife	Hope Lange
Bernie Davis, Dick's agent and business manager	Marty Brill
Carol Davis, Bernie's wife	Nancy Dussault
Michele (Mike) Preston, Dick's sister and secretary	Fannie Flagg
Annie Preston, Dick and Jenny's daughter	Angela Powell
Lucas Preston,	

Dick and Jenny's
son   Michael Shea
Ted Atwater, Dick's
  boss, the president of
  the Compton Broadcasting
  Company   David Doyle

Music: Jack Elliott, Allyn Ferguson.

Format Two:

The New Dick Van Dyke Show—30
minutes—CBS—September 10, 1973 -
September 2, 1974.

Background: 747 Bonnie Vista
Road, Tarzana, California. Relocating
after his show is cancelled, Dick
acquires the role of Dr. Brad Fair-
mont, a surgeon at Pleasant Valley
Hospital on the mythical daytime TV
soap opera, "Those Who Care."
Stories relate his home and working
life.

CAST

Dick Preston   Dick Van Dyke
Jenny Preston   Hope Lange
Annie Preston   Angela Powell
Max Mathias,
  the program's
  producer   Dick Van Patten
Alex Montez, the
  director   Henry Darrow
Dennis Whitehead, the
  script writer   Barry Gordon
Richard Richardson,
  Dick's neighbor, the
  star of the mythical
  TV series "Harrigan's
  Holligans"   Richard Dawson
Connie Richardson, his
  wife   Chita Rivera
Margot Brighton,
  the serial lead,
  playing Dr. Susan
  Allison   Barbara Rush

Music: Jack Elliott, Allyn Ferguson.

THE NEW HOWDY DOODY SHOW

Children. A spin-off from "Howdy
Doody" (which see for story line
information). The updated version
features puppets, guest performers,
and sketches geared for children.

CAST

Buffalo Bob Smith, the
  host   Bob Smith
Clarabell Hornblow, the
  clown   Lou Anderson
Happy Harmony, the schoolteacher   Marilyn Patch
Cornelius Cobb, the prop
  man   Bill LeCornec
Nicholson Muir, the
  mythical
  producer   Nick Nicholson
Jackie Davis, a
  singer   Himself

Puppets: Howdy Doody (voiced by
  Bob Smith), Phineas T. Bluster
  (voiced by Dayton Allen), Dilly
  Dally, The Flubadub, Outer Or-
  bit, the flying saucer (voiced by
  Nick Nicholson).

Music: The Doodyville Doodlers, conducted by Jackie Davis.

Executive Producer: Nick Nicholson,
  E. Roger Muir.

Producer: Ronald Wayne.

Director: Errol Falcon.

THE NEW HOWDY DOODY SHOW
—30 minutes—Syndicated 1976.

THE NEW LAND

Drama. Background: Minnesota,
1858. The life and struggles of the
Larsen family, Scandinavian immigrants attempting to carve a life and
share in the American Dream.

CAST

Christian Larsen, the father	Scott Thomas
Ann Larsen, his wife	Bonnie Bedelia
Tuliff Larsen, their son	Todd Lookinland
Anneliese Larsen, their daughter	Debbie Lytton
Bo Larsen, Christian's brother	Kurt Russell
Mr. Lundstrom, their neighbor	Donald Moffat
Molly Lundstrom, his wife	Gwen Arner

Music: The Orphanage.

THE NEW LAND—60 minutes—ABC—September 14, 1974 - October 19, 1974. 4 episodes.

THE NEW MICKEY MOUSE CLUB

Children. An updated version of the 1950s "Mickey Mouse Club" (which see), featuring twelve new Mouseketeers in songs, dances, and sketches, and an array of never-before televised Disney cartoons and films.

The Mouseketeers: Kelly Parsons, Lisa Whelchel, Mindy Feldman, Nita (DiGiampaolo) Dee, Curtis Wong, Julie Piekarski, Scott Craig, Shawnte Northcutte, Allison Fonte, Todd Turquand, Angel Florez, William "Pop" Attmore.

Voice of Mickey Mouse: Wayne Allwine (for the series; Walt Disney's voice is heard in the cartoons prior to 1949).

Voice of Jiminy Cricket: Cliff Edwards.

Music: Buddy Baer, Robert F. Brunner, William Schaefer.

Executive Producer: Ron Miller.

Producer: Ed Ropolo, Mike Wuergler.

Director: John Tracy, Dick Amos, James Field, Dick Krown.

THE NEW MICKEY MOUSE CLUB—30 minutes—Syndicated 1977. 130 tapes.

The New Mickey Mouse Club. The new Mouseketeers: bottom, left to right: Todd, Curtis, Julie, Nita, Lisa, Pop; top row, left to right: Allison, Scott, Mindy, Shaunte, Angel, Kelly. © *Walt Disney Productions.*

THE NEW NEWLYWED GAME

Game. A spin-off from "The Newlywed Game," which see for format.

Host: Bob Eubanks.

Announcer: Johnny Jacobs.

Music: Lee Ringuette.

Executive Producer: Chuck Barris.

Producer: Mike Metzger.

Director: John Dorsey.

Creator: Roger Muir.

THE NEW NEWLYWED GAME—30 minutes—Syndicated 1977.

THE NEW, ORIGINAL WONDER WOMAN

See title: "Wonder Woman."

THE NEW PEOPLE

Drama. Enroute from Southeast Asia to the mainland, a small inner island charter is caught in a fierce storm. Damaged, and unable to maintain a steady flight pattern, the plane crash lands on Buamo, a remote Pacific island once chosen as a hydrogen bomb test site by the Atomic Energy Commission, but abandoned due to a fear of contamination by the trade winds.

Of the fifty passengers, forty young adults, American college students on a cultural exchange program, survive. Stories depict: Their struggle for survival; and, having a completely provisioned city on the island, their attempts to establish a society untouched by the destruction of modern man.

CAST

Susan Bradley	Tiffany Bolling
Robert Lee	Zooey Hall
Eugene "Bones" Washington	David Moses
George Potter	Peter Ratray
Errol "Bull" Wilson	Lee Jay Lambert
Dexter	Kevin Michaels
Barbara	Brenda Sykes
Gloria	Nancy DeCarol
Stanley	Dennis Olivieri Kevin O'Neal
Ginny	Jill Jaress
Laura	Elizabeth Berger
Jack	Clive Clerk
Wendy	Donna Baccala
Dan Stoner	Carl Reindel

Music: Earle Hagen.

THE NEW PEOPLE—45 minutes— ABC—September 22, 1969 - January 12, 1970. 13 episodes.

NEWSSTAND THEATRE

A series of thirty minute dramas broadcast on ABC from January 23, 1952 - February 6, 1952.

THE NEW STU ERWIN SHOW

See title: "Trouble With Father."

THE NEW SUPER FRIENDS HOUR

Animated Cartoon. A spin-off from "Super Friends." Background: The Hall of Justice in Washington, D.C., an organization formed by the world's mightest super heroes to battle injustice. The series depicts their individual and/or joint ventures.

The Super Friends: Superman, Batman and Robin, Wonder Woman, Aquaman, Rima the Jungle Queen, The Black Vulcan, Samural the Apache Chief, and Space Twins Zan and Jana, and their space monkey Gleek.

Voices: Sherry Alberoni, Danny Dark, Casey Kaseem, Olan Soule, Ted Knight, John Stevenson, Franklin Rucker, Frank Welker, Shannon Farnon, Norman Alden.

Music: Hoyt Curtin, Paul DeKorte.

Executive Producer: William Hanna, Joseph Barbera.

Producer: Iwao Takamoto.

Director: William Hanna, Joseph Barbera.

THE NEW SUPER FRIENDS HOUR

—55 minutes—ABC—Premiered: September 10, 1977.

THE NEW TEMPERATURES RISING SHOW

See title: "Temperatures Rising."

THE NEW TREASURE HUNT

Game. A spin-off from "Treasure Hunt." Three contestants are chosen from the studio audience. Brought on stage, each selects one of three boxes. The contestant whose box contains a "Treasure Hunt" card receives the opportunity to seek $25,000 in cash. The player chooses one of thirty boxes that are displayed on stage. The box, which contains a cash amount (two hundred to two thousand dollars), is offered to the player to forfeit whatever the box contains. If the player refuses the money she receives the contents of the box—cash (five thousand to twenty-five thousand dollars), valuable merchandise (cars, airplanes, furniture), or a clunk (inexpensive prizes). Two such rounds are played on each program.

Host: Geoff Edwards.

Assistants: Jane Nelson, Joey Faye.

Announcer: Johnny Jacobs.

Music: Frank Jaffe; Lee Ringuette.

Check Guard: Emil Arture, a bonded security agent.

Model: Sivi Aberg.

Executive Producer: Chuck Barris.

Producer: Michael J. Metzger.

Director: John Dorsey.

Creator: Jan Murray.

THE NEW TREASURE HUNT—30 minutes—Syndicated 1973.

THE NEW TRUTH OR CONSEQUENCES

See title: "Truth Or Consequences."

NEW YORK CONFIDENTIAL

Crime Drama. Background: New York City. The investigations of newspaper reporter-columnist Lee Cochran. Based on the book by Lee Mortimer and Jack Lait.

Starring: Lee Tracy as Lee Cochran.

NEW YORK CONFIDENTIAL—30 minutes—Syndicated 1958. 39 episodes.

THE NEW ZOO REVUE

Educational. Background: A zoo. Various aspects of the world are related to children via songs, dances, sketches, and stories.

CAST

Doug	Doug Momary
Emmy Jo	Emily Peden
Charlie, the wise owl	Sharon Baird
Freddie, the frog	Yanco Inone
	Scutter McKay
Henrietta, the hippo	Thomas Carri
	Larri Thomas
Mr. Dingle, the general-store owner	Chuck Woolery

Voices for the costumed characters (Freddie, Charlie, and Henrietta): Bob Holt, Hazel Shermit, Joni Robbins, Bill Callaway.

Orchestra: Denny Vaughn; Milton Greene.

THE NEW ZOO REVUE—30 minutes—Syndicated 1972.

THE NEWLYWED GAME

Game. Four husband-and-wife couples compete. The husbands appear before camera; the wives are isolated backstage in a soundproof room. The host asks each husband three five-point questions. The couples are reunited and the questions are restated one at a time. If the wife matches her husband's answer, they receive the points. There is no penalty for an incorrect response.

The second half is played in reverse. The wives are asked three ten-point questions and one twenty-five point bonus question. The husbands have to match their wives' answers.

Winners, the highest point scorers, receive a specially selected merchandise prize.

Host: Bob Eubanks.

Announcer: Johnny Jacobs.

Music: Frank Jaffe; Lee Ringuette.

THE NEWLYWED GAME–30 minutes–ABC. Daytime version: July 11, 1966 - December 20, 1974. Evening version: January 7, 1967 - August 30, 1971.

NICHOLS

Western. Background: Nichols, Arizona, 1914. Returning to his home town after an eighteen-year absence, Nichols finds that the town, homesteaded from his mother, no longer belongs to him. Drowning his sorrows at the Salter House bar, he begins talking to its beautiful barmaid, Ruth, and enrages her jealous boyfriend, Ketchum. A fight ensues, and Nichols is held responsible for three hundred dollars in damages. Unable to pay it, he is sentenced to six months duty as sheriff by Sara Ketchum, Ketchum's mother, the self-appointed law.

Stories depict his reluctant attempts to maintain law and order.

Last episode. Nichols, in an attempt to stop a barroom brawl, is killed. Several days following, his twin brother, Jim Nichols, arrives in town. After discovering what has happened, he apprehends his brother's killer. Refusing to accept the position of sheriff, he parts town, never to darken its path again.

Expected to have been renewed, "Nichols" was cancelled at the last minute after the aforedescribed episode evolved to establish a more courageous and forceful hero, Jim Nichols.

CAST

Nichols (not identified by a first name)	James Garner
Jim Nichols	James Garner
Mitchell, the deputy	Stuart Margolin
Sara Ketchum (Ma)	Neva Patterson
Ruth	Margot Kidder
Ketchum	John Beck
Salter, the owner of the bar	John Harding
Johnson, a con-artist	Paul Hampton
Bertha, the saloon keeper	Alice Ghostley
Judge Thatcher	Richard Bull
Gabe, the general-store owner	M. Emmett Walsh
Scully One, the owner of the town	John Quade
Scully Two, his brother	Jesse Wayne
Mitchell's dog: Slump.	

NICHOLS–60 minutes–NBC–September 16, 1971 - August 8, 1972. 29 episodes. Also known as: "James Garner As Nichols."

NIGHT COURT

Courtroom Drama. Dramatizations based on the files of New York and Los Angeles Night Court hearings.

Judge: Jay Jostyn.

Public Defenders: Sandy Spillman, Barney Biro.

NIGHT COURT–30 minutes–Syndicated 1965. 78 episodes.

NIGHT EDITOR

Anthology. Dramatizations depicting the struggles of newspapermen.

Host: Hal Burdick.

NIGHT EDITOR–30 minutes– DuMont 1949.

NIGHT LIFE

Variety. Celebrity guests and interviews.

Hosts: Les Crane, Nipsey Russell.

Announcer: Nipsey Russell.

Orhcestra: Elliot Lawrence.

NIGHT LIFE–1 hour, 45 minutes– ABC–March 4, 1965 - October 22, 1965.

NIGHT GALLERY

See title: "Four-In-One," *Night Gallery* segment.

NIGHTMARE

Anthology. Dramatizations depicting the plight of people suddenly involved in unexpected and perilous situations.

Included:

Magic Formula. The story of an actress who finds herself trapped in a plane after a crash.

Starring: Claudette Colbert, Patric Knowles.

High Adventure. The story concerns a woman and her attempts to find help for her ill son after they are marooned in a mountain lodge.

Starring: Virginia Carroll, Gordon Gebert.

Turn Back The Clock. The story concerns a war verteran who is suffering from amnesia and his attempts to discover who he is.

Starring: Richard Carlson.

NIGHTMARE–30 minutes–Syndicated 1958.

THE NIGHT STALKER

Mystery. Background: Chicago. The investigations of Carl Kolchak, a reporter for the *Independent News Service* (I.N.S.). Stories relate his attempts to solve baffling, bizarre, and supernatural crimes.

CAST
Carl Kolchak	Darren McGavin
Tony Vincenzo, his editor	Simon Oakland
Ron Updyke, an I.N.S. reporter	Jack Grinnage
Monique Marmelstein, an I.N.S. reporter	Carol Ann Susi
Gordon Spangler (Gordy the Goul), the mortician	John Fiedler
Emily Cowles, the advice columnist	Ruth McDevitt

Narrator: Darren McGavin.

Music: Gil Mellé.

Executive Producer: Cy Chermak.

Producer: Paul Playdon.

Director: Seymour Robbie, Doug McDougall, Allen Baron, Alex Grassoff.

Creator: Jeff Rice.

THE NIGHT STALKER—60 minutes —ABC—September 13, 1974 - August 30, 1975. 20 episodes. Original title: "Kolchak: The Night Stalker."

THE NINE LIVES OF ELFEGO BACA

See title: "Walt Disney Presents," *The Nine Lives of Elfego Baca* segment.

NINETY BRISTOL COURT

Comedy. The overall title for three family comedies: "Harris Against the World"; "Karen"; and "Tom, Dick, and Mary."

Background: Ninety Bristol Court in Southern California, the address and name of a fashionable but fictitious apartment-motel. Through the eavesdropping of Cliff Murdock, the superintendant, segments are introduced and scenes are established.

Harris Against The World. The trials and tribulations of Alan Harris, a businessman struggling to survive the constant barrage of everyday problems.

CAST

Alan Harris	Jack Klugman
Kate Harris, his wife	Patricia Barry
Billy Harris, their son	David Macklin
Dee Dee Harris, their daughter	Claire Wilcox
Cliff Murdock	Guy Raymond

Karen. The life of Karen Scott, a beautiful, delightful, and resourceful high-school girl; a carbonated teenager with an unquenchable thirst for life and an uncontrollable penchant for mischief.

CAST

Karen Scott	Debbie Watson
Steve Scott, her father, a lawyer	Richard Denning
Barbara Scott, her mother	Mary La Roche
Mimi Scott, Karen's sister	Gina Gillespie
Mrs. Rowe, the Scott housekeeper	Grace Albertson
Cliff Murdock	Guy Raymond

Ninety Bristol Court. Mary La Roche and Debbie Watson of "Karen."

KAREN'S FRIENDS:

Candy	Trudi Ames
Janis	Bernadette Winters
Spider	Murray MacLeod
David	Richard Dreyfuss

Music: Jack Marshall.

Theme: "Karen" sung by the Beachboys.

Tom, Dick, And Mary. Unable to afford a flat at Ninety Bristol Court, intern Tom Gentry and his wife Mary solve their problem by arranging to share an apartment and expenses with their bachelor-intern friend, Dick Moran. Stories depict: Dick's endless romantic entanglements; and Tom and Mary's attempts to regain their cherished privacy.

CAST

Tom Gentry	Don Galloway
Mary Gentry	Joyce Bulifant
Dick Moran	Steve Franken
Dr. Kievoy, their supervisor	John Hoyt
Cliff Murdock	Guy Raymond

NINETY BRISTOL COURT—90 minutes (thirty minutes per segment)—NBC—October 5, 1964 - January 4, 1965. Spin-off: "Karen"—30 minutes —NBC—January 11, 1965 - September 6, 1965.

NOAH'S ARK

Drama. The struggles of two dedicated veterinarians: Dr. Sam Rinehart, the wiser, ill and aging; and Dr. Noah McCann, the younger, eager and progressive.

CAST

Dr. Noah McCann	Paul Burke
Dr. Sam Rinehart	Vic Rodman
Liz Clark, a nurse	May Wynn
Glenn White	Russell Whitney
Agnes Marshall	Natalie Masters
Davey Marshall	Paul Engle

NOAH'S ARK—30 minutes—NBC— February 26, 1957 - September 1957. 23 episodes.

NO HIDING PLACE

A nine-episode crime series, produced in England, and starring Raymond Francis. Syndicated 1960.

NO—HONESTLY

Comedy. Background: London, England. A thirteen-part series that follows the courtship and early married life of the Danbys: Charles, an actor, and his scatterbrained wife, Clara, the author of "Ollie the Otter" childrens stories. Produced in England.

CAST

Charles Danby (C. D.)	John Alderton
Clara Danby	Pauline Collins
Lord Burrell, Clara's absent-minded father	James Berwick
Lady Burrell, Clara's mother	Franny Rowe
Royal, the Burrell's butler	Kenneth Benda

Music: Lynsey De Paul.

Producer: Humphrey Barclay.

Director: David Askey.

NO—HONESTLY—25 minutes—PBS —July 9, 1975 - September 3, 1975.

THE NOONDAY SHOW

Variety. Comedy skits, interviews,

guests. Broadcast each day at 12:00 p.m., E.T.

Host: David Steinberg.

Regulars: Stan Cann, Jane Dulo, Caroline Grosky, Gaillard Sartaine.

Orchestra: David Foster.

Producer: Marty Pasetta.

Director: Eric Lieber.

THE NOONDAY SHOW—NBC— December 15, 1975 - December 19, 1975. 5 shows; three were 25 minutes; two were 55 minutes each.

N.O.P.D.

Crime Drama. Background: New Orleans, Louisiana. The investigations of Detectives Beaujac and Conroy, law enforcers attached to the New Orleans Police Department (N.O.P.D.).

CAST

Senior Detective Beaujac	Stacy Harris
Detective Conroy	Lou Sirgo

N.O.P.D.—30 minutes—Syndicated 1956. 39 episodes.

NORBY

Comedy. Background: Pearl River, New York. Events in the lives of the Norby family: Pearson, the vice-president of small loans at the First National Bank; his wife, Helen; and their children, Diane (age eleven) and Hank (six).

CAST

Pearson Norby	David Wayne
Helen Norby	Joan Lorring
Diane Norby	Susan Holloran
Hank Norby	Evan Elliott
Bobo, their friend and neighbor	Jack Warden
Maureen, his wife	Maxine Stuart
Wahleen Johnson, the bank telephone operator	Janice Mars
The bank president	Paul Ford

Also: Carol Vegazie; Ralph Dunn.

NORBY—30 minutes—NBC—January 5, 1955 - April 6, 1955.

NORMAN CORWIN PRESENTS

Anthology. Original dramatic presentations.

Host: Norman Corwin.

NORMAN CORWIN PRESENTS—30 minutes—Syndicated 1971.

NORTHWEST PASSAGE

Adventure. Background: New York State, 1754, during the era of the French and Indian War. The story of Major Robert Rogers, and his search for the fabled Northwest Passage, a waterway that supposedly links the East and West.

CAST

Major Robert Rogers	Keith Larsen
Sergeant Hunk Marriner, a master woodsman	Buddy Ebsen
Ensign Langdon Towne, a mapmaker	Don Burnett

NORTHWEST PASSAGE—30 minutes—NBC—September 14, 1958 - September 7, 1959. 26 episodes. Syndicated.

NOT FOR HIRE

Crime Drama. Background: Honolulu, Hawaii. The investigations of Sergeant Steve Dekker, U.S. Army Criminal Investigations Division, into crimes associated with the military: desertion, sabotage, and hijacking.

CAST

Sgt. Steve Dekker   Ralph Meeker
Sonica Zametoo, his WAC
    aide   Lizabeth Rush
Corporal Zimmerman, his
    aide   Ken Drake

Music: Joseph Hooven.

NOT FOR HIRE—30 minutes—Syndicated 1959. 39 episodes. Also known as: "Sgt. Steve Dekker."

NOT FOR PUBLICATION

Crime Drama. Background: New York City. The investigations of reporter Collins of the *New York Ledger*. Stories reveal the facts hidden behind headline-making stories.

Starring: Jerome Cowan as Collins.

NOT FOR PUBLICATION—30 minutes—DuMont 1951. Also known as "Reporter Collins."

NOT FOR WOMEN ONLY

Discussion. A panel of five guests discuss current topical issues.

Hostesses: Aline Saarinen, Barbara Walters, Polly Bergen, Lynn Redgrave.

Hosts: Hugh Downs, Frank Field.

Music: Recorded.

NOT FOR WOMEN ONLY—30 minutes—Syndicated 1972. Originally aired locally in New York (WNBC-TV, Ch. 4) under the title: "For Women Only."

NOTHING BUT THE BEST

A thirty-minute variety series, broadcast on NBC in 1953, and starring Eddie Albert.

NOTHING BUT THE TRUTH

Game. Three contestants appear, each laying claim to the same identity. The host reads a short biography concerning one of the contestants who is the person involved. Through a series of question-and-answer probe rounds with the contestants, a panel of three celebrities have to determine the purveyor of the truth.

Host: John Cameron Swayze.

Panel: Polly Bergen, Dick Van Dyke, Hildy Parks.

NOTHING BUT THE TRUTH—30 minutes—CBS—December 18, 1956 - December 25, 1956.

NO TIME FOR SERGEANTS

Comedy. Background: Andrews Air Force Base. The misadventures of Private Will Stockdale, a reluctant and naive Georgia farm boy who was drafted into the Air Force. Stories relate his attempts to adjust to military life, and the trials and tribulations of his superior officers who are plagued by his philosophy of kindness. Based on the movie.

CAST

Private Will
    Stockdale   Sammy Jackson
Sgt. Orville King, Will's
    superior   Harry Hickox

Captain Paul Martin	Paul Smith
Private Ben Whitledge, Will's friend	Kevin O'Neal
Millie Anderson, Will's romantic interest; operates the camp supply store	Laurie Sibbald
Grandpa Anderson, her grandfather, a farmer	Andy Clyde
Colonel Farnsworth	Hayden Rorke
Private Irving Blanchard, Will's nemesis	Greg Benedict
Private Jack Langdon	Michael McDonald
Private Neddick	Joey Tata
Pa Stockdale, Will's father	Frank Ferguson
Tilda Jay Stockdale, Will's sister	Stacey Maxwell
General Thomas	Bill Zuckert

Will's dog: Blue.

NO TIME FOR SERGEANTS—30 minutes—ABC—September 14, 1964 - September 6, 1965. 34 episodes. Syndicated.

NO WARNING

Anthology. Dramatic presentations that depict the plight of people whose lives are suddenly thrown into turmoil by an unexpected crisis.

Narrator: Westbrook Van Voorhis.

Included:

Fire Lookout Post. The story of a woman who is held prisoner by an arsonist amid the rages of a raging forest fire.

Starring: Ann Rutherford, Strother Martin, Wheaton Chambers.

Stranded. The story concerns a couple's attempts to find help after their car stalls, stranding them in the Mojave Desert.

Starring: Marsha Hunt, Walter Coy.

The Prisoner. A man, sentenced to life imprisonment, requests permission to see his dying wife, an inmate of a women's prison. When his request is refused, he vows to escape and free his wife so she will not die in the penitentiary.

Starring: Kenneth Tobey, Jaclynne Greene, Tim Powers, Vivi Janiss.

NO WARNING—30 minutes—NBC—April 6, 1958 - September 7, 1958.

THE NOW EXPLOSION

Variety. Prerecorded Rock music is coupled with the appearance of the actual performer. Visual and audio effects prevail in an attempt to televise a radio program.

Local station personalities serve as hosts, who, using the voice-over technique, conduct the show as if it were a radio program.

THE NOW EXPLOSION—7 hours, 30 minutes—Syndicated 1970.

NOW YOU SEE IT

A fifteen minute variety series that features performances by magicians. *Host:* Andre Baruch. CBS 1949.

NOW YOU SEE IT

Game. Two competing teams each composed of two members.

Round One: The "Now You See It" board is displayed, which contains four vertical lines of run-on letters. The four vertical lines, which are numbered one to four, become the line; and the fourteen letters each line contains (numbered one to fourteen across the top) become the position. Teams compete one at a time. One player sits with his back to the board; the host reads a question; and the other player has to locate the answer on the board by calling the line (one, two, three, or four). If correct, his partner, seated on a swivel chair, faces the board and has to call the position of the answer (one to fourteen). Points are awarded according to the line and position total (e.g., line, 3; position 10; points: 13). The remaining team competes in the same manner. Winners are the highest point scorers.

Round Two: The members of the winning team compete against each other. One blank line containing fourteen spaces is displayed. After the host reads a question, two letters to the answer appear. The player first to sound his buzzer receives a chance to answer. If correct, the three- or four-letter answer appears on the board and the player receives one point. Another question is asked, and the last letter of the previous answer becomes the first letter of the new answer. The player first to acquire four points is the winner.

The Solo Round: The champion competes. The game follows the format of round one wherein the player has to locate ten answers within sixty seconds. One hundred dollars is awarded for each correct answer; five thousand dollars if locating all ten.

Host: Jack Narz.

Announcer: Johnny Olsen.

Music: Michael Malone.

NOW YOU SEE IT—30 minutes—CBS —Premiered: April 1, 1974.

NUMBER PLEASE

Game. A line of twenty spaces is placed before each player. After a clue is given, the host calls a number. Players then remove that number, which reveals a letter, and attempt to identify the concealed phrase that the line contains. The game continues until one player correctly identifies the message. Incorrect answers disqualify players from that particular round. Winners, the highest scorers (most correct identifications), receive merchandise prizes.

Host: Bud Collyer.

NUMBER PLEASE—30 minutes— ABC—January 30, 1961 - December 21, 1961.

THE NURSES
THE DOCTORS AND THE NURSES

Medical Drama. Background: Alden General Hospital in New York City. The personal and professional lives of nurses Liz Thorpe and Gail Lucas.

CAST

Nurse Liz Thorpe	Shirl Conway
Nurse Gail Lucas	Zina Bethune
Dr. Ted Steffen	Joseph Campanella
Dr. Alexander Tazinski	Michael Tolan
Nurse Ayres	Hilda Simms
Dr. Lowry	Stephen Brooks
Dr. Kiley	Edward Binns

The Nurses. Zina Bethune and Shirl Conway.

Producer: Herbert Brodkin, Robert Costello, Arthur Lewis.

THE NURSES–CBS–September 27, 1962 - September 17, 1964. As "The Doctors and the Nurses"–60 minutes –CBS–September 22, 1964 - September 7, 1965. Syndicated. 103 episodes.

THE NURSES

Serial. A daily afternoon version based on the prime-time series. Background: Alden General Hospital. Continued events in the working lives of nurses Liz Thorpe and Gail Lucas.

CAST

Liz Thorpe	Mary Fickett
Gail Lucas	Melinda Plank
Brenda	Patricia Hyland
Nurse Dorothy Warner	Leonie Norton
Dr. John Crager	Nat Polen
Donna	Carol Gainer
Mrs. Grassberg	Polly Rowles
Mike	Darryl Wells
Hugh	Arthur Franz
Cora	Mauriel Kirkland
Paul	Paul Stevens
Martha	Joan Wetmore

Also: Alan Yorke, Nicholas Pryor, John Beal.

THE NURSES–30 minutes–ABC– September 27, 1965 - March 31, 1967.

N.Y.P.D.

Crime Drama. Background: New York City. The investigations of Mike Haines, Johnny Corso, and Jeff Ward, plainclothes police detectives attached to Manhattan's 27th precinct (N.Y.P.D.: New York Police Department).

CAST
Mike Haines	Jack Warden
Johnny Corso	Frank Converse
Jeff Ward	Robert Hooks

Music: Charles Gross.

Executive Producer: Daniel Melnick, Bob Markell.

Producer: Robert Butler.

Director: Daniel Petrie, Robert Butler, David Pressman, Joshua Shelley, Reza S. Badiyi, Robert Gist, Alex March, Lawrence Dobkin.

Creator: David Susskind, Arnold Perl.

N.Y.P.D.—30 minutes—ABC—September 5, 1967 - September 16, 1969. 49 episodes. Syndicated.

THE OBJECT IS

Game. Six players compete: three celebrity guests and three studio audience members. The format involves identifying personalities from object clues.

Host: Dick Clark.

THE OBJECT IS—30 minutes—ABC—December 30, 1963 - March 24, 1964.

OCCASIONAL WIFE

Comedy. Background: New York City. Seeking an executive position with his company that is only available to a married man, Peter Christopher, a swinging young bachelor, solves his problem by proposing to a girlfriend, a beautiful hat check girl: "Greta, I want you to be my wife . . . occasionally." The agreement: She will pose as his wife whenever the situation warrants; and he will pay for her rent and art lessons. Living in the same apartment house, and on different floors (he, the seventh; she, the ninth), stories depict the chaos that ensues as two unmarried people struggle to affect a normal, happy marriage.

CAST
Peter Christopher	Michael Callan
Greta Patterson	Patricia Harty
Mr. Brahms, Peter's employer, the owner of Brahm's Baby Foods Company	Jack Collins
Mrs. Brahms, his wife	Joan Tompkins
Mrs. Christopher, Peter's mother	Sara Seeger
The man-in-the-middle, residing in an apartment on the eighth floor	Bryan O'Byrne
Bernie, Greta's jealous boyfriend	Stuart Margolin
Wally	Jack Riley
Vera	Susan Silo

OCCASIONAL WIFE—30 minutes—NBC—September 13, 1966 - August 29, 1967. 30 episodes.

THE ODDBALL COUPLE

Animated Cartoon. The misadventures

of two trouble-prone, free-lance magazine writers: Fleabag the dog, a natural-born slob; and Spiffy, a perfectionist cat. A spin-off from "The Odd Couple."

Characters' Voices

Fleabag	Paul Winchell
Spiffy	Frank Nelson
Goldie, their secretary	Joan Gerber

Additional Voices: Frank Welker, Sarah Kennedy, Joe Besser, Don Messick, Bob Holt, Ginny Tyler.

Music: Doug Goodwin.

THE ODDBALL COUPLE—30 minutes—ABC—Premiered: September 6, 1975.

THE ODD COUPLE

Comedy. Background: New York City; 1049 Park Avenue, Apartment 1102, the residence of two divorced men: Oscar Madison, sportswriter for the *New York Herald,* an irresponsible slob; and Felix Unger, a commercial photographer, an excessively neat perfectionist. Stories depict the chaos that ensues as they struggle to live together. Based on the play by Neil Simon.

CAST

Felix Unger	Tony Randall
Oscar Madison	Jack Klugman
Police Officer Murray Grechner, their friend	Al Molinaro
Speed, a poker-playing friend	Gary Walberg
Vinnie, a poker-playing friend	Larry Gelman
Roy, a poker-playing friend	Ryan MacDonald
Dr. Nancy Cunningham, Oscar's romantic interest	Joan Hotchkis
Cecily Pigeon, Felix and Oscar's upstairs neighbor	Monica Evans
Gwen Pigeon, her sister	Carole Shelley
Miriam Welby, Felix's romantic interest	Elinor Donahue
Myrna Turner, Oscar's secretary	Penny Marshall
Gloria Unger, Felix's ex-wife	Janis Hansen
Edna Unger, Felix's daughter	Pamelyn Ferdin
	Doney Oatman
Blanche Madison, Oscar's ex-wife	Brett Somers Klugman

Music: Neil Hefti; Kenyon Hopkins.

Music Supervision: Leith Stevens.

Executive Producer: Garry Marshall, Jerry Belson, Harvey Miller, Sheldon Keller.

Producer: Tony Marshall.

Director: Mel Ferber, Jerry Paris, Frank Buxton, Dan Dailey, Hal Cooper, Charles R. Rondeau, Jay Sandrich, Jack Winter, Garry Marshall, Jack Donohue, Harvey Miller, Jerry Belson.

Program Open:

Announcer: "On November thirteenth Felix Unger was asked to remove himself from his place of residence. That request came from his wife. Deep down he knew she was right. But he also knew that someday he would return to her. With no where else to go, he appeared at the home of his childhood friend, Oscar Madison. Sometime earlier, Madison's wife had thrown him out, requesting that he never return. Can two divorced men share an apartment without driving each other crazy?"

THE ODD COUPLE—30 minutes—
ABC—September 24, 1970 - July 4,
1975.

ODYSSEY

Documentary. Dramatizations based
on the events that shaped the world.

Host-Narrator: Charles Collingwoood.

ODYSSEY—30 minutes—CBS—January 6, 1957 - June 16, 1957.

OFFICIAL DETECTIVE

Anthology. Dramatizations based on
stories that appear in *Official Detective* magazine.

Host-Narrator: Everett Sloane.

OFFICIAL DETECTIVE—30 minutes
—Syndicated 1957. 39 episodes.

OFF THE RECORD

A comedy series starring Zero Mostel
and Joey Faye. Producer: Martin
Gosch; Director: Tony Kraber. 30
minutes—DuMont 1949.

OFF TO SEE THE WIZARD

Anthology. Adventure films geared
for children.

Hosts: Animated "Wizard of Oz"
    characters: Dorothy, The Scare-
    crow, The Tin Woodman, The
    Cowardly Lion, and the Wizard.

Included:

Island of the Lost. Shipwrecked off an
uncharted island, an anthropologist
and his family struggle for survival.

CAST
Josh MacRae: Richard Green; Stu:
Luke Halpin; Gabe: Mart Hulswit;
Liz: Robin Mattson.

The Hellcats. An unsold pilot film.
Coming to the aid of a beautiful
woman, three pilots attempt to re-
cover the money left to her by her
father who lived on a remote South
American island.

CAST
Melinda: Barbara Eden; Lee Ragdon:
George Hamilton; El Primero:
Nehemiah Persoff; Bugs: John Craig;
Ripple: Warren Berlinger.

Gypsy Colt. The story of a young
girl's devotion to an orphaned colt.

CAST
Frank MacWarde: Ward Bond; Meg:
Donna Corcoran; Em: Frances Dee.

Mike and the Mermaid. An unsold
pilot film. Background: Florida. The
complications that ensue when a
young boy discovers a beautiful mermaid in a river.

CAST
The Mermaid: Jeri Lynn Fraser; Mike
Malone: Kevin Brodie; Jim Malone:
Ned Foley, Nellie Malone: Rachel
Ames.

OFF TO SEE THE WIZARD—60 minutes—ABC—September 8, 1967 - September 20, 1968.

OF LIFE AND LOVE

Anthology. Rebroadcasts of dramas
that were originally aired via other
filmed anthology programs. Stories
emphasize the struggles of man and

nature.

OF LIFE AND LOVE—30 minutes—
ABC 1960.

OH, BABY!

Baby Talk. The host talks with infants
who respond via voice-over dubbing.

Host: Jack Barry.

OH, BABY!—05 minutes—Syndicated
1952.

OH, BOY!

Musical Variety. Performances by
Country and Western artists.

Host: Tony Hall.

Regulars: Brenda Lee, Cherry Warner,
Don Lang, Cudley Dudley
Helsop, Dickie Pride, Lorie
Mann, Mike Preston, Dene Webb,
Red Price, Chris Andrews,
Neville Taylor, The Cutters, Lord
Rockingham's XI; The Vernons,
Tony Sheridan, The Wreckers.

OH, BOY!—30 minutes—ABC—July
16, 1954 - September 3, 1959.

OH, KAY!

Variety. Music, songs, and interviews.

Hostess: Kay Westfall.

Regulars: Jim Dimitri, Ellen White.

Pianist: David le Winter.

OH, KAY!—30 minutes—ABC—
February 24, 1951 - May 26, 1951.

OH! SUSANNA

See title: "The Gale Storm Show."

OH, THOSE BELLS!

Comedy. Background: The Hollywood Prop Shop, a theatrical warehouse in California. The misadventures of its financially insecure custo-
dians, the Bell Brothers: Harry,
Sylvester, and Herbert.

CAST

Herbert Bell	Herbert Wiere
Harry Bell	Harry Wiere
Sylvester Bell	Sylvester Wiere
Mr. Slocum, their employer	Henry Morgan
Kitty, his secretary	Carol Byron

OH! THOSE BELLS—30 minutes—
CBS—March 8, 1962 - May 31, 1962.
13 episodes.

Oh, Those Bells! Left to right: Harry Wiere,
Jessie White (guest), Herbert Wiere, and
Sylvester Wiere.

O'HARA,
UNITED STATES TREASURY

Crime Drama. Background: Washington, D.C. The investigations of James O'Hara, United States Treasury Department agent, into crimes perpetrated against customs, secret service, and internal revenue.

Starring: David Janssen as James O'Hara.

O'HARA, UNITED STATES TREASURY—60 minutes—CBS—September 17, 1971 - September 8, 1972. 22 episodes.

THE O'HENRY PLAYHOUSE

Anthology. Dramatizations based on the stories of William Sydney Porter, who, while in prison, wrote under the pen name of O'Henry.

Host-Narrator: Thomas Mitchell.

Included:

Hearts and Hands. The story of a safecracker who marries the girl who sent him to prison.

CAST
Marueen Stephenson, Lester Matthews, Frank Kreig.

Between Rounds. The story of a street cleaner who recounts heroic tales of General Custer and the Battle of Little Big Horn to an eight-year-old admirer.

CAST
Thomas Mitchell, Paul Engle.

Georgia's Ruling. The story of a U.S. land commissioner and his struggles to perform his job after the death of his young daughter.

CAST
Thomas Mitchell, Richard Arlen.

THE O'HENRY PLAYHOUSE—30 minutes—Syndicated 1957. 39 episodes.

OKAY MOTHER

Testimonial tributes to mothers of celebrities or mothers who have become famous on their own. With Dennis James as host, the series was first broadcast on DuMont in 1950.

O.K. CRACKERBY!

Comedy. Background: California. Settling in Palm Springs, O.K. Crackerby, a rough and ready Oklahoman, widower, father of three children, Cynthia, Hobart, and O.K., Jr., and the world's richest man, finds that he is not acceptable to the genteel society circle. Determined to change matters, he hires St. John Quincy, a penniless Harvard graduate, to tutor his children in the ways of society. Stories depict O.K.'s battle of wits against snobbery.

CAST
O.K. Crackerby	Burl Ives
St. John Quincy	Hal Buckley
Cynthia Crackerby	Brooke Adams
Hobart Crackerby	Joel Davison
O.K. Crackerby, Jr.	Brian Corcoran
The chauffeur	John Indrisano
Susan Wentworth, Quincy's girlfriend	Laraine Stephens
Slim, O.K.'s friend	Dick Foran

Creator: Abe Burrows, Cleveland Amory.

O.K. CRACKERBY!—30 minutes—ABC—September 16, 1965 - January 6, 1966. 17 episodes.

THE OLDSMOBILE MUSIC THEATRE

Anthology. Dramatizations interwoven with songs of the past and present.

Hosts: Florence Henderson, Bill Hayes.

Included:

The Almost Perfect Plan. Background: Japan. Adopting western ways, a young man attempts to court the niece of an old-fashioned businessman.

CAST

Jimmy Kimura: James Shigeton; Kinirme Sagoyan: Michi Kobi; Kasho Eguchi: Richard Loo.

Too Bad About Sheila Troy. After the death of her father, her guiding light, an actress attempts to adjust to life without him.

CAST

Sheila Troy: Carol Lawrence; Tom Walker: Roddy McDowall.

A Kiss Before Leaving. A lonely girl attempts to impress a visiting stranger she has become infatuated with.

CAST

Gabrielle: Florence Henderson; Nick: Bill Hayes; Adrian: Ernest Truex.

THE OLDSMOBILE MUSIC THEATRE—30 minutes—NBC—March 26, 1959 - May 7, 1959.

THE OLSEN AND JOHNSON SHOW

Variety. Music, songs, dances, blackouts, and slapstick comedy.

Hosts: John "Ole" Olsen, Harold "Chic" Johnson.

Regulars: Marty May, June Johnson.

Orchestra: Milton DeLugg.

Producer: Ezra Stone.

Director: Frank Burns, Ezra Stone.

THE OLSEN AND JOHNSON SHOW —60 minutes—NBC Summer of 1949.

OMNIBUS

Educational. Programs devoted to people and "living ideas"; dramatic presentations; explanations, discussions, and demonstrations concerning music, dance, history, theatre, opera, ballet, and literature.

Host: Alistair Cooke.

Music: Merrill Slanton; Milton Weinstein.

OMNIBUS—60 minutes. CBS-November 9, 1952 - April 1, 1956; ABC—October 7, 1956 - March 3, 1957; NBC—October 20, 1957 - May 10, 1959.

ON BROADWAY TONIGHT

Variety. Performances by undiscovered professional talent.

Host: Rudy Vallee.

Orchestra: Harry Zimmerman; Harry Sosnick.

ON BROADWAY TONIGHT—60 minutes—CBS—July 8, 1964 - September 16, 1964.

ONCE UPON A CLASSIC

Children. Adaptations of classic children's stories.

Host: Bill Bixby.

Included:

Heidi. The heartwarming story of a lovable Swiss Orphan named Heidi.

CAST

Heidi: Emma Blake; Grandfather: Hans Meyer; Peter: Nicholas Lyndhurst.

The Prince and the Pauper. The story of two lookalike boys, Tom Canty, the impoverished son of a petty thief, and Edward, the Prince of Whales, and the chaos that results when they switch roles.

CAST

Tom/Edward: Nicholas Lyndhurst; Charles: Donald Eccles.

ONCE UPON A CLASSIC—30 minutes—PBS—Premiered: October 11, 1976.

ONCE AN EAGLE

See title: "Best Sellers."

ONCE UPON A TUNE

Variety.

Host: Phil Hanna.

Regulars: Sondra Lee, Holly Harris.

Pianist: Reggie Bean.

ONCE UPON A TUNE—30 minutes—DuMont 1950.

One Day at a Time. Pat Harrington and Bonnie Franklin.

ONE DAY AT A TIME

Comedy. Background: Indianapolis, Indiana. The story of Ann Romano, a thirty-four-year-old divorcee whose transition from wife to working mother is complicated by her two headstrong daughters, Julie and Barbara Cooper (Ann retains her maiden name).

CAST

Ann Romano	Bonnie Franklin
Julie Cooper	Mackenzie Phillips
Barbara Cooper	Valerie Bertinelli
Dwayne Schneider, the building super	Pat Harrington
David Kane, Ann's romantic interest	Richard Masur
Ginny Wrobliki, Ann's friend	Mary Louise Wilson
Ed Cooper, Ann's ex-husband	Joseph Campanella

Music: Jeff Barry, Nancy Barry.

Executive Producer: Norman Lear, Mort Lachman, Norman Paul, Jack Elinson.

Producer: Allan Manings.

Director: Hal Cooper, Don Richardson, Norman Campbell, Howard Morris, Sandy Kenyon, Herbert Kenwith.

Creator: Whitney Blake, Allan Manings.

ONE DAY AT A TIME—30 minutes—CBS—Premiered: December 16, 1975.

THE ONEDIN LINE

Drama. Background: Liverpool, England, 1860. The exploits of tradesman James Onedin, captain of the *Charlotte Rhodes,* a three-masted topsail schooner, as he seeks to maintain a cargo transporting business.

CAST

Captain James Onedin	Peter Gilmore
Anne Onedin, his wife	Anne Stallybrass
Robert Onedin, James's brother	Brian Rawlinson
Elizabeth Onedin, James's sister	Jessica Benton
Captain Joshua Webster, Anne's father	James Hayter
Sara Onedin, Robert's wife	Mary Webster
Albert Frazer, Elizabeth's romantic interest	Philip Bond

Music: Anthony Isaac.

Producer: Peter Graham Scott.

THE ONEDIN LINE—60 minutes—Syndicated 1976. Produced in England.

ONE HAPPY FAMILY

Comedy. Marrying, but unable to afford their own home, Dick and Penny Cooper move in with her parents, Barney and Mildred Hogan; and her grandparents, Charley and Lovey Hackett. Stories depict the trials and tribulations that befall the families as generations clash.

CAST

Dick Cooper	Dick Sargent
Penny Cooper	Jody Warner
Barney Hogan	Chick Chandler
Mildred Hogan	Elizabeth Fraser
Charley Hackett	Jack Kirkwood
Lovey Hackett	Cheerio Meredith

ONE HAPPY FAMILY—30 minutes—NBC—January 13, 1961 - September 8, 1961.

ONE HUNDRED GRAND

Game. One contestant, possessing knowledge in at least one specific field, is placed opposite a panel of five professional authorities. The panelists then ask him questions. Each correct response awards a large amount of cash. The player is permitted to continue or quit and leave with his earnings at any time. One incorrect response and the player is defeated. If the player survives several of these knowledge battles, he then faces the final competition: to answer five questions compiled from questions sent in by home viewers. If he is successful, he receives $100,000; if he is incorrect, he is defeated and loses his earnings.

Host: Jack Clark.

ONE HUNDRED GRAND—30 minutes—ABC—September 15, 1963 - September 29, 1963.

THE $100,000 BIG SURPRISE

Game. Contestants first choose a subject category, then select one of two types of questions, the "easy" or the "difficult." Related questions are asked of the player, and each correct response awards a large amount of cash. The player is permitted to continue or depart after any question with his accumulated earnings. Players are defeated and lose their money if they incorrectly answer a question. Players vie for the opportunity to win $100,000 by answering increasingly difficult questions in their chosen subject category.

Hosts: Jack Barry; Mike Wallace.

Assistants: Sue Oakland, Mary Gardiner.

THE $100,000 BIG SURPRISE—30 minutes—CBS—September 18, 1956 - April 2, 1957.

THE $100,000 NAME THAT TUNE

See title: "Name That Tune."

THE $128,000 QUESTION

Game. An updated version of "The $64,000 Question." Players, who possess knowledge in at least one specific field, compete. Each is asked a series of questions ranging from $64 doubled to $64,000. The contestant, who risks loss of everything if, at any time he should give an incorrect response, can either continue playing or quit after answering a question. His decision determines his earnings, if any. For players who continue, the first plateau is reached when the $4,000 question is answered. A 1977 car becomes the player's prize—and he continues because he has nothing to lose. If a player successfully answers the $16,000 question he reaches the second plateau and again continues, as

this money is his and he has nothing to lose. The next series of questions, if successfully answered, earns the player $64,000 and the opportunity to return at a later date and compete further with the object being to win another $64,000. Failure to correctly answer the $32,000 or $64,000 questions earns a player his second plateau winnings.

Host: Mike Darrow; Alex Trebek.

Models: Lauri Locks, Cindy Reynolds, Pattie Lee.

Announcer: Alan Calter.

Music: Recorded.

Security Director: Michael O'Rourke.

Executive Producer: Steve Carlin.

Producer: Willie Stein.

Director: Dick Schneider, George Choderker.

THE $128,000 QUESTION—30 minutes—Syndicated 1976.

THE O'NEILLS

Serial. The dramatic story of Peggy O'Neill, fashion designer.

CAST
Peggy O'Neill	Vera Allen
Bill O'Neill	Ian Martin
Mrs. Levy	Celia Budkin
Mr. Levy	Ben Fishbern

Also: Janice Gilbert, Michael Lawson, Jane West, Maurice Franklen.

Producer: Ed Wolf.

Director: Jack Rubin.

THE O'NEILLS—30 minutes— DuMont 1949.

ONE IN A MILLION

Game. Through a series of question-

and-answer probe rounds, contestants have to discover the secrets shared by a panel of four guest celebrities. Winners, those who identify the most secrets, receive merchandise prizes.

Host: Danny O'Neil.

ONE IN A MILLION—30 minutes—ABC—April 3, 1967 - June 16, 1967.

ONE LIFE TO LIVE

Serial. Background: Philadelphia. The dramatic story of two families, each from different sides of the tracks: The Woleks, first generation Americans struggling for a position on top of the social ladder; and the Lords, an established family entrenched in the dominant social and economic milieu. Episodes present an insight into life in contemporary America, and the problems faced by the underprivileged, the uneducated, the nonwhite, and the non-Angelo Saxon Protestant.

CAST

Cathy Craig	Amey Levitt
	Dorrie Kavanaugh
	Jane Alice Brandon
	Jennifer Harmon
Dr. James Craig	Nat Polen
Victoria Lord	Erika Slezak
	Gillian Spencer
Dr. Mark Toland	Tom Lee Jones
Anna Wolek	Doris Belack
Meredith Lord Wolek	Lynn Benesch
	Trish Van Devere
Bert Skelly	Herb Davis
Stephen Burke	Bernard Grant
Dr. Larry Wolek	Michael Storm
Daniel Lord Wolek	Justin White
Vince Wolek	Anthony Ponzini
	Jordan Charney
Joe Riley	Lee Patterson
Eileen Riley	Patricia Roe
	Alice Hirson
Dave Siegal	Allan Miller
Julie Siegal	Lee Warrick
Carla Gray	Ellen Holly
Dr. Marcus Polk	Norman Rose
	Donald Moffat
Victor Lord	Ernest Graves
	Shepperd Strudwick
Dr. Joyce Brothers	Herself
Lt. Ed Hall	Al Freeman, Jr.
Sadie Gray	Lillian Hayman
Susan Barry	Lisa Richards
Jack Dawson	Jack Ryland
Wanda Webb	Marilyn Chris
Joshua West	Laurence Fishburne
	Todd Davis
Dr. Dorian Cramer	Nancy Pinkerton
	Claire Malis
Melinda Cramer	Patricia Pearcy
Rachel Wilson	Nancy Barrett
Karen Martin	Niki Flacks
Tom Edwards	Joe Gallison
Merry	Lynn Benish
Millie Parks	Millee Taggart
Dr. Price Trainor	Peter DeAnda
Jenny Siegal	Kathy Glass
Mario Dane	Gerald Anthony
Peggy Filmore	Valerie French
Timmie Siegal	Tom Berenger
Eileen Siegal	Alice Hirson
Julie Toland	Leonie Norton
Tony Lord	George Reinholt
John Douglas	Donald Madden
Sheila Rafferty	Christine Jones
Peter Blair	Peter Brouwer
Michiko	Lani Gerrie Miyazaki
Dr. Will Vernon	Farley Granger
	Bernie McInerney
Lana	Jackie Zeman
Also	Peggy Wood

Music: Aeolus Productions.

Music Theme: George Reinholt.

Producer: Doris Quinlan, Joseph Stuart.

Creator: Agnes Nixon.

ONE LIFE TO LIVE—30 minutes—

ABC—July 15, 1968 - July 23, 1976. 45 minutes—ABC—Premiered: July 26, 1976.

ONE MAN'S EXPERIENCE

Serial. Human-interest accounts depicting the joys and sorrows of men. Guests appear in stories that run four days each.

ONE MAN'S EXPERIENCE—15 minutes—DuMont 1952 - 1953.

ONE MAN'S FAMILY

Serial. Background: The swank Sea Cliff section of Bay City in San Francisco, California. The dramatic story of the Barbour family: Henry, a stockbroker; his wife, Frances; and their children, Paul, Hazel, Clifford and Claudia (twins), and Jack. Episodes depict the life, sex values, and worthiness of the family. Created by Carlton E. Morse.

CAST

Henry Barbour	Bert Lytell
	Theodore Von Eltz
Frances (Fanny)	
Barbour	Marjorie Gateson
	Mary Adams
Hazel Barbour	Lilian Schaff
	Linda Reighton
Jack Barbour	Robert Wigginton
	Martin Dean
	Arthur Cassell
Claudia Barbour	Eva Marie Saint
	Anne Whitfield
Clifford Barbour	James Lee
Paul Barbour	Russell Thorson
Bob	Walter Brooke
John Roberts	Jack Edwards
Beth Holly	Susan Shaw
Mac	Tony Randall
Joe	Jim Boles
Teddy Barbour	Medaline Bugard

Also: Billy Idelson, Patricia Robbins, Nancy Franklin.

Announcer: Bob Sheppard.

Music: Paul Watson.

Producer: Carleton E. Morse, Richard Clemmer.

Director: Edgar Kahn.

Sponsor: Sweetheart Soap.

ONE MAN'S FAMILY—15 and 30 minute versions—NBC—November 4, 1949 - April 1, 1955.

ONE MAN SHOW

Variety. Performance by guest comedians. "Wherever laughter is king, it's One Man Show."

Hosts: Including Bob and Ray (Bob Elliott and Ray Goulding), Morey Amsterdam, Rip Torn, Groucho Marx.

ONE MAN SHOW—30 minutes—Syndicated 1969.

ONE MINUTE PLEASE

Game. Two teams, each composed of three members. The host states a topic (e.g., raccoon coats; the perfect woman; how to make glue); and each panelist then has to incorporate it in conversation for one minute without undue repetition, hesitation, or straying from the point. Winners are the wordiest talkers. Prizes are awarded to studio audience members who are represented by the individual players. Based on the B.B.C. radio and television program.

Host: John K. M. McCaffery.

Panel: Ernie Kovacs, Beatrice Straight,

Hermione Ginggold, Alice Pearce, Cleveland Amory, Jimmy Cannon.

Announcer: Don Russell.

ONE MINUTE PLEASE—30 minutes —DuMont 1954.

ONE NIGHT STAND

A variety series featuring performances by musical groups. 24 minutes—Syndicated 1969.

ONE STEP BEYOND

Anthology. Dramatizations based on true events that are strange, frightening, and unexplainable in terms of normal human experience.

Host: John Newland, "Our guide into the world of the unknown."

Music: Harry Lubin.

Executive Producer: Larry Marcus.

Producer: Collier Young.

Included:

The Clown. Infatuated with Pippo, a deaf-mute clown, a young woman, Nonnie, follows him to his trailer. Found by her jealous husband, Tom, she is accidentally killed when he picks up a pair of scissors and attempts to stab Pippo. Found with the dead girl in his arms, Pippo is blamed for the murder. Police are summoned and he is locked in and guarded. Tom, though free, is haunted by visions of Pippo choking him. Standing by a small bridge overlooking a river, Tom falls in when he believes Pippo is choking him. Screaming for help, he is rescued and con-

fesses to killing Nonnie. Back at the fair grounds, Pippo's trailer is unlocked, and Pippo, constantly under guard, is soaking wet. How?

CAST

Nonnie: Yvette Mimieux; Pippo: Mickey Shaughnessey; Tom: Christopher Dark.

The Hand. Background: New Orleans. When piano player Tom Brandt discovers that his girl friend, Alma, is no longer interested in him, he picks up a bottle, breaks it, and kills her by jabbing its sharp edges into her stomach. His hand, though uncut, continually bleeds. Unable to stop the bleeding, and driven to the point of hysteria, he confesses—and the bleeding stops.

CAST

Tom Brandt: Robert Loggia; Alma: Miriam Colon; Johnny: Pete Candall; Harmon: Joseph Sullivan.

Night of the Kill. Found safe and well after being lost in the woods for three days, a young boy relates the story of his being found and cared for by a huge, friendly beast. His parents and friends are disbelieving until the following day when huge footprints, a strange odor, and a sighting of the creature convinces them otherwise. Wanting only to visit his young friend, the creature, supposedly sixteen feet tall, is tracked and trapped in a box canyon. The canyon is set ablaze, but no trace has ever been found of the creature, who, according to the story, escaped, still roams a backwoods area in America, and has been sighted since on several occasions.

CAST

Ann Morris: Ann McCrea; John Morris: Fred Beir; Danny Morris:

Dennis Holmes.

Program Open:

Host: "Have you ever been certain the telephone would ring within the next ten seconds? Or have you ever walked down a street and had the feeling you knew what lay beyond the unturned corner? Yes? Then you've had a brief encounter with the world of the unknown. . .a small step beyond. Now take a giant one."

ONE STEP BEYOND—30 minutes—Syndicated 1962. Originally broadcast as "Alcoa Presents"—30 minutes—ABC—January 26, 1959 - October 3, 1961. 94 episodes.

ONE, TWO THREE—GO!

Educational. Through filmed and taped explorations to places of interest, various aspects of the world are explained to children.

Host: Jack Lescoulie.

Assistant: Richard Thomas.

ONE, TWO THREE—GO!—30 minutes—NBC—October 8, 1961 - May 27, 1962.

ONE WOMAN'S EXPERIENCE

Serial. Human interest accounts depicting the joys and sorrows of women. Guests appear in stories that run four days each.

ONE WOMAN'S EXPERIENCE—15 minutes—DuMont—1952 - 1953.

ON OUR OWN

Comedy. Background: New York City. The story of two women in the creative department of the Madison Avenue Bedford Advertising Agency: Julia Peters, a copywriter, and Maria Bonino, an art director.

CAST

Julia Peters	Bess Armstrong
Maria Teresa Bonino	Lynnie Greene
Toni McBain, the head of the agency	Gretchen Wyler
April Baxter, a copywriter	Dixie Carter
Eddie Barnes, the producer of TV commericals	John Christopher Jones
Craig Boatwright, the agency's salesman	Dan Resin
Mrs. Oblenski, Julia and Maria's landlady	Sasha Van Scherler

Also: Flotsam the dog.

Executive Producer: David Susskind.

Producer: Sam Denoff.

Creator: Bob Randall.

ON OUR OWN—30 minutes—CBS—Premiered: October 9, 1977.

ON PARADE

Variety. The series consists of musical programs that were produced by the C.B.C. and first shown in Canada.

The Performers: Rosemary Clooney (7-17-64); Tony Bennett (7-24); Henry Màncini (7-31); Phil Ford and Mimi Hines (8-7); Juliet Prowse (8-14); Diahann Carroll (8-21); Julius La Rosa (8-28); Jane Morgan (9-4); The Limelighters (9-11); Steve Lawrence and Eydie Gormé (9-18).

ON PARADE—30 minutes—NBC—July 17, 1964 - September 18, 1964.

ON STAGE

Anthology. Stories written, produced, directed, and performed by Canadian actors.

ON STAGE—60 minutes—Syndicated 1962.

ON THE BOARDWALK

Musical Variety. Background: The Steel Pier in Atlantic City, New Jersey.

Host: Paul Whiteman.

Orchestra: Paul Whiteman.

ON THE BOARDWALK—30 minutes —ABC—May 30, 1954 - August 1, 1954.

ON THE GO

Variety. Guests, interviews, and visits to various areas around Los Angeles.

Host: Jack Linkletter.

Announcer: Johnny Jacobs.

ON THE GO—30 minutes—CBS—April 27, 1959 - July 8, 1960.

ON THE ROCKS

Comedy. Background: Alamesa State Prison. Life in a minimum security prison as seen through the eyes of convict Hector Fuentes, a streetwise and wisecracking petty thief. Based on the British television series "Porridge."

CAST

Hector Fuentes	Jose Perez
Mr. Gibson, a correctional officer	Mel Stewart
Mr. Sullivan, a correctional officer	Tom Poston
The Warden	Logan Ramsey
Dorothy Burgess, the warden's secretary	Cynthia Harris

The Convicts:

DeMott	Hal Williams
Cleaver	Rick Hurst
Nick Palik	Bobby Sandler
Gabby	Pat Cranshaw

Music: Jerry Fielding.

Producer: John Rich, H.R. Poindexter.

Director: John Rich, Dick Clement.

ON THE ROCKS—30 minutes—ABC —September 11, 1975 - May 17, 1976.

ON TRIAL

Anthology. Dramatizations based on actual courtroom trials.

Host-Occasional performer: Joseph Cotten.

Included:

The Case of the Jealous Bomber. After a businessman discovers that his partner is secretly seeing his wife, he plots to kill him.

CAST
Joseph Cotten, Audrey Totter, William Hopper.

The Case of the Abandoned Horse. An Indian girl, a lawyer, attempts to defend her people against government attempts to force her tribe off their land.

CAST
Eva Bartok, Hugh Marlowe.

Alibi for Murder. After three partners discover uranium, one is killed. The story relates police efforts to discover which partner is the murderer.

CAST
Macdonald Carey, Peggy Knudsen, John Vivyan, Morris Ankrum.

ON TRIAL—30 minutes—CBS—September 14, 1956 - September 13, 1957; July 6, 1959 - September 21, 1959. 27 episodes. Also known as "The Joseph Cotten Show."

ON YOUR ACCOUNT

Game. Contestants appear on stage and bear their sorrows. A panel then questions them to determine the seriousness of their individual situations. Each question asked deposits five dollars in a bank. After a specified time, the panel chooses the person they feel is the most desperate. The contestant receives the money that has been deposited in the bank.

Hosts: Eddie Albert; Win Elliot; Dennis James.

Producer: Bob Quigley.

Sponsor: Procter and Gamble.

ON YOUR ACCOUNT—30 minutes—CBS—June 1953 - September 1954.

ON YOUR MARK

Game. Children, aged from nine to thirteen, and who are pursuing the same career goal, compete. A series of question and answer rounds, based on the contestants career potential, follow, with the player scoring the highest being declared the winner.

Host: Sonny Fox.

ON YOUR MARK—30 minutes—CBS—September 23, 1961 - December 30, 1961.

ON YOUR WAY

Game. Selected studio-audience members compete. The host reads a general-knowledge type of question. The player who first identifies himself through a buzzer signal receives a chance to answer. If correct he is awarded points. The winner, the highest scorer, receives an all-expense-paid trip to his place of desire.

Hosts: Bud Collyer; John Reed King; Kathy Godfrey.

Producer: Larry White.

Sponsor: Welch's Wines.

ON YOUR WAY—30 minutes—DuMont 1953.

OPEN END

See title: "The David Susskind Show."

OPENING NIGHT

Anthology. Retitled episodes of "Ford Theatre."

Hostess: Arlene Dahl.

Included:

Strange Disappearance. After his wife leaves him, a man is accused of murdering her. The story depicts his attempts to find her and clear his name.

CAST
Stephen McNally, June Vincent, Peggy Knudsen.

Sometimes it Happens. Living in Manhattan with her aunt and uncle, a Welsh girl believes in the Old World legend that says that a love that proves itself three times will last forever. When she meets a man in a train, she is certain that she is in love with him, but they are separated before she can learn his name. The story concerns her frantic search to find him.

CAST

Dianne Foster, Guy Madison, Jeanne Cooper.

The Gentle Deceiver. The story of a hobo who is mistaken for an eccentric millionaire.

CAST

Keenan Wynn, Lucy Marlow, Lucien Littlefield.

OPENING NIGHT—30 minutes—NBC —June 14, 1958 - September 6, 1958.

OPERA CAMEOS

Music. Condensed versions of operas. Background information and anecdotes are presented before the actual performance.

Host: Giovanni Martinelli.

OPERA CAMEOS—30 minutes— DuMont—1953 - 1954.

OPERA VS. JAZZ

Musical Symposium. Discussions and demonstrations of opera and jazz.

Hostess: Nancy Kenyon.

Jazz Representative: Don Cornell.

Opera Representatives: Jan Peerce, Robert Merrill.

Regulars: Alan Dale, The Strawhatters.

Orchestra: Johnny Reo.

OPERA VS. JAZZ—30 minutes—ABC —May 25, 1953 - September 21, 1953.

OPERATION: ENTERTAINMENT

Variety. U.S.O.-type performances geared to American servicemen.

Host: Jim Lange.

Singers/Dancers: The Operation Entertainment Girls.

Music: The Terry Gibbs Quartet.

OPERATION: ENTERTAINMENT— 60 minutes—ABC—January 5, 1968 - January 31, 1969. 39 tapes.

OPERATION: NEPTUNE

Adventure. Background: Nadiria, a kingdom thirty-two thousand feet beneath the surface of the sea. The battle against evil as undertaken by Commander Hollister, the skipper of a United States government submarine, who is known and feared as Captain Neptune.

CAST

Commander Hollister	Tod Griffin
Dink, his assistant	Humphrey Davis
Thirza, the empress of Nadiria	Margaret Stewart
Dick Saunders, his assistant	Richard Holland
Mersenus, a villain	Harold Conklin

OPERATION: NEPTUNE—30 minutes—NBC—June 28, 1953 - August 16, 1953. Also known as: "Captain Neptune."

OPERATION PETTICOAT

Comedy. Background: The South Pacific during World War II. The series revolves around the misadventures of the officers and crew of the jerry-built Navy submarine *USS Sea Tiger*—a pink* sub, captained by Matthew Sherman, whose crew includes five sexy Army Nurses (Edna Hayward, Ruth Colfax, Barbara Duran, Claire Reid, and Dolores Crandall), who, stranded on and rescued from a Pacific Island, are now trapped aboard the *Tiger* as it roams the seas.

CAST

Lt. Cmdr. Matthew Sherman	John Astin
Lt. Nick Holden, the supply officer	Richard Gilliland
Major Edna Hayward	Yvonne Wilder
Lt. Dolores Crandall	Melinda Naud
Lt. Barbara Duran	Jamie Lee Curtis
Lt. Ruth Colfax	Dorrie Thompson
Lt. Claire Reid	Bond Gideon
Yeoman Alvin Hunkle	Richard Brestoff
Ensign Stovall	Christopher J. Brown
Seaman Dooley	Kraig Cassity
Chief Herbert Molumphrey	Wayne Long
Seaman Gossett	Michael Mazes
Chief Tostin	Jack Murdock
Seaman Horwich	Peter Schuck
Lt. Watson	Raymond Singer
Seaman Broom	Jim Varney
Seaman Williams	Richard Marion

Narrator: John Astin.

Music: Artie Butler.

Executive Producer: Leonard B. Stern.

Producer: David J. O'Connell, Si Rose.

*Only a shocking pink undercoat was possible due to an enemy plane destroying the sub's supply of gray paint.

OPERATION PETTICOAT—30 minutes—ABC—Premiered: September 17, 1977. Based on the film of the same title.

THE ORCHID AWARD

Variety. Show business achievement awards. Selected personalities are first interviewed then perform their material.

Host: Bert Lytell.

Announcer: John Heistand.

Orchestra: Paul Weston.

Included award receivers: Rex Harrison, Lilli Palmer, Eddie Fisher, Teresa Brewer, Marguerite Piazza.

THE ORCHID AWARD—30 minutes —ABC—May 24, 1953 - January 24, 1954. Also broadcast under the title: "The Orchid Room."

THE OREGON TRAIL

Western. Era: 1842. The story follows the journey of a group of pioneers traveling by wagon train from Illinois to Oregon; people seeking the free land offered by the government to settlers willing to farm it.

CAST

Evan Thorpe, a widower, the wagon master	Rod Taylor
Andrew Thorpe, his son	Andrew Stevens
William Thorpe, his son	Tony Becker
Rachel Thorpe, his daughter	Gina Marie Smika
Margaret Devlin, a young pioneer	Darleen Carr
Luther Sprague, the trail scout	Charles Napier

Mr. Cutler, the
        captain   Ken Swofford

Music: Dick De Benedictis.

Theme Vocal: Danny Darst.

Executive Producer: Michael Gleason.

Producer: Richard Collins, Carl Vitale.

THE OREGON TRAIL—60 minutes—NBC—Premiered: September 21, 1977.

THE ORIENT EXPRESS

Anthology. Dramatizations set against the background of the Old East.

Included:

Portrait of a Lady. The effect of malicious gossip on a happily married couple.

CAST
Colette Marchand, Peter Walker, Roger Treville.

One in a Million. Suspecting her daughter-in-law is involved in a shoddy operation, a woman intervenes and attempts to find out.

CAST
Gertrude Flynn, Espanita Cortes.

Uppercut. The story of a boxing champion who loses everything when a combination of love, arrogance, and selfishness interferes with his rigid life as a prizefighter.

CAST
Steve Barclay.

Disaster. The Orient Express, on which a spoiled American is traveling to meet her husband, crashes between Rome and Florence. The story relates her discovery of her faults while awaiting rescue.

CAST
Patricia Roc, Philip Reed.

THE ORIENT EXPRESS—30 minutes—ABC—1953 - 1954. Syndicated.

ORSON WELLES' GREAT MYSTERIES

Anthology. Mystery presentations.

Host: Orson Welles.

Music: John Barry.

Included:

The Dinner Party. Having swindled a million dollars from his company, a man attempts to conceal the fact by attending a dinner party in which he is being considered for a promotion, and have his rude and vicious wife jeopardize all his chances of promotion out of the bookkeeping department.

CAST
Jane Blake: Joan Collins; Edmond Blake: Anton Rodgers.

The Ingenious Reporter. Posing as the sought murderer of young women, a newspaper reporter attempts to acquire an exclusive story on the mysterious killings.

CAST
David Birney, Peter Madden, Pam St. Clement, Geoffrey Blenden.

Ice Storm. The story of a woman who is trapped with a would-be thief who is posing as one of three experts invited to view a valuable manuscript collection.

CAST
Claire Bloom, Donald Eccles.

ORSON WELLES' GREAT MYS-TERIES—30 minutes—Syndicated 1973. 26 episodes.

THE OSMONDS

Animated Cartoon. Appointed as goodwill ambassadors by the United States Music Committee, the Osmond Brothers Rock group begins a round-the-world concert tour to promote understanding between nations. Stories depict their various misadventures as they become involved in intrigues in foreign lands.

Characters' Voices
Allen Osmond	Himself
Jay Osmond	Himself
Jimmy Osmond	Himself
Donny Osmond	Himself
Merril Osmond	Himself
Wayne Osmond	Himself
Fugi, their dog	Paul Frees

Background Orchestrations: Maury Laws.

THE OSMONDS—30 minutes—ABC—September 9, 1972 - September 1, 1974.

O.S.S.

Adventure. Background: Europe during World War II. The behind-enemy-lines assignments of Frank Hawthorn, an agent for the United States Intelligence Office of Strategic Services (O.S.S.).

CAST
Frank Hawthorn	Ron Rondell
The O.S.S. chief	Lionel Murton

O.S.S.—30 minutes—ABC—September 20, 1957 - March 14, 1958. Syndicated.

OUR FIVE DAUGHTERS

Serial. The dramatic story of Jim and Helen Lee and their five daughters: Ann, Marjorie, Barbara, Jane, and Mary.

CAST
Jim Lee	Michael Keene
Helen Lee	Esther Ralston
Mary Lee Weldon	Wynne Miller
Barbara Lee	Patricia Allison
Jane Lee	Nuella Dierking
Marjorie Lee	Iris Joyce
Anne Lee	Jacqueline Courtney
Don Weldon	Ben Hayes
Uncle Charlie	Robert W. Stewart
Kyle Townsend	Randy Kraft
Dr. Briggs	Allen Nourse
Joe Tully	Earl Muron
Evvy	Susan Halloran
Thelma	Melinda Plank
Bob Purdon	Bill Tabbert
Mort Lucas	Duke Farley
Greta	Janis Young
Lucy	Ann Hillary
Ed Lawson	Michael Higgins
Mary Lawson	Kay Lyder
Bill Cannon	Alfred Sandor
Pat	Ed Griffith
Peter Stevens	Ronn Cummings
George Barr	Ralph Ellis
Cynthia Dodd	Joan Anderson
Randy	Carlton Coyler
Driscoll	Jon Cypher
Ginny	Suzanne Tripp
Mrs. Hess	Claudia Morgan
Mr. Hess	Douglas Gregory
Gil Morton	Alan Bergman

OUR FIVE DAUGHTERS—30 minutes—NBC—January 2, 1962 - September 28, 1962.

OUR MAN HIGGINS

Comedy. Background: New York State. Inheriting a rare and expensive silver service from a titled British relative, the MacRobertses, a middle-class American family, also inherit a high-tone English butler named Higgins whom they must retain to keep the silver service. Stories depict the problems that befall both Higgins and the MacRoberts family as they struggle to rearrange their lives and adjust to each other. Based on the radio program "It's Higgins, Sir."

CAST

Higgins	Stanley Holloway
Duncan MacRoberts, the father	Frank Maxwell
Alice MacRoberts, his wife	Audrey Totter
Tommy MacRoberts, their son	Rickey Kelman
Joanne MacRoberts, their daughter	Regina Groves
Dinghy MacRoberts, their son	K. C. Butts

OUR MAN HIGGINS—30 minutes—ABC—October 3, 1962 - September 11, 1963. 34 episodes.

OUR MISS BROOKS

Comedy. Distinguished by two formats.

Format One: 10-3-52 - 10-7-55.

Background: Madison High School in the town of Madison. The trials and tribulations of Connie Brooks, the English teacher. Stories depict her romantic misadventures as she struggles to impress Philip Boynton, the biology instructor; and her continual clash with Osgood Conklin, the principal.

CAST

Connie Brooks	Eve Arden
Osgood Conklin	Gale Gordon
Philip Boynton	Robert Rockwell
Walter Denton, the main problem student	Richard Crenna
Harriet Conklin, Osgood's daughter	Gloria McMillan
Mrs. Davis, Connie's landlady	Jane Morgan
Stretch Snodgrass, a student	Leonard Smith

Mrs. Davis's cat: Minerva.

Music: Lud Gluskin.

Orchestra: Wilbur Hatch.

Announcer: Bob Lemond.

Producer: Larry Berns.

Creator: Eddie Bracken.

Sponsor: General Foods.

Format Two: 10-14-55 - 9-21-56.

Background: The San Fernando Valley in California. Relocating after Madison High is demolished for a highway, Connie acquires a position as English teacher at Mrs. Nestor's Private Elementary School. Stories depict her continued clash with Osgood Conklin, who, also relocating, acquired the position of principal; and her romantic misadventures as she becomes involved with two suitors: Gene Talbot, the gym instructor, and Clint Albright, the athletic director.

CAST

Connie Brooks	Eve Arden
Osgood Conklin	Gale Gordon
Gene Talbot	Gene Barry
Clint Albright	William Ching
Angela Nestor,	

the owner of the
school   Nana Bryant
                           Jesslyn Fax
Oliver Munsey,
  Angela's eccentric
  brother   Bob Sweeney
Mrs. Nestor, Angela's
  sister   Isobel Randolph
Benny Romero, the
  ten-year-old problem
  child   Ricky Vera
Mrs. Davis, also
  relocating, Connie's
  landlady   Jane Morgan

Music: Lud Gluskin.

OUR MISS BROOKS—30 minutes—
CBS—October 3, 1952 - September
21, 1956. 127 episodes. Based on the
radio program.

OUR PLACE

Musical Variety.

Hosts: Jack Burns and Avery
  Schreiber.

Regulars: The Doodletown Pipers,
  Rowlf (the hound-dog muppet
  from "The Jimmy Dean Show").

Orchestra: George Wilkins.

OUR PLACE—60 minutes—CBS—July
2, 1967 - September 3, 1967.

OUR PRIVATE WORLD

Serial. A prime-time verison of the
afternoon serial "As the World
Turns." Background, from the previous Oakdale: New York City. The
dramatic story of Lisa Hughes, a nurse
struggling to readjust to life after a
deeply affecting divorce.

CAST

Lisa Hughes   Eileen Fulton

Eve   Julienne Marie
Brad   Robert Drivas
Helen   Geraldine Fitzgerald
Dick   Ken Tobey
John   Nicholas Coster
Sandy   Sandra Scott
Tom   Sam Groom
Franny   Pamela Murphy
Tony   David O'Brien

Music: Charles Paul.

OUR PRIVATE WORLD—30 min-
utes—CBS—May 5, 1965 - September
10, 1965.

OUR STREET

Serial. Background: Our Street, an
any street in an any city. A street
filled with the hopes and the despairs
of any family caught in the echos of
slow-dying prejudice. The dramatic
story of one such family, the Robinsons, a black family searching for
dignity and respect.

CAST

Mae Robinson, the
  mother   Barbara Mealy
Bull Robinson, her
  husband   Gene Cole
                          Clayton Corbin
Jet Robinson, their eldest
  son   Curt Stewart
Slick Robinson, the middle
  child   Darryl F. Hill
                          Howard Rollins
Tony Robinson, the youngest
  son   Tyrone Jones
Kathy Robinson, their
  daughter   Sandra Sharp
J. T. Robinson, Mae's half
  brother   Arthur French
Grandma Robinson Alfredine Parham
Cynthia, a friend   Janet League
Emily, a friend   Frances Foster
Mrs. Ryder, Grandma's
  friend   Birdie Hale

Pearlina, Slick's
  girlfriend   Pat Picketts

Music: Don Schwartz.

OUR STREET—30 minutes—PBS (not all markets)—October 4, 1971 - October 10, 1974.

THE OUTCASTS

Western. Background: The post-Civil War West. Bound to an alliance of survival, two outcasts, Earl Corey, an uprooted Virginian Aristocrat, and Jemal David, an ex-slave freed by the Proclamation, team and become bounty hunters. Stories depict their exploits, distrustful of each other because of their respected backgrounds, but standing together in times of duress. The overall series underlines the general feeling of prejudice and animosity toward blacks in the West of the 1860s.

CAST
Earl Corey   Don Murray
Jemal David   Otis Young

THE OUTCASTS—60 minutes—ABC —September 23, 1968 - September 15, 1969. 26 episodes.

THE OUTER LIMITS

Anthology. Science-fiction presentations.
Creator: Leslie Stevens.
Music: Dominic Frontiere; Harry Lubin.
The Control Voice: Vic Perrin.
Executive Producer: Joseph Stefano.
Producer: Sam White, Ben Brady.
Director: John Brahm, Gerd Oswald, Charles Haas, Byron Haskin, Laslo Benedek, Leon Benson, James Goldstone, Paul Stanley, Felix Feist, John Erman, Alan Crosland, Jr.
Included:

The Tumbleweeds. A couple's efforts to escape from tumbleweeds that seem to possess intelligence and seek to kill them.

CAST
Eddie Albert, June Havoc.

The Guests. Five people, mysteriously transported to a home where times stands still, attempt to escape.

CAST
Florida: Gloria Graham; Norton: Geoffrey Horne; Tess: Luana Anders.

The Chameleon. An intelligence agent attempts to infiltrate a party of creatures from another world.

CAST
Louis Mace: Rober Duvall; Chambers: Howard Caine; General Crawford: Henry Brandon.

Fun and Games. Transported to a distant planet and placed in a contest of death with creatures from another world, two Earthlings struggle to save the planet Earth from the destruction it will face if they should lose.

CAST
Nancy Malone, Nick Adams, Bill Hart.

The Galaxy Being. The disaster that results when a scientist invents three-dimensional television and contacts a creature from another galaxy.

CAST
Cliff Robertson, Jacqueline Scott.

Program Open: A distorted picture appears, followed by a control voice: "There is nothing wrong with your television set, do not attempt to adjust the picture. We are controlling transmission. . . . For the next hour sit quietly and we will control all that you see and hear. You are about to participate in a great adventure, you are about to experience the awe and mystery which reaches from the inner mind to the Outer Limits."

Program Close: The Control Voice: "We now return control of your television set to you, until next week at this same time when the Control Voice will take you to the Outer Limits."

THE OUTER LIMITS—60 minutes—ABC—September 16, 1963 - January 16, 1965. 49 episodes. Syndicated.

THE OUTLAWS

Western. Background: The Oklahoma Territory during the nineteenth century. The events surrounding the apprehension of wanted outlaws by U.S. Marshal Frank Caine and his deputies Will Foreman, Heck Martin, and Chalk Breeson.

CAST

Marshal Frank Caine	Barton MacLane
Deputy Heck Martin	Jack Gaynor
Deputy Marshal Will Foreman	Don Collier
Constance, Will's romantic interest	Judy Lewis
Deputy Chalk Breeson	Bruce Yarnell
Slim, a town character	Slim Pickens

Music: Joseph Hooven; Vic Mizzy.

THE OUTLAWS—60 minutes—NBC—September 29, 1960 - September 13, 1962. 50 episodes. Syndicated.

OUT OF THE INKWELL

Animated Cartoon. The antics of Koko the Clown and his friends, Kokonut, Mean Moe, and Kokete.

Voice characterizations: Larry Storch.

Creator: Max Fleischer.

OUT OF THE INKWELL—05 minutes—Syndicated 1961. 100 episodes.

OUTRAGEOUS OPINIONS

Discussion. Celebrity guests discuss various topical issues.

Hostess: Helen Gurley Brown.

Music: Recorded.

OUTRAGEOUS OPINIONS—30 minutes—Syndicated 1967.

THE OUTSIDER

Crime Drama. Background: Los Angeles, California. The investigations of David Ross, an embittered ex-con turned private detective.

Starring: Darren McGavin as David Ross.

Music: Stanley Wilson.

THE OUTSIDER—60 minutes—NBC—September 18, 1968 - September 10, 1969. 26 episodes.

OUT THERE

Anthology. Science-fiction presentations. Stories are culled from originals and pulp magazines.

Producer: John Haggatt.

Director: Byron Paul, Andrew McCullough.

OUT THERE—30 minutes—CBS—1951 - 1952.

OVERLAND TRAIL

Western. Era: The nineteenth century. The saga of the Overland Stage, the first complete coach line to run from Missouri to California and back.

CAST

Frederick Thomas Kelly, the superintendant	William Bendix
Frank "Flip" Flippen, his assistant	Doug McClure

OVERLAND TRAIL—30 minutes—Syndicated 1960. 17 episodes.

OVERSEAS ADVENTURE

See title: "Foreign Intrigue."

OWEN MARSHALL: COUNSELOR AT LAW

Crime Drama. Background: Santa Barbara, California. The cases and courtroom defenses of attorney Owen Marshall.

CAST

Owen Marshall (widower)	Arthur Hill
Jess Brandon, his assistant	Lee Majors
Melissa Marshall, Owen's daughter	Christine Matchett
Frieda Krause, Owen's secretary	Joan Darling
Danny Paterno, Owen's colleague	Reni Santoni
Ted Warrick, Owen's colleague	David Soul

Music: Elmer Bernstein; Richard Clements.

OWEN MARSHALL: COUNSELOR AT LAW—60 minutes—ABC—September 16, 1971 - August 24, 1974. 69 episodes.

OZARK JUBILEE

See title: "Jubilee U.S.A."

OZMOE

Children. Background: Studio Z, a storeroom in the sub-sub-basement of the ABC television center. The misadventures of electronically operated puppets: Ozmoe, a lighthearted monkey; Roderick Dhon't, the leprechaun; Horatio, the caterpillar; Misty Waters, a curvaceous mermaid; Poe the Crow; Sam the Clam; and Throckmorton the Sea Serpent.

Voices: Bradley Bolke, Jack Urbant, Elinor Russell, Alan Stapleton, Jan Kindler.

Producer: Henry Banks.

Director: Carl Shain, Richard Ward.

OZMOE—15 minutes—ABC—March 6, 1951 - April 12, 1951.

OZZIE AND HARRIET

See title: "The Adventures of Ozzie and Harriet."

OZZIE'S GIRLS

Comedy. A spin-off from "The Adventures of Ozzie and Harriet." Background: 822 Sycamore Street, Hillsdale, the residence of Ozzie and Harriet Nelson. With their children, Dave and Ricky, grown and married, Ozzie and Harriet rent the boys' room to two college girls, Susan Hamilton and Brenda MacKenzie. Stories depict the trials and tribulations of the four members of the Nelson household. (Ozzie's occupation, as in the original series, is not identified.)

CAST

Ozzie Nelson	Himself
Harriet Nelson	Herself
Susan Hamilton	Susan Sennett
Brenda MacKenzie (first introduced as Jennifer MacKenzie)	Brenda Sykes
Lenore Morrison, their neighbor	Lenore Stevens
Alice Morrison, her daughter	Joie Guercio
The mailman	Jim Begg
Professor McCutcheon, the girl's psychology instructor	David Doyle

Also, portraying various friends of Susan and Brenda: Mike Wagner, Gaye Nelson, Tom Harmon.

Music: Frank McKelvey.

OZZIE'S GIRLS—30 minutes—Syndicated 1973. 24 episodes.

THE PACKARD SHOWROOM

See title: "The Martha Wright Show."

PADDY THE PELICAN

Children. Background: Pelicanland. The misadventures of Paddy, the mischievous pelican. Stories unfold through comic-strip drawings.

Hostess: Mary Frances Desmond, as Pam, Paddy's assistant.

Paddy's voice and manipulation: Helen York.

The Artist and creator: Sam Singer.

Other character voices (puppets): Ray Suber.

PADDY THE PELICAN—15 minutes —ABC—1950 - 1951.

THE PALLISERS

Drama. Background: Victorian England. Based on the novels by Anthony Trollope, the series chronicles twenty-five years in the lives of Plantagenet Palliser, a respected member of Parliament, and his wife, Lady Glencora M'Clockie Palliser. Produced by the B.B.C.

CAST

Plantagenet Palliser	Philip Latham
Glencora Palliser	Susan Hampshire
The Duke of Omnium	Roland Culver
Alice	Caroline Mortimer
George	Gary Watson
Lady Dumbello	Rachel Herbert
John Gray	Bernard Brown
Burgo Fitzgerald	Barry Justice
Phineas Finn	Donal McCann
Slide	Clifford Rose
Laura Kennedy	Anna Massey
Lizzie Eustace	Sarah Badel
Mme. Max Goesler	Barbara Murphy

Music: Herbert Chappel, Wilfred Joseph.

Music Played By: The New Philharmonic Orchestra, conducted by Marcus Dods.

Producer: Martin Lisemore, Roland Wilson.

THE PALLISERS—60 minutes—PBS —January 31, 1977 - June 20, 1977. 22 episodes.

PALL MALL PLAYHOUSE

Anthology. Dramatic presentations.

Included:

Square Shootin'. An eastern city newspaper reporter attempts to adjust to life on the Western range.

CAST
Jim Caltin: John Newland; Polly Dorman: Marcia Patrick.

Reunion at Steepler's Hill. A reformed outlaw attempts to persuade his former partner in crime to surrender.

CAST
Billy Bob Jackson: John Ireland; Luke Powers: John Larch; Beth Powers: Dorothy Patrick.

No Compromise. A Texas Ranger struggles to face a difficult assignment: bring in his childhood friend who is now wanted for murder.

CAST
Pvt. Earl Webb: Stephen McNally; John Fenner: Robert Strauss; Judge Fenner: Fay Roope.

Prisoners in Town. A deputy sheriff attempts to defend a beautiful woman accused of murder.

CAST
June Sando: Carolyn Jones; Jim Regan: John Ireland; Cal York: Carleton Young.

PALL MALL PLAYHOUSE—30 minutes—ABC—July 20, 1955 - September 9, 1955.

PANHANDLE PETE AND JENNIFER

Children. Background: A ranch in Chickamoochie Country (the Old South). Incorporating a cartoon story format, yarns told by Johnny Coons, Jennifer Holt, and her life-size dummy, Panhandle Pete, are illustrated by an artist.

Starring: Jennifer Holt, Johnny Coons.

Cartoonist: Bill Newton.

Organist: Adele Scott.

PANHANDLE PETE AND JENNIFER —15 minutes—NBC 1950.

PANIC

Anthology. Suspense dramatizations. Stories of people confronted with sudden, unexpected, and perilous situations.

Host-Narrator: Westbrook Van Voorhis.

Included:

Airline Hostess. On an airline flight across America's Southwest, the pilot informs stewardess Janet Hunter of a radio message that a foreign agent, fleeing the country is aboard the plane and may attempt to divert the flight to Mexico. The story depicts Janet's attempts to discover the spy without alarming the passengers.

CAST
Janet Hunter: Carolyn Jones.

The Moth and the Flame. The story of June Sullivan, a vaudeville dancer who is threatened by a maniacal knife-thrower, a man who believes that she is the reincarnation of his wife—a dancer he murdered years before and plans to kill again.

CAST
June Sullivan: June Havoc; the knife-thrower: Alan Napier; the stage manager: Norman Alden.

May Day. Trapped in his burning home, a paraplegic radio "ham" is unable to reach his transmitter set to summon help. The story depicts the worldwide short-wave rescue search.

CAST
Steve Bridges: Richard Jaeckel; Charlene: Kathy Garver; Honolulu: Keye Luke; Loretta: Florence Shaen; Tokyo: Dale Ishimoto.

Love Story. The time: December 24, 1957. Two lonely people, a discouraged boy and a desperate girl, meet by chance on a wharf where each had contemplated suicide. Being Christmas Eve, the couple agree to meet for a Yuletide celebration at her apartment in one hour. The story depicts the boy's frantic efforts to find the girl after he loses her address.

CAST
The boy: Darryl Hickman; the girl: Mary Webster; the storekeeper: Lila Lee.

PANIC—30 minutes—NBC—September 1957 - September 1958. 31 episodes.

PANTOMIME QUIZ

Game. Two competing teams, the Home and the Visiting, each composed of four members. The host presents one member of one team with a charade. The player than has to perform the charade, which has a two-minute time limit, to his team. The amount of time accumulated before the charade is identified is calculated. All remaining players compete in the same manner. Teams who accumulate the least amount of over-all time are the winners. Home viewers, who submit charades, receive merchandise prizes if the team fails to identify their charade.

Host: Mike Stokey.

Regulars: Dorothy Hart, Angela Lansbury, Rocky Graziano, Carol Haney, Robert Clary, Hans Conried, Jackie Coogan, Milt Kamen, Howard Morris, Carol Burnett, Stubby Kaye, Denise Darcell, Tom Poston, Vincent Price, Coleen Gray, Robert Stack, Sandra Spence, Dave Willock, Fred Clark, George O'Brien, George Macready, Frank DeVol, Beverly Tyler, Virginia Field.

Announcers: Ken Niles; Art Fleming; Ed Reimers.

Orchestra: Frank DeVol.

PANTOMIME QUIZ—30 minutes. CBS—October 4, 1949 - December 1954; ABC—January 22, 1955 - March 6, 1955; ABC—April 8, 1958 - October 4, 1959.

PAPA CELLINI

Comedy. Background: New York

City. The trials and tribulations of the Cellinis, an Italian-American family.

CAST

Papa Cellini	Tito Virolo
	Carlo DeAngelo
Mama Cellini	Ada Ruggeri
Nita Cellini, their daughter	Carol Sinclair
Antino Cellini, their son	Aristide Sigismondi

PAPA CELLINI—30 minutes—ABC—September 28, 1952 - November 16, 1952.

PAPER MOON

Comedy. Background: The Midwest during the 1930s. The story of Moses "Moze" Pray, conartist, a fast-talking salesman for the Dixie Bible Company, and a precocious eleven-year-old-girl, Addie Pray, who believes, that because he looks like her, he is her father. Traveling in a 1931 roadster, they struggle to survive the Depression through imaginative swindles. Based on the motion picture.

CAST

Moze Pray	Christopher Connelly
Addie Pray	Jodie Foster

Music: Harold Arlen.

Theme: "Paper Moon."

PAPER MOON—30 minutes—ABC—September 12, 1974 - January 2, 1975. 13 episodes.

PARADISE BAY

Serial. Background: Paradise Bay, a small coastal community in Southern California. The impact of the new-world standards as experienced by the Morgan family: Jeff, a radio-station manager; his wife, Mary; and their teenage daughter, Kitty.

CAST

Jeff Morgan	Keith Andes
Mary Morgan	Marion Ross
Kitty Morgan	Heather North
Duke Spalding	Dennis Cole
Walter	Walter Brooke

Also: Barbara Boles, Paulie Clark, Steve Mines.

PARADISE BAY—30 minutes—NBC—September 27, 1965 - July 1, 1966.

PARAGON PLAYHOUSE

Anthology. Rebroadcasts of dramas that were originally aired via "Douglas Fairbanks, Jr., Presents."

Host: Walter Abel.

PARAGON PLAYHOUSE—30 minutes—CBS—June 1953 - September 1953.

THE PARENT GAME

Game. Three married couples compete. Object: To match their ideas in raising children with those of a child psychologist. The host reads a question relating to children and reveals four possible answers. Each couple chooses the answer it believes is correct. The correct answer is revealed and points are awarded accordingly (round one: five points per correct choice; round two: ten; round three: fifteen; the finale: thirty). Winners, the highest point scorers, receive a specially selected merchandise prize.

Host: Clark Race.

Announcer: Johnny Jacobs.

Music: Frank Jaffe.

THE PARENT GAME—30 minutes—Syndicated 1972.

PARENTS, PLEASE!

Information. Discussions on the problems faced by parents in the raising of children. A trio of performers enact a situation that is the incorrect approach to raising a child. Three studio-audience members appear on stage and suggest the proper techniques. After the approaches are discussed, the situation is reenacted in correct fashion.

Hostess: Mrs. Bess B. Lane, of the N.Y. State Board of Regents.

Father: Jim Daly.

Mother: Helen Mary.

Daughter: Patsy Cooper.

PARENTS, PLEASE!—30 minutes—DuMont 1947.

PARIS CAVALCADE OF FASHION

See title: "Faye Emerson."

PARIS PRECINCT

Crime Drama. Background: Paris, France. The investigations of Surete (French police department) Inspectors Bolbec and Beaumont.

CAST
Inspector Bolbec   Claude Dauphin
Inspector Beaumont   Louis Jourdan

PARIS PRECINCT—30 minutes—ABC—April 3, 1955 - June 20, 1955;

September 25, 1955 – December 18, 1955. 26 episodes. Syndicated title: "World Crime Hunt."

PARIS 7000

Mystery. Background: The American Consulate in Paris, France. The investigations of Jack Brennan, a troubleshooter who aides distressed U.S. citizens. Paris 7000: the consulate telephone number.

CAST
Jack Brennan   George Hamilton
Jules Maurois, the Surete
   chief   Jacques Aubuchon
Robert Stevens, Brennan's
   assistant   Gene Raymond
Music Supervision: Lionel Newman.

PARIS 7000—60 minutes—ABC—January 22, 1970 - June 4, 1970. 10 episodes.

THE PARTNERS

Comedy. Background: Los Angeles, California. The fumbling investigations of inept Sergeant Lennie Crooke, and his level-headed partner, Sergeant George Robinson, plainclothes police detectives attached to the Los Angeles thirty-third precinct.

CAST
Sgt. Lennie Crooke   Don Adams
Sgt. George
   Robinson   Rupert Crosse
Captain Aaron William
   Andrews   John Doucette
Sergeant Nelson
   Higgenbottom   Dick Van Patten
Freddie Butler, the
   man with the compulsion
   to confess to every
   crime   Robert Karvelas

Music: Lalo Schifrin.

THE PARTNERS—30 minutes—NBC —September 18, 1971 - January 8, 1972. Rebroadcasts (NBC): July 28, 1972 - September 8, 1972. 20 episodes.

THE PARTRIDGE FAMILY

Comedy. Background: 698 Sycamore Road, San Pueblo, California, the residence of a show-business Rock group, the Partridge Family: Shirley, a widow; and her children: Keith, Laurie, Danny, Tracy, and Chris. Stories depict the home and working lives of an ordinary family who became prominent when Danny, their ten-year-old manager, organized the family into a Rock group, recorded a song, and talked agent Reuben Kinkade into hearing the demonstration tape, which lead to a recording contract and fame.

CAST

Shirley Partridge	Shirley Jones
Keith Partridge	David Cassidy
Laurie Partridge	Susan Dey
Danny Partridge	Danny Bonaduce
Tracy Partridge	Suzanne Crough
Chris Partridge	Jeremy Gelbwaks
	Brian Foster
Reuben Kinkade	Dave Madden
Alan Kinkade, his nephew	Alan Bursky
Ricky Stevens, the neighbor's four-year-old son	Ricky Segal
Walter Renfrew, Shirley's father	Ray Bolger
	Jackie Coogan
Amanda Renfrew, Shirley's mother	Rosemary DeCamp

Partridge Family dog: Simon.

Music: Hugo Montenegro.

The Partridge Family. Bottom, left to right: Suzanne Crough, Shirley Jones, Susan Dey. Top, left to right: Brian Foster, David Cassidy, Danny Bonaduce. © *Screen Gems.*

Additional Music: Shorty Rogers, George Duning, Benny Golson.

Executive Producer: Bob Claver.

Producer: Larry Rosen, Mel Swope, Paul Junger Witt.

Director: Ralph Senesky, Lee Philips, E.W. Swackhamer, Russ Mayberry, Jerry London, Herb Wallerstein, Lou Antonio, Christopher Morgan, Bob Claver, Jerry Berstein, Claudio Guzman, Herbert Kenwith, Richard Kinon, Earl Bellamy, Peter Baldwin.

Creator: Bernard Slade.

Background voices (additional to Shirley Jones and David Cassidy) who comprise the Partridge Family: John Bahler, Tom Bahler, Jackie Ward, Ron Hicklin.

THE PARTRIDGE FAMILY—30 minutes—ABC—September 25, 1970 -

September 7, 1974. 96 episodes. Syndicated. Spin-off series: "Partridge Family: 2200 A.D."

PARTRIDGE FAMILY: 2200 A.D.

Animated Cartoon. A spin-off from "The Partridge Family." Background: Earth, 2200 A.D. The misadventures of the traveling (to other planets) show-business Rock group, the Partridge Family: Shirley, Keith, Laurie, Danny, Tracy, and Chris.

Additional characters: Reuben Kinkade, their manager; and their friends: Judy, Beannie, and Marion.

Voices: Sherry Alberoni, Danny Bonaduce, Suzanne Crough, Susan Dey, Brian Foster, Joan Gerber, Dave Madden, Chuck McLennan, Julie McWhirter, Allan Melvin, Alan Oppenheimer, Mike Road, Hal Smith, John Stephenson, Lennie Weinrib, Franklin Welker.

Music: Hoyt Curtin.

PARTRIDGE FAMILY: 2200 A.D.— 25 minutes—CBS—September 7, 1974 - March 9, 1975. 16 episodes.

PARTY TIME AT CLUB ROMA

Variety. The series, filmed in San Francisco, features performances by guest artists.

Host: Ben Alexander.

Producer: Ben Alexander.

Sponsor: Roma Wines.

PARTY TIME AT CLUB ROMA—30 minutes—NBC 1950.

THE PASSING PARADE

Anthology. Reedited theatrical shorts. Touching dramas revealing the lives of people and events of the past.

Narrator: John Nesbitt.

Included:

The Immortal Blacksmith. The story of blacksmith Tom Davenport and his invention of the printing-press motor.

The Giant of Norway. The efforts of statesman Fridtjof Nansen to assist refugees as they return home after World War II.

Magic on a Stick. John Walker's discovery of the safety match.

My Old Town. Life in a small American town before the invention of the automobile.

People on Paper. A history of the comic strip, beginning with *"The Yellow Kid."*

Stairway to Light. French doctor Philippe Pinel's efforts in the treatment of the mentally ill.

THE PASSING PARADE—15 minutes—Syndicated 1961.

PASSPORT 7

Travel. The filmed expeditions of various explorers.

Host-Narrator: Bob Maxwell.

PASSPORT 7—30 minutes—Syndicated 1964.

PASSPORT TO DANGER

Adventure. The global assignments of

Steve McQuinn, a United States diplomatic courier, and the unwitting decoy of the Hungarian Secret Police.

Starring: Cesar Romero as Steve McQuinn.

PASSPORT TO DANGER—30 minutes—CBS 1956. 39 episodes.

PASSWORD

Game. Distinguished by four formats.

Format One:

Password—30 minutes—CBS—October 2, 1961 - September 15, 1967. Syndicated.

Two competing teams, each composed of two members—one celebrity and one noncelebrity contestant. Each member of one team is handed a concealed password (e.g., "discover"). The player then relates a one word clue to his partner, who must identify the password. If he is unable, their opponents then receive a chance to identify it. The word is played until it is identified or until it is voided by the use of ten clues. Words start at ten points and diminish one point with each additional clue. Winners are the teams first to score twenty-five points. The champions then compete in the bonus "Lightning Round." Object: to identify five words within sixty seconds. Fifty dollars is awarded for each correct identification.

Host: Allen Ludden.

Announcer: Jack Clark; John Harlan.

Music: Recorded.

Format Two:

Password—30 minutes—ABC—April 5, 1971 - November 15, 1974.

The same as format one.

Host: Allen Ludden.

Announcer: John Harlan.

Music: Recorded.

Format Three:

Password All Stars—30 minutes—ABC—November 18, 1974 - February 21, 1975.

Six celebrities compete. Four at a time play, divided into two teams of two. One player on each team receives a password and through one-word clues has to relate its meaning to his partner. Words start at ten points and diminish one point with each clue to a limit of five clues. The team first to score twenty-five or more points is the winner. Each member of the team receives that amount of points and a chance to double it via "20-20 Password." Within a twenty-second time limit, each player has to identify one word. The time one player uses is deducted from the total time and becomes the amount of time the remaining player has.

To determine who will compete as partners with each member of the winning team, "The Qualifying Game" is played. The four remaining players compete. The two champions rotate, each giving one word clues to the identification of a password. The player first to press a button and sound a buzzer receives a chance to answer. If correct, he scores one password. The first two players to score two passwords each qualify. The first player to qualify selects his partner from the previous winning team. The remaining two players, the champion and the second to qualify, form the opposing team.

The game plays as such, four days, Monday through Thursday. The four players with the highest point scores compete in the fifth day tournament segment wherein the highest scoring player receives a silver master award and five thousand dollars for purposes of donation to a favorite charity.

Host: Allen Ludden.

Announcer: John Harlan.

Music: Recorded.

Format Four:

Password—30 minutes—ABC—February 24, 1975 - June 27, 1975.

The same as Format One.

Host: Allen Ludden.

Announcer: John Harlan.

Music: Recorded.

PAT BOONE

Listed: The television programs of singer-actor Pat Boone.

The Pat Boone Show—Musical Variety—30 minutes—ABC—October 3, 1957 - June 25, 1959 (1958 title: "The Pat Boone Chevy Show").

Host: Pat Boone.

Regulars: The Artie Malvin Chorus, The Jada Quartet, The McGuire Sisters.

Orchestra: Mort Lindsey.

The Pat Boone Show—Musical Variety (Daily)—30 minutes—NBC—October 17, 1966 - March 31, 1967.

Host: Pat Boone.

Pat Boone in Hollywood—Talk-Variety—90 minutes—Syndicated 1969.

Host: Pat Boone.

Announcer: Jay Stewart.

THE PATCHWORK FAMILY

Children. Songs, games, sketches, and related educational entertainment geared to children.

Hostess (Portraying Carol): Carol Corbett.

Voice of Rags the puppet: Cary Antebi.

Regulars: Joanna Pang, John Canemaker, Arlene Thomas, Elaine Lefkowits.

Music: Recorded.

Executive Producer: Linda Allen.

Producer-Director: Bill Bryan.

THE PATCHWORK FAMILY—60 minutes—Premiered: January 1, 1974. Broadcast on CBS owned and operated stations.

PAT PAULSEN'S HALF A COMEDY HOUR

Comedy. A satire of the contemporary scene.

The Patchwork Family. Carol Corbett with Rags the puppet.

Host: Pat Paulsen.

Regulars: Jean Byron, Sherry Miles, Bob Einstein, Peppe Brown, Vanetta Rogers, Pedro Regas (as Mrs. Buffalo Running Schwartz, an eighty-seven-year-old Indian).

Announcer: Billy Sands.

PAT PAULSEN'S HALF A COMEDY HOUR—30 minutes—ABC—January 22, 1970 - March 9, 1970. 13 tapes.

THE PATRICE MUNSEL SHOW

Musical Variety.
Hostess: Patrice Munsel.
Featured: The Martins Quartet.
Orchestra: Charles Sanford.

THE PATRICE MUNSEL SHOW—30 minutes—ABC—October 18, 1957 - July 18, 1958.

THE PATRICIA BOWAN SHOW

Musical Variety.
Hostess: Patricia Bowan.
Regulars: Paul Shelly, Maureen Cannon, The Pastels.
Music: The Norman Paris Trio.

THE PATRICIA BOWAN SHOW—15 minutes—CBS 1951.

PATROL CAR

Rebroadcasts of "Inspector Fabian of Scotland Yard" (which see).

PATTI PAGE

Listed: The television programs of

The Patti Page Show. Patti Page.

singer-actress Patti Page.

The Scott Music Hall—Musical Revue —30 minutes—CBS—July 15, 1952 - September 25, 1952.
Hostess: Patti Page.
Regulars: Frank Fontaine, Mary Ellen Terry.
Orchestra: Carl Hoff.

The Patti Page Show—Musical Variety —15 minutes—NBC—July 3, 1955 - July 7, 1956.
Hostess: Patti Page.
Featured: The Page Five Singers.
Orchestra: Jack Rael.

The Patti Page Show—Musical Variety (summer replacement for "The Perry Como Show")—30 minutes—NBC— June 16, 1956 - July 16, 1956.
Hostess: Patti Page.
Featured: The Spellbinders.
Orchestra: Jack Rael.

The Patti Page Show—Musical Variety —15 minutes—CBS— February 9, 1957 - June 11, 1958.

Hostess: Patti Page.

Orchestra: Jack Rael.

The Big Record—Musical Variety—60 minutes—CBS—September 18, 1957 - June 11, 1958 (see title).

The Patti Page Show—Musical Variety —30 minutes—ABC—September 24, 1958 - March 16, 1959.

Hostess: Patti Page.

Regulars: The Jerry Packer Singers, The Matt Mattox Dancers.

Orchestra: Vic Schoen.

THE PATTY DUKE SHOW

Comedy. Background: Number Eight Remsen Drive, Brooklyn Heights, Brooklyn, New York, the residence of the Lane family: Martin, the managing

The Patty Duke Show. Patty Duke as Patty Lane.

The Patty Duke Show. Patty Duke as Cathy Lane, her European cousin.

editor of the *New York Chronicle;* his wife, Natalie; their daughter, Patty; their son, Ross; and their glamorous European cousin, Cathy Lane, who is residing with them until she completes her high school education and is able to rejoin her father, Kenneth Lane, a foreign correspondent for the *Chronicle.*

Stories depict the lives of two pretty high school girls, sixteen-year-old identical cousins, Patty and Cathy Lane. Patty, the average American girl, possesses an unquenchable thirst for life and the ability to complicate matters that are seemingly uncomplicatable; and Cathy, shy, warm, and sensitive, possesses a love for the arts, and, treasuring her European upbringing, sometimes encounters difficulty as she struggles to adjust to the American way of life.

CAST

Patty Lane	Patty Duke
Cathy Lane	Patty Duke
Martin Lane	William Schallert

Natalie Lane	Jean Byron
Ross Lane	Paul O'Keefe
Richard Harrison, Patty's boyfriend	Eddie Applegate
Sue Ellen Turner, Patty's rival for Richard	Kitty Sullivan
Ted Brownley, Cathy's boyfriend	Skip Hinnant
Gloria, Patty's rival for Richard (later episodes)	Kelly Wood
J.R. Castle, Martin's employer	John McGiver
Nikki Lee Blake, Ross's girlfriend	Susan Melvin
William Smithers, Martin's employer (later episodes)	Ralph Bell
Mr. Brewster, the principal of Brooklyn Heights High School	Charles White
Sammy, the owner of the Shake Shop, the after-school hangout	Sammy Smith
Jonathan Harrison, Richard's father	David Doyle
Mrs. Harrison, Richard's mother	Amzie Strictland
Kenneth Lane, Cathy's father	William Schallert
T. J. Blodgett, the publisher of the *Chronicle*	Alan Bunce Robert Carson Jerry Hauser
Mrs. Marlow, Natalie's friend	Natalie Masters
Miss Gordon, J.R.'s secretary	Phyllis Coates
Louie, the waiter at Leslie's Ice Cream Parlor (the hangout in later episodes)	Bobby Diamond
Monica Robinson, Patty's friend	Laura Barton
	Kathy Garver
Mrs. MacDonald, the Lane housekeeper	Margaret Hamilton
Alice, Patty's friend	Alice Rawlings
Rosiland, Patty's friend	Robyn Millan
Alfred, Patty's friend	Jeff Siggins

Patty Duke's stand-in: Rita McLaughlin (portraying Cathy when Miss Duke is portraying Patty; Patty when Miss Duke is portraying Cathy).

Lane family dog: Tiger.

Music: Sid Ramin; Harry Geller.

THE PATTY DUKE SHOW—30 minutes—ABC—September 18, 1963 - August 31, 1966. 104 episodes. Syndicated.

PAULA STONE'S TOY SHOP

Children. Music, comedy, and fantasy set against the background of a toy store.

Hostess: Paula Stone.

Regulars: Tim Herbert (as Freddie Fun) and dancers Howard and Marge as Pitter and Patter.

Producer-Director: Paula Stone.

PAULA STONE'S TOY SHOP—60 minutes—ABC 1955.

PAUL BERNARD—PSYCHIATRIST

Drama. Background: Canada, the office of psychiatrist Paul Bernard. The session between doctor and patient is dramatized. The patient relates her elements of distress; and, in the final moments of the program, Dr. Bernard analizes her seemingly uncomplicated and innocent thoughts. Produced with the cooperation of the Canadian Mental Health Association.

CAST

Paul Bernard, Psychiatrist	Chris Wiggins
Regular Patients:	
Mrs. Alice Talbot	Dawn Greenhalgh
Mrs. Howard	Tudi Wiggins
Mrs. Finley	Marcia Diamond
Miss Parker	Valerie-Jean Hume
Mrs. Connie Walker	Phyllis Maxwell
Mrs. Katie Conner	Nuala Fitzgerald
Mrs. Wilkins	Vivian Reis
Miss Barbara Courtney	Sheley Sommers
Mrs. Bradshaw	Diane Polley
Mrs. Collins	Kay Hawtrey
Mrs. Donaldson	Gale Garnett
Mrs. Roberts	Paisley Maxwell
Mrs. Patterson	Josephine Barrington
Mrs. Johnson	Anna Commeron
Miss Michaels	Peggy Mahon
Mrs. Karen Lampton	Barbara Kyle
Mrs. Brookfield	Carol Lazare
Mrs. Jennifer Barlow	Micki Moore
Mrs. Vickie Lombard	Arlene Meadows

Music: Milani Kymlicka.

PAUL BERNARD—PSYCHIATRIST—30 minutes—Syndicated 1972. 195 tapes.

PAUL DIXON

Listed: The television programs of singer Paul Dixon.

The Paul Dixon Show—Variety—60 minutes—ABC—August 8, 1951 - November 15, 1951.

Host: Paul Dixon.

Regulars: Wanda Lewis, Dottie Mack, Lennie Gorrian.

The Paul Dixon Show—Variety—30 minutes—Syndicated 1974. Music, songs, and conversation geared to women.

Host: Paul Dixon ("Paul baby.")

Regulars: Coleen Sharp, Bonnie Lou ("Star of the now defunct Midwestern Hayride.")

Music: The Bruce Brownfield Band.

THE PAUL LYNDE SHOW

Comedy. Background: Ocean Grove, California, the residence of the Simms family: Paul, an attorney with the firm of McNish and Simms; his wife, Martha; and their children, Barbara (twenty-one), and Sally (fourteen).

Completing her studies at college, Barbara Simms and Howie Dickerson, a penniless former graduate studying for his Masters degree in oceanogrophy, elope, return to Ocean Grove from Las Vegas, and establish housekeeping in the Simms home, where Howie encounters Paul's objections—concerned over Barbara's welfare and Howie's inability to support her. Stories depict the bickering relationship between Paul and Howie; and Paul's desperate attempts to find Howie (a genius with an I.Q. of 185 who can't function properly in the business world) suitable employment. Based on the stage play, "Howie."

CAST

Paul Simms	Paul Lynde
Martha Simms	Elizabeth Allen
Barbara Dickerson (Simms)	Jane Actman
Howie Dickerson	John Calvin
Sally Simms	Pamelyn Ferdin
J.J. McNish, Paul's business partner	Herb Voland
Barney Dickerson, Howie's	

father, a butcher
in Eagle Rock
California   Jerry Stiller
Grace Dickerson, Howie's
mother   Anne Meara
Alice, Paul's
secretary   Allison McKay
Jimmy Fowler, Sally's
boyfriend   Anson Williams
Jimmy Lyons, Sally's
boyfriend   Stuart Getz

Music: Shorty Rogers.

THE PAUL LYNDE SHOW—30 minutes—ABC—September 13, 1972 -
September 8, 1973. 26 episodes.

PAUL WHITEMAN'S SATURDAY NIGHT REVUE

Musical Variety.

Host: Paul Whiteman.

Regulars: Linda Romay, Eric Viola,
Joe Young, Duffy Otel.

Orchestra: Paul Whiteman.

Choreographer: Frank Westbrook.

Producer: Tony Stanford, Ward Byron, Dick Eckler.

Director: William H. Brown.

Sponsor: Goodyear.

PAUL WHITEMAN'S SATURDAY
NIGHT REVUE—30 minutes—ABC—
November 6, 1949 - October 29,
1950. Also titled: "The Paul Whiteman Goodyear Revue."

PAUL WHITEMAN'S TEEN CLUB

Variety. Performances by teenage
talent discoveries.

Host: Paul Whiteman.

Regulars: Nancy Lewis, June Keegan,
Maureen Cannon, The Ray
Porter Singers.

Orchestra: Paul Whiteman.

Producer: Jack Sleck, Skipper Dawes,
Paul Whiteman.

Director: Herb Horton.

Sponsor: Griffin Shoe Polish.

PAUL WHITEMAN'S TEEN CLUB—
60 minutes—ABC—April 2, 1949 -
March 28, 1954.

PAUL WINCHELL AND JERRY MAHONEY

Listed: The television programs of
ventriloquist Paul Winchell.

Winchell and Mahoney—Children—30
minutes—NBC 1947.

Background: Jerry Mahoney's Club
House. Twenty Children from
the studio audience compete in
various games for prizes.

Host: Paul Winchell.

His Dummies: Jerry Mahoney,
Knucklehead Smith.

Regulars: Dorothy Claire, Hilda
Vaughn.

Orchestra: John Gart.

Dunninger and Winchell—Variety—30
minutes. NBC—October 14, 1948 -
September 28, 1949; CBS—October 5,
1949 - December 28, 1949. Also
known as "The Bigelow Show."

Format: Demonstrations on the art of
mind reading.

Hosts: Paul Winchell, Jerry Mahoney.

Starring: Joseph Dunninger, the
"master mentalist."

The Paul Winchell and Jerry Mahoney Show.
Paul Winchell and his dummy friend, Jerry
Mahoney.

**The Paul Winchell and Jerry Mahoney
Speidel Show**—Variety—30 minutes—
NBC—1950 - 1953.

Hosts: Paul Winchell, Jerry Mahoney.

Regulars: Dorothy Claire, Hilda
Vaughn, Jimmy Blaine, Patricia
Bright, Sid Raymond.

Announcer: Ted Brown.

Orchestra: John Gart.

**Paul Winchell and Jerry Mahoney's
What's My Name**—Game—30 minutes
—NBC—January 1952 - May 22, 1954.

Format: Object: For players to
identify the name of a famous
person through clues provided by
Paul and his dummies as they
dramatize an incident in the subject's life. War bonds are awarded
to winners.

Hosts: Paul Winchell, Jerry Mahoney.

Regulars: Maybin Hewe, Mary Ellen
Terry.

Orchestra: Milton DeLugg.

Toyland Express—Children—30 minutes—ABC—November 7, 1955 -
December 12, 1955.

Hosts: Paul Winchell, Jerry Mahoney.

Orchestra: Ralph Herman.

Circus Time—Circus Variety Acts—60
minutes—ABC—October 4, 1956 -
June 27, 1957.

Ringmasters: Paul Winchell, Jerry Mahoney.

Orchestra: Ralph Herman.

The Paul Winchell Show—Variety—30 minutes—ABC—September 29, 1957 - April 3, 1960.

Hosts: Paul Winchell, Jerry Mahoney.

Featured: Frank Fontaine.

Orchestra: Milton DeLugg.

The Paul Winchell Show—Variety—30 minutes—ABC—December 25, 1960 - April 16, 1961.

Hosts: Paul Winchell, Jerry Mahoney.

Music: Milton DeLugg.

Cartoonsville—Cartoons—30 minutes—ABC—April 6, 1963 - September 28, 1963.

Hosts: Paul Winchell, Jerry Mahoney, Knucklehead Smith.

Cartoons: "Sheriff Saddle Head"; "Goodie the Gremlin"; "Scatt Skit."

Winchell and Mahoney Time —Children—60 minutes—Syndicated 1965.

Background: Jerry's Club House. Selected members of the studio audience compete in games for prizes.

Hosts: Paul Winchell, Jerry Mahoney, Knucklehead Smith.

Runaround—Game—30 minutes—NBC —September 9, 1972 - September 1, 1973. See title.

PAY CARDS

Game. Three contestants compete in a game of poker. Twenty cards, which contain singles, pairs, and three and four of a kind, are displayed face down on an electronic board. By selecting the numbered cards (one to twenty) players have to build a five-card hand better than their opponents. Players begin by selecting three cards, then two on their next turn. The player with the best hand is the winner.

Cash: a pair: ten dollars; three of a kind or a full house: thirty dollars; four of a kind: one hundred dollars.

Rounds Two and Three: "Joker's Wild." The format and the payoffs are the same as round one.

Round Four: "The Jackpot." The winner, the highest cash scorer, is shown the faces of twelve cards for twelve seconds. At the end of the time the cards are hidden by overlaying numbers. The host spins a wheel which when stopping pinpoints one of the twelve cards. If the player can guess the number that the card is hidden under, he wins a new car.

Host: Art James.

Announcer: Fred Collins.

PAY CARDS—30 minutes—Syndicated 1968. 260 tapes.

P.D.Q.
(PLEASE DRAW QUICKLY)

A game show, hosted by Ed Cooper, that features players competing in a drawing type of guessing game for prizes. 30 minutes—ABC 1950.

P.D.Q.

Game. Two competing teams, "The Home Team" and "The Challengers." The Home Team is composed of two celebrities; and the Challengers comprise one celebrity and one non-celebrity contestant. One member of each team is placed in a soundproof isolation booth. As the sound is turned off in one booth, the other team competes. Standing before a phrase that is spelled out in large plastic letters, the outside player has to place letters on a wall rack within six second intervals and induce his partner into identifying it. The amount of letters used until the phrase is guessed is calculated. The sound is turned on in the other booth and the team competes in the same manner with the same phrase. The team using the fewest letters is the winner of that round. If it is the contestant's team, she wins a merchandise prize. A two-out-of-three-game competition is played.

If the challengers accumulate the least amount of overall time, the contestant receives the opportunity to win five hundred dollars and a new car. The player is shown three letters of one word (e.g., WTR-- WATER) and has to identify ten words within sixty seconds. For each correct identification she receives fifty dollars. If she guesses all ten she wins five hundred dollars and a new car. Should the contestant have scored lower than the Home Team, each correct identification awards twenty-five dollars.

Host: Dennis James.

Announcer: Kenny Williams.

P.D.Q.—30 minutes—Syndicated 1965-1970. Withdrawn. Revised as: "Baffle" (see title).

PEABODY'S IMPROBABLE HISTORY

See title: "Rocky and His Friends."

PEANUTS

Animated Cartoon. The misadventures of the Peanuts gang: eight children (Charlie Brown, Linus, Lucy, Schroeder, Pig Pen, Frieda, Peppermint Patty, and Sally), and one mischievous dog, Snoopy, who believes he is a World War I flying ace in battle with the Red Baron. Stories depict their attempts to solve problems without help from the adult world. Created by Charles Schultz.

Characters' Voices

Charlie Brown	Peter Robbins
	Chad Webber
	Duncan Watson
Snoopy	Bill Melendez
Lucy	Sally Dryer
	Tracy Stratford
	Pamelyn Ferdin
	Robin Kohn
Linus	Christopher Shea
	Stephen Shea
Pig Pen	Jeff Orstein
	Thomas A. Muller
Peppermint Patty	Gail De Faria
	Kip De Faria
	Maureen McCormick
	Donna Forman
Schroeder	Glenn Mendelson
	Danny Hjelm
	Brian Kayanjian
	Greg Felton
Sally	Kathy Steinberg
	Hilary Momberger
	Lynn Mortensen
Frieda	Ann Altieri

Music composed by: Vince Guaraldi.

Orchestra: John Scott Trotter.

Animation: Bill Melendez.

The Series:

A Charlie Brown Christmas. With the Christmas season approaching, Charlie, disillusioned by the commer-

© 1969 by United Feature Syndicate, Inc.

SCHULZ

Peanuts. The cast of "Peanuts." Created by Charles Schultz. © *United Features Syndicate, Inc.*

cialism of the holiday, attempts to relay his feelings to his friends who are eagerly awaiting the big day.

A Charlie Brown Thanksgiving. Charlie's efforts to organize a Thanksgiving feast.

Be My Valentine, Charlie Brown. The episode focuses on several characters: Sally, who thinks Linus's purchase of a box of candy is for her, when in reality it is for his homeroom teacher; Lucy, who seeks Schroeder's attention; and Charlie Brown, who begins a vigil by his mailbox, hoping for a valentine.

Charlie Brown's All Stars. With 999 straight losses, and 3000 runs given up by its pitcher, Charlie Brown, the All Stars baseball team, which is composed of five boys, three girls, and a dog, play—and lose—their thousandth game.

He's Your Dog, Charlie Brown. Charlie's efforts to curtail the antics of his mischievous dog, Snoopy.

It's a Mystery, Charlie Brown. Donning the guise of Sherlock Holmes, Snoopy attempts to solve the case of Woodstock's missing nest.

It's Arbor Day, Charlie Brown. The

chaos that results when the students of the Birchwood School decide to observe Arbor Day and proceed to beautify the world.

It's The Easter Beagle, Charlie Brown. The story focuses on the Peanuts gang as they prepare for the Easter Beagle, a mythical dog who magically appears to hand out candy and decorate eggs on Easter Sunday Morning.

It's the Great Pumpkin, Charlie Brown. The saga of Linus's vigil in a pumpkin field where he eagerly awaits the arrival of the Great Pumpkin, a mythical being who is supposed to give toys to good girls and boys.

It Was a Short Summer, Charlie Brown. Charlie and the gang recall a summer at camp where the boys were pitted against the girls in various sports events.

Play it Again, Charlie Brown. Through Lucy's meddling, Schroeder, the gifted pianist, is booked to play his toy piano for the P.T.A. The story focuses on his efforts to please an audience who are expecting a rock concert from a boy who is strictly a Beethoven man.

There's No Time For Love, Charlie Brown. A hectic day in the lives of the Peanuts gang is recalled through essay tests, Peppermint Patty's crush on Charlie, and a misguided field trip.

You're a Good Sport, Charlie Brown. The story focuses on a cross-country race with the Peanuts characters as the main competitors.

You're Elected, Charlie Brown. Charlie's disastrous campaign against Linus for the presidency of the sixth grade.

You're In Love, Charlie Brown. With only two days left before the end of the term, Charlie attempts to acquire the affections of the red-haired girl who sits in front of him.

PEANUTS—30 minutes—CBS. First broadcast as a series of specials during the 1965-1966 season.

THE PEARL BAILEY SHOW

Musical Variety.
Hostess: Pearl Bailey.
Announcer: Roger Carroll.
Orchestra: Louis Bellson.

THE PEARL BAILEY SHOW—60 minutes—ABC—January 23, 1971 - May 5, 1971. 13 episodes.

PEBBLES AND BAMM BAMM

See title: "The Flintstones."

PECK'S BAD GIRL

Comedy. The misadventures of twelve-year-old Torey Peck.

CAST

Torey Peck	Patty McCormack
Steve Peck, her father, a lawyer	Wendell Corey
Jennifer Peck, her mother	Marsha Hunt
Roger Peck, her seven-year-old brother	Roy Ferrell
Francesca, her girlfriend	Reba Waters

PECK'S BAD GIRL—30 minutes—CBS—May 5, 1959 - August 4, 1959.

Rebroadcasts: CBS—June 28, 1960 - September 20, 1960.

THE PEE WEE KING SHOW

Musical Variety. Performances by Country and Western entertainers.

Host: Pee Wee King.

Regulars: Chuck Wiggins, Neal Burris, Redd Stuart, Ellen Long, The Cleveland Jamboree, The Golden West Cowboys.

Orchestra: Pee Wee King.

THE PEE WEE KING SHOW—30 minutes—ABC—May 23, 1955 - September 5, 1955.

THE PENDULUM

Anthology. Retitled episodes of "The Vise."

Host: John Bentley.

Producer: Bob Breckner.

Director: Dean Reed.

THE PENDULUM—30 minutes—Syndicated 1956. 65 episodes.

PENNY TO A MILLION

Game. Two competing teams, each composed of five members. Through general-knowledge question-and-answer rounds, eight of the ten players are eliminated. An incorrect response defeats a player. The remaining two players, one per team, compete in a spelling bee wherein they receive one penny doubled to a possible million ($10,000). The surviving player receives what money he has won, and returns the following week, competes again in the question-answer session, and if successful again, competes in the spelling bee to increase the money he has already won.

Host: Bill Goodwin.

PENNY TO A MILLION—30 minutes —ABC—June 1955 - September 1955.

PENTAGON CONFIDENTIAL

Drama. Background: Washington, D.C. Factual dramatizations based on the files of the United States Army Criminal Investigation Division.

CAST
The C.I.D. colonel   Addison Richards
The police detective   Gene Lyons
The army investigator   Edward Binns
The army investigator   Larry Fletcher

PENTAGON CONFIDENTIAL—30 minutes—CBS 1953.

PENTAGON U.S.A.

See title: "Pentagon Confidential." (One week after the premiere of "Pentagon Confidential," the title changed to "Pentagon U.S.A.".)

PENTHOUSE PARTY

Variety. Music, songs, and celebrity interviews.

Hostess: Betty Furness.

Vocalist: Don Cherry.

Music: The Buddy Weed Trio.

Producer: Lester Lewis.

Director: Alex Segal.

Sponsor: Best Foods.

PENTHOUSE PARTY—30 minutes—ABC—September 15, 1950 - June 8, 1951.

PENTHOUSE SONATA

Classical Music.

Hostess: June Browne.

Music: The Fine Arts Quartet (Leonard Sorkin, George Sopkin, Sheppard Lehnoff, Joseph Stepansky).

PENTHOUSE SONATA—30 minutes —ABC—June 19, 1949 - June 26, 1949.

PEOPLE ARE FUNNY

See title: "Art Linkletter."

THE PEOPLE'S CHOICE

Comedy. Background: New City, California. The trials and tribulations of Socrates "Sock" Miller, a Bureau of Fish and Wildlife Ornithologist studying to become a lawyer.

Stranded on a country road by an inoperative car, Amanda "Mandy" Peoples, the mayor's daughter, is assisted by Sock, who, after fixing the flat tire, befriends her. Feeling that he is the right man for a city-council vacancy, she delivers a television speech and urges a write-in vote for Miller. An overwhelming voter response elects Sock as a city councilman and as the head of Barkerville, a housing development.

Following the format of a serial, episodes depict: Sock and Mandy's secret marriage—eloping after her father, John Peoples, refused to grant his permission (feeling Sock is not worthy, as yet, not a lawyer); their attempts to conceal their marriage, which after several months is discovered by John, who, though bitter, accepts Sock; the struggles of newly-

weds; and Sock's attempts to promote Barkerville.

Through voice-over dubbing, the proceedings are observed and commented on by Cleo, Sock's bassethound dog.

CAST

Socrates "Sock" Miller	Jackie Cooper
Amanda "Mandy" Peoples (Miller)	Patricia Breslin
Mayor John Peoples	Paul Maxey
Augusta "Gus" Miller, Sock's aunt	Margaret Irving
Hex Hexley (Rollo), Sock's friend	Dick Wesson
Miss Larson, Sock's employer	Elvia Allman
Pierre, a penniless artist, a friend of Sock's	Leonid Kinskey

Cleo's Voice: Mary Jane Croft.

Music: Raven Kosakoff.

THE PEOPLE'S CHOICE—30 minutes—CBS—October 6, 1955 - September 25, 1958. Syndicated. 104 episodes.

THE PEOPLE'S COURT OF SMALL CLAIMS

Courtroom Drama. Dramatic reenactments of small-claims court hearings.

Judge: Orrin B. Evans.

THE PEOPLE'S COURT OF SMALL CLAIMS—30 minutes—Syndicated 1958.

PEOPLE WILL TALK

Game. Two competing contestants. The host reads a yes-or-no type of answerable question to a panel of fifteen selected studio audience members who lock in an answer of the corresponding type. Contestants, one at a time, choose a panelist and predict his or her answer. The panelist reveals his answer and if it is in accord with the contestant's, he receives one point. Winners, the highest scoring contestants, receive merchandise prizes.

Host: Dennis James.

PEOPLE WILL TALK—25 minutes—NBC—July 1, 1963 - December 27, 1963.

PEPSI-COLA PLAYHOUSE

Anthology. Dramatic presentations.
Hostesses: Anita Colby; Polly Bergen.

Included:

One Thing Leads to Another. The trials and tribulations of a young lawyer and his fiancée.

CAST
Patrick O'Neal, Bridgett Carr.

Adopted Son. A mother attempts to reconstruct her adopted, musically inclined son into the image of her deceased, athletic son.

CAST
Frances Gifford.

Bachelor's Week. The story of a bachelor's doubts about marriage.

CAST
Robert Paige.

Playmates. The life of a lonely girl whose world is dominated by invisible playmates.

CAST
Natalie Wood, Alan Napier.

PEPSI-COLA PLAYHOUSE—30 minutes—ABC—October 2, 1953 - June 26, 1955. Also titled: "Playhouse '54."

THE PERFECT MATCH

Game. Two three-member teams, the men and the women. Object: For the men to discover which female a computer has matched him with and vice versa.

Round One: The host presents a romantic situation to the men who then answer and attempt to solve it. Choosing any of the men, each woman is permitted to question him concerning his answers.

Round Two: The reverse of round one. The men are permitted to question the women concerning their responses to a romantic problem.

Round Three: Varies greatly in presentation, but the basic format is an exchange of questions and answers between the two teams to determine the romantic natures of each individual.

Finale: Each male chooses the girl he feels he is best suited for, and vice versa. Players who match receive fifty dollars. The computer choices, which are validated by the Computer Match Company, are revealed, and the couples who paired themselves as did the computer, have a perfect match and each receive two hundred dollars.

Host: Dick Enberg.

Music: Score Productions.

THE PERFECT MATCH—30 minutes—Syndicated 1967.

THE PERILS OF PENELOPE PITSTOP

Animated Cartoon. Becoming the legal guardian of Penelope Pitstop, a young and vulnerable female racer, Sylvester Sneekly dons the guise of the Hooded Claw and sets his goal to acquire her wealth by killing her. Traveling around the world in her car, the *Compact Pussycat,* Penelope and her protectors, the Ant Hill Mob, struggle to foil the Hooded Claw's sinister efforts. A Hanna-Barbera Production.

Characters' Voices
Penelope Pitstop   Janet Waldo
Sylvester Sneekly   Paul Lynde
Chugaboom   Mel Blanc
Yak Yak   Mel Blanc
The Bully Brothers   Mel Blanc

The Ant Hill Mob:
Clyde   Paul Winchell
Softly   Paul Winchell
Zippy   Don Messick
Pockets   Don Messick
Dum Dum   Don Messick
Snoozy   Don Messick

Narrator: Gary Owens.

Music: Hoyt Curtin.

Musical Director: Ted Nichols.

Producer-Director: William Hanna, Joseph Barbera.

THE PERILS OF PENELOPE PIT-STOP—30 minutes—CBS—September 13, 1969 - September 4, 1971. 26 episodes. Syndicated.

PERRY COMO

Listed: The television programs of singer Perry Como.

The Chesterfield Supper Club—Musical Variety—15 minutes—NBC—December 24, 1948 - May 28, 1950.

Host: Perry Como.

Regulars: The Fontaine Sisters (Geri, Margie, and Bea), Martin Block.

Orchestra: Mitchell Ayres.

Sponsor: Chesterfield Cigarettes.

The Perry Como Show—Musical Variety—15 minutes—CBS—October 4, 1950 - June 24, 1955.

Host: Perry Como.

Regulars: The Ray Charles Singers, The Fontaine Sisters.

Announcer: Frank Gallop.

Orchestra: Mitchell Ayres.

The Perry Como Show—Musical Variety—60 minutes—CBS—September 17, 1955 - June 6, 1959.

Host: Perry Como.

Regulars: The Fontaine Sisters, Mindy Carson, Don Adams, Sandy Stewart, Joey Heatherton, Kaye Ballard, Milt Kamen, The Ray Charles Singers, The Louis Da Pron Dancers.

Announcer: Frank Gallop.

Orchestra: Mitchell Ayres.

PERRY MASON

Crime Drama. Background: Los Angeles, California. The cases and courtroom defenses of criminal attorney Perry Mason. Based on the character created by Erle Stanley Gardner.

Versions:

Perry Mason—60 minutes—CBS—Sep-

tember 21, 1957 - September 4, 1966.
271 episodes. Syndicated.

CAST

Perry Mason	Raymond Burr
Della Street, his secretary-Girl Friday	Barbara Hale
Paul Drake, a private investigator	William Hopper
Lieutenant Arthur Tragg, L.A.P.D.	Ray Collins
Hamilton Burger, the state prosecuting attorney	William Talman
Lieutenant Steve Drumm, L.A.P.D.	Richard Anderson
Gertie Lade, Mason's receptionist	Connie Cezon
Margo, Drake's secretary	Paula Courtland
Drake's operator	Lyn Guild
David Gideon, a law student, Mason's associate	Karl Heid
Anderson, Mason's associate	Wesley Lau
Sgt. Brice	Lee Miller
Clay	Dan Tobin

Music: Richard Shores, Fred Steiner.

Executive Producer: Gail Patrick Jackson, Arthur Marks.

Producer: Art Seid, Sam White, Ben Brady.

Director: Jerry Hopper, John Peyser, Arthur Marks, Christian Nyby, Gordon Webb, Francis D. Lyon, Anton Leader, Lalso Benedek, Ted Post.

The New Adventures Of Perry Mason —60 minutes—CBS—September 16, 1973 - January 27, 1974. 15 episodes.

CAST

Perry Mason	Monte Markham
Della Street	Sharon Acker
Hamilton Burger	Harry Guardino

Paul Drake	Albert Stratton
Lt. Arthur Tragg	Dane Clark
Gertie Lade	Brett Somers

Music: Earle Hagen; Lionel Newman.

PERRY PRESENTS

Musical Variety. A summer replacement for "The Perry Como Show."

Hosts: Teresa Brewer, Jaye P. Morgan, Tony Bennett.

Regulars: Hans Conried, The Four Lads, The Modernaires, The Mel Pahl Chorus, The Louis Da Pron Dancers.

Orchestra: Mitchell Ayres; Jimmy Lytell.

PERRY PRESENTS—60 minutes—NBC—June 13, 1959 - September 5, 1959.

PERSON TO PERSON

Interview. Cameras are established in the home of a celebrity, a world leader, or a political figure. Seated in a studio-set living room, the host chats with prominent people who relate aspects of their private lives.

Hosts: Edward R. Murrow (10/2/53 - 7/2/59).
Charles Collingwood (6/23/61 - 9/16/61).

Announcer: Bob Dixon.

Producer: Jesse Zousmer, Robert Sammon, Charles Hill, John Aaron.

PERSON TO PERSON—30 minutes—CBS—October 2, 1953 - July 2, 1959; June 23, 1961 - September 16, 1961.

PERSONAL APPEARANCE

Anthology. Rebroadcasts of dramas that were originally aired via other filmed anthology programs.

Included:

The Brush Roper. An elderly cowpoke struggles to prove his tall tales are true.

Starring: Walter Brennan.

The Girl Who Scared Men Off. A hillbilly schoolmarm attempts to acquire the affections of her British exchange professor.

Starring: Phyllis Avery, Hans Conried.

Waiting House. The story of a young woman's fears about moving into a house with an accident reputation.

Starring: Phyllis Kirk, Paul Langton, Dorothy Green.

PERSONAL APPEARANCE—30 minutes—CBS—June 1958 - September 1958.

PERSONALITY

Game. Basis: The individual personalities of show business celebrities. Three celebrities appear, playing for members of the home audience (post card selection).

Round One: "Awareness." Celebrities have to determine how well they know each other. The host reads one question, which refers to one of the celebrities, and reveals three answers, only one of which is his. The remaining two players have to determine the correct response. A prerecorded video tape is played to reveal the answer.

The manner of play is the same regarding the remaining two celebrities. Correct guesses score twenty-five dollars.

Round Two: "Self Public Image Awareness." Questions that were asked of a studio audience of three hundred regarding the celebrities, are restated, one at a time, with three possible answers, of which only one is correct. Celebrities have to determine the correct responses. Twenty-five dollars is scored for each correct guess.

Round Three: "Finale." A prominent personality is asked three questions (prerecorded on tape). The host reveals question one and three possible answers, one of which is correct. Celebrities have to determine the correct response. The tape is played to reveal the answers. Twenty-five dollars is scored for each correct guess.

The money each celebrity has accumulated is awarded to the home-audience players.

Host: Larry Blyden.

Announcer: Jack Clark.

PERSONALITY—30 minutes—NBC—July 3, 1967 - September 26, 1969. 500 tapes.

PERSONALITY PUZZLE

Game. Four competing contestants who comprise the panel. Seated with their backs to a celebrity guest, panelists are handed articles of clothing and tools of their guest's trade. Through their examination and indirect question and answer probe rounds, panelists have to establish the celebrity's identity. Correct identifications score points. Winners, who receive merchandise prizes, are the highest point scorers.

Hosts: John Conte; Robert Alda.

PERSONALITY PUZZLE—30 minutes—ABC 1953.

PERSPECTIVE ON GREATNESS

Documentary. Through film clips and interviews, the lives of celebrated individuals are recalled (e.g., Babe Ruth, John Wayne, Barbara Stanwyck, Lee Marvin).

Host-Narrator: Pat O'Brien.

Music Score: Music for Films.

Producer-Director: Harry Rasky.

PERSPECTIVE ON GREATNESS—60 minutes—Syndicated 1961.

THE PERSUADERS

Adventure. Background: Europe. The hectic exploits of two handsome young playboys: Brett Sinclair, a wealthy and debonair British Lord; and Daniel Wilde, a self-made American millionaire from the Bronx. Tricked into becoming justice-seeking partners by a retired judge, Fulton, the two reluctant troubleshooters encounter beautiful women, misadventure, and trouble as they seek to uncover the facts behind the criminal cases that Judge Fulton feels warrant further investigation. Spiced with light humor. Produced in Europe by I.T.C.

CAST

Lord Brett Sinclair	Roger Moore
Daniel Wilde	Tony Curtis
Judge Fulton	Laurence Naismith

The Persuaders. Tony Curtis and Roger Moore. *Courtesy Independent Television Corporation; an ATV Company.*

Music: John Barry.

THE PERSUADERS!—60 minutes—ABC—September 18, 1971 - June 14, 1972. 24 episodes. Syndicated.

PETE AND GLADYS

Comedy. Background: Los Angeles, California. The trials and tribulations of the Porters: Pete, an insurance salesman, and his beautiful but scatterbrained wife, Gladys. A spin-off from "December Bride." Portraying Gladys, Cara Williams became Pete's never-before-seen, but often-referred-to wife.

CAST

Gladys Porter	Cara Williams
Peter Porter	Harry Morgan
Hilda Crocker, their friend	Verna Felton
Peggy Briggs, the Porter's friend	Mina Kobb

Pete and Gladys. Harry Morgan and Cara Williams.

Ernie Briggs, her husband	Joe Mantell
Paul Porter, Pete's uncle	Gale Gordon
Howie, the Porters' friend	Alvy Moore
Alice, his wife	Barbara Stuart
Gladys's father	Ernest Truex
Bruce, Gladys's nephew, a college student who is residing with her	Bill Hinnait
Mr. Slocum, Pete's employer	Barry Kelly
Mrs. Slocum, his wife	Helen Kleeb
George Colton, a neighbor	Peter Leeds
Janet Colton, his wife	Shirley Mitchell

Music: Wilbur Hatch.

Producer: Devery Freeman, Parke Levy.

Director: James V. Kern.

PETE AND GLADYS—30 minutes—CBS—September 19, 1960 - September 10, 1962. Syndicated. 70 episodes.

PETE KELLY'S BLUES

Drama. Background: Kansas City during the 1920s. Events in the lawless era of prohibition and gangsterism as seen through the eyes of Pete Kelly, coronet player, and leader of "The Big Seven," a jazz band that steadily plays at 17 Cherry Street, a brownstone-turned-funeral-parlor-turned-speakeasy. Based on the motion picture.

CAST

Pete Kelly	William Reynolds
Savannah Brown, the	

band's songstress   Connee Boswell
George Lupo, the club
    owner   Phil Gordon
Police Officer Johnny
    Cassino   Anthony Eisley

The Band: Johnny Silver, Thann Wyenn, Fred Beems, Rickey Allen, Dick Cathcart.

Music for the club scenes: The Matty Matlock Combo.

Background Music: Frank Comstock.

Off-screen coronet player for Kelly: Dick Cathcart.

PETE KELLY'S BLUES—30 minutes —NBC—April 5, 1959 - September 4, 1959. 13 episodes. Syndicated.

PETE SMITH SPECIALTIES

Comedy. Theatrical shorts. Humorous glimpses depicting the problems that befall people in everyday life.

Narrator: Pete Smith.

CAST
Dave O'Brien, Don DeFore.

PETE SMITH SPECIALTIES—10 minutes—Syndicated 1968. 101 episodes.

THE PETER AND MARY SHOW

Comedy. A domestic comedy series that focuses on the misadventures of a man, his wife, and a friend who "sort of comes for dinner and stays on to become a perpetual scavenger."

CAST
Peter, the
    husband   Peter Lind Hayes
Mary, his wife   Mary Healy
The friend   Claude Stroud
Their housekeeper   Mary Wickes

Music: Bert Farber.

Producer: Allen Ducovny.

Director: Theodore Sills.

THE PETER AND MARY SHOW—30 minutes—NBC 1950.

PETER GUNN

Crime Drama. Background: Los Angeles, California. The investigations of private detective Peter Gunn.

CAST
Peter Gunn   Craig Stevens
Edie Hart, his
    girlfriend, a
    singer at Mother's
    Night Club   Lola Albright
Lieutenant Jacoby   Herschel Bernardi
Mother, the nightclub
    owner   Hope Emerson
                         Minerva Urecal
Leslie   James Lamphier
Emmett   Bill Chadney

Gunn's hangout: Mother's, a waterfront nightclub.

Music: Henry Mancini.

Producer: Blake Edwards.

Gunn's Address: 351 Ellis Park Road.

PETER GUNN—30 minutes—NBC— September 22, 1958 - September 1960. ABC—30 minutes—October 3, 1960 - September 21, 1961. 114 episodes. Syndicated.

THE PETER LIND HAYES SHOW

Musical Variety.

Host: Peter Lind Hayes.

Regulars: Mary Healy, Don Cherry, John Bubbles, The Four Voices, The Malagon Sisters.

Orchestra: Bert Farber.

THE PETER LIND HAYES SHOW—
60 minutes—ABC—October 31, 1958 - April 10, 1959.

PETER LOVES MARY

Comedy. Background: Connecticut, the residence of Peter and Mary Lindsey, a show-business couple, and their children Leslie and Steve. Stories depict Peter and Mary's attempts to divide their time between a career on Broadway and a home life in the country.

CAST

Peter Lindsey	Peter Lind Hayes
Mary Lindsey	Mary Healy
Leslie Lindsey	Merry Martin
Steve Lindsey	Gil Smith
Wilma, their housekeeper	Bea Benaderet
Happy Richman, their agent	Alan Reed
Charlie, Wilma's boy-friend	Arch Johnson

Music: Bert Farber.

PETER LOVES MARY—30 minutes —NBC—October 12, 1960 - May 31, 1961. 32 episodes.

THE PETER MARSHALL VARIETY SHOW

Variety. Music, songs, interviews, and comedy sketches.

Host: Peter Marshall.

Regulars: Rod Gist, Denny Evans, The Chapter 5.

Orchestra: Alan Copeland.

Choreographer: Kevin Carlisle.

Executive Producer: David Salzman.

Producer: Rocco Urbisci, Neil Marshall, Beth Uffner.

Director: Jeff Margolis.

THE PETER MARSHALL VARIETY SHOW—90 minutes—Syndicated 1976.

PETER POTTER'S JUKE BOX JURY

Discussion. Guest Hollywood personalities judge and discuss the merits of just and/or prereleased recordings; "Will it be a hit (Bong!) or a miss (Clunk!)."

Host: Peter Potter.

Producer: Peter Potter.

Sponsor: Hazel Bishop Cosmetics.

PETER POTTER'S JUKE BOX JURY—30 minutes—ABC—September 6, 1953 - October 4, 1953. 42 episodes.

THE PETER POTAMUS SHOW

Animated Cartoon. The global adventures of Peter Potamus, the purple hippo, and his assistant, So So the monkey.

Character segments:
"Breezly," the polar bear; "Sneezly," the seal; and "Yippie, Yappie, and Yahooey," three mischievous dogs.

Characters' Voices

Peter Potamus	Daws Butler
So So	Don Messick
Breezly	Howard Morris
Sneezly	Mel Blanc
The Colonel	John Stephenson
Yippie	Hal Smith
Yahooey	Daws Butler

The King   Hal Smith

Music Supervision: Hoyt Curtin.

THE PETER POTAMUS SHOW—30 minutes—Syndicated 1964. A Hanna-Barbera Production.

PETROCELLI

Crime Drama. Background: San Remo, a Southwestern cattle town. The cases and courtroom defenses of Tony Petrocelli, an Italian, Harvard-educated attorney.

CAST
Tony Petrocelli   Barry Newman
Maggie Petrocelli, his
  wife   Susan Howard
Pete Toley, his
  investigator   Albert Salmi
Frank Kaiser, the assis-
    tant D.A.   Michael Bell
Lt. John Clifford   David Huddleston

Music: Lalo Schifrin.

Executive Producer: Thomas L. Miller, Howard Milkis.

Producer: Leonard Katzman.

PETROCELLI—60 minutes—NBC—September 11, 1974 - March 2, 1976. 48 episodes.

THE PET SET

Discussion. Discussions concerning pet care, ecology, and wildlife preservation.

Hostess: Betty White.

Assistants: Ralph Helfer, of Africa, U.S.A. (Calif.); Dare Miller, a dog psychiatrist.

Announcer: Allen Ludden.

Appearing: Doris Day, Mary Tyler Moore, Barbara Bain, Amanda Blake, Barbara Eden, Barbara Feldon, Lorne Greene, Paul Lynde, Bob Barker, Eva Gabor, Michael Landon, Johnny Mathis, Shirley Jones, James Stewart, Peter Lawford.

Music: Recorded.

THE PET SET—30 minutes—Syndicated 1971. 39 tapes.

PETTICOAT JUNCTION

Comedy. Background: Hooterville, a rural farm valley. A depiction of life in a small American town as seen through the activities of Kate Bradley, widow, proprietress of the Shady Rest Hotel; her three beautiful daughters, Billie Jo, Bobbie Jo, and Betty Jo; and their uncle, the hotel's self-proclaimed manager, Joe Carson.

Recurring story line: Discovering a long-abandoned, but still operational railroad branch line in Hooterville, Homer Bedlow, the vice president of the C.F. & W. Railroad, sets his goal to scrap the Cannonball (an 1890s steam engine, coal car, and mail/passenger coach) and discharge its engineers, Charlie Pratt and Floyd Smoot. Though continually encountering Kate's objections, Bedlow deviously schemes to achieve his goal in hopes of becoming a company big shot.

Changes: After crash landing near the Shady Rest Hotel, pilot Steve Elliott is rescued and nursed back to health by the Bradley girls. Seemingly in love with Billie Jo, he finds an attraction to and later marries Betty Jo. Establishing housekeeping a short distance from the hotel, they are pre-

Petticoat Junction. The original Bradley girls: (left to right) Pat Woodell (Bobbie Jo), Jeannine Riley (Billie Jo), and Linda Kaye (Betty Jo).

sented with a daughter, Kathy Jo.

Bea Benaderet's untimely death in 1968 ended the characterization of Kate Bradley. The need for an understanding and comforting mother figure evolved the character of Janet Craig, a doctor who assumes the practice of the valley's retiring physician, Barton Stuart.

Stories depict: the struggles of young marrieds; Janet's attempts to acquire the trust of people who are distrustful of women doctors; Joe's endless money-making ventures; and the romantic heartaches of Billie Jo and Bobbie Jo.

CAST

Kate Bradley	Bea Benaderet
Joe Carson	Edgar Buchanan
Billie Jo Bradley	Jeannine Riley
	Gunilla Hutton
	Meredith MacRae
Bobbie Jo Bradley	Pat Woodell
	Lori Saunders
Betty Jo Bradley (Elliott)	Linda Kaye Henning
Charley Pratt	Smiley Burnette
Floyd Smoot	Rufe Davis
Sam Drucker, the general-store owner	Frank Cady
Steve Elliott	Mike Minor

Homer Bedlow	Charles Lane
Norman Curtis, the railroad president	Roy Roberts
Fred Ziffel, a pig farmer	Hank Patterson
Ben Miller, a farmer	Tom Fadden
Newt Kiley, a farmer	Kay E. Kuter
Dr. Janet Craig	June Lockhart
Dr. Barton Stuart	Regis Toomey
Wendell Gibbs, the Cannonball engineer (later episodes)	Byron Foulger
Orrin Pike, the game warden	Jonathan Daly
Doris Ziffel, Fred's wife	Barbara Pepper
Selma Plout, Kate's nemesis, the woman determined to snag Steve for her daughter	Elvia Allman
Henrietta Plout, her daughter	Lynette Winter
Kathy Jo Elliott	Elaine Daniele Hubbel
Herby Bates, a friend of the girls	Don Washbrook

Also appearing: the "Green Acres" regulars:

Oliver Douglas, a farmer	Eddie Albert
Lisa Douglas, his wife	Eva Gabor
Eb Dawson, their handyman	Tom Lester
Cousin Mae*	Shirley Mitchell
Aunt Helen*	Rosemary DeCamp

Bradley family dog: Boy.

Music: Curt Massey.

*Both actresses temporarily replaced Bea Benaderet during her illness.

PETTICOAT JUNCTION—30 min-utes—CBS—September 24, 1963 - September 12, 1970. 148 episodes. Syndicated.

PEYTON PLACE

Serial. Background: The small New England town of Peyton Place. Dramatic incidents in the lives of its townspeople.

CAST

Dr. Michael Rossi	Ed Nelson
Constance Mac-Kenzie	Dorothy Malone
	Lola Albright
Alison MacKenzie	Mia Farrow
Rodney Harrington	Ryan O'Neal
Matthew Swain	Warner Anderson
Leslie Harrington	Paul Langton
Laura Brooks	Patricia Breslin
Betty Anderson	Barbara Parkins
Rita Jacks Harrington	Patricia Morrow
Norman Harrington	Christopher Connelly
David Schuster	William Smithers
Doris Schuster	Gail Kobe
Clair	Mariette Hartley
Elliot Carson (Connie's husband)	Tim O'Connor
Dr. Morton	Kent Smith
Julie Anderson	Kasey Rogers
George Anderson	Henry Beckman
Paul Hanley	Richard Evans
Kim	Kimberly Beck
Sherwood Price	Roy Roberts
Fowler	John Kerr
Martin Peyton	George Macready
Hannah Cord	Ruth Warrick
Steven Cord	James Douglas
Eli Carson	Frank Ferguson
Miss Nolan	Penelope Gillette
Lee	Stephen Oliver
Sandy	Lana Wood
Chris	Gary Haynes
Susan Winter	Diana Hyland
Dr. Miles	Percy Rodriques

Marsha Russell	Barbara Rush
Lew Miles	Glynn Turmann
The Reverend	
Mr. Bedford	Ted Hartley
Alma Miles	Ruby Dee
Joanne Walker	Jeanne Buckley
Carolyn Russell	Elizabeth Walker
Jeff	John Findlater
Tom	Robert Hogan
Fred	Joe Maross
Maggie Riggs	Florida Friebus
Nurse Jennifer Ivers	Myrna Fahey
Atwell	Mario Alcalde
Vickie	Judy Pace
Nurse Choate	Erin O'Brien-Moore
The Judge	Michael Strong
	John Lormer
Sgt. Walker	Morris Buchanan
Ada Jacks	Evelyn Scott
Jill	Joyce Jillson
Joe	Michael Christian
Stella	Lee Grant
Richard	Don Gordon
Russ	David Canary
Adrienne	Gena Rowlands
Eddie	Dan Duryea
Ted	Patrick Whyte
Mrs. Dowell	Heather Angel
Mrs. Chernak	Anna Karen
Donna Franklin	Sharon Hugueny
Gus	Bruce Gordon
Marian	Joan Blackman
Rachel	Leigh Taylor-Young
Chandler	John Kellogg
Joe	Don Quine

Music: Arthur Morton; Lionel Newman.

Additional Music: Cyril Mockridge, Lee Holdridge.

Music Theme: Franz Waxman.

Executive Producer: Paul Monash.

Producer: Everett Chambers, Richard Goldstone, Felix Feist, Richard DeRoy.

Director: Walter Doniger, Ted Post.

PEYTON PLACE—30 minutes—ABC —September 15, 1964 - June 2, 1969. 514 episodes. Syndicated. Spin-off series: "Return to Peyton Place" (see title).

PHILBIN'S PEOPLE

Discussion. Five guest panelists discuss controversial topical issues.

Host: Regis Philbin.

Music: Recorded.

PHILBIN'S PEOPLE—90 minutes (12:30 a.m. -2:00 a.m)—1969-1970. Aired over the R.K.O. General owned stations in New York and Los Angeles.

PHILCO TELEVISION PLAYHOUSE

Anthology. Dramatic presentations. Created by Fred Coe.

Producer: Fred Coe, Gordon Duff, Garry Simpson.

Director: Delbert Mann, Fred Coe, Garry Simpson.

Sponsor: Philco (also Goodyear when broadcast as "The Philco-Goodyear Playhouse").

Included:

A Room in Paris. The tender love affair between a young American girl and an ex-G.I. studying abroad.

CAST
Stan Kagen: John Cassavetes; Janet Wells: Kathleen Maguire; Buzz Shapion: Al Markin.

The Takers. A police chief struggles to break the city's numbers racket.

CAST

Bernard Zysski: Ed Begley; Walter Gregg: Martin Balson; Edna Zysski: Peggy Allenby.

Gretel. The difficulties that arise when the son of a socially prominent family marries a teenage refugee.

CAST

Gretel: Eva Stein; Alan Putnam: Geoffrey Horne.

Marty. Paddy Chayefsky's heart-warming story of a lonely Bronx butcher who is goaded by his mother and friends to find himself a girl.

CAST

Marty: Rod Steiger; Clara: Nancy Marchand.

The Rich Boy. An adaption of the F. Scott Fitzgerald novel. The story of a neurotic flapper during the 1920s.

CAST

Phyllis Kirk (her first televison appearance).

Friday the 13th. Of the three women involved in an automboile accident, one is killed. When their husbands are informed, the identity of the dead woman is not revealed. Arriving at the hospital, the husbands find numerous obstacles as they attempt to discover who the dead woman is.

CAST

Brett Somers, Julie Follansbee, Rebecca Sands, Mark Roberts.

PHILCO TELEVISION PLAY-HOUSE–60 minutes–NBC–October 3, 1948 - October 2, 1955. Also known as "The Philco-Goodyear Play-house."

THE PHIL DONAHUE SHOW

Discussion. Discussions on the contemporary issues that affect women in their daily lives. Representative guests appear.

Host: Phil Donahue.

Music: Recorded.

THE PHIL DONAHUE SHOW–60 and 30 minute versions (depending on the local station)–Syndicated 1969.

PHIL SILVERS

Listed: The television programs of comedian Phil Silvers.

Welcome Aboard–Musical Variety–30 minutes–NBC 1948.

Host: Phil Silvers.

Featured: The Four Step Brothers.

Orchestra: Russ Morgan.

Producer-Director: Vic McLeod.

Sponsor: Admiral.

The Phil Silvers Arrow Show–Variety–30 minutes–NBC 1949.

Host: Phil Silvers.

Regulars: Connie Sawyer, Jerry Hausner, Len Hale, Herbert Coleman, The Mack Triplets.

Orchestra: Harry Salter.

Producer: Wes McKeeb.

Director: Hal Keith.

Sponsor: Arrow Shirts.

You'll Never Get Rich–Comedy–30 minutes–CBS–1955-1959. (See title.)

The Phil Silvers Show–Comedy–30 minutes–CBS–1963 - 1964.

The story of Harry Grafton, a

factory foreman for Brink Enterprises; a conartist who manipulates men and machines for the benefit of himself.

CAST
Harry Grafton	Phil Silvers
Mr. Brink, Harry's employer	Stafford Repp
Harry's co-workers, dupes for the master mind:	
Waluska	Herbie Faye
Lester	Jim Shane
Roxy	Pat Renella
Scarpitta	Norman Grabowski
	Henry Scott
Starkey	Steve Mitchell
Audrey, Harry's sister	Elena Verdugo
Susan, Audrey's daughter	Sandy Descher
Andy, Audrey's son	Ronnie Dapo

Music: Harry Geller.

Producer: Nat Hiken, Rod Amateau.

Note: Harry is also known to be associated with Osborne Industries.

PHILIP MARLOWE

Crime Drama. The investigations of private detective Philip Marlowe. Based on the character created by Raymond Chandler.

Starring: Philip Carey as Philip Marlowe.

PHILIP MARLOWE—30 minutes— ABC—September 29, 1959 - March 29, 1960. 26 episodes.

THE PHILIP MORRIS PLAYHOUSE

Anthology. Dramatic presentations.

Host: Charles Martin.

Announcer: Joe King.

Music: Ray Bloch.

Producer: Charles Martin.

Sponsor: Philip Morris Cigarettes.

THE PHILIP MORRIS PLAYHOUSE —30 minutes—CBS 1953.

PHOTOPLAY TIME

A series of thirty minute anthology dramas, produced by Perry Lafferty, and first broadcast on ABC in 1949.

PHYLLIS

Comedy. A spin-off from "The Mary Tyler Moore Show." Following the death of her husband, Lars, Phyllis Lindstrom, a self-satisfied woman, leaves Minneapolis and relocates to San Francisco where she acquires a job as assistant to commercial photographer Julie Erskine, the owner of Erskine's Commercial Photography Studio.

Stories relate the misadventures of a glamorous widow as she struggles to begin a new life.

CAST
Phyllis Lindstrom	Cloris Leachman
Bess Lindstrom, her daughter	Lisa Gerritsen
Julie Erskine	Barbara Colby
	Liz Torres
Leo Heatherton, the photographer employed by Julie	Richard Schaal
Audrey Dexter, Lars's scatterbrained mother (recently remarried)	Jane Rose
Jonathan Dexter, her husband	Henry Jones

Sally Dexter, Jonathan's
  mother   Judith Lowry
Dan Valenti, Phyllis'
  employer, later
  episodes*   Carmine Caridi
Leonard Marsh, Dan's
  associate   John Lawlor
Harriet Hastings, Leonard's
  assistant   Garn Stephens
Mark Valenti, Dan's
  nephew, married Bess on
  2-27-77   Craig Wasson
Arthur Lanson, married
  Mother Dexter on
  12-13-76   Burt Mustin
Van Horn, the park wino,
  Phyllis' confidante Jack Elam

Music: Dick De Benedictis.

Executive Producer-Creator: Ed Weinberger, Stan Daniels.

Director: Jay Sandrich, Joan Darling, James Burrows, Harry Mastrogeorge, Asaad Keleda.

Phyllis's Address: 4482 Bayview Drive.

*A cast change during the second season dropped the Julie Erskine role. Julie, who supposedly married, closed the studio, leaving Phyllis unemployed—temporarily, that is—until she found employment as administrative assistant to Dan Valenti, a supervisor for the San Francisco Board of Supervision.

PHYLLIS—30 minutes—CBS—Premiered: September 8, 1975.

THE PHYLLIS DILLER SHOW

See title: "The Pruitts of Southhampton."

PICCADILLY PALACE

Musical Variety. Songs and comedy sketches set against the background of London's Piccadilly Palace.

Hostess: Millicent Martin.

Regulars: Eric Morecambe, Ernie Wise, The Paddy Stone Dancers, The Michael Sammes Singers.

Orchestra: Jack Parnell.

PICCADILLY PALACE—60 minutes —ABC—May 26, 1967 - September 9, 1967.

PICTURE THIS

Game. Two competing teams, each composed of one celebrity and one noncelebrity contestant. One member of each team is presented with a phrase that is concealed from his partner. The player then directs his partner by telling him what clues to draw to its identity. The "artist" first to identify the phrase receives points for his team. The game is played to enable all players to share equally on directing and drawing. Winners, the highest scoring teams, receive cash.

Host: Jerry Van Dyke.

Announcer: Art Baker.

Premiere guests: Gretchen Wyler, Orson Bean.

PICTURE THIS—30 minutes—CBS— June 25, 1963 - September 17, 1963.

THE PINK PANTHER SHOW

Animated Cartoon. The misadventures of a nontalking, nondiscouraging Pink Panther.

Hosts: Lennie Schultz; The Ritts Puppets.

Puppeteers: Paul and Mark Ritts.

Voices: John Byner, Dave Barry, Paul Frees, Rich Little, Marvin Miller,

Athena Forde.

Music: William Lava, Doug Goodwin, Walter Green.

The Pink Panther theme: Henry Mancini.

THE PINK PANTHER—30 minutes—NBC—Premiered: September 6, 1969.

THE PINKY LEE SHOW

Variety. Music, songs, circus variety acts, and burlesque comedy skits.

Host: Pinky Lee, vaudeville comedian.

Regulars: Roberta Shore, Jane Howard (as Lily Chrysanthemum), Mel Knootz, Jimmy Brown.

Music: The Charlie Couch Trio.

THE PINKY LEE SHOW—30 minutes —NBC—1950 - 1955.

THE PIONEERS

Western Anthology. Retitled episodes of "Death Valley Days."

Host: Will Rogers, Jr.

Music: Marlen Skiles.

Included:

Man on the Run. Broke, a tenant attempts to sneak out of town and away from his landlady.

CAST
Billy Nelson, Mary Field.

Death and Taxes. A young deputy attempts to collect taxes from a gang of outlaws.

CAST
Wayne Mallory, Jean Lewis.

The Million Dollar Wedding. The story of a miner who is offered a large sum of money to marry a homely waitress.

CAST
James Best, Virginia Lee.

THE PIONEERS—30 minutes—Syndicated 1964. 104 episodes.

PIP THE PIPER

Children. Mythical adventures set against the background of Pipertown, a magic and musical city in the clouds.

CAST
Pip the Piper	Jack Spear
Miss Merrynote	Phyllis Spear
Mr. Leader, a pompous buffoon	Lucien Kaminsky

PIP THE PIPER—30 minutes—ABC—December 5, 1960 - June 6, 1961. NBC—30 minutes—July 7, 1961 - September 1962. 52 episodes. Syndicated.

PISTOLS 'N' PETTICOATS

Western Comedy. Background: Wretched, Colorado, 1871. The saga of the gun-carrying Hanks family: Henrietta, a widow; her father, Andrew; his wife, referred to as Grandma; and, opposed to violence, Henrietta's twenty-one-year-old daughter, Lucy. Stories depict their attempts to maintain law and order in a restless territory.

CAST
Henrietta (Hank) Hanks	Ann Sheridan
Andrew Hanks	Douglas Fowley
Lucy Hanks	Carole Wells

Grandma Hanks	Ruth McDevitt
Harold Sikes, the town's inept sheriff	Gary Vinson
Bernard Courtney, a land baron seeking to acquire the Hanks ranch	Robert Lowery
Mark Hangman, his gunman	Morgan Woodward
Jed Timmins, a lawyer working for Courtney	Stanley Adams
Eagle Shadow, Chief of the Kiowa Indians	Lon Chaney, Jr.
Gray Hawk, his son	Mark Cavell
Great Bear, Chief of the Atona Indians	Jay Silverheels
Little Bear, his son	Alex Hentlehoff
Town Drunk	Gil Lamb
Mrs. Tinsley, a townsperson	Eleanor Audley
The W.C. Fields type of character who hangs out in the bar	Bill Oberlin
Cyrus Breech, the double-crossing gun smuggler	Leo Gordon

Hanks family dog: Bowzer.

Music: George Tibbles; Jack Elliott; Stanley Wilson.

Executive Producer: Joe Connelly.

Producer: Irving Paley.

Director: Joe Connelly, Lou Watts

PISTOLS 'N' PETTICOATS—30 minutes—CBS—September 17, 1966 - August 26, 1967. 26 episodes.

PITCHING HORSESHOES

See title: "Billy Roses Playbill."

PITFALL

Anthology. Dramatizations depicting the plight of people caught in a web of concealed danger.

Included:

Agent From Scotland Yard. A British agent attempts to capture a wanted criminal in San Francisco's China-town.

CAST
Lynn Bari, Patric Knowles.

The Hot Welcome. The story of an eccentric old woman who changes the destinies of a beautiful girl and two men.

CAST
Gale Storm, Richard Denning, Elizabeth Patterson.

Hit and Run. The story of a man and his attempts to clear himself of a false hit-and-run charge.

CAST
Robert Hutton, Bonita Granville.

PITFALL—30 minutes—Syndicated 1955.

PLACES PLEASE

Variety. The setting is the backstage of a television studio where the performances of bit players and chronies from Broadway shows and nightclubs are featured.

Host: Barry Wood.

Producer: Barry Wood.

Director: Ralph Levy.

PLACES PLEASE—15 minutes—CBS 1948.

PLACE THE FACE

Game. Specially selected contestants are placed opposite someone from their past. Through clues that are provided by the host, players have to associate each other's faces. Prizes are awarded to the player who is first to make the association.

Hosts: Jack Smith; Jack Paar; Bill Cullen

PLACE THE FACE—30 minutes—CBS—August 27, 1953 - August 26, 1954. NBC—30 minutes—June 28, 1955 - September 1955.

THE PLAINCLOTHESMAN

Crime Drama. Background: New York City. The subjective camera method is incorporated to detail the investigations of a never-seen police lieutenant. By use of the subjective camera, which enacts emotion and becomes the eyes of the lieutenant, the viewer hears the actor's voice and experiences situations as if he were actually present.

CAST
The Unseen Lieutenant   Ken Lynch
Sergeant Brady, his
    assistant   Jack Orrison

Producer: John L. Clark, John Clarol.

Director: William Marclare, Charles Harrell.

Sponsor: Edgeworth.

THE PLAINCLOTHESMAN—30 minutes—DuMont—September 1950 - September 12, 1954.

PLANET OF THE APES

Science Fiction Adventure. Penetrating a radioactive turbulence area, a United States Air Force space capsule passes through the time barrier and is hurled from the present 1988 to Earth in the year 3085.

In the crash-landing, one of the three astronauts aboard the craft is killed. Discovering themselves in an era ruled by intellectual apes (humans, treated as a lesser species, serve as laborers), the survivors, Alan Virdon and Pete Burke, are captured and imprisoned due to a fear among the ape leaders that awareness of their presence may inaugurate a revolt among the other humans.

Intrigued by the intelligence of the astronauts, Galen, an intellectual ape, befriends them, seeking to absorb their knowledge. However, distrustful of the astronauts, Veska, one of the ape leaders, plans their demise.

Finding their cell door unlocked, Pete and Alan escape. Arriving to speak with the astronauts, Galen spots Veska in the bushes with a gun aimed at the front door of the prison. As Pete and Alan open the door, Galen yells, warns them, and in the attempt to thwart Veska's plan, accidentally kills him. The three, branded dangerous fugitives, are sought for murder.

Stories depict their struggle for survival; and Pete and Alan's attempts, assisted by Galen, to return to the Earth of the 1980s. Adapted from the motion picture.

CAST
Galen	Roddy McDowall
Alan Virdon	Ron Harper
Pete Burke	James Naughton
Zaius, the ape leader	Booth Colman
Urko, his assistant	Mark Lenard
Veska (first episode)	Woodrow Parfrey

Music: Lalo Schifrin; Lionel Newman.

Executive Producer: Herbert Hirschman.

Producer: Stan Hough.

PLANET OF THE APES—60 minutes —CBS—September 13, 1974 - December 27, 1974. 13 episodes.

PLANET PATROL

Marionette Adventure. Era: Twenty-first-century Earth. The work of the agents of the Galasphere Patrol, an interplanetary police force established to protect the planets of a united solar system.

Characters:
Colonel Raeburn, the Galasphere leader
Captain Larry Dart
Husky, the Martian
Slim, the Venusian
Berridge, an enemy

PLANET PATROL—30 minutes—Syndicated 1963.

PLAYBOY'S PENTHOUSE
PLAYBOY AFTER DARK

Variety. Background: The Chicago penthouse apartment of *Playboy* magazine publisher Hugh Hefner. Guests, conversation, and entertainment.

Playboy's Penthouse—60 minutes—Syndicated 1960.
Host: Hugh Hefner.
Hostesses: The Playboy Bunnies.
Music: The Marty Ruberstein Trio.

Playboy After Dark—60 minutes—Syndicated 1969.

Host: Hugh Hefner.
Hostesses: The Playboy Bunnies.
Music: Provided by guests.

PLAY YOUR HUNCH

Game. Two husband-and-wife couples compete. Object: To solve problems by instinct. Three sets that pertain to one subject are displayed (e.g., three sets of eyes, X, Y, and Z). Couples have to determine the factor that distinguishes one from the others (e.g, "Which eyes are Marilyn Monroe's?"). The couple first to score three correct identifications are the winners and receive merchandise prizes.

Hosts: Merv Griffin; Robert Q. Lewis.
Assistant: Liz Gardner.
Producer: Bob Rowe, Ira Skutch.
Director: Mike Gargiulo.

PLAY YOUR HUNCH—30 minutes—CBS—June 30, 1958 - June 17, 1962. NBC—30 minutes—June 20, 1962 - September 27, 1963. Evening run: NBC—April 15, 1960 - June 25, 1960.

PLAYHOUSE

Anthology. Dramatic presentations.

Included:

Tourists Overnight. The story revolves around two women travelers who stop at a tourist home only to find themselves held captive by a criminal.

CAST
Dorothy Lee: Barbara Hale; Aunt Ella: Norma Varden; Eddie: Donald Murphy; Mrs. Welkins: Frances Bavier.

Ambitious Cop. The story concerns a policeman's efforts to overcome the resentment that occurs after he kills an old friend turned mobster in a gun duel.

CAST

Joe Devlin: Gene Evans; Arthur Healy: Dayton Lummis; Dr. Gerski: John Stephenson.

PLAYHOUSE—30 minutes—NBC—May 13, 1958 - July 1, 1958.

PLAYHOUSE '54

See title: "Pepsi Cola Playhouse."

PLAYHOUSE 90

Anthology. Dramatic presentations.

Music: George Smith; Robert Allen.

Producer: Martin Manulis, John Houseman, Russell Stoneham, Fred Coe, Arthur Penn.

Included:

Seven Against the Wall. Chicago, 1928. Al Capone's revenge against the Bugs Moran gang when they begin to muscle in on his lucrative bootleg business. A recreation of the famed St. Valentine's Day Massacre.

CAST

Al Capone: Paul Lambert; Bugs Moran: Dennis Patrick; Nick Serrello: Frank Silvera; Pete Gusenberg: Dennis Cross.

A Marriage of Strangers. The trials and tribulations of a newlywed couple. Adapted from the play by Reginald Rose.

CAST

Red Buttons, Diana Lynn.

The Helen Morgan Story. A biographical drama based on the life of torch singer Helen Morgan.

CAST

Helen Morgan: Polly Bergen.

Rumors of Evening. England, World War II. The story of U.S. Air Force Captain Neil Dameron and his attempts to impress a girl in a visiting U.S.O. show.

CAST

Capt. Neil Dameron: John Kerr; Sidney Cantrell: Barbara Bel Geddes; General Strayer: Robert F. Simon; Irma-Jean Deever: Pat Hitchcock; Major Woulman: Robert Loggia.

PLAYHOUSE 90—90 minutes—CBS—October 4, 1956 - September 19, 1961.

PLAYHOUSE OF MYSTERY

Anthology. Rebroadcasts of mystery dramas that were originally aired via "Schlitz Playhouse of Stars."

Included:

Vol Turio Investigates. The story of a suave jewel thief and his attempts to track down three accomplices after a jewel robery.

CAST

Basil Rathbone, Edward Ashley, Melville Cooper.

The Menace of Hasty Heights. The story of a woman who is held hostage in her home by an escaped criminal.

CAST

Jean Hagen, Steve Cochran, Kent Taylor.

The Quiet Stranger. When the new school teacher arrives in Three Forks, he discovers that the school has burned down and that the citizens have done nothing about it. The story relates his struggles to rebuild it.

CAST

George Montgomery, Forrest Tucker, Bobby Clark.

PLAYHOUSE OF MYSTERY—60 minutes—CBS—September 3, 1957 - September 24, 1957.

PLAYHOUSE OF STARS

Anthology. Dramatic presentations.

Hostess: Irene Dunne.

PLAYHOUSE OF STARS—30 minutes—CBS—May 30, 1952 - September 1952.

PLAYHOUSE OF STARS

Anthology. Rebroadcasts of dramas that were originally aired via other filmed anthology programs.

Included:

O'Connor and the Blue-Eyed Felon. The story of a man, alone in his fishing lodge, who is confronted by a girl intent on shooting him for a past grievance.

CAST

Diana Lynn, Chuck Connors, Bob Nichols.

The Breaking Point. The story of a man and wife, the owner-operators of a service-station café The husband is satisfied; the wife is not and constantly complains about the situation, hoping he'll sell the business so they can begin life elsewhere.

CAST

Carolyn Jones, Dane Clark, Doris Singleton, Philip Reed.

The Night They Won the Oscar. The story of a movie director and his attempts to save his rocky marriage.

CAST

Richard Carlson, June Lockhart, Hayden Rorke, Dorothy Green.

PLAYHOUSE OF STARS—30 minutes—NBC—June 1960 - September 1960.

PLAY OF THE WEEK

Anthology. Dramatic presentations.

Included:

Archy and Mehitabel. A musical fantasy. A pensive cockroach with a flair for free verse tries to reform his flamboyant friend, a cat with a penchant for free love.

CAST

Tammy Grimes, Eddie Bracken, Jules Munshin.

Mary Stuart. The dramatic story of Mary, the deposed Queen of Scotland.

CAST

Signe Hasso, Eva Le Gallienne, Staats Cotsworth.

The Grass Harp. The story of an old

lady, a rebellious boy, and a Negro servant who, finding themselves badgered by the forces of order, take to a home in the trees.

CAST

Lillian Gish, Nick Hyams, Russell Collins, Georgia Burke.

PLAY OF THE WEEK–2 hours– Syndicated 1960.

PLAYWRIGHTS '55 ('56)

Anthology. Dramatic adaptations of stories by famous authors. Broadcast live from New York.

Producer: Fred Coe.

Director: Delbert Mann, Arthur Penn, Vincent Donehue.

Sponsor: Pontiac.

Included:

The Battler. The story concerns a young fighter's decision not to enter the ring after he meets a down-and-out former champ. Adapted from Ernest Hemmingway's story by A.E. Hockner and Sidney Carroll.

Starring: Paul Newman, Phyllis Kirk.

The Answer. During a nuclear-bomb test, an army general discovers that an angel has been shot down and mortally wounded. Feeling that the angel was bearing an important message, the story follows his efforts to find "The Answer." Adapted from Philip Wylie's story by Donald Davidson.

Starring: Paul Douglas, Nina Foch, Albert Dekker, Conrad Nagel.

PLAYWRIGHTS '55 ('56)–60 minutes–NBC–October 4, 1955 - June 19, 1956.

PLEASE DON'T EAT THE DAISIES

Comedy. Background: 228 Circle Avenue, Ridgemont, New York. The trials and tribulations of the Nash family: James, an English professor at Ridgemont College; his wife, Joan, a free-lance magazine writer (pen name: Joan Holliday); and their children: Kyle, Joel, and Trevor and Tracy (twins). Based on the book by Jean Kerr.

CAST

Joan Nash	Patricia Crowley
Jim Nash	Mark Miller
Kyle Nash	Kim Tyler
Joel Nash	Brian Nash
Tracy Nash	Joe Fithian
Trevor Nash	Jeff Fithian
Marge Thorton, their neighbor	Shirley Mitchell
Herb Thorton, her husband, a lawyer	King Donovan
Ed Hewley, the repairman	Dub Taylor
Gerald Carter, the college dean	Bill Quinn
Martha O'Reilly, the Nash maid	Ellen Corby
Ethel Carter, the dean's wife	Jean VanderPyl

Nash family dog: Lad (a sheep dog).

Music: Jeff Alexander.

Producer: Paul West.

Director: Peter Baldwin, David Alexander, Richard Whorf, Tay Garnett, Gary Nelson, John Erman, Alvin Ganzer.

PLEASE DON'T EAT THE DAISIES –30 minutes–NBC–September 14, 1965 - September 2, 1967. 58 episodes. Syndicated.

P.M. EAST . . . P.M. WEST

Talk-Variety. Specific topics of discussion (e.g., violence, Rock and Roll, jazz) are coupled with entertainment performances. Broadcast from both New York and San Francisco.

Hosts (New York): Mike Wallace, Joyce Davidson.

Host (San Francisco): Terrence O'Flatherty.

P.M. EAST . . . P.M. WEST—90 minutes—Syndicated—1960 - 1961. Withdrawn.

POLICE CALL

Anthology. Dramatizations based on the files of various law enforcement agencies throughout the country.

Included:

The Alleghanny County Story. The story of detective James McGinley and his attempts to track down a ring of blackmailers.
Starring: Russell Hardie.

The Dallas, Texas Story. The story of Sheriff Decker and his attempts to track down confidence men who are swindling elderly women.
Starring: Robert Emhardt.

Switzerland. Police efforts to track down a handsome ladies man who earns his living by swindling the women who fall for him.
Starring: Philip Reed, Adam Gannette, Anna Korda.

POLICE CALL—30 minutes—Syndicated 1955.

POLICE STORY

Anthology. Criminal case dramatizations based on the files of the Nashville, Tennessee Police Department.
Narrator: Norman Rose.

POLICE STORY—30 minutes—CBS 1952.

POLICE STORY

Anthology. Dramatizations depicting the day-to-day struggles of police officers. Based on the files of various law-enforcement agencies throughout the country.

Music: Jack Elliott, Allyn Ferguson, Jerry Goldsmith, Richard Markowitz.

Executive Producer: Stanley Kallis.

Producer: Liam O'Brien, David Gerber, Christopher Morgan.

Director: Corey Allen, Vince Edwards, Barry Shear, Gary Nelson, Seymour Robbie, Alex March, Lee H. Katzin, Arthur Kean, John Badham.

Creator: Joseph Wambaugh.

Included:

Collison Course. The problems of an experimental patrol are depicted as a male officer, Vincent LaSorda, and a beautiful police woman, June Culhane, are teamed.

CAST
Vincent LaSorda: Hugh O'Brian; June Culhane: Sue Ane Langdon.

Dangerous Games. Posing as a producer, a vice-squad detective attempts to apprehend the leader of a prostitution racket.

CAST

Charlie Czonka: James Farentino; Janette Johnson: Elizabeth Ashley; Snake McKay: Fred Williamson.

The Big Walk. A realistic portrayal of the complex pressures, harassment, and dangers of the cop on the neighborhood beat.

CAST

Jack Bonner: Don Murray; Harriet Bonner: Dorothy Provine; Hecker: Noah Beery; Angela Wilson: Lynda Day George.

The Gamble. Posing as a prostitute, vice-squad detective Lisa Beaumont attempts to infiltrate and expose the ranks of a gambling syndicate. The pilot film for "Police Woman."

CAST

Lisa Beaumont: Angie Dickinson; Carl Vitalle: Joseph Campanella; Sgt. William Crowley: Bert Convy.

POLICE STORY—60 minutes—NBC— Premiered: October 2, 1973.

POLICE SURGEON

Crime Drama. Background: Toronto, Canada. The cases of Simon Locke, a surgeon with the Emergency Medical Unit of the Metropolitan Police Department, a "doctor with the mind of a detective." A spin-off from "Dr. Simon Locke."

CAST

Dr. Simon Locke	Sam Groom
Lt. Dan Palmer	Len Birman
Lt. Jack Gordon	Larry Mann
Police radio dispatcher	Nerene Virgin
Tony, Locke's ambulance driver	Marc Hebet

Music: Lewis Helkman; Score Productions.

POLICE SURGEON—30 minutes— Syndicated 1972. 76 episodes.

POLICE WOMAN

Crime Drama. Background: Los Angeles, California. The cases of Sergeant Suzanne "Pepper" Anderson, divorcée, a sensual, brassy, compassionate, sincere, and beautiful undercover police woman with the Criminal Conspiracy division of the Los Angeles Police Department.

Stories, which are adult and open minded about sex and marriage, realistically depict the life of a police woman. A spin-off from "Police Story," wherein the pilot episode, "The Gamble," aired.

CAST

Sgt. Suzanne "Pepper" Anderson	Angie Dickinson
Sgt. William Crowley	Earl Holliman
Sgt. Pete Royster	Charles Dierkop
Sgt. Joe Styles	Ed Bernard
Lt. Paul Marsh	Val Bisoglio

Police Woman. Left to right: Angie Dickinson, Ed Bernard, Earl Holliman, Charles Dierkop.

Cheryl, Pepper's
sister, enrolled at the
Austin School for the
Handicapped   Nichole Kallis

Music: Jerry Goldsmith; Morton Stevens; Geroge Romanis; Pete Rugolo; Jeff Alexander.

Executive Producer: David Gerber.

Producer: Douglas Benton.

Director: Barry Shear, John Newland, Alf Kjellin, Corey Allen, Alvin Ganzer, Alexander Singer, Douglas Benton, Herschel Daugherty, Barry Crane, Robert Vaughn, David Moessinger.

Creator: Robert Collins.

Pepper's Address: 102 Crestview Drive.

Note: Pepper's first name is also known to be Lee Anne.

POLICE WOMAN—60 minutes—NBC —Premiered: September 13, 1974.

POLICE WOMAN DECOY

See title: "Decoy."

POLKA-GO-ROUND

Variety. Polka songs and dances.

Host: Bob Lewandowski.

Regulars: Carolyn De Zurick, Rusty Gill, Jimmy Hitchinson, Jack Cordaro, Lenny Druss, John Hunt, Lou Prout, Georgia Drake, The Polka Rounders, Tom Fouts, The Singing Waiters.

POLKA-GO-ROUND—60 minutes— ABC—June 23, 1958 - September 14, 1959.

POLKA PARTY

Variety. Polka songs and dances.

Host: Eddie Gronet.

Featured: Dolores Ann Duda.

Orchestra: Stan Jaworski; Al Siszeski.

POLKA PARTY—30 minutes—Syndicated 1958. Withdrawn.

POLKA TIME

Variety. Polka songs and dances.

Host: Bruno Junior Zienlinski.

Regulars: Carolyn De Zurik, The Polka Chips, The Kenal Siodmy Folk Dancers.

Music: Stan Wolowic's Seven Man Instrumental Group.

POLKA TIME—60 minutes—ABC— July 13, 1956 - August 31, 1956.

THE POLLY BERGEN SHOW

Musical Variety.

Hostess: Polly Bergen.

Orchestra: Luther Henderson, Jr.

Producer: Irving Mansfield.

THE POLLY BERGEN SHOW—30 minutes—NBC—September 21, 1957 - May 3, 1958.

PONDEROSA

See title: "Bonanza."

PONY EXPRESS

Western. Background: Sacramento, California, 1860s. The investigations of Brett Clark, a troubleshooter for the Central Overland Express Company, better know as the Pony Express.

CAST

Brett Clark	Grant Sullivan
Tom Clyde	Bill Cord
Donovan	Don Dorell

PONY EXPRESS—30 minutes—Syndicated 1960. 39 episodes.

POPEYE THE SAILOR

Animated Cartoon. The endless battle between love-hungry sailors Popeye and Bluto over the long-sought affections of Olive Oyl, a skinny, fickle woman. Their bickering usually begins verbally, then becomes violent as Popeye, the underdog, removes a can of spinach from his blouse, devours it, acquires incredible strength, and, as good triumphs over evil, deals justice to Bluto.

Characters' Voices

Popeye	Det Poppen
	Floyd Buckley
	Jack Mercer
Bluto	Jackson Beck
Olive Oyl	Olive La Moy
	Mae Questel
Wimpy, a friend, forever seeking hamburgers	Charles Lawrence
	Jack Mercer
Swee' pea, Olive's nephew	Mae Questel

Popeye The Sailor. © *King Features Syndicate, Inc.*

Shorty, a sailor
  friend of
  Popeye's   Arnold Stang

Additional characters: Popeye's nephews: Pupeye, Peepeye, Poopeye, Pipeye; Popeye's father: Grandpappy; Popeye's dog: The visible/invisible Jeep.

Music: Winston Sharples.

Additional Music: Sam Lerner, Sammy Timberg, Bob Loymberg, Tot Seymour, Vee Lawnhurst.

Producer: Associated Artists Productions.

Director: Seymour Kenietel, I. Sparber, Dave Fleischer.

POPEYE THE SAILOR—06 minutes —Syndicated 1958. 200 Theatrical Cartoons, 1933-1954; 220 televison produced episodes, 1961-1963.

POP GOES THE COUNTRY

Musical Variety. Performances by Country and Western entertainers.

Host: Ralph Emery.

Music: Jim Malloy.

POP GOES THE COUNTRY—30 minutes—Syndicated 1974.

POPPI

Comedy. Background: New York City. The misadventures of Abraham Rodriquez, the Puerto Rican widower of two children, Abraham Junior and Luis, as he struggles to hold down several part time jobs and raise his mischievous sons.

CAST

Abraham Rodriquez   Hector Elizondo
Abraham Rodriquez,
  Jr.   Anthony Perez
Luis Rodriquez   Dennis Vasquez
Lupe, Abraham's
  girlfriend   Edith Diaz
Angelo Maggio, Abraham's
  friend   Lou Criscuolo

Music: George Del Barrio.

Executive Producer: Herbert B. Leonard, Arne Sultan.

Producer: Nick Anderson, A.J. Nelson.

Director: Hy Averback, Al Viola.

Creator: Tina and Lester Pine.

POPPI—30 minutes—CBS—January 20, 1976 - March 2, 1976; July 20, 1976 - August 24, 1976.

THE PORKY PIG SHOW

Animated Cartoon. The misadventures of the stuttering Porky Pig.

Additional segments: "Daffy Duck"; "Bugs Bunny"; "Sylvester and Tweety"; "Foghorn Leghorn"; "Pepe le Pew."

Voice characterizations: Mel Blanc.

Music: Carl Stalling; Milt Franklin.

THE PORKY PIG SHOW—30 minutes—ABC—1964 - 1965. Syndicated. Also known as "Porky Pig and His Friends."

THE PORTER WAGONER SHOW

Musical Variety. Background: The Wagon House. Performances by Country and Western entertainers.

Host: Porter Wagoner.

Regulars: Dolly Parton, Bruce Osborne, Barbara Lee, Spec Rose.

Announcer: Don Housner.

Music: The Wagon Masters.

THE PORTER WAGONER SHOW—30 minutes—Syndicated 1960.

PORTIA FACES LIFE

Serial. The dramatic story of Portia Manning, attorney and mother, who struggles to divide her time between the demands of work and the necessities of a home and a family.

CAST

Portia Manning	Fran Carlon
	Frances Reid
Walter Manning, her husband	Karl Swenson
	Donald Woods
Shirley Manning, their daughter	Ginger McManus
	Renne Jarrett
Dick Manning, their son	Charles Taylor
Karl Manning, Walter's brother	Patrick O'Neal

Also: Elizabeth York, Richard Kendrick.

Music: Tony Mottola.

PORTIA FACES LIFE—15 minutes—

Portia Faces Life. Left to right: Charles Taylor, Fran Carlon, Ginger McManus, Karl Swenson.

CBS—April 4, 1954 - March 11, 1955. Also known as: "The Inner Flame."

PORTRAIT

Celebrity Interview.

Host: Harry Reasoner.

PORTRAIT—30 minutes—CBS—January 30, 1963 - September 13, 1963.

THE PRACTICE

Comedy. Background: New York City. The trials and tribulations of Dr. Jules Bedford, a gruff but lovable West Side Manhattan physician. The series focuses on the running battle that exists between Jules, who practices on the Lower East Side, and his son, Dr. David Bedford, a Park Avenue physician, who objects to his father's methods and longs for him to join him on Park Avenue.

CAST
Dr. Jules Bedford   Danny Thomas
Dr. David Bedford   David Spielberg
Jenny Bedford, David's
    wife   Shelley Fabares
Molly Gibbons, Jule's
    nurse   Dena Dietrich
Helen, Jule's
    receptionist   Didi Conn
Paul Bedford, David and
    Jenny's son   Allen Price
Tony Bedford, David and
    Jenny's son   Damon Raskin
Nate, the hospital restaurant
    waiter   Sam Laws
Dr. Roland Caine, David's
    partner   John Byner
Lenny, an intern   Mike Evans
Dr. Byron Fisk   Barry Gordon
Music: David Shire, James DiPasquale.

Executive Producer: Danny Thomas, Paul Junger Witt.

Producer: Steve Gordon, Tony Thomas.

Director: Lee Philips, Noam Pitlik, Bill Persky, Tony Mordente, George Tyne.

Creator: Steve Gordon.

THE PRACTICE—30 minutes—NBC—January 30, 1976 - August 6, 1976; October 13, 1976 - January 20, 1977.

PREMIERE

Pilot Films. Proposed dramas for the 1968-1969 season.

Included:

Lassiter. A magazine writer's probe of corruption in a large Midwestern city.

CAST
Lassiter: Burt Reynolds; Stan Marchek: Cameron Mitchell; Joan Mears: Sharon Farrell; Russ Faine: James MacArthur.

The Search. Background: Switzerland. Probing a supposed accidental drowning, an American private detective attempts to prove that it was murder.

CAST
Paul Cannon: Mark Miller; Inspector Sheppard: Barry Foster; Molly: Julie Sommars.

Call to Danger. A federal troubleshooter's efforts to retrieve stolen Treasury Department currency plates. The pilot film for "Mission: Impossible." (Filmed in 1966.)

CAST
Jim Kingsley: Peter Graves; Paul

Wilkins: James Gregory; John Hinderson: Dan Travanty; Andre Kellman: Albert Paulsen.

Crisis. A psychiatrist struggles to locate a man who phones him and threatens to commit suicide.

CAST

Frank Chandler: Carl Betz; Lisa Edwards: Susan Strasberg; Art Winters: Robert Drivas; June Fielding: Davey Davison.

PREMIERE—60 minutes—CBS—July 1, 1968 - September 9, 1968. Rebroadcast as "Suspense Theatre"—60 minutes—CBS—May 24, 1971 - July 5, 1971.

PREVIEW

Previews of forthcoming Broadway plays and films. Hosts: Tex McCrary, Jinx Falkenberg. 30 minutes—CBS 1949.

PREVIEW THEATRE

Pilot Films. Proposed comedy series for the 1961-1962 season.

Included:

I Married a Dog. Marrying Joyce Nicoll, Peter Chance suddenly finds his life hindered by Noah, her extremely jealous French poodle.

CAST

Peter Chance: Hal March; Joyce Nicoll: Marcia Henderson; Madge Kellogg: Mary Carver.

Five's a Family. The misadventures of Harry Canover, a retired detective who can't resist the urge to solve crimes.

CAST

Harry Canover: Joe E. Brown; Bill Hewitt: Dick Foran; Peg Hewitt: Hollis Irving; Bobby Hewitt: Michael Petit.

Picture Window. The trials and tribulations of a suburban couple.

CAST

Joe Saxon: Charles Stewart; Amy Saxon: Mary La Roche.

Innocent James. The misadventures of a footloose, free-lance magazine writer.

CAST

Innocent James: Chris Warfield; Prudence Brown: Merry Anders.

PREVIEW THEATRE—30 minutes—CBS—July 14, 1961 - September 1961.

PREVIEW TONIGHT

Pilot Films. Proposed series for the 1966-1967 season.

The Complete Series:

Somewhere in Italy, Company B. Comedy. Background: Italy, World War II. The misadventures of a foul-up squadron cut off from its battalion command.

CAST

Lt. John Leahy: Robert Reed; Sgt. Wilkie Krantz: Harold J. Stone; Paulo Pietri: Vassili Lambrinos; Selena: Barbara Shelly.

Roaring Camp. Western. Background:

Roaring Camp, a mining town struck by gold fever. Teaming with a U.S. marshall, a gunslinger attempts to maintain law and order.

CAST

Marshall Walker: Richard Bradford; Cain: Jim McMullan; Rachel: Katherine Justice; Angus: Ian Hendry.

Great Bible Adventures. "Seven Rich Years. . .And Seven Lean." The dramatic story of Joseph, tracing his rise out of bondage to his reign as the pharaoh's minister.

CAST

Joseph: Hugh O'Brian; Pharaoh: Joseph Wiseman; Aton: Eduardo Ciannelli; Asenath: Katherine Ross.

Program Open:

Announcer: "Each year many of the new shows developed for television fail to make the network grade even though they are entertaining and well produced. Tonight's pilot film is one of these. We invite you behind the scenes to see what you think of [name of show] on Preview Tonight. . . ."

PREVIEW TONIGHT–60 minutes–ABC–August 14, 1966 - September 11, 1966.

THE PRICE IS RIGHT

Game. Four studio-audience members compete. The game varies greatly in presentaiton, but the basic format for each version and each segment is to price merchandise items exactly or as close as possible to the manufacturer's suggested retail selling price. Players who surpass the selling price forfeit their chance to win that particular item; the contestant whose bid comes closest to the selling price receives the item as her gift.

Versions:

The Price Is Right–30 minutes–NBC –September 1956 - September 9, 1963; ABC–30 minutes–September 18, 1963 - September 3, 1965.

Host: Bill Cullen, Jack Clark.

Assistants: Beverly Bently, Toni Wallace, June Ferguson.

The New Price Is Right–30 minutes–CBS–September 4, 1972 - October 31, 1975. 60 minutes–CBS–Premiered: November 3, 1975.

Host: Bob Barker.

Assistants: Nancy Myers, Pamela Parker.

Models: Anitra Ford, Holly Hallstrom, Janice Pennington, Dian Parkinson.

Announcer: Johnny Olsen.

Music: Ed Kalehoff.

The New Price Is Right–30 minutes–Syndicated 1972.

Host: Dennis James.

Assistants: Nancy Myers, Pamela Parker.

Models: Anitra Ford, Holly Hallstrom, Janice Pennington, Dian Parkinson.

Announcer: Johnny Olsen.

Music: Ed Kalehoff.

PRIDE OF THE FAMILY

Comedy. The trials and tribulations of the Morrison family: Albie, the advertising head of a small-town newspaper;

his wife, Catherine; their daughter, Ann; and their son, Albie, Jr.

CAST
Albie Morrison	Paul Hartman
Catherine Morrison	Fay Wray
Ann Morrison	Natalie Wood
Albie Morrison, Jr.	Bobby Hyatt

PRIDE OF THE FAMILY—30 minutes—ABC—October 9, 1953 - September 24, 1954. 40 episodes. Also known as "The Paul Hartman Show."

PRIMUS

Adventure. Background: Nassau. The cases of oceanographer Carter Primus, a global underwater troubleshooter.

His equipment: Big Kate, an underwater robot; the *Pegasus,* an exploration and photography vehicle; *Tegtight,* his operational base; *Dagat,* the mother ship; and the *Orka,* his patrol boat.

CAST
Carter Primus	Robert Brown
Toni Hyden, his assistant	Eva Renzi
Charlie Kingman, his assistant	Will Kuluva

Narrator: Robert Brown.

Music: Leonard Rosenman.

PRIMUS—30 minutes—Syndicated 1971. 26 episodes.

PRINCE DINOSAUR

A science fiction series, set on a prehistoric island in the South Pacific, that details the exploits of a jungle boy as he battles evil. 30 minutes—Syndicated 1967, 26 episodes.

PRINCE PLANET

Animated Cartoon. Background: Twenty-first-century Earth; the city of New Metropolis. The battle against evil as undertaken by Prince Planet, a youngster from the Universal Peace Corps of the planet Radion. Produced in Japan.

Characters:
Prince Planet, known as Bobby
Diana, his girlfriend, forever in distress
Haja Baba, a friend
Dynamo, a friend
Warlock, the evil Martian

PRINCE PLANET—30 minutes—Syndicated 1966. 52 episodes. Also known as "The Prince of Planets."

THE PRISONER

Adventure. Assigned to locate a missing scientist, secret agent John Drake* permits him to defect to Russia when he discovers the nature of the doctor's work: to complete a deadly mind transference device. Returning to England and reprimanded for his actions, Drake resigns, feeling it is a matter of principal.

Leaving the Ministry building, he is unknowingly followed by a mysterious black-clothed gentleman. Entering the hallway of the apartment, the gentleman places a nozzle in the keyhole and releases gas that knocks Drake unconscious.

Awakening, Drake finds himself in a strange room. He discovers that he is no longer a man, but a number—Number Six—and the prisoner of a self-contained community known as The Village, a flowery, courtyarded,

*The agent's name is not revealed, but is assumed to be John Drake as "The Prisoner" is a continuation from the last episode of "Secret Agent."

fantasylike area boarded by mountains and ocean—a place from which there is no escape.

Continuing his probe, he enters the Green Dome and meets one of the leaders, Number Two. Though unable to discover who his captors are, or where The Village is, he learns the reason for his abduction: "It's a question of your resignation. . .a lot of people are curious about. . .why you suddenly left. . .the information in your head is priceless. . .a man like you is worth a great deal on the open market. . .it's my job to check your motives."

Stories depict his attempts to discover the identity of Number One and who his captors are; and his desperate attempts to escape from The Village.

Last episode. Proving himself extraordinary—unable to be broken by exhaustive mind-bending experiments—Drake, after defeating Number Two, is led to an area below The Village. There, he is presented to an assembly, recognized as an individual—a man superior to them—and given a choice: leave or remain and lead the people of The Village. Undecided, he is taken to see Number One.

Met by his only friend, The Silent Butler, he is led through a heavily guarded hallway and to a room, containing highly complex machinery, that is designed to destroy him. Discovering that the room is a trap, he, The Silent Butler, and two system revolters, Number Two (imprisoned for failing to defeat Number Six), and Number Forty-eight join forces. Overpowering the guards, the machines are disengaged and reset to destruct. Boarding a truck, the four escape through an underground tunnel as the inner workings of The Village are destroyed.

Approaching London** the truck stops. Numbers Two and Forty-eight depart; Number Six, a free man, and The Silent Butler remain a team.

Intriguing, highly imaginative, and at times complex, "The Prisoner" requires one's full and uninterrupted attention to appreciate it.

CAST

Number Six	Patrick McGoohan
The Silent Butler	Angelo Muscat
Number Two	Colin Gordon
	Clifford Evans
	Mary Morris
	John Sharpe
	Peter Wyngarde
	Guy Doleman
	Leo McKern
Number Forty-eight	Alexis Kanner
The President	Kenneth Griffith

Orchestra: Albert Elms.

Prisoner Theme: Ron Grainer.

**Though not revealed, the location of The Village is assumed to be within fifty miles of London by the last episode. The series is filmed in North Wales.

THE PRISONER—60 minutes—CBS— June 1, 1968 - September 21, 1968. CBS—June 1969 - September 1969 (rebroadcasts). 17 episodes.

PRIVATE SECRETARY

Comedy. Background: New York City. The misadventures of Susie McNamara, private secretary to theatrical agent Peter Sands.

CAST

Susie McNamara	Ann Sothern
Peter Sands	Don Porter
Vi Praskins, the office receptionist	Ann Tyrrell
Cagey Calhoun, a rival talent agent	Jesse White
Sylvia, Susie's	

secretarial
friend   Joan Banks
The drugstore boy   Joseph Nartocana

Producer: Jack Chertok.

Sponsor: American Tobacco.

PRIVATE SECRETARY—30 minutes
—CBS—September 12, 1954 - September 10, 1957. 104 episodes. Syndicated title: "Susie." Also known as "The Adventures of Susie."

PRIZE PERFORMANCE

Variety. Performances by undiscovered professional talent.

Hostess: Arlene Francis.

Regulars: Cedric Adams, Peter Donald.

PRIZE PERFORMANCE—30 minutes—CBS—July 3, 1950 - September 1950.

PRIZE STORY

Anthology. Dramatizations depicting the plight of people confronted with everyday emotional problems.

PRIZE STORY—30 minutes—NBC 1952.

PROBE

Discussion. In-depth discussions on worldly affairs.

Host: Dr. Albert E. Burke.

PROBE—30 minutes—Syndicated—1961 - 1964. Withdrawn.

PRODUCERS' CHOICE

Anthology. Dramatic presentations.

Included:

The Last Rodeo. The story concerns a girl who, after witnessing a fatal rodeo accident, attempts to convince her fiancé to give up his career as a rodeo performer.

Starring: Robert Horton, Nancy Olson, Stacy Harris, Claude Akins.

Battle for a Soul. The story of a man who plots revenge against his former fiancée for framing him for a jewel theft he never committed.

Starring: Ray Milland, Lisa Daniels.

Long Distance. Minutes before her husband's scheduled execution, a wife finds a letter that proves his innocence. The story concerns her hysteria as she tries to reach the governor.

Starring: Jessica Tandy, Isobel Elsom, Carl Benton Reid.

PRODUCERS' CHOICE—30 minutes —NBC—March 31, 1960 - September 22, 1960.

PRODUCERS' SHOWCASE

Anthology. Lavish adaptations of stories by noted authors.

Included:

Peter Pan. A musical adaptation of the Barrie fantasy. Peter Pan's battle against the evil Captain Hook.

CAST
Peter Pan: Mary Martin; Captain Hook: Cyril Ritchard.

Our Town. A musical adaptation of the Thornton Wilder play. The story of life in a small American town.

CAST

Eva Marie Saint, Paul Newman, Frank Sinatra.

Music: Sammy Cahn, James Van Heusen.

The Sleeping Beauty. An adaptation of the Sadler Wells Ballet. When a young girl is cursed to a lifetime of sleep, a handsome young prince is sought to awaken her.

CAST

Sleeping Beauty: Margot Fonteyn; Prince Charming: Michael Somes.

Jack and the Beanstalk. The story of a poor farm family and the problems that ensue when Jack, the son, trades their milk cow for some magic beans.

CAST

Joel Gray, Billy Gilbert, Celeste Holm, Peggy King, Cyril Ritchard, Dennis King.

PRODUCERS' SHOWCASE—60 and 90 minutes (depending on the production)—NBC—October 18, 1954 - June 24, 1957.

PROFESSIONAL FATHER

Comedy. The trials and tribulations of the Wilson family: Thomas, a child psychologist; his wife, Helen; and their two mischievous children, Kit and Twig.

CAST

Dr. Thomas Wilson	Steve Dunne
Helen Wilson	Barbara Billingsley
Kit Wilson	Beverly Washburn
Twig Wilson	Ted Marc
Nana, their house-keeper	Ann O'Neal
Fred, their neighbor	Joseph Kearns
Madge, his wife	Phyllis Coates
Mr. Boggs, the handyman	Arthur Q. Bryan

Also: Sammy Ogg, Harry Cheshire.

PROFESSIONAL FATHER—30 minutes—CBS—January 8, 1955 - September 1955. 13 episodes.

PROFILES IN COURAGE

Documentary. Dramatizations based on events in past American history. Stories stress the valor of political figures who risked their careers, reputations and even lives to undertake unpopular causes. Based on the book, *Profiles in Courage,* by John F. Kennedy.

Program open: an excerpt from the book's prologue.

Program close: the words that close the final chapter: "The stories of past courage can define that ingredient—they can teach, they can offer hope, they can provide inspiration. But they cannot supply courage itself. For this, each man must look into his own soul."

PROFILES IN COURAGE—60 minutes—NBC—November 8, 1964 - September 1965. Syndicated.

THE PROJECTION ROOM

Anthology. Mystery presentations.

Hostess: Ruth Gilbert.

THE PROJECTION ROOM—30 minutes—ABC—March 19, 1952 - March 26, 1952.

THE PROTECTORS

See title: "The Bold Ones," *The Protectors* segment.

THE PROTECTORS

Adventure. Background: London, England. The investigations of Harry Rule, American; Contessa Caroline di Contini, British; and Paul Buchet, French—private detectives, members of the Protectors, an international organization of the world's finest investigators united in the battle against crime in the capitols of Europe.

CAST
Harry Rule	Robert Vaughn
Contessa Caroline di Contini, widow of a wealthy Italian	Nyree Dawn Porter
Paul Buchet	Tony Anholt
Suki, Harry's Japanese housekeeper	Yasuko Nagazumi
Chino, a Protector	Anthony Chinn
Harry's dog: Gus.	

Music: John Cameron.

Executive Producer: Sherwood Price.

Producer: Gerry Anderson, Reg Hill.

THE PROTECTORS—30 minutes—Syndicated 1972. 52 episodes.

PRUDENTIAL FAMILY THEATRE

Anthology. Dramatic presentations.

Producer: Donald Davis.

Sponsor: Prudential Life Insurance Company.

PRUDENTIAL FAMILY THEATRE

The Protectors. Left to right: Robert Vaughn, Nyree Dawn Porter, Tony Anholt. *Courtesy Independent Television Corp.; an ATV Company.*

—60 minutes—CBS—1950 - 1951.

THE PRUITTS OF SOUTHAMPTON

Comedy. Background: Southampton, Long Island, New York. Forced to drastically reduce her living standards when an Internal Revenue investigation discloses that she owes ten million dollars in back taxes, society matron Phyllis Pruitt struggles to maintain the appearance of wealth and social status, while at the same time attempting to adjust to the squalid life of a family, a home with eight rooms, one car, and a butler.

CAST

Phyllis Pruitt	Phyllis Diller
Ned Pruitt, her uncle	Reginald Gardiner
Stephanie Pruitt, her daughter	Pamela Freeman
Sturgis, the butler	Grady Sutton
Regina, Phyllis's social rival	Gypsy Rose Lee
Suzy, Regina's daughter	Lisa Loring
Internal Revenue Agent Baldwin	Richard Deacon
General Cannon, a friend of Phyllis's	John McGiver
Mr. Krump, the repairman	Marty Ingels
Vernon Bradley, the stuffy boarder	Billy DeWolfe
Rudy	John Astin
Maxwell	Charles Lane

Music: Vic Mizzy.

THE PRUITTS OF SOUTHAMPTON —30 minutes—ABC—September 6, 1966 - January 6, 1967. As "The Phyllis Diller Show"—30 minutes— ABC—January 13, 1967 - September 1, 1967. 30 episodes.

THE PSYCHIATRIST

See title: "Four-in-One," *The Psychiatrist* segment.

PUBLIC DEFENDER

Drama. The cases and courtroom defenses of Bart Matthews, a public defender of indigent people.

Starring: Reed Hadley as Bart Matthews.

PUBLIC DEFENDER—30 minutes— CBS—March 11, 1954 - June 23, 1955. 69 episodes.

PUBLICITY GIRL

A comedy series starring Jan Sterling as a publicity girl for a P.R. firm in Southern California. 30 minutes— Syndicated 1956.

THE PUBLIC LIFE OF CLIFF NORTON

Comedy. Capsule skits depicting one man's approaches and solutions to everday problems (e.g., "Table Manners"; "Police Your Bureau Drawer"; "Disposal of Your Christmas Tree"; "Building a Fruit Bowl").

Host-Demonstrator: Cliff Norton.

THE PUBLIC LIFE OF CLIFF NORTON—05 minutes—NBC—1950 - 1952.

PUBLIC PROSECUTER

Game. Three competing players who are designated detective-fiction experts. A fifteen-minute whodunit film is played and stopped prior to the denouement. Players have to determine who the culprit is. The film is played to reveal the answer. Winners receive a merchandise prize.

Host: John Howard.

Announcer: Bob Shepard.

Film Performers: John Howard, Anne Gwynne, Walter Sande.

PUBLIC PROSECUTER—30 minutes —DuMont 1947.

PUD'S PRIZE PARTY

Variety. Nonprofessional child entertainers perform and compete against each other for merchandise prizes and a title that names one individual the most talented child of the week.

Host: Todd Russell.

PUD'S PRIZE PARTY—30 minutes— ABC 1952.

PULSE OF THE CITY

Anthology. Dramatizations set against the background of New York City.

PULSE OF THE CITY—30 minutes— DuMont 1952.

PULITZER PRIZE PLAYHOUSE

Anthology. Dramatic adaptations of Pulitzer Prize-winning stories.

Producer: Edgar Peterson, Lawrence Carra.
Director: Charles S. Dubin, Alex Segal.

PULITZER PRIZE PLAYHOUSE—60 minutes—ABC—October 6, 1950 -

June 29, 1951.

PUPPET PLAYHOUSE

See title: "Howdy Doody."

PURSUIT

Anthology. Dramatizations depicting the plight of people pursued by others.

Producer: Peter Kortner, Norman Felton, Charles Russell.

Included:

Tiger on a Bicycle. After his friend, a policeman, is killed while attempting to stop an armored-car robbery, a man sets out to find the murderers.

CAST
Matt Shaw: Dan Duryea; Kathy Nelson: Laraine Day; Mood: Chester Morris.

Kiss Me Again Stranger. Assisting the local sheriff, a lieutenant attempts to discover the murderer of a young airman.

CAST
Lt. Aaron Gibbs: Jeffrey Hunter; Mara: Margaret O'Brien; Skip: Mort Sahl; Evelyn: Mary Beth Hughes.

The Dark Cloud. Suspended from the force on false charges, a police detective attempts to uncover the facts behind a bookie's death and clear his name.

CAST
Det. Eddie Hackett: Gary Merrill; Sunny: Ann Sheridan; Det. Mike Robbins: Darryl Hickman; Andrea: Fay Spain.

PURSUIT—60 minutes—CBS—October 22, 1958 - January 14, 1959.

Producer-Director: Ralph Levy.

15 minutes—CBS 1949.

℥

Q.E.D.

Game. Object: For a celebrity panel to solve mystery stories that are submitted by members of the viewing audience. The facts are relayed by the host, and panelists each receive one guess. If mysteries remain unsolved, the sender receives a merchandise prize.

Host: Fred Uttal.

Panel: Nina Foch, Hy Brown, plus guests.

Q.E.D.—30 minutes—ABC—April 13, 1951 - September 1951. Also known as "Mystery File."

Q.T. HUSH

Animated Cartoon. The investigations of Q.T. Hush, a fumbling private detective.

His assistants: Shamus, his dog; and Quincy, his shadow, which is able to operate independently of him.

Q.T. HUSH—30 minutes—Syndicated 1960. 100 episodes.

QUADRANGLE

A comedy game show with Beverly Fite, Frank Stevens, Burt Taylor, Dean Campbell, Bob Burkhardt, Ray Kirschner, Claire Granville.

THE QUEEN AND I

Comedy. Background: New York Harbor. The story of master schemer Duffy, the first mate of the *Amsterdam Queen,* an old and decrepit ocean liner, and his attempts to save the ship, a floating paradise for his money-making schemes.

CAST
Mr. Duffy	Larry Storch
First Officer Nelson	Billy De Wolfe
Captain Washburn	Liam Dunn
Commodore Dodds, the ship's owner	Reginald Owen

Duffy's Crew:
Seaman Becker	Carl Ballantine
Wilma, Duffy's romantic interest	Barbara Stuart
Ozzie	Dave Willock
Max Kowalski	Dave Morick
Barney Cook	Pat Morita

THE QUEEN AND I—30 minutes—CBS—January 16, 1969 - May 1, 1969. 13 episodes.

QUEEN FOR A DAY

Contest. Four women appear and bare their souls, stating their single most needed object. Through electronic voting machines, the audience then selects the one woman they feel is the most needy. The woman is crowned "Queen For A Day," and receives, in addition to the requested gift, various merchandise prizes.

Versions:

Queen For A Day—30 minutes—NBC - April 28, 1955 - September 25, 1960; ABC—September 28, 1960 - October 2, 1964.

Host: Jack Bailey.

Fashion Commentator: Jeanne Cagney.

Announcer: Gene Baker.

Queen For A Day—30 minutes—Syndicated 1970.

Host: Dick Curtis.

Fashion Commentator: Nancy Myers.

QUENTIN DERGENS, M.P.

Drama. Background: London, England. The story of Quentin Dergens, a Member of Parliment (M.P.) who crusades against British government apathy and red tape.

Starring: Gordon Pinsent as Quentin Dergens.

QUENTIN DERGENS, M.P.—60 minutes—Syndicated 1966. 9 episodes.

THE QUEST

Western. Background: The Frontier during the last quarter of the 19th Century. Eight years after being captured and raised by the Cheyenne Indians who attacked the wagon train on which he was traveling, Morgan "Two Persons" Baudine is freed by the army. Shortly after, as he begins to search for his sister, Patricia, who is reputed to be living among the Cheyenne, he meets his long-lost brother, Quentin, a young medical student who, raised by an aunt in San Francisco, has also begun a search for Patricia. Reunited by a common goal, they begin a hazardous quest to find their sister. The series concerns their adventures as they travel throughout the rugged West following new leads.

CAST

Morgan Baudine   Kurt Russell
Quentin Baudine   Tim Matheson

Music: Richard Shores.

Executive Producer: David Gerber.

Producer: Mark Rogers, James H. Brown.

Director: Earl Bellamy, Michael O'Herlihy, Corey Allen, Bernard McEveety.

THE QUEST—60 minutes—NBC—September 22, 1976 - December 22, 1976.

QUEST FOR ADVENTURE

Travel. Excursions to various areas around the globe via the *Quest,* a sixty foot sailing vessel.

Host: Michael O'Toole.

QUEST FOR ADVENTURE—30 minutes—Syndicated 1966. 20 episodes.

QUICK AS A FLASH

Game. Two competing teams, each composed of one celebrity and one studio-audience contestant. A specially prepared film sequence, that describes a person, place, or event is played. The player first to identify himself by a flashing light signal (pressing a button), receives a chance to answer. If he identifies the subject, he receives one point; if he fails, he and his partner are disqualified from that particular round. The opposing team then views the entire film before hazarding a guess. Winners, the highest point scorers, receive merchandise prizes.

Host: Bobby Sherwood.

QUICK AS A FLASH—30 minutes—ABC—March 12, 1953 - September 10, 1953.

QUIET, PLEASE

Anthology. Mystery and adventure presentations.

Narrator: Ernest Chappel.
Announcer: Ed Michael.
Music: Albert Buhrmann.
Producer: Wyllis Cooper.

QUIET, PLEASE—30 minutes—ABC —June 16, 1949 - July 21, 1949.

QUICK DRAW McGRAW

Animated Cartoon. A spoof of the adult westerns of the 1950s. Background: The territory of New Mexico. The exploits of Marshal Quick Draw McGraw, a dim-witted horse who, assisted by Baba Looey, the Mexican burro, struggles to maintain law and order. A Hanna-Barbera production.

Additional segments:
"Snagglepuss." The misadventures of a trouble-prone lion.
"Snooper and Blabber." The antics of a mischievous cat and mouse.
"Augie Doggie and Doggie Daddy." The efforts of a father to control his potentially juvenile deliquent son.

Characters' Voices
Quick Draw McGraw	Daws Butler
Baba Looey	Daws Butler
Snooper	Daws Butler
Blabber	Daws Butler

Quick Draw McGraw. Quick Draw McGraw. *Courtesy Hanna-Barbera Productions.*

Augie Doggie	Daws Butler
Doggie Daddy	Doug Young
Snagglepuss	Daws Butler

Music Supervision: Hoyt Curtin.

QUICK DRAW McGRAW—30 minutes—Syndicated 1959. 195 episodes.

QUICK ON THE DRAW

Game. Object: For contestants to identify phrases that are presented by a series of cartoon drawings.

Hostess: Eloise McElhone.
Artist: Bob Dunn.

QUICK ON THE DRAW—30 minutes —NBC 1950.

QUINCY, M.E.

Crime Drama. Background: Los Angeles, California. The story of Dr.

Quincy, a medical examiner (M.E.) for the coroner's office, who prefers to probe as a detective rather than just working in a lab.

CAST

Dr. Quincy   Jack Klugman
Lee Potter, his
    girlfriend   Lynnette Mettey
Dr. Robert Astin, his
    superior   John S. Ragin
Dr. Sam Fugiyama, his
    assistant   Robert Ito
Lt. Frank Monahan, the homicide
    detective   Garry Walberg
Danny Tarvo, Quincy's
    friend, the owner of Danny's
    Place, a bar   Val Bisoglio

Music: Stu Philips.

Theme: Glen A. Larson.

Executive Producer: Glen A. Larson.

Producer: Lou Shaw, Robert O'Neil, Michael Star.

Director: E.W. Swackhamer, Stephen Stern, Noel Black, Bruce Kessler, David Moessinger, Corey Allen, Ronald Stalof, Alvin Ganzer, Jackie Cooper.

QUINCY, M.E.—60 minutes—NBC— Premiered: February 4, 1977. Broadcast as part of "The NBC Sunday Mystery Movie" from October 3, 1976 to January 2, 1977.

THE QUIZ KIDS

Panel. Five exceptionally intelligent children attempt to answer difficult questions. Based on the radio program.

Host: Joe Kelly; Clifton Fadiman.

Producer: Louis G. Cowan, John LeWellen.

Director: Don Meler.

Sponsor: Alka Seltzer; Miles Labs; Cat's Paw.

THE QUIZ KIDS—30 minutes—CBS— November 13, 1952 - September 27, 1956.

QUIZZING THE NEWS

Game. Object: For a panel to identify news events through a series of three cartoon drawings.

Host: Allan Prescott.

Panel: Arthur Q. Bryan, Ray Joseph, Mary Hunter, Milton Coniff.

Artist: Albee Treider.

QUIZZING THE NEWS—30 minutes —ABC—August 16, 1948 - March 5, 1949.

R

RACKETS ARE MY RACKET

Drama. Dramatizations exposing confidence games—"The tricks of the tricky traders."

Host: Sgt. Audley Walsh, of the Ridgefield, New Jersey, Police Department.

RACKETS ARE MY RACKET—15 minutes—DuMont 1947.

RACKET SQUAD

Crime Drama. Background: San Francisco, California. Dramatizations exposing the confidence game and its organizers.

Detailing the investigations of Captain John Braddock of the San Francisco Racket Squad, the series presents the step-by-step methods taken to expose rackets.

Starring: Reed Hadley as Captain John Braddock.

Narrator: Reed Hadley.

Music: Joseph Mullendore.

Producer: Hal Roach, Jr., Carroll Chase.

Director: Frank McDonald.

Sponsor: Philip Morris Cigarettes.

Program open:
Capt. Braddock: "What you are about to see is a real life story taken from the files of police racket and bunco squads, business protective associations, and similar sources all over the country. It is intended to expose the confidence game, the carefully worked out frauds by which confidence men take more money each year from the American public than all the bank robbers and thugs with their violence."

Program close:
Capt. Braddock: "I'm closing this case now, but they'll be others because that's the way the world is built. Remember there are people who can slap you on the back with one hand and pick your pocket with the other—and it could happen to you."

RACKET SQUAD—30 minutes. Syndicated 1950; CBS—June 7, 1951 - September 28, 1953. 98 episodes. Syndicated (again after the network run).

RAFFERTY

Medical Drama. Background: Cali-

fornia. The story of Sid Rafferty, M.D., a former army doctor turned brilliant diagnostician in private practice; a doctor who, working part time in City General Hospital, "believes in healing people, not in setting himself up in a fancy business just to make money."

CAST

Dr. Sid Rafferty   Patrick McGoohan
Dr. Daniel Gentry, his
   associate   John Getz
Vera Wales, his office
   nurse   Millie Slavin
Beryl Keynes, the hospital admissions nurse   Joan Pringle

Music: Leonard Rosenman, Richard Clements.

Executive Producer: Jerry Thorpe.

Producer: James Lee, Norman S. Powell.

Director: Jerry Thorpe, Barry Crane, Alexander Singer.

Creator: James Lee.

RAFFERTY—60 minutes—CBS—Premiered: September 5, 1977.

RAMAR OF THE JUNGLE

Adventure. Background: Nairobi, Africa. The experiences of Dr. Thomas Reynolds, a research scientist known as Ramar—White Witch Doctor.

CAST

Dr. Thomas Reynolds   Jon Hall
Professor Ogden, his
   assistant   Ray Montgomery

RAMAR OF THE JUNGLE—30 minutes—Syndicated 1952. 52 episodes.

RANCH PARTY

Musical Variety. Performances by Country and Western entertainers.

Host: Tex Ritter.

Regulars: Jim Reeves, Bonnie Guitar.

RANCH PARTY–30 minutes–Syndicated 1957. 39 episodes.

THE RANGE RIDER

Western. Background: California, 1860s. The exploits of the Range Rider, a wandering defender of justice, and his sidekick, Dick West, "the all-American boy."

CAST
The Range Rider   Jock Mahoney
Dick West   Dick Jones

Program Open:

Song: "Home, home on the range, where the deer and the antelope play . . .

Announcer (over music): And who could be more at home on the range than the Range Rider, with his exciting experiences, rivaling those of Davy Crockett, Daniel Boone, Buffalo Bill, and other pioneers of this wonderful country of ours."

THE RANGE RIDER–30 minutes–Syndicated 1951. 76 episodes.

RANGO

Western Comedy. Background: Gopher Gulch, Texas, 1870s. The exploits of Rango, a fumbling, dim-witted Texas Ranger who struggles to successfully carry out his assignments and glorify the dignity of the Texas Rangers.

CAST
Rango   Tim Conway
Pink Cloud, his Indian assistant   Guy Marks
Captain Horton   Norman Alden

Music: Earle Hagen.

RANGO–30 minutes–ABC–January 13, 1967 - June 25, 1967.

THE RANSOM SHERMAN SHOW

Variety. Music, songs, and comedy sketches.

Host: Ransom Sherman.

Regulars: Johnny Bradford, Nancy Wright.

Music: The Art Damme Quintet.

THE RANSOM SHERMAN SHOW– 30 minutes–NBC 1950.

THE RAT CATCHERS

Mystery. The global activities of a group of London based spies. Stories detail their battle against criminal masterminds.

CAST
Glyn Owen, Gerald Flood, Philip Stone.

THE RAT CATCHERS–50 minutes– Syndicated 1965. 13 episodes.

THE RAT PATROL

Adventure. Background: North Africa during World War II. The exploits of the Rat Patrol, a squadron of four desert allies assigned to harass and demoralize Rommel's Afrika Korps.

CAST

Sgt. Sam Troy   Christopher George
Sgt. Jack Moffitt   Gary Raymond
Pvt. Tully Pettigrew   Justin Tarr
Pvt. Mark Hitchcock   Larry Casey
Captain Hans Dietrich,
  their German
  nemesis   Hans Gudegast

Music: Dominic Frontiere.

Producer: Mark Weingart.

THE RAT PATROL—30 minutes—ABC—September 12, 1966 - September 16, 1968. 58 episodes. Syndicated.

RAWHIDE

Western. Era: The 1860s. The struggles and hardships faced by the men of the cattle drive from San Antonio, Texas, to Sedalia, Kansas.

CAST

Gil Favor, the trail
  boss   Eric Fleming
Rowdy Yates, the
  ramrod   Clint Eastwood
Pete Nolan, the trail
  scout   Sheb Wooley
Wishbone, the
  cook   Paul Brinegar

The Drovers:
Mushy   James Murdock
Clay Forrester   Charles Gray
Joe Scarlett   Rock Shahan
Quince   Steve Raines
Hey Soos   Robert Cabal
Simon Blake   Raymond St. Jaques
Ian Cabot   David Watson

Music: Dimitri Tiomkin.

Theme: "Rawhide," by Ned Washington, Dimitri Tiomkin; Recorded by Frankie Laine.

Producer: Charles Warren, Endre Bohem, Vincent M. Fennelly.

Program Open:
Announcer (over music and scene of a cattle drive): "This is the landscape of Rawhide: desert, forest, mountain and plains; it is intense heat, bitter cold, torrential rain, blinding dust; men risking their lives, earning small reward—a life of challenge—Rawhide. It is men like trail scout Pete Nolan, the cantankerous Wishbone, Ramrod Rowdy Yates, good natured Mushy, and trail boss Gil Favor —these men are Rawhide!"

RAWHIDE—60 minutes—CBS—January 1, 1959 - January 4, 1966. 144 episodes. Syndicated.

RAY ANTHONY

Listed: The television programs of band leader Ray Anthony.

The Ray Anthony Show—Musical Variety—ABC—60 minutes—1949.

Host: Ray Anthony.

Regulars: Frank Leahy, The Four Freshman, The Belvaders.

Orchestra: Ray Anthony.

The Ray Anthony Show—Musical Variety—60 minutes—Syndicated 1956.

Host: Ray Anthony.

Regulars: The Four Freshman, The Bookends (singers, dancers), Don Durant, Med Flory, Frank Leahy.

Orchestra: Ray Anthony.

The Ray Anthony Show—Musical

Variety—60 minutes—Syndicated 1962.

Host: Ray Anthony.

Regulars: Vikki Carr, Lisa Marne, Kellie Greene, The Bookends.

Orchestra: Ray Anthony.

THE RAY BOLGER SHOW

See title: "Where's Raymond?"

THE RAY KNIGHT REVUE

Musical Variety.

Host: Ray Knight.

Regulars: Phyllis Gehrig, Don Weismuller, Jonathan Lucas, Harry Archer, Ernie Burtis, Tony Craig, Kaye Conner, Joan Fields, Adam Carroll, Frank Seporelli.

Orchestra: Ray Knight.

Producer: Michael Cramoy.

Director: Howard Cordery.

THE RAY KNIGHT REVUE—30 minutes—ABC—May 15, 1949 - September 1949.

THE RAY MILLAND SHOW

Comedy. Distinguished by two formats.

Format One:

Meet Mr. McNutly—30 minutes—CBS—September 17, 1953 - July 15, 1954. Also known as: "Meet Mr. McNutley."
    Background: The town of Lynnhaven. The trials and tribulations of Ray McNutly (McNutley), a drama professor at Lynnhaven, an all-girl college.

CAST

Professor Ray McNutly	Ray Milland
Peggy McNutly, his wife	Phyllis Avery
Dean Bradley	Minerva Urecal
Pete Thompson, Ray's friend	Gordon Jones
Ruth Thompson, his wife	Jacqueline de Wit

Announcer: Del Sharbutt.

Format Two:

The Ray Milland Show—30 minutes—CBS—September 16, 1954 - September 30, 1955. Syndicated.
    Background: Los Angeles, California. The trials and tribulations of Ray McNutly, a drama professor at Comstock, a coeducational college.

CAST

Professor Ray McNutly	Ray Milland
Peggy McNutly, his wife	Phyllis Avery
Dean Dodsworth	Lloyd Corrigan

Announcer: Del Sharbutt.

THE RAY STEVENS SHOW

Variety. Music, songs, and comedy sketches.

Host: Ray Stevens.

Regulars: Lulu, Dick Curtis, Steve Martin, Carol Robinson, Florian Carr, Billy Van, Max Elliott, Cass Elliott.

Orchestra: Jimmy Dale.

THE RAY STEVENS SHOW—60 minutes—NBC—July 1970 - September 1970. Original title: "Andy Williams Presents the Ray Stevens Show."

THE R.C.A. VICTOR SHOW

See title: "The Dennis Day Show."

REACH FOR THE STARS

A game show wherein contestants have to perform stunts in return for merchandise prizes. Hosted by Bill Mazer, the thirty minute series ran on NBC from January 3, 1967 to March 31, 1967.

THE REAL McCOYS

Comedy. Background: The San Fernando Valley in California. The struggles of a poor farm family, the McCoys: Grandpa Amos, widower, the head of the clan; Luke, his grandson; Kate, Luke's wife; and Hassie and Little Luke, Luke's sister and brother (their parents, deceased).

CAST

Amos McCoy	Walter Brennan
Luke McCoy	Richard Crenna
Kate McCoy ("Sugar Babe")	Kathleen Nolan
Hassie McCoy	Lydia Reed
Little Luke McCoy	Michael Winkleman
Pepino Garcia, their hired hand	Tony Martinez
George MacMichael, Amos's friend	Andy Clyde
Flora MacMichael, George's sister	Madge Blake
Mac Maginnis, Amos's friend	Willard Waterman
Lela Maginnis, Mac's wife	Shirley Mitchell
Mrs. Jensen, the McCoy housekeeper	Connie Gilchrist
Helga, replaced Mrs. Jensen	Eva Norde
Frank Grant, Helga's boyfriend	James Lydon
Louise Howard, the owner of the ranch next to the McCoys (CBS episodes)	Janet De Gore
Gregg Howard, her son	Butch Patrick
Frank, their handyman	John Qualen
Winifred Jordan, Louise's aunt	Joan Blondell
Hank Johnson, Amos's friend	Lloyd Corrigan
Harry Purvis, Amos's partner in the roadside egg business	Charles Lane
"Rightly" Ralph McCoy, Luke's uncle	Jack Oakie
Mr. Taggart, the Grand Pharoah of Amos's lodge	Frank Ferguson
Mrs. Purvis, Kate's mother	Lurene Tuttle

Music: Billy Loose; Ed Norton; Harry Ruby.

Executive Producer: Irving Pincus, Danny Thomas.

Producer: Danny Arnold, Norman Pincus, Charles Isaacs.

Director: Danny Arnold, David Alexander, Sidney Miller, Richard Crenna, Hy Averback, Sheldon Leonard.

Creator: Irving Pincus.

Note: Amos's fraternity: The Royal Order of the Mystic Nile Lodge; The McCoys car: Gertrude, a Model T Ford.

THE REAL McCOYS–30 minutes. ABC–October 3, 1957 - September 20, 1962. CBS–September 24, 1962 - September 22, 1963. 224 episodes. Syndicated.

THE REAL TOM KENNEDY SHOW

Talk-Variety.

Host: Tom Kennedy.

Regulars: Kelly Garrett, John McCormick, Foster Brooks.

Announcer: Tom Kennedy.

Orchestra: Dave Pell.

THE REAL TOM KENNEDY SHOW
—60 minutes—Syndicated 1970. 45 tapes.

THE REBEL

Western. Era: The post-Civil War West. The exploits of Johnny Yuma, an embittered, leather-tough young Confederate who journeys West after the Civil War to seek self-identify.

Starring: Nick Adams as Johnny Yuma.

Music: Richard Markowitz.

Theme: "Johnny Yuma," sung by Johnny Cash.

THE REBEL—30 minutes—ABC—October 4, 1959 - September 24, 1961. 76 episodes. Syndicated.

THE REBUS GAME

Game. Two competing teams, each composed of two contestants. One member of each team receives a secret name or phrase. Each partner in turn then draws pictures on a board and attempts to relate its meaning. A player is only permitted to guess when his partner is drawing. Each correct identification scores one point. Winners, the highest scorers, receive merchandise prizes.

Host: Jack Linkletter.

THE REBUS GAME—30 minutes—ABC—March 29, 1965 - September 24, 1965.

RECKONING

Anthology. Rebroadcasts of dramas that were originally aired via "Climax," "Pursuit," and "Studio One."

Included:

Tongues of Angels. The story of a young man who pretends to be a deaf mute to get a job working on a farm.

CAST
Ben Adams: James MacArthur; Jenny Walker: Margaret O'Brien; Cyrus Walker: Leon Ames; Mrs. Walker: Frances Farmer.

The Vengeance. The story of a young man who is hounded by the father of a boy he accidentally crippled in his youth.

CAST
Richie Rogart: Sal Mineo; Harry Talback: Macdonald Carey; Elaine Hermann: Carol Lynley; Detective Fraelich: Stu Erwin.

A Leaf Out of the Book. The story of two women, one successful, the other ambitious.

CAST
Diana Lynn, Sylvia Sidney.

RECKONING—60 minutes—CBS—June 1959 - September 1959; June 1960 - September 1960; June 1961 - September 1961; June 1962 - September 1962; June 1963 - September 1963.

THE RED BUTTONS SHOW

Variety. Music, songs, dances, and

comedy sketches.

Host: Red Buttons.

Regulars: Phyllis Kirk, Paul Lynde, Beverly Dennis, Jean Carson, Sara Seeger, Jimmy Little, Ralph Stanley, Sonny Birch, Dorothy Jolliffee, Howard Smith, Allan Walker, Bobby Sherwood, Joe Silver, Betty Ann Grove, The Ho Ho Kids (named after Red's hit recording, "The Ho Ho Song.")

Announcer: Nelson Case.

Producer: Don Appel, Ben Brady, Leo Morgan.

Sponsor: Pontiac; General Foods.

Orchestra: Elliott Lawrence.

Characters portrayed by Red: Keeglefarven, the knucklehead German; Rocky Buttons, the punch-drunk prizefighter; Buttons the bellboy; Razzberry Buttons; The Kupke Kid; The Sad Sack.

THE RED BUTTONS SHOW—60 minutes—CBS—October 14, 1952 - June 14, 1953.

THE REDD FOXX COMEDY HOUR

Variety. Basically, a series of comedy sketches spotlighting the talents of comedian Redd Foxx.

Host: Redd Foxx.

Regulars: Murray Langston, Deborah Pratt, Hal Smith, Dick Owens, Walt Hanna, Andrew Johnson.

Announcer: Roger Carroll.

Orchestra: Gerald Wilson.

Producer: Allyn Blye, Bob Einstein.

Director: Donald Davis.

Choreographer: Lester Wilson.

THE REDD FOXX COMEDY HOUR —60 minutes—ABC—Premiered: September 15, 1977.

THE RED HAND GANG

Children. The adventures of five preteen city children, members of the Red Hand Gang club, as they stumble upon and seek to solve crimes. Stories are episodic.

CAST
Frankie	Matthew La Borteaux
J. R.	J. R. Miller
Joannie	Jolie Neman
Lil Bill	Johnny Brogna
Doc	James Bond III

Music: Score Productions.

Executive Producer: William P. D'Angelo, Ray Allen, Harvey Bullock.

Producer-Director: William P. D'Angelo.

THE RED HAND GANG—30 minutes—NBC—Premiered: September 10, 1977.

REDIGO

Drama. Background: Mesa, New Mexico. The story of Jim Redigo, a rancher struggling to maintain a vast cattle spread. A spin-off from "Empire."

CAST
Jim Redigo	Richard Egan
Gerry, the assistant manager of the Gold Hotel	Elena Verdugo
Linda Franks, the ranch cook	Mina Martinez
Mike, a ranch hand	Roger Davis

Frank, a ranch
hand   Rudy Solari

REDIGO—30 minutes—NBC—September 24, 1963 - December 31, 1963. 15 episodes.

RED RYDER

Western. Era: The nineteenth century. The exploits of Red Ryder and his Indian friend, Little Beaver, as they struggle to maintain law and order throughout the West.

CAST

Red Ryder   Rocky Lane
Little Beaver   Louis Letteri
The Dutchess   Elizabeth Slifer

RED RYDER—30 minutes—Syndicated 1956. 39 episodes. Withdrawn. Based on the radio program.

THE RED SKELTON SHOW

Variety. Music, songs, dances, and comedy sketches.

Host: Red Skelton.

Regulars: Chinan Hale, Sheila Rogers, Jan Arvin, Helen Funai, Lloyd Kino, Jan Davis, Billy Barty, Beverly Powers, Ida Moe McKenzie, Elaine Joyce, Jimmie Cross, Lester Mathews, Kathryn Cord, Stanley Adams, Peggy Rae, Mike Wagner, Dorothy Love, Bob Duggan, Adam Kaufman, Stuart Lee, Linda Sue Risk, The Tom Hanson Dancers, The Alan Copeland Singers, The Skeltones (Dancers); The Burgandy Street Singers.

Announcer: Art Gilmore.

Orchestra: David Rose.

Characters portrayed by Red: Freddie the Freeloader; Clem Kaddiddlehopper (the farm boy); Sheriff Deadeye (the corrupt lawman); Junior, the Mean Widdle Kid; Cauliflower McPugg (the punchy boxer); George Appleby (the henpecked husband); San Fernando Red (the con artist); Ludwick von Humperdoo (the scientist); Bolivar Shagnasty; Willy Lump Lump (the drunk).

THE RED SKELTON SHOW—30 minutes—NBC—September 30, 1951 - June 1953; CBS—30 and 60 minute versions—September 22, 1953 - June 1970; NBC—30 minutes—September 14, 1971 - August 29, 1972. Also known as "The Red Skelton Hour."

THE REEL GAME

Game. Three competing contestants, each beginning with two hundred and fifty dollars bidding money.

The Film Clip Round: The host states a category topic (e.g., "comedy teams") and players wager any amount of their money on their ability to answer the forthcoming question. The question is then read (e.g., "For years the team of George Burns and Gracie Allen ended their comedy routine by George telling Gracie to do something. What?"). After players write their answers on a card, a film clip is shown that reveals the answer ("Say goodnight, Gracie.") Contestants whose answers are correct receive the wagered amount of money; if incorrect, it is deducted.

Each of the three film clip rounds are divided by a question-and-answer session wherein three questions are asked regarding the subject of the film clip round. Players first to sound a buzzer receive a chance to answer. Twenty-five dollars are either deducted from or added to a player's score.

The Grand Finale: The category question is stated. Each player secretly writes his answer and his wager on a card. A film clip reveals the correct answer. Winners, who receive their earnings, are the highest cash scorers.

Host: Jack Barry.

Announcer: Jack Clark.

THE REEL GAME—30 minutes—ABC—January 18, 1971 - May 3, 1971. 13 tapes.

THE REGIS PHILBIN SHOW

Talk-Variety.

Host: Regis Philbin.

Music: The Terry Gibbs Sextet.

THE REGIS PHILBIN SHOW—90 minutes—Syndicated 1964. 100 tapes.

REHEARSAL CALL

Variety. The series features music, songs, and a behind-the-scenes look, as "Rehearsal Call" takes viewers backstage at TV productions.

Hostess: Dee Parker.

Music: The Leonard Stanley Trio.

Producer: John Pival.

REHEARSAL CALL—15 minutes—ABC 1949.

THE RELUCTANT DRAGON AND MR. TOAD

Animated Cartoon. Based on the novel *The Wind in the Willows.*

The Reluctant Dragon. Background: The Willowmarsh Village in England. The story of Sir Malcolm and his struggles to protect Tobias, a four-hundred-year-old dragon cursed to breathing fire, from the little girl (not identified by a name) who delights in causing misery by presenting Tobias with daisies—which cause him to sneeze, breathe fire, and disrupt life in the village.

Mr. Toad. The adventures of a carefree, gadabout frog, Mr. Toad.

THE RELUCTANT DRAGON AND MR. TOAD—30 minutes—ABC—September 12, 1970 - September 3, 1972. 52 episodes.

RENDEZVOUS

Drama. Background: The Chez Nikki, a sophisticated nightclub in Paris, France. The story of its proprietress, a beautiful woman who, supposedly engaged in underground activities during World War II, involves herself in and attempts to solve the problems of others.

Starring: Ilona Massey.

Music: Edward Vito.

RENDEZVOUS—30 minutes—ABC—February 13, 1952 - March 12, 1952.

RENDEZVOUS

Anthology. Dramatic presentations.

Host-Narrator: Charles Drake.

RENDEZVOUS—30 minutes—Syndicated 1958.

RENDEZVOUS WITH ADVENTURE

Adventure. Films revealing the hazardous expeditions of explorers.

Host-Narrator: Lee Green.

RENDEZVOUS WITH ADVENTURE—30 minutes—Syndicated 1963.

RENDEZVOUS WITH MUSIC

Musical Variety.

Hostess: Carol Reed.

Regulars: Rosemary Bangham, Andy McCann, Mary Jane Boone, Tommy Johnson, Teddy Katz.

Music: The Tony DeSimone Trio.

RENDEZVOUS WITH MUSIC—30 minutes—NBC 1950.

RENFREW OF THE ROYAL MOUNTED

Adventure. Background: Canada. The investigations of Douglas Renfrew, a Royal Canadian Mounted Policeman.

CAST

Douglas Renfrew	James Newell
Constable Kelly	Dave O'Brien
Carol Girard, Renfrew's romantic interest	Louise Stanley

RENFREW OF THE ROYAL MOUNTED—30 minutes—Syndicated 1953. 13 episodes.

THE REPORTER

Drama. Background: Manhattan. The investigations of Danny Taylor, a newspaper reporter-columnist for the *New York Globe.*

CAST

Danny Taylor	Harry Guardino
Lou Sheldon, the city editor	Gary Merrill
Artie Burns, a friend of Danny's	George O'Hanlon
Ike Dawson, the bartender, a friend of Danny's	Remo Pisani

Music: Kenyon Hopkins.

Executive Producer: Keefe Brasselle.

Producer: John Simon.

THE REPORTER—60 minutes—CBS—September 25, 1964 - December 15, 1964. 15 episodes.

RESCUE 8

Drama. Background: California. The experiences of Wes Cameron and Skip Johnson, paramedics with the Rescue 8 Division of the Los Angeles County Fire Department. Stories depict their attempts to rescue people trapped in unusual predicaments.

CAST

Wes Cameron	Jim Davis
Skip Johnson	Lang Jeffries
Patty Johnson, their dispatcher	Nancy Rennick

Producer: Herbert B. Leonard.

RESCUE 8—30 minutes—Syndicated 1958. 73 episodes.

THE RESTLESS GUN

Western. "I ride with the wind, my eyes on the sun, and my hand on my Restless Gun." Background: The West of the 1860s. The exploits of Vint Bonner, a wandering ex-gunfighter ("The Six Gun") who aides people in distress.

Starring: John Payne as Vint Bonner.

Narrator: John Payne.

Bonner's horse: Scar.

Music: Stanley Wilson.

Producer: John Payne, David Dortort.

THE RESTLESS GUN—30 minutes. NBC—September 1957 - September 14, 1959; ABC—October 12, 1959 - September 30, 1960. 77 episodes. Syndicated.

RETURN ENGAGEMENT

Anthology. Rebroadcasts of dramas that were originally aired via other filmed anthology programs.

RETURN ENGAGEMENT—30 minutes—ABC—June 1953 - September 1953.

RETURN TO PEYTON PLACE

Serial. A spin-off from "Peyton Place." Background: The small New England town of Peyton Place. Continued events in the turmoil-ridden lives of its citizens.

CAST

Constance MacKenzie Carson, the owner of the town bookstore	Bettye Ackerman
Elliot Carson, her husband; the editor-publisher of the *Peyton Place Clarion*	Warren Stevens
Alison MacKenzie, their illegitimate daughter	Kathy Glass
Eli Carson, Elliot's father, the owner of the general store	Frank Ferguson
Rodney Harrington, the nephew of Martin Peyton, the founder of Peyton Place	Yale Summers
	Lawrence Casey
Norman Harrington, Rodney's brother	Ron Russell
Betty Anderson Harrington, Rodney's wife	Julie Parrish
	Lynn Loring
Rita Jacks Harrington, Norman's wife	Patricia Morrow
Leslie Harrington, the father of Rodney and Norman	Stacy Harris
Ada Jacks, Rita's mother, the owner of Ada Jack's Tavern, a waterfront bar	Evelyn Scott
Dr. Michael Rossi, the town physician	Guy Stockwell
Stephen Cord, the illegitimate son of Martin Peyton's daughter	Joe Gallison
Hannah Cord, one time mistress and housekeeper for Martin Peyton; raised Stephen Cord	

as her own
son   Mary K. Wells
Benny Tate,
   a mysterious,
   menacing figure
   from Alison's
   past   Ben Andrews
Matthew Carson,
   the three-year-old
   son of Constance
   and Elliot   John Levin
Martin Peyton, the
   founder of Peyton
   Place   John Hoyt
Dr. Wells   Alex Nicol
Lt. Ed Riker   Chuck Daniel
Judge Foster   Anne Seymour
Seena Cross   Margaret Mason
Monica Bell, a
   waitress   Betty Ann Carr
The Attorney   Rudy Solari

Music: Linda Line.

RETURN TO PEYTON PLACE–30 minutes–NBC–April 3, 1972 - January 4, 1974.

RETURN TO THE PLANET OF THE APES

Animated Cartoon. A spin-off from "Planet of the Apes." Traveling aboard the NASA space craft *Venture,* three astronauts, Bill, Judy, and Jeff, penetrate a time vortex and are hurled from their present day Earth (1975) to Earth in the year A.D. 3979–into a world that is ruled by intellectual apes (humans, treated as a lesser species, serve as pets, servants, and sport for hunters). Seeking shelter after their ship crash lands, the astronauts find refuge in the humanoid colony of New City. As they learn what fate has befallen the Earth, the colony is raided by an army of apes; Bill is captured and brought to ape scientists Cor-neileus and Zera for experimentation purposes. In his attempt to communicate with them, Bill speaks, shocking Corneileus and Zera, who held a mis-belief that humans were incapable of speech.* Realizing that Bill will be killed by the ape leaders if they learn of his capability, Corneileus and Zera set him free.

Stories follow the astronauts adventures as they struggle for survival and seek a way to return to the Earth of their time.

Characters' Voices:

Bill   Tom Williams
Judy   Claudette Nevins
Jeff   Austin Stoker
Corneileus   Henry Corden
Dr. Zera   Phillipa Harris

Additional Voices: Richard Black-burn, Edwin Mills.

Music: Dean Elliot, Eric Rogers.

*The few elder ape leaders are the only ones who know that humans once ruled the planet Earth. Humanoid greed, folly, and lust for power caused him to destroy his civilization in a cataclysmic war. From his ruins, the ape society emerged. It is written that if the humanoids were to regain the intelligence of language, they would once again become the masters of the planet and would once again destroy it. Thus, the intelligence possessed by the humans has been kept secret from the ape population to prevent panic.

RETURN TO THE PLANET OF THE APES–30 minutes–NBC–September 6, 1975 - September 4, 1976.

REVLON MIRROR THEATRE

Anthology. Dramatic presentations.

Hostess–Commercial Spokeswoman: Robin Chandler.

REVLON MIRROR THEATRE–30 minutes–NBC–June 23, 1953 - September 1953.

RHEINGOLD THEATRE

Anthology. Dramatic presentations.

Hosts: Henry Fonda; Douglas Fairbanks, Jr.

Included:

Louise. Fearing to lose her daughter to a struggling young lawyer, a domineering mother attempts to prevent their marriage.
Starring: Judith Anderson.

The Norther. A sheriff attempts to track a gang of outlaws through a blistering heat wave ("Norther").
Starring: Stephen McNally.

End Of Flight. A fugitive's flight from justice.
Starring: Edmond O'Brien.

Honolulu. When the captain of a ship discovers that his first mate has fallen in love with his wife, he attempts to destroy him through voodoo.
Starring: Frank Lovejoy.

RHEINGOLD THEATRE—30 minutes—NBC—1955 - 1956.

RHODA

Comedy. A spin-off from "The Mary Tyler Moore Show," wherein the character of Rhoda Morganstern was portrayed as a plumpish brunette whose main challenges were to land an occasional date and, with some will power, slim down so as not to eat her heart out everytime she looked at her attractive friend, confidante, and neighbor, Mary Richards (Mary Tyler Moore).

Now, four years later, slim, glamorous, and single, Rhoda leaves Minneapolis for a two-week vacation and returns to home of her birth, New York City (born in the Bronx), where she moves in with her sister, Brenda, an overweight bank teller.

Preparing for a date her mother has arranged for her, Rhoda meets and falls in love with Joe Gerard, the head of the New York Wrecking Company, when he comes to the apartment to leave his ten-year-old son, Donny (by a former marriage which ended in divorce), with Brenda, his baby-sitter.

Cancelling her plans to return to Minneapolis, Rhoda secures employment as a store window dresser and, shortly after, accepts Joe's proposal of marriage.

Married, Rhoda and Joe establish housekeeping in the same apartment house as Brenda. Stories depict the trials and tribulations of newlyweds as they struggle to survive the trying first years in difficult times.

CAST

Rhoda Morganstern (Gerard)	Valerie Harper
Joe Gerard	David Groh
Brenda Morganstern	Julie Kavner
Ida Morganstern, Rhoda's mother	Nancy Walker
Martin Morganstern, Rhoda's father	Harold Gould
Voice of Carlton, the never seen, intoxicated doorman	Lorenzo Music
Mae, Joe's secretary-bookkeeper	Cara Williams
Justin Culp, Joe's partner	Scoey Mitchlll
Donny Gerard	Todd Turquand
Alice, Joe's secretary-bookkeeper (later episodes)	Candy Azzara
Sally Gallagher, Rhoda's	

friend   Anne Meara
Myrna Morganstein, Rhoda's
    friend   Barbara Sharma
Nick Lobo, Brenda's
    friend   Richard Masur
Lenny Fielder, Brenda's
    friend   Wes Stern

Music: Billy Goldenberg.

Executive Producer-Creator: James L. Brooks, Allan Burns.

Producer: Charlotte Brown, David Davis, Lorenzo Music.

Director: Robert Moore, Tony Mordente, Howard Storm, Jay Sandrich.

Program Open:

Rhoda: "My name is Rhoda Morganstern. I was born in the Bronx, New York in December of 1941. I've always felt responsible for World War II. The first thing that I remember liking that liked me back was food. I had a bad puberty, it lasted seventeen years. I'm a high school graduate. I went to art school—my entrance exam was on a book of matches. I decided to move out of the house when I was twenty-four. My mother still refers to this as the time I ran away from home. Eventually I ran to Minneapolis where it's cold, and I figured I'd keep better. Now I'm back in Manhattan. New York, this is your last chance."

RHODA—30 minutes—CBS—Premiered: September 9, 1974.

RHYME AND REASON

Game. Six celebrity guests and two contestants are involved. The host reads a rhyming phrase (e.g., "I did a double take when I first met Mae West..."). The contestants then write a word that rhymes with the last word of the phrase. One player selects a celebrity who must then make up a rhyme to complete the phrase. If he uses the same word as the contestant, the contestant scores two points; if the celebrity matches the opponent, the opponent scores one point. Three points are played per game and the first player to win two games is the champion and receives five hundred dollars.

Host: Bob Eubanks.

Announcers: Johnny Jacobs, Jack Clark.

Regular Panelist: Nipsey Russell.

Semiregular Panelists: Conny Van Dyke, Jaye P. Morgan, Charlie Brill, Mitzi McCall, Pat Harrington, Frank Gorshin, Jamie Farr.

Music: Recorded.

RHYME AND REASON—30 minutes—ABC—July 7, 1975 - July 9, 1976.

THE RICHARD BOONE SHOW

Anthology. Dramatic presentations. A regular cast of players appear in non-continuing roles.

Host-Performer: Richard Boone.

Repertory Company: Harry Morgan, Laura Devon, Robert Blake, June Harding, Warren Stevens, Bethel Leslie, Guy Stockwell, Lloyd Bochner, Jeanette Nolan, Ford Rainey.

Music: Vic Mizzy.

Producer: Mark Goodson, Bill Todman, Buck Houghton.

Included:

First Sermon. A priest's fears and doubts about his abilities to address his parishioners.

CAST

Guy Stockwell, Robert Blake, Richard Boone.

Where Did You Hide An Egg? Three unqualified safecrackers attempt a bank robbery.

CAST

Richard Boone, Harry Morgan, Robert Blake.

Don't Call Me Dirty Names. The struggles of an unwed mother to be.

CAST

June Harding, Lloyd Bochner.

Where's The Million Dollars? Pursuing an underworld character, federal authorities attempt to learn the whereabouts of a million dollars.

CAST

Guy Stockwell, Harry Morgan.

THE RICHARD BOONE SHOW—60 minutes—NBC—September 24, 1963 - September 15, 1964. 25 episodes.

RICHARD DIAMOND, PRIVATE DETECTIVE

Crime Drama. Distinguished by two formats.

Format One:

Background: New York City. The investigations of private detective Richard Diamond. Operating without police assistance, his life rests solely in the hands of a woman identified only as Sam, a beautiful, sexy-voiced telephone operator who is aware of his presence at all times and possesses the ability to sense endangering situations and summon help. Operating from a small room in Manhattan, Sam, who is never fully seen, is situated in a dimly lit atmosphere designed to display her shapely figure, notably her legs.

CAST

Richard Diamond   David Janssen
Sam   Mary Tyler Moore
                         Roxanne Brooks

Music: Pete Rugolo; Richard Shores.

Format Two:

Background: Hollywood, California. The investigations of private detective Richard Diamond.

CAST

Richard Diamond   David Janssen
Karen Wells, his
  girlfriend   Barbara Bain
Lieutenant McGouh,
  L.A.P.D.   Regis Toomey
Lt. Pete Kile   Russ Conway
Sgt. Alden   Richard Devon

Music: Pete Rugolo; Richard Shores.

RICHARD DIAMOND, PRIVATE DETECTIVE—30 minutes—CBS—July 1, 1957 - September 30, 1957; December 2, 1958 - September 25, 1958; February 15, 1959 - September 20, 1959; NBC—October 5, 1959 - January 25, 1960. 51 episodes. Syndicated. Also known as "Call Mr. D."

THE RICHARD PRYOR SHOW

Variety. Basically, a series of comedy sketches spotlighting the talents of comedian Richard Pryor.

Host: Richard Pryor.

Regulars: Paula Kelly, Jeff Corey, Sam Laws, Juanita Moore, Charles Fleischer, Jimmy Martinez, The Chuck Davis Dance Company.

Orchestra: Johnny Pate.

Special Musical Material: Lenny La-Crox.

Executive Producer: Burt Sugarman.

Producer: Rocco Urbisci.

Director: John Moffitt.

Choreographer: Chuck Davis.

THE RICHARD PRYOR SHOW—60 minutes—NBC—September 13, 1977 - October 18, 1977.

RICHARD THE LION HEART

History. Background: Eleventh-century England. The life of King Richard the Lion Heart—from his participation in the Crusades, to his capture in Austria, to his final return to England.

Starring: Dermot Walsh as King Richard.

RICHARD THE LION HEART—30 minutes—Syndicated 1963. 39 episodes.

THE RICH LITTLE SHOW

Variety.

Host: Rich Little.

Regulars: Julie McWhirter (as "The Family Hour Fairy"), Charlotte Rae, Joe Baker, R.G. Brown, Mel Bishop.

Orchestra: Robert E. Hughes.

Executive Producer: Jerry Goldstein.

Producer: Al Rogers, Rick Eustis.

Director: Lee Bernhardi.

THE RICH LITTLE SHOW—60 minutes—NBC—February 2, 1976 - May 18, 1976.

RICH MAN, POOR MAN, BOOK I

Drama. A miniseries that follows the lives of the Jordache brothers: Rudy, the straight one who moves up the establishment ladder; and Tom, the troublemaker. The series also simultaneously covers the changes that occur in America from World War II through the mid-1960s. Based on the novel by Irwin Shaw.

CAST

Tom Jordache	Nick Nolte
Rudy Jordache	Peter Strauss
Julie Prescott	Susan Blakely
Axel Jordache	Edward Asner
Mary Jordache	Dorothy McGuire
Kate Jordache	Kay Lenz
Wesley Jordache	Willie Aames
	Michael Morgan
Sue Prescott	Gloria Grahame
Bill Falconetti	William Smith
Willie Abbott	Bill Bixby
Duncan Calderwood	Ray Milland
Virginia Calderwood	Kim Darby
Teddy Boylan	Robert Reed
Linda Quales	Lynda Day George
Brad Knight	Tim McIntire
Smitty	Norman Fell
Gloria	Jo Ann Harris
Marsh Goodwin	Van Johnson
Irene Goodwin	Dorothy Malone
Rod Dwyer	Herbert Jefferson, Jr.
Sid Gossett	Murray Hamilton
Colonel Bainbridge	Andrew Duggan
Bayard Nichols	Steve Allen
Teresa Santoro	Talia Shire

Muisc: Alex North.

Executive Producer: Harve Bennett.

Producer: Jon Epstein.

Director: David Greene, Boris Sagal.

RICH MAN, POOR MAN, BOOK I—12 hours—ABC—February 1, 1976 - March 15, 1976. Rebroadcasts: ABC—May 10, 1977 - June 21, 1977.

RICH MAN, POOR MAN, BOOK II

Drama. A continuation of the miniseries "Rich Man, Poor Man, Book I." Continued events in the life of Rudy Jordache, now a United States Senator. Serial-type episodes.

CAST

Rudy Jordache	Peter Strauss
Maggie Porter, his lawyer	Susan Sullivan
Wesley Jordache, Rudy's ward (Tom had been killed off)	Gregg Henry
Ramona Scott, Wesley's girlfriend	Penny Peyser
Billy Abbott, Rudy's stepson	James Carroll Jordan
Kate Jordache, Tom's widow	Kay Lenz
Bill Falconetti, the man seeking to destroy Rudy	William Smith
Diane Porter, Maggie's daughter	Kimberly Beck
Mr. Scott, Ramona's father	John Anderson
Charles Estep, the ruthless billionaire	Peter Haskell
Rod Dwyer, Wesley's friend	Herbert Jefferson, Jr.
Claire Estep, Charles's wife	Laraine Stephens
Marsh Goodwin	Van Johnson
Annie	Cassie Yates
Vickie St. John	Collen Camp

Music: Alex North, Michael Isaacson.

Music Supervision: Stanley Wilson.

Executive Producer: Michael Gleason.

Producer: Jon Epstein.

Director: Alex Segal, Bill Bixby, Karen Arthur, Paul Stanley.

RICH MAN, POOR MAN, BOOK II—60 minutes—ABC—September 21, 1976 - March 8, 1977.

THE RIFLEMAN

Western. Background: North Fork, New Mexico, 1888. The story of Lucas McCain, widower, "The Rifleman" (the fastest man with a .44-40 hair-trigger action rifle), and his young son, Mark, ranchers, and their struggles to maintain a small cattle spread.

CAST

Lucas McCain	Chuck Connors
Mark McCain	Johnny Crawford
Marshal Micah Torrance	Paul Fix
Hattie Denton, the owner of the general store (early episodes)	Hope Summers
Millie Scott, the	

The Rifleman. Left to right: Chuck Connors, Johnny Crawford, Joan Taylor.

owner of the
general store
(later episodes)   Joan Taylor
Eddie Holstead,
the owner of
the Madera House
Hotel   Larry Perron
Lou Mallory, the
owner of the
Mallory House
Hotel   Patricia Blair
Nils Svenson, the
blacksmith   Joe Higgins
Sweeney, the Last
Chance Saloon
bartender   Bill Quinn
Jay Burrage,
the town
doctor   Edgar Buchanan
                                Jack Kruschner
                                Ralph Moody
Angus Evans, the
gunsmith   Eddie Quinlan
Ruth, a hotel
waitress   Amanda Ames
Betty Lind,
a hotel
waitress   Carol Leigh
John Hamilton, the
banker   Harlan Warde
Aggie Hamilton, his
wife   Sarah Selby

Music: Herschel Burke Gilbert.

THE RIFLEMAN—30 minutes—ABC
—September 30, 1958 - July 1, 1963.
Syndicated. 168 episodes.

RIN TIN TIN

See title: "The Adventures Of Rin Tin
Tin."

RIPCORD

Adventure. The experiences of Jim
Buckley and Ted McKeever, sky-diving instructors for Ripcord, Incorporated, a sky-diving school.

CAST

Jim Buckley	Ken Curtis
Ted McKeever	Larry Pennell

Program Open:

Announcer: "This is the most danger-packed show on television. Every aerial manuver is real, photographed just as it happened, without tricks or illusions. All that stands between a jumper and death is his Ripcord."

RIPCORD—30 minutes—Syndicated
1961. 76 episodes.

RIPTIDE

Adventure. Background: Bermuda. The experiences of Moss Andrews, the captain of the charter boat service Riptide, Incorporated.

CAST

Moss Andrews	Ty Hardin
His secretary	Jacki Hickmont

RIPTIDE—60 minutes—Syndicated
1965.

THE RIVALS OF
SHERLOCK HOLMES

Anthology. Mystery presentations depicting incidents in the lives of fictional detectives who were popular in Europe at the time of Sherlock Holmes. Produced in England.

Music: Robert Sharples.

Executive Producer: Kim Mills, Lloyd Shirley.

Producer: Jonathan Alwyn, Robert

Lane, Reginald Collen.

Director: Reginald Collen, Bill Bain.

THE RIVALS OF SHERLOCK HOLMES—60 minutes—PBS—1975 - 1976.

RIVERBOAT

Adventure. Background: Areas along the Mississippi and Missouri Rivers during the 1840s. The experiences of Grey Holden, the captain of the riverboat *Enterprise.*

CAST

Grey Holden	Darren McGavin
Ben Frazer, the pilot (early episodes)	Burt Reynolds
Bill Blake, the pilot (later episodes)	Noah Beery, Jr.
Brad Turner, the captain (later episodes)	Dan Duryea

The Crew:

Joshua	Jack Lambert
Chip	Mike McGreevy
Carney	Dick Wessell
Pickalong	John Mitchum
Terry Blake	Bart Patton

Music: Elmer Bernstein; Richard Sendry; Leo Shuken.

RIVERBOAT—60 minutes—NBC— September 13, 1959 - January 16, 1961. 44 episodes.

RIVIERA POLICE

A crime drama series, set on the French Riviera. 13 films. 60 minutes— Syndicated 1965.

R.J. AND COMPANY

Music. Borrowing its format from "American Bandstand," the show features teenagers dancing to popular music.

Host: Ron Joseph (R.J.).

Announcer: Jim Bacon, Mark Anthony, Gene Arnold.

Musical Director: Marty Morley, Glen Rosewald.

Executive Producer: Ron Joseph.

R.J. AND COMPANY—30 minutes— Syndicated 1976. Originally, aired locally over WTAF-TV, Channel 29 in Philadelphia.

ROAD OF LIFE

Serial. Background: The town of Merimac. The dramatic story of Doctor Jim Brent and his wife, Joycelyn. Episodes relate the conflicts and tensions that befall three generations of two families: the Brents and the Overtons (Joycelyn's family). Based on the radio program.

CAST

Jim Brent	Don McLaughlin
Joycelyn Brent	Virginia Dwyer
Malcolm Overton	Harry Holcombe
Sybil Overton	Barbara Becker
Conrad Overton	Charles Dingle
Aunt Reggie	Dorothy Sands

Also: Bill Lipton, Elizabeth Lawrence, Michael Kane, Elspeth Eric, Hollis Irving, Jack Lemmon.

Narrator: Nelson Case.

ROAD OF LIFE—15 minutes—CBS —December 13, 1954 - June 24, 1955.

ROAD OF ROMANCE

Anthology. Rebroadcasts of romantic dramas originally aired via other filmed anthology programs.

ROAD OF ROMANCE—30 minutes—ABC 1955.

THE ROAD RUNNER SHOW

Animated Cartoon. Background: The desert. Using defective Acme Warehouse products, Wile E. Coyote, a scavenger, endlessly attempts to catch himself a decent meal: a foxy, outsmarting bird, the Road Runner. Composed of both theatrical and made-for-television cartoons.

Voice characterizations: Mel Blanc.

Music: William Lava.

THE ROAD RUNNER SHOW—30 minutes—CBS—September 2, 1967 - September 7, 1968.

THE BUGS BUNNY/ROAD RUNNER HOUR—60 minutes—CBS —September 14, 1968 - September 4, 1971.

THE ROAD RUNNER SHOW—30 minutes—ABC—September 11, 1971 - September 2, 1972. Syndicated. Theatrical shorts syndicated prior to the network run.

THE ROADS TO FREEDOM

Serial. Background: Europe. The collapse of pre-world War II France is dramatized as it is seen through the eyes of three people: Mathieu, an intellectual college professor; Daniel, a homosexual; and Brunet, a Communist—men unable to act or think definitively. Based on Jean Paul Sarte's *The Roads To Freedom* Trilogy: *The Age of Reason; Loss of Innocense;* and *The Awakening.* Produced by the B.B.C.

CAST

Mathieu De LaRue	Michael Bryant
Marcelle, his mistress	Rosemary Leach
Daniel	Daniel Massey
Lola Montero, a singer in a Paris night club	Georgia Brown
Boris, her romantic interest	Anthony Corlan
Ivich, his sister	Alison Fiske
Jacques De LaRue, Mathieu's brother	Clifford Rose
Odette De LaRue, his wife	Anna Fox
Sarah	Heather Canning
Rose	Bella Amberg
Brunet	Donald Burton
Andre Pinette	Donald Burnet
Emil	Tom Marshall
Chamberlain	Michael Goodlife
Hitler	Tenniel Edans
Phillipe	Simon Ward
The Mayor	George Roderick
Fiske	Dick Allison
Laytex	Peter Wyatt
Longin	John Carter
Nippert	Christian Rodska
Gomez	Andrew Faulds
Schoolmaster	Blake Butler
Clipot	Donald Webster
Post girl	Claire Sutcliffe
Sgt. Clossom	James Appleby
Blonde woman	Kate Brown

Dramatization: David Turner.

Music (theme only): "La Route Est Dure." Arranged by Richard Holmes; vocal (in French): Georgia Brown.

THE ROADS TO FREEDOM—45 minutes. Imported and presented to PBS stations in 1972 by WNET-TV, Channel 13, New York. Official title: "La Route Est Dure."

ROAD TO REALITY

Serial. The program dramatizes what happens at a group therapy session. With the help of a doctor, six people discuss their emotional problems.

CAST

Dr. Lewis	John Beal
Vic	Robert Drew
Rosalind	Robin Howard
Margaret	Eugena Rawls
Joan	Judith Braun
Lee	James Dimitri
Chris	Kay Doubleday

ROAD TO REALITY—30 minutes—ABC—October 17, 1960 - March 31, 1961.

THE ROAD WEST

Western. Background: Lawrence County, Kansas, 1860. The struggles of a family of homesteaders, the Prides, as they attempt to establish a new life.

CAST

Ben Pride, the father	Barry Sullivan
Elizabeth Pride, Ben's wife	Kathryn Hays
Tim Pride, Ben's son	Andrew Prine
Midge Pride, Ben's daughter	Brenda Scott
Chance Reynolds, Elizabeth's brother	Glen Corbett
Christopher (Kip) Pride, Ben's son	Kelly Corcoran
Thomas Jefferson (Tom) Pride, Ben's father	Charles Seel

Music: Leonard Rosenman.

THE ROAD WEST—60 minutes—NBC—September 12, 1966 - September 4, 1967. 26 episodes.

THE ROARING TWENTIES

Drama. Background: Manhattan, 1920s. The investigations of Scott Norris and Pat Garrison, newspaper reporter-columnists for the *New York Record.* Assisted by Pinky Pinkham, a beautiful singer at The Charleston Club, they strive to acquire the headline-making stories by infiltrating the

The Roaring 20's. Guest Maxie Rosenbloom and star Dorothy Provine. Episode: "Asparagus Tips."

rackets and exposing the racketeers. Through rear-screen projection and intercutting of newsreel film of the era, an illusion of authenticity is presented.

CAST

Pinky Pinkham	Dorothy Provine
Pat Garrison	Donald May
Scott Norris	Rex Reason
Chris Higbee, the copy boy	Gary Vinson
Jim Duke Williams, a reporter	John Dehner
McDonald, the city editor	Emile Meyer
Dixie, the hat check girl at The Charleston Club	Carolyn Komant
Chauncey Kowalski, the bartender at The Charleston Club	Wally Brown
Lt. Joe Switolski, N.Y.P.D.	Mike Road

Background Music: Sandy Courage.

Miss Provine's musical accompaniment: Pinky and Her Playboys—a re-created Syncopation Dance Orchestra composed of Pinky's Playboys (a cabaret band) and six squeaky-voiced chorus girls, "And the Girls."

THE ROARING TWENTIES—60 minutes—ABC—October 15, 1960 - September 2, 1962. 45 episodes. Syndicated.

ROAR OF THE RAILS

Model Railroads. Stories of railroading told via narration over scenes of model railroads in operation.

Hostess: Mimi Strangin.

Narrator: Rusty Slocum.

Producer: Ray Nelson.

Sponsor: A.C. Gilbert Electric Trains.

ROAR OF THE RAILS—15 minutes —CBS—1948-1949.

THE ROBBINS NEST

Variety. Various comedy sketches satirizing life.

Host: Fred Robbins.

Regulars: Nat Cantor, Fran Gregory.

Announcer: Cynthia Carlin.

THE ROBBINS NEST—15 minutes— ABC—September 29, 1950 - December 22, 1950.

THE ROBERT HERRIDGE THEATRE

Anthology. Dramatic presentations. Adaptations of short stories and plays by noted authors.

Host: Robert Herridge.

Included:

The World Of Irving Harmon. Screen comedian Irving Harmon enacts a series of sketches that tell about himself and the people he has encountered during his career.

CAST
Irving Harmon, Sandra Lee, Joe Silver, Lee Sherman.

The Tell-Tale Heart. A servant kills his master because he is haunted by the old man's pale blue eyes. Believing that he has committed the perfect murder, he allows police to search the room in which the body is hidden. Suddenly, the servant hears the old man's heart beat—louder and louder until it causes him to confess.

CAST

Michael Kane.

The Story of a Gunfighter. The story of a gunfighter who is hired to kill the town sheriff.

CAST

William Shatner, Philip Coolidge, Dennis Kohler.

THE ROBERT HERRIDGE THEATRE—30 minutes—CBS—July 7, 1960 - September 1960.

ROBERT MONTGOMERY PRESENTS

Anthology. Dramatic presentations.

Host-Narrator-Producer-Occasional Performer: Robert Montgomery.

Included:

Bella Fleace Gave a Party. Despising her heirs, a woman decides to spend her money on one last, lavish ball.

CAST

Bella Fleace: Fay Bainter; Riley: J. Pat O'Malley.

The Tall Dark Man. After witnessing a murder, a young girl, who is addicted to telling tall tales, struggles to prove her story truthful.

CAST

Sarah Grass: Robin Morgan; Mrs. Everett: Margaret Warwick; Mrs. Grass: Mary Jackson.

P.J. Martin and Son. Realizing that she can't run her family as she does her successful construction company, a woman struggles to regain their love.

CAST

Pauline Martin: Edna Brent; David Martin: Lin McCarthy; Tommy Martin: Jack Mullaney; Joan Martin: Gloria Strovck.

ROBERT MONTGOMERY PRESENTS—60 minutes—NBC—January 30, 1950 - June 24, 1957. Also known as "The Lucky Strike Theatre."

THE ROBERTA QUINLAN SHOW

Musical Variety.

Hostess: Roberta Quinlan.

Announcer: Bob Stanton.

Music: The Harry Clark Trio; The Tony Mottola Trio; The Elliott Lawrence Orchestra.

Versions:

THE ROBERTA QUINLAN SHOW—15 minutes—NBC—May 3, 1949 - November 23, 1951. Also known as "Especially For You."

ROBERTA Q'S MATINEE—30 minutes—NBC—1952 - 1956.

THE ROBERT Q. LEWIS SHOW

Musical Variety.

Host: Robert Q. Lewis.

Regulars: Jaye P. Morgan, Rosemary Clooney, Merv Griffin, Jan Ardan, Earl Wrightson, Jill Corey, Lois Hunt, Pat Lytell, Nat Cantor.

Orchestra: Ray Bloch; George Wright.

Producer: Rai Purdy, Lester Gottlieb.

Director: Jerome Schnur.

THE ROBERT Q. LEWIS SHOW—30 minutes—CBS—January 11, 1954 - May 25, 1956.

ROBERT YOUNG, FAMILY DOCTOR

See title: "Marcus Welby, M.D."

ROBIN HOOD

See title: "The Adventures of Robin Hood."

ROBINSON CRUSOE

Adventure Serial. Background: Somewhere off the coast of South America during the seventeenth century. Caught in a tropical storm at sea, a young Englishman, Robinson Crusoe, is shipwrecked on an uncharted island from which there is no escape. The thirteen-part dramatization depicts his first day of life on the island to his rescue twenty-eight years later. Based on the novel by Daniel Defoe.

Starring: Robert Hoffman as Robinson Crusoe.

ROBINSON CRUSOE—30 minutes—Syndicated 1964.

ROCKET ROBIN HOOD

Animated Cartoon. Background: New Sherwood Forest, A.D., 3000 a floating, solar-powered asteroid—the headquarters of Rocket Robin Hood and his band of Merry Men: Will Scarlet, Little John, Allen, Jiles, and Friar Tuck—the futuristic defenders of justice. Stories depict their battle against the forces of villainy throughout the universe, namely, the evils of the Sheriff of Knott.

Music: Winston Sharples.

ROCKET ROBIN HOOD—30 minutes—Syndicated 1967. 156 episodes.

THE ROCK FOLLIES

Musical Drama. Background: London, England. A penetrating satire that follows the careers of "The Little Ladies" (Anna Wynd, Devonia "Dee" Rhoades, and Nancy "Q" Qunard), a three girl British Rock Group, as they struggle to succeed in the world of Pop music.

CAST

Anna Wynd	Charlotte Cornwell
Devonia "Dee" Rhoades	Julie Covington
Nancy "Q" Qunard	Rula Lenska
Derek Huggin, Q's romantic interest	Emlyn Price
Spike, Dee's romantic interest	Billy Murray
Jack, Anna's romantic interest	Stephen Moore
Gloria, a friend	Angela Bruce
Bob, a friend	Bob Stewart
Mrs. Wynd, Anna's mother	Vivienne Burgess

The Little Ladies Rock Band: Brian Chatton, Peter Hooke, Tony Stevens, Ray Russell.

Music: Andy Mackay.

Producer: Andrew Brown.

Director: Jon Scoffield, Brian Farnum.

THE ROCK FOLLIES—60 minutes—

PBS—March 5, 1977 - March 10, 1977. 6 episodes. Produced in England.

THE ROCKFORD FILES

Crime Drama. Background: Los Angeles, California. The investigations of Jim Rockford, the chief operative of the Rockford Private Detective Agency, as he attempts to solve criminal cases that are considered unsolvable and labled inactive by police.

CAST

Jim Rockford	James Garner
Joseph (Rocky) Rockford, his father	Noah Beery
Beth Davenport, a lawyer	Gretchen Corbett
Sergeant Dennis Becker, L.A.P.D.	Joe Santos
Angel Martin, Jim's friend	Stuart Margolin
Peggy Becker, Dennis's wife	Pat Finley

Executive Producer: Meta Rosenberg, Stephen J. Cannell.

Producer: Charles Johnson, David Chase.

Creator: Roy Huggins, Stephen J. Cannell.

Music: Mike Post, Pete Carpenter.

THE ROCKFORD FILES—60 minutes—NBC—Premiered: September 13, 1974.

ROCKY AND HIS FRIENDS

Animated Cartoon. A battle against evil as seen through the activities of Rocky the flying squirrel and his simple-minded friend, Bullwinkle the moose. Stumbling upon the evils of Mr. Big, the midget, they struggle to thwart his plans by foiling the work of his agents, Boris Badenov, "International Bad Guy," and his aide, the deadly Natasha Fataly.

Additional segments:

Fractured Fairy Tales. Modern adaptations of childrens fables.

Aesop's Fables. The wise Aesop's efforts to explain the aspects of a changing world to his impressionable son.

Peabody's Improbable History. Through the use of their Way Back Machine, Mr. Peabody, the intelligent dog, and his friend, Sherman, a young boy, travel throughout history to help famous people achieve their fame.

Dudley Do-Right. The efforts of a simple-minded Mountie to apprehend the notorious Snively Whiplash.

Bullwinkle's Corner. Ninety seconds of nonsense poetry.

Characters' Voices

Rocky	June Foray
Bullwinkle	Bill Scott
Boris Badenov	Paul Frees
Natasha Fataly	June Foray
Snively Whiplash	Hans Conried
Peabody	Bill Scott
Sherman	June Foray
Aesop	Charlie Ruggles

Narrator of the Rocky and Bullwinkle Segment: Paul Frees.

Narrator of "Fractured Fairy Tales:" Edward Everett Horton.

Additional Voices: Bill Conrad, Walter Tetley, Skip Craig, Barbara Baldwin, Adrienne Diamond.

Music: Fred Steiner; Frank Comstock.

Producer: Jay Ward, Bill Scott.

Note: The character voiced by Hans Conried, is also known to be Snidely Whiplash.

ROCKY AND HIS FRIENDS–30 minutes–ABC–September 29, 1959 - September 3, 1961. Syndicated. Spin-off series: "Bullwinkle"–30 minutes –NBC–September 1961 - September 1962; ABC–30 minutes–September 20, 1964 - September 2, 1973. Syndicated.

ROCKY JONES, SPACE RANGER

Adventure. Era: Twenty-first-century Earth. The battle against interplanetary evil as undertaken by Rocky Jones, chief of the Space Rangers, an organization of men and women established to protect the planets of a united solar system.

CAST
Rocky Jones	Richard Crane
Winky, his assistant	Scott Beckett
Vena Ray, his assistant	Sally Mansfield
Bobby, his junior assistant	Robert Lyden
Professor Newton	Maurice Cass
Yarra, the ruler of the planet Medina	Dian Fauntelle

Rocky's ship: The *Orbit Jet.*

Producer: Roland Reed.

Director: William Beaudine, Hollingsworth Morse.

ROCKY JONES, SPACE RANGER– 30 minutes–NBC–1954 - 1955. 31 episodes. Syndicated.

ROCKY KING, DETECTIVE

Crime Drama. Background: New York City. The investigations of Rocky King, a plainclothes police detective with the Manhattan 24th precinct.

CAST
Rocky King	Roscoe Karns
Sergeant Hart	Todd Karns

Producer: Lawrence Menkin, Charles Speer, Jerry Layton.

Director: Dick Sandwick.

Sponsor: American Chicle.

ROCKY KING, DETECTIVE–30 minutes–DuMont–1950 - 1951. Original title: "Inside Detective."

ROD BROWN OF THE ROCKET RANGERS

Adventure. Era: Twenty-second-century Earth. The battle against interplanetary evil as undertaken by the Rocket Rangers, a celestial defense organization established on Omega Base. Stories relate the work of Ranger Rod Brown as he explores the unknown realms of outer space.

CAST
Ranger Rod Brown	Cliff Robertson
Ranger Frank Boyle	Bruce Hall
Commander Swift	John Boruff
Ranger Wilbur Wormser (Wormsey)	Jack Weston
Also	Shirley Standlee

Rod's rocket ship: The *Beta.*

Program Open:

Announcer: "CBS Television presents Rod Brown of the Rocket Rangers. Surging with the power of the atom, gleaming like great silver bullets, the mighty Rocket

Rangers space ships, stand by for blast-off. [Rockets are seen blasting off.] Up, up, rockets blazing with white hot fury, the man-made meteors ride through the atmosphere, breaking the gravity barrier, pushing up and out, faster and faster and then outer space and high adventure for the Rocket Rangers."

ROD BROWN OF THE ROCKET RANGERS—30 minutes—CBS—April 18, 1953 - May 29, 1954.

ROD ROCKET

A cartoon series, based on space travel, that details the adventures of Rod Rocket, his sidekick Joey, and Professor Argus. 130 five minute films, Syndicated 1962.

ROD SERLING'S NIGHT GALLERY

See title: "Four-In-One," *Night Gallery* segment.

THE ROGER MILLER SHOW

Musical Variety.

Host: Roger Miller.

Regulars: Arthur Godfrey, The Doodletown Pipers.

Orchestra: Eddie Karam.

THE ROGER MILLER SHOW—30 minutes—NBC—September 12, 1966 - January 3, 1967. 16 tapes.

ROGER RAMJET

Animated Cartoon. Experimenting, scientist Roger Ramjet discovers a pill that, when taken, endows him with the power of twenty atom bombs for twenty seconds. Incorporating its power, he battles the sinister forces of evil.

ROGER RAMJET—05 minutes—Syndicated 1965. 150 episodes.

THE ROGUES

Drama. Background: London, England. The saga of the Fleming-St. Clairs, a family of con artists who devise ingenious schemes to steal treasures from those who can afford to be robbed, or deserve to be.

CAST

Alec Fleming, British, the head of the family	David Niven
Marcel St. Clair, the Suave French cousin	Charles Boyer
Tony Fleming, the American cousin	Gig Young
Timmy Fleming, an English cousin	Robert Coote

The Rogues. Left to right: Gig Young, Charles Boyer, David Niven.

Margaret Fleming, an
English cousin   Gladys Cooper
Scotland Yard Inspector
Briscoe   John Williams.

Music: Nelson Riddle.

THE ROGUES—60 minutes—NBC—
September 13, 1964 - September 5,
1965. 29 episodes. Syndicated.

ROLL OUT!

Comedy. Background: World War II
France (1944). The saga of the men
assigned to the 5050th Quartermaster
Trucking Company of the U.S. Third
Army's Red Ball Express, the mostly
black American trucking company
designed to deliver supplies to the
front lines, swing around, and return
for more.

CAST

Cpl. Carter "Sweet"
Williams, a
smooth-talking, conniving
draftee from
Harlem   Stu Gilliam
Pfc. Jed Brooks,
his sidekick, a
Southern draftee, a
country boy
responsive to the
system   Hilly Hicks
Sgt. B.J. Bryant   Mel Stewart
Captain Rocco Calvelli,
the C.O.   Val Bisoglio
Lt. Robert Chapman   Ed Begley, Jr.
Madame Delacourt, the
owner of the
restaurant   Penny Santon
Wheels Dawson   Garrett Morris
High Strung   Theodore Wilson
Jersey Hampton   Darrow Igus
Phone Booth   Rod Gist
Focus   Jeff Burton
Sergeant Grease, the
cook   Sam Laws

Music: Dave Grusin; Benny Golson.

ROLL OUT!—30 minutes—CBS—
October 5, 1973 - January 4, 1974. 13
episodes.

ROLLIN' ON THE RIVER

Musical Variety. Background: The
Mississippi River Boat, the *River
Queen.*

Host: Kenny Rodgers.

Regulars: The First Edition: Mary
Arnold, Terry Williams, Kin
Vassey, Mickey Jones.

Musical Direction: Larry Cansler.

ROLLIN' ON THE RIVER—30 minutes—Syndicated 1971. 26 tapes. Also
titled: "Rollin' with Kenny Rodgers
and The First Edition."

ROMAN HOLIDAYS

Animated Cartoon. Twentieth-century
life is depicted in Ancient Rome.
Background: 4960 Terrace Drive, the
Venus DiMillo Arms apartment house
in Pastafasullo, Rome, A.D. 63—the
residence of the Holidays: Gus, an
engineer with the Forum Construction
Company; his wife, Laurie; and their
children Precocia and Happius. Stories
depict the trials and tribulations of a
family as they struggle to cope with
the endless problems of a changing
world. A Hanna-Barbera production.

Characters' Voices
Gus Holiday   Dave Willock
Laurie Holiday   Shirley Mitchell
Precocia Holiday   Pamelyn Ferdin
Happius Holiday
(Happy)
                      Stanley Livingston
Mr. Evictus, the
Landlord   Dom De Luise

Mr. Tycoonius, Gus's Employer	Hal Smith
Brutus, the Holiday pet lion	Daws Butler
Groovia, Happy's girlfriend	Judy Strangis
Herman, Gus's friend	Hal Peary
Henrietta, his wife	Janet Waldo

Music: Hoyt Curtin.

ROMAN HOLIDAYS–30 minutes–NBC–September 9, 1972 - September 1, 1973.

ROMANTIC INTERLUDE

Anthology. Rebroadcasts of dramas that were originally aired via other filmed anthology programs.

Included:

The Perfect Gentleman. The story of a self-made man who tries to make himself over to please his fiancée.
Starring: Bruce Cabot.

Angel. The story of a man who pretends to be the guardian angel of a little girl to escape from the police.
Starring: Steve Brodie.

The Return of Van Sickle. An elderly man tries to teach his vicious son-in-law the meaning of kindness.
Starring: Cliff Arquette.

ROMANTIC INTERLUDE–30 minutes–ABC 1955.

ROMPER ROOM

Educational. Entertainment geared to preschoolers. A basic format, which includes sets, games, songs, stories, and activities, is syndicated to local stations to allow the inclusion of their own instructresses.

Hostesses-Instructresses, including: Gloria Flood (WABC-TV, New York); Jean Mosley (WBAC-TV, Baltimore); Rosemary Rapp (WGN-TV, Chicago); Joan Thayer (WNEW-TV, New York); Connie Sullivan (WCDA-TV, Albany, N.Y.); June Hurley (WLCY-TV, Tampa-St. Petersberg, Florida); Louise Redfield (WOR-TV, New York).

ROMPER ROOM–60 minutes–Syndicated 1953.

RONA BARRETT'S HOLLYWOOD

Hollywood Gossip Reports.
Hostess-Commentator: Rona Barrett.

RONA BARRETT'S HOLLYWOOD –2 minutes, 30 seconds (five times weekly)–Syndicated 1969.

THE ROOKIES

Crime Drama. Background: California. The investigations of William Gillis, Terry Webster, Michael Danko, and Chris Owens, Rookies attached to Station Number Seven of the Southern California Police Department. Reluctant to use firearms, they represent the new breed of law enforcer and the nonviolent approach to crime control.

CAST

Lieutenant Edward Ryker	Gerald S. O'Loughlin

Patrolman William
Gillis   Michael Ontkean
Patrolman Terry
Webster   Georg Stanford Brown
Patrolman Michael
Danko   Sam Melville
Jill Danko,
Mike's wife,
a nurse   Kate Jackson
Patrolman Chris
Owens   Bruce Fairbairn
The Police Radio
Dispatcher   Darlyn Ann Lindley

Music: Elmer Bernstein; Lawrence Rosenthal; Pete Rugolo; Jack Elliott, Allyn Ferguson.

Executive Producer: Aaron Spelling, Leonard Goldberg.

Producer: Rick Husky, Skip Webster, William Blinn, Paul Junger Witt, Hal Sitowitz.

Director: E.W. Swackhamer, Phil Bondelli, Alvin Ganzer, Leonard Horn, Lee Philips, Gene Nelson, Harry Falk, Gerald S. O'Loughlin, Ralph Senesky, Jerry Jamison, Walter Claxton, Michael Caffrey, Ivan Dixon, Fernando Lamas.

Creator: Rita Lakin.

Note: Jill works at Memorial Hospital.

THE ROOKIES—60 minutes—ABC—September 11, 1972 - June 15, 1976. 68 episodes.

ROOM FOR ONE MOORE

Comedy. Background: Los Angeles, California. Incidents in the lives of the Rose family: George, an engineer; his wife, Anna; and their children, Laurie and Flip (their own); and Jeff and Mary (adopted). Stories depict Anna's fond love of children and her attempts to help the misplaced and lonely. Based on the film, "The Easy Way."

CAST

George Rose   Andrew Duggan
Anna Rose   Peggy McCay
Laurie Rose   Carol Nicholsen
Flip Rose   Ronnie Dapo
Jeff Rose   Timmy Rooney
Mary Rose   Anna Capri
Walter Burton, their
neighbor   Jack Albertson
Ruth Burton, his
wife   Marine Stuart
Elsie, Anna's
friend   Sara Seeger

Rose Family Dog: Tramp.

Music: Paul Sawtell, Frank Perkins.

ROOM FOR ONE MORE—30 minutes—ABC—January 27, 1962 - September 22, 1962. 26 episodes. Syndicated.

ROOM 222

Comedy-Drama. Background: Walt Whitman High School in Los Angeles, California. Life in an integrated urban high school as seen through the eyes of Pete Dixon, a black American History instructor whose classes are held in Room 222.

CAST

Pete Dixon   Lloyd Haynes
Seymour Kaufman, the
principal   Michael Constantine
Liz Macintyre,
the guidance counselor,
Pete's romantic
interest   Denise Nicholas
Alice Johnson,
a student
teacher   Karen Valentine
Miss Evans   Hollis Irving
Miss Hogarth   Patsy Garret
Miss Portnoy   Carol Worthington

Room 222. Left to right: Lloyd Haynes, Karen Valentine, Michael Constantine.

Students:

Richie Lane	Howard Rice
Jason Allen	Heshimu
Larry	Eric Laneuville
Pamela	Ta Tanisha
Helen Loomis	Judy Strangis
Bernie	David Jolliffe
Laura	Pamela Peters

Music: Richard La Salle.

Additional Music: Jerry Goldsmith, Lionel Newman, Benny Golson.

Executive Producer: William P. D'Angelo.

Producer: Gene Reynolds, Jon Kubichan, Ronald Rubin.

Director: Allen Baron, Seymour Robbie, Lee Philips, Hal Cooper, Herman Hoffman, James Sheldon, Leslie H. Martinson, Richard Michaels, Charles R. Rondeau, William Wiard, Gene Reynolds.

Creator: James L. Brooks.

ROOM 222–30 minutes–ABC–September 17, 1969 - January 11, 1974. Syndicated.

ROOTIE KAZOOTIE

Children. Puppet antics set against the background of the Rootie Kazootie Club.

Host: Todd Russell.

Assistant: John Schoepperle as Mr. Deetle Dootle.

Puppet characters: Rootie Kazootie, a freckle-faced little boy; Gala

Poochie Pup, his wide-eyed dog; Polka Dottie, Rootie's girlfriend; El Squeako the mouse; Nipper, Catador, and Poison Sumac.

Producer: Steve Carlin.

Director: Dwight Hemion.

ROOTIE KAZOOTIE—30 minutes—ABC—January 3, 1952 - February 5, 1954. NBC run: October 13, 1951 - November 21, 1952.

ROOTS

Drama. An eight-part adaptation of the novel by Alex Haley, which dramatizes a century in Haley's family history—from his ancestors' life in 18th-century tribal Africa to their emancipation in the post-Civil War South.

CAST

Kunta Kinte	LeVar Burton
	John Amos
Binta, Kunta's mother	Cicely Tyson
Omoro, Kunta's father	Thalmus Rasulala
Capt. Thomas Davies	Edward Asner
Slater	Ralph Waite
Brima Cesay	Harry Rhodes
Fanta	Ren Woods
	Beverly Todd
Nyo Boto	Maya Angelou
Kintango	Moses Gunn
Reynolds	Lorne Greene
Fiddler	Louis Gossett, Jr.
Ames	Vic Morrow
Dr. William Reynolds	Robert Reed
Mrs. Reynolds	Lynda Day George
Kizzy	Leslie Uggams
Missy Anne Reynolds	Sandy Duncan
Mrs. Moore	Carolyn Jones
Noah	Lawrence-Hilton Jacobs
Tom Moore	Chuck Connors
Sam Bennett	Richard Roundtree
Kadi Touray	O.J. Simpson
Tom	Georg Stanford Brown
Chicken George	Ben Vereen
Irene	Lynne Moody
Evan Brent	Lloyd Bridges
Jeremy Brent	Doug McClure
Ol' George	Brad Davis
Virgil	Austin Stoker
Senator Justin	Burl Ives

Also: Todd Bridges, Robert Phalen, Macon McColman, Lillian Randolph, Wally Taylor, William Watson.

Music: Gerald Fried.

Executive Producer: David L. Wolper.

Producer: Stan Margulies.

Director: David Greene, John Erman, Gilbert Moses, Marvin Chomsky.

ROOTS—12 hours—ABC—January 23, 1977 - January 30, 1977.

ROSEMARY CLOONEY

Listed: The television programs of singer Rosemary Clooney.

The Rosemary Clooney Show—Musical Variety—30 minutes—Syndicated—1956 - 1957.

Hostess: Rosemary Clooney.

Vocalists: The Hi-Lo's.

Orchestra: Nelson Riddle.

The Rosemary Clooney Show—Musical Variety—30 minutes—NBC—September 26, 1957 - June 19, 1958.

Hostess: Rosemary Clooney.

Vocalists: Paul Kelly and The Modernaires.

Orchestra: Frank DeVol.

ROSETTI AND RYAN

Drama. Background: California. The cases of Joseph Rosetti and Frank Ryan, a playboy and an ex-cop, now freewheeling attorneys who incorporate unorthodox methods as they strive to seek justice for their clients.

CAST

Joseph Rosetti	Tony Roberts
Frank Ryan	Squire Fridell
Jessica Hornesby, the assistant D.A.	Jane Elliot
Rocky (originally Georgia), Joe's secretary	Randi Oakes
Rosa Rosetti, Joe's mother	Penny Santon

Music: Peter Matz, Gordon Jenkins.

Executive Producer: Leonard B. Stern.

Producer: Jerry Davis.

ROSETTI AND RYAN—60 minutes—NBC—Premiered: September 22, 1977.

THE ROSEY GRIER SHOW

Variety.

Host: Rosey Grier.

Featured: Charles Brown, columnist.

THE ROSEY GRIER SHOW—30 minutes—Syndicated 1969. 52 tapes.

THE ROUGH RIDERS

Western. Background: Various areas between the Great Smokies and the High Sierras during the 1860s. Following the surrender at Appomattox, two Union officers, Captain Jim Flagg and Sergeant Buck Sinclair, and one Confederate, Lieutenant Kirby, team and journey West to begin a new life. Seeking land on which to settle, they involve themselves in and attempt to solve the problems of others.

CAST

Captain Jim Flagg	Kent Taylor
Lieutenant Kirby	Jan Merlin
Sergeant Buck Sinclair	Peter Whitney

THE ROUGH RIDERS—30 minutes—ABC—October 2, 1958 - September 24, 1959. 39 episodes. Syndicated.

THE ROUNDERS

Comedy. Background: The J. L. Cattle Ranch. The saga of two dim-witted cowboys, hired hands, Ben Jones and Howdy Lewis.

CAST

Jim Ed Love, the ranch owner	Chill Wills
Ben Jones	Ron Hays
Howdy Lewis	Patrick Wayne
Sally, Ben's girlfriend	Janis Hansen
Ada, Howdy's girlfriend	Bobbi Jordan
Vince, Jim Ed's right-hand man	J. Pat O'Malley
Shorty Davis, a ranch hand	Jason Wingreen

Music: Jeff Alexander.

THE ROUNDERS—30 minutes—ABC—September 6, 1966 - January 3, 1967. 17 episodes.

ROUTE 66

Adventure. Left penniless after the death of his wealthy father, Tod

Route 66. George Maharis and Martin Milner. © *Screen Gems.*

THE ROWAN AND MARTIN SHOW

Variety. Music, songs, and comedy sketches.

Hosts: Dan Rowan, Dick Martin.

Regulars: Frankie Randall, Lainie Kazan, Judi Rolin, The Wisa D'Orso Dancers.

Orchestra: Les Brown.

THE ROWAN AND MARTIN SHOW —60 minutes—NBC—June 16, 1966 - September 8, 1966.

ROYAL CANADIAN MOUNTED POLICE

Adventure. Background: Shamattawa, Canada, a base of the Royal Canadian Mounted Police. Stories depict the investigations of three Canadian policemen and the methods incorporated in the battle against crime.

CAST

Corporal Jacques Gagnier	Gilles Pelletier
Constable Scott	John Perkins
Constable Mitchell	Don Francks

ROYAL CANADIAN MOUNTED POLICE—30 minutes—Syndicated 1960. 39 episodes. Also known as "R.C.M.P."

ROYAL PLAYHOUSE

Anthology. Retitled episodes of dramas originally aired via "Fireside Theatre" during its 1949 - 1950 season.

Producer: Bing Crosby Enterprises.

ROYAL PLAYHOUSE—30 minutes— DuMont 1953. 32 episodes.

Stiles, and Buzz Murdock, an employee of Tod's father, a poor boy from New York's Hell's Kitchen, pool their resources, purchase a 1960 Chevrolet, and begin an uncertain journey, wandering along the highway of Route 66.

Seeking work and eventually a place to settle down, they involve themselves in and attempt to solve the problems of others.

CAST

Tod Stiles	Martin Milner
Buzz Murdock	George Maharis
Linc Case, a Vietnam war veteran, Tod's partner in later episodes	Glen Corbett

Music: Nelson Riddle.

Producer: Herbert B. Leonard, Jerry Thomas, Leonard Freeman, Sam Manners.

ROUTE 66—60 minutes—CBS—October 7, 1960 - September 18, 1964. 116 episodes. Syndicated.

ROYAL SHOWCASE

Variety. Performances by an established or up and coming comic, movie figure, or recording personality.

Host: George Abbott.

Announcer: Ben Grauer.

Orchestra: Gordon Jenkins.

ROYAL SHOWCASE—30 minutes—NBC 1952.

THE ROY ROGERS AND DALE EVANS SHOW

Musical Variety. Performances by Country and Western entertainers.

Hosts: Roy Rogers and Dale Evans (Mrs.)

Regulars: Pat Brady, Cliff Arquette, The Sons of the Pioneers, and the Rogers's children: Dodie, Debbie, Dusty, and Sandy.

Orchestra: Ralph Carmichael.

Producer: Ralph Wonders, Bob Henry.

Director: Bob Henry.

THE ROY ROGERS AND DALE EVANS SHOW—60 minutes—ABC—September 29, 1962 - December 23, 1962.

THE ROY ROGERS SHOW

Modern Western. Background: The Double R Bar Ranch in Mineral City. The exploits of Roy Rogers and Dale Evans, ranchers and the owners of a diner, as they strive to maintain law and order. Spiced with light comedy.

CAST

Roy Rogers, "King of the Cowboys"	Himself
Dale Evans, "Queen of the West"	Herself
Pat Brady, the diner cook	Himself
Mayor Ralph Cotton	Harry Lauter
Sheriff Potter	Harry Harvey, Sr.

Also: The Sons of the Pioneers: Bob Nolan, Karl Farr, Lloyd Perryman, Hugh Farr.

Orchestra: Lou Bring.

Theme: "Happy Trails To You."

Producer: Jack Lacey, Bob Henry, Roy Rogers, Leslie H. Martinson.

Sponsor: General Foods.

Roy's horse: Trigger.

Dale's horse: Buttercup.

Pat's jeep: Nellybelle.

Roy's dog: Bullet.

Program Open:

Announcer: "The Roy Rogers Show, starring Roy Rogers, king of the cowboys; Trigger, his golden Palomino; and Dale Evans, queen of the West. With Pat Brady, his comical sidekick; and Roy's wonder dog, Bullet."

THE ROY ROGERS SHOW—30 minutes—CBS—October 4, 1951 - September 19, 1964. 100 episodes. Syndicated.

THE RUFF AND READY SHOW

Animated Cartoon. The adventures of Ruff the cat and Ready the dog as they unite to battle the sinister forces of evil. A Hanna-Barbera Production.

Host: Jimmy Blaine.

Characters' Voices

Ruff	Don Messick
Ready	Daws Butler

Additional characters: Professor Gismo, Captain Greedy, Killer and Diller, Salt Water Daffy, Harry Safari.

THE RUFF AND READY SHOW—30 minutes—NBC—December 14, 1957 - September 1964. Syndicated.

THE RUGGLES

Comedy. The trials and tribulations of the Ruggles family.

CAST

Charlie Ruggles	Himself
Mrs. Ruggles	Erin O'Brien Moore
	Ruth Tedrow
Sharon Ruggles, their daughter	Margaret Kerry

Also: Judy Nugent, Jimmy Hawkins, Tommy Bernard.

Music: Fred Howard

Producer: Robert Raisbeck.

Director: George M. Cahan.

THE RUGGLES—30 minutes—ABC— January 1, 1950 - April 1, 1950.

RUN, BUDDY, RUN

Comedy. Background: Los Angeles, California. In a clouded steam room, the unsuspecting meeting place of gangland hoods, Buddy Overstreet, a mild-mannered accountant, overhears their plotting of the killing of "The Man in Chicago," and the mysterious words, "Chicken Little." Spotted by Mr. Devere, the underworld boss, Buddy is chased, but escapes capture. Considered a threat to their plan of operation, Devere orders Buddy's apprehension. Endlessly pursued by the mob, Buddy struggles to avoid being captured and to resolve the differences between him and Devere.

CAST

Buddy Overstreet	Jack Sheldon
Mr. Devere	Bruce Gordon
Junior Devere	Jim Connell

Devere's Aides:

Harry	Gregg Palmer
Wendell	Nick Georgiade
Joseph	Dort Clark

RUN, BUDDY, RUN—30 minutes— CBS—September 12, 1966 - January 2, 1967. 16 episodes.

RUN FOR YOUR LIFE

Adventure. Discovering he has only a short time to live when a medical report reveals he is dying of an incurable disease, attorney Paul Bryan decides to cram a lifetime of living into his remaining one or two years. Clinging to the slim hope of a medical breakthrough, he travels around the world and involves himself in and attempts to solve the problems of others.

CAST

Paul Bryan	Ben Gazzara
The doctor (program opening)	John Hoyt

Music: Pete Rugolo.

RUN FOR YOUR LIFE—60 minutes —NBC—September 13, 1965 - September 11, 1968. 85 episodes. Syndicated.

RUN, JOE, RUN

Adventure. Distinguished by two formats.

Format One:

Falsely accused of attacking his master, Joe, a black and tan army trained German Shepherd dog, escapes before he is able to be destroyed. Declared an army fugitive, a two hundred dollar reward is posted for his capture. Able to prove his innocence, his master, Sergeant William Corey, begins a cross-country trek and, against numerous obstacles, attempts to capture Joe and clear his name.

Starring: Arch Whiting as Sgt. William Corey.

Music: Richard La Salle.

RUN, JOE, RUN—30 minutes—NBC —September 7, 1974 - August 30, 1975. Returned: NBC—December 6, 1975 - September 4, 1976.

Format Two:

Before he is able to prove Joe's innocence, Sgt. Corey is ordered back to active duty. Still wandering, Joe meets and befriends Josh McCoy, a backpacker who is unaware of Joe's past. Stories depict their adventures as they travel across the country.

Starring: Chad States as Josh McCoy.

Music: Richard La Salle.

RUN, JOE, RUN—30 minutes—NBC —September 6, 1975 - November 29, 1975.

RUNAROUND

Game. Nine children compete. After the host reads a question, three answers appear on stage. On the word "go" the players run to the lane that they each believe is the correct answer. A light reveals the correct answer, and players standing on that particular lane receive one token. Other players are placed in a penalty box. The game continues until two players remain. Each is then asked a question. The player who correctly answers it is the winner and receives one additional token. The players are removed from the penalty box and a new game begins. Winners, the highest token accumulators, receive merchandise prizes.

Host: Paul Winchell.

Assistants: His dummy friends, Jerry Mahoney and Knucklehead Smith.

Announcer: Kenny Williams.

Music: Mort Garson.

RUNAROUND—30 minutes—NBC— September 9, 1972 - September 1, 1973.

THE RUSS MORGAN SHOW

Musical Variety.

Host: Russ Morgan.

Vocalist: Helen O'Connell.

Orchestra: Russ Morgan.

THE RUSS MORGAN SHOW—60 minutes—CBS—July 7, 1956 - September 1, 1956.

RUTHIE ON THE TELEPHONE

Comedy. Via a split-screen effect, which is accomplished through mirrors, a girl relentlessly pursues a guy, who'd rather be left alone, by telephone. Adapted from a sketch on the CBS radio program, "The Robert Q. Lewis Show."

CAST

Ruthie	Ruth Gilbert
The guy	Philip Reed

RUTHIE ON THE TELEPHONE—05 minutes—CBS 1948.

RUTH LYONS 50 CLUB

Variety. Music, songs, guests, interviews, and household tips.

Hostess: Ruth Lyons.

Regulars: Dick Noell, Bill Thall.

Orchestra: Bert Farber.

RUTH LYONS 50 CLUB—60 minutes—NBC 1951.

RYAN'S HOPE

Serial. Background: The upper West Side in New York City. The triumphs and tragedies of three generations of an Irish-American family, the Ryans.

CAST

John Ryan	Bernard Barrow
Mary Ryan	Kate Mulgrew
Maeve Ryan	Helen Gallagher
Frank Ryan	Michael Hawkins
	Andrew Robinson
Delia Ryan	Ilene Kristen
Dr. Pat Ryan	Malcolm Groome
Jack Fenelli	Michael Levin
Jillian Coleridge	Nanci Addison
Dr. Clem Moultrie	Hannibal Penney
Nell Baulac	Diana van der Vlis
Dr. Roger Coleridge	Ron Hale
Faith Coleridge	Faith Catlin
	Nancy Barrett
	Catherine Hicks
Ramona Gonzalez	Rosalinda Guerra
Dr. Edward Coleridge	Frank Latimore
Dr. Bucky Carter	Justin Deas
Bob Reid	Earl Hindman
Nick Szabo	Michael Fairman
Seneca Baulac	John Gabriel
Annie Burney	Jody Catlin
Tom Desmond	Tom MacGreevey
Alicia	Anita Ortiz
Father Richards	Bernie McInerney
Alex Webster	Ed Evanko

Music: Aelous Productions.

Music Supervision: Sybil Weinberger.

Additional Music: Carey Gold.

Producer: Robert Costello, Monroe Carroll.

Director: Lela Swift.

RYAN'S HOPE—30 minutes—ABC— Premiered: July 7, 1975.

S

SABER OF LONDON

See title: "Mark Saber."

SABRINA, THE TEEN-AGE WITCH

Animated Cartoon. Background: The town of Riverdale. The misadventures of Sabrina, a high school student and apprentice witch who struggles to conceal the existence of her powers. A spin-off from "The Archie Show."

Characters:
Sabrina, Aunt Hilda, Aunt Zelda, Archie Andrews, Jughead Jones, Reggie Mantle, Veronica Lodge, Valerie, Hot Dog (the Archie gang

pet), Salem (Sabrina's cat), Harvey, Mr. Weatherby (the school principal), Miss Grundy (a teacher), Cousin Ambrose, The Groovie Goolies.

Voices: Larry Storch, Jane Webb, Dallas McKennon, John Erwin, Don Messick, Howard Morris.

Music: George Blais, Jeff Michael.

SABRINA, THE TEEN-AGE WITCH —30 minutes—CBS—September 11, 1971 - September 1, 1973. Originally broadcast as "Sabrina and the Groovie Goolies"—60 minutes—CBS—September 12, 1970 - September 4, 1971. 35 episodes.

SAFARILAND

Documentary. Film studies of the animals and people of Africa.

Host-Guide: Jim Stewart.

SAFARILAND—30 minutes—Syndicated 1963.

SAFARI TO ADVENTURE

Documentary. Films exploring the world of man and animal.

Host-Narrator: Bill Burrud.

SAFARI TO ADVENTURE—30 minutes—Syndicated 1971.

SAILOR OF FORTUNE

Adventure. Background: The Mediterranean. The assignments of Grant Mitchell, the captain of an American motor freighter.

CAST
Grant Mitchell   Lorne Greene

His assistant   Jack McGowran

SAILOR OF FORTUNE—30 minutes —Syndicated 1957.

THE SAINT

Adventure. The global exploits of Simon Templar, alias The Saint, a dashing dare-devil free-lance troubleshooter. Wealthy, young, handsome, suave, and sophisticated, he possesses rich and fancy tastes in wine and women; is cunning, ingenious, and a master among thieves; and, though considered criminal by police, assists them in his quest to aid people in distress. Created by Leslie Charteris. An I.T.C. Production.

CAST
Simon Templar, The
    Saint   Roger Moore

The Saint. Roger Moore. *Courtesy Independent Television Corporation; an ATV Company.*

Claude Eustace Teal,
the Chief Inspector
of Scotland
Yard   Winsley Pithey
                        Norman Pitt
                        Ivor Dean

Hoppy, Simon's
houseboy   Percy Herbert

Music: Edwin Astley.

THE SAINT–60 minutes. Syndicated
–1963 - 1966; NBC–May 21, 1967 -
September 2, 1967; NBC–February
18, 1968 - September 14, 1968;
NBC–April 11, 1969 - September 12,
1969. 114 episodes. Syndicated.

SAINTS AND SINNERS

Drama. Background: Manhattan. The
investigations of Nick Alexander,
newspaper reporter-columnist for the
New York Record. Stories present a
behind-the-scenes insight into the
world of newspaper men and women.

CAST
Nick Alexander   Nick Adams
Mark Grainger, the
city editor   John Larkin
Dave Tobak, the
copyeditor   Robert F. Simon
Staff photographer
Klugie   Richard Erdman
Liz Hogan,
the Washington
correspondent   Barbara Rush

SAINTS AND SINNERS–60 minutes
–NBC–September 18, 1962 - January
28, 1963. 18 episodes.

SALE OF THE CENTURY

Game. Three competing contestants
who each receive twenty-five dollars
bidding cash.

Round One: The host reads a general-
knowledge type of question. The first
player to identify himself through a
buzzer signal receives a chance to
answer. If he is correct he scores five
dollars; incorrect, the amount is
deducted. After several questions an
"Instant Bargain" (e.g., "For only
$27.95 you can buy an $800 mink
coat") appears. The player first to
sound his buzzer receives the merchandise; the amount, rounded off to
the nearest dollar, is deducted from
his score.

Round Two: Played the same. Values
or deductions are ten dollars per
question.

Round Three: Played the same.
Values or deductions are twenty-five
dollars per question.

The highest cash scorer is the
winner, and, brought downstage, he is
shown five bargains (e.g., "A $2,400
car for $239"). He is permitted to
purchase any one of the five, providing it is with money earned on the
program. If an item is desired, but the
money is lacking, he is permitted to
compete further to earn the additional
resources.

Host: Jack Kelly; Joe Garagiola.

Announcer: Bill Wendell.

Music: Al Howard, Irwin Bazelon.

SALE OF THE CENTURY–30 minutes–NBC–September 29, 1969 -
July 13, 1973. Syndicated first run
during the 1973-1974 season.

SALLY

Comedy. Distinguised by two formats:

Format One: September 15, 1957 -
February 9, 1958.

The story concerns the global travels of Myrtle Banford, a rich, elderly widow, part owner of the Banford and Bascomb Department Store, and Sally Truesdale, her pretty, young traveling companion.

Format Two: February 16, 1958 - March 30, 1958.

The format change focuses on the misadventures of Sally as she begins work as a salesgirl in Mrs. Banford's store after returning to the U.S.

CAST
Sally Truesdale	Joan Caulfield
Myrtle Banford	Marion Lorne
Bascomb Bleacher, Sr., Sally's employer	Gale Gordon
Jim Kendall, Sally's romantic interest	Johnny Desmond
Junior Bleacher, Bascomb's son	Arte Johnson

Producer: Frank Ross.

SALLY—30 minutes—NBC—September 15, 1957 - March 30, 1958.

SALTY

Adventure. Background: The Cove Marina in Nassau. When their parents are killed by a hurricane in the Bahamas, Taylor Reed and his brother, Tim, are unofficially adopted by their rescuer, Clancy Ames a retired lawyer, now the owner of the marina. Stories depict the difficulties in operating a marina, and the adventures shared by Tim and his pet sea lion, Salty. Filmed in the Bahamas.

CAST
Clancy Ames	Julius Harris
Taylor Reed	Mark Slade
Tim Reed	Johnny Doran
Rod Porterfield, Tim's friend	Vincent Dale

Music: Samuel Matlovsky.

Executive Producer: Kobi Jaeger.

Producer: Monroe Carroll.

Director: Ricou Browning.

SALTY—30 minutes—Syndicated 1974. 26 episodes.

SAM BENEDICT

Crime Drama. Background: San Francisco, California. The cases and courtroom defenses of attorney Sam Benedict. Based on the files of criminal attorney Jacob Ehrlich.

CAST
Sam Benedict	Edmond O'Brien
Hank Tabor, his assistant	Richard Rust
Trudy Warner, his secretary	Joan Tompkins

Music: Nelson Riddle; Jeff Alexander.

SAM BENEDICT—60 minutes—NBC—September 15, 1962 - September 7, 1963. 28 episodes. Syndicated.

THE SAM LEVENSON SHOW

Discussion. Celebrities appear with their children and discuss the problems that exist between them.

Host: Sam Levenson.

Orchestra: Henry Sylvern.

Producer: Irving Mansfield.

Director: Byron Paul.

THE SAM LEVENSON SHOW—30 minutes—CBS—January 27, 1951 - June 30, 1951.

SAMMY AND COMPANY

Variety. Music, songs, dances, interviews, and comedy sketches.

Host: Sammy Davis, Jr.

Regulars: Avery Schreiber, Johnny Brown, Joyce Jillson, Kay Dingle.

Announcer: William B. Williams.

Orchestra: George Rhodes.

SAMMY AND COMPANY—90 minutes—Syndicated 1975.

THE SAMMY DAVIS, JR. SHOW

Musical Variety.

Host: Sammy Davis, Jr.

Featured: The Lester Wilson Dancers.

Orchestra: George Rhodes.

Premiere guests: Richard Burton, Elizabeth Taylor, Nancy Wilson, Corbett Monica, The Will Martin Trio.

THE SAMMY DAVIS, JR. SHOW—60 minutes—NBC—January 7, 1966 - May 1966.

SAMMY KAYE'S MUSIC FROM MANHATTAN

Musical Variety.

Host: Sammy Kaye.

Regulars: Ray Michaels, Hank Kanui, Larry O'Brien, Charles Roder, Johnny McAfee, Joe Mack, Teddy Auletto, Larry Ellis, Lynn Roberts, J. Blasingame Bond, Toby Wright, Joe Macchiaverna, Janice Jones, Harry Reser, Jack Jennings, Richard Dini, Johnny

Amorosa, The Dixieland Quartet, The Kaydettes.

Orchestra: Sammy Kaye.

SAMMY KAYE'S MUSIC FROM MANHATTAN—30 minutes—ABC—September 20, 1958 - June 13, 1959.

SAMSON AND GOLIATH

Animated Cartoon. A battle against crime and corruption as undertaken by a young boy, Samson, and his dog, Goliath. Whenever trouble becomes evident, the boy raises his wrists, touches his bracelets, and utters, "I need Samson power." Instantly he is transformed into the mighty Samson, and his dog into the vicious lion, Goliath.

Characters' Voices
Samson   Tim Matthieson

Music: Hoyt Curtin.

SAMSON AND GOLIATH—30 minutes—NBC—September 9, 1967 - September 7, 1968. 26 episodes. Syndicated.

SAN FRANCISCO BEAT

See title: "Line-Up."

SAN FRANCISCO INTERNATIONAL AIRPORT

See title: "Four-In-One," *San Francisco International Airport* segment.

THE SAN PEDRO BEACH BUMS

Comedy. Background: San Pedro,

Samson and Goliath. The mighty Samson and his lion, Goliath. *Courtesy Hanna-Barbera Productions.*

California. The misadventures of five knockabout young men (Buddy, Boychick, Dancer, Stuf, and Moose), who live on the *Our Boat* (originally called the *Challenger*), an old fishing boat docked in the San Pedro harbor.

CAST

Buddy Binder	Christopher Murney
Boychick	Jeff Druce
	Christopher DeRose
Edward "Dancer" McClory	John Mark Robinson
Stuf Danelli	Stuart Pankin
Moose	Darryl McCullough
Suzi Camelli, their friend, the operator of a sight-seeing boat	Susan Mullen
Louise, the waitress at Tiny Teena's, the beach café	Louise Hoven
Marge, Moose's girlfriend, the lifeguard	Lisa Reeves
Julie, a friend	Nancy Morgan
Ralphie Walker, a friend	Christoff St. John

Music: Pete Rugolo, Mark Snow.

Executive Producer: Aaron Spelling, Douglas S. Cramer.

Producer: E. Duke Vincent, Earl Barret, Simon Munter.

Creator: E. Duke Vincent.

THE SAN PEDRO BEACH BUMS—60 minutes—ABC—Premiered: September

19, 1977. Originally titled "The San Pedro Bums."

THE SANDY DUNCAN SHOW

Comedy. Background: 130 North Weatherly, the Royal Weatherly Hotel, Apartment 2-A, the residence of Sandy Stockton, a student teacher enrolled in U.C.L.A., and a part-time secretary employed with the advertising agency of Quinn and Cohen. Stories depict her misadventures as she struggles to divide her time between work, school, and studies. A spin-off from "Funny Face."

CAST

Sandy Stockton	Sandy Duncan
Bert Quinn, her employer	Tom Bosley
Kay Fox, Sandy's neighbor	Marian Mercer
Hilary, the agency receptionist	Pamela Zarit
Alex Lembert, Sandy's neighbor, a police officer	M. Emmet Walsh
Leonard Cohen, Bert's partner	Alfie Wise
Ben Hampton, the building janitor	Eric Christmas

Music: Pat Williams.

THE SANDY DUNCAN SHOW—30 minutes—CBS—September 17, 1972 - December 31, 1972. 13 episodes.

SANDY STRONG

A fifteen minute puppet show first seen on ABC in 1950.

SANFORD AND SON

Comedy. Background: 9114 South Central, Los Angeles, California, the residence and business address of Fred and Lamont Sanford, black junk dealers. Fred, a sixty-five-year-old widower who refuses to retire, is satisfied with the business; Lamont, his thirty-four-year-old son, a bachelor, is dissatisfied with existing conditions and wants to better himself by beginning a new life on his own. Fearing his life will be meaningless without Lamont, Fred struggles to keep him with him by feigning illness, usually heart attacks, and calling on his deceased wife—"Elizabeth, I'm coming Elizabeth." Aware of his pretense, Lamont remains, saving his money, and hoping one day to establish a life of his own.

Stories depict their continual bickering and their misadventures as they struggle to operate a junk business. Based on the British series "Steptoe and Son."

CAST

Fred Sanford	Redd Foxx
Lamont Sanford	Demond Wilson

The Sandy Duncan Show. Sandy Duncan.

Grady Wilson, Fred's
friend   Whitman Mayo

Aunt Esther, Elizabeth's
sister   LaWanda Page

Rollo Larson, Lamont's
friend   Nathaniel Taylor

Julio, the Sanfords'
neighbor   Gregory Sierra

Melvin, Fred's
friend   Slappy White

Officer Swanhauser,
L.A.P.D.   Norman Pitlik

Officer Smith (Smitty),
L.A.P.D.   Hal Williams

Officer Hoppy,
L.A.P.D.   Howard T. Platt

Bubba, Fred's
friend   Don Bexley

Donna Harris,
Fred's romantic
interest   Lynn Hamilton

Leroy, Fred's
friend   Leroy Daniels

May Hopkins, Hoppy's
mother   Nancy Kulp

Woody Anderson, Esther's
husband   Raymond Allen

Janet, Lamont's
girlfriend   Marlene Clark

Roger, Janet's son, from
a marriage that ended
in divorce   Edward Crawford

Frances Victor, Fred's
sister   Mary Alice

Rodney Victor, Frances's
husband   Allan Drake

Music: Quincy Jones.

Executive Producer: Norman Lear, Bud Yorkin.

Producer: Bernie Orenstein, Saul Turteltaub.

Director: Norman Abbott, Chick Liotta, Peter Baldwin, Russ Petranto, Mike Warren, Alan Rafkin.

British Cast ("Steptoe and Son"):
Albert Steptoe   Wilfred Bramwell

Harold Steptoe   Harry H. Corbett

SANFORD AND SON—30 minutes—NBC—Premiered: January 14, 1972.

SANFORD ARMS

Comedy. A spin-off from "Sanford and Son." Background: 9114 South Central, Los Angeles, California, the address of the Sanford Arms, a junkyard turned rooming house owned and operated by Phil Wheeler, a widower and retired Army man with two children who purchased the residence from Fred Sanford as an investment to enable him to remain home and raise his children, Angie and Nat. The series focuses on his attempts to cope with the numerous problems associated with running a rooming house.

CAST

Phil Wheeler   Theodore Wilson
Angie Wheeler   Tina Andrews
Nat Wheeler   John Earl
Esther Anderson, the
landlady   LaWanda Page
Woody Anderson, Esther's
husband   Raymond Allen
Jeannie, Phil's
girlfriend   Bebe Drake-Hooks
Grady Wilson, a
tenant   Whitman Mayo
Bubba, the handyman-
bellboy   Don Bexley

Music: Henry Mancini.

Executive Producer: Bud Yorkin, Saul Turteltaub, Bernie Orenstein.

Producer: Woody Kling.

SANFORD ARMS—30 minutes—NBC—Premiered: September 16, 1977.

Sara. Brenda Vaccaro.

SARA

Western Drama. Background: Independence, Colorado, 1870. The story of Sara Yarnell, a pretty schoolteacher who leaves what she considers to be a dull existence in Philadelphia to teach school in the West. Episodes revolve around her difficulties as she struggles to educate the town of Independence.

CAST

Sara Yarnell	Brenda Vaccaro
Emmett Ferguson, her friend, a rancher	Bert Kramer
Martin Pope, publisher of the *Bulletin,* the town newspaper	Albert Stratton
Julia Bailey, Sara's friend	Mariclare Costello
George Bailey, Julia's husband, the owner of the bank	William Wintersole
Claude Barstow, the mayor	William Phipps
Martha Higgins, the owner of the boarding house	Louise Latham
Emma Higgins, her daughter	Hallie Morgan
Deborah Higgins, her daughter	Debbie Leyton
Samuel Higgins, Martha's husband	Al Henderson
Georgie Bailey, Julia's son	Kraig Metzinger
Claranet, the Bailey's housekeeper	Silva Soares
Frank Dixon, a rancher	Jerry Hardin
Jimmy Waggins, a student of Sara's	Stephen Manley

Music: Lee Holdridge.

Music Supervision: Hal Mooney.

Executive Producer: George Eckstein.

Director: Judd Taylor, Stuart Margolin, Gordon Hessler, Alf Kjellin, William F. Claxton, Michael Preece, William Wiard, Daniel Haller.

Creator: Richard Collins.

SARA—60 minutes—CBS—February 13, 1976 - July 30, 1976.

SARGE

Drama. Background: California. Shattered emotionally after his wife is killed by an assassin's bullet that was meant for him, veteran detective Sarge Swanson enters the priesthood. Three years later he is ordained Father Samuel Patrick Cavanaugh and assigned to the Saint Aloysius Parish in San Diego. Still referred to as "Sarge," and using unorthodox methods, he attempts to solve the problems of his urban community.

CAST

Father Samuel Patrick Cavanaugh	George Kennedy
Valerie, his	

secretary   Sallie Shockley
Lieutenant Barney
    Verick   Ramon Bieri
Kenji Takichi,
    the parish athletic
    coach   Harold Sakata

SARGE—60 minutes—NBC—September 21, 1971 - January 11, 1972.

THE SATURDAY NIGHT DANCE PARTY

Variety. Music and comedy set against the background of a country club.

Host: Jerry Lester.

Music: Guest orchestra leaders, including: Ray Malone, Louis Prima, Billy May, Stan Kenton, Lionel Hampton, Ray Anthony.

THE SATURDAY NIGHT DANCE PARTY—60 minutes—NBC—June 7, 1952 - September 1952.

SATURDAY NIGHT LIVE WITH HOWARD COSELL

Variety. Appearances and/or performances by major stars, front-page newsmakers, and celebrities from every continent. Broadcast live from the Ed Sullivan Theatre in New York City.

Host: Howard Cosell.

Regulars: The Peter Gennaro Dancers.

Announcer: John Bartholomew Tucker.

Orchestra: Elliott Lawrence.

Executive Producer: Roone Arledge.

Producer: Rubert Hitzig.

Director: Don Mischer.

SATURDAY NIGHT LIVE WITH HOWARD COSELL—60 minutes—ABC—September 20, 1975 - January 17, 1976.

THE SATURDAY NIGHT REVUE

Variety. Name bands, filmed European variety acts, and performances by show business personalities. Broadcast live from the Studebaker Theatre in Chicago, and the International Theatre on Columbus Circle in New York.

Host (Chicago): Jack Carter.

Host (New York): Sid Caesar.

Also hosting: Eddie Albert, Hoagy Carmichael, Alan Young, Ben Blue.

Regulars: Donald Richards, Jackie Lockridge, Susan Stewart, Misha Elman, Jackie Kannon, Betty Bruce, Anita Dorian, Andy Roberts, Hoctor and Byrd, Lou Wills, Jr., Pat Carroll, Hy Averback, The Bill Callahan Dance Troupe.

Orchestra: Lou Breese; Sauter-Finegan.

THE SATURDAY NIGHT REVUE—2 hours, 30 minutes—NBC—1950 - 1954.

SATURDAY PLAYHOUSE

Anthology. Retitled episodes of "Schlitz Playhouse of Stars."

SATURDAY PLAYHOUSE—30 minutes—CBS 1957.

THE SATURDAY SUPERSTAR MOVIE

Animated Cartoon Features. Subjects

are drawn from real life, TV, literature, films, and comic strips.
Included:

Nanny and the Professor. A spin-off
from the series of the same title. After
the Everett children find a microdot,
Nanny struggles to prevent its theft
until it is returned to the proper
authorities.

Voices: Nanny: Juliet Mills; Professor
    Everett: Richard Long; Hal:
    David Doremus; Prudence: Kim
    Richards; Butch: Trent Lehman.

Gidget Makes the Wrong Connection.
Gidget and her friends attempt to
expose a ring of gold smugglers.

Voices: Gidget: Kathy Gori; Jud:
    David Lander; Steve: Denny
    Evans.

**Lassie and the Secret of Thunder
Mountain.** Lassie's efforts to thwart
plans to build an amusement park on
sacred Indian Lands.

Voices: Father: Ted Knight; Mother:
    Jane Webb; Little Ben: Keith
    Allen.

THE SATURDAY SUPERSTAR
MOVIE—60 minutes—ABC—September 9, 1972 - August 31, 1974.

SAY IT WITH ACTING

Game. Object: For contestants to
identify charades that are performed
on stage.

Hostess: Maggie McNellis.

Performers: Robert Alda, Bud
    Collyer.

SAY IT WITH ACTING—30 minutes
—NBC 1951.

SAY WHEN

Game. Two competing contestants. A
specific amount of money (up to two
thousand dollars) is established, and
various merchandise items are displayed on stage. Unaware of their
selling prices, players have to select
items that add up to, but do not
surpass the established amount. When
both players stop, the value of their
items are totaled, and the player who
has come the closest to the established
amount is the winner and receives the
merchandise items.

Host: Art James.

Producer: Ron Kweskin, Robert S.
    Rowe.

Director: Don Bohl.

SAY WHEN—30 minutes—NBC 1961.

THE SCARLET PIMPERNEL

Adventure. Background: England,
1792. The exploits of Sir Percy
Blakeney, a man of wealth and social
status who adopts the guise of the
mysterious Scarlet Pimpernel (named
after a small, red, star-shaped flower
that is common to the English
countryside). Appearing as the Scarlet
Pimpernel whenever trouble is appar-
ent, he battles injustice in his
endeavor to aid the oppressed.

Starring: Marius Goring as Sir Percy
    Blakeney, The Scarlet Pimpernel.

Orchestra: Sidney Torch.

THE SCARLET PIMPERNEL—30
minutes—Syndicated 1954.

SCARLETT HILL

Serial. Background: The Russell

Boarding House in Scarlett Hill, New York. The dramatic story of three people: Kate Russell, widow, its proprietress; Ginny Russell, her rebellious teenage daughter; and Janice Turner, a young girl residing at the inn.

CAST

Kate Russell	Beth Lockerbie
Ginny Russell	Lucy Warner
Janice Turner	Suzanne Bryant
David Black	Gordon Pinsent
Walter Pendleton	Ivor Barry
Harry Russell	Ed McNamara
Pearl	Cosette Lee
Tom Harvey	Marty Stetrop
Sidney	Alan Pearce
Sandy	Norman Ettlinger
Dr. Spangle	Tony Kramriether

SCARLETT HILL—30 minutes—Syndicated 1965. 260 tapes.

SCENE 70

Musical Variety. Performances by Rock Personalities.

Host: Jay Reynolds.

Featured: The Scene 70 Action Dancers.

Music: Recorded.

SCENE 70—60 minutes—Syndicated 1970.

THE SCHAEFER CENTURY THEATRE

Anthology. Dramatic presentations.

THE SCHAEFER CENTURY THEATRE—30 minutes—NBC 1950.

SCENES FROM A MARRIAGE

Drama. Background: Sweden. A penetrating study of the incidents that break up and lead to a couple divorcing after ten years of marriage. Produced in Sweden; expertly dubbed in English.

CAST

Marianne, the wife	Liv Ullman
Johan, the husband	Eriand Josephson

Hostess: Liv Ullman.

Producer: Lars-Owe Carlberg.

Director: Ingmar Bergman.

English Version Producer: Paulette Rubinstein.

Director of Liv Ullman's Segments: John Marden.

Series Producer: David Griffiths.

SCENES FROM A MARRIAGE—60 minutes—PBS—March 9, 1977 - April 20, 1977. 6 episodes. Originally aired in Sweden in 1973. Broadcast on some PBS stations in both English and Swedish.

SCHLITZ PLAYHOUSE OF STARS

Anthology. Dramatic presentations.

Hostess: Irene Dunne.

Producer: Joseph T. Naar, William Self, Edward Lewis, Felix Jackson, Jules Bricker.

Director: Frank Telford, William H. Brown, Jr., Edward Lewis.

Sponsor: Schlitz Beer.

Included:

For Better or Worse. Accused of a

hit-and-run accident, a woman, a pathological liar, attempts to prove her innocence.

CAST
Irene Wagner: Bette Davis; Van Wagner: John Williams.

The Restless Gun. The pilot film for the series of the same title. A wandering cowboy attempts to save an old friend from a ruthless bounty hunter.

CAST
Britt Pinsett (later changed to Vint Bonner): John Payne; Don Maler: William Hopper; Red Dawson: Andrew Duggan.

The Traveling Corpse. A criminologist professor attempts to solve the mysterious case of a vanishing corpse.

CAST
Prof. Stephen Bolt: Dennis O'Keefe; Doctor: John Baragrey; Mrs. Ditwiter: Leora Dana.

SCHLITZ PLAYHOUSE OF STARS —60 minutes—CBS—1951 - 1955.

SCIENCE FICTION THEATRE

Anthology. Though science fiction in nature, stories present an insight into the problems man faces as he ventures to unravel the mysteries of science and nature.

Host-Narrator: Truman Bradley.

Producer: Ivan Tors.

Director: Leigh Jason, Leon Benson, Jack Arnold.

Included:

Gravity Zero. The work of two scientists as they attempt to discover a method for neutralizing gravity.

CAST
Lisa Gaye, Percy Hilton.

The Legend of Carter Mountain. The story of a school teacher who is confronted with three pupils who possess the power to move objects by thought.

CAST
Marilyn Erskine.

The Miracle of Doctor Dove. A security officer attempts to locate three missing scientists.

CAST
Gene Lockhart.
The Sound of Murder. A scientist attempts to clear himself of a murder charge.

CAST
Howard Duff, Russell Collins.

The Dark Side. The story of an astronomer's efforts to construct a telescopic camera that is capable of photographing the dark side of the moon.

CAST
Skip Homeier.

SCIENCE FICTION THEATRE—30 minutes—Syndicated 1955-1957. 78 episodes.

SCHOOLHOUSE

Variety. Comedy, songs, and performances by undiscovered professional talent. Based on the vaudeville routine "School Days."

Host: Kenny Delmar.

Regulars: Arnold Stang, Maureen Cannon, Betty Ann Morgan, Wally Cox, Tommy Dix, Mary Ann Reeves.

SCHOOLHOUSE – 30 minutes – DuMont 1947.

SCOOBY-DOO, WHERE ARE YOU?

Animated Cartoon. Traveling throughout the country in their car, the *Mystery Machine,* four teenagers, Freddy, Daphne, Velma, and Shaggy, and their Great Dane, Scooby-Doo, a dog who is afraid of his own shadow, all members of a mystery club, involve themselves in and attempt to solve supernatural-based mysteries. A Hanna-Barbera production.

Characters' Voices

Scooby-Doo	Don Messick
Freddy	Frank Welker
Daphne	Heather North
Shaggy	Casey Kaseem
Velma	Nichole Jaffe

Additional Voices: John Stephenson, Henry Cardin, Ann Jillian, Joan Gerber, Ted Knight, Olan Soule, Vincent Van Patten, Cindy Putman, Pat Harrington, Frances Halop, Jim McGeorge, Mike Road.

Music: Hoyt Curtin.

Musical Director: Ted Nichols.

Executive Producer: William Hanna, Joseph Barbera.

Director: Charles A. Nichols.

Scooby-Doo, Where Are You? Left to right: Daphne Blake, Shaggy, Freddy, and Scooby-Doo. *Courtesy Hanna-Barbera Productions.*

SCOOBY-DOO, WHERE ARE YOU?
–30 minutes–CBS–September 13,
1969 - September 2, 1972; 60 minutes–CBS–September 9, 1972 -
August 31, 1974.

THE SCOOBY-DOO/ DYNOMUTT HOUR

Animated Cartoon. Exactly the same
story line, cast, and credits as the
previous title, "Scooby-Doo, Where
Are You?" (which see) with the only
difference being a segment detailing
the exploits of the Blue Falcon and
his assistant, Dynomutt, a mechanical
dog.

THE SCOOBY-DOO/DYNOMUTT
HOUR–55 minutes–ABC–Pre-
miered: September 11, 1976.

SCOOBY'S ALL STAR LAFF-A-LYMPICS

Animated Cartoon.

Segments:

The Laff-A-Lympics. Features three
teams (The Yogi Yahooes; The
Scooby Dooies; and The Really Rot-
tens) competing in wild olympiclike
games throughout the world.

Captain Caveman and the Teenangels.
The story of a fumbling prehistoric
caveman and his three female helpers,
the Teenangels, as they battle crime.

Scooby Doo. The misadventures of a
cowardly dog detective. See title:
"Scooby Doo, Where Are You?" for
information.

The Blue Falcon and Dynomutt. The
adventures of super crime-fighter Blue
Falcon (voiced by Gary Owens) and
his robot dog, Dynomutt.

Announcer: Gary Owens.

Voices: Don Messick, Joan Gerber,
Julie McWhirter, Pat Harrington,
Daws Butler, John Stephenson,
Alan Oppenheimer, Vic Perrin,
Janet Waldo, Frank Welker,
Nichole Jaffe, Heather North,
Casey Kaseem, Jim MacGeorge,
Mike Road.

Music: Hoyt Curtin, Paul DeKorte.

Executive Producer: William Hanna,
Joseph Barbera.

Producer: Iwao Takamoto.

Director: Charles A. Nichols.

SCOOBY'S ALL STAR LAFF-A-
LYMPICS–2 hours–ABC–Premiered:
September 10, 1977. The first two-
hour Saturday morning series.

SCOTLAND YARD

Crime Drama. Background: London,
England. Dramatizations based on the
files of Scotland Yard's Criminal
Investigation Division.

CAST
Host-Narrator	Edgar Lustgarten
Inspector Duggan	Russell Napier
Inspector Ross	Ken Henry
Sergeant Mason	Arthur Mason

SCOTLAND YARD–30 minutes–
Syndicated 1955. ABC run: November 17, 1957 - April 6, 1958. 39
episodes.

SCOTT ISLAND

See title: "Adventures at Scott Island."

SCOTT MUSIC HALL

See title: "Patti Page."

SCREEN DIRECTORS PLAYHOUSE

Anthology. Dramatic and comedic presentations.

Included:

Meet The Governor. The struggles of a mid-west lawyer as he attempts to become the governor of the state.

CAST
Clem Waters: Herb Shriner; June Walo: Barbara Hale; Sonny Waters: Bobby Clark.

The Life of Vernon Hathaway. The story of a meek watch repairman who daydreams himself into exciting adventure.

CAST
Ernest Stockhaffer: Alan Young; Irma: Cloris Leachman; Red Beecham: Douglas Dumbrille.

The Brush Roper. Prone to telling tall tales, an elderly cowpoke attempts to prove his stories true by roping a dangerous bull that is loose in the brush.

CAST
Grandpa Atkins: Walter Brennan; Grandma Jenny: Olive Carey; Cowhide: Lee Aaker; Royal: Edgar Buchanan.

SCREEN DIRECTORS PLAYHOUSE—30 minutes—NBC—October 5, 1955 - September 26, 1956. 35 episodes.

SEA HUNT

Adventure. Background: The Pacific. The investigations of Mike Nelson, an ex-Navy frogman turned underwater troubleshooter. Underwater sequences filmed at Silver Springs, Florida; above-water sequences filmed at Marineland of the Pacific.

Starring: Lloyd Bridges as Mike Nelson.
Music: Ray Llewellyn.

SEA HUNT—30 minutes—Syndicated 1958. 155 episodes

SEALAB 2020

Animated Cartoon. Era: Earth A.D. 2020. The struggles of two hundred fifty men, women, and children, pioneers, as they attempt to maintain sealab 2020, a complex, scientific experimental city constructed beneath the ocean floor. A Hanna-Barbera production.

Characters' Voices
Captain Mike Murphy	John Stephenson
Dr. Paul Williams	Ross Martin
Hal, a diver	Jerry Dexter
Gail, a diver	Ann Jillian
Ed, a diver	Ron Pinckard
Bobby Murphy, the captain's nephew	Josh Albee
Salli Murphy, the captain's	

niece   Pamelyn Ferdin
Sparks, the radio
    dispatcher   Bill Callaway
Jamie   Gary Shapiro
Mrs. Thomas   Olga James

Gail's pet dolphin: Tuffy.

Music: Hoyt Curtin.

SEALAB 2020–30 minutes–NBC–
September 9, 1972 - September 1,
1973. 24 episodes.

SEA WAR

Documentary. Films depicting
Britian's naval battles during World
War II.

Host-Narrator: Rear Admiral Ray
    Foster Brown.

Introductions: Admiral Sir Caspor
    John.
SEA WAR–30 minutes–Syndicated
1963. 13 episodes

SEARCH

Adventure. Background: World Secur-
ities Corporation in Washington,
D.C.–the headquarters of Probe, a
supercomputerized detective agency.
Stories relate the investigations of its
three top operatives: Hugh Lockwood, Probe One; Nick Bianco,
Omega Probe; and Christopher Grove.
Standby Probe–agents who incorporate the ultimate in electronic wizardry:
a super miniaturized two-way radio
that is implanted in the ear; a ring that
houses a miniaturized TV camera and
a scanner; and delicate and highly
sensitive body detectors (implanted
under the skin) that enable whereabouts, heartbeat, and brainwaves to
be transmitted to Probe Control, who
monitor their agents at all times.

CAST
Hugh Lockwood   Hugh O'Brian
Nick Bianco   Tony Franciosa
Christopher R. Grove   Doug McClure
B.C. Cameron,
    the head of
    Probe   Burgess Meredith
Dr. Barnett,
    the senior
    director   Ford Rainey

Probe Control Agents:

Gloria Harding   Angel Tompkins
Kuroda   Byron Chung
Miss Keach   Ginny Golden
Miss James   Pamela Jones
Harris   Tom Hallick
Anna Mulligan   Ann Prentiss
Carlos   Ron Costro
Ramos   Tony DeCosta
Griffin   Albert Popwell
Amy   Cheryl Stoppelmoor

Music: Dominic Frontiere.

SEARCH–60 minutes–NBC–September 12, 1972 - August 29, 1973. 26
episodes.

SEARCH AND RESCUE: THE
ALPHA TEAM

Adventure. Background: The Alpha
Ranch in Canada. The exploits of the
Ganelle family–Bob, a widower, and
his teenage children, Katie and Jim, as
they train wild animals for difficult
rescue missions.

CAST
Bob Ganelle   Michael J. Reynolds
Katie Ganelle   Donann Cavin
Jim Ganelle   Michael Tough

Music: Lew Lehman.

Executive Producer: Seymour Berns, Will Lorin.

Producer: Lew Lehman.

Director: Peter Carter, Lawrence Dobkin.

Creator: Seymour Berns, Ray Freeman, Will Lorin.

SEARCH AND RESCUE: THE ALPHA TEAM—30 minutes—NBC—Premiered: September 10, 1977.

SEARCH FOR BEAUTY

Women. Beauty tips and advice.

Host: Ern Westmore.

Announcer: Dick Hageman.

SEARCH FOR BEAUTY—30 minutes—NBC 1955.

SEARCH FOR THE NILE

Documentary. Through on-location filming, old journals, and letters, the 1857 explorations of Sir Richard Francis Butler and John Hanning Speke, members of the Royal Geographical Society, are recounted as they attempt to uncover the source of the Nile River—the mysterious life source for Africa.

CAST

Sir Richard Butler	Kenneth Haigh
John Hanning Speke	John Quentin
David Livingston	Michael Gough
Henry Stanley	Keith Buckley
Isabel	Barbara Leigh-Hunt
James Grant	Ian McCulloch
Mutesa	Oliver Litondo
Samuel Baker	Norman Rosington
Florence	Catherine Schell

Narrator: James Mason.

Music: Joseph Horowitz.

SEARCH FOR THE NILE—60 minutes—NBC—January 25, 1972 - February 29, 1972. Syndicated.

SEARCH FOR TOMORROW

Serial. Background: The town of Henderson. The dramatic story of Joanne Barron.* Episodes depict the conflicts and tensions that arise from the interactions of the characters.

CAST

Joanne Barron	Mary Stuart
Victor Barron	Cliff Hall
Keith Barron	John Sylvester
Patty Barron	Lynn Loring
	Abigail Kellogg
	Patricia Harty
	Trish Van Devere
	Gretchen Walther
	Melissa Murphy
	Melinda Plank
	Leigh Lassen
	Tina Sloan
Irene Barron	Bess Johnson
Marge Bergman	Melba Raye
Henri Cartier	John LaGioia
Grace Boulton	Jill Clayburgh
Arthur Tate	Terry O'Sullivan
Susan Carter	Sharon Smyth
Ida Weston	Vera Allen
Andrea Whiting	Virginia Gilmore
	Joan Copeland
Dr. Wade Collins	John Cunningham
Stu Bergman	Larry Haines
Doug Martin	Ken Harvey

*Originally Joanne Barron. After her husband, Keith, is killed in an automobile accident, she secures employment in Henderson Hospital where she meets, falls in love with, and marries Arthur Tate. After Arthur's death years later, she marries Dr. Tony Vincente. Her daughter, Patty, also marries a physician, Dr. Len Whiting.

Dr. Dan Walton	Martin Brooks
	Philip Abbott
	Ron Husmann
Dr. Bob Rogers	Carl Low
Dr. Len Whiting	Dino Narizzano
	Jeff Pomerantz
Liz Walton	Denise Nickerson
Gary Walton	Tom Nordon
	John Driver
Scott Phillips	Peter Simon
Jim McCarren	Michael Shannon
Kathy Parker	Courtney Sherman
Carl Devlin	David Ford
Marcy	Jeanne Carson
Eunice Gardiner	Marion Brash
	Ann Williams
Lauri Phillips	Kelly Wood
Eric Lawson	Chris Lowe
Liza Walton	Kathy Beller
Emily Rogers Hunter	Kathryn Walker
Nick Hunter	Ken Kercheval
Helen	Sandy Duncan
Wilbur	Don Knotts
Dr. Murphy	Charles Siebert
Ross Cavanaugh	Keith Charles
Bruce Carson	Bobby Benson
	Garry Tomlin
Sam Reynolds	Robert Mandan
	George Gaynes
	Ray Shuman
Bill Lang	Tom Ewell
Dr. Tony Vincente	Anthony George
Chris	Daniel Leddy
Dr. Facciola	Conrad Bain
Rose Peabody	Lee Grant
	Constance Ford
	Nita Talbot
Dr. Wheeler	Roy Scheider
Dr. Joe Foster	Joe Morton
John Wyatt	Val Dufour
Stephanie Wilkins	Marie Cheatham
Dr. Walter Osmond	Byron Sanders
Miss Markham	Sharon Spellman
Ralph Hayward	James O'Sullivan
Harriet Kane	Chase Crosley
Monica Bergman	Barbara Baxley
Larry Carter	Hal Linden
Hazel	Mary Patton
Rex Twining	Laurence Hugo

Frank Gardiner	Eric Dressler
	Harry Holcombe
Mrs. Millie	Freida Allman
The social worker	Margaret Draper
Agnes Lake	Ann Revere
Fred Metcalf	David O'Brien
Janet Bergman	Ellen Spencer
	Sandy Robinson
	Fran Sharon
	Marian Hailey
	Millee Taggart
Tom Bergman	Peter Broderick
	Ray Bellaran
Nathan Walsh	George Petrie
Ellie Harper	Billie Lou Watt
Brette Moore	Martin Brooks
Allison Simmons	Ann Pearson
Harriet Baxter	Viki Viola
Budd Gardner	George Maharis
Kathy Merritt	Donna Theodore
Ed Minter	Richard Cox
Jennifer Phillips	Morgan Fairchild
Walter Pace	Tom Klunis
Gail Caldwell	Sherry Rooney
Greg Hartford	Robert Rockwell
Ralph Haywood	James O'Sullivan
Wendy Wilkins	Lisa Peluso
	Andrea McArdle
Sam Hunter	Stephen Joyce
Wade Collins	John Cunningham
Dave Wilkins	Dale Robinette
Clay Collins	Brett Halsey

Also: Ross Martin, Margaret Hamilton, Louise Larabee, Lenka Peterson, House Jameson, Sara Anderson, Martin Rudy, Robert Gentry, Audra Lindly, Jan Miner, Ken Rabat.

Announcer: Dwight Weist.

Organists: Chester Kingsbury; Ashley Miller.

SEARCH FOR TOMORROW—15 and 30 minute versions—CBS—Premiered: September 3, 1951.

SEAWAY

Adventure. Background: Montreal, Canada. The investigations of Nick King, an agent for the Ship Owners Association, an organization responsible for security along the Saint Lawrence Seaway.

CAST

Nick King	Stephen Young
Admiral Fox, the head of the Ship Owners Association	Austin Willis

Music: Edwin Astley.

SEAWAY—60 minutes—Syndicated (United States) 1969. Produced in Canada in 1965. 30 episodes.

SECOND CHANCE

Game. Three contestants compete. After a question is read, each player writes his answer on a card, which he places before him. Three possible answers to the question are now revealed and players receive a second chance with which to change their original answers if they wish to. The correct answer is then revealed and points are scored accordingly: three points for an original answer; one point for a second chance answer. Three such questions are played. The number of points earned are now used by the players for spins on a large, electronic prize board (which is divided into a series of small squares containing cash amounts, merchandise prizes, and devils). The machine, which is characterized by flashing lights (to indicate individual boxes) is started. When a player pushes a button, the machine stops and the lights pinpoint one box. Cash or merchandise prizes are added to the players score; a devil erases all earnings up to that point. The second half of the game is played in the same manner and the player who scores the highest cash value is the winner.

Host: Jim Peck.

Announcer: Joe Sider, Jay Stewart, Jack Clark.

Music: Score Productions.

Executive Producer: Bill Carruthers.

Producer: Joel Stein.

Director: Chris Darley.

SECOND CHANCE—30 minutes—ABC—March 7, 1977 - July 15, 1977.

SECOND CITY TELEVISION

Comedy. Background: The ficticious Second City Television Station, Channel 109, in Canada. The program satirizes life at a "typical" television station by spoofing, via short sketches, the programs broadcast throughout the day.

Starring: Andrea Martin, Dave Thomas, John Candy, Catherine O'Hara, Joe Flaherty, Eugene Levy, Harold Ramis.

Music: Recorded.

Producer: Bernard Sahlins, Miland Bessada.

Director: Miland Bessada.

SECOND CITY TELEVISION—30 minutes—Syndicated 1977.

THE SECOND HUNDRED YEARS

Comedy. Alaska, 1900. Prospecting for gold, Luke Carpenter, thirty-three

The Second Hundred Years. Arthur O'Connell and Monte Markham. © *Screen Gems.*

years of age, is buried and frozen alive when caught in an avalanche.

Series background: Woodland Oaks, California, 1967. Summoned to the office of Air Force Colonel Garroway, Edwin Carpenter, sixty-seven years of age, widower and retired businessman, is informed of a recent avalanche in Alaska and of a find—his father, alive, and, though chronologically one hundred years old, physically and mentally unchanged since 1900.

Remaining top secret, the concern of cryogenicists (scientists involved with the study of deep cold), he is released to his son, Edwin, and, returning home, Luke meets his thirty-three-year-old grandson, Ken, his exact double. Stories depict the struggles of a turn-of-the-century prospector to adjust to life in the late 1960s.

CAST

Luke Carpenter	Monte Markham
Ken Carpenter	Monte Markham
Edwin Carpenter	Arthur O'Connell
Colonel Garroway	Frank Maxwell
Erica, Ken's girlfriend	Kay Reynolds
Mr. Tolliver, Ken's employer	Don Beddoe

THE SECOND HUNDRED YEARS— 30 minutes—ABC—September 6, 1967 - September 19, 1968. 26 episodes.

SECRET AGENT

Adventure. The investigations of British Intelligence agent John Drake into situations that endanger world security. A spin-off from "Danger Man."

Starring: Patrick McGoohan as John Drake.

Music: Edwin Astley.

SECRET AGENT–60 minutes–CBS –April 1965 - September 11, 1965; December 4, 1965 - September 10, 1966. 45 episodes. Syndicated.

SECRET FILE, U.S.A.

Adventure. The investigations of American espionage agent Major Bill Morgan and his female assistant Colonel Custer into situations that threaten U.S. security.

CAST

Major Bill Morgan	Robert Alda
Colonel Custer	Lois Hensen
Mrs. Morgan	Kay Callard

Narrator: Frank Gallop.

Music: Ella Sacco.

Producer-Director: Arthur Dreifuss.

SECRET FILE, U.S.A.–30 minutes– Syndicated 1954. 26 episodes.

THE SECRET FILES OF CAPTAIN VIDEO

See title: "Captain Video and His Video Rangers."

THE SECRET LIVES OF WALDO KITTY

Animated Cartoon. The program begins to establish three live-action animals: Waldo, a cat; Felicia, a cat, his girlfriend; and Tyrone, their nemesis, a mean bulldog. When Tyrone becomes a threat to Felicia's safety, Waldo, who is a coward at heart, imagines himself as her heroic savior. The program then becomes animated and each week features Waldo as a different hero struggling to protect Felicia from harm.

Characters' Voices

Waldo Kitty	Howard Morris
Felicia	Jane Webb
Tyrone	Allan Melvin

Music: Yvette Blais, Jeff Michael.

THE SECRET LIVES OF WALDO KITTY–30 minutes–NBC–Premiered: September 6, 1975.

THE SECRETS OF ISIS

CBS's Fall 1977 title for "Isis," which see for information.

SECRETS OF THE DEEP

Documentary. Films exploring mans final frontier–the oceans and seas of the world.

Host-Narrator: Scott Carpenter.

Music: Ugo Calise, Danielle Palucchi.

SECRETS OF THE DEEP–30 minutes–Syndicated 1974.

SECRET SQUIRREL

See title: "The Atom Ant/Secret Squirrel Show."

THE SECRET STORM

Serial. Background: The town of Woodridge. Dramatic incidents in the lives of the Ames family.

CAST

Peter Ames	Peter Hobbs	Keefer	Troy Donahue
	Cec Linder	Kip Ripdale	Don Galloway
	Ward Costello	Ann Wicker	Diana Muldaur
Amy Ames	Jada Rowland	Bob Hill	Roy Scheider
	Lynn Adams	Tim Brannigan	Anthony Herrera
Susan Ames	Jean Mowry		Nicholas Lewis
	Judy Lewis	The Assistant D.A.	Gary Campbell
Jerry Ames	Warren Berlinger	Irene Simms	Jennifer Darling
	Wayne Tippert	Cecilia	Kathleen Cody
Pauline Rysdale	Haila Stoddard	Herbie Vail	Noel Craig
Mr. Tyrell	Russell Hicks	Nola Hollister	Rosemary Murphy
Hugh Clayborn	Peter MacLean		Mary K. Wells
Dan Kincaid	Bernard Barrow	Myra Lake	Joan Hotchkis
Mickey Potter	Larry Block		June Graham
Valerie Northcote	Lori March	Alan Dunbar	Liam Sullivan
Jill Stevens	Barbara Rodell		James Vicary
Kevin Kincaid	David Ackroyd	Frank Carver	Jack Ryland
Belle Clements	Marla Adams		Robert Loggia
Nancy Vallin	Iris Braun		Laurence Luckinbill
Ursula Winthrope	Jacqueline Brooks	Cassie	Mildred Clinton
Paul Britton	Nick Coster	Mark Reddin	David Gale
	Linden Chiles	Dr. Brian Neeves	Jeff Pomerantz
Ken Stevens	Joel Crothers		Keith Charles
Lisa Britton	Judy Safran	Clay Stevens	Jamie Grover
	Diane Dell	Jason Ferris	Robert Alda
	Terri Falis	Robert Landers	Dan Hamilton
Kitty Styles	Diane Ladd	Monsignor Quinn	Sidney Walker
Jonathan Styles	Scott Mefford	Joanna Morrison	Audrey Landers
Peter Dunbar	Donnie Melvin		Ellen Barber
Grace Tyrell	Marjorie Gateson		
	Eleanor Phelps		
Dr. Ian Northcote	Gordon Rigsby		
	Alexander Scourby		
Doug Winthrope	Bruce Sherwood		
Tom Gregory	Richard Venture		
Aggie Parsons	Jane Rose		
Reilly	Joe Ponazecki		
Laurie Stevens	Stephanie Braxton		
Polly	Susan Oakes		
Phil Forrestor	Patrick Fox		
Mike	Devin Goldenberg		
Alden	Cliff de'Young		
Martha Ann			
Ashley	Audre Johnson		
Freddy	Roberta Royce		
Charlotte	Susan Sudert		
Mulholland	Mike Galloway		
Andrea	Roberta Rickett		

Also: Virginia Dwyer, Robin Strasser, Charles Baxter.

Announcer: Ken Roberts.

Music: Carey Gould.

THE SECRET STORM—30 minutes—CBS—February 1, 1954 - February 15, 1974.

SEE IT NOW

Documentary. An in-depth analysis of news-making stories. The program led television news out of infancy and into maturity.

Host: Edward R. Murrow.

Also: Eric Sevaried, Howard K. Smith.

Producer: Edward R. Murrow, Fred W. Friendly, Palmer Williams.

Director: Don Hewitt.

Sponsor: Alco.

SEE IT NOW—30 minutes—CBS—December 2, 1951 - July 7, 1958.

THE SEEKING HEART

Serial. The dramatic story of John Adams, general practitioner and criminologist.

CAST

John Adams	Scott Forbes
Grace Adams	Dorothy Lovett
Dr. McKay	Flora Campbell

Producer: Minerva Ellis.

Sponsor: Procter and Gamble.

THE SEEKING HEART—15 minutes—CBS—July 5, 1954 - December 10, 1954.

THE SENATOR

See title: "The Bold Ones," *The Senator* segment.

SENSE AND NONSENSE

Game. Two competing teams, each composed of three members. Basis: The testing of the five senses (sight, hearing, taste, touch, and smell). Players each compete in rounds that are designed to test one sense without the assist of the others. Points are awarded for each problem that is solved by each sense. Winners, the highest scorers, receive merchandise prizes.

Versions:

Sense and Nonsense—30 minutes—NBC 1952.

Host: Bob Kennedy.

Assistant: Vivian Farrar.

Sense and Nonsense Junior—30 minutes—NBC 1952. A children's version of the adult game.

Host: Ralph Paul.

Assistant: Vivian Farrar.

THE SENTIMENTAL AGENT

Adventure. The global investigations of Carlos Borella, an agent-troubleshooter for an import-export company.

Starring: Carlos Thompson as Carlos Borella.

THE SENTIMENTAL AGENT—60 minutes—Syndicated 1962.

SERGEANT BILKO

See title: "You'll Never Get Rich."

SERGEANT PRESTON OF THE YUKON

Adventure. Era: The 1890s. Completing his college studies, William Preston receives word from the Yukon of his father's death. So as to have the legal authority to apprehend his father's murderer, he journeys to Alaska and joins the ranks of the Northwest Mounted Police. After months of hardships and deprivation, his search ends when the culprit, Spike Wilson, is apprehended.

Shortly after, Constable Preston

intervenes in a lynx attack and rescues a husky puppy that had been raised by a female wolf. Naming the dog Yukon King, he teaches it to command a team, respect good men, and hate evil ones.

Months following, after Spike Wilson escapes from prison, Preston is again assigned to capture him. Succeeding, he is promoted to Sergeant.

Stories depict Sergeant Preston's attempts to maintain law and order in the early Gold Rush days of the Yukon.

Starring: Richard Simmons as Sergeant William Preston.

Preston's horse: Rex.

Program Open:

Announcer: "Sergeant Preston of the Northwest Mounted Police, with Yukon King, swiftest and strongest lead dog, breaking the trail in the relentless pursuit of lawbreakers in the wild days of the Yukon."

SERGEANT PRESTON OF THE YUKON—30 minutes—Syndicated 1955. 78 episodes.

SERGEANT STEVE DEKKER

See title: "Not For Hire."

SERPICO

Crime Drama. Background: New York City. The investigations of Frank Serpico, a daring undercover patrolman with the 22nd Police Precinct.

CAST

Frank Serpico (Badge
No. 21049)   David Birney
Lt. Sullivan, his
superior   Tom Atkins

Music: Robert Dransin, Elmer Bernstein.

Executive Producer: Emmet G. Larvey, Jr.

Producer: Don Ingalls, Barry Oringer.

Director: Reza S. Badiyi, Michael Caffrey, Art Fisher, Sigmund Neufeld, Jr., Robert Markowitz, Alex March, Paul Stanley.

SERPICO—60 minutes—NBC—September 24, 1976 - January 28, 1977.

SESAME STREET

Educational. Entertainment geared to preschoolers. Background: Sesame Street—an anywhere street of learning in an anywhere city or town. Live action is coupled with cartoons, puppets, stories, and songs to help children solve problems, reinforce their reading skills, and assist them as they attempt to learn the alphabet and count from one to twenty.

Starring: Jim Henson's Muppets, Bob McGrath, Matt Robinson, Loretta Long, Will Lee, Charlotte Rae, Elmo Delgado, Roscoe Orman, Alaina Reed, Clarice Taylor, Anne Revere, Paul B. Brice, Raul Julia, Larry Block, Northern J. Calloway.

Music: Joe Raposo.

Musical Director: Sam Pottle.

Executive Producer: Jon Stone.

Producer: Dulcy Singer.

Director: Robert Myhrum.

SESAME STREET—60 minutes. NET —November 10, 1969 - November 6,

1970; PBS—Premiered: November 9, 1970.

SEVEN AT ELEVEN

Variety. Broadcast on an alternating basis with "Broadway Open House."

Host: George de Witt.

Regulars: Sid Gould, Denise Lor, Betty Luster, Jack Stanton.

Orchestra: Milton DeLugg.

Producer: Hal Friedman.

Director: Douglas Rodgers.

SEVEN AT ELEVEN—60 minutes—NBC—May 28, 1951 - August 1951. Broadcast from 11:00 p.m.-12:00 a.m.

SEVEN KEYS

Game. Two competing contestants. A picture, which represents a person, place, event, or object, is flashed on a screen. The player who is first to identify himself via a buzzer signal, receives a chance to answer. If correct, one point is scored. Winners, the highest scorers, receive merchandise prizes and one key. If the player is successful and wins seven straight games, he acquires seven keys and is awarded a merchandise showcase.

Host: Jack Narz.

SEVEN KEYS—30 minutes—ABC—April 3, 1961 - March 27, 1964.

SEVEN LEAGUE BOOTS

Travel. Films depicting the life styles and customs of people around the world.

Host-Narrator: Jack Douglas.

SEVEN LEAGUE BOOTS—30 minutes—Syndicated 1959. 38 episodes.

THE SEVEN LIVELY ARTS

Anthology. Dramatizations based on literary works and events of past and present history.

Host: John Crosby.

Orchestra: Alfredo Antonino.

Producer: Jud Kinberg, Robert Herridge, Robert Goldman.

THE SEVEN LIVELY ARTS—60 minutes—CBS—November 3, 1957 - February 16, 1958.

SEVENTH AVENUE

See title: "Best Sellers."

77 SUNSET STRIP

Mystery. Background: Hollywood, California. The investigations of Stuart Bailey and Jeff Spencer, private detectives operating from plush offices at 77 Sunset Strip.

CAST

Stuart Bailey	Efrem Zimablist, Jr.
Jeff Spencer	Roger Smith
Gerald Lloyd Kookson III (Kookie), their parking-lot attendant; later a detective	Edward Byrnes
Detective Rex Randolph	Richard Long
Suzanne Fabray, their switchboard operator	Jacqueline Beer

Roscoe, their junior partner, an ex-Broadway horse player — Louis Quinn

Lieutenant Gilmore, Hollywood Police Department — Byron Keith

J. R. Hale, the parking lot attendant at Dino's, the bar next to 77 Sunset Strip — Robert Logan

Hannah, Stu's secretary — Joan Staley

Music: Warren Barker; Frank Ortega; Frank Perkins; Paul Sawtell; Jay Livingston, Ray Evans.

Producer: William T. Orr, Roy Huggins, William Conrad, Howie Horwitz, Fenton Earnshaw.

77 SUNSET STRIP—60 minutes—ABC—October 10, 1958 - February 26, 1964. 205 episodes. Syndicated (excluding twenty 1961 episodes with star Efrem Zimbalist, Jr. and Joan Staley; available for export use only).

79 PARK AVENUE

Drama. A three-part miniseries based on the novel by Harold Robbins. The story, which spans thirteen years beginning in New York in August 1935, focuses on the life of Marja Fludjicki, a high-priced call girl, and the two men who love her: Ross Savitch, the rich son of a syndicate boss; and Mike Koshko, a poor, hard-working young man. (The series title is derived from the address of a modeling agency that fronts for high-priced call girls.)

CAST

Marja Fludjicki	Lesley Ann Warren
Ross Savitch	Marc Singer
Mike Koshko	David Dukes
Kaati Fludjicki, Marja's mother	Barbara Barrie
Ben Savitch, Ross's father	Michael Constantine
Myrna Savitch, Ross's mother	Margaret Fairchild
Peter Markevich, Marja's step-father	Albert Salmi
Paulie Fludjicki, Marja's brother	Scott Jacoby
Vera Keppler, the madam	Polly Bergen
Harry Vito	John Saxon
Armond Perfido	Raymond Burr
Joker	Jack Weston
Brian Whitfield	Peter Marshall

Music: Nelson Riddle.

Executive Producer: George Eckstein.

Producer-Director: Paul Wendkos.

79 PARK AVENUE—6 hours (total)—NBC—October 16, 1977 - October 18, 1977.

SHADDER BOY

An animated series that follows the exploits of Shadder Boy, a daring crusader for justice. 286 five minute films, Syndicated 1968.

SHADOW OF THE CLOAK

Spy Drama. A private detective's battle against espionage rings.

Starring: Helmut Dantine as the private detective.

SHADOW OF THE CLOAK—30 minutes—DuMont 1951.

SHAFT

Crime Drama. Background: New York

City. The investigations of John Shaft, a hip black private detective who strives to solve complex and baffling crimes. Based on the movie of the same title with sex and violence curtailed for television.

CAST
John Shaft	Richard Roundtree
Lt. Al Rossi, N.Y.P.D.	Ed Barth

Music: Johnny Pate.

Theme: Isaac Hayes.

SHAFT–90 minutes–CBS–October 9, 1973 - September 3, 1974. 8 episodes.

SHA NA NA

Variety. Musical numbers, blackouts, and comedy sketches set against the background of a city neighborhood in the 1950s.

Starring: Sha Na Na, a ten-member Rock group.

Regulars: Avery Schreiber, Kenneth Mars, Pamela Myers, Jane Dulo, Phil Roth, Jack Wohl.

Announcer: Pamela Myers.

Musical Director: Ray Charles.

Executive Producer: Pierre Cossette.

Producer: Bernard Rothman, Jack Wohl.

Director: Walter Miller.

Choreography: Walter Painter.

Additional Music/Choreography: Sha Na Na.

SHA NA NA–30 minutes–Syndicated 1977.

SHANE

Western. Background: Wyoming, 1900. The story of Shane, a mysterious wandering ex-gunman who, for reasons that are unknown, sides with homesteaders against cattlemen in the bloodthirsty quest for land. Hooking on as a rancher for the Starrett family –Marian, a widow who is drawn to the stranger; Joey, her young son who idolizes him; and Tom, the boy's grandfather–Shane strives to peacefully resolve the difficulties that arise over cattle baron Rufe Ryker's attempts to acquire land.

CAST
Shane	David Carradine
Marian Starrett	Jill Ireland
Tom Starrett	Tom Tully
Joey Starrett	Christopher Shea
Rufe Ryker	Bert Freed
Grafton, Ryker's assistant	Sam Gilman

SHANE–60 minutes–ABC–September 10, 1966 - December 31, 1966. 17 episodes.

SHANNON

Adventure. The cases of Joe Shannon, an insurance investigator for the Transport Bonding and Surety Company.

CAST
Joe Shannon	George Nader
Bill Cochran, his employer	Regis Toomey

SHANNON–30 minutes–Syndicated 1961. 36 episodes.

SHARI LEWIS

Listed: The television programs of ventriloquist Shari Lewis.

Facts 'N' Fun—Children—15 minutes—Local New York (WNBT-TV)—1953. Also known as "The Shari Lewis Show."

Hostess: Shari Lewis.

Shari and Her Friends—Children—30 minutes—Local New York (WPIX-TV)—1954. Also known as "Kartoon Kapers."

Hostess: Shari Lewis.

Puppets: Lamb Chop, Charlie Horse, Hush Puppy.

Format: Songs, stories, and sketches geared to children.

Shariland—Children—30 minutes—NBC—1957.

Hostess: Shari Lewis.

Puppets: Lamb Chop, Charlie Horse, Hush Puppy.

Format: Songs, stories, and sketches geared to children.

Hi Mom—Information-Variety—60 minutes—NBC—1957-1959. See title.

The Shari Lewis Show—Children—30 minutes—NBC—October 1, 1960 - September 28, 1963.

Hostess: Shari Lewis.

Her Assistant: Ronald Radd as Mr. Goodfellow.
Shari's puppets and format are the same as "Shariland."

The Shari Lewis Show—Children—10 minutes to one hour—B.B.C.-TV, London, England—1967-Present.

Hostess: Shari Lewis.

The puppets and format are the same as "Shariland."

The Shari Show—Children—30 minutes—NBC—Premiered: October 7, 1975. Broadcast as a series of monthly specials on NBC's five owned and operated stations.

Background: The Bearly Broadcasting Company, a television station that is run by twenty-five animal puppets. The series, which features Shari Lewis as the human assistant station manager, deals with people and how they relate to one another; how they create problems, and how they resolve them.

Starring: Shari Lewis.

Shari's Partner: Ron Martin.

Puppeteers: Shari Lewis, Mallory Tarcher, Bill Jackson, Nancy Wettler.

Musical Director: Bob Alberti.

Voices: Shari Lewis.

SHAZAM!

Adventure. Selected by the immortal elders — Solomon, Mercury, Zeus, Achilles, and Atlas—Billy Batson, a radio station broadcaster, is endowed with the ability to transform himself into Captain Marvel, a daring crusader for justice.

Stories relate Billy's battle against evil as the mysterious crime fighter, Captain Marvel. (When Billy utters the word "Shazam!" he is transformed into Captain Marvel.) Based on the comic strip, "Shazam!"

CAST
Billy Batson	Michael Gray
Mentor, his assistant	Les Tremayne
Captain Marvel	Jackson Bostwick
	John Davey

Music: Yvette Blais, Jeff Michael.

Executive Producer: Norm Prescott, Lou Scheimer, Dick Rosenbloom.

Producer: Arthur H. Nadel, Robert Chenault.

Director: Hollingsworth Morse, Robert Chenault, Harry Lange, Jr., Arnold Laven, Arthur H. Nadel.

SHAZAM!–30 minutes–CBS–Premiered: September 7, 1974.

THE SHAZAM!–ISIS HOUR

See individual titles: "Shazam!" and "Isis."

SHAZZAN!

Animated Cartoon. Finding two ring halves, twins Nancy and Chuck place them together, completing the word "Shazzan." Instantly they are transported from America to the age of the Arabian Knights, where they command the powerful sixty-foot genie, Shazzan. Stories depict their battle against evil. A Hanna-Barbera production.

Characters' Voices

Shazzan	Barney Phillips
Nancy	Janet Waldo
Chuck	Jerry Dexter

Music: Hoyt Curtin.

SHAZZAN!–30 minutes–CBS–September 9, 1967 - September 6, 1969. 26 episodes.

SHEENA, QUEEN OF THE JUNGLE

Adventure. Background: Africa. Having survived a plane crash as a child, and growing up in the savage continent, Sheena, a beautiful and courageous white jungle goddess, struggles to protect her adopted homeland from the forces of evil. Filmed on location in Mexico.

CAST

Sheena	Irish McCalla
Bob, her friend, a white trader	Christian Drake

Sheena's assistant: Chim (a chimpanzee).

Irish McCalla's stand-in: Raul Gaona, a Mexican acrobat. Unable to find a woman tall enough, a man, dressed in tiger skin and wig, was selected to perform the stunts that are unable to be performed by Irish McCalla (seventy-three-inches tall).

SHEENA, QUEEN OF THE JUNGLE –30 minutes–Syndicated 1955. 26 episodes.

Shazzan! The genie Shazzan and his masters Nancy and Chuck. *Courtesy Hanna-Barbera Productions.*

THE SHEILA GRAHAM SHOW

Celebrity Interview.

Hostess: Sheila Graham, Hollywood gossip columnist.

THE SHEILA GRAHAM SHOW—15 minutes—NBC 1951.

THE SHEILA MacRAE SHOW

Interview. Interviews with guests on topical issues.

Hostess: Sheila MacRae.

Co-Hostesses: Meredith MacRae and Heather MacRae (her daughters).

THE SHEILA MacRAE SHOW—30 minutes—Syndicated 1971.

SHENANAGANS

Game. Two children compete. Background: A three-dimensional game board. Players' moves are determined by the roll of two dice. Players move space by space and perform whatever is printed on the square on which they fall (either answer a question or perform a stunt). Each correct answer or performance awards Shenanagans play money. The first player to complete the board is the winner and is permitted to trade his play money for merchandise prizes.

Host: Stubby Kaye.

Announcer: Kenny Williams.

SHENANAGANS—30 minutes—ABC —September 26, 1964 - September 1965.

THE SHERIFF OF COCHISE
U.S. MARSHAL

Western. Background: Cochise, Arizona. Law enforcer Frank Morgan's battle against the modern-day breed of criminal. In 1956, under the title "Sheriff of Cochise," as sheriff; and in 1958, under the title "U.S. Marshal," as marshal.

CAST

Sheriff, then Marshal Frank Morgan	John Bromfield
Rafe Patterson, his deputy	Stan Jones

THE SHERIFF OF COCHISE—30 minutes—Syndicated 1956 - 1958.

U.S. MARSHAL—30 minutes—Syndicated 1958.

SHERLOCK HOLMES

Mystery. Background: 221-B Baker Street, London, England, the residence of Sherlock Holmes, a consulting detective (a man who intervenes in baffling police matters), and his roommate, Dr. John H. Watson. Stories depict their investigations into and attempts to solve baffling acts of criminal injustice through deductive reasoning and scientific evaluation. Based on the character created by Sir Arthur Conan Doyle.

CAST

Sherlock Holmes	Ronald Howard
Dr. John H. Watson	H. Marion Crawford
Inspector Lestrade	Archie Duncan

Music: Claude Durant.

SHERLOCK HOLMES—30 minutes— Syndicated 1954. 39 episodes.

SHIELDS AND YARNELL

Variety. Music, comedy, songs, dances,

and mime.

Hosts: Robert Shields, Lorene Yarnell.

Regulars: Ted Zeigler, Joanna Cassidy.

Orchestra: Norman Mamey.

Executive Producer: Steve Binder.

Director: Steve Binder.

SHIELDS AND YARNELL—30 minutes—CBS—June 13, 1977 - July 25, 1977.

SHINDIG

Musical Variety. Performances by Rock, Folk, and Country and Western entertainers.

Host: Jimmy O'Neal.

Regulars: Bobby Sherman, Ray Pohlman, The Blossoms, The Shindig Dancers, The Shindogs.

Music: The Shin-Diggers.

SHINDIG—60 minutes—ABC—September 16, 1964 - January 5, 1966.

THE SHIRLEY MacLAINE SHOW

See title: "Shirley's World."

SHIRLEY TEMPLE'S STORYBOOK

Anthology. Musical adaptations of fairytales.

Hostess-Frequent Performer: Shirley Temple.

Music: Vic Mizzy; Vic Schoen; Mack David; Walter Scharf.

Included:

Land of Oz. A sequel to L. Frank Baum's *The Wizard of Oz.* The evil Lord Nikidik's efforts to control the kingdom of Oz.

CAST

Princess Ozma: Shirley Temple; Mombi the Witch: Agnes Moorehead; Lord Nikidik: Jonathan Winters; Scarecrow: Ben Blue; Pumpkinhead: Sterling Holloway; Tin Woodman: Gil Lamb; Glinda: Frances Berger.

Kim. Background: India. The adventures of Rudyard Kipling's young hero, Kim O'Hara.

CAST

Captain Creighton: Michael Rennie; Kim: Tony Haig; White Suit: Arnold Moss.

Tom and Huck. Mark Twain's classic of life along the Mississippi River. The story of Tom Sawyer and his friend Huckleberry Finn and their involvement with Muff, the gravedigger.

CAST

Tom Sawyer: David Ladd; Huck Finn: Teddy Rooney; Aunt Polly: Janet Blair; Muff: Dan Duryea; Becky Thatcher: Ruthie Robinson; Injun Joe: Paul Stevens.

Little Men. An adaptation of the story by Ed James and Louisa May Alcott. Background: The Plumfield School for Boys in New England. The story of Professor Fritz Bhaer and his wife Jo as they attempt to solve the problem of a new arrival, Dan Baker, a lad who has a habit of running away from home.

CAST

Professor Bhaer: Fernando Lamas; Jo Bhaer: Shirley Temple; Dan Baker: Bobby Crawford.

SHIRLEY TEMPLE'S STORYBOOK

—60 minutes. NBC—January 12, 1958 - September 12, 1958; ABC—January 12, 1959 - June 8, 1959; NBC—September 18, 1960 - September 10, 1961. 27 episodes. Syndicated.

SHIRLEY'S WORLD

Comedy. Background: London, England, the offices of *World Illustrated* magazine. The assignments of Shirley Logan, a beautiful, wanderlust photojournalist who possesses an insatiable curiosity and a warm-hearted nature that involves her with other people's problems.

CAST

Shirley Logan   Shirley MacLaine
Dennis Croft, her
    editor   John Gregson

Music: John Barry.

Shirley's World. Shirley MacLaine. *Courtesy Independent Television Corporation; an ATV Company.*

Executive Producer: Sheldon Leonard, Ronald Rubin.

Producer: Barry Delmaine, Ray Austin.

SHIRLEY'S WORLD—30 minutes—ABC—September 15, 1971 - January 5, 1972. 17 episodes.

SHIVAREE

Musical Variety. Performances by Rock personalities.

Host: Gene Weed.

Featured: The Shivaree Dancers.

Music: Recorded.

SHIVAREE—30 minutes—Syndicated 1965. 26 tapes.

SHOOT FOR THE STARS

Game. Two teams compete, each composed of one celebrity and one noncelebrity contestant. Each team begins with $100. From a board that contains twenty-four numbered boxes, a player chooses one. A phrase is revealed (e.g., "Cleaver as a lash") and has to be unscrambled as follows: the contestant has to give the first half ("Smart as) and the celebrity the second half (a whip"). Each phrase is worth money and is added to a player's score only if both halves of the phrase are correctly answered. Turns alternate back and forth between the teams and the first team to score $1500 is the winner.

Host: Geoff Edwards.

Announcer: Bob Clayton.

Music: Bob Cobert.

Executive Producer: Bob Stewart.

Producer: Bruce Burmester.

Director: Mike Gargiulo.

SHOOT FOR THE STARS—30 minutes—NBC—Premiered: January 3, 1977.

SHORT STORY DRAMA

Anthology. Dramatic presentations.

Hostess: Ruth Woods.

Producer: Bernard Prockter.

Sponsor: Pepsi Cola.

SHORT STORY DRAMA—15 minutes—NBC 1952.

SHORT STORY THEATRE

Anthology. Dramatic presentations.

Hostess: Mary Kay.

Producer: Ted Mills.

Director: Dave Brown.

SHORT STORY THEATRE—15 minutes—ABC 1952.

SHOTGUN SLADE

Western. Background: The Frontier, 1860s. The exploits of Shotgun Slade, a wandering detective who, possessing a unique two-in-one shotgun, struggles to enforce justice.

CAST
Shotgun Slade	Scott Brady
Monica, his romantic interest	Monica Lewis

SHOTGUN SLADE—30 minutes—Syndicated 1959. 78 episodes.

SHOW BUSINESS INCORPORATED

Variety. Highlights of past Broadway shows are spotlighted with performances by the original cast members.

Host: Danton Walker.

Producer: Martin Jones.

Director: Ralph Nelson.

SHOW BUSINESS INCORPORATED—30 minutes—NBC 1949.

SHOWCASE '68

Variety. Performances by undiscovered professional talent. Taped on various college campuses throughout the country.

Host: Lloyd Thaxton.

SHOWCASE '68—60 minutes—NBC—June 11, 1968 - September 10, 1968.

SHOWDOWN

A game show wherein two three member teams compete in a series of question and answer rounds.

Host: Joe Pyne.

Music: The Bantams.

30 minutes—NBC—July 4, 1966 - October 4, 1966.

SHOWER OF STARS

Musical Variety. Broadcast once a month in place of "Climax."

Host: Jack Barry.

Orchestra: David Rose.

Premiere Guests: Betty Grable, Harry James, Mario Lanza.

SHOWER OF STARS—60 minutes—CBS—1954 - 1955.

THE SHOW GOES ON

Variety. Undiscovered professional talent acts perform with the hope of receiving bookings from talent buyers who are present.

Host: Robert Q. Lewis.

Producer: Lester Gottlieb, Lou Melamed.

Director: Alexander Leftwich.

Sponsor: American Safety Razor; Columbia Records.

THE SHOW GOES ON—60 minutes—CBS 1950.

SHOWOFFS

Game. Two teams, each composed of two celebrities and one noncelebrity contestant, compete. One team is placed in a sound-proof isolation booth while the other team is at play. One player is made the guesser; the other two the actors. The object is for the actors to pantomime as many words as possible during a sixty-second time limit. Each word that is identified by the guesser scores one point. At the end of the round the other team is brought out and the game is played in the same manner. The team with the highest score is the winner of round one. A two-out-of-three match competition is played (the roles of actor and guesser alternate). The winner receives a thousand dollars in merchandise prizes.

Host: Bobby Van.

Announcer: Gene Wood.

Music: Recorded.

Executive Producer: Mark Goodson, Bill Todman.

Producer: Howard Flesher.

Director: Paul Alter.

SHOWOFFS—30 minutes—ABC—June 30, 1975 - December 26, 1975.

SHOWROOM

Variety. Interviews and entertainment acts.

Host: Cesar Romero.

SHOWROOM—30 minutes—ABC—1953 - 1954.

SHOW STREET

Variety. Performances by undiscovered professional talent.

Hostess: Phyllis Diller.

SHOW STREET—30 minutes—Syndicated 1964.

SHOWTIME

Musical Variety. Produced in England.

Showoffs. Left to right: Studio contestant, host Bobby Van and guests Dick Gautier, Sally Struthers, Ron Masak, and Joyce Bulifant.

Hosts: American guests including Juliet Prowse, Bill Dana, Liberace.

Regulars: The Mike Sammes Singers, The London Line Dancers.

Orchestra: Jack Parnell.

SHOWTIME—60 minutes—CBS—June 11, 1968 - September 17, 1968. 12 tapes. Syndicated.

SHOWTIME AT THE APOLLO

Variety. Celebrity performances set against the background of the Apollo Theatre.

Host: Willie Bryant.

Appearing: Nat King Cole, Count Basie, Dinah Washington, Cab Calloway, Sarah Vaughn, Herb Jeffries, Martha Davis, Bill Bailey, Amos Millburn, Nipsey Russell, Mildred Melvin, The Larks.

SHOWTIME AT THE APOLLO—30 minutes—Syndicated 1954.

SHOWTIME, U.S.A.

Musical Variety. Scenes from Broadway plays are presented and performed by the original cast members.

Hosts: Henry Fonda; Vinton Freedly.

Announcer: Tom Gilbert.

Orchestra: Nathan Kroll.

SHOWTIME, U.S.A.—30 minutes—ABC 1951.

SHOW WAGON

Variety. The series spotlights entertainment figures who received their first break on Horace Heidt's talent programs of the past. The program also travels from state to state to showcase native talent.

Host: Horace Heidt.

Orchestra: Fran DeVol.

SHOW WAGON—30 minutes—NBC—January 8, 1955 - October 1, 1955.

SID CAESAR

Listed: The television programs of comedian Sid Caesar.

The Admiral Broadway Revue—Variety—60 minutes—NBC—January 28, 1949 - June 17, 1949.

Host: Sid Caesar.

Regulars: Imogene Coca, Mary McCarthy, Marge and Gower Champion, Roy Atwill, Bobby Van, Coren Welch.

Choreography: James Starbuch.

Orchestra: Charles Sanford.

Sponsor: Admiral.

Your Show of Shows—Variety—90 minutes—NBC—February 25, 1950 - June 5, 1954.

Host: Sid Caesar.

Regulars: Imogene Coca, Carl Reiner, Howard Morris, Judy Johnson, Cliff Norton, Robert Merrill, Marguerite Piazza, Bill Hayes, Nellie Fisher, Bambi Linn, Rod Alexander, The Bob Hamilton Trio, the Billy Williams Quartet, The Chandra Kaly Dancers.

Announcer: Vaughn Monroe.

Orchestra: Charles Sanford; Tony Romano.

Creator: Pat Weaver.

Producer: Max Liebman.

The Saturday Night Revue—Variety—NBC—1950. See title.

Caesar's Hour—Variety—60 minutes—NBC—September 27, 1954 - May 25, 1957.

Host: Sid Caesar.

Regulars: Carl Reiner, Howard Morris, Nanette Fabray, Janet Blair, Ellen Parker, Earl Wild, William Lewis, Sondra Dell, Cliff Norton, Virginia Curtis, Shirl Conway. The Ted Cappy Dancers.

Announcer: Vaughn Monroe; Joe De Santis.

Orchestra: Bernie Green.

The Sid Caesar Show—Comedy—30 minutes—ABC—January 20, 1958 - May 25, 1958.

Host: Sid Caesar.

Regulars: Imogene Coca, Carl Reiner, Howard Morris, Jeanne Bal, Paul Reed, Milt Kamen, The Kirby Stone Four.

Orchestra: Paul Weston.

The Sid Caesar Show—Comedy—30 minutes—ABC—September 19, 1963 - March 14, 1964.

Host: Sid Caesar.

Regulars: Gisele MacKenzie, Joey Forman.

Orchestra: Peter Matz.

SID CAESAR PRESENTS COMEDY PREVIEW

Comedy. The summer replacement for "Caesar's Hour.."

Hosts: Phil Foster, Bobby Sherwood.

Regulars: Barbara Nichols, Cliff Norton, Sid Gould, The Ted Cappy Dancers.

Music: Bill Hayes, Judy Tyler.

SID CAESAR PRESENTS COMEDY PREVIEW—60 minutes—NBC—July 4, 1955 - September 1955.

SIERRA

Drama. Background: Sierra National Park (fictional). The rescue operations of the park rangers—men and women dedicating their lives to protecting people from nature—and nature from people.

CAST

Ranger Tim Cassidy	James C. Richardson
Ranger Matt Harper	Ernest Thompson
Ranger Julie Beck	Susan Foster
Ranger P.J. Lewis	Mike Warren
Chief Ranger Jack Moore	Jack Hogan

Music: Lee Holdridge.

SIERRA—60 minutes—NBC—September 12, 1974 - December 12, 1974. 13 episodes.

SIGMUND AND THE SEA MONSTERS

Comedy. Background: 1730 Ocean Drive, Cyprus Beach, California, the residence of brothers Johnny and Scott Stuart and their pet sea monster, Sigmund, who, when disowned by his family for his inability to scare humans, was found and befriended by Johnny and Scott, taken home, and concealed in their club house. Stories depict Johnny and Scott's attempts to conceal Sigmund's presence and protect him from the devious efforts of his family, who seek to retrieve him when emergencies arise that require his presence at home (a cave at Dead Man's Point).

CAST

Sigmund Ooz	Billy Barty
Johnny Stuart	Johnny Whitaker
Scott Stuart	Scott Kolden
Zelda Marshall, their housekeeper; caring for Scott and Johnny whilst their parents are away on business	Mary Wickes
Sheriff Chuck Bevins, Zelda's boyfriend	Joe Higgins
Sheldon, the Sea Genie	Rip Torn
Miss Eddels, the Stuart's nosey neighbor	Margaret Hamilton
Shelby, Sheldon's nephew	Sparky Marcus
Gertrude Gouch, the housekeeper, later episodes	Fran Ryan

Also: Sharon Baird, Van Snowden, Paul Gale, Walter Edmonds, Larry Larson.

Additional characters (not given screen credit): Big Daddy, Sigmund's father; Sweet Mama, Sigmund's mother; Blurp Ooz, Sigmund's brother; Slurp Ooz, Sigmund's brother.

Ooz family pet: Prince (a barking lobster).

Characters: The Sid and Marty Krofft Puppets.

Music: Jimmie Haskell, Wes Farrell.
Additional Music: Michael Lloyd.

Producer: Sid and Marty Krofft.

Director: Dick Darley, Murray Golden.

SIGMUND AND THE SEA MONSTERS—30 minutes—NBC—September 8, 1973 - October 18, 1975.

THE SILENT FORCE

Crime Drama. Background: Washington, D.C. The investigations of Amelia Cole, Jason Hart, and Ward Fuller, undercover agents for the Federal government who comprise The Silent Force, a secret organization designed to corrupt the inner workings of organized crime.

CAST

Amelia Cole	Lynda Day
Jason Hart	Percy Rodrigues
Ward Fuller	Ed Nelson

THE SILENT FORCE—30 minutes—ABC—September 21, 1970 - January 11, 1971. 13 episodes.

The Silent Force. Left to right: Ed Nelson, Percy Rodrigues, Lynda Day.

THE SILENT SERVICE

Anthology. Backgrounds: World War II; and the Korean War. Dramatizations based on incidents in the lives of the officers and men of the submarine division of the U.S. Navy.

Host-Narrator: Rear Admiral Thomas Dykers, U.S.N.

Included:

The Ugly Duckling. Ridiculed because their sub, the USS *Nautilus,* is oversized and ungainly, its crew bet a month's pay that she'll score the biggest hit on her first patrol. The story follows the maiden voyage of the atomic-powered submarine.

CAST
Carl Betz, Peter Hansen.

The Unsuccessful Patrol. The story of the maiden voyage of the S-34, which runs aground on her first patrol.

CAST
Richard Carlyle, Robert Knapp.

The Sculpin Story. The story of a submarine captain who elects to go down with his ship rather than to fall into enemy hands.

CAST
Ray Montgomery, Leon Sullivan.

THE SILENT SERVICE—30 minutes—Syndicated 1957. 78 episodes.

THE SILENT YEARS

Movies. Silent film classics.
Host-Narrator: Orson Welles.

THE SILENT YEARS—90 minutes—PBS—July 6, 1971 - September 24, 1971.

SILENTS PLEASE

Documentary. A history of the silent era of motion pictures—"The great stars, the excitement, the thrills, the laughter, and the heartbreak of Hollywood's Golden Era."

Host: Ernie Kovacs.

SILENTS PLEASE—30 minutes—ABC—August 4, 1960 - October 13, 1960; March 23, 1961 - October 5, 1961. Syndicated. 40 episodes.

SILVER THEATRE

See title: "Conrad Nagel."

SING ALONG

Musical Variety. The lyrics of familiar songs are rolled across the bottom of the screen to enable home viewers to participate.

Host: Jim Lowe.

Regulars: Florence Henderson, Tina Robin, June Roselle, Somethin' Smith and the Red Heads.

Orchestra: Harry Sosnick.

Featured Segment: "The Money Song." A limerick melody is played. Home audience members whose lyrics (which are sent to the program) best fit the music, receive merchandise prizes.

SING ALONG—30 minutes—CBS—June 4, 1958 - September 1958.

SING ALONG WITH MITCH

Musical Variety. The lyrics of familiar songs are rolled across the bottom of the screen to enable home viewers to sing along.

Host: Mitch Miller.

Regulars: Gloria Lambert, Louise O'Brien, Victor Griffin, Paul Friesen, Keith Booth, Gloria Chu, Bill Ventura, Phil Okon, Leslie Uggams, Frank Raye, Len Stokes, Bob McGrath, Mary Lou Rhyal, Hubie Hendrie, Tommy Nordon, Stan Carlson, Diana Trask, Jack Brown, Rita McLaughlin.

Musical Director: Jimmy Carroll.

SING ALONG WITH MITCH—60 minutes—NBC—September 28, 1962 - September 21, 1964. Rebroadcasts: NBC—May 1966 - September 1966. Several episodes (holiday broadcasts) are syndicated.

SING IT AGAIN

Musical Quiz. Object: For contestants to identify mystery song titles after hearing only several notes. Prizes are awarded to those who score the most correct identifications.

Home audience segment: "The Phantom Voice." The host places four telephone calls during one program and if recipients are able to identify a famous but unknown voice, they are awarded a fifty-dollar bond.

Hosts: Dan Seymour (1950); Jan Murray(1951).

Regulars: Alan Dale, Judy Lynn, Jack Stanton, Larry Douglas, Betty Luster, Bob Howard, The Riddlers.

Orchestra: Ray Bloch.

Producer: Lester Gottlieb, Louis Cowan, Herb Moss.

Director: Bob Bleyer.

SING IT AGAIN—60 minutes—CBS—1950 - 1951.

THE SINGING LADY

Children. Music, songs, stories, and marionette sketches.

Hostess: Irene Wicker, The Singing Lady.

Puppets: The Suzarri Marionettes.

Announcer: Walter Herlihy.

Orchestra: Allen Gart.

Producer: Blair Wallister.

Sponsor: Kellogg's.

THE SINGING LADY—30 minutes—ABC—August 12, 1948 - January 26, 1949.

SIR FRANCIS DRAKE

Adventure. Background: Sixteenth-century England. The exploits of Sir Francis Drake, an admiral of the Queen's Navy, as he defends the crown against warring marauders.

CAST

Sir Francis Drake	Terrence Morgan
Queen Elizabeth I	Jean Kent
Mindoza	Roger Delgado
Trevelyan	Patrick McLaughlen
John Drake	Michael Crawford

Drake's ship: the *Golden Hind.*

SIR FRANCIS DRAKE—30 minutes—NBC—June 24, 1962 - September 1962. 23 episodes.

SIROTA'S COURT

Comedy. Background: An unidentified American City. A comical look at life in a night court as seen through the hectic experiences of Matthew J. Sirota, a compassionate judge.

CAST

Judge Matthew
    Sirota   Michael Constantine
Maureen O'Connor, the
    court clerk   Cynthia Harris
Gail Goodman, the public
    defender   Kathleen Miller
Sawyer Dabney, the
    private attorney   Ted Ross
Bud Nugent, the
    assistant D.A.   Fred Willard
John Belson, the
    U.S. Marshal   Owen Bush

Music: David Shire.

Theme Vocal: Ted Ross.

Producer: Harvey Miller, Peter Engel.

Director: Mel Ferber, Tom Trobrich.

SIROTA'S COURT—30 minutes— NBC—December 1, 1976 - January 26, 1977.

THE SIX MILLION DOLLAR MAN

Adventure. Seriously injured after crashing in an Air Force research jet that malfunctioned, civilian astronaut Steve Austin becomes the immediate concern of the Office of Strategic Operations, a U.S. government organization that requires an extraordinary agent and spends six million dollars to reconstruct Austin to their specifications.

Through biotic and cybernetic surgery, both of Austin's legs, one arm and one eye are replaced with synthetic, nuclear-powered mechanisms

The Six Million Dollar Man. Richard Anderson (left) and Lee Majors.

that produce superhuman abilities and make him something that has never before existed: a cyborg (cybernetic organism), part human and part machine.

Stories detail Austin's attempts on behalf of the O.S.O. to resolve situations that pose a threat to humanity.

CAST

Steve Austin   Lee Majors
Dr. Rudy Wells,
    the aeromedical
    surgeon   Alan Oppenheimer
                 Martin E. Brooks
Oscar Goldman, Austin's
    superior   Richard Anderson
Jaime Sommers, the Bionic
    Woman (recurring
    role)   Lindsay Wagner
Janet Callahan, Oscar's
    secretary   Jennifer Darling
Miss Johnson, Oscar's
    secretary   Susan Keller

Music: Stu Phillips; Gil Mellé.

Additional Music: J.J. Johnson, Richard Clements.

Executive Producer: Harve Bennett.

Producer: Kenneth Johnson, Lionel E. Siegel.

Director: Richard Moder, Jerry London, Alan Crosland, Barry Crane, Richard Doner, John Lucas, Cliff Bole, Phil Bondelli, James Lydon, Arnold Laven, Lawrence Dohney.

Note: In later episodes, the organization Steve works for, had become the O.S.I. (Office of Scientific Intelligence).

Vocal: "The Six Million Dollar Man" sung by Dusty Springfield.

THE SIX MILLION DOLLAR MAN —90 and 60 minute versions—ABC— Premiered: October 20, 1973.

THE SIXTH SENSE

Suspense Drama. Background: Los Angeles, California. The investigations of Michael Rhodes, professor of parapsychology at the University School, as he attempts to aid people threatened by "ghosts" and solve crimes that are linked to supernatural occurrences.

CAST

Michael Rhodes	Gary Collins
Nancy Murphy, his assistant	Catherine Farrar

Music: Billy Goldenberg.

THE SIXTH SENSE—60 minutes— ABC—January 15, 1972 - December 30, 1972. 25 episodes.

THE $64,000 QUESTION

Game. One contestant competes at a time. The player begins by selecting one category from a list. The host then asks him a question for one dollar. If he responds correctly, he receives the money. Each succeeding question doubles the previous amount of money if the player successfully answers it. Incorrect answers defeat a player, and players are permitted to leave at any established amount of money.

After ten questions are asked, the player reaches the first plateau of $512. The money is frozen and remains his.

The player continues for he has nothing to lose. He is then asked the one thousand dollar question. If he decides to continue, the two thousand dollar question is stated. Should the player decide to try to double the previous amount, the second plateau is reached if he correctly answers the four thousand dollar question. Once again, the money remains frozen and his, and he continues because he has nothing to lose.

For the eight thousand dollar question, he is placed in the Revlon Isolation Booth. The question is stated and the player receives thirty seconds with which to answer. If correct, he is then asked the sixteen thousand dollar question. Should he win the money he is given one week to decide if he wishes to continue or quit.

If he continues, he is again placed in the booth. The player selects one of two question that are held by the host. The question is read, and the player, if correct, wins $32,000. The player then receives another week to decide if he wants to quit or gamble it on a chance to answer the $64,000 question. Should he decide to continue, he is permitted to bring an expert in his category field into the booth with him. However, should both fail to correctly answer the question, the player receives his second plateau earnings.

Host: Hal March.

Assistant: Lynn Dollar.

Announcer: Wayne Howell.

Judge: Dr. Bergen Evans.

Music: Norman Leyden.

Question Guard: Mr. Harrington, of the Bankers Trust Co. in N.Y. who assures "no one has had previous access to questions."

Producer: Merrill Heatter, Mert Hoplin.

Sponsor: Revlon.

Note: During one stage of the series, a 1955 Cadillac was also the consolation prize.

THE $64,000 QUESTION—30 minutes—CBS—June 7, 1955 - November 2, 1958.

THE $64,000 CHALLENGE

Game. A spin-off from "The $64,000 Question." Three contestants compete, one "$64,000 Question" champion and two challengers. Each has to answer questions based on the subject chosen by the champion. Each is placed in a separate isolation booth, and all three players are asked the same question, one at a time (the sound is turned off in two when one is in use). Incorrect answers defeat a player, and money doubles in the same manner as "The $64,000 Question." If successful, previous champions can win as much as $128,000. Players who are defeated receive a Cadillac as a consolation prize.

Hosts: Sonny Fox; Ralph Story.

Announcer: Bill Rogers.

Music: Norman Leyden.

THE $64,000 CHALLENGE—30 minutes—CBS—April 8, 1956 - September 14, 1958.

THE SIX WIVES OF HENRY VIII

Historical Drama. Chronicled: The life and six marriages of Henry VIII (1491-1547), the ruler of England during the fifteenth century.

CAST

Henry VIII	Keith Michell
Princess Catherine of Aragon, his first wife	Annette Crosbie
Anne Boleyn, his second wife	Dorothy Tutin
Jane Seymour, his third wife	Anne Stallybrass
Anne of Cleves, his fourth wife	Elvi Hale
Catherine Howard, his fifth wife	Angela Pleasence
Catherine Parr, his sixth wife	Rosalie Crutchley
Wolsey	John Baskcomb
Maria	Margaret Ford
The Duke of Norfork	Patrick Troughton
Chapuys	Edward Atienza
Princess Mary	Verina Greenlaw
Thomas Seymour	John Ronane
Lady Rochford	Shelia Burrell
Cromwell	Wolfe Morris
Archbishop Cranmer	Bernard Hepton
Mark Smeaton	Michael Osborne
Bishop Gardiner	Basil Dignam
Lord Hertford	Daniel Moynihan
Thomas Wriothesley	Patrick Godfrey
Francis Dereham	Simon Prebble

Dowager, Dutchess of
Norfolk   Catherine Lacey

Narrator: Anthony Quayle.

Music: David Munrow.

THE SIX WIVES OF HENRY VIII—90 minutes—CBS—August 1, 1971 - September 5, 1971. Syndicated. Produced by the B.B.C.

THE SKATEBIRDS

Children. A series of cartoons hosted by three roller skating birds—Sach, Knock Knock, and Scooter.

Animated Segments:
The Robonic Stooges. A take-off on the 1940s "Three Stooges" wherein a Space Age Moe, Larry, and Curly, constructed from the finest parts available, battle evil throughout the universe.

Wonder Wheels. The story of Wheelie, the owner of a decrepit motorcycle, which, when the need arises, he transforms into Wonder Wheels to battle evil. His girlfriend: Doolie.

Woofer and Wimper. The misadventures of detective dogs Woofer and Wimper and their human masters, the teenage members of the Clue Club, a professional investigative organization. See title "Clue Club" for further information.

Live Action Segment:
Mystery Island. Retreating to an uncharted island, the evil Dr. Strenge establishes a base where he constructs his diobolical machines to control the world. His device, however, is incomplete and needs the aide of Paups, a sophisticated computer robot to fully activate it. Discovering that the robot is being transported, Dr. Strenge forces the plane carrying Paups to crash land on his island, marooning scientists Chuck Kelly, Sue Corwin, her brother, Sandy—and Paups. Stories concern Chuck, Sue, and Sandy's attempts to safeguard Paups from Dr. Strenge and escape from the island.

Music: Hoyt Curtin.

Executive Producer: William Hanna, Joseph Barbera.

Producer (of "Mystery Island"): Terry Morse, Jr.

Film Director: Hollinsworth Morse, Sidney Miller.

Animation Director: Charles A. Nichols.

Skatebirds Director: Sidney Miller.

THE SKATEBIRDS—55 minutes—CBS—Premiered: September 10. 1977.

THE SKIP FARRELL SHOW

Variety.

Host: Skip Farrell.

Featured: The Honeydreamers Quintet.

Announcer: Jack Lester.

Music: The George Baines Trio.

THE SKIP FARRELL SHOW—15 minutes—ABC—January 17, 1949 - August 28, 1949.

SKIPPY, THE BUSH KANGAROO

Adventure. Background: The Waratah National Park in Australia. Crossing the path of an injured and orphaned baby kangaroo, Sonny Hammond, the son of the chief park ranger, takes her home, cares for her, and, adopting her, names her Skippy. Stories depict the efforts of park rangers to maintain a game reserve; and the adventures shared by a young boy and his tame and intelligent pet kangaroo.

CAST
Matt Hammond, the
  chief ranger,
  Sonny's father   Ed Devereaux
Sonny Hammond   Garry Pankhurst
Mark Hammond, Sonny's
  brother, the
  river-patrol
  ranger   Ken James
Jerry King, the
  flight ranger   Tony Bonner
Clarissa (Clancy) Merrick,
  a pretty teenager
  residing with Hammonds
  while her parents
  are away on a
  business trip   Liza Goddard
Dr. Alexander Stark Frank Thring

SKIPPY, THE BUSH KANGAROO—30 minutes—Syndicated 1969. 91 episodes.

SKYERS 5

The animated exploits of a quintet of crime fighters. 30 minutes—Syndicated 1967. 39 episodes.

SKYHAWKS

Animated Cartoon. The assignments of Skyhawks, Incorporated, a daredevil air transport and rescue service owned and operated by the Wilson family.

Characters: The Wilson family: Mike Wilson, widower, former Air Force colonel; his children: Steve, and Carolyn; his father: Patty Wilson, a World War I air ace; and his foster children: Red Hughes and Little Cindy.

Music: Jack Fascinato.

SKYHAWKS—30 minutes—ABC—September 6, 1969 - September 2, 1971.

SKY KING

Adventure. Background: The Flying Crown Ranch in Grover City. The exploits of rancher Sky King, a former World War II naval aviator who struggles to maintain law and order in the California ranch country.

CAST
Sky King   Kirby Grant
Penny King, his
  niece   Gloria Winters
Clipper King, his
  nephew   Ron Hagerthy
The sheriff   Ewing Mitchell

Producer: Jack Chertok.

Sponsor: Derby Foods; Nabisco.

Sky's plane: The *Songbird*.

SKY KING—30 minutes—CBS—September 1952 - September 3, 1966. 72 episodes. Syndicated.

THE SKY'S THE LIMIT

Game. Selected studio-audience members compete in various contests, both question-and-answer and stunt rounds. Prizes are awarded to players in accord with their ability to complete tasks.

Host: Gene Rayburn.

Assistants: Hope Lange, Marilyn Cantor.

THE SKY'S THE LIMIT—15 minutes —NBC—November 1, 1954 - August 19, 1955; 30 minutes—NBC—August 22, 1955 - June 1, 1956.

SLATTERY'S PEOPLE

Drama. The story of James Slattery, politician, lawyer, and minority leader in the state legislature who crusades against the injustices of government.

CAST

James Slattery	Richard Crenna
B. J. Clawson	Maxine Stuart
Bert Metcaff	Tol Avery
Mike Valera	Alejandro Rey
Wendy Wendkoski	Francine York
Liz Andrews	Kathie Brown
Frank Radcliffe	Edward Asner
Johnny Ramos	Paul Geary

Program Open:

Announcer: "Democracy is a very bad form of government, but I ask you never to forget it, all the others are so much worse."

SLATTERY'S PEOPLE—60 minutes —CBS—September 21, 1964 - November 26, 1965. 30 episodes.

THE SMALL FRY CLUB

Children. Stories, game contests, audience participation, magic tricks and other related entertainment for children.

Host: Bob Emery.

Producer: Bob Emery, Kay Emery.

Sponsor: General Foods.

THE SMALL FRY CLUB—60 and 30 minute versions—DuMont—1948-1951.

SMILIN' ED'S GANG

See title: "Andy's Gang."

THE SMITH FAMILY

Comedy-Drama. Background: 219 Primrose Lane, the residence of the Smith family: Chad, a twenty-five-year veteran detective sergeant, L.A.P.D.; his wife, Betty; and their children: Cindy, Bob, and Brian. Stories depict: the home and working life of a law enforcer; and the conflicts and crises that face a family in everyday life.

CAST

Chad Smith	Henry Fonda
Betty Smith	Janet Blair
Cindy Smith	Darleen Carr
Bob Smith	Ronny Howard
Brian Smith	Michael-James Wixted
Ray Martin, Chad's partner	John Carter

Slattery's People. Richard Crenna.

Captain Hughes   Charles McGraw

Music: Frank DeVol.

THE SMITH FAMILY—30 minutes—ABC—January 20, 1971 - September 8, 1971; April 12, 1972 - June 14, 1972. 39 episodes.

THE SMOKEY THE BEAR SHOW

Animated Cartoon. The adventures of Smokey the Bear, as both a bear and cub, as he struggles to protect the forests and their creatures from fire. Stories are conservative in nature and relate the careful use of fire and the importance of nature's woodlands to children.

Music: Maury Laws.

THE SMOKEY THE BEAR SHOW—30 minutes—ABC—September 6, 1969 - September 12, 1971. 17 episodes.

THE SMOTHERS BROTHERS

Listed: The television programs of comedians Tom and Dick Smothers.

The Smothers Brothers Show—Comedy—30 minutes—CBS—September 17, 1965 - September 9, 1966.
  Background: Los Angeles, California. Drowned at sea many years ago, Tom Smothers returns to Earth as an apprentice angel and takes up residence in the bachelor apartment of his brother, Dick. Inept, and ordered to assist people in distress, Tom, reluctantly assisted by Dick, struggles to complete his assignments and acquire the status needed to become a full-fledged angel.

CAST
Dick Smothers   Himself

Tommy Smothers   Himself
Leonard J. Costello,
  Dick's boss   Roland Winters
Diane Costello, his
  daughter   Marilyn Scott
Mrs. Costello, his
  wife   Harriet MacGibbon
Janet, Dick's
  girlfriend   Ann Elder

Music: Alfred Perry; Perry Botkin, Jr.

The Smothers Brothers Comedy Hour—Variety—60 minutes—CBS—February 5, 1967 - June 8, 1969.

Format: Controversial humor, satire, songs, and topical sketches.

Hosts: Tom and Dick Smothers.

Regulars: Pat Paulsen, John Hartford, Jennifer Warren, Murray Romas, Leigh French, Mason Williams, Bob Einstein (as Officer Judy), Don Wyatt, Carl Gottlieb, Cathy Cahill, Jessica Myerson, The Jimmy Joyce Singers, The Anita Kerr Singers, The Ron Poindexter Dancers, The Louis Da Pron Dancers.

Announcer: Roger Carroll.

Orchestra: Nelson Riddle.

The Smothers Brothers Comedy Hour—Variety—60 minutes—ABC—July 15, 1970 - September 16, 1970.

Format: Same as the CBS sixty minute version.

Hosts: Tom and Dick Smothers.

Regulars: Sally Struthers, Spencer Quinn.

Announcer: Roger Carroll.

Orchestra: Denny Vaughn.

The Smothers Organic Prime Time Space Ride—Variety—30 minutes—Syndicated 1971.
Format: Offbeat, controversial

comedy. The Space Ride: Performances by new talent finds.

Host: Tom Smothers.

Occasional co-host: Dick Smothers.

The Smothers Brothers Show—Variety—60 minutes—NBC—January 13, 1975 - May 26, 1975.

Hosts: Tom and Dick Smothers.

Regulars: Pat Paulsen, Don Novello, Pete Smith, Betty Aberlain, Evelyn Russell.

Orchestra: Marty Paich.

SNAP JUDGEMENT

Game. Two competing two-member teams. One member of each team is presented with a concealed word. The player then relates a one-word clue to his partner, who must identify the word. If he is unable, their opponents then receive a chance to identify it. The word is played until it is identified or until it is voided by the use of ten clues. Words start at ten points and diminish one point with each clue. Winners, the highest scoring teams, receive both cash and merchandise prizes.

Hosts: Ed McMahon; Gene Rayburn.

Announcer: Johnny Olsen.

Music: Recorded.

SNAP JUDGEMENT—30 minutes—NBC—April 3, 1967 - March 28, 1969.

SNEAK PREVIEW

Pilot Films. Proposed comedy series for the 1956 - 1957 season.

Included:

Calling Terry Conway. The misadven-tures of Terry Conway, a public relations director in a glamorous Las Vegas Hotel.

CAST
Terry Conway: Ann Sheridan; Pearl McGrath: Una Merkel; Stan: Philip Ober.

Carolyn. Named the guardian of three children after their parents' death, an actress struggles to win their affection.

CAST
Carolyn: Celeste Holm; Mrs. Little: Jeanette Nolan; Smattering: Parley Baer.

Real George. The misadventures of George Gidley, a junior salesman in a department store.

CAST
George Gidley: George O'Hanlon; Mr. Tutwiter: Ray Collins; Janet: Gloria Henry.

Just Plain Folks. The misadventures of a Hollywood couple who are type cast as an actress and writer.

CAST
Zsa Zsa Gabor, Cy Howard.

SNEAK PREVIEW—30 minutes—NBC—July 3, 1956 - August 24, 1956.

THE SNOOKY LANSON SHOW

Musical Variety.

Host: Snooky Lanson.

Vocalists: The Mellow-Larks.

THE SNOOKY LANSON SHOW—15 minutes—NBC—July 17, 1956 - September 26, 1956.

THE SNOOP SISTERS

See title: "NBC Wednesday Mystery Movie," *Snoop Sisters* segment.

SOAP

Satire. Background: Dunn's River, Connecticut. Spoofing afternoon soap operas, the series focuses on the lives of two sisters: the wealthy Jessica Tate, and the not-so-rich Mary Campbell, and the outlandish activities of their families—who live on opposite sides of the town. The stories, which are adult, are episodic.

CAST

Jessica Tate	Cathryn Damon
Mary Campbell	Katherine Helmond
Chester Tate, Jessica's husband	Robert Mandan
Corinne Tate, Jessica's daughter	Diana Canova
Eunice Tate, Jessica's daughter	Jennifer Salt
Billy Tate, Jessica's son	Jimmy Baio
Burt Campbell, Mary's husband	Richard Mulligan
Jodie Campbell, Mary's son	Billy Crystal
Danny Campbell, Mary's son	Ted Wass
Benson, the Tate's butler	Robert Guillaume

Soap. From far left: Diana Canova (seated), Robert Mandan (next to Diana), Katherine Helmond (seated on arm of chair); top, left: Arthur Peterson (in military uniform), Jennifer Salt (behind Miss Helmond), and Robert Guillaume (center). Right side: Cathryn Damon (seated); standing, left to right: Ted Wass, Richard Mulligan, Robert Urich, Billy Crystal. *Courtesy of the Call-Chronicle Newspapers, Allentown, Pa.*

The Major, Jessica's
   crazed father (believes
   he is living World
   War II)   Arthur Peterson
Peter, Jessica's lover;
   Corinne's
   boyfriend   Robert Urich
Godfather, the head of the
   local Mafia in which
   Danny is
   involved   Richard Libertini

Announcer-Narrator: Rod Roddy.

Music: George Tipton.

Executive Producer: Paul Junger Witt, Tony Thomas.

Producer: Susan Harris.

Director: Jay Sandrich.

Creator: Susan Harris.

SOAP—30 minutes—ABC—Premiered: September 13, 1977.

SOLDIER PARADE

Variety. Performances by army talent. Broadcast from military bases throughout the country.

Hostesses: Arlene Francis; Martha Wright.

Co-Emcee: Pfc. Richard Hayes.

Vocalists: The Ford Dix Chorus.

Music: The Ford Dix Band.

SOLDIER PARADE—30 minutes—ABC—1949 - 1955.

THE SOLDIERS

Comedy. The misadventures of two reluctant G.I.s: Hal March and Tom D'Andrea—soldiers conducting a private battle with the U.S. army.

CAST

Private Hal March	Himself
Private Tom D'Andrea	Himself
The captain	John Dehner
The sergeant	Red Pearson

THE SOLDIERS—30 minutes—NBC—June 25, 1955 - September 3, 1955.

SOLDIERS OF FORTUNE

Adventure. The exploits of American globetrotters Tim Kelly and Toubo Smith as they battle the forces of injustice throughout the world.

CAST

Tim Kelly	John Russell
Toubo Smith	Chick Chandler

SOLDIERS OF FORTUNE—30 minutes—Syndicated 1955. 52 episodes.

SOMERSET

Serial. A spin-off from "Another World." Background: The town of Somerset. The dramatic story of three families: the Lucases, the Grants, and the Delaneys. Episodes depict the conflicts and tensions that arise from the interactions of the characters.

CAST

Sam Lucas	Jordan Charney
Lahoma Lucas	Ann Wedgeworth
Missy Lucas	Carol Roux
Robert Delaney	Nicholas Coster
Laura Cooper	Dorothy Stinnette
Randy Buchanan	Gary Sandy
Ben Grant	Ed Kemmer
Jill Grant	Susan McDonald
David Grant	Ron Martin
Peter Delaney	Len Gochman
Marsha Davis	Alice Hirson
Ellen Grant	Georgann Johnson
Gerald Davis	Walter Matthews

Jessica Buchanan	Wynn Miller	Jerry Kane	James O'Sullivan
India Delaney	Marie Wallace	Lena Andrews	Abby Lewis
Rex Cooper	Paul Sparer		
Tom Cooper	Ernest Thompson		

Music: Chet Kingsbury.

Chuck Hillman — Ed Winter

Additional Music: Charles Paul.

Dr. Stan Kurtz — Michael Lipton

Announcer: Bill Wolff.

Ginger Kurtz — Meg Winter

Fawne Harriman

Renne Jarrett

Executive Producer: Lyle B. Hill, Sid Sirulnik.

Leo Kurtz	Gene Fanning
Eve Lawrence	Bibi Besch

Director: Jack Coffey, Bruce Minnix.

Julian Cannel	Joel Crothers
Dr. Terri Martin	Gloria Hoy
Frieda Lang	Polly Rowles
Becky Winkle	Jane Rose
Doris Hiller	Gretchen Wyler
Mark Mercer	Stanley Grover
Edith Mercer	Judy Searle
Tony Cooper	Barry Jenner
	Doug Chapin
Mrs. Benson	Eleanor Phelps
Greg Mercer	Gary Swanson
Pamela Davis	Pamela Toll
Crystal Ames	Diahn Williams
Danny Catsworth	Melinda Plank
Mitch Farmer	Dick Shoberg
Bill Greeley	Bill Hunt
Andrea Moore	Harriet Hall
Emily Moore	Lois Kibbee
Phil	Bob Gabriel
Kenny	Ed Bryce
Philip Matson	Frank Scofield
Dana Moore	Chris Pennock
Karen MacMillan	Nancy Pinkerton
Jasper Delaney	Ralph Clanton
Zoe Cannel	Lois Smith
Rafe Carter	Phil Sterling
Carter Matson	Jay Gregory
Virgil Paris	Marc Alaimo
Heather Lawrence	AudreyLanders
Luke MacKenzie	Robert Burr
Lai Ling	Helen Funai
Bobby Hanson	Matthew Greene
Joey Cooper	Sean Wood
Buffy	Roxanne Gregory
Carrie Wheeler	Jobeth Williams
Chip Williams	Roger Rathburn
Heather Kane	Audrey Landers
Kate Cannell	Tina Sloan

SOMERSET—30 minutes—NBC— March 30, 1970 - December 31, 1976. Original title: "Another World in Somerset."

THE SOMERSET MAUGHAM THEATRE

See title: "Teller of Tales."

SOMETHING ELSE

Musical Variety. Performances by the recording industry's top artists.

Host: John Byner.

Featured: The Action Faction Dancers.

SOMETHING ELSE—30 minutes— Syndicated 1969. 68 tapes.

SOMETHING SPECIAL

Musical Variety.

Hosts, monthly guests: Barbara McNair, Patti Page, Peggy Lee, The New Christy Minstrels, Pearl Bailey, Allan Sherman, Julie London, The Young Americans, Ethel Waters.

Orchestra: Marty Paich.

SOMETHING SPECIAL—60 minutes —Syndicated 1966. 10 tapes.

SONG SNAPSHOTS ON A SUMMER HOLIDAY

See title: "Merv Griffin."

SONGS FOR SALE

Variety. The material of four songwriters (per show) is performed, then judged and evaluated by professional authorities.

Hosts: Jan Murray; Steve Allen.

Vocalists: Margaret Whiting, Rosemary Clooney, Richard Hayes, Toni Arden, Betty Clooney, Bob Carroll, Martha Stewart, Don Cherry, Eileen Burton, Helen Forrest, Joan Edwards, Johnny Johnston, Jack Robbins, Tony Bennett, Dorothy Field, The Four Aces, The Ink Spots, Richard Himber.

Judges: Mitch Miller, Morey Amsterdam, Bob Hillard, Martin Block, Duke Ellington, Dorothy Loudon.

Orchestra: Ray Bloch.

Producer: Al Span, Herb Morse, Bob Bleyer.

Director: John Morse.

SONGS FOR SALE—30 minutes—CBS 1951.

THE SONNY AND CHER SHOW

Variety. Music, songs, dances, and comedy sketches.

Hosts: Sonny and Cher (Salvatore

The Sonny and Cher Show. Cher (left) and Sonny.

Bono and his wife Cher—Cheryl La Piere).

Regulars: Chastity Bono (their daughter), Peter Cullen, Clive Clerk, Murray Riff, Teri Garr, Freeman King, Steve Parker, Ted Zeigler, Ted Bickle, Tom Filari, Ralph Morrow, Billy Van, Murray Langston, The Jaime Rogers Dancers, The Tony Mordente Dancers, The Earl Brown Singers.

Announcer: Peter Cullen.

Orchestra: Jimmy Dale; Marty Paich.

THE SONNY AND CHER SHOW—60 minutes—CBS—August 1, 1971 - September 5, 1971; December 27, 1971 - May 29, 1974. Also titled: "The Sonny and Cher Comedy Hour." Spin-offs: "Cher" and "The Sonny Comedy Revue."

THE SONNY AND CHER SHOW

Variety. Music, songs, dances, and comedy sketches.

Hosts: Sonny and Cher.

Regulars: Ted Zeigler, Billy Van, Peter

Cullen, Jack Harnell, Richard Lewis, Felix Silla.

Orchestra: Harold Battiste.

Special Musical Material: Billy Barnes, Earl Brown.

Choreographer: Jaime Rogers.

Producer: Nick Vanoff.

Director: Tim Kiley.

THE SONNY AND CHER SHOW—60 minutes—CBS—February 1, 1976 - March 18, 1977.

THE SONNY COMEDY REVUE

Variety. Music, songs, dances, and comedy sketches.

Host: Sonny Bono.

Regulars: Teri Garr, Freeman King, Ted Zeigler, Peter Cullen, Billy Van, Murray Langston.

Announcer: Peter Cullen.

Orchestra: Lex DeAzevedo.

THE SONNY COMEDY REVUE—60 minutes—ABC—September 22, 1974 - December 29, 1974.

SONS AND DAUGHTERS

Drama. Background: Stockton, California, 1956. A depiction of the last innocence of American youth as seen through the eyes of Anita Cramer and Jeff Reed, Southwest High School seniors who are steadily dating and struggling to cope with difficult family readjustments: Jeff, to his father's recent passing; and Anita, to her mother's decision to live with another man.

CAST

Anita Cramer	Glynnis O'Connor
Jeff Reed	Gary Frank
Lucille Reed, Jeff's mother	Jay W. Macintosh
Walter Cramer, Anita's father	John S. Ragin
Ruth Cramer, Anita's mother	Jan Shutan
Danny Reed, Jeff's brother	Michael Morgan

Jeff and Anita's friends:

Murray "Moose" Kerner	Barry Livingston
Stash	Scott Colomby
Charlie	Lionel Johnston
Evie Martinson	Debralee Scott
Mary Anne	Laura Siegel

Music: James Di Pasquale.

SONS AND DAUGHTERS—60 minutes—CBS—September 12, 1974 - November 6, 1974.

SOS FREQUENCY 17

A six-episode series of fifty-two-minute mystery films first syndicated to the U.S. in 1968.

SO THIS IS HOLLYWOOD

Comedy. Background: The LaPaloma Courts, the residence of Kim Tracy, an aspiring actress, and her roommate, Queenie Dugan, a stunt girl. The hopes and heartaches of two young show business hopefuls are seen through the eyes of Kim Tracy as she and Queenie struggle to make their mark on the movie capital.

CAST

Queenie Dugan	Mitzi Green
Kim Tracy	Virginia Gibson
Hubie Dodd, Queenie's boyfriend	Gordon Jones

Andy Boone, Kim's agent	James Lydon
April Adams, Kim's friend, an actress	Peggy Knudsen
Mr. Snead, their landlord	Charles Lane

Narrator: Virginia Gibson.

Mitzi Green's stand-in: Shirley Lucas.

SO THIS IS HOLLYWOOD—30 minutes—NBC—January 1, 1955 - August 19, 1955. 24 episodes. Syndicated.

SOUL TRAIN

Musical Variety. Performances by Soul personalities.

Host: Don Corneileus.

Announcer: Don Cobb.

Music: Recorded.

SOUL TRAIN—60 minutes—Syndicated 1971.

SOUND OFF TIME

Variety. Music, songs, performances by guests, and comedy sketches.

Hosts, on an alternating basis: Bob Hope, Fred Allen, Jerry Lester.

Announcer: Hy Averback.

Orchestra: Les Brown.

Producer: Doug Coulter, Monroe Hack.

Director: Warren Jacober, Ezra Stone.

Sponsor: Chesterfield Cigarettes.

SOUND OFF TIME—30 minutes—NBC —1951 - 1952.

THE SOUNDS OF SUMMER

See title: "Steve Allen."

SOUPY SALES

Listed: The television programs of comedian Soupy Sales.

Program background: Soupy's house.

Characters: White Fang (represented by a white paw), "The biggest and meanest dog in the United States"; Black Tooth (a brown paw), "The kindest dog in the United States."

Puppets: Pookie, the whistling lion; Hippie, the silent hippopotamus; Herman, the flea; Willie, the worm.

Other characters: Marilyn Monwolf, a curvaceous friend of White Fang and Black Tooth; Peaches, Soupy's flirtatious friend; and salesmen and irate neighbors who are seen only by their hands and arms as they talk from the side of the house near an open door.

Programs:

Soupy's On—Children—30 minutes—Local Detroit—1953.

Host: Soupy Sales.

Assistant: Clyde Adler.

The Soupy Sales Show—Children—30 minutes—ABC—July 4, 1955 - August 26, 1955.

Host: Soupy Sales.

Assistant: Clyde Adler.

The Soupy Sales Show—Children—30 minutes—ABC—October 3, 1959 - June 25, 1960. Based on his local Los Angeles show which is aired over

KABC-TV, Ch. 7.

Host: Soupy Sales.

Assistant: Clyde Adler.

The Soupy Sales Show—Children—30 minutes—Syndicated—1966 - 1968. Originally a local New York program aired over WNEW-TV, Ch. 5.

Host: Soupy Sales.

Assistant: Clyde Adler.

Sketch: "The Adventures of Philo Kvetch." A cliff-hanger type of serial wherein private detective Philo Kvetch (Soupy) attempts to apprehend the notorious Mask and his henchman, Onions Oregano (Clyde).

SO YOU WANT TO LEAD A BAND

Variety. Music, comedy vignettes, and songs.

Quiz segment: Four members of the studio audience are selected to lead the orchestra. Studio audience applause determines the winner (the best conductor), who receives a merchandise prize.

Host: Sammy Kaye.

Regulars: Jeffrey Clay, Barbara Benson, Tony Alamo, The Kaydettes, The Kay Choir.

Orchestra: Sammy Kaye.

The Band Boy (brings the baton to the contestant): Chubby Silvers.

Producer: Jim Lichtman, Vic McLeod.

Director: Vic McLeod.

Sponsor: Brillo.

SO YOU WANT TO LEAD A BAND —30 minutes. CBS—1951 - 1954; ABC—1954.

SPACE ACADEMY

Science Fiction Adventure. Era: Earth in the year 3732. The story of the Nova Blue Team, a group of young cadets assigned to the man-made planetoid Space Academy for training. Their experiences, as they patrol, protect, and explore the universe are dramatized.

CAST

Commander Gampu	Jonathan Harris
Cadet Laura Gentry	Pamelyn Ferdin
Captain Chris Gentry	Ric Carrott
Adrian, a cadet	Maggie Cooper
Lt. Paul Jerome	Ty Henderson
Tee Gar Sume, a cadet	Brian Tochi
Loki, the alien	Eric Greene

The Robot: Peepo.

Music: Yvette Blais, Jeff Michael.

Executive Producer: Norm Prescott, Lou Scheimer.

Producer: Arthur H. Nadel.

Director: Jeffrey Hayden, George Tyne.

SPACE ACADEMY—25 minutes— CBS—Premiered: September 10, 1977.

SPACE ACE

Science fiction blended with animation as a superboy from outer space assists Earth in its battle against evil. 30 minutes—Syndicated 1968. 39 episodes.

SPACE ANGEL

Animated Cartoon. The exploits of Scott McCloud, Interplanetary Space Force agent, as he protects the planets of a united solar system from the sinister forces of evil.

Music: Paul Horn.

SPACE ANGEL—05 minutes—Syndicated 1964. 260 episodes.

SPACE GHOST

Animated Cartoon. The exploits of Space Ghost, an interplanetary crime fighter. (Through the use of a magic belt he receives the gift of invisibility.)

Additional characters: Jan and Jayce, his teenage wards; and Blip, their pet space monkey.

Additional segment: "Dino Boy."

Characters' Voices

Space Ghost	Gary Owens
Jan	Ginny Tyler
Jayce	Tim Matthieson
Dino Boy	
(Tod)	Johnny Carson
Ugh	Mike Road

Music: Hoyt Curtin.

Musical Director: Ted Nichols.

Producer-Director: William Hanna, Joseph Barbera.

SPACE GHOST—30 minutes—CBS—September 10, 1966 - September 7, 1968. 48 episodes. A Hanna-Barbera production.

SPACE GIANTS

Science Fiction Adventure. Background: Tokyo, Japan. Seeking to control the planet Earth, Rodak, an evil, alien scientist, appears to Tomoko Mura, a newspaper reporter, and relates the details of his plans.

The published story brings Matuslah, an old, white-bearded alien scientist to Earth. Seeking and finding Tomoko, Matuslah tells him about the evils of Rodak and of his own battle to destroy him. To assist the Earth in its soon to ensue war against Rodak, Matuslah constructs Goldar, a fifty-foot golden robot; Silva, his fifty-foot silver robot wife, and their gold son, Gam.

The series depicts Earth's battle against Rodak, who, by establishing a base in an orbiting spaceship with an advanced laboratory, manufactures and sends to Earth giant, prehistoric type monsters to carry out his plan of domination. Produced in Japan; dubbed in English.

CAST

Tomoko	Mayako Yashiro
Mikko, his wife	Toshio Egi
Itomura	Masumi Okada
Gam	Hideki Ninomiya

Music: Naozumi Yamamoto.

Producer: Kazuo Kamuima.

Writer: Osamu Tezuka.

Program Open:
Announcer: "From the far reaches of outer space comes a threat to planet Earth. Mankind faces its most powerful enemy—the mastermind Rodak. The Space Giants."

SPACE GIANTS—30 minutes—Syndicated 1969. 52 episodes.

SPACE G-MEN

A futuristic space drama about an interplanetary protection organization. 30 minutes—Syndicated 1963. 13 episodes.

SPACE KIDDETTES

Animated Cartoon. The battle against celestial evil as undertaken by the Space Kiddettes, a group of space-age youngsters. A Hanna-Barbera production.

Characters' Voices

Scooter	Chris Allen
Snoopy	Lucille Bliss
Countdown	Don Messick
Jenny	Janet Waldo
Captain Sykhook	Daws Butler
Pupstar	Don Messick

Music: Hoyt Curtin.

SPACE KIDDETTES—30 minutes—NBC—September 10, 1966 - September 2, 1967.

SPACE: 1999

Science Fiction Adventure. Establishing an early warning system on the Moon to repel invaders, three hundred men and women, from all nations on Earth, are assigned to man it. Accidentally blasted out of its orbit due to a radioactive chain reaction, the Moon begins to wander in space, seeking a new planet on which to afix itself. Considered the invaders by the inhabitants of other planets, the marooned Earthlings struggle to combat the life forms of distant worlds, the elements of outer space, and sustain life on their new world as it wanders on its unexpected odyssey across the universe. An I.T.C. production.

Space: 1999. Left to right: Barbara Bain, Catherine Schell, Martin Landau.

CAST

Commander John Koenig	Martin Landau
Dr. Helena Russell	Barbara Bain
Professor Victor Bergman	Barry Morse
Maya, the beautiful alien, a metamor* from the planet Psychon	Catherine Schell
Tony Verdeschi, the security officer	Tony Anholt
Captain Alan Carter	Nick Tate
Sandra Benes, a communications officer (a.k.a. San)	Zienia Merton
Yasko, a communications officer	Yasuko Nagazumi
Dr. Bob Mathias	Anton Phillips
Dr. Ben Vincent	Jeffrey Kisson
Bill Fraser	John Hug
Peter Irving	Michael Culver
Dr. Ed Spencer	Sam Destor
Nurse	Hazel McBride
David Kano	Clifton Jones
Paul Morrow	Prentis Hancock
Commissioner Simmonds	Roy Dotrice

Opening Narration: Barbara Bain.

Music: Barry Gray, Vic Elms, Derek Wadsworth.

* A woman who is capable of transforming herself into any form on which she concentrates.

Executive Producer: Gerry Anderson.

Producer: Sylvia Anderson, F. Sherwin Greene, Fred Freiberger.

Director: Lee H. Katzin, Val Guest, Robert Lynn, Kevin Connor, Tom Clegg, Bob Brooks, Peter Medak, David Tomblin, Ray Austen, Bob Kellett, Charles Crichton.

SPACE: 1999—60 minutes—Syndicated 1975.

SPACE PATROL

Adventure. Era: Twenty-first-century Earth. The battle against celestial dangers as seen through the assignments of Buzz Corey, the commander-in-chief of the Space Patrol, an Earth-based organization responsible for the safety of the United Planets (Earth, Mars, Venus, Jupiter, and Mercury).

CAST

Commander Buzz Corey	Ed Kemmer
Cadet Happy, his co-pilot	Lyn Osborn
Carol Karlyle, the daughter of the Secretary General of the United Planets	Virginia Hewitt
Dr. Von Meter, a Space Patrol scientist	Rudolph Anders
Tonga, a Space Patrol ally	Nina Bara

Also: Jack Narz.

Corey's Rocket Ship: The *X-R-Z.*

Producer: Mike Mosser, Mike Devery, Helen Mosser.

Director: Dick Darley.

Sponsor: Nestle; Ralston.

Program Open:

Announcer: "High adventure in the wild vast regions of space. Missions of daring in the name of interplanetary justice. Travel into the future with Buzz Corey, commander-in-chief of the Space Patrol."

SPACE, PATROL—30 minutes—ABC —September 11, 1950 - December 29, 1956.

SPARRING PARTNERS

Game. Background: A simulated boxing ring. Contestants, who are drawn from business arts and professions, comprise two three member teams— the men vs. the women. The basis is a question and answer game with the team scoring the most correct answers being declared the winner.

Host: Walter Kiernan.

SPARRING PARTNERS—30 minutes —ABC 1949.

SPEAKEASY

Interview. Performances by and interviews with Rock personalities.

Host: Chip Monck.

SPEAKEASY—60 minutes—Syndicated 1973.

SPECIAL AGENT 7

Drama. The investigations of Treasury Agent Conroy as he probes the elements behind crimes perpetrated against the U.S. Department of Internal Revenue. Based on official files.

Starring: Lloyd Nolan as Treasury Agent Conroy.

SPECIAL AGENT 7—30 minutes—Syndicated 1958. 26 episodes.

SPECIAL BRANCH

Crime Drama. Background: London, England. The cases of the Special Branch, an elite team of Scotland Yard undercover agents. Produced in London by Thames TV.

CAST
Chief Inspector
    Craven   George Sewell
Chief Inspector Tom
    Haggerty   Patrick Mower
Chief Inspector
    Strand   Paul Eddington
Commander Fletcher Frederick Jaeger
Music: Robert Earley.

Executive Producer: George Taylor.

Producer: Ted Childs.

SPECIAL BRANCH—60 minutes—Syndicated 1976.

SPECIAL EDITION

Documentary. Filmed versions of magazine stories.

Hostess: Barbara Feldon.

Music: Richard LaSalle.

Producer: Alan Sloan.

Director: Steve Kattin.

SPECIAL EDITION—30 minutes—Syndicated 1977.

SPECIAL FOR WOMEN

Anthology. Sympathetic dramatizations based on the problems faced by women. Following the drama, brief discussions are held with guest doctors and pyschiatrists.

Hostess: Pauline Fredericks.

Producer: George Lefferts.

Sponsor: Purex.

SPECIAL FOR WOMEN—60 minutes —NBC—October 14, 1960 - August 29, 1961.

SPEED BUGGY

Animated Cartoon. Traveling throughout the country in their car, *Speed Buggy*, which possesses a Saint Bernard-like personality, teenagers Debbie, Tinker, and Mark, involve themselves in and attempt to solve the problems of others.

Voices: Chris Allen, Arlene Golonka, Mel Blanc (as *Speed Buggy*), Phil Luther, Jr., Hal Smith, Michele Road, Sid Miller, Ron Feinberg, Virginia Gregg, John Stephenson, Ira Paran.

Music: Hoyt Curtin, Paul DeKorte.

SPEED BUGGY—30 minutes—CBS— September 8, 1973 - August 31, 1974.

SPEED RACER

Animated Cartoon. The exploits of Speed Racer, a daring young racing-car driver. Produced in Japan; dubbed in English.

Characters:

Speed Racer.
Trixie, his girlfriend.

Spridal, Speed's kid brother.

Chim Chim, Spridal's pet monkey.

Speed's car: The *Special Formula Mark Five.*

SPEED RACER—30 minutes—Syndicated 1967. 52 episodes.

SPENCER'S PILOTS

Adventure. Background: California. The exploits of Cass Garrett and Stan Lewis, charter pilots for Spencer Aviation, an organization that undertakes hazardous assignments.

CAST
Cass Garrett	Christopher Stone
Stan Lewis	Todd Susman
Spencer Parish, their employer	Gene Evans
Linda Dann, Spencer's secretary	Margaret Impert
Wig Wiggins, the mechanic	Britt Leach

Music: Bruce Broughton, Morton Stevens, Jerrold Immel.

Executive Producer: Bob Sweeney, Edward H. Feldman.

Producer: Larry Rosen.

Director: Bill Bixby, Marc Daniels, Don Weis, Ernest Pintoff, Bruce Bilson, Gordon Hessler.

SPENCER'S PILOTS—60 minutes—CBS—September 17, 1976 - November 19, 1976.

SPIDER-MAN

Animated Cartoon. Background: New York City. Completing his notes following a demonstration on radioactivity, Central High School student Peter Parker is bitten by a spider that has been exposed to the deadly effects of the demonstration.

Returning home, he realizes that the spider's venom has become a part of his bloodstream and that he has absorbed the proportionate power and ability of a living spider.

Experimenting, he develops his webbed feeler (a liquid that enables him to spin a web) and the costume of Spider-Man to conceal his real identity.

Acquiring a position as reporter for the *New York Daily Bugle,* he institutes a battle against crime, dispensing justice as the mysterious Spider-Man.

Characters' Voices
Peter Parker/ Spider-Man	Bernard Cowan
	Paul Sols
Betty Brandt, a reporter	Peg Dixon
J. Jonah Jameson, the editor	Paul Kligman

Music: Ray Ellis.

Theme: Bob Harris, Paul Francis Webster.

Executive Producer: Robert L. Lawrence, Ralph Bakshi.

Producer: Ray Patterson.

Director: Ralph Bakshi.

Note: On September 14, 1977, CBS presented a ninety-minute live action pilot film, titled "Spider-Man," with Nicholas Hammond in the title role and David White as J.J. Jameson.

SPIDER-MAN—30 minutes—ABC—September 9, 1967 - August 30, 1969; March 22, 1970 - September 6, 1970. 52 episodes. Syndicated.

SPIKE JONES

Listed: The television programs of

comic Spike Jones.

The Spike Jones Show—Variety—60 minutes—NBC 1951.

Host: Spike Jones.

Regulars: Helen Grayco, Jan Peerce, The Wayne Marlin Trio.

Orchestra: The City Slickers.

The Spike Jones Show—Variety—60 minutes—NBC—January 2, 1954 - May 8, 1954.

Host: Spike Jones.

Regulars: Helen Grayco, George Rock, Freddie Morgan, Sir Frederick Gar.

Orchestra: The City Slickers.

The Spike Jones Show—Variety—30 minutes—CBS—April 2, 1957 - June 25, 1957.

Host: Spike Jones.

Regulars: Helen Grayco, Billy Barty, The Dixie Pixies, The Polka Dots, The Clypso Kings, The Rock 'N' Rollers.

Orchestra: The City Slickers.

Club Oasis—Variety—30 minutes—ABC—June 1958-September 6, 1958.

Host: Spike Jones.

Regulars: Helen Grayco, Joyce Jameson, Billy Barty, Georgia Rock, Gil Bernard, Carl Fortina, Joel Paul.

Orchestra: The City Slickers.

The Spike Jones Show—Variety—60 minutes—CBS—August 1, 1960 - September 19, 1960; July 17, 1961 - September 1961.

Host: Spike Jones.

Vocalist: Helen Grayco.

Orchestra: The City Slickers.

SPIN-OFF

Game. Before each of the two husband-and-wife teams that compete are five wheels that each contain numbers (1 to 6) and spin at the rate of seventeen numbers per second. The game begins when the host reads a question. The team that is first to identify themselves through a buzzer signal receives a chance to answer. If correct, they receive a chance to play the spinning wheels. One player activates the wheels by pressing a green plunger. The other player presses a red plunger to stop one of the wheels. A number is then revealed. Since scoring follows the rules of poker, they can either keep it or spin it off and try for a different number (only three spins are permitted per wheel). Once the decision is made, another question is asked and the game follows in the same manner (five questions are played per game). The team that scores the highest number values (as in cards) wins the game and the money associated with the numbers (1 pair: $50; 2 pair: $75; 3 of a kind: $100; straight: $125; full house: $150; 5 of a kind: $200).

Host: Jim Lange.

Music: Recorded.

SPIN-OFF—30 minutes—CBS—June 16, 1975 - September 5, 1975.

SPIN THE PICTURE

Game. Object: For players to identify photographs of famous celebrities. A rapidly spun picture is flashed on a screen and is accompanied by a verbal clue. A telephone call is then placed to a home viewer. If the home viewer can identify the picture, he receives the merchandise prizes that have been accumulated to date. If not, an additional prize is added to the jackpot and the player receives a consolation prize.

Hostess: Kathi Norris.

Assistant: Eddie Dunn.

SPIN THE PICTURE—60 minutes—DuMont 1949.

SPLIT PERSONALITY

Game. Two competing contestants. Two sets of clues, each depicting one facet of a celebrity's life, are related by the host. The player who is first to identify the represented personality is the winner of that round and receives points. Winners, the highest point scorers, receive merchandise prizes.

Host: Tom Poston.

Producer: Mark Goodson, Bill Todman, Robert Rowe.

SPLIT PERSONALITY—30 minutes —NBC—September 28, 1959 - February 5, 1960.

SPLIT SECOND

Game. Three competing contestants.

Round One: Three topics are displayed (e.g., *Mad* magazine, *Playboy* magazine, and *World* magazine). The host then reads a question that refers to the topic. ("Pick one of these current magazines and tell me did it begin publishing before or after 1960.") Players each sound a bell and receive a chance to answer as they are recognized. Each player chooses one of the three topics and states his answer. If all three responses are correct, the players each receive five

dollars; if only two are correct, these players receive ten dollars each; should only one player correctly respond, he receives twenty-five dollars. (Answers: *Mad* and *Playboy*, before 1960; *World*, after 1960.)

Round Two: Played in the same manner with larger cash amounts: one correct response, fifty dollars; two correct answers, twenty-five dollars; three correct, ten dollars each.

Round Three: Each player is assigned a specific number of questions to answer. The highest cash scorer has to answer three questions; the second -place contestant, four questions; and the lowest scorer, five questions. The topics are displayed followed by their questions. The first player to be recognized is permitted to answer one or all parts of the question. The player who is first to answer all his questions is the winner. Losers receive their accumulated earnings.

The champion is brought downstage and placed opposite five new automobiles—only one of which will start. He selects one, and turns the ignition key. 'If the car starts he wins it; if not, he is permitted to return and compete again.

Host: Tom Kennedy.

Announcer: Jack Clark.

SPLIT SECOND—30 minutes—ABC—March 20, 1972 - June 27, 1975.

SPORTS CHALLENGE

Game. Two competing teams, each composed of three sports personalities. Basis: Sports-related question-and-answer rounds.

Rounds One and Two: "Break the Record." A film clip is shown, followed by a question that relates to it.

The team that is first to identify itself through a buzzer signal receives a chance to answer. If correct, twenty-five points are scored.

Round Three: "Unforgettable Moments." Same format as above; sixty points are scored for correct answers.

Finale: "The Biography Round." The biography of a prominent sports figure is read. The team that correctly identifies the personality receives sixty points.

Winners, the highest point scorers, receive AMF sports equipment for purposes of donation to worthy causes.

Host: Dick Enberg.

Announcer: Johnny Gilbert.

SPORTS CHALLENGE—30 minutes —Syndicated 1971.

SPOTLIGHT

A daily dramatic series that adopts stories from all fields including plays and novels. Each play stars three actors, one of whom narrates, and uses no sets and few props. The use of music, rear-screen projection and sound-effects, coupled with the viewer's imagination, provides the setting. 30 minutes—Syndicated 1954.

SPOTLIGHT

Variety. Produced in England. Guest celebrities host.

Regulars: The Lionel Blair Dancers.

Orchestra: Jack Parnell.

Producer-Director: Ian Scofield.

SPOTLIGHT—60 minutes—CBS—July 4, 1967 - August 29, 1967.

SPOTLIGHT ON THE STARS

Anthology. Rebroadcasts of dramas originally aired via other filmed anthology programs.

SPOTLIGHT ON THE STARS—30 minutes—CBS—June 1958 - September 1958.

SPOTLIGHT PLAYHOUSE

Anthology. Rebroadcasts of dramas originally aired via other filmed anthology programs.

Included:

The Net Draws Tight. The story of a roadside diner owner who suspects and attempts to discover if his teenage helper is robbing him.

CAST
Edmond O'Brien, Skip Homeier, Paul Bryar.

Something Wonderful. The story of an actress who decides to take one final fling at a stage career before marrying and settling down.

CAST
Marcia Patrick, Claude Dauphin, John Bryat.

The Long Trail. The struggles faced by a Texas Ranger as he attempts to bring a murder suspect to Oregon.

CAST
Anthony Quinn, Robert Armstrong, Maxine Cooper, John Bryat.

SPOTLIGHT PLAYHOUSE–30 minutes–CBS–June 21, 1955 - September 21, 1955.

SPOTLIGHT PLAYHOUSE

Anthology. Retitled episodes of "Ford Theatre."

Included:

Four Things He'd Do. Background: The Old West. When ridiculed by the townspeople for his inability to find gold, a young Irishman becomes even more determined to find gold and show them he's a man to be reckoned with.

CAST
Michael O'Shea.

Model Wife. The story of a model who struggles to acquire the attentions of a photographer who couldn't care less about her.

CAST
Ralph Bellamy, Felica Farr, Emlen Davis, Pat Conway.

The Man Across the Hall. Discovering that a friend of her mother's is coming to visit, a young woman, who is not a successful television star and lives in a run-down apartment, acquires the keys to the glamorous apartment of the man who lives across the hall and attempts to impress the friend by saying that she lives there. Complications ensue when the man, who cut his weekend short, returns home.

CAST
Robert Sterling, Vera-Ellen, Marga Deighton.

SPOTLIGHT PLAYHOUSE–30 minutes–CBS–July 2, 1957 - September 1957.

SPOTLIGHT PLAYHOUSE

Anthology. Retitled episodes of "The Loretta Young Theatre." Selected dramas do not star Loretta Young.

Hostess: Anita Louise.
Music: Harry Lubin.

Included:

Power Play. The story of a coach who believes his lifelong dream has been fulfilled when he is asked to coach a college football team.

CAST
Anita Louise, James Daly.

Man On A String. A wife's difficulties as she struggles to understand her husband, a writer, and his preoccupation with work.

CAST
Laraine Day, Kim Spaulding.

The Defense. Accepting the case of a delinquent, an attorney attempts to prevent him from making the same mistakes that he made as a youth.

CAST
Mark Stevens, Addison Richards.

SPOTLIGHT PLAYHOUSE–30 minutes–CBS–July 1, 1958 - September 1958.

SPOTLIGHT PLAYHOUSE

Anthology. Rebroadcasts of dramas originally aired via other filmed anthology programs.

Hostess: Julia Meade.

Host: Zachary Scott.

Included:

The Dead Are Silent. Infatuated with a young admirer, a woman, the beautiful wife of a tyrannical man, plots to leave her husband.

CAST

Susan Hobson: Glynis Johns; Aaron Hobson: Robert Middleton; Mary Lee: Sandy Descher.

That's The Man. The effect of a false robbery charge accusation on the life of an innocent man.

CAST

Russell Kent: Ray Milland; Evelyn Kent: Nancy Davis.

Tunnel Eight. Era: The 1860s. The obstacles that plague railroad officials as they attempt to lay track.

CAST

Preston Foster.

A Question Of Survival. Surrounded by Commanche Indians, a cavalry captain faces a difficult decision: to let the doctor, a man he despises, operate on the chief's fatally injured son, which would mean his certain death, but an escape for his men; or risk the lives of his squad in one inevitable battle.

CAST

Capt. John Arnette: Ronald Reagan; Dr. Towne: Kevin McCarthy; Charlie Taney: Arthur Space.

SPOTLIGHT PLAYHOUSE—30 minutes—CBS—June 1959 - September 1959.

SPREAD OF THE EAGLE

Anthology. Dramatizations based on the Roman plays of William Shakespeare: *Anthony and Cleopatra, Coriolanus* and *Julius Caesar.* Produced by the B.B.C.

Performers:. Paul Eddington, Barry Jones, Peter Cushing, Keith Michell, Mary Morris, David Williams, Jerome Willis.

SPREAD OF THE EAGLE—60 minutes—Syndicated 1964. 9 episodes.

SPUNKY AND TADPOLE

Animated Cartoon. The adventures of Spunky, a young boy, and his come-to-life teddy bear, Tadpole, as they battle evil.

Voices: Joan Gardner.

SPUNKY AND TADPOLE—05 minutes—Syndicated 1960. 150 episodes.

THE SQUARE WORLD OF ED BUTLER

Discussion. Discussions with concerned guests on topical issues.

Host: Ed Butler.

Music: Recorded.

THE SQUARE WORLD OF ED BUTLER—30 minutes—Syndicated 1970.

S.R.O. PLAYHOUSE

Anthology. Retitled episodes of "Schlitz Playhouse of Stars."

Included:

Two Bit Gangster. Traveling to a small town to cover what appears to be a routine robbery, a reporter discovers that a master thief has killed an ex-con who interfered with the getaway. The story depicts the reporter's attempts to find the murderer and the reason why the ex-con risked his life to foil the robbery.

CAST
Keenan Wynn, Robert Wilke, Addison Richards.

Moment Of Triumph. The story of a college professor who is unjustly discharged because he refuses to give a wealthy man's son the passing grade he does not deserve.

CAST
Kevin McCarthy, Eduard Franz, Angela Greene.

Foolproof. After an accident, a woman awakens in a hospital bed. Her eyes are covered with bandages and, unknown to her, she has been kidnapped and is being held hostage. The story relates the attempts of the kidnappers to fool her long enough to collect the ransom.

CAST
Claire Trevor, Walter Coy, Christopher Dark.

S.R.O. PLAYHOUSE—60 minutes—CBS—May 11, 1957 - September 1957.

THE S.S. HOLIDAY

Musical Variety.
Host: Phil Hanna.

Regulars: Ralph Stanley, Marya, Joe Curtis, Hollis Harris.
Musical Interlude: Reginald Beane, pianist.

THE S.S. HOLIDAY—30 minutes—DuMont 1950.

THE S.S. TELE CRUISER

Variety. Musical numbers played against photographic backgrounds.
Host: Jack Steck.
Regulars: Eddie Roecker, Carol Wynne, Bon Bon, The Thomas Cannon Ballet, The Crewman.
Music: The Dave Appel Trio.

THE S.S. TELE CRUISER—2 hours—ABC—April 28, 1951 - September 1951.

STAGECOACH WEST

Western. Background: Areas between California and Missouri during the 1860s. The experiences of Luke Perry and Simon Kane, drivers for the Overland Stage Coach Lines.

CAST
Luke Perry	Wayne Rogers
Simon Kane (a widower)	Robert Bray
David Kane, Simon's son	Richard Eyer

STAGECOACH WEST—60 minutes—ABC—October 4, 1960 - September 26, 1961. Syndicated. 38 episodes.

STAGE DOOR

A dramatic series that focuses on

show-business life. Starring Louise Albritton and Scott McKay. 30 minutes—CBS 1950.

STAGE ENTRANCE

Variety. Performances by undiscovered professional talent.
Host: Earl Wilson.

STAGE ENTRANCE—15 minutes—DuMont 1951.

STAGE 7

Anthology. Dramatic presentations.

Included:

Appointment In Highbridge. The romance between a British army captain and an American nurse is recalled when the two meet ten years later in New York City.
Starring: Dan O'Herlihy.

The Legacy. After her grandmother's death, a young woman, who had unselfishly cared for her for three years, struggles to claim her share of the inheritance from a greedy cousin who wants it all.
Starring: Vanessa Brown, Elizabeth Patterson, George Nader.

Debt Of Honor. The difficult assignment of a detective: the man he is ordered to bring in is the man who saved his daughter's life.
Starring: Edmond O'Brien.

The Deceiving Eye. Incorporating unorthodox methods, a criminology professor attempts to prove that the eye never accurately records what it sees.
Starring: Frank Lovejoy.

STAGE 7—30 minutes—CBS—January 30, 1955 - September 25, 1955.

STAGE SHOW

Musical Variety.
Hosts: Tommy and Jimmy Dorsey.
Featured: The June Taylor Dancers.
Music: The Dorsey Orchestra.

STAGE SHOW—60 minutes—CBS—July 2, 1954 - September 18, 1954; March 12, 1955 - March 19, 1955; 30 minutes—October 1, 1955 - September 26, 1956.

STAGE 13

A thirty-minute anthology series, produced and directed by Wyllis Cooper, that, geared to children, was first broadcast by CBS in 1950.

STAGE TWO REVUE

Musical Revue.
Hostess: Georgia Lee.
Regulars: Arlene Harris, Bob Harris.
Orchestra: Buzz Adlam.

STAGE TWO REVUE—60 minutes—ABC—1949 - 1951.

STAND UP AND BE COUNTED

Advice. Basis: The solving of problems. Participants, who are selected via letters, appear on stage and state the specific problems that confront them. Selected studio-audience members then suggest solutions. Through an audience vote, the most feasible advice is tried by the participants. At a later date, he returns and states the results of the advice.

Host: Bob Russell.

STAND UP AND BE COUNTED—30 minutes—CBS 1956.

STAND UP AND CHEER

See title: "Johnny Mann's Stand Up and Cheer."

STANLEY

Comedy. Background: New York City. The misadventures of Stanley, the sloppy, nonaggressive proprietor of a hotel-lobby newsstand.

CAST

Stanley	Buddy Hackett
Celia, his girlfriend	Carol Burnett
Mr. Phillips, the hotel manager	Frederic Tozere
Jane, Celia's girlfriend	Jane Connell

STANLEY—30 minutes—NBC—September 24, 1956 - March 11, 1957.

STAR ATTRACTION

Anthology. Rebroadcasts of dramas originally aired via other filmed anthology programs.

STAR ATTRACTION—30 minutes—ABC—June 1958 - September 1958.

STAR FOR TODAY

Anthology. Retitled episodes of "Telephone Time."

Hosts: John Nesbitt, Dr. Frank Baxter.

Included:

Campaign For Marriage. The story of a young woman who plots to acquire the proposal of her employer, the attorney general of Montana.

CAST
Robert Sterling, Anne Jeffreys.

She Sette. Her Little Foote. The story of a group of women from London sent to become the wives of Virginia colonists.

CAST
Barbara Baxley, Ron Randall.

Smith of Ecuador. A dramatization recounting the disastrous 1949 earthquake that struck Ecuador.

CAST
Harold J. Stone.

STAR FOR TODAY—30 minutes—Syndicated 1963.

THE STARLAND VOCAL BAND

Musical Variety.

Starring: The Starland Vocal Band: Bill Danoff, Taffy Danoff, Margot Chapman, Jon Carroll.

Regulars: Mark Russell, David Letterman.

Announcer: David Letterman.

Musical Director: Eddie Karam.

Executive Producer: Jerry Weintraub.

Producer: Al Rogers.

Director: Rick Bennewitz.

THE STARLAND VOCAL BAND—30 minutes—CBS—July 31, 1977 - September 2, 1977. 6 tapes.

STARLIT TIME

Musical Revue.

Host: Phil Hanna.

Regulars: Bill Williams, Gordon Dilworth, Holly Harris, Alan Prescott, Ed Holmes, Bibi Osterwald, The Reggie Beane Dancers.

Music: The Reggie Beane Trio.

STARLIT TIME—45 minutes—DuMont 1950.

THE STARLOST

Science Fiction. Era: Earth, A.D. 2790. Unable to marry Rachel, the girl he loves, because he is the son of a poor farmer, Devon defies the law and speaks in protest. Deemed unsuitable by the elders, he is sentenced to death. Escaping their grasp, he enters a forbidden cave wherein the Earth Ship Ark lies. Approaching a control board, he accidentally activates a computer and learns of the fate of Earth from Mulander One Sixty-Five, a recorded image: "In the year A.D. 2285, a catastrophe...threatened all Earth life with extinction...so the Committee of Scientists...set about selecting desireable elements of Earth life to seed other planets...to do this, the committee between Earth and the Moon had to build Earth Ship Ark...an organic cluster of environ-mental domes called biospheres, looped to each other through tubular corridors for life support power and communication. In the biospheres we have representative segments of Earth's population, three million souls in all. Whole, separate ecologies sealed from each other and isolated to preserve their characteristics...Earth Ship Ark was launched...to seek out and find a solar system of a class six star...Earth Ship Ark traveled for one hundred years before...there was an accident...Earth Ship Ark locked in collision course with class G solar star, an unidentified sun...no further data recorded."

Returning to his home in Cypress Corners, Devon seeks Rachel, but when returning to the ship, they are followed by Garth, the man who is pledged to marry her. Unable to persuade Rachel to return with him, Garth remains, determined to protect Rachel from Devon.

Drifting in space for eight hundred years and containing the sole survivors of the dead planet Earth—beings locked in separate worlds—Devon Rachel, and Garth begin their exploration of the various biospheres seeking to find someone or something to explain the mystery of the great catastrophe and save the remains of Earth life by locating a class six star. The Starlost. Produced in Canada.

CAST

Devon	Keir Dullea
Rachel	Gay Rowan
Garth	Robin Ward
Mulander One Sixty-five, the computer host	William Osler

Music: Score Productions.

THE STARLOST—60 minutes—Syndicated 1973. 16 episodes.

STAR MAIDENS

Science Fiction Adventure. Faraway, in the solar system Proxsema Centauri, there exists the planet Medusa— a world of advanced, humanlike life in which women are the rulers and men subservient. For one thousand orbits the populace enjoyed a life of peace and serenity. Then suddenly, the great comet Dioneses, with its awesome force, passes over the planet; Medusa's orbit is altered and the planet is slowly dragged toward the frozen regions of outer space. Before its final destination—a planet of ice—the Medusians plan and construct a new world beneath the surface.

Now, frozen, and having drifted for generations, the planet locks itself onto a solar system in which another life supporting planet—Earth—is discovered. The Earth, however, contridicts the Medusians programmed society and is declared out of bounds to all its citizens.

As with all laws, it, too, is violated, when two Medusian men, Adam and Shem, escape to Earth and thus open the doorway for the inhabitants of the two worlds to meet. The series depicts incidents in the lives of the Earthlings and Medusians as they meet and interact for the first time.

CAST

Fulvia, a Medusian leader	Sally Geeson
Octavia, a Medusian leader	Christiane Kruger
Liz, the Earth scientist	Lisa Harrow
Adam, Fulvia's servant	Pierre Brice
Shem, the mechanic, Adam's friend	Gareth Thomas
The Medusian Announcer	Penelope Horner
Evans	Derek Farr
Kate Moss	Jenny Morgan
Rudi	Christian Quadflieg

Music: Patrick Aulton.

Producer-Director: James Gatward.

Creator: Eric Paice.

STAR MAIDENS—30 minutes—Syndicated 1977. Produced in England.

STAR OF THE FAMILY

Variety. Music and songs coupled with performances by selected members of American families (preselected by letters that are written to the program by members of the individual's family).

Host: Morton Downey.

Regulars: Peter Lind Hayes, Mary Healy, The Beatrice Kroft Dancers.

Announcer: Frank Waldeeker.

Orchestra: Carl Hoff.

Producer: Perry Lafferty, Coby Ruskin, Newt Stammer.

Director: John Wray.

Sponsor: Ronson Lighters; Kelvinator.

STAR OF THE FAMILY—60 minutes—CBS 1952.

STAR ROUTE

Musical Variety. Performances by possessors of gold records in Country and Western music.

Host: Rod Cameron.

Regulars: Glenn Campbell, Lorrie Collins, The Collins Kids.

Orchestra: Gene Davis.

STAR ROUTE—30 minutes—Syndicated 1964. 26 tapes.

STARRING BORIS KARLOFF

Anthology. Mystery presentations.

Host-Performer: Boris Karloff.

Announcer: George Gunn.

Organist: George Henniger.

STARRING BORIS KARLOFF–30 minutes–ABC 1949.

STARSKY AND HUTCH

Crime Drama. The investigations of Dave Starsky and Ken "Hutch" Hutchinson, plainclothes police detectives.

CAST

Dave Starsky	Paul Michael Glaser
Ken "Hutch" Hutchinson	David Soul
Captain Dobey, their superior	Bernie Hamilton
Huggy Bear, their information man	Antonio Fargas

Starsky and Hutch. David Soul (left) and Paul Michael Glaser.

Music: Lalo Schifrin, Tom Scott, Jack Elliott, Allyn Ferguson.

Executive Producer: Aaron Spelling, Leonard Goldberg.

Producer: Joseph T. Naar.

Creator: William Blinn.

STARSKY AND HUTCH–60 minutes–ABC–Premiered: September 10, 1975.

STAR SPANGLED REVUE

A series of lavish variety hours produced by Max Liebman and directed by Hal Keith. First broadcast on NBC in 1950, the series would later emerge into television's first specials series, "Max Liebman Presents," which see for information.

STAR STAGE

Anthology. Dramatic presentations.

STAR STAGE–30 minutes–NBC–September 9, 1955 - September 7, 1956.

STAR THEATRE

Anthology. Rebroadcasts of dramas that were originally aired via other filmed anthology programs.

Included:

Passport To Life. The story of a Russian commissar who reverts to slave practices in a small Hungarian town.

Starring: William Campbell.

Fortunatus. A French immigrant's

search for gold in California.

Starring: Jacques Sernas.

Recipe For Success. The story of Henri Charpentier, the creator of the crêpe suzette.

Starring: Walter Slezak.

The Hole in the Wall. Era: World War II Germany. Trapped in a farmhouse occupied by a German patrol, two members of the Italian underground desperately attempt to escape unnoticed.

Starring: Paul J. Cessari, Joseph Vitale.

Away Boarders. A redramatization of the capture of a German submarine that was captured by boarding in 1944.

Starring: Arthur Space, Robert Brubaker.

Program Open:

Announcer: "From the world's most exotic cities, from Paris, London, Shanghai, New York, stories of the people who give these cities life on Star Theatre."

STAR THEATRE—30 minutes—Syndicated 1963.

STARTIME

Musical Variety.

Hosts: Frances Langford, Don Ameche.

Regulars: Lew Parker, Ben Blue, Phil Regan, Kathryn Lee, The Benny Goodman Sextet, The Don Liberti Chorus.

Orchestra: Artego.

Producer: Hubbell Robinson, Robert Wright.

Director: George Forbes, Robert Wright.

STARTIME—60 minutes—DuMont—1950-1951.

STAR TIME PLAYHOUSE

Anthology. Dramatic presentations.

STAR TIME PLAYHOUSE—30 minutes—CBS 1954.

STAR TONIGHT

Anthology. Dramatic presentations. Scripts are suited to the talents of young performers.

Included:

Giants' Star. A sheriff's efforts to locate a missing woman's husband during the rages of a rain storm.

Starring: Bruce Gordon.

You Need Me. The fears of a reformed alcoholic as he prepares to meet his wife's family for the first time.

Starring: Jacqueline Holt, Kevin McCarthy, Joanna Ross, Fred Stewart.

Uppercut. The influence of a beautiful woman on the rigid life of a prizefighter.

Starring: Steve Barclay.

STAR TONIGHT—30 minutes—ABC —February 3, 1955 - August 9, 1956.

Star Trek. Nichelle Nichols (top, left), DeForest Kelley (top, right), Leonard Nimoy (bottom left), William Shatner (bottom right).

STAR TREK

Science Fiction Adventure. Era: The twenty-second century. The voyages of the starship U.S.S. *Enterprise,* representing the United Federation of Planets, as it explores the endless universe, seeking new life, new worlds, and new civilizations. Created by Gene Roddenberry.

CAST

Captain James Kirk, commander of the *Enterprise*	William Shatner
Science Officer Spock, half Earthling, half Vulcan	Leonard Nimoy
Dr. Leonard McCoy ("Bones"), the chief medical officer	DeForest Kelley
Lieutenant Uhura, the communications officer	Nichelle Nichols
Lt. Commander Montgomery Scott ("Scotty"), the chief engineer	James Doohan
Yeoman Janice Rand	Grace Lee Whitney
Nurse Christine Chapel, McCoy's assistant	Majel Barrett
Mr. Sulu, a navigator	George Takei
Ensign Paval Chekov, a navigator	Walter Koenig
Mr. Farrell, a navigator	Jim Goodwin
Lt. Starnes	James Wellman

Narrator: William Shatner.

Music: Alexander Courage; Fred Steiner; Gerald Fried; Wilbur Hatch; George Duning; Sol Kaplan.

Executive Producer: Gene Roddenberry.

Producer: John Meredyth Lucas, Gene L. Coon, Fred Freiberger.

Director: Marc Daniels, Herschel Daugherty, Ralph Senesky, Harvey Hart, James Komack, John Meredyth Lucas, John Newland, Joseph Pevney, Jud Taylor, Robert Sparr, Michael O'Herlihy, Herb Wallerstein, Murray Golden, David Alexander, Marvin Chomsky, Joseph Sargent, Herbert Kenwith, Don McDougall, Gerd Oswald, Robert Gist, James Goldstone, Vincent McEveety, Tony Leader, Lawrence Dobkin, Leo Penn.

The Enterprise identification number: NCC 1701.

STAR TREK—60 minutes—NBC—September 8, 1966 - April 4, 1969. Rebroadcasts: NBC—June 3, 1969 -

September 9, 1969. 78 episodes. Syndicated.

Animated Version:

STAR TREK. The further explorations of the starship *Enterprise*.

Characters' Voices

Captain James
   Kirk   William Shatner
Science Officer
   Spock   Leonard Nimoy
Dr. Leonard
   McCoy   DeForest Kelley
Lieutenant Uhura   Nichelle Nichols
Mr. Sulu   George Takei
Chief Engineer Montgomery
   Scott   James Doohan
Ensign Paval
   Chekov   Walter Koenig
Nurse Christine
   Chapel   Majel Barrett

Music: Yvette Blais, Jeff Michael.

Producer: Norm Prescott, Lou Scheimer.

Director: Hal Sutherland.

STAR TREK—30 minutes—NBC—September 8, 1973 - August 30, 1975.

STARS OVER HOLLYWOOD

Anthology. Dramatic presentations.

STARS OVER HOLLYWOOD—30 minutes—NBC 1950.

STATE TROOPER

Crime Drama. Background: Nevada. The investigations of Rod Blake, chief of the Nevada State Troopers.

Starring: Rod Cameron as Rod Blake.

Music: Stanley Wilson; Maury Leaf.

STATE TROOPER—30 minutes—Syndicated 1957. 104 episodes.

STEP THIS WAY

Dance Contest. Selected studio-audience couples compete in two phases of a dance contest: their own specialty dances and "The Dance of the Week Selection." Couples are judged and the winners receive merchandise gifts.

Versions:

Step This Way—30 minutes—ABC—July 25, 1955 - April 14, 1956.

Host: Bobby Sherwood.

Judges: Zedan and Carol, professional dancers.

Orchestra: Nat Brandywyne; Buddy Weed.

Step This Way—30 minutes—Syndicated 1966.

Hostess: Gretchen Wyler.

Announcer: Jim Lucas.

Judges: Guest celebrities (three per show).

Orchestra: Warren,Covington.

STEVE ALLEN

Listed: The television programs of author-comedian-composer-pianist Steve Allen.

Songs For Sale—Variety—30 minutes—CBS—1951. See title.

Talent Patrol—Variety—30 minutes—ABC—1953.

Format: Performances by servicemen.

Host: Steve Allen.

Hostess: Arlene Francis.

The Tonight Show—Variety—40 minutes (11:20 p.m.-12:00 a.m.)—Local New York (WNBT-TV, Ch. 4)—July 27, 1953 - September 24, 1954.

Host: Steve Allen.

Regulars: Steve Lawrence, Helen Dixon, Pat Kirby.

Announcer: Gene Rayburn.

Orchestra: Bobby Byrne.

The Tonight Show—Variety—90 minutes—NBC—September 27, 1954 - January 25, 1957 (Steve's appearance as the host).

Host: Steve Allen.

Regulars: Steve Lawrence, Eydie Gormé, Pat Marshall, Helen Dixon, Andy Williams, Don Knotts, Tom Poston, Louis Nye.

Announcer: Gene Rayburn.

Orchestra: Skitch Henderson.

The Steve Allen Show—Variety—60 minutes—NBC—June 24, 1956 - May 3, 1959.

Host: Steve Allen.

Regulars: Don Knotts (as The Nervous Chap), Louis Nye (as Gordon Hathaway), Tom Poston (as The Perennial Amnesiac), Skitch Henderson (The Man from the Bronx), Dayton Allen (as The Why Not Man), Gabe Dell, Pat Harrington, Jr., Bill Dana (as Jose Jiménez).

Announcer: Gene Rayburn.

Orchestra: Skitch Henderson.

Commercial Spokesman: John Cameron Swayze; Erin O'Brian.

The New Steve Allen Show—Variety—60 minutes—NBC—1959 - 1960.

Host: Steve Allen.

Regulars: Louis Nye, Don Knotts, Dayton Allen, Gabe Dell, Pat Harrington, Jr.

Orchestra: Les Brown.

The New Steve Allen Show—Variety—60 minutes—ABC—September 27, 1961 - December 27, 1961.

Host: Steve Allen.

Regulars: Louis Nye, Pat Harrington, Jr., Joey Forman, Bill Dana, The Smothers Brothers (Tom and Dick), Tim Conway.

Orchestra: Les Brown.

The Steve Allen Show—Variety—90 minutes—Syndicated 1963.

Host: Steve Allen.

Announcer: Johnny Jacobs.

Orchestra: Donn Trenner.

I've Got a Secret—Game—30 minutes—CBS—1964 - 1967. See title.

The Steve Allen Comedy Hour—Comedy—60 minutes—CBS—July 1967 - September 1967.

Host: Steve Allen.

Regulars: Jayne Meadows, Ruth Briggs, Louis Nye, The David Winters Dancers.

Music: The Terry Gibbs Band.

The Steve Allen Show—Variety—90- and 60-minute versions (pending local stations)—Syndicated 1968. Also known as "The Allen Show" and "The New Steve Allen Show."

Host: Steve Allen.

Orchestra: Paul Smith.

The Sounds of Summer—Music—2 hours—NET—June 1, 1969 - August 1969.

Format: Jazz, Folk, and Symphonic concerts.

Host: Steve Allen.

Music: Provided by guest performers.

I've Got a Secret–Game–30 minutes –Syndicated 1972. See title.

Steve Allen's Laugh-Back–Variety– 90 minutes–Syndicated 1976. The series combines new material with clips from Steve's previous series.

Host: Steve Allen.

Regulars: Jayne Meadows, Louis Nye, Bill Dana, Martha Raye, Don Knotts, Skitch Henderson, Pat Harrington.

Music: The Terry Gibbs Sextet.

Executive Producer: Jerry Harrison.

Producer: Rogers Ailes.

Director: John Rumbaugh.

Meeting of the Minds–History–60 minutes–PBS–January 15, 1977 - February 19, 1977. In an intimate party setting, several historical figures meet to discuss their lives, careers and the world situation.

Host: Steve Allen.

Featured: Jayne Meadows.

Music: Steve Allen.

Creator-Writer: Steve Allen.

Producer: Perry Rosemond.

STEVE CANYON

Adventure. Background: Big Thunder Air Force base. The investigations of Lieutenant Colonel Stevenson B. Canyon, pilot-troubleshooter, as he probes the elements behind crimes perpetrated against the U.S. government. Based on the comic strip by Milton Coniff.

CAST

Lt. Col. Steve Canyon	Dean Fredericks
Major Willie Williston, his superior	Jerry Paris

Music: Walter Schumann, Nathan Scott.

STEVE CANYON–30 minutes–NBC –September 13, 1958 - September 7, 1959.

STEVE DONOVAN, WESTERN MARSHAL

Western. Background: The Frontier during the latter nineteenth century. The exploits of U.S. Marshal Steve Donovan and his deputy, Rusty Lee, as they attempt to maintain law and order.

CAST

Steve Donovan	Douglas Kennedy
Rusty Lee	Eddy Waller

STEVE DONOVAN, WESTERN MARSHAL–30 minutes–Syndicated 1955. 39 episodes.

THE STEVE LAWRENCE AND EYDIE GORMÉ SHOW

Musical Variety.

Hosts: Steve Lawrence, Eydie Gormé.

Vocalists: The Artie Malvin Singers.

Announcer: Gene Rayburn.

Orchestra: Jack Kane.

THE STEVE LAWRENCE AND

EYDIE GORMÉ SHOW—60 minutes —NBC—July 13, 1958 - September 1958.

THE STEVE LAWRENCE SHOW

Musical Variety.

Host: Steve Lawrence.

Regulars: Charles Nelson Reilly, Donna Mills, Betty Walker, The Pussycat Dancers.

Orchestra: Joe Guercio.

THE STEVE LAWRENCE SHOW—60 minutes—CBS—September 13, 1965 - December 13, 1965.

STINGRAY

Marionette Adventure. Era: Earth, A.D. 2000. The battle against the destructive forces of evil as undertaken by the World Aquanaut Security Patrol, an international organization established on the ocean floor. Filmed in Supermarionation. An I.T.C. presentation.

Characters' Voices

Troy Tempest, the
captain of the
submarine *Stingray*   Don Mason
Atlanta, the Earth
girl   Lois Maxwell
Sam Shore, the
commander of the
Marineville base   Ray Barrett
Phones, the hydrophonic
operator   Robert Easton
X-20   Robert Easton
Titan   Ray Barrett

Additional characters: Marina, the enchanting girl from the sea (nonspeaking).

Music: Barry Gray.

STINGRAY—30 minutes—Syndicated

1965. 39 episodes.

STONEY BURKE

Adventure. The experiences of Stoney Burke, a champion rodeo rider, as he travels from rodeo to rodeo seeking to secure "The Gold Buckle," the trophy that is awarded to the world's best saddle bronco buster.

CAST
Stoney Burke   Jack Lord
E.J. Stocker, a
rodeo performer   Bruce Dern
Wes Paineter, a
rodeo performer   Warren Oates
Cody Bristal, a
rodeo performer   Robert Dowdell

Music: Dominic Frontiere.

STONEY BURKE—60 minutes—ABC —October 1, 1962 - September 2, 1963. 32 episodes. Syndicated.

STOP THE MUSIC

Musical Game. As the orchestra plays a song, three girls place telephone calls. When a call is completed, she yells "Stop the Music." Taking the phone, the host asks the viewer to identify the song that was just played. If the participant is able, he receives the prizes that have been accumulated to date; if not, another prize is added to the jackpot, and he receives a home appliance as a consolation prize.

Studio Audience Competition:

Selected members have to identify song titles. Each correct identification awards fifty dollars, to a maximum of four hundred dollars. Players are defeated by incorrect responses.

Hosts: Bert Parks; Jimmy Blaine.

Regulars: Jaye P. Morgan, Jack Haskell, Betty Ann Grove, Jimmy Blaine, Estelle Loring, Sonya and Courtney Van Horne, Don Little, Wayne Lamb, Martin Croft, Maureen Palmer, Ruth Ostrander, Harriet Roeder, Charles Luchsinger, Kay Armen.

Announcer: Jack Haskell.

Orchestra: Harry Sosnick.

Producer: Louis Cowan, Steve Carlin, Joe Cates, Mark Goodson.

Director: Ralph Warren.

Sponsor: Admiral; Old Golds; Exquisite Form Bras.

STOP THE MUSIC—60 minutes—ABC—May 5, 1949 - June 14, 1956.

STOP ME IF YOU'VE HEARD THIS ONE

Game. The emcee reads an incomplete joke that has been submitted by a home viewer. A panel of four comics then have to complete it with an original, funny punch line. The sender receives five dollars for submitting the joke, and an additional five dollars if the panel fails to complete it.

Emcee: Leon Janney.

Panelists: Mae Questel, Cal Tinney, Benny Rubin, George Givot.

STOP ME IF YOU'VE HEARD THIS ONE—30 minutes—NBC 1949.

THE STOREFRONT LAWYERS

Crime Drama. Background: The Neighborhood Legal Services in Century City (downtown Los Angeles, California). The cases and courtroom defenses of attorneys David Hansen, Deborah Sullivan, and Gabriel Kay, representatives of indigent clients.

CAST
David Hansen	Robert Foxworth
Deborah Sullivan	Sheila Larken
Gabriel Kay	David Arkin
Attorney Roberto Barelli	A. Martinez
Mr. Thatcher, the defense attorney	Gerald S. O'Loughlin
Rachel, the N.L.S. secretary	Royce Wallace

THE STOREFRONT LAWYERS—60 minutes—CBS—September 16, 1970 - January 13, 1971. 13 episodes. Spin-off series: "Men At Law" (see title).

STORIES OF THE CENTURY

Western. Era: The 1890s. The investigations of Matt Clark and his female assistant, Frankie Adams, detectives for the Southwestern Railroad. Based on official newspaper files and records.

CAST
Matt Clark	Jim Davis
Frankie Adams	Mary Castle
Jonsey Jones, his female assistant in later episodes	Kristine Miller

STORIES OF THE CENTURY—30 minutes—Syndicated 1956. 39 episodes. Also known as "The Fast Guns."

THE STORK CLUB

Interview. Celebrity interviews are conducted against the background of the Stork Club.

Host: Sherman Billingsley.

Hostesses: Virginia Peine, Betty Ann Grove.

Announcer: George Byran.

Producer: Irving Mansfield, Mike Dutton.

Director: Fred Rickey.

Sponsor: Fatima Cigarettes.

THE STORK CLUB—CBS—1950 - 1953; ABC—30 minutes—1953.

THE STORYBOOK SQUARES

Game. A spin-off from "The Hollywood Squares." Two children compete, designated as Player X and Player O. Nine guest celebrities, who each occupy one of the squares on a huge Tic Tac Toe board, are attired in costumes representing children's literary characters. Object: To win two out of three Tic Tac Toe games.

The first player begins by choosing one of the characters who is then asked a question by the host. The player must determine whether the answer is correct or a bluff, i.e., agree or disagree. If the player is correct, the appropriate letter is lit on the board; incorrect, the opponent receives the square. Exception: Should the square complete a Tic Tac Toe game for the opponent, he does not receive it. Players have to earn essential squares by themselves.

Winners, those who acquire three squares in a row, up and down or diagonally, receive cash and prizes.

Host: Peter Marshall.

Announcer (Town Crier): Kenny Williams.

Music: Recorded.

THE STORYBOOK SQUARES—30 minutes—NBC—January 1968 - August 31, 1968.

STORY FOR AMERICANS

Anthology. Dramatic delineations of America's past.

Performers: Carmen Andrews and Eugene Lee.

STORY FOR AMERICANS—30 minutes—CBS—June 1952 - September 1952.

THE STORY OF—

Anthology. Dramatizations depicting the events that spark the lives of interesting individuals.

Host-Narrator: John Willis.

THE STORY OF— —30 minutes—Syndicated 1962.

STORY THEATRE

Fables. Stories, based on tales by Aesop and The Brothers Grimm, are dramatized against the background of an improvosational theater with performers speaking their lines in narrative, as if reading from a book, and providing their own narration.

CAST
Paul Sills Broadway Repertoire Company: Bob Dishy, Mina Kolb, Peter Bonerz, Judy Graubart, Richard Libertini, Melinda Dillon, Paul Sand, Hamid Hamilton Camp, Ann Sweeny, Severn Darden, Peter Bones, Dick Schall, Eugene Troabnick, Mickey

LaGare, Heath Lambertal, Jeff Brownstein.

STORY THEATRE—30 minutes— Syndicated 1971. 26 episodes.

STRAIGHTAWAY

Adventure. The experiences of Scott Ross and Clipper Hamilton, the owners and operators of the Straightaway Garage, as they become involved with professional drivers and races.

CAST

Scott Ross	Brian Kelly
Clipper Hamilton	John Ashley

STRAIGHTAWAY—30 minutes— ABC—October 6, 1961 - July 4, 1962. 26 episodes. Original title: "The Racers."

STRANGE PARADISE

Serial. Background: The forbidding Caribbean island of Maljardin (French for "Garden of Evil"). Once thriving on rare wine, exotic food, and beautiful women, Jean Paul Desmond, after meeting the beautiful Erica Kerr, retreats to the island after they are married.

After one year, Erica is stricken with an unknown disease and mysteriously dies. Unable to accept her death, and determined to bring her back to life, he places her body in a metal casing and preserves her through the process of cryogenics.

Hoping to achieve his goal by summoning the powers of darkness, he breaks the ancient spell that has ruled the island and cursed his family when he conjures up the spirit of Jacques Eloi De Monde, an ancestor who, three hundred years before, also lost his wife. To conceal and protect himself, the spirit takes refuge in a portrait of Jacques that hangs over a fireplace. Discovering Jean Paul's act, Raxil, priestess and Desmond family servant, vows to return Jacques to hell.

As the powers of evil work to restore Erica's life, seven people arrive on the island—each to meet bizarre destinies: Alison Kerr, Erica's sister; Dan Forest, Jean Paul's business manager; Tim Stanton, an artist hired by Alison to paint Erica's portrait; Holly Marshall, a beautiful young heiress; Elizabeth Marshall, her mother; and Reverend Matthew Dawson, a friend of the Marshalls'.

Alive, but evil and deadly, Erica, to exist, must kill all visitors to the island, pierce Holly's heart with a silver pin, then possess her body.

Through Jacques's possession of Jean Paul, the murders are committed: Vangie (a medium incorporated by Raxil to help rid Jacques); Tim, Reverend Dawson, Dan, and Alison.

A fire, started by Jacques in the boathouse, leaves Elizabeth, Holly, and Erica alone in the mansion, while Jean Paul, Raxil and Quito, her assistant, battle the blaze.

Overtaken by her will, Holly stands before Erica, who with a large silver pin, is about to pierce her heart. Spotting the two, Elizabeth pushes Holly aside—and is herself killed when stabbed. Entering the house, and in possession of his own will, Jean Paul awakens Holly, who is taken to safety by Raxil, and, approaching Jacques's portrait, sets it on fire. Spreading, the flames engulf the house, wherein Erica perishes.

Safely outside, Jean Paul looks back and hears the final words of Jacques echoing the atmosphere: "Whether you live or die Jean Paul

Desmond, wherever you choose to run, your curse will follow you, and life will be for you always a Strange Paradise. Aha ha ha ha ha ha ha ha."

CAST

Jean Paul Desmond	Colin Fox
Jacques Eloi De Monde	Colin Fox
Holly Marshall	Sylvia Feigel
Erica Desmond	Tudi Wiggins
Alison Kerr	Dawn Greenhalgh
Raxil	Cosette Lee
Quito	Kurt Schiegl
Elizabeth Marshall	Paisley Maxwell
Vangie	Angela Roland
Reverend Matthew Dawson	Dan McDonald
Tim Stanton	Bruce Gray
Dan Forrest	John Granik

Also: Patricia Collins, Trudy Young.

Music: Score Productions.

STRANGE PARADISE—30 minutes —Syndicated 1969. 195 episodes. Produced in Canada.

STRANGE PLACES

Documentary. Films exploring various remote regions of the world.

Host-Narrator: Peter Graves.

Music: Gerherd Trede.

STRANGE PLACES—30 minutes— Syndicated 1973. Produced by the B.B.C. Also known as "Other People, Other Places."

THE STRANGE REPORT

Mystery. Background: London, England. The investigations of criminologist Adam Strange as he intervenes in domestic and international crises and attempts to solve ingenious criminal acts of injustice.

CAST

Adam Strange	Anthony Quayle
Evelyn McLane, his assistant	Anneke Wells
Ham Gynt, his assistant	Kaz Garas

Music: Edwin Astley.

THE STRANGE REPORT—60 minutes—NBC—January 8, 1971 - September 12, 1971. 16 episodes.

THE STRANGER

Drama. The story of The Stranger, an unknown man who, whenever innocent people are threatened by unscrupulous individuals, mysteriously appears, assists, and when completing his task, vanishes, accepting no fees for his services.

Starring: Robert Carroll as The Stranger.

Producer: Frank Telford.

THE STRANGER—30 minutes— DuMont—June 25, 1954 - September 1954.

THE STRAUSS FAMILY

Biography. A seven-part dramatization depicting the lives of composers Johann Strauss and his son, Johann Strauss, Jr., "The Waltz Kings of the nineteenth century."

CAST

Johann Strauss	Eric Woolfe
Anna Strauss	Anne Stallybrass
Johann Strauss, Jr.	Stuart Wilson
Josef Lanner	Derek Jacobi

Emilie Trampusch	Barbara Ferris
Olga	Ania Marson
Madamee Smirnitska	Jill Balcon
Hirsh	David de Keyser
Dommayer	Christopher Benjamin
Lucari	Sonia Dresdel
Hetti	Margaret Whiting
Edi	Tony Anholt
Josef Strauss	Nikolas Simmonds
Lili	Georgina Hale
Annele	Hilary Hardiman
Theresa	Amanda Walker
Max Steiner	William Dexter
Adele	Lynn Farleigh

Music: The London Symphony Orchestra.

Conductor: Cyril Ornadel.

THE STRAUSS FAMILY—60 minutes—ABC—May 5, 1973 - June 16, 1973.

STRAWHAT MATINEE

Women. Music, songs, variety acts, and fashion shows.

Host: Mel Martin.

Music: Ernie Lee's Hillbilly Band.

STRAWHAT MATINEE—30 minutes——NBC 1951.

THE STRAWHATTERS

Musical Variety. Background: Palisades Amusement Park, Palisades New Jersey. Performances by: Country and Western bands, guest vocalists, and acrobats.

Host: Johnny Olsen.

THE STRAWHATTERS—30 minutes—DuMont—May 27, 1953 - September 1953.

STRAWHAT THEATRE

Musical Variety. Performances by Country and Western artists.

Hosts: Mel Martin, Rosemary Olberding.

Regulars: June Pickens, Marian Spellman, Lee Jones, Dick and Pat, The Log Jammers, The Pine Mountain Boys.

Orchestra: Ernie Lee.

STRAWHAT THEATRE—60 minutes—NBC 1951.

STRAWHAT THEATRE

Anthology. Dramatic presentations.

STRAWHAT THEATRE—30 minutes—ABC—July 5, 1953 - September 20, 1953.

STREETS OF DANGER

See title: "The Lone Wolf."

THE STREETS OF SAN FRANCISCO

Crime Drama. Background: San Francisco, California. The investigations of Lieutenant Mike Stone, "a street smart homicide detective," and his impulsive, college-trained partner, Steve Keller.

CAST

Lt. Mike Stone	Karl Malden
Detective Steve Keller	Michael Douglas
Lt. Lessing	Lee Harris
Officer Haseejian	Vic Tayback

Inspector Dan Robbins	Richard Hatch
Jean Stone, Mike's daughter	Darleen Carr
Sgt. Sekulovich	Art Passarella

Music: John Elizade; Pat Williams.

Executive Producer: Quinn Martin.

Producer: John Wilder, Cliff Gould, William Yates.

Director: Virgil W. Vogel, Walter Grauman, William Wiard, Barry Crane, Robert Day, John Badham, Paul Stanley, Harry Falk, George McCowan, Kenneth Gilbert, William Hale.

THE STREETS OF SAN FRANCISCO—60 minutes—ABC—September 16, 1972 - June 23, 1977.

STRICTLY SKITCH

See title: "Faye Emerson."

STRIKE IT RICH

Game. Contestants stand before the studio audience and relate their hardluck stories, stating their single most needed possession. Home viewers are then permitted to call the program and donate money. The saddest storytellers, as determined by the studio audience, receive the program's "heartline," a cash bonanza.

Host: Warren Hull.

Substitute Host: Monty Hall.

Assistant: Jack Carson.

Commercial Spokeswoman: Virginia Graham.

Announcer: Ralph Paul.

Producer: Walt Framer.

Director: Matthew Harlib.

Sponsor: The Colgate-Palmolive Company.

STRIKE IT RICH—30 minutes—CBS—May 7, 1951 - January 3, 1958.

STRYKER OF SCOTLAND YARD

Crime Drama. Background: London, England. The investigations of Robert Stryker, the chief inspector of Scotland Yard, into cases wherein innocent people have become the pawns of master criminals.

Starring: Clifford Evans as Inspector Robert Stryker.

STRYKER OF SCOTLAND YARD—30 minutes—NBC 1957. 39 episodes.

THE STU ERWIN SHOW

See title: "Trouble with Father."

STUDIO '57

Anthology. Dramatic presentations.

Included:

The Haven Technique. A skilled surgeon attempts to perform a difficult and revolutionary type of operation on the son of a former sweetheart.

CAST
Dr. Glenn Haven: Brian Keith; Helen Blaine: Sallie Brophy; Ann Randall: Irene Hervey.

The Bitter Rival. A wife's efforts to end her husband's unfounded jealousy.

CAST

Beryl Miller: Margaret Field; Harry Miller: Larry Dobkin; Joe Perry: Don Haggerty; Margaret Perry: Ann Robinson.

The Engagement Ring. When an heiress hears a rumor that her fiancé is marrying her for her money, she begins an investigation to uncover the truth.

CAST

Hugh O'Brian, K.T. Stevens, Lili Fontaine.

Hazel Crane. Believing his wife is a murderess, a lawyer begins an investigation to uncover her past.

CAST

Hazel Crane: Eleonara Tanin; Ben Crane: Walter Reed.

STUDIO '57—60 minutes—DuMont—1954 - 1956.

STUDIO ONE

Anthology. Dramatic presentations.

Producer: Worthington Miner, Fletcher Markle, Felix Jackson, Norman Felton, Gordon Duff, William Brown, Paul Nickell, Franklin Schaffner, Charles Schultz.

Director: John Peyser, Paul Nickell, Charles Schultz, Worthington Miner.

Sponsor: Old Golds; Westinghouse.

Included:

Signal Thirty-Two. The story of a rookie policeman's misuse of his position as he succumbs to the temptations of bribes.

CAST

Joe Maross, Gene Lyons.

The Walsh Girls. A psychological study of the relationship between two sisters.

CAST

Jane Wyatt.

The Trial of John Titler Zenger. The true story of John Zenger, a printer who was imprisoned for publishing the truth about the corrupt administration of a colonial government.

CAST

Eddie Albert, Marian Selder.

The Incredible World of Horace Ford. The story of a man who escapes the pressures of business by daydreaming himself into adventures.

CAST

Art Carney, Leora Dana.

STUDIO ONE—60 minutes—CBS—November 17, 1948 - September 16, 1957. Also known as "Studio One in Hollywood" (from September 23, 1957 to September 29, 1958).

STUD'S PLACE

Comedy. Background: Stud's Place, a restaurant-bar in Chicago. The misadventures of its owner-operator, Studs Terkel, as he becomes involved with staff and clientele difficulties.

CAST

Studs Terkel — Himself
The waitress — Beverly Younger
The Folk-singing handyman — Win Strackle

The blues-singing
pianist   Chet Robel

Music: Chet Robel.

Producer: Biggie Levin, Norman Felton, Dan Petrie, Ben Paric.

Director: Dick Locke, Norman Felton.

STUD'S PLACE—30 minutes—ABC 1950.

STUMPERS

Game. Two teams compete, each composed of one celebrity captain and one noncelebrity contestant. A stumper, which contains three clues to the identity of a person, place, or thing, is revealed to one member of one team. That player then relates one of the clues to one member of the opposing team. If the player identifies the stumper he scores fifteen points. If, within five seconds, he is stumped, a second clue is given (worth ten points) and finally a third clue (worth five points). If he is still stumped, the team at play is given a chance to solve it and win fifteen points. Each player receives two turns at giving and guessing stumpers per round. Two such rounds are played, the second being the double up round (points are 30, 15, and 10). The winner is the highest scoring team.

Host: Allen Ludden.

Music: Alan Thicke.

Executive Producer: Lin Bolen.

Producer: Walt Case, Noreen Colen.

Director: Marty Pasetta, Jeff Goldstein.

STUMPERS—30 minutes—NBC—October 4, 1976 - December 31, 1976.

STUMP THE STARS

Game. Two competing teams, the Regulars and the Visitors, each composed of four Hollywood celebrities. Object: The performance of charades. One member of one team is handed a charade. Within a two-minute time limit, he has to perform it and relay its meaning to his teammates. The amount of time consumed until it is identified is calculated. Each player competes in the same manner. The team accumulating the least amount of overall time is the winner. Prizes are awarded to home viewers whose charades are selected to be played.

Versions:

Stump The Stars—30 minutes—CBS—September 17, 1962 - September 16, 1963. Syndicated. Withdrawn (due to poor audio and video quality).

Host: Mike Stokey.

Regulars: Beverly Garland, Ross Martin, Diana Dors, Sebastian Cabot, Ruta Lee, Hans Conried.

Stump The Stars—30 minutes—Syndicated 1969.

Host: Mike Stokey.

Regulars: Vera Miles, Deanna Lund, Roger C. Carmel, Dick Patterson.

SUCCESS STORY

Interview. Interviews with people who have struggled for and achieved success.

Hostess: Betty Furness.

SUCCESS STORY—15 minutes—ABC 1951.

SUGARFOOT

Western. Background: The Frontier during the 1860s. The exploits of Tom Brewster, Sugarfoot,* student of law, and wanderer who encounters and reluctantly aids people in distress.

Starring: Will Hutchins as Tom Brewster.

Music: Paul Sawtell.

*A cowboy designated one grade lower than a tenderfoot.

SUGARFOOT—60 minutes—ABC— September 17, 1957 - September 13, 1960. Syndicated.

SUGAR TIME

Comedy. Background: Los Angeles, California. The heartaches, loves, struggles, and misadventures of Maxx, Diane, and Maggie, three starry-eyed Rock singers, who comprise the act "Sugar," hoping to make the big time.

CAST

Maxx Douglas	Barbi Benton
Diane Zukerman	Didi Carr
Maggie Barton	Marianne Black
Al Marks, the owner of the Tryout Room Night Club	Wynn Irwin
Paul Landson, Diane's boyfriend	Mark Winkworth
Lightning Jack Rappaport, a performer at the Tryout Room	Charles Fleischer

Musical Director: David Garland.

Musical Supervision: Paul Williams.

Executive Producer-Creator: James Komack.

Producer: Hank Bradford, Martin Cohan.

Director: Bill Hobin, Howard Storm.

Choreography: Helen Funai.

SUGAR TIME—30 minutes—ABC— August 13, 1977 - September 3, 1977. 4 episodes.

THE SUMMER SMOTHERS BROTHERS SHOW

Musical Variety. The summer replacement for "The Smothers Brothers Comedy Hour."

Host: Glen Campbell.

Regulars: Sally Struthers, Pat Paulsen, Jack Burns, John Hartford.

Announcer: Roger Carroll.

Orchestra: Nelson Riddle.

THE SUMMER SMOTHERS BROTHERS SHOW—60 minutes—CBS—June 23, 1968 - September 8, 1968. 13 tapes. Spin-off series: "The Glen Campbell Goodtime Hour."

SUMMER FUN

Pilot Films. Proposed comedy series for the 1966-1967 season.

Included:

McNab's Lab. The misadventures of Andrew McNab, small town druggist and amateur inventor.

CAST
Andrew McNab: Cliff Arquette; Harvey Barter: Paul Smith; Ellen McNab: Sherry Alberoni; Timmy McNab: David Bailey.

Little Leatherneck. Fascinated by her father, a marine drill sergeant, a young girl decides to follow in his footsteps—and become a leatherneck.

CAST

Cindy Fenton: Donna Butterworth; Sgt. Mike Fenton: Scott Brady; Dolores: Sue Ane Langdon; Mess Sgt.: Ned Glass.

Meet Me in Saint Louis. Background: Saint Louis, 1903. The misadventures of Esther Smith, a beautiful young debutante from New York.

CAST

Esther Smith: Shelley Fabares; Anne Smith: Celeste Holm; Glenn Smith: Larry Merrill.

The Pirates of Flounder Bay. Era: The 1800s. The effort of the son of the infamous Captain Kidd, Barnaby Kidd, to achieve fame.

CAST

Capt. Barnaby Kidd: William Cort; Governor: Basil Rathbone; Capt. Jack Slash: Keenan Wynn; Mayor Abner Bunker: Harold Peary; Molly Bunker: Bridget Hanley; Sidney: Jack Soo.

Thompson's Ghost. The misadventures of Henry Thompson, a four-thousand, seven-hundred-year-old ghost who is conjured up by a ten-year-old girl.

CAST

Henry Thompsonn: Bert Lahr; Annabel Thompson: Pamela Dapo; Milly Thompson: Phyllis Coates; Sam Thompson: Robert Rockwell.

SUMMER FUN—30 minutes—ABC— July 22, 1966 - September 2, 1966.

SUMMER IN THE CITY

Variety. The summer replacement for "Faye Emerson's Wonderful Town."

CAST

Bob Sweeney, Hal March, Nancy Kelly, Gladys Swarthout, Virginia Conwell, Bobby Scheer.

SUMMER IN THE CITY—30 minutes—CBS—August 18, 1951 - August 25, 1951.

SUMMERTIME U.S.A.

Musical Variety.

Hosts: Teresa Brewer, Mel Tormé.

Featured: The Honeydreamers.

Orchestra: Ray Bloch.

SUMMERTIME   U.S.A.—15 minutes—CBS—July   9,   1953 - September 1, 1953.

SUNDAY AT THE BRONX ZOO

Educational. Background: The Bronx (New York) Zoological Garden. Visits to and facts about the various exhibits.

Host: William Bridges.

Announcer: Durwood Kirby.

Producer: Louis Cowan.

Director: Gail Compton.

SUNDAY AT THE BRONX ZOO—30 minutes—ABC 1950.

SUNDAY DATE

Musical Variety.

Hostess: Helen Lee.

Regulars: Dick Style, Paulette Seslan, Shirley Levitt, Joe E. Marks.

Music: The Cavalier Trio.

SUNDAY DATE—15 minutes—NBC 1949.

SUNDAY MYSTERY

Anthology. Mystery presentations.

Host: Walter Slezak.

Included:

Dead Man's Walk. An amnesiac's search for his past.

CAST
Abel: Robert Culp; Karen Prescott: Abby Dalton; Lt. Spear: Bruce Gordon; Florence: Barbara Stuart.

Trial By Fury. A woman attempts to prove that her daughter's fiancé is her husband's murderer.

CAST
Elizabeth Marshall: Agnes Moorehead; Jim Powell: Warren Stevens; Joanna Marshall: Louise Carroll.

Femme Fatale. Police efforts to prove that a famous movie queen is responsible for the deaths of two of her husbands.

CAST
Lisa Townsend: Janet Blair; Claire Bradford: Tracey Roberts; Daniel Otis: Joe DeSantis.

Murder Me Nicely. Detesting a student, a teacher sets out to destroy the young man's career.

CAST
Alfred Emerson: Everett Sloane; Peter: Mark Goddard; Carolyn: Yvonne Craig.

SUNDAY MYSTERY—60 minutes—NBC—July 2, 1961 - September 17, 1961.

SUNSHINE

Comedy-Drama. Background: Van Couver, California. The story of Sam Hayden, a happy-go-lucky musician who is left in charge of his young daughter, Jill, after the death of his wife. Episodes focus on his attempts to fill the maternal void left in Jill's life.

CAST
Sam Hayden	Cliff De Young
Jill Hayden	Elizabeth Cheshire
Nora, Sam's girlfriend	Meg Foster
Weaver, Sam's friend, a musician	Bill Mumy
Corey Givits, Sam's friend, a musician	Corey Fischer
Ms. Cox, Jill's teacher	Barbara Bosson

Music: Hal Mooney.

SUNSHINE—30 minutes—NBC—March 6, 1975 - June 19, 1975. 13 episodes.

THE SUPER

Comedy. Background: A less-than-fashionable apartment building in New York City. The trials and tribulations of Joe Girelli, its two-hundred-and-forty-pound Italian-American superintendant. Plagued by tenant complaints, building condemnation threats, and a family "which ain't got no respect," he struggles to solve problems, survive the daily tensions of city living, and enjoy what simple pleasure life affords him.

CAST

Joe Girelli   Richard S. Castellano
Francesca Girelli, his
   wife   Ardell Sheridan
Joanne Girelli, their
   daughter   Margaret E. Castellano
Anthony Girelli, their
   son   B. Kirby Jr.
Frankie Girelli, Joe's
   brother, studying to
   become a
   lawyer   Phil Mishkin
Officer Clark, a
   tenant   Ed Peck
Dottie Clark, his
   wife   Virginia Vincent
Sylvia Stein, a
   tenant   Janet Brandt
Janice Stein, her
   daughter   Penny Marshall
Pizuti, Joe's friend,
   owner of a
   neighborhood bar   Vic Tayback
Fritz, Joe's
   friend   John Lawrence
Herbie, Joe's
   friend   Wynn Irwin
Louie, Joe's
   friend   Louis Basile

Music: Larry Grossman.

THE SUPER—30 minutes—ABC—June 21, 1972 - August 23, 1972. 13 episodes.

SUPERCAR

Marionette Adventure. The battle against crime as undertaken by Supercar, Incorporated, an international anti-crime organization.

Characters:

Mike Mercury, the pilot of *Supercar*, an indestructible automobile
Dr. Beeker.
Professor Popkiss.
Jimmy, Mike's ward.

Mitch, Jimmy's pet monkey.
Masterspy, a criminal.
Zorin, a criminal.

Voices: Paul Maxwell, David Graham, John Bluthal, Sylvia Anderson.

Music: Barry Gray.

SUPERCAR—30 minutes—Syndicated 1962. 39 episodes.

SUPER CIRCUS

Circus Variety Acts.

Ringmasters: Claude Kirchner; Jerry Colonna.

Regulars: Mary Hartline ("Queen of the Super Circus"), Cliff Soubier, Bordie Patton, Nick Francis, C. D. Charlie, Sandy Wirth, Will "Blooper" Able, Otto Griebling.

Clowns: Nicky, Scampy, and Cliffy.

Orchestra: Bruce Case.

Producer: Jack Gibney, Phil Patton, Morton Stone.

Director: Ed Skotch.

Sponsor: Kellogg's; Mars Candies.

SUPER CIRCUS—60 minutes—ABC—January 16, 1949 - June 3, 1956.

SUPER FRIENDS

Animated Cartoon. Background: The Hall of Justice in Washington, D.C.—the headquarters of the Super Friends: Batman and Robin, Superman, Wonder Woman, Aquaman, Marvin, Wendy, and Wonder Dog—indestructible crusaders who've united to form the Justice League of America. Stories depict their battle against the sinister forces of evil.

Character evolvement:

Batman and Robin: See title: "Batman."

Aquaman: See title: "Aquaman."

Superman: See title: "The Adventures of Superman."

Wonder Woman: See title: "Wonder Woman."

Marvin, Wendy and Wonder Dog: Details not related.

Voices: Sherry Alberoni, Danny Dark, Casey Kaseem, Olan Soule, Ted Knight, John Stephenson, Franklin Rucker, Frank Welker, Shannon Farnon, Norman Alden.

Music: Hoyt Curtin, Paul DeKorte.

SUPER FRIENDS—55 minutes—ABC—September 8, 1973 - August 30, 1975.

SUPERMAN

See title: "The Adventures of Superman."

SUPERMARKET SWEEP

Game. Three competing husband-and-wife couples. Background: A supermarket. Couples, each with shopping carts, stand before a white line. A specific amount of time is established, and on the word "go," players run up and down the aisles, cramming grocery items into their carts. At the end of the time, the items are totaled, and the couple with the largest cash amount are the winners and receive the items and the opportunity to compete again.

Host: Bill Malone.

SUPERMARKET SWEEP—30 minutes—ABC—December 20, 1965 - July 17, 1967.

SUPER PRESIDENT

Animated Cartoon. Background: Washington, D.C. The exploits of James Norcross, Chief Justice of the United States, possessing unique powers as the result of a cosmic storm, as he battles the sinister forces of evil.

Additional segment:

Spy Shadow. The crime-battling exploits of private detective Richard Vance and, able to operate independently of himself, his shadow.

SUPER PRESIDENT—30 minutes—NBC—September 16, 1967 - September 14, 1968. 15 episodes.

THE SUPER SIX

Animated Cartoon. The exploits of the Super Six, futuristic crime fighters.

Characters: Super Bwoing; The Super Services Incorporated; and The Brothers Matzoriley.

THE SUPER SIX—30 minutes—NBC—September 10, 1966 - September 6, 1969. 26 episodes.

SUPERSONIC

Music. Performances by Rock Personalities. The program does not include a host, announcer, regulars, or a studio orchestra (guests provide their own music). Produced in England.

Producer-Director: Mike Mansfield.

SUPERSONIC—30 minutes--Syndicated 1976.

SUPER WITCH

Animated Cartoon. Background: The town of Riverdale. The misadventures of Sabrina, a beautiful, but mischievous teenage witch. See also: "Sabrina, the Teenage Witch."

Additional Characters: The Archies (Archie, Jughead, Betty, Veronica, Reggie, and Hot Dog) and The Groovie Goolies.

Voice of Sabrina: Jane Webb.

Additional Voices: Dallas McKennon, Don Messick, John Erwin, Jose Flores, Howard Morris.

Music: Yvette Blais, Jeff Michael.

Executive Producer: Lou Scheimer, Norm Prescott.

Producer: Don Christensen.

SUPER WITCH—30 minutes—NBC— Premiered: November 11, 1977.

SURE AS FATE

Anthology. Dramatic presentations.

SURE AS FATE—30 minutes—CBS— 1950 - 1951.

SURFSIDE SIX

Mystery. Background: Miami Beach, Florida. The investigations of private detectives Dave Thorne, Ken Madison, and Sandy Winfield, into society- -based crimes. (Surfside Six: The address of their houseboat.)

CAST

Dave Thorne	Lee Patterson
Ken Madison	Van Williams
Sandy Winfield	Troy Donahue
Daphne DeWitt Dutton, their girlfriend	Diane McBain
Cha Cha O'Brien, a friend, a nightclub singer	Margarita Sierra
Lieutenant Snediger	Donald Barry
Lieutenant Plehn	Richard Crane

Music: Frank Ortega; Frank Perkins; Paul Sawtell; Mack David, Jerry Livingston.

SURFSIDE SIX—60 minutes—ABC— October 3, 1960 - September 24, 1962. 74 episodes. Syndicated.

SURF'S UP

Documentary. Backgrounds: Hawaii and California. Films depicting the lives and world of surfers.

Host: Stan Richards.

SURF'S UP—30 minutes—Syndicated 1965.

SURVIVAL

Documentary. Filmed coverage of both natural and human-caused disasters.

Host-Narrator: James Whitmore.

SURVIVAL—30 minutes—Syndicated 1964. 38 episodes.

THE SURVIVORS

Serial. Background: New York City. The struggles and emotional problems of the rich as seen through the activi-

The Survivors. Louise Sorel and Kevin McCarthy.

ties of the wealthy Carlyle family, the owners of a Wall Street banking empire. Created by Harold Robbins.

CAST

Baylor Carlyle, the head of the empire	Ralph Bellamy
Tracy Carlyle Hastings, his daughter	Lana Turner
Philip Hastings, her greedy husband	Kevin McCarthy
Duncan Carlyle, Baylor's son	George Hamilton
Jeffrey Carlyle, Tracy's illegimite son	Jan-Michael Vincent
Jonathan	Louis Hayward
Belle	Diana Muldaur
Jean Vale	Louise Sorel
Riakos	Rossano Brazzi
Miguel Santerra	Robert Viharo
Marguerita	Donna Baccalor
Sheila	Kathy Cannon

Tom	Robert Lipton
Rosemary	Pamela Tiffin
Corbett	Michael Bell

THE SURVIVORS—60 minutes— ABC—September 22, 1969 - September 17, 1970. 15 episodes.

SUSAN'S SHOW

Children. An imaginative program that features songs, stories, and "Popeye" cartoons.

Hostess: Susan Heinkel (twelve years old).

Characters: Rusty, her terrier; a magic flying stool from her mother's kitchen; and Mr. Pegasus, a talking table.

Producer: Paul Frumkin, Frank Atlass.

SUSAN'S SHOW—30 minutes—CBS— May 4, 1957 - January 18, 1958.

SUSIE

See title: "Private Secretary."

SUSPENSE

Anthology. "Well-calculated tales to keep you in Suspense." Based on the radio classic.

Included:

I, Christopher Bell. Despite a recent heart attack, a man attempts to prove that he is capable of living a strenuous life.

CAST

Christopher Bell: Charles Bickford;

Anna: Lila Skala; Betty: Kathleen McGuire.

I, Bradford Charles. After an alligator kills his father, a seventeen-year-old boy begins to hunt for it, determined to kill it.

CAST

Bradford Charles: Andrew Prine; Sheriff: Victor Jory; Reporter: Norman Fell; Brad's mother: Doreen Long.

Web of Circumstance. Embezzling pennies for years, a bank teller plots to escape from his shrewd wife and retreat to a South Seas paradise. Complications ensue when a shortage is discovered.

CAST

Carl Smith: Thomas Mitchell; Elva Smith: Jeanette Nolan; Tom Sutton: Hugh Beaumont; Fred Carlson: Lyle Talbot.

Witness to Condemn. Witnessing a murder and psychologically losing her sight as the result of an attack by the killer, a young woman struggles to overcome the fear that is blocking her sight.

CAST

Laurie Savage: Teresa Wright; Peter Jordan: Warren Stevens.

Fast Break. Once jailed for accepting a bribe, a former basketball player struggles to settle down and end his life of running, despite his constant fear of his record catching up with him.

CAST

Bill Harlow: Jackie Cooper; Lois Harlow: Betty Lynn; Joey Harlow: Michael Winkleman; Pastor Thompson: Hayden Rorke.

Versions:

Suspense—30 minutes—CBS—March 1, 1949 - August 17, 1954.

Voice of Suspense (Narrator): Paul Frees.

Music: Wilbur Hatch.

Producer: Robert Stevens, Martin Manulis.

Director: Robert Stevens.

Sponsor: Auto-Lite.

Suspense—30 minutes—CBS—March 25, 1964 - September 9, 1964.

Host: Sebastian Cabot.

Producer: Fred Hendrickson.

SUSPENSE PLAYHOUSE

Pilot films. Rebroadcasts of series projects originally aired via "Premiere" (see title).

SUSPENSE PLAYHOUSE—60 minutes—CBS—May 24, 1971 - July 5, 1971.

SUSPENSE THEATRE

Anthology. Retitled episodes of "The Bob Hope Chrysler Theatre" and "The Kraft Suspense Theatre" (see titles for examples of the type of dramas presented).

SUSPENSE THEATRE—60 minutes— Syndicated 1969.

SUSPICION

Anthology. Suspense mysteries.

Hosts: Dennis O'Keefe; Walter Abel.

Producer: Mort Abrams, Robert Fashko, Mark Smith, Frank Rosenberg, Richard Lewis, William Frye, Allan Miller.

Included:

The Other Side of the Curtain. A psychiatrist attempts to discover the reason behind a woman's recurring dream of a dark hallway, a curtain, and the unsuspecting fear that lurks behind it.

CAST

Donna Reed, Herbert Anderson, Jeff Richards, Ainsile Pryor.

Hand in Glove. Aiding a Scotland Yard inspector, a woman attempts to find the man who framed her nephew for murder.

CAST

Ramskill: Burgess Meredith; Aunty B.: Cathleen Nesbitt; Hughie: Fred Gwynne.

The Story of Margery Reardon. Returning home from an evening party, a young woman is attacked by a psycopath. Developing a strong distrust of men, she moves to the city to begin a new life. The story revolves around her struggles to overcome her fears when she meets a handsome young man.

CAST

Margery: Margaret O'Brien; Jim: Rod Taylor: Dick: Henry Silva.

Diary of Death. Journeying to New York City, a young man attempts to avenge the death of his sister.

CAST

Jeremiah Taylor: Macdonald Carey;

Ralph Storkey: Everett Sloane.

SUSPICION—60 minutes—NBC—September 30, 1957 - September 6, 1959. 21 episodes available for syndication.

SWAMP FOX

See title: "Walt Disney Presents, *Swamp Fox* segment.

S.W.A.T.

Crime Drama. Background: California. The cases of the Special Weapons and Tactics Unit (S.W.A.T.) of the West California Police Department, a group of five men who assist police who are in trouble.

CAST

Lieutenant Hondo Harrelson	Steve Forrest
Sergeant Deacon Kay	Rod Perry
Officer James Street	Robert Urich
Officer T. J. McCabe	James Coleman
Officer Dominic Luca	Mark Shera

Music: Barry De Vorzon; John Parker.

Executive Producer: Aaron Spelling, Leonard Goldberg.

Producer: Robert Hamner, Barry Shear, Gene Levitt.

Director: George McCowan, Richard Benedict, Earl Bellamy, William Crane, Bruce Bilson, Harry Falk, Dick Moder, Reza S. Badiyi.

Creator: Robert Hamner.

S.W.A.T.—60 minutes—ABC—February 24, 1975 - June 26, 1976.

THE SWEENEY

Crime Drama. Background: London, England. The cases of the Flying Squad, an elite team of specially trained Scotland Yard police detectives.

CAST
Inspector Jack Regan   John Thaw
Sergeant Carter   Dennis Waterman
Chief Inspector
     Haskins   Garfield Morgan

Music: Harry South.

Executive Producer: Lloyd Shirley, George Tayler.

Producer: Ted Childs.

THE SWEENEY—60 minutes—Syndicated 1976.

THE SWIFT SHOW

Variety. Music, songs, fashion, cooking, and interviews.

Host: Tex McCrary.

Hostess: Jinx Falkenberg.

Music: The Swift Foods Orchestra.

Additional Music: The Johnny Guarnieri Quintet.

Vocalists: Helen Carroll and the Escorts.

Announcer: Dan Seymour.

Producer: Lee Cooley.

Sponsor: Swift Foods.

THE SWIFT SHOW—30 minutes—NBC 1946. Also known as "The Tex and Jinx Swift Show." In 1948, Lanny Ross became the host (see title "The Lanny Ross Show").

THE SWIFT SHOW WAGON WITH HORACE HEIDT AND THE AMERICAN WAY

Musical Variety. Musical salutes to the cities and states that comprise the United States.

Host: Horace Heidt.

Orchestra: Horace Heidt.

THE SWIFT SHOW WAGON WITH HORACE HEIDT AND THE AMERICAN WAY—30 minutes—CBS—1954 - 1955.

SWINGING COUNTRY

Musical Variety. Performances by Country and Western entertainers.

Host: Roy Clark.

Substitute Host: Minnie Pearl.

Regulars: Molly Bee, Rusty Draper, The Swinging Countrymen, The Hometown Singers.

SWINGING COUNTRY—25 minutes —NBC—July 4, 1966 - December 30, 1966.

SWISS FAMILY ROBINSON

Adventure. Era: The nineteenth century. The series follows the adventures of the Robinson family, shipwrecked on an almost deserted tropical island, as they struggle for survival and seek a way to escape. Based on the story by Johann Wyss.

CAST
Karl Robinson, the
    father   Martin Milner
Lotte Robinson, his
    wife   Pat Delany
Fred Robinson, their
    son   Willie Aames

Ernie Robinson, their
son   Eric Olson

Jeremiah Worth,
a marooned,
loud-mouthed
sea dog   Cameron Mitchell

Helga Wagner, the
Robinson's adopted
daughter   Helen Hunt

Music: Lionel Newman, Richard La Salle.

Producer: Irwin Allen.

Director: Harry Harris, Leslie H. Martinson, George Fenady.

SWISS FAMILY ROBINSON—60 minutes—ABC—September 14, 1975 - April 11, 1976. 26 episodes.

THE SWISS FAMILY ROBINSON

Adventure. Background: An uncharted island in the year 1881. The series follows the adventures of the Robinsons, a Swiss family who were shipwrecked on a deserted island, which they name New Switzerland, after their ship was destroyed during a tropical storm at sea. Closely follows the novel by Johann Wyss; more so than the previous title. Produced in Canada.

CAST

Johann Robinson, the
father   Chris Wiggins

Elizabeth Robinson, his
wife   Diana Leblanc

Marie Robinson, their
daughter   Heather Graham

Franz Robinson, their
son   Micky O'Neill

Ernest Robinson, their
son   Michael Duhig

Narrator: Chris Wiggins.

Music: Score Productions.

Music Supervision: Lewis Lehman.

Producer: Gerald Mayer.

Director: Peter Carter, Gerald Mayer, Don Haldane.

THE SWISS FAMILY ROBINSON—30 minutes—Syndicated 1976.

SWITCH

Crime Drama. Background: Los Angeles, California. The story of Frank MacBride, a tough, retired bunco cop; and Pete Ryan, his partner, a soft-soap ex-con, the owner-operators of the Ryan-MacBride Private Detective Organization. Episodes relate their investigations as they attempt to beat swindlers at their own game.

CAST

Frank MacBride   Eddie Albert

Pete Ryan   Robert Wagner

Maggie, their
secretary   Sharon Gless

Malcolm, their
con-artist friend   Charlie Callas

Revel, the waitress
at Malcolm's
bar   Mindi Miller

Lt. Schiller   William Bryant

Music: Stu Phillips, Glen A. Larson.

Executive Producer: Glen A. Larson, Matthew Rapf.

Producer: Leigh Vance, Jack Laird, John Guss, Paul Playdon, John Peyser.

Director: Noel Black, Bruce Kessler, John Peyser, Sutton Roley, Leo Penn, Sigmund Neufeld, Jr., Bruce Evans, Glen A. Larson, E.W. Swackhamer, Walter Doniger.

SWITCH—60 minutes—CBS—Premiered: September 9, 1975.

THE SWORD OF FREEDOM

Adventure. Background: Florence, Italy, during the Renaissance period of the fifteenth century. The exploits of Marco del Monte, swordsman, painter, and lover, as he attempts to defend the Free Republic against the iron-hand rule of the Medicis.

Starring: Edmund Purdom as Marco del Monte.

THE SWORD OF FREEDOM—30 minutes—Syndicated 1957. 39 episodes.

SYLVESTER AND TWEETY

Animated Cartoon. The series, composed of various Warner Brothers theatrical cartoons, most often features the antics of Sylvester and Tweety—a cat (Sylvester) who relentlessly pursues one goal—to catch himself a decent meal, that being Tweety, the foxy bird.

Voice Characterizations: Mel Blanc.

Music: William Lava, Milt Franklin, John Seely, Carl W. Stalling.

Director: Robert McKimson, Friz Freeling, Chuck Jones.

SYLVESTER AND TWEETY—30 minutes—CBS—Premiered: September 11, 1976.

SZYSZNYK

Comedy. Background: Washington, D.C. The story of Nick Szysznyk (pronounced Ziznik), an ex-Marine

sergeant turned playground supervisor, as he attempts to salvage the financially troubled Northeast Community Center.

CAST

Nick Szysznyk	Ned Beatty
Ms. Harrison, the district supervisor	Olivia Cole
Sandi Chandler, Nick's assistant	Susan Lanier
Leonard Kriegler, the assistant to the director; in charge of sports equip.	Leonard Barr
Ray Gun, one of the teen-agers at the center	Thomas Carter
Ralph, same as Ray	Jarrod Johnson
Tony, same as Ray	Scott Colomby
Fortwengler, same as Ray	Barry Miller

Music: Doug Gilmore.

Theme Vocal: Sonny Curtis.

Executive Producer: Jerry Weintraub.

Producer: Rich Eustis, Michael Elias.

Director: Peter Bonerz.

Creator: Jim Mulligan, Ron Landry.

SZYSZNYK—30 minutes—CBS—August 1, 1977 - August 29, 1977. 5 episodes.

J

THE TAB HUNTER SHOW

Comedy. Background: Malibu Beach, California. The romantic misadventures of Paul Morgan, playboy, and creator-artist of the comic strip "Bachelor at Large."

CAST

Paul Morgan	Tab Hunter
Peter Fairfield III, his friend	Richard Erdman
John Larsen, the publisher of *Comics Incorporated,* Paul's employer	Jerome Cowan

Music: Pete Rugolo.

THE TAB HUNTER SHOW—30 minutes—NBC—September 20, 1960 - September 10, 1961. 32 episodes.

TABITHA

Comedy. A spin-off from "Bewitched." Background: Los Angeles, California. Events in the life of Tabitha Stevens, a witch (the daughter of Samantha and Darrin Stevens), now a beautiful young woman employed by ABC affiliated station KXLA-TV; a young woman who frequently resorts to bits of conjured magic to achieve her goal.

CAST

Tabitha Stevens	Lisa Hartman
Adam Stevens, her brother	David Ankrum
Paul Thurston, the star of his own program on KXLA	Robert Urich
Marv, Paul's producer	Mel Stewart
Minerva, Tabitha's aunt	Karen Morrow
Dr. Bombay, the warlock doctor	Bernard Fox

Music: Dick De Benedictis.

Executive Producer: Jerry Mayer.

Producer: George Yanok.

Director: Charles S. Dubin.

Creator: Jerry Mayer.

TABITHA—30 minutes—ABC—Premiered: September 10, 1977. Broadcast on an irregular basis throughout the 1977-1978 season.

TAG THE GAG

Game. Selected members of the studio audience compete. A group of actors pantomime a joke on stage and stop prior to its punch line. The player who is able to verbally complete it is the winner of that round. Cash prizes are awarded to players who most often tag the gag.

Host: Hal Block.

Producer: Ray Buffum.

Director: Jack Hein.

TAG THE GAG—30 minutes—NBC—August 20, 1951 - September 1951.

TAKE A CHANCE

Game. A player, who is given five dollars, is either able to leave with it or risk it in an attempt to answer a question. If choosing the latter, he is asked a general-knowledge type of question. A correct response awards the player a gift and a choice: to continue or leave. A maximum of four questions are asked and prizes range from gags to costly items. An incorrect answer defeats a player, who then loses his money and prizes.

Host: Don Ameche.

Producer: Dick Lewis.

Sponsor: Nestle.

TAKE A CHANCE—30 minutes—ABC 1950.

TAKE A GIANT STEP

Discussion. Teenagers (thirteen to fifteen years of age) discuss personal and social matters. The program attempts to help children between the ages of seven and fourteen develop their own sense of judgment.

Revised title and format "Talk to a Giant."

Teenagers discuss various aspects of the world with celebrities—giants in their respected fields.

Hosts (chosen from a group of twenty-five teenagers): Andrea Mays, Nancy Melendez, Nancy Wemmer, John Rucker, Bill Bliss, Linda Lloyd da Silva, Heather Thomas, Chip Portocarrero, Scott Falloner, Rinky Favor, Linda Lagisola, David Kollack, Sherry Shapiro.

Music: Recorded.

TAKE A GIANT STEP—60 minutes—NBC—September 11, 1971 - August 26, 1972.

TALK WITH A GIANT—30 minutes—NBC—September 9, 1972 - September 1, 1973.

TAKE A GOOD LOOK

Game. Distinguished by two formats.

Format One:

Three contestants compete. Object: To identify prominent news figures from film clips and sound recordings.

Format Two:

A celebrity panel of three compete. A cast performs a dramatic sketch on stage that relates clues to a mystery guest. The panelist who first associates the clues and identifies the celebrity guest is the winner of that round. Winners are the highest-scoring players. Prizes are awarded to home viewers who are represented by panelists.

Host: Ernie Kovacs.

Panelists: Edie Adams, Cesar Romero, Carl Reiner.

Dramatic Cast: Ernie Kovacs, Peggy Connelly, Bob Lauher.

TAKE A GOOD LOOK—30 minutes—ABC—October 22, 1959 - July 21, 1960; October 27, 1960 - March 16, 1961.

TAKE A GUESS

Game. Selected members of the studio audience compete. Through question-and-answer probe rounds with a celebrity panel, players have to uncover a mystery phrase that is known only to the host and panel. Players start with $150. Each "yes" answer by a panelist deducts five dollars from that player's total. The round continues until a player, who receives four guesses, identifies the phrase. The player then receives the total amount of money deducted from all the scores added to his total. The winner, the highest cash scorer, receives his accumulated earnings as a prize.

Host: John K. M. McCaffery.

Panelists: Ernie Kovacs, John Crawford, Dorothy Hart, Margaret Lindsey.

TAKE A GUESS—30 minutes—CBS—June 18, 1953 - September 1953.

TAKE ANOTHER LOOK

Game. Contestants compete in a fashion quiz for prizes.

Host: Sonny Mars.

Vocalist: Peggy Taylor.

Music: The Bill Otto Band.

TAKE ANOTHER LOOK—60 minutes—CBS 1950.

TAKE FIVE WITH STILLER AND MEARA

Comedy. A series of humorous black-out type skits satirizing various aspects of everyday life.

Starring: Jerry Stiller and Anne Meara.

Music: Recorded.

Executive Producer: John Davis.

Producer: William Watts.

Director: Ivan Curry.

TAKE FIVE WITH STILLER AND MEARA—05 minutes—Syndicated 1977.

TAKE IT FROM ME

Comedy. Background: The Bronx, New York. The life of the average American housewife as interpreted by comedienne Jean Carroll.

CAST

The housewife	Jean Carroll
Her husband	Alan Carney
Their daughter	Lynn Loring
Their neighbor	Alice Pearce

Orchestra: Bernie Greene.

TAKE IT FROM ME—30 minutes— ABC—November 4, 1953 - January 13, 1954. Also known as: "The Jean Carroll Show."

TAKE MY ADVICE

Discussion. Four celebrity guests discuss and suggest answers to problems sent in by viewers.

Hostess: Kelly Lange.

Announcer: Bill Armstrong.

Music: Score Productions.

Executive Producer: Burt Sugarman.

Producer: Mark Massari, Ken Salter.

Director: Hank Behar.

Creator: Armand Grant.

TAKE MY ADVICE—25 minutes— NBC—January 5, 1976 - June 11, 1976.

TAKE TWO

Game. Four celebrity guests, divided into two teams of two. Four pictures are flashed on a screen (e.g., Marilyn Monroe, Amy Vanderbilt, Jayne Mansfield, and a cat). The team that is first to identify themselves receives a chance to answer. If they are able to identify two pictures related to one set (Monroe and Mansfield, actresses), they receive points. Winners are the highest scorers. Selected members of the studio audience, who are represented by the celebrities, receive merchandise prizes.

Host: Don McNeil.

TAKE TWO—30 minutes—ABC—May 5, 1963 - August 11, 1963.

TALENT PATROL

See Title: "Steve Allen."

TALENT VARIETIES

Musical Variety. Performances by Country and Western entertainers.

Host: Slim Wilson.

Announcer: Chuck Hesington.

Music: The Tall Timber Trio; The Country Rhythm Boys.

TALENT VARIETIES—30 minutes—ABC—June 28, 1955 - September 6, 1955.

TALES OF THE BLACK CAT

Anthology. Horror, suspense, and mystery presentations.

Host: James Monks.

Assisting: Thanatopsis, his black siamese cat.

TALES OF THE BLACK CAT—30 minutes—CBS 1950.

TALES OF THE CITY

Anthology. Dramatizations set against the background of New York City.

Host: Ben Hect.

Included:

Miracle In The Rain. The tender and heartwarming story of a lonely girl who keeps a spiritual vigil for her sweetheart who was killed in the war.

CAST
William Prince, Phyllis Thaxter.

Blackie Gagin. The story of Blackie Gagin, one of the dumbiest crooks who ever lived, is told via song and story by Burl Ives.

CAST
Blackie Gagin: Dane Clark.

TALES OF THE CITY—30 minutes—CBS—June 25, 1953 - September 16, 1953.

TALES OF MYSTERY

A thirty-minute anthology series, first syndicated in 1954, that delves into the world of the supernatural.

TALES OF THE 77th BENGAL LANCERS

Adventure. Background: India. The saga of the British forces, 77th Bengal Lancers, as they battle the constant Afrid uprisings.

CAST
Lieutenant Rhodes	Philip Carey
Lieutenant Storm	Warren Stevens
Colonel Standish	Pat Whyte
Captain Scott Ellis	John Hubbard
Captain Clary	Sean McClory

TALES OF THE 77th BENGAL LANCERS—30 minutes—NBC—October 21, 1956 - June 2, 1957. 26 episodes. Syndicated.

TALES OF THE TEXAS RANGERS

Western. Background: Texas. Dramatizations based on the files of the Texas Rangers, North America's oldest law-enforcement organization. Stories detail the investigations of Rangers Jace Pearson and Clay Morgan, and the time-honored methods of crime control from the 1830s to the 1950s.

CAST

Ranger Jace Pearson	Willard Parker
Ranger Clay Morgan	Harry Lauter

Producer: Colbert Clark, Jonal Seinfield, Harry Ackerman.

TALES OF THE TEXAS RANGERS—30 minutes—ABC—September 21, 1957 - May 25, 1959. 52 episodes. Syndicated.

TALES OF THE UNEXPECTED

Anthology. Suspense and mystery presentations.

Host-Narrator: William Conrad.

Music: Richard Markowitz, David Shire.

Executive Producer: Quinn Martin.

Producer: John Wilder.

Included:

The Mark of Adonis. The story concerns an aging producer who relies on the mysterious rejuvenation process of a doctor to maintain the appearance of a young man.

CAST

Alexander Cole: Robert Foxworth; Viviana: Marlyn Mason; Gerry: Linda Kelsey; Davidion: Victor Jory.

Devil Pack. The story of a small, isolated community terrorized by fearce wild dogs.

CAST

Jerry Colby: Ronny Cox; Ann Colby: Christine Belford; Sheriff: Van Johnson.

The Final Chapter. The story of Frank Harris—a crusading newspaper reporter who has himself placed on death row in an attempt to write about capital punishment. The unexpected occurs when he is scheduled for execution and cannot convince anyone of his masquerade.

CAST

Frank Harris: Roy Thinnes; Warden Greer: Ramon Bieri; Chaplain: Brendon Dillon.

TALES OF THE UNEXPECTED—60 minutes—NBC—February 2, 1977 - March 9, 1977.

TALES OF THE UNKNOWN

Anthology. Science fiction tales enacted by a single actor or actress.

TALES OF THE UNKNOWN—30 minutes—Syndicated 1954.

TALES OF THE VIKINGS

Adventure. Background: Scandinavia, A.D. 1000. Episodes of conflict and conquest in the lives of Leif Ericson and his sea raiders, the Vikings.

CAST

Leif Ericson	Jerome Courtland
Finn	Walter Barnes
Firebeard	Stefan Schnabel
Haldar	Peter Bull
Jessica	June Thorburn

TALES OF THE VIKINGS—30 minutes—Syndicated 1960. 39 episodes.

TALES OF TOMORROW

Anthology. Stories of the supernatural.

Music: Bobby Christian.

Producer: Mort Abrams.

Director: Leonard Valenta.

Sponsor: Kreisler Products.

Included:

Ahead of His Time. The story of an ordinary man who becomes extraordinary when he invents a time machine.

Starring: Paul Tripp.

Discovered Heart. The story of a young girl who makes a playmate of a visitor from outer space.

Starring: Susan Holloran.

Dark Angel. The story of a woman who never grows old.

Starring: Meg Mundy, Sidney Blackmer.

TALES OF TOMORROW—30 minutes—ABC—August 3, 1951 - September 18, 1953.

THE TALES OF WELLS FARGO

Western. Background: The Frontier during the 1860s. The investigations of Jim Hardie, agent-troubleshooter for Wells Fargo, Incorporated, gold transporters.

Revised Format:
   Background: San Francisco, California. The series focuses on both Jim Hardie's home life, now the owner of a ranch, and his experiences as a Wells Fargo Troubleshooter.

CAST

Jim Hardie	Dale Robertson
Jeb Gane, the foreman	William Demarest
Beau McCloud, Hardie's assistant	Jack Ging
Widow Ovie, Jim's neighbor	Virginia Christine
Mary Gee, Ovie's daughter	Mary Jane Saunders
Tina, Ovie's daughter	Lory Patrick

Narrator: Dale Robertson.

Music: Stanley Wilson; Melvyn Lenard; Morton Stevens.

Producer: Nat Holt, Earl Lyon.

THE TALES OF WELLS FARGO—30 minutes (first format)—NBC—March 18, 1957 - August 28, 1961. 60 minutes (revised format)—NBC—September 30, 1961 - September 8, 1962. 167 episodes. Syndicated.

TALES OF THE WIZARD OF OZ

An animated series, produced in Canada, that follows the further adventures of L. Frank Baum's memorable "Wizard of Oz" characters. 130 five minute films, syndicated 1961.

TALK TO A GIANT

See title: "Take A Giant Step."

TALLAHASSEE 7000

Crime Drama. Background: Miami Beach, Florida. The investigations of Lex Rogers, special agent-troubleshooter for the Florida Sheriff's

Tallahassee 7000. Walter Matthau. © *Screen Gems.*

Bureau. (Tallahasse 7000: The Florida Sheriff's Bureau telephone number.)

Starring: Walter Matthau as Lex Rogers.

Narrator: Walter Matthau.

Music: Irving Friedman.

TALLAHASSEE 7000—30 minutes—Syndicated 1961. 39 episodes.

THE TALL MAN

Western. Background: Lincoln County, territory of New Mexico, 1879. The relationship between a law enforcer, Sheriff Pat Garrett, and his captor, William Bonney, alias Billy the Kid, now released in the custody of an English rancher. Stories detail Garrett's attempts, helped and hindered by Billy, to maintain law and order.

CAST

Sheriff Pat Garrett	Barry Sullivan
William Bonney	Clu Gulager

Music: Esquivel.

THE TALL MAN—30 minutes—NBC —September 10, 1960 - September 1, 1962. 75 episodes. Syndicated.

TAMMY

Comedy. Background: Louisiana. Raised in the desolate Bayou country by her grandfather after her parents' death, Tammy Tarleton, a young and

Tammy. Left to right: Frank McGrath, Denver Pyle, Debbie Watson.

lonely riverboat girl, enrolls as a student in a secretarial school after completing special educational courses at nearby Seminola College.

Completing the course, she applies for a position as secretary to John Brent, a wealthy widower.

Shortly after, while milking her goat, Nan, a telegram arrives at the *Ellen B,* her houseboat, informing her of an appointment for an interview with Mr. Brent at Brentwood Hall.

Interviewed and impressing Mr. Brent with her ability to type approximately two hundred words a minute, she is hired as his secretary-receptionist. Immediately, she encounters the wrath of Lavinia Tate, an attractive widow who had hoped to acquire the position for her daughter, Gloria, and further her own plans to acquire John's long-sought proposal of marriage. With her chances ruined, Lavinia sets her goal to acquire the secretarial position for Gloria by disgracing Tammy in the hope that it will either cause her to quit or be dismissed.

Having lived a sheltered life, and conveying a philosophy of love and understanding, Tammy struggles to overcome the situations that arise as Lavinia deceitfully attempts to achieve her goal. Based on the motion

pictures *Tammy and the Bachelor,* which stars Debbie Reynolds, and *Tammy Tell Me True* which stars Sandra Dee.

CAST

Tammy Tarleton	Debbie Watson
Mortecai Tarleton, her grandfather	Denver Pyle
Lucius Tarleton, her uncle	Frank McGrath
John Brent	Donald Woods
Lavinia Tate	Dorothy Green
Gloria Tate	Linda Marshall
Dwayne Witt, John's associate	George Furth
Peter Tate, Lavinia's son	David Macklin
Stephen Brent, John's son	Jay Sheffield
Cletus Tarleton, Tammy's cousin	Dennis Robertson

Theme: "Tammy," composed by Jay Livingston and Ray Evans.

Background music composed by: Frank Skinner.

Series music supervision: Stanley Wilson.

Series Music: Jack Marshall.

Producer: Dick Wesson.

Director: Ezra Stone, Sidney Miller, Harry Keller, Leslie Goodwins.

TAMMY—30 minutes—ABC—September 17, 1965 - July 15, 1966. 26 episodes. Theatrical version culled from the series: "Tammy and the Millionaire."

THE TAMMY GRIMES SHOW

Comedy. Background: New York City. The story of Tammy Ward, a young heiress who is restricted to a tight budget by her stingy Uncle Simon, and who is unable to claim her

The Tammy Grimes Show. Tammy Grimes.

multi-million dollar inheritance because she has not yet reached the age of thirty. Episodes depict her misadventures as she struggles to finance her expensive tastes through elaborate schemes.

CAST
Tammy Ward	Tammy Grimes
Simon Ward	Hiram Sherman
Terence Ward, Tammy's brother	Dick Sargent

THE TAMMY GRIMES SHOW—30 minutes—ABC—September 8, 1966 - September 29, 1966. 10 episodes (only four of which aired).

TARGET

Anthology. High-tension, impact dramas that depict the conflicting forces that drive men and women.

Host: Adolphe Menjou.

Included:

The Last Stop. The story focuses on the desperation of two kidnappers as they flee from a police agent.
Starring: Neville Brand.

Backfire. The story of a nurse who is kidnapped and forced to treat a wounded criminal.
Starring: Pat O'Brien.

Unreasonable Doubt. The story of a man and his attempts to clear himself of a false murder charge.
Starring: Macdonald Carey.

Fateful Decision. The story of a man and his attempts to kill his wife's supposed lover.
Starring: Marshall Thompson.

TARGET—30 minutes—Syndicated 1951. 38 episodes.

TARGET: THE CORRUPTORS

Crime Drama. The investigations of Paul Marino, a racket reporter, and Jach Flood, a federal undercover agent, as they attempt to infiltrate the rackets and expose the methods of organized crime through the power of the press.

CAST
Paul Marino	Stephen McNally
Jach Flood	Robert Harland

Music: Herschel Burke Gilbert; Rudy Schrager.

TARGET: THE CORRUPTORS—60 minutes—ABC—September 29, 1961 - September 20, 1962. 34 episodes. Syndicated.

TARO, GIANT OF THE JUNGLE

An animated series about Taro, a jungle boy who, to battle evil, acquires his powers from a radioactive tree. 30 minutes—Syndicated 1969. 39 episodes.

TARZAN

Adventure. Background: Africa. Put ashore by the mutinous crew of a ship bound for England, Lord John Greystoke and his wife Alice, left with tools and firearms, construct a small shack near the coast when all attempts to escape fail. One year later, a son is born to them.

Shortly after, the cabin is attacked by a tribe of bull apes. John and Alice are savagely slaughtered, and little Lord Greystoke is taken by Kalah, a young female. ape, who raises him as Tarzan, Lord of the Jungle.

Twenty years later, after a safari is marooned on the island, Tarzan befriends a Frenchman who, teaching him to speak English, persuades him to return to England. Educated in the finest finishing schools, but unable to adjust to civilized life, he returns to the land of his birth.*

Stories relate Tarzan's attempts to protect his beloved homeland from the sinister forces of evil. His female companion, Jane,** and his poor English are deleted from the story and character created by Edgar Rice Burroughs.

*One of two versions relating Tarzan's education.
**Separated from a safari, Jane Parker is suddenly propelled amid a web of pending death: a rampaging elephant and savage Pygmies. Rescued by Tarzan, she befriends him and teaches him to talk. The "Me Tarzan, you Jane" type of dialogue prevails through many of the features.

CAST

Tarzan   Ron Ely
Jai, an orphaned jungle
    boy   Manuel Padilla, Jr.
Jason Flood, Jai's
    tutor   Alan Caillou
Rao, the village
    veterinarian   Rockne Tarkington
Tall Boy, his
    assistant   Stewart Rafill

Music: Walter Greene, Nelson Riddle.

Producer: Maurice Unger.

Tarzan's chimpanzee: Cheetah.

TARZAN—60 minutes—NBC—September 8, 1966 - September 13, 1968. CBS (rebroadcasts): June 4, 1969 - September 10, 1969. 57 episodes. Syndicated.

TARZAN: LORD OF THE JUNGLE

Animated Cartoon. Background: Africa. The further adventures of Tarzan as he battles the evils of man and beast.

Tarzan's assistant: Nakima, the monkey.

Voices: Bob Ridgley, Linda Gray, Joan Gerber, Ted Cassidy, Barry Gordon, Alan Oppenheimer, Jane Webb.

Music: Yvette Blais, Jeff Michael.

Executive Producer: Norm Prescott, Lou Scheimer.

Director: Don Christensen.

TARZAN: LORD OF THE JUNGLE —25 minutes—CBS—Premiered: September 11, 1976.

TATE

Western. Background: The Frontier during the 1870s. The saga of Tate, a wandering one-armed (the left, smashed during the Civil War is preserved in a black leather casing) ex-gunfighter who sides with justice against criminal elements.

Starring: David McLean as Tate.

TATE—30 minutes—NBC—June 8, 1960 - September 28, 1960.

TATTLETALES

Game. Three celebrity couples compete, each representing one third of the studio audience.

Round One: The husbands are isolated offstage; the wives are before camera. The host reads a question (e.g., "It happened on vacation"). The player who first sounds her buzzer receives a chance to answer. She then relates a situation that concerns her marriage and a one- or two-word clue that summarizes the answer. The host then presses a button and airs the husbands, who appear on monitors placed before each of their mates. The question is restated and the one- or two-word clue is given. The husband who believes it is his wife's response sounds a bell. He then has to relate a similar story. If correct, one hundred dollars is scored.

Round Two: The reverse of round one: wives have to recognize and match what their husbands have said regarding their marriage. One hundred dollars is scored for each correct association.

Winners are the highest scoring teams. The program adds one thousand dollars to the total and it is then divided between the studio audience members who are represented by that celebrity couple.

Host: Bert Convy.

Announcer: Jack Clark.

Music: Recorded.

TATTLETALES—30 minutes—CBS—Premiered: February 18, 1974.

TED MACK

Listed: The television programs of Ted Mack.

Ted Mack And The Original Amateur Hour—Variety—30 minutes. NBC—October 4, 1949 - September 11, 1954; ABC—October 30, 1955 - June 23, 1957; NBC—September 1957 - October 4, 1958; CBS—October 1958 - September 1971.

Host: Ted Mack.

Announcers: Dennis James; Roy Greece.

Orchestra: Lloyd Marx.

Format: Performances by undiscovered professional talent.

Ted Mack's Family Hour—Variety—30 minutes—ABC—January 7, 1951 - November 25, 1954.

Host: Ted Mack.

Vocalist: Andy Roberts.

Announcer: Dennis James.

Orchestra: Lloyd Marx.

Format: Performances by professional entertainers.

Ted Mack's Matinee—Variety—30 minutes—NBC—1954 - 1955.

Host: Ted Mack.

Regulars: Elsie Rhodes, Dick Lee and the Honeydreamers.

Orchestra: Lloyd Marx.

Format: Performances by professional entertainers.

THE TED STEELE SHOW

Musical Variety.

Host: Ted Steele.

Regulars: Helen Wood, Michael Rich, Nola Day, Mardi Bryant, Charles Danford.

Orchestra: Ted Steele.

THE TED STEELE SHOW—30 minutes—DuMont 1949.

THE TELECOMICS

Animated Cartoon. The overall title for four rotating series: "Danny March"; "Johnny and Mr. Do-Right"; "Kid Champion"; and "Space Barton." The first cartoons made especially for television. Character credits are not given.

Danny March. Background: Metro City. Shortly after his parents are killed in an automobile accident, young Danny March is sent to live with his uncle, a shady character who soon meets with a violent end. Sent to an orphanage, he grows up as one of the toughest kids in town.

But instead of turning to a life of crime, he decides to devote his life to combatting crime. Rejected by the Metro City police force when he falls short of height requirements, he becomes a private detective and soon afterward, because of his heroic exploits, is appointed as the mayor's personal detective. Stories depict his investigations.

Johnny And Mr. Do-Right. The adventures shared by a young boy and his dog.

Kid Champion. Dreaming of becoming a musician, Eddie Hale relinquishes his desire and begins to train as a prize-fighter to please his father, a once-famous boxer who has only one year to live.

Passing a gas station, and witnessing a robbery, Eddie, in an attempt to save the attendant, accidentally knocks him to the ground. Fearing to have killed the man, he flees, drops his real name and adopts the alias of Kid Champion. Sometime later, when crossing the path of Lucky Skinner, a manager, he is persuaded to further his career as a boxer. Stories depict his attempts to become a champion.

Space Barton. Fascinated by space, Horace Barton, Jr., sets his goal to become the world's greatest pilot. His ambition, which is reflected in everything he does, earns him the nickname of "Space."

After three years of college, and just prior to World War II, he joins the army air corps. Assigned to test the first U.S. jet, he receives his first experience with outer space. Stories relate his attempts to achieve a dream.

THE TELECOMICS—15 minutes—NBC—1950-1951. CBS—15 minutes—1951. Syndicated. Withdrawn. Also known as "The NBC Comics."

TELEDRAMA

Anthology. Dramatizations based on stories by leading playwrights.

Included:

Pier 23. The story of a San Francisco storekeeper who turns detective to track down two murderers.

CAST
Richard Travis, Hugh Beaumont, Ann Savage.

Traffic In Crime. A police spy attempts to break up two gambling syndicates that are operating in a small town.

CAST
Kane Richmond, Ruth Terry, Adele Mara.

Tales Of Robin Hood. A video adaptation of the classic folk tale. The story of Robin Hood, an outlaw who stole from the rich to give to the poor.

CAST
Robert Clark.

TELEDRAMA—30 minutes—CBS 1953.

TELEPHONE TIME

Anthology. Dramatizations depicting the events that spark the lives of ordinary people.
Hosts: John Nesbitt, Frank Baxter.

Included:

The Golden Junkman. The story of a junkman with an amazing ability to make money.

CAST
Lon Chaney, Jr.

Harry In Search Of Himself. The story of the founder of the American Society for the Prevention of Cruelty to Animals.

CAST
Edgar Buchanan, Frances Reid, Philip Bourneuf.

Time Bomb. The true story of the manager of a Shanghai textile factory and his diabetic wife who are trapped in the city by the Japanese occupation at the beginning of World War II.

CAST
Steven Geary, Terie Shimada, Osa Massen, Keye Luke.

TELEPHONE TIME—30 minutes—CBS—1956 - 1958.

TELE PUN

Game. Standing before the studio audience, a player has to perform a pun, which represents geographical locations, songs, people, proverbs, or titles, through charades to their satisfaction. If he is successful (rarely) he receives a prize. However, should he make a mistake, he is charged with "punning in public places" and arrested. Taking on the atmosphere of a courtroom hearing, the player is then comically defended by an attorney. When the judge dismisses the case, the player receives a consolation prize and the crime, "the errant pun"is performed in the correct manner.

Home participation segment: "The Tele Pun of the Week." A pun is enacted during the course of the program. Left unanswered, it is offered for solution to home viewers who respond via post cards. Answers are judged and prizes are awarded accordingly.

Host-Judge: Johnny Bradford.

Announcer-Attorney: Ray Michael.

TELE PUN—30 minutes—NBC 1948.

TELL IT TO THE CAMERA

Comedy. A spin-off from "Candid Camera." People, who are aware of a camera, speak directly into it and reveal their thoughts concerning personal and/or wordly problems. Created by Allen Funt.

Host: Red Rowe.

Music: Sid Ramin.

TELL IT TO THE CAMERA—30 minutes—CBS—January 11, 1962 - May 24, 1962.

TELL IT TO GROUCHO

Interview-Quiz. Two contestants are first comically interviewed by the host, then compete in a quiz wherein they attempt to identify persons, places, or objects from pictures that are rapidly flashed on a screen. Players earnings, which are divided, are based on the number of correct identifications. A spin-off from "You Bet Your Life."

Host: Groucho Marx.

Assistants: Patty Harmon, Jack Wheels.

Announcer: George Fenneman.

Orchestra: Jerry Fielding.

TELL IT TO GROUCHO—30 minutes—CBS 1962.

TELL US MORE

Documentary. The careers of famous celebrities are recalled through film clips, photographs, letters, and newspaper clippings. Two biographies of similar personalities are presented on each program.

Host-Narrator: Conrad Nagel.

Included Biographies: Marilyn Monroe, Elizabeth Taylor; Bing Crosby, Bob Hope; Spencer Tracy, Pat O'Brien; Joan Fontaine, Olivia De Havilland; Grace Kelly, Audrey Hepburn; Bud Abbott and Lou Costello, Stan Laurel and Oliver Hardy; Kate Smith, Marian Anderson; Johnny Weissmuller, Buster Crabbe; Lon Chaney, Boris Karloff; Jackie Robinson, Joe Dimaggio.

TELL US MORE—30 minutes—NBC —September 9, 1963 - March 16, 1964.

TELLER OF TALES

Anthology. Dramatizations based on stories by author William Somerset Maugham.

Host: William Somerset Maugham.

Producer: John Gibbs, Anne Marlowe, Martin Ritt.

Director: David Alexander, Martin Ritt.

Sponsor: Tintair

TELLER OF TALES—30 minutes—CBS—1950 - 1951. Also known as "The Somerset Maugham Theatre."

THE TELLTALE CLUE

Crime Drama. Background: New York

City. The investigations of Detective Captain Richard Hale, of the Metropolitan Homicide Squad, as he attempts to solve crimes through one seemingly insignificant piece of evidence: The Telltale Clue.

Starring: Anthony Ross as Richard Hale.

THE TELLTALE CLUE—30 minutes —CBS—July 15, 1954 - September 23, 1954.

TEMPERATURES RISING

Comedy. Distinguished by two formats.

Format One:

Background: Capitol General Hospital in Washington, D.C. A comical portrait of life in a hospital as seen through the eyes—and antics—of Dr. Jerry Noland, a gambling-inclined intern who, with his cohorts, Nurses Ann Carlisle, Mildred MacInerney, and Ellen Turner, struggles to aid patients who are in need of financial assistance.

Upsetting normal hospital routines by his endless attempts to raise money, he encounters the wrath of Dr. Vincent Campanelli, the chief of surgery, who attempts, but fails to keep him in line, and struggles to return the hospital to normalcy.

CAST

Dr. Vincent Campanelli	James Whitmore
Dr. Jerry Noland	Cleavon Little
Nurse Ann Carlisle	Joan Van Ark
Nurse Mildred MacInerney	Reva Rose
Nurse Ellen Turner	Nancy Fox
Miss Liewellen, Dr. Campanelli's secretary	Olive Dunbar

Music: Shorty Rogers.

TEMPERATURES RISING—30 minutes—ABC—September 12, 1972 - September 4, 1973.

Format Two:

Background: Capitol General Hospital in Washington, D.C. The harassed life of Paul Mercy, its administrator, a nonpracticing doctor who struggles to solve endless patient and staff difficulties.

CAST

Dr. Paul Mercy	Paul Lynde
Wendy Winchester, R.N.	Jennifer Darling
Miss Tillis, the admissions nurse	Barbara Cason
Dr. Jerry Noland	Cleavon Little
Dr. Charles Claver	John Dehner
Dr. Lloyd Axton	Jeff Morrow
Edwina Mercy, Paul's sister	Alice Ghostley
Agatha Mercy, Paul's mother	Sudie Bond
Nurse Kelly	Barbara Rucker
Haskell, the orderly	Jerry Houser

Music: Vic Mizzy.

THE NEW TEMPERATURES RISING SHOW—30 minutes—ABC—September 25, 1973 - January 8, 1974. Returned (ABC): July 28, 1974 - August 30, 1974.

TEMPLE HOUSTON

Western. Background: The post-Civil War Southwest. The cases of Temple Houston, a circuit-riding attorney, and his partner, an ex-gunslinger turned law enforcer, George Taggert, as they attempt to defend unjustly accused people before circuit-riding judges.

CAST

Temple Houston Jeffrey Hunter
George Taggert   Jack Elam

TEMPLE HOUSTON—60 minutes—NBC—September 19, 1963 - September 17, 1964. 26 episodes.

TEMPTATION

Game. Three female contestants compete. Each player chooses one of three merchandise showcases, the contents of which are unknown, that are displayed on stage. Object: For the player to identify the contents of their selection. A general-knowledge type of question is asked. The player who is first to identify herself by a buzzer signal receives a chance to answer. If correct, she is permitted to ask the host a question regarding the contents of the showcase. To sway players from the showcase, tempting and expensive merchandise items are offered to them after every several questions. If a player chooses to have the article, she forfeits her chances at the showcase. The game continues until one player correctly identifies the showcase, which is then awarded to her.

Host: Art James.

TEMPTATION—30 minutes—ABC—December 4, 1967 - July 2, 1968.

TENAFLY

See title "NBC Wednesday Mystery Movie," *Tenafly* segment.

TENNESSEE ERNIE FORD

Listed: The television programs of singer Tennessee Ernie Ford.

The Kollege Of Musical Knowledge—Variety-Quiz—30 minutes—NBC 1954. See title: "Kay Kyser's Kollege of Musical Knowledge."

The Tennessee Ernie Ford Show—Musical Variety—30 minutes—NBC—January 3, 1955 - June 28, 1957.

Host: Tennessee Ernie Ford.

Regulars: Molly Bee, Doris Drew, Reginald Gardiner, The Voices of Walter Schumann.

Announcer: Skip Farrell.

Orchestra: Walter Schumann.

The Tennessee Ernie Ford Show—Musical Variety—30 minutes—NBC—1958 - 1960.

Host: Tennessee Ernie Ford.

Announcer: Jack Narz.

Orchestra: Harry Geller.

The Tennessee Ernie Ford Show—Musical Variety—30 minutes—ABC—April 2, 1961 - March 26, 1965.

Host: Tennessee Ernie Ford.

Regulars: Dick Noel, Anita Gordon, Billy Strange.

Announcer: Jim Lange.

Orchestra: Jack Fascinato.

TENNESSEE TUXEDO AND HIS TALES

Animated Cartoon. Background: The Megopolis Zoo. The misadventures of Tennessee Tuxedo, a penguin, and his friend, Chumley, the walrus, as they struggle to improve living conditions against the objections of Stanley Livingstone, the curator.

Additional characters: Mr. Whoopie, a friend of Tennessee's, a professor who teaches him and Chumley to apply scientific principles in everyday life; and Flunkey, Stanley's assistant.

Additional segments:

Tutor The Turtle. Background: The Great Forest. The story of Tutor, a turtle who becomes whatever he wishes through the magic of Mr. Wizard, the lizard.

The World Of Commander McBragg. A retired naval officer's tall tales concerning his experiences while in the service.

The Hunter. A Beagle detective's relentless pursuit of the cunning criminal, the Fox.

Voices: Don Adams (Tennessee), Jackson Beck, Bradley Bolke, Larry Storch, Ben Stone, Allen Swift, Delo Stokes, Norman Rose, Mort Marshall, Kenny Delmar, George S. Irving.

Music: Not credited.

TENNESSEE TUXEDO AND HIS TALES—30 minutes—Syndicated 1963. 70 episodes.

THE $10,000 PYRAMID

Game. Two competing teams, each composed of one celebrity and one noncelebrity contestant. One team chooses one subject from six categories that are displayed on a board (e.g., "Keep Going"). A question is then read that states its purpose ("Describe things that go from one place to another."). One player has a small monitor before him on which the key words appear, one at a time.

Through one-word clues, he has to relate the meaning to his partner. One point is scored for each correct identification. Rounds are limited to thirty seconds each, and each team competes in three games. The highest scoring team is the winner, and the contestant receives the opportunity to win ten thousand dollars.

The contestant and his partner are escorted to the Winner's Circle. One player sits with his back to a large pyramid that contains six subject categories, each designated by a cash value—fifty to two hundred dollars. The player who is facing the pyramid relates clues to the identity of each of the subjects. If the player guesses all six within one minute, he receives ten thousand dollars. If not, he receives what money is represented by the subjects he correctly identifies.

Host: Dick Clark.

Announcer: Bob Clayton.

Music: Recorded.

Executive Producer: Bob Stewart.

Producer: Anne Marie Schmitt.

Director: Mike Gargiulo.

THE $10,000 PYRAMID—30 minutes—CBS—March 26, 1973 - March 29, 1974. ABC—30 minutes—May 6, 1974 - January 16, 1976. On January 19, 1976, the title changed to "The $20,000 Pyramid," which is played in the same manner and permits players to win $20,000 instead of ten.

TEN WHO DARED

Documentary. A ten-episode series that re-creates the explorations of ten explorers: Christopher Columbus (portrayed by Carlos Ballesteros), Francisco Pizarro (Francisco Cordova), James Cook (Dennis Burgess), Alexander von Humboldt (Matthias Fuchs), Jebediah Smith (Richard Clark), Robert Burke and William Wills (Martin Shaw and John Bell), Henry Morton Stanley (Sean Lynch), Charles Doughty (Paul Chapman), Mary Kingsley (Penelope Lee), and Roald Amundsen (Per Theodor Haugen).

Host-Narrator: Anthony Quinn.

Producer: The B.B.C, Michael Latham.

Sponsor: Mobil Oil.

Note: European title: "The Explorers" (narrated by David Attenborough).

TEN WHO DARED—60 minutes—Syndicated 1977.

TERROR

A thirty-minute anthology series, based on the world of the supernatural, which was first syndicated in 1952.

TERRY AND THE PIRATES

Adventure. Inheriting an abandoned gold mine from his grandfather, Terry Lee, a colonel in the U.S. Air Force, journeys to the Orient, where he begins his search for it. Captured by a sinister band of cutthroats, he is taken to a secret mountain hideaway. Standing at the end of a long line of prisoners, he meets his evil Eurasian captor, Lai Choi San, alias The Dragon Lady, who plans to enslave him.

Resisting, and escaping her bounds, he remains in the Orient, where, while searching for the gold mine, he attempts to battle the evils of The Dragon Lady.

CAST

Terry Lee	John Baer
Lai Choi San, The Dragon Lady	Gloria Saunders
Burma	Sandra Spence
Hot Shot Charlie	Walter Tracy
Chopstick Joe	Jack Reitzen

TERRY AND THE PIRATES—30 minutes—DuMont—1952 - 1953.

TESTIMONY OF TWO MEN

Drama. A six-hour, three-part adaptation of Taylor Caldwell's novel. Background: Hamilton, Pennsylvania. The story, which begins with the end of the Civil War and ends at the turn of the century, focuses on the lives of the Ferrier brothers: Jonathan, a crusading physician, and Harald, who seeks an easy life and ready money. This is the first series to be produced by Operation Prime Time, a project that allows independent stations to pool their resources and purchase excellent quality, first-run programs.

CAST

Jonathan Ferrier	David Birney
Harald Ferrier	David Huffman
Mavis Ferrier, Jonathan's wife	Linda Purl
Dr. Martin Eaton	Steve Forrest
Marjorie Ferrier	Barbara Parkins
Hilda	Barbara Parkins
Adrian Ferrier	William Shatner
Flora Eaton	Margaret O'Brien
Louis Hedler	Tom Bosley

Narrator: Tom Bosley.

Music: Leonard Rosenman, Gerald Fried.

Producer: Jack Laird.

Director: Leo Penn.

TESTIMONY OF TWO MEN—6 hours—Operation Prime Time—1977.

TEXACO STAR THEATRE

See Title: "Milton Berle."

THE TEXAN

Western. Background: Texas during the 1870s. The exploits of Bill Longley, a wandering ex-gunfighter who aides people in distress.

Starring: Rory Calhoun as Bill Longley.

Narrator: Rory Calhoun.

THE TEXAN—30 minutes. CBS—September 29, 1958 - September 1959; ABC—October 3, 1960 - January 6, 1961; September 4, 1961; - May 12, 1962. Syndicated.

THE TEX AND JINX SHOW

See title: "The Swift Show."

TEXAS JOHN SLAUGHTER

See title: "Walt Disney Presents," *Texas John Slaughter* segment.

THE TEXAS WHEELERS

Comedy. Background: Lamont, Texas. Deserting his family after the death of his wife, Zack Wheeler, a lazy good for nothing, returns to his children eight months later, intent on sponging off them. Disliked by his elder offspring, Truckie, twenty-four, a general contractor, and Doobie, seventeen; and loved by the younger, Boo, twelve, and T. J., ten, he struggles to revert to his previous, shiftless life,

The Texas Wheelers. From bottom, then left to right: Tony Becker, Mark Hamill, Jack Elam, Gary Busey, Karen Oberdiear.

and solve the problems that ensue from four independent children who can't wait to grow up.

CAST

Zack Wheeler	Jack Elam
Truckie Wheeler	Gary Busey
Doobie Wheeler	Mark Hamill
Boo Wheeler	Karen Oberdiear
T. J. Wheeler	Tony Becker
The Sheriff	Noble Willingham

Music: Mike Post, Pete Carpenter.

THE TEXAS WHEELERS—30 minutes—ABC—September 13,. 1974 - October 4, 1974. Returned: ABC—June 26, 1975 - July 24, 1975.

THAT GIRL

Comedy. Background: New York City. Talented, young, and beautiful, and hoping to embark on a career as an actress, Ann Marie leaves her home in Brewster, New York and moves to Manhattan, where she acquires Apart-

That Girl. Ted Bessell and Marlo Thomas.

ment 4-D at 344 West 78th Street.*

Stories tenderly depict her world of joys and sorrows as she struggles to further a dream, supporting herself by taking various part-time jobs, cope with parents who don't understand her, and share the interests of her boyfriend, Don Hollinger, a reporter for *Newsview* magazine.

CAST

Ann Marie	Marlo Thomas
Don Hollinger	Ted Bessell
Lou Marie, Ann's father, the owner of the Le Parisienne restaurant	Lew Parker
Helen Marie, Ann's mother	Rosemary DeCamp
Jules Benedict, Ann's drama coach	Billy De Wolfe

*Her address in early episodes. In later episodes; 627 East 54th Street.

Judy Bessimer, Ann's neighbor	Bonnie Scott
Leon Bessimer, Judy's husband, a doctor	Dabney Coleman
Jerry Myer, Don's co-worker, Ann's neighbor (early episodes)	Bernie Kopell
Jerry Bauman, Don's co-worker (later episodes)	Bernie Kopell
Margie Myer, Jerry's wife (early episodes)	Arlene Golonka
Ruth Bauman, Jerry's wife (later episodes)	Carolyn Daniels Alice Borden
Marcy, Ann's friend	Reva Rose
Pete, Ann's friend	Ruth Buzzi
Gloria, Ann's telephone answering service girl	Bobo Lewis
Jonathan Adams, the publisher of *Newsview*	Forrest Compton James Gregory
Agnes Adams, his wife	Phyllis Hill
Bert Hollinger, Don's father	Frank Faylen
Mildred Hollinger, Bert's wife	Mabel Albertson
Nino, the owner of the Italian restaurant frequented by Ann and Don	Gino Conforti
Mr. Brantano, Ann's landlord	Frank Puglia
Mrs. Brantano, his wife	Renata Vanni

Ann's agents (the Gilliam & Norris Theatrical Agency):

Seymour Schwimmer	Don Penny

Harvey Peck   Ronnie Schell
Sandy Stone   Morty Gunty
George Lester   George Carlin

Music: Walter Scharf; Earle Hagen; Warren Barker; Harry Geller.

Executive Producer-Creator: Bill Persky and Sam Denoff.

Producer: Bernie Orenstein, Saul Turteltaub, Jerry Davis.

Director: Jay Sandrich, Homer Powell, James Sheldon, Danny Arnold, Alan Rafkin, Bob Sweeney, Sidney Miller, David MacDearmon, Jeff Hayden, Ted Bessell, John Rich, Roger Dochaway, Bill Persky, Saul Turteltaub, Russ Mayberry, Hal Cooper, Harry Falk, John Erman, James Frawley, Jerry Davis.

THAT GIRL—30 minutes—ABC—September 8, 1966 - September 10, 1971. 136 episodes. Syndicated.

THAT GOOD OLD NASHVILLE MUSIC

A thirty-minute Country and Western variety series, hosted by Dave Dudley, and first syndicated in 1975.

THAT REMINDS ME

Game. Through a series of question-and-answer probe rounds, a celebrity panel has to uncover the identity of celebrity guests who appear in elaborate disguises.

Hostess: Arlene Francis.

Panelists: Nina Foch, Roger Price, Robert Coates.

THAT REMINDS ME—30 minutes—NBC 1952.

THAT SHOW

Talk-Variety.

Hostess: Joan Rivers.

Announcer: Jim Perry.

Music: Recorded.

THAT SHOW—30 minutes—Syndicated 1968. 260 tapes. Also known as "That Show Starring Joan Rivers."

THAT'S HOLLYWOOD!

Documentary. Various aspects of films produced by 20th Century-Fox—from leading ladies, to westerns, to disaster epics—are showcased with on camera performances and behind-the-scenes preparations.

Narrator: Tom Bosley.

Music: Ruby Raksin.

Executive Producer: Jack Haley, Jr.

Producer: Lawrence Einhorn, Phillip Savenick.

Associate Producer: Eytan Keller, Draper Lewis.

Executive In Charge Of Production: David Lawrence.

THAT'S HOLLYWOOD!—30 minutes—Syndicated 1977.

THAT'S LIFE

Musical Comedy. Background: New York. Combining the format of a serial, and the Broadway paced blend of romance, music, comedy, song, and dance, the series depicts the meeting and courtship of Robert Dickson, a junior executive with a chalk company, and Gloria Quigley, and their later marriage, struggle as newly-weds, and attempts to adjust to parenthood when presented with a son, Robert Dickson, Jr.

CAST

Robert Dickson	Robert Morse
Gloria Quigley (Dickson)	E. J. (Edra Jeanne) Peaker
Mr. Quigley, Gloria's father	Shelly Berman
Mrs. Quigley, Gloria's mother	Kay Medford

Choreography: Tony Mordente; The Tony Mordente Dancers.

Orchestra: Elliott Lawrence.

THAT'S LIFE—60 minutes—ABC—September 24, 1968 - May 19, 1969. 26 tapes.

THAT'S MY BOY

Comedy. Background: Rossmore, Ohio, the residence of the Jackson family: "Jarrin" Jack, businessman, ex-college athlete; his wife, Alice, a former Olympic swimming champion; and their son, Jack Junior, a near-sighted bookworm who is prone to hayfever and sinus attacks.

Stories depict the elder's attempts to relive his college youth through Junior by instilling him with the sports spirit and broadening his character; and Junior's attempts to pursue his own goals as he enters his freshman year at Rossmore College. Based on the motion picture.

CAST

Jack Jackson, Sr.	Eddie Mayehoff
Alice Jackson	Rochelle Hudson
Jack Jackson, Jr.	Gil Stratton, Jr.
Henrietta Patterson, Jack's employer's wife	Mabel Albertson
Sam Baker, their neighbor	Larry Blake

Announcer: Bill Baldwin.

Producer: Cy Howard.

Sponsor: The Chrysler Corporation, Plymouth Division.

THAT'S MY BOY—30 minutes—CBS —April 10, 1954 - January 1, 1955. Rebroadcasts: CBS—30 minutes—June 1959 - September 1959.

THAT'S MY MAMA

Comedy. Background: Oscar's Barber Shop in Washington, D.C. Events in the lives of the Curtis family as seen through the eyes of Clifton Curtis, the eldest child, a twenty-five-year-old bachelor who, while attempting to operate his late father's business and live his own life, constantly finds his life being run by his meddling, well-meaning mother, Eloise.

CAST

Clifton Curtis	Clifton Davis
Eloise "Mama" Curtis	Theresa Merritt
Tracy Taylor, her married daughter	Lynne Moody
	Joan Pringle
Leonard Taylor, Tracy's husband	Illunga Adell
Earl Chambers, their friend, the postman	Ed Bernard
	Theodore Wilson
Wildcat, a friend of the family	Jester Hairston
Junior, a friend of Clifton's	Ted Lange
Josh, a	

friend of the
family   DeForest Covan

Music: Jack Eskew.

Additional Music: Lamont Dozier.

Producer: David Pollock.

Director: Herbert Kenwith, Mort Lachman, Arnold Margolin.

Address of Oscar's Barber Shop: 14th and Grant Street.

THAT'S MY MAMA—30 minutes—ABC—September 4, 1974 - December 24, 1975.

THAT WAS THE WEEK THAT WAS

Satire. Utilizing the format of a news program, sketches, blackouts, and commentary are used to satirize the news events of the week preceding the broadcast. Unlike its sophisticated parent show, the British "That Was the Week That Was," the American version suffers from an uneven flow of material and a constant degrading of major political parties.

American Version:

Host: Elliott Reid.

TW3 Girl: Nancy Ames (introducing each broadcast with a musical commentary of the preceding week's events).

CAST
Henry Morgan, Phyllis Newman, Pat Englund, David Frost, Doro Merande, Buck Henry, Burr Tillstrom, Bob Dishy.

THAT WAS THE WEEK THAT WAS—30 minutes—NBC—September 29, 1964 - May 4, 1965. Also known as "TW3."

British Version:

Host: David Frost.

TW3 Girl: Millicent Martin.

CAST
Lance Percival, Roy Kinnear, William Rushton, Kenneth Cope, David Kernan, Ned Sheriin.

Orchestra: Dave Lee.

THAT WAS THE WEEK THAT WAS—30 minutes—B.B.C. TV 1963.

THAT WONDERFUL GUY

Comedy. Background: New York City. The romantic and business misadventures of Harold, a would-be actor who is employed by a sophisticated drama critic.

CAST
Harold   Jack Lemmon
The drama critic   Neil Hamilton
Harold's girlfriend   Cynthia Stone

Orchestra: Bernard Green.

Producer: Charles Irving.

Director: Babette Henry.

THAT WONDERFUL GUY—30 minutes—ABC 1950.

THEATRE '58

Anthology. Rebroadcasts of dramas that were originally aired via other filmed anthology programs.

Included:

Always The Best Man. The story of a man who falls in love with his friend's ex-fiancée.

CAST
Angie Dickinson, Don Taylor, Adam Kennedy, Greta Tyssen.

The House That Jackson Built. Fed up with manhunting, a career girl purchases a house and decides to settle down to a life as a spinster. The story relates the changes that occur in her life when she falls in love with the designer of the house.

CAST

Diana Lynn, Arthur Franz, Jean Carson.

A Mule For Santa Fe. Because he is short one mule, a man finds that he cannot join a wagon train destined for Santa Fe. The story relates his desperate attempts to secure the money he needs to buy one.

CAST

Will Rogers, Jr., Stephen Woolton.

THEATRE '58—30 minutes—CBS— June 18, 1958 - September 1958.

THEATRE '59

Anthology. Rebroadcasts of dramas that were originally aired via other filmed anthology programs.

Included:

A Very Fine Deal. The problems that arise when a New York City transit walker discovers a diamond mine beneath Central Park.
Starring: Bert Lahr.

Markheim. A lawyer's defense of a man who is accused of committing murder.
Starring: Charles Drake.

Too Early Spring. The story of two young lovers confused by the complications of the adult world.
Starring: Burt Brinckerhoff, Jan Norris.

The Wonderful Ice Cream Suit. Pooling their resources, six men purchase a white suit. The story depicts the changes in their lives as each takes a turn wearing it.
Starring: Mike Kellin, Lou Nova.

Alone. The fear that grips a woman who lives alone in a house in a neighborhood where police are searching for an escaped murderer.
Starring: Laraine Day, Joseph Wiseman.

THEATRE '59—30 minutes—Syndicated 1959.

THE THEATRE HOUR

Anthology. Dramatic presentations.

THE THEATRE HOUR—60 minutes —CBS 1949.

THEATRE '60

Anthology. Varying dramatic and musical presentations that feature guest hosts and performers.
Music: The CBS Symphonic Orchestra, conducted by Alfredo Antonini.

Included:

The Treasure. The story of an eccentric French nobleman who prefers his friend's treasured wine celler to that of his beautiful wife.

CAST

Charles Drake, Francios Christophe.

Cotch's Catch. The story of a young American actor who, in order to get a good part in an English film, agrees to a marriage of convenience.

CAST

Charles Drake, Dora Bryan.

An Early Winter. The trials and tribulations of a young bride and groom.

CAST
Kim Hunter, Pat Hingle.

THEATRE '60—60 minutes—CBS 1960.

THEATRE TIME

Anthology. Retitled episodes of "Fireside Theatre" and "The General Electric Theatre."

Hostess: Anita Louise.

Included:

Father Happe. The story of a spinster who finds a new lease on life when a priest encourages her to take up painting.

CAST
Mercedes McCambridge, Rommey Brent.

Louise. The story of a woman who struggles to aid European children following World War II.

CAST
Viveca Lindfors, Herbert Marshall, Norma Varden.

A Shadow Believes. The story of a psychiatrist who seeks to discover whether a patient of his, an amnesiac, is the former fiance' of the woman he loves.

CAST
Marjorie Lord, Stephen McNally, Mary Sinclair.

THEATRE TIME—30 minutes—ABC— July 25, 1957 - September 26, 1957.

T.H.E. CAT

Adventure. Background: A contemp-

orary metropolis. The cases of Thomas Hewitt Edward (T.H.E.) Cat, aerialist turned cat burglar turned professional bodyguard.

CAST

Thomas Hewitt Edward Cat	Robert Loggia
Pepe, the owner of the Casa de Gate cafe	Robert Carricart
William McAllister, the police captain	R.G. Armstrong
Maria, Cat's romantic interest	Norma Bengell

T.H.E. CAT—30 minutes—NBC—September 16, 1966 - September 8, 1967. 26 episodes. Syndicated.

THEN CAME BRONSON

Adventure. Disillusioned after his friend commits suicide, Jim Bronson, a newspaper reporter, resigns, and, inheriting his friend's motorcycle, begins his travels across the United States to discover the meaning of life. Stories depict his involvement with the people he meets and the effect in their lives as the result of his intervention.

Starring: Michael Parks as Jim Bronson.

Music: George Duning.

THEN CAME BRONSON—60 minutes—NBC—September 17, 1969 - September 9, 1970. 26 episodes. Syndicated.

THERE'S ONE IN EVERY FAMILY

Variety. The series spotlights members of a family who are outstandingly different. Several such people appear on each telecast to relate their stories (why they are different) to the studio audience. The audience then votes on each subject by applauding, which is registered on a meter. The person whose score registers the highest is judged the winner and receives the opportunity to win prizes for his family by competing in a question-and-answer session.

Host: John Reed King.

THERE'S ONE IN EVERY FAMILY—30 minutes—CBS—September 29, 1952 - June 18, 1953.

THESE ARE MY CHILDREN

Serial. The struggles of a mother as she attempts to raise her fatherless children.

CAST

The Mother	Alma Platto

Her children: Jane Brooksmith, George Kluge, Martha McCain, Joan Alt, Eloise Kunner.

THESE ARE MY CHILDREN—15 minutes—NBC 1949.

THESE ARE THE DAYS

Animated Cartoon. Background: The town of Elmsville during the early 1900s. Life in America at the turn of the century as seen through the experiences of the Day family: Martha, a widow; her children, Ben, Cathy, and Danny; and their grandfather, Jeff Day, the owner of the Day General Store.

Characters' Voices

Martha Day	June Lockhart
Cathy Day	Pamelyn Ferdin

These Are the Days. Left to right: Martha, Cathy, Jeff (center), Ben, and Danny. © *Hanna-Barbera Productions.*

Danny Day	Jackie Haley
Ben Day	Andrew Parks
Jeff Day	Henry Jones
Homer, Jeff's friend	Frank Cady

Music: Hoyt Curtin.

Executive Producer: William Hanna, Joseph Barbera.

Director: Charles A. Nichols.

THESE ARE THE DAYS—30 minutes—ABC—September 7, 1974 - September 5, 1976.

THEY STAND ACCUSED

Courtroom Drama. Dramatizations based on actual court records.

Judge: Charles Johnson.

Announcer: Harry Creighton.

Lawyers and Defenders: Guest actors.

Jurists: The studio audience.

Producer: William Wines, Richard Albrecht.

Director: Sheldon Cooper.

Sponsor: Crawford Clothes.

THEY STAND ACCUSED—60 minutes—DuMont 1948.

THEY WENT THAT'A WAY

Documentary. The role of the western film on American cultural history is explained and illustrated through the use of film clips.

Hosts: Ruane Hull, Jon Tuska.

THEY WENT THAT'A WAY—30 minutes—PBS—February 16, 1971 - April 20, 1971.

THICKER THAN WATER

Comedy. Aging, and critically ill for the past ten years, Jonas Paine, the founder of Paine's Pure Pickles, stipulates that for his children (Nellie, a forty-year-old spinster, and Ernie, a thirty-four-year-old penniless playboy, who dislike each other) to receive an inheritance, they must live together in the family residence for a period of five years and operate the family pickle factory.

Stories depict: the impatient wait of two feuding siblings as they struggle to live together, operate the business, and care for a father who just won't kick the bucket. Based on the British TV series, "Nearest and Dearest."

CAST

Nellie Paine	Julie Harris
Ernie Paine	Richard Long
Jonas Paine	Malcolm Atterbury
Lily Paine, a cousin	Jessica Myerson
Walter Paine, Lily's husband	Lou Fant
Bert Taylor, the factory foreman	Pat Cranshaw
Lyle Woodstock, Jonas's lawyer	Jim Connell
Agnes Dorsell, a factory employee	Dolores Albin

Music: Michael Melvoin.

THICKER THAN WATER—30 minutes—ABC—June 13, 1973 - August 8, 1973. 13 episodes.

THINK FAST

Game. Object: For celebrity panelists to reach a throne by out-talking each other on topics that are relayed by the host (or hostess). Winners are the wordiest talkers.

Host (1949): Mason Gross.

Hostess (1950): Gypsy Rose Lee.

Panelists: Lois Wilson, Leon Janney, Eloise McElhone, Vivian della Chiesa, David Broekman.

Orchestra: David Broekman.

THINK FAST—30 minutes—ABC—March 26, 1949 - October 8, 1950.

THE THIN MAN

Mystery. Background: Greenwich Village in New York City, the residence of the Charleses: Nick, a former private detective turned mystery editor for a publishing house; and his beautiful, trouble-prone wife, Nora. Stories depict their investigations when Nora accidentally stumbles upon and involves Nick in crimes. Based on the characters created by Dashiell Hammett.

The Thin Man. Peter Lawford and Phyllis Kirk (holding Asta).

CAST

Nick Charles	Peter Lawford
Nora Charles	Phyllis Kirk
Beatrice Dean, alias Blondie Collins, a beautiful con-artist and friend of Nick's who arouses Nora's jealous streak	Nita Talbot
Lt. Jack Evans, N.Y.P.D.	Jack Albertson
Mrs. Durkem, the Charles's neighbor	Blanche Sweet

The Charles dog: Asta.

Music: Pete Rugolo.

THE THIN MAN—30 minutes—NBC —September 20, 1957 - June 26, 1959. 72 episodes. Syndicated.

THE THIRD MAN

Mystery. Background: London, England. The exploits of Harry Lime, business tycoon, troubleshooter, and private detective, as he aides people in distress.

CAST

Harry Lime	Michael Rennie
Bradford Webster, his assistant	Jonathan Harris

THE THIRD MAN—30 minutes—Syndicated 1960. 77 episodes.

THIS COULD BE YOU

Game. Three married couples compete. Couples are first interviewed, then in return for prizes, each reenacts a personal situation in their lives that was brought about as the result of a popular song.

Host: Bill Gwinn.

THIS COULD BE YOU—30 minutes —ABC 1951.

THIS IS ALICE

Comedy. The misadventures of nine-year-old Alice Holliday.

CAST

Alice Holliday	Patty Ann Gerrity
Mr. Holliday, her father	Tommy Farrell
Mrs. Holliday, her mother	Phyllis Coates
Also	Stephen Woolton

THIS IS ALICE—30 minutes—Syndicated 1958. 39 episodes.

THIS IS CHARLES LAUGHTON

Readings. Selections from the Bible and classical and modern stories are read.

Host: Charles Laughton, "The man of many moods."

THIS IS CHARLES LAUGHTON—60 minutes—Syndicated 1952.

THIS IS GALEN DRAKE

Variety. Music, songs, and celebrity interviews.

Host: Galen Drake.

Regulars: Rita Ellis, Stuart Foster.

THIS IS GALEN DRAKE—30 min-

utes—ABC—January 12, 1957 - May 11, 1957.

THIS IS MUSIC

Musical Variety.

Hostess: Alexandra Gray.

Host: Colin Male.

Regulars: Jacqueline James, Bruce Foote, Jackie Van, Bill Snarz.

Orchestra: Robert Trendler.

THIS IS MUSIC—30 minutes—ABC— June 6, 1958 - May 21, 1959.

THIS IS SHOW BUSINESS

Variety. Guest celebrities entertain then air their problems to a panel, who in turn offer advice.

Host: Clifton Fadiman.

Panelists: Sam Levenson, George S. Kaufman, Abe Burrows.

Regulars: Toni Arden, Jack E. Leonard, Lou Willis, Jr., Russell Arms, Dorothy Collins.

Orchestra: Ray Bloch, Hank Sylvern.

Producer: Irving Mansfield.

Director: Alexander Leftwich, Paul Byron.

Sponsor: American Tobacco Company.

THIS IS SHOW BUSINESS—30 minutes—CBS—July 15, 1949 - September 11, 1956. Also known as "This Is Broadway."

THIS IS TOM JONES

Musical Variety.

Host: Tom Jones.

Regulars: Big Jim Sullivan, The Norman Maen Dancers, The Mike Sammes Singers.

Orchestra: Jack Parnell; Johnnie Spence.

THIS IS TOM JONES—60 minutes—ABC—February 7, 1969 - January 1971. 27 tapes. Syndicated.

THIS IS YOUR LIFE

Variety-Interview. A semidocumentary-style presentation wherein the lives of show-business personalities, who appear as guests, are relived through the testimonies of friends and family.

Appearing: Marilyn Monroe, Jayne Mansfield, Stan Laurel, Jack Benny, Hugh O'Brian, Andy Griffith, Barbara Eden, Carol Channing, Ruth Gordon, Irene Ryan, Jackie Cooper, Pearl Bailey, Shirley Jones, Florence Henderson, Pat Boone, Nanette Fabray, Bette Davis, Johnny Cash, Ann-Margret, Bob Hope, Cliff Robertson, Totie Fields.

Versions:

This Is Your Life—30 minutes—NBC —October 2, 1952 - September 10, 1961.

Host: Ralph Edwards.

Announcer: Bob Warren.

Orchestra: Von Dexter.

This Is Your Life—30 minutes—Syndicated 1971.

Host: Ralph Edwards.

Announcer: Bob Warren.

Orchestra: Nelson Riddle.

THIS IS YOUR MUSIC

Musical Variety.

CAST
Byron Palmer, Joan Weldon, David Lechine, Jana Ecklund, Rita Walsh, Betty Wand, Suzie Baree, Mary Margaret Gelden, The Pied Pipers.

Choreography: David Lechine.

Orchestra: Nelson Riddle.

THIS IS YOUR MUSIC—30 minutes —Syndicated 1955.

THIS MAN DAWSON

Crime Drama. Background: A large unidentified urban community. The methods incorporated in the battle against crime as seen through the investigations of Colonel Frank Dawson, the police chief.

Starring: Keith Andes as Colonel Frank Dawson.

THIS MAN DAWSON—30 minutes—Syndicated 1959. 39 episodes.

THOSE ENDURING YOUNG CHARMS

Comedy. The trials and tribulations of the Charms, an American family.

CAST
The father	Maurice Copeland
His wife	Betty Arnold
Their daughter	Pat Matthews
Their son	Gerald Garvey
The uncle	Clarence Hartzell
The delivery boy	Norm Gottschalk

Also: Everett Clark, Helen Barrett.

THOSE ENDURING YOUNG

CHARMS–30 minutes–NBC–1951 - 1952.

THOSE TWO

Variety. Music, songs, dances, and vaudeville routines.

Host: Pinky Lee.

Co-hostesses: Martha Stuart, Vivian Blaine.

Orchestra: Harry Lubin.

Producer: Olive Barbour, Walter Craig.

Director: William Slate.

Sponsor: Procter and Gamble.

THOSE TWO–15 minutes–NBC– November 20, 1951 - April 24, 1953.

THOSE WHITING GIRLS

Comedy. Background: Hollywood, California. The romantic misadven-

Those Whiting Girls. Margaret (top) and Barbara Whiting.

tures of the Whiting sisters: Barbara, an actress; and Margaret, a songstress.

CAST

Barbara Whiting	Herself
Margaret Whiting	Herself
Mrs. Whiting, their mother	Mabel Albertson
Artie, Margaret's accompanist	Jerry Paris
Daisy Dunbar, Barbara's friend	Beverly Long

Orchestra: Eliot Daniel.

THOSE WHITING GIRLS–30 minutes–CBS–July 4, 1955 - September 26, 1955.

THREE FOR THE MONEY

Game. Two three-member teams, each composed of one celebrity captain and two noncelebrity contestants, compete for five days, Monday through Friday. Three categories, each containing three questions, are revealed. One team, as determined by the flip of a coin, receives a chance at play. The captain either selects himself or his teammates. to compete against the opposing team. If he chooses to match one player from his team against one opponent, the question is worth $100; should he choose to play one against two, the question value is $200; if one player is pitted against three, the question is worth $300 for the team at play. A question, chosen from one of the categories, is then read by the host and clues to its answer appear on an electronic board. The player who is first to sound a buzzer signal stops the clues from progressing and receives a chance to answer. If the question is correctly answered by the member of the team at play, the money is scored accordingly; however, should the opposing team respond first, or supply a correct answer for an incorrect response on the part of the team at play, they score $100. The remaining categories are played in the same manner. The game itself continues in this same manner with a final two round contest played on the Friday program. The team whose accumulative five day score is the highest is the winner (the money is divided between the two contestants).

Host: Dick Enberg.

Announcer: Jack Clark.

Model: Jane Nelson.

Executive Producer: Stefan Hatos, Monty Hall.

Producer: Stu Billett.

Director: Hank Behar.

THREE FOR THE MONEY—25 minutes—NBC—September 29, 1975 - November 28, 1975.

THREE FOR THE ROAD

Drama. The assignments of photographer Pete Karras, a widower who roams the country in his motor home, the *Zebec,* with his two sons John and Endy.

CAST

Pete Karras	Alex Rocco
John Karras	Vincent Van Patten
Endy Karras	Leif Garrett

Music: James Di Pasquale, David Shire.

THREE FOR THE ROAD—60 minutes—CBS—September 14, 1975 - November 30, 1975.

THREE GIRLS

A live situation comedy series that features the misadventures of three beautiful career girls (played by Janis Carter, Barbara Gayelord, and Jeannie Johnson). Broadcast on ABC in 1955.

3 GIRLS 3

Variety. A musical comedy series that spotlights the talents of three unknown "but terribly talented girls doing a variety series about three unknown but terribly talented girls."

Starring: Mimi Kennedy, Ellen Foley, Debbie Allen.

Regulars: Oliver Clark, Richard Byrd.

Orchestra: Marvin Laird.

Executive Producer: Gary Smith, Dwight Hemion.

Producer: Kenny Solms, Gail Parent.

Director: Tony Mordente, Tim Kiley.

Choreography: Alan Johnson.

3 GIRLS 3—60 minutes—June 15, 1977 - June 29, 1977. One episode was previously seen on March 30, 1977. 3 tapes.

THE THREE MUSKETEERS

Adventure. Background: Paris during the 1620s. The exploits of the Three Musketeers, D'Artagnan, Porthos, and Aromas, as they struggle to protect the thrown of France from the machinations of the evil Prime Minister Richelieu. Based on the story by Alexandre Dumas.

CAST

D'Artagnan	Jeffrey Stone
Porthos	Peter Trent

Aromas	Paul Campbell
Jacqueline	Marina Berti
The Count of Brisemont	Sebastian Cabot
Sasquinet	Alan Furlan
Captain De Treville	George Conneaur

THE THREE MUSKETEERS—30 minutes—Syndicated 1956. 26 episodes.

THREE ON A MATCH

Game. Three competing contestants. Three topic categories are revealed. Players each press a button and lock in the number of questions they wish to answer (one to four). Their choices are revealed, and each bet scores ten dollars, which becomes the money that is available for that round. If each player has chosen a different amount of questions, the highest bidder chooses one of the categories. He is then asked true-and-false type of questions. If he correctly answers his bet amount of questions, he wins the money and a new round begins. If he fails to answer correctly, the second highest player chooses one of the remaining categories. Should he fail, the lowest bidder receives a chance to win the money. Exception: Should all players bid the same amount, they cancel each other out and rebid; if two bid the same amount, they cancel each other out and the remaining player automatically receives a chance to win the money.

When a player scores at least one hundred and fifty dollars, he is permitted to play "Three On a Match." A large game board is displayed. The board is composed of twelve squares that are divided into three horizontial rows of four vertical squares each. Each horizontal row is marked by a color: red, green, yellow, or blue; the vertical rows represent the cash values of each square: twenty, thirty, or forty dollars. The player purchases a square by naming a color and an amount. A merchandise prize or a cash value is revealed. If the player is able to match the first square with two identical squares, he receives the prize that is represented, becomes the champion, and faces two new challengers. If he is unsuccessful, the game continues and follows the previous format until one player matches three squares (the prizes change position with each player's gamble).

Host: Bill Cullen.

Announcers: Roger Tuttle; Don Pardo.

Music: Bob Cobert.

THREE ON A MATCH—30 minutes—NBC—August 2, 1971 - June 28, 1974.

THREE PASSPORTS TO ADVENTURE

Travel. Films depicting the global travels of the Hinker Family.

Hosts-Narrators: Hal Halla, and David Hinker.

THREE PASSPORTS TO ADVENTURE—30 minutes—Syndicated 1970. 39 tapes.

THREE STEPS TO HEAVEN

Serial. Background: New York City. The dramatic story of Poco Thurman, a young model frought with romantic heartaches.

CAST

Pqco Thurman	Phyllis Hill
	Kathleen McGuire

Bill Morgan	Mark Roberts
	Walter Brooks
Mike	Joe Brown, Jr.
Jennifer	Lori March
Alice	Laurie Vendig
Angela	Ginger McManus
Mrs. Doane	Doris Rich
Barry Thurmond	Roger Sullivan
Laura	Inge Adams
Uncle Frank	Frank Twedell
Pigeon Malloy	Eata Linden
Walter Jones	Earl George
Charlotte Doane	Mona Burns
Jason Cleve	Lauren Gilbert
Nan	Beth Douglas
Vince Bannister	John Marley
Alice	Laurie Ann Vendig
Alan Anderson	Dort Clark

Also: Diana Douglas, Mercer McCloud, Irving Taylor.

Producer: Caroline Burke.

Creator: Irving Vendig.

Sponsor: Miles Laboratories.

THREE STEPS TO HEAVEN—15 minutes—NBC—July 31, 1953 - December 31, 1954.

THE THREE STOOGES

Comedy. The misadventures of Moe Howard, Larry Fine, and Curly Howard, three misfits plagued by life's abounding obstacles.

CAST

Moe Howard	Himself
Larry Fine	Himself
Curly Howard	Himself
Shemp Howard (replaced Curly)	Himself
Joe De Rita (replaced Shemp)	Himself

Also: Joe Besser, who replaced Joe DeRita during the 1950s.

Producer-Director: Jules White.

The Three Stooges. Bottom to top: Larry Fine, Moe Howard, Curly Howard. © *Screen Gems.*

THE THREE STOOGES—20 minutes (approximately)—Syndicated 1959. 190 episodes.

THREE'S COMPANY

Musical Variety.

Host: Cy Walters.

Regulars: Stan Freeman, Judy Lynn.

THREE'S COMPANY—30 minutes— CBS 1950.

THREE'S COMPANY

Comedy. Background: Los Angeles, California. Finding that the high cost of apartment rent is preventing them from living comfortably, working girls Janet Wood and Chrissy Snow resolve their problem by taking in a male roommate—Jack Tripper, a culinary student whom they find sleeping in

Three's Company. Left to right: Joyce DeWitt, Suzanne Somers, John Ritter. *Courtesy of the Call-Chronicle Newspapers, Allentown, Pa.*

their bathtub after a wild party. The series focuses on the misadventures that occur in such a situation as Janet, Chrissy, and Jack struggle to live their own lives while attempting to maintain a strictly platonic relationship.

CAST

Janet Wood, runs a flower shop	Joyce DeWitt
Chrissy Snow, a typist	Suzanne Somers
Jack Tripper	John Ritter
Stanley Roper, the landlord	Norman Fell
Helen Roper, his wife	Audra Lindley

Music: Joe Raposo.

Producer: Don Nicholl, Bernie West, Michael Ross.

Director: Bill Hobin.

THREE'S COMPANY—30 minutes— ABC—March 15, 1977 - April 21, 1977. Returned: ABC—Premiered: August 11, 1977.

British Version, upon which "Three's Company" is based:

Man About The House. Background: London, England. The story of two working girls, Jo and Chrissy, and their ensuing misadventures when they decide to share a flat with Robin Tripp, a male catering student, in an attempt to resolve the housing problem.

CAST

Jo	Sally Thomsett
Chrissy	Paula Wilcox
Robin Tripp	Richard O'Sullivan
George Roper, the landlord	Brian Murphy
Mrs. Roper, his wife	Yotta Joyce

Producer-Director: Peter Jones.

THRILL HUNTERS

Adventure. Films depicting the perilous occupations of people (e.g., mountain climbers, racers, test pilots).

Host-Narrator: Bill Burrud.

THRILL HUNTERS—30 minutes— Syndicated 1966.

THRILL SEEKERS

Adventure. Films examining the perilous occupations of people.

Host-Narrator: Chuck Connors.

Music: David Davis.

THRILL SEEKERS—30 minutes— Syndicated 1973.

THRILLER

Anthology. Mystery and suspense presentations. Twisted tales of people who are suddenly trapped in unexpected situations that are fostered through emotion, greed, or the threat of crime.

Host-Occasional Performer: Boris Karloff.

Music: Pete Rugolo; Jerry Goldsmith.

Musical Supervision: Stanley Wilson.

Executive Producer: Hubbell Robinson.

Producer: Fletcher Markle, William Frye.

Director: Ida Lupino, Herschel Daugherty, John Brahm, Arthur Hiller.

Included:

Mr. George. The story of a young heiress who is protected from harm by a friendly spirit (Mr. George).

CAST
Priscilla: Gina Gillespie; Edna: Virginia Gregg; Laura: Joan Tompkins; Jarrad: Howard Freeman.

Parasite Mansion. Knocked unconscious during a minor automobile accident, a woman is taken prisoner by the owners of a decrepit mansion. Attempting to escape, she learns of a spirit that holds the family in a grip of fear. The story revolves around her attempts to expose it.

CAST
Marcia: Pippa Scott; Harrod: James Griffith; Lollie: Beverly Washburn; Granny (the spirit): Jeannette Nolan.

The Finger Of Fate. A detective's efforts to apprehend a psychopathic child killer.

CAST
Nehemiah Persoff, Robert Middleton, Kevin Hagen.

The Fatal Impulse. The frantic police search for a woman who, unbeknown to her, carries a live and ticking bomb in her pocketbook.

CAST
Rome: Robert Lansing; Jane: Whitney Blake; Mary: Mary Tyler Moore; Secretary: Cynthia Pepper; Elser: Elisha Cook.

THRILLER—60 minutes—NBC—September 10, 1960 - July 9, 1962. 67 episodes. Syndicated.

THRILLER

Anthology. Mystery and suspense presentations. Out-of-the-ordinary stories about chilling and eerie events that could happen to anyone. An ATV/I.T.C. production (British).

Producer: John Sichel.

Director: Peter Jeffries, John Sichel, Bill Hayes, John Cooper, Robert Tronson, Shaun O'Riordan, Alan Gibson.

Included:

Possession. Turning to the occult, a terrified young woman attempts to combat a sinister spirit that has possessed her husband.

CAST
John Carson, Joanna Dunham, Hilary Hardiman.

An Echo Of Theresa. Honeymooning in London, an American couple is suddenly plunged into a nightmare world when Brad, the husband, witnesses an event that triggers memories hidden deeply in the recesses of his mind. Imagining himself as someone else, and married to a woman

Thriller. Polly Bergen and Paul Burke in "An Echo of Theresa." *Courtesy of Independent Television Corp.; an ATV Company.*

named Theresa, he believes his wife, Suzy, is an enemy and plots to kill her. The story depicts the conflict that ensues when the past and present merge into one.

CAST

Brad Hunter: Paul Burke; Suzy Hunter: Polly Bergen; Earp: Dinsdale Landen; Trasker: William Job.

File It Under Fear. An amateur detective attempts to solve the baffling murders of several young women.

CAST

Liz: Maureen Lipman; George: Richard O'Callaghan; Superintendent: James Grout.

Lady Killer. A husband's careful planning and attempts to murder his wife.

CAST

Barbara Feldon, Robert Powell, Linda Thorson, T. P. McKenna, Mary Wimbush, Jessie Evans.

THRILLER–66/68 minutes (actual running time, less commercials)– Syndicated 1973. Telecast in the United States via "ABC Wide World of Entertainment."

THROUGH THE CRYSTAL BALL

A variety series, hosted by Anita Alvarez, and first broadcast by CBS in 1949.

THROUGH WENDY'S WINDOW

Interview.

Hostess: Wendy Barrie.

THROUGH WENDY'S WINDOW—15 minutes—NBC—December 22, 1949 - February 16, 1950.

THUNDER

Adventure. The story of a semiwild black stallion named Thunder and the adventures of the young girl, Cindy Prescott, who befriends him.

CAST
Bill Prescott, Cindy's father	Clint Ritchie
Ann Prescott, Cindy's mother	Melissa Converse
Cindy Prescott	Melora Hardin
Willie Williams, Cindy's friend	Justin Randi

Also: Cupcake the mule.

Music: Ray Ellis.

Producer-Creator: Irving Cummings, Charles Marion.

Director: Sigmund Neufeld, Jr., William Beaudine, Jr.

THUNDER—30 minutes—NBC—Premiered: September 10, 1977.

THUNDERBIRDS

Marionette Adventure. Background: A remote island in the Pacific, the headquarters of International Rescue (I.R.), a global organization of highly complex machinery, the Thunderbirds, and skillfully trained men who

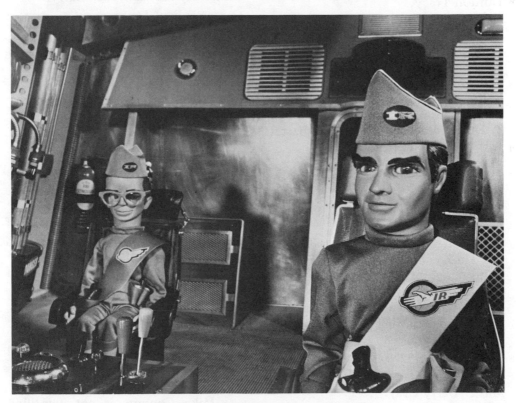

Thunderbirds. A Supermarionation series. The figures are electronic marionettes, members of International Rescue.

are dedicated to rescuing people trapped in unusual predicaments. Stories depict I.R.'s rescue operations. Filmed in Supermarionation. An I.T.C. presentation.

Characters' Voices

Jeff Tracy, the head of I.R.	Peter Dyneley
Scott Tracy, his son, the pilot of *Thunderbird I*	Shane Rimmer
Virgil Tracy, his son, the pilot of *Thunderbird II*	David Holliday
Alan Tracy, his son, the pilot of *Thunderbird III*	Matt Zimmerman
Gordon Tracy, his son, the pilot of Aquanaut *Thunderbird IV*	David Graham
John Tracy, his son, the pilot of Space Monitor *Thunderbird V*	Ray Barrett
Lady Penelope Creighton-Ward, the London agent	Sylvia Anderson
Professor Brains, an I.R. scientist	David Graham
Kyrano, Jeff's servant	David Graham
Tin Tin Kyrano, his daughter	Christine Finn
The Hood, a diabolical fiend bent on acquiring I.R.'s secrets	Ray Barrett
Parker, Lady Penelope's chauffeur	David Graham

Music: Barry Gray.

THUNDERBIRDS—60 and 30 minute versions—Syndicated 1968. Episodes are available complete in one hour, or in two thirty minute cliff-hanger installments.

TIC TAC DOUGH

Game. Two competing contestants, Player X and Player O; basis: the game of Tic Tac Toe. A general-knowledge type of question is read. The player who first identifies himself through a buzzer signal receives a chance to answer. If correct, he is permitted to choose one square on a Tic Tac Toe board that is displayed on stage. The game continues until one player wins by acquiring three squares in a row, up and down, or diagonally. Cash prizes are awarded.

Hosts: Jay Jackson; Jack Barry.

Organist: Paul Taubman.

Producer: Stan Greene, Hudson Faussett, Robert Noah, Howard Flesher.

TIC TAC DOUGH—30 minutes—NBC —July 30, 1956 - October 30, 1959.

TIGHTROPE

Crime Drama. The investigations of Nick Stone, undercover police agent, as he attempts to infiltrate the underworld and expose the ranks of organized crime.

Starring: Mike Connors as Nick Stone.

Music: George Duning.

Producer: Clarence Greene, Russell Rouse.

Note: The character portrayed by Mike Connors is not identified by a name in some sources; he is referred to as "The Unnamed

Tightrope. Mike Connors as Nick Stone, police agent, demonstrating his special gun draw. © *Screen Gems.*

Agent" or "The Undercover Agent."

TIGHTROPE—60 minutes—CBS—September 8, 1959 - September 13, 1960. 37 episodes. Syndicated.

TIM CONWAY

Listed: The television programs of comedian Tim Conway.

RANGO—Comedy—30 minutes—ABC—1967. See title.

THE TIM CONWAY SHOW—Comedy—30 minutes—CBS—January 30, 1970 - June 19, 1970.

Background: Crawford Airport in Los Angeles, California, the business and operations base of Timothy "Spud" Barrett, pilot, and Herbert Kenworth, executive officer, the owners of the *Lucky Linda,* a decrepit plane that comprises Triple A Airlines. Unable to pay creditors, and threatened by eviction, they struggle to acquire passengers, relieve monetary burdens and maintain an airline.

CAST

Timothy "Spud" Barrett	Tim Conway
Herbert Kenworth	Joe Flynn
Mrs. Crawford, the owner of the airport	Anne Seymour
Ronnie Crawford, her son	Johnnie Collins III
Becky, the Crawford Airlines reservationist, Spud's girlfriend	Emily Banks
Sherman, the radio-control-tower operator	Dennis Robertson

Harry, the owner of
the airport coffee
shop   Fabian Dean

THE TIM CONWAY COMEDY HOUR—Variety—60 minutes—CBS—September 20, 1970 - December 28, 1970.

Host: Tim Conway.

Regulars: Sally Struthers, McLean Stevenson, Art Metrano, Bonnie Boland, Belland and Somerville, The Tom Hanson Dancers.

Orchestra: Nelson Riddle.

TIME FOR BEANIE

See title: "The Beanie and Cecil Show."

TIME TO REMEMBER

Documentary. Through re-creations and available material (film, newspaper files, stills, and drawings) events that sparked the world from 1895-1945 are recalled.

Narrators: Guest actors.

TIME TO REMEMBER—30 minutes —Syndicated 1963. 39 episodes.

A TIME FOR US

Serial. The dramatic story of two sisters, Linda and Jane Driscoll. Breaking her engagement to Steve Reynolds, Linda Leaves home and travels to New York City, where she hopes to further her acting career. Jane, who is secretly in love with Steve, remains behind, hoping to one day marry her sister's fiancé.

CAST

Linda Driscoll	Joanna Miles
Jane Driscoll	Beverly Hayes
Steve Reynolds	Gordon Gray
Martha	Lenka Peterson
Al	Roy Poole
Jason	Walter Coy
Chris	Richard Thomas
Kate Austen	Kathleen Maguire
Elizabeth	Nancy Franklin
Roxanne Reynolds	Maggie Hayes
Ted	John McMartin
Linda Skerba	Jane Elliot
Paul	Conrad Fowkes
Nick	Jon Stone
Louise	Josephine Nichols
Tony Grey	Morgan Sterne
Flora	Jacqueline Brooks
Dave	Terrence Logan
Craig Reynolds	Frank Schofield
Sue Michaels	Jill O'Hara
Jane Skerba	Margaret Ladd
Leslie Farrell	Rita Lloyd
Fran	Elaine Hymas
Gillespie	Robert Hogan
Doug	Ira Berger
Nancy	Lynn Rogers

A TIME FOR US—30 minutes— ABC—June 28, 1965 - December 16, 1966. Original title: "Flame In the Wind.

A TIME TO LIVE

Serial. Background: A small Midwestern town. The dramatic story of Julie Byron, newspaper proofreader and occasional reporter.

CAST

Julie Byron	Patricia Sully
Don Riker, a reporter	Larry Kerr
Madge Byron	Viola Berwick
Chic	Len Wayland
Carl Sherman	Jack Lester
Justin	John Devoe
Lenore	Barbara Foley

Lucy   Nell Clark
Miles Dow   Dort Clark
Daphne   Toni Gilman
Ann   Rosemary Kelly
Rudy   Zachary Charles
Patricia   Beverly Younger
Dr. Clay   Dana Elcar

Executive Producer-Creator: Adrian Samish.

Producer-Director: Alan Beaumont.

A TIME TO LIVE—15 minutes—NBC—July 5, 1954 - December 31, 1954.

THE TIME TUNNEL

Science Fiction Adventure. Background: Tic Toc Base, a concealed underground lab, the secret location of the Time Tunnel, a seven and one half billion dollar U.S. government project concerned with time displacement.

Discovering that government officials, who are considering scrapping the project, are dissatisfied with their inability to send a man through time, scientist Tony Newman takes matters into his own hands and enters the Time Tunnel's psychedelic portal chamber. Within seconds he disappears and is sent into time—"yesterday, today, tomorrow, or a million years from now."

Because Tony has previously taken a radioactive bath, engineers are able to pinpoint his whereabouts and receive his voice and image through the Tunnel's recorders. However, their

The Time Tunnel. Left to right: James Darren, Robert Colbert, and guest Victor Jory. Episode: "Pirates of Deadman's Island."

ability to control his destiny or return him to the present (1968) has not been mastered.

When discovering that Tony has been sent back in time to April 14, 1912, as an unregistered passenger on the disaster bound *Titanic,* scientist Doug Phillips enters the Time Tunnel in an attempt to save Tony who, though of the present, is effected by events of the past—or future.

Meeting with Tony, the two are frozen by Tunnel engineers, removed from danger, and sent into time.

Stories depict the experiences of scientists Tony Newman and Doug Phillips, travelers lost in time.

CAST

Tony Newman	James Darren
Doug Phillips	Robert Colbert
General Heywood Kirk, the Time Tunnel's supervisor	Whit Bissell
Dr. Ann McGregor, a Time Tunnel engineer	Lee Meriwether
Dr. Raymond Swain, a scientist	John Zaremba
Sergeant Jiggs, the security guard	Wesley Lau
Jerry, a Time Tunnel engineer	Sam Groom

Music: Lionel Newman.

Additional Music: Joseph Mullendore, Lyn Murray, Robert Dransin, Johnny Williams, George Duning.

Producer-Creator: Irwin Allen.

Director: Herschel Daugherty, Harry Harris, William Hale, Sobey Martin, Murray Golden, Nathan Juran, Paul Stanley.

Program Open:

Announcer: "Two American scientists are lost in the swirling maze of past and future ages during the first experiments on America's greatest and most secret project—The Time Tunnel. Tony Newman and Doug Phillips now tumble helplessly toward a new fantastic adventure somewhere along the infinite corridors of time."

THE TIME TUNNEL—60 minutes— ABC—September 9, 1966 - September 1, 1967. 30 episodes. Syndicated.

TIMES SQUARE PLAYHOUSE

Anthology. Rebroadcasts of dramas that were originally aired via other filmed anthology programs.

Host-Narrator: Herbert Marshall.

Included:

His Name Is Jason. The story of a woman's unselfish devotion to her alcoholic husband.

CAST
John Warburton, Gertrude Michael.

The Hitchhiker Was A Lady. After picking up a woman hitchhiker, a truck driver is accused of attempting to murder her. The story concerns his efforts to prove his innocence.

CAST
Jane Nigh, John Kellogg.

Call Me Irving. By changing his name an actor attempts to acquire a part in a play.

CAST
Johnny Johnston, Jean Byron.

The Biggest Little Theatre. The story

of a counterfeiter who uses a theater as a front for his illegal undertaking.

CAST

Paul Bryar.

TIMES SQUARE PLAYHOUSE–30 minutes–Syndicated 1963. 39 episodes.

TIMMIE AND LASSIE

See title: "Lassie."

TIN PAN ALLEY TV

Musical Variety.
Host: Johnny Desmond.
Orchestra: Gloria Van.

TIN PAN ALLEY TV–30 minutes–ABC 1950.

TIN TIN

Animated Cartoon. The adventures of Tin Tin, a twelve-year-old boy, and his dog, Snowy, as they become involved with and attempt to solve crimes. Based on the European comic strip, *The Adventures of Tin Tin.* Voices, music, and announcer credits are not given screen or verbal credit.

Additional characters: The Thompson Brothers, detectives; Professor Calculis; and Captain Haddock, the skipper of the ship, *Karaboudjan.*

TIN TIN–30 minutes–Syndicated 1961. Also known as: "Herge's Adventures of Tin Tin" and "The Adventures of Tin Tin."

TOAST OF THE TOWN

See title: "The Ed Sullivan Show."

TODAY IS OURS

Serial. Background: The town of Bolton. The dramatic story of Laura Manning, assistant principal at Bolton Central High School. Episodes depict her conflicts and tensions: divorced, the mother of a young son, and romantically involved with a married man, architect Glenn Turner.

CAST

Laura Manning	Patricia Benoit
Nick Manning	Peter Lazer
Glenn Turner	Patrick O'Neal
Laura Turner	Joyce Lear

Also: Ernest Graves, Tom Carlin, Nancy Sheridan, Chase Crosley, Joanna Roos, Martin Blaine, Eugene Roos, John McGovern, Nelson Olmstead, Barry Thompson, Eugenia Raivis.

TODAY IS OURS–30 minutes–NBC –August 30, 1958 - January 27, 1959.

THE TODAY SHOW

Information. News, weather, sports, politics, fashion, and entertainment.

Host: Dave Garroway (1952-1961); John Chancellor (1961-1962); Hugh Downs (1962-1971); Frank McGee (1971-1974); Jim Hartz (1974-1976); Lloyd Dobbins (7-19-76 – 8-27-76); Tom Brokaw (8-30-76).
Hostess: Barbara Walters; Jane Pauley
Substitute Host: Jim Backus.
Regulars: Charles Van Doren, Betsy Palmer, Robin Chandler, Judith

Crist, Frank Blair, Louise O'Brien, Bob Elliott, Ray Goulding, Margaret O'Sullivan, Estelle Parsons, Helen O'Connell, Barbara Walters, Pat Fontaine, Martin Agronsky, Joe Garagiola, Paul Cunningham, Florence Henderson, Anita Colby, Robbin Bain, Lee Ann Meriwether, Gene Shalit, Beryl Pfizer, James Fleming, Jack Lescoulie, Lew Wood, The Muppets, J. Fred Muggs (a chimpanzee), Roberta MacDonald.

Music Theme: "This Is Today" by Ray Ellis.

THE TODAY SHOW—2 hours (7:00 a.m.-9:00 a.m., E.S.T.)—NBC—Premiered: January 14, 1952.

TODAY WITH MRS. ROOSEVELT

Interview. Guests are first interviewed then asked to answer questions that were submitted by home viewers.

Hostess: Elinor Roosevelt.

TODAY WITH MRS. ROOSEVELT—30 minutes—NBC—1950 - 1955. Also known as: "Mrs. Roosevelt Meets the Public."

TOMA

Crime Drama. Background: Newark, New Jersey. The investigations of Dave Toma, undercover police agent, and master of disguise, as he attempts to infiltrate and expose the "Organization," which is responsible for numerous illegal rackets. Based on the real-life exploits of David Toma, Newark detective.

CAST

Dave Toma	Tony Musante
Patty Toma, his wife	Susan Strasberg
Inspector Spooner	Simon Oakland
Donna Toma, their daughter	Michele Livingston
Jimmy Toma, their son	Sean Mannering
Also, various parts	David Toma

Music: Mike Post, Pete Carpenter.

TOMA—60 minutes—ABC—October 4, 1973 - September 6, 1974.

TOMAHAWK

Adventure. Background: America's Northwest during the seventeenth century. The exploits of Pierre Radisson and his partner, Medard, as they assist pioneers in their attempts to settle in new and unexplored territory.

CAST

Pierre Radisson	Jacques Godin
Medard	Rene Caron

TOMAHAWK—30 minutes—Syndicated 1957. 26 episodes.

TOM AND JERRY

Animated Cartoon. The misadventures of two non-talking animals: Tom the cat, and Jerry the mouse.

Vocal Effects: June Foray, Mel Blanc.

Music: Scott Bradley, Eugene Poddany.

Producer: Fred Quimby.

Director: William Hanna, Joseph Barbera, Chuck Jones.

TOM AND JERRY—30 minutes—CBS—September 1965 - September 17, 1972.

Tom and Jerry. Tom the cat and Jerry the mouse.

THE TOM AND JERRY/ GRAPE APE SHOW

Cartoon. The overall title for two animated series: "Tom and Jerry" and "The Grape Ape."

Tom and Jerry. The misadventures of the mischievous cat and mouse team of Tom and Jerry. The main characters are nonspeaking.

The Grape Ape. The misadventures of the Grape Ape, a forty-foot purple gorilla, and his fast-talking friend, Beagle the dog.

Characters' Voices

Beagle	Marty Ingels
The Grape Ape	Daws Butler

Additional Voices: Henry Corden, Joan Gerber, Bob Holt, Bob Hastings, Virginia Gregg, Cathy Gori, Don Messick, Alan Oppenheimer, Allan Melvin, Hal Smith, Joe E. Ross, John Stevenson, Jean VanderPyl, Janet Waldo, Lurene Tuttle, Paul Winchell, Frank Welker, Lennie Weinrib.

Music: Hoyt Curtin, Paul DeKorte.

THE TOM AND JERRY/GRAPE APE SHOW—55 minutes—ABC—Premiered: September 6, 1975.

TOMBSTONE TERRITORY

Western. Background: Tombstone, Arizona, 1880s. The exploits of Harris Clayton, editor of the *Tombstone*

Epitaph as he attempts to establish peace through the power of the press in "the town too tough to die."

CAST

Harris Clayton	Richard Eastham
Sheriff Clay Hollister	Pat Conway
Deputy Charlie Riggs	Gil Ranken

Producer: Andy White, Frank Pittman.

Program Open:

Clayton: "An actual account from the pages of my newspaper, the *Tombstone Epitaph*. This is the way it happened in the town too tough to die."

TOMBSTONE TERRITORY—30 minutes—ABC—October 16, 1957 - October 9, 1959. 91 episodes. Syndicated.

TOM CORBETT, SPACE CADET

Adventure. Era: Earth, A.D. 2350. The exploits of Tom Corbett, a Space Cadet at Space Academy, U.S.A., an Earth-based West Point wherein young men and women train to become Solar Guards, the agents of a celestial police force established to protect Earth, Mars, Venus, and Jupiter, the planets that comprise a universal council of peace known as the Solar Alliance.

CAST

Tom Corbett	Frankie Thomas
Cadet Roger Manning	Jan Merlin
Astro, the Venusian	Al Markhim
Captain Larry Strong	Michael Harvey
Dr. Joan Dale, a Space Academy instructress	Patricia Ferris
	Margaret Garland
Cadet T. J. Fissell	Jack Grimes
Commander Arkwright, the head of Space Academy	Carter Blake
Betty, a teacher	Beryl Berney
Gloria, a teacher	Marian Brash

Announcer: Jackson Beck.

Producer: Al Ducovny, Leonard Carlton.

Director: George Gould.

Sponsor: Kellogg's; Kraft.

Corbett's rocket ship: the *Polaris.*

Program Open:

Announcer: "Space Academy, U.S.A., in the world beyond tomorrow. Here the Space Cadets train for duty on distant planets. In roaring rockets they blast through the millions of miles from Earth to far-flung stars and brave the dangers of cosmic frontiers, protecting the liberties of the planets, safeguarding the cause of universal peace in the age of the conquest of space."

TOM CORBETT, SPACE CADET—15 and 30 minute versions—NBC—1950 - 1956.

TOM, DICK AND MARY

See title: "Ninety Bristol Court," *Tom, Dick and Mary* segment.

THE TOM EWELL SHOW

Comedy. Background: Los Angeles, California. The trials and tribulations of the Potter family: Tom, a real-estate salesman; his wife, Frances; their daughters, Debbie, Carol, and Cissy; and Tom's mother-in-law, Irene Brady.

CAST

Tom Potter	Tom Ewell
Frances Potter	Marilyn Erskine
Debbie Potter	Sherry Alberoni
Carol Potter	Cindy Robbins
Cissy Potter	Eileen Chesis
Irene Brady	Mabel Albertson

Music: Jerry Fielding.

THE TOM EWELL SHOW—30 minutes—CBS—September 27, 1960 - September 1961. Syndicated. Also known as "The Trouble with Tom."

TOMFOOLERY

Animated Cartoon. Sketches, songs, and poetry based on children's literature.

Characters: The Youngie Bungi Bow (a creature whose head is bigger than his body), The Scroovy Snake, The Umbrageous Umbrella Maker, Fastidious Fish, and The Enthusiastic Elephant.

TOMFOOLERY—30 minutes—NBC—September 12, 1970 - September 4, 1971. 17 episodes.

THE TOMMY HUNTER SHOW

Musical Variety. Performances by Country and Western entertainers.

Host: Tommy Hunter.

Regulars: The Rhythm Pals, The Allen Sisters.

Orchestra: Bert Niosi.

THE TOMMY HUNTER SHOW—60 minutes—Syndicated 1966. 125 tapes. Produced in Canada.

TOMORROW

Discussion. Interviews with people rarely seen on television and for the most part nonshow business, who have a story to tell.

Host: Tom Snyder.

Announcers: Frank Barton: Bill Wendell.

Music: Recorded.

TOMORROW—60 minutes—NBC—Premiered: October 15, 1973. Broadcast from 1:00 a.m.-2:00 a.m., E.S.T.

TOM TERRIFIC

A cartoon series that details the adventures of a small boy named Tom Terrific. 130 four minute films, syndicated in the early 1960s.

TONIGHT ON BROADWAY

Variety. Condensed versions of Broadway plays are presented.

Host: Martin Gosch.

TONIGHT ON BROADWAY—30 minutes—CBS 1949.

THE TONIGHT SHOW

Talk-Variety. Television's first late-night entertainment series. The series first began as "Broadway Open House," then continued as "Seven At Eleven" and "The Left Over Revue" (see titles) before becoming "The Tonight Show."

Versions:

The Tonight Show—40 minutes—

Local New York (WNBT-TV, Channel 4)—July 27, 1953 - September 24, 1954. Broadcast from 11:20 p.m. - 12:00 a.m.

Host: Steve Allen.

Regulars: Steve Lawrence, Helen Dixon, Pat Kirby.

Announcer: Gene Rayburn.

Orchestra: Bobby Byrne.

The Tonight Show—105 minutes—NBC—September 27, 1954 - January 25, 1957.

Host: Steve Allen.

Regulars: Steve Lawrence, Edyie Gormé, Pat Marshall, Helen Dixon, Andy Williams.

Announcer: Gene Rayburn.

Orchestra: Skitch Henderson.

The Tonight Show—105 minutes—NBC—October 1, 1956 - January 22, 1957. Broadcast twice a week for a period of four months, preempting version two (above) on Monday and Tuesday evenings.

Host: Ernie Kovacs.

Vocalists: Maureen Arthur, Pete Hanley.

Announcer: Bill Wendell.

Orchestra: Leroy Holmes.

Tonight! America After Dark—News -Entertainment—NBC—105 minutes—January 28, 1957 - July 26, 1957.

Format: Live interviews coupled with on-the-spot news coverage.

Hosts: Jack Lescoulie; Al "Jazzbo" Collins.

Vocalist: Judy Johnson.

Newsmen: Hy Gardner, Bob Con-

sidine, Earl Wilson (New York); Irv Kupcinet (Chicago); Vernon Scott, Paul Coates, Lee Giroux (Los Angeles).

Music: The Lou Stein Trio (January -March); The Mort Lindsey Quartet (March-June); The Johnny Guarnieri Quartet.

The Tonight Show—105 minutes—NBC—July 29, 1957 - March 30, 1962.

Host: Jack Paar.

Regulars: Cliff Arquette (as Charlie Weaver); Pat Harrington, Jr. (as Guido Panzini), Peggy Cass, Alexander King, Mary Margaret McBride, Dodie Goodman, Betty Johnson, Elsa Maxwell, Tedi Thurman (the weather girl), The Bil and Cora Baird Puppets.

Announcers: Hugh Downs; Art James.

Orchestra: Jose Melis.

The Tonight Show (Interim)—105 minutes—NBC—April 2, 1962 - September 28, 1962.

Hosts: Guests, including Bob Cummings, Jan Murray, Jack Carter, Peter Lind Hayes, Art Linkletter, Joey Bishop, Merv Griffin, Steve Lawrence, Jerry Lewis, Arlene Francis, Jimmy Dean, Jack E. Leonard, Hal March, Groucho Marx, Soupy Sales, Mort Sahl.

Announcers: Hugh Downs; Ed Herlihy.

Orchestra: Skitch Henderson.

The Tonight Show—105 and 90 minute versions—NBC—Premiered: October 1, 1962.

Host: Johnny Carson.

Announcers: Jack Haskell; Durwood

Kirby; Ed McMahon.

Featured in sketches: Carol Wayne (as "The Tea Time Movie Girl").

Orchestra: Skitch Henderson; Milton DeLugg; Doc Severinsen.

Substitute Orchestra Leader: Tommy Newson.

THE TONY BENNETT SHOW

Musical Variety.

Host: Tony Bennett.

Regulars: The Spellbinders, The Frank Lewis Dancers.

Premiere Guests: June Valli, Ben Blue, and George Reeves (as a singer-guitarist).

THE TONY BENNETT SHOW—60 minutes—NBC—August 11, 1956 - September 8, 1956.

THE TONY MARTIN SHOW

Musical Variety.

Host: Tony Martin.

Vocalists: The Interludes.

Orchestra: Hal Bourne; David Rose.

THE TONY MARTIN SHOW—15 minutes—NBC—April 26, 1954 - February 26, 1956.

TONY ORLANDO AND DAWN

Variety. Various comedy sketches and musical numbers.

Hosts: Tony Orlando and Dawn (a singing duo comprising Joyce Vincent Wilson and Telma Hopkins).

Regulars: Steve Franken, Susan Tolsky, George Carlin, Bob Holt.

Featured: The Jerry Jackson Singers.

Announcer: Roger Carroll, Dick Tufeld.

Orchestra: Bob Rozario.

TONY ORLANDO AND DAWN—60 minutes—CBS—July 3, 1974 - July 24, 1974. Returned: CBS—December 4, 1974 - December 28, 1976. Also titled: "The Tony Orlando and Dawn Rainbow Hour."

THE TONY RANDALL SHOW

Comedy. Background: Philadelphia. The home and working life of widower Walter Franklin, a less-than-magisterial judge of the Court of Common Pleas.

CAST

Judge Walter O. Franklin	Tony Randall
Roberta "Bobby" Franklin, his daughter	Devon Scott
	Penny Peyser
Oliver Franklin, Jr., his son	Brad Savage
Janet Reubner, his secretary	Allyn Ann McLerie
Mrs. McClellan, his housekeeper	Rachel Roberts
Judy Trowbridge, his law clerk	Brooke Adams
Jack Terwilliger, the court stenographer	Barney Martin
Mr. Franklin, Walter's father	Hans Conried

Music: Patrick Williams.

Producer-Creator: Tom Patchett, Jay Tarses.

Director: Jay Sandrich, James Burrows, Hugh Wilson.

THE TONY RANDALL SHOW—30 minutes—ABC—September 23, 1976 - March 10, 1977. Returned: CBS—Premiered: September 1977.

TOOTSIE HIPPODROME

Variety. Entertainment geared to children: circus variety acts and telephone quizzes (a prize is awarded to the child who is able to answer a question correctly).

Host: John Reed King.

Producer: Vernon Becker, Eli Broidy, Whitey Carson, Milton Stanson.

Sponsor: Sweets Company.

TOOTSIE HIPPODROME—15 minutes—ABC—February 3, 1952 - August 19, 1953.

TOO YOUNG TO GO STEADY

Comedy. The innocent romantic misadventures of fifteen-year-old Pamela Blake, a tomboy who suddenly discovers the opposite sex and is endowed with an urge to date.

CAST

Pamela Blake	Brigid Bazlen
Tom Blake, her father, a lawyer	Don Ameche
Mary Blake, her mother	Joan Bennett
John Blake, her older brother	Martin Huston

TOO YOUNG TO GO STEADY—30 minutes—NBC—May 14, 1959 - June 25, 1959.

Top Cat. Top Cat and his gang. *Courtesy Hanna-Barbera Productions.*

TOP CAT

Animated Cartoon. A spin-off from the Phil Silvers character, Sgt. Bilco (see title: "You'll Never Get Rich"). Background: The alley way of the 13th police precinct in New York City, the residence of Top Cat, a master conartist, and his feline dupes: Choo Choo, Benny the Ball, Spook, The Brain, Fancy Fancy, Pierre, and Goldie. Stories depict their attempts to enjoy a carefree, easy life despite the constant threats of eviction and arrest by Officer Dibble, the cop upon whose beat Top Cat enacts his ingenious money-making ventures.

Characters' Voices

Top Cat (T.C.)	Arnold Stang
Choo Choo	Marvin Kaplan
Benny the Ball	Maurice Gosfield
Spook	Leo de Lyon
The Brain	Leo de Lyon
Officer Dibble	Allen Jenkins
Goldie	Jean VanderPyl
Fancy Fancy	John Stephenson
Pierre	John Stephenson

Additional Voices: Paul Frees.

Music: Hoyt Curtin.

TOP CAT—30 minutes—ABC—September 27, 1961 - March 30, 1962. 30 episodes. Syndicated.

TOP DOLLAR

Game. Three competing contestants. Object: To form words. A line that contains blank spaces is displayed. Clues to the identity of a word (eight letters or more) are relayed by the host. Players then contribute three letters each to its formation. For each additional letter that a player contributes that is correct, he receives one hundred dollars. Players suggest letters in turn and are disqualified if they complete the unknown word by supplying the last letter. The first player to identify the word is the winner of that round. The highest cash scorer is the overall champion and competes until he is defeated.

Home participation segment: The first eight letters that are created by players are matched with the digits on a telephone dial. The number that appears represents serial numbers and are flashed on a screen. Home viewers who possess matching dollar bills receive one hundred dollars if they submit them to the program.

Host: Toby Reed.

Judge: Dr. Bergen Evans.

TOP DOLLAR—30 minutes—CBS—March 29, 1958 - August 30, 1958 (evening run); September 1, 1958 - October 23, 1959 (daytime run).

TOPPER

Comedy. Background: New York City. Purchasing a home, Cosmo Topper, the henpecked vice-president of the National Security Bank, inherits three ghosts: George and Marian Kirby, its previous owners, man and wife, who were killed while skiing in Switzerland, and a liquor-consuming Saint Bernard dog, Neil, who was also the victim of the avalanche. Stories depict Topper's attempts to cope with the situations that result as three ghosts, who appear and only talk to him, interfere in his personal and business life. Based on the motion picture.

CAST

Cosmo Topper	Leo G. Carroll
Marian Kirby	Anne Jeffreys
George Kirby	Robert Sterling
Henrietta Topper, Cosmo's wife	Lee Patrick
Mr. Schuyler, the bank president	Thurston Hall
Katie, the Topper's maid	Kathleen Freeman
Maggie, the Topper's housekeeper, later episodes	Edna Skinner
Thelma Gibney, Henrietta's friend	Mary Field
Buck	Neil

Music: Charles Koff.

Producer: John W. Loveton, Bernard L. Schubert.

Director: Leslie Goodwins, Lew Landers, Philip Rapp, James V. Kern, Richard L. Bare.

Sponsor: R.J. Reynolds.

Topper's Address: 101 Maple Drive.

Note: Throughout the run of the series Topper is also known to be associated with these additional banks: City Bank, Gotham Trust Company, City Trust and Savings Bank.

Program Open:

Announcer: "Anne Jeffreys as Marian Kirby, the ghostess with the mostess; Robert Sterling as George Kirby, that most sporting spirit; and Leo G. Carroll, host to said ghosts as Topper."

TOPPER—30 minutes. NBC—October 9, 1953 - September 30, 1955. ABC—October 3, 1955 - September 17, 1956. 78 episodes. Syndicated.

TOP OF THE MONTH

Variety. Highlights of the months of the year are saluted through songs, sketches, and dances.

Host: Tony Randall.

Co-hostess: E. J. (Edra Jeanne) Peaker.

Regulars: Anson Williams, Tina Andrews, The Anita Mann Dancers, The Alan Copeland Singers.

Orchestra: Alan Copeland.

TOP OF THE MONTH—30 minutes—Syndicated 1972.

TOP PLAYS OF 1954

Anthology. Rebroadcasts of outstanding dramas that were originally aired via other filmed anthology programs.

Included:

A Season To Love. The story of a plain-looking girl who falls in love with a disreputable vagrant.

CAST
Ida Lupino, Howard Duff, Sara Hoden.

Wonderful Day For A Wedding. The story of a bride who changes her mind at the last minute and refuses to make the march to the altar.

CAST
Scott Brady, Joan Leslie, Spring Byington.

Keep It In The Family. An episode in the hectic life of the Warren family. The story centers on the chaos that results when teenage daughter Peggy announces that she has been discovered by a talent agent and will star on Broadway.

CAST
Robert Young, Ellen Drew, Sally Foster, Tina Thompson.

TOP PLAYS OF 1954—30 minutes—June 1954 - August 24, 1954.

TOP SECRET

Adventure. The exploits of Peter Dallas, a British agent of law and order in South America.

Starring: William Franklyn as Peter Dallas.

TOP SECRET—30 minutes—Syndicated 1961.

TOP SECRET U.S.A.

Drama. The work of United States government undercover agents in conjunction with the Bureau of Scientific Information (B.S.I.).

CAST
Professor Brand   Paul Stewart
Powell, his
    assistant   Gena Rowlands

TOP SECRET U.S.A.—30 minutes—Syndicated 1954.

TO ROME WITH LOVE

Comedy. Background: Rome, Italy. Hired to teach at the American School in Europe, Professor Michael Endicott, widower, and his three daughters, Alison, Penny, and Mary Jane (Pokey), leave Iowa and, relocating in the Eternal City, take up residence at Mama Vitale's Boarding House.

Stories depict the trials and tribulations of an American family as they struggle to adjust to a new homeland.

CAST

Michael Endicott	John Forsythe
Alison Endicott	Joyce Menges
Penny Endicott	Susan Neher
Pokey Endicott	Melanie Fullerton
Andy Pruitt, the girls' grandfather	Walter Brennan
Harriet Endicott, Mike's sister	Kay Medford
Gino Mancini, their friend, a cab driver	Vito Scotti
Mama Vitale, their landlady	Peggy Mondo
Nico, a friend of Penny's	Gerald Michenaud
Margot, a friend	Brioni Farrell
Tina, a friend of Alison's	Brenda Benet

Music: Frank DeVol.

TO ROME WITH LOVE—30 minutes —CBS—September 28, 1969 - September 1, 1971. 48 episodes.

TO SAY THE LEAST

Game. Two teams, each composed of three players—two celebrities and one noncelebrity contestant—compete. Two players from each team are placed backstage and isolated so as not to be able to see or hear. A phrase is then shown to the on stage players (e.g., "Dutch girls clop around in them"); on an alternating basis, the players eliminate words from it. At any time, the contestant at play can challenge or take out a word. When a challenge is made, the opposing team must attempt to identify the meaning of the phrase. The backstage players are brought out and the challenged player's teammates are shown the remaining words to the phrase. If they can identify it ("Wooden shoes" for the given example) they score one point; if not, the opposing team scores the point. If a challenge is not made the game continues until only two words remain. At this point, the contestant at play has to either challenge or take out a word. If he takes out a word then his teammates have to attempt to answer; if not, then the challenge is made and the opposing team has to guess it. The first team to score two points is the winner and the noncelebrity player receives merchandise prizes.

Host: Tom Kennedy.

Announcer: Kenny Williams.

Producer: Merrill Heatter, Bob Quigley.

TO SAY THE LEAST—30 minutes— NBC—Premiered: October 3, 1977.

TO TELL THE TRUTH

Game. Three people appear, each laying claim to the same identity. Through question-and-answer probe rounds, a celebrity panel of four have to determine which person is telling the truth. Cash prizes are awarded to players depending on the number of incorrect guesses on the part of the panel.

Versions:

To Tell The Truth—30 minutes—CBS—January 1, 1957 - May 22, 1967 (evening run); June 18, 1962 - September 6, 1968 (daytime run).

Moderator: Bud Collyer.

Regular Panelists: Phyllis Newman, Peggy Cass, Sally Ann Howes, Tom Poston, Orson Bean, Kitty Carlisle, Milt Kamen, Bess Myerson, Joan Fontaine, Sam Levenson, Barry Nelson, Dr. Joyce Brothers, Polly Bergen, Dick Van Dyke, John Cameron Swayze, Hildy Parks.

Announcer: Johnny Olsen.

To Tell The Truth—30 minutes—Syndicated 1969.

Moderator: Garry Moore.

Regular Panelists: Orson Bean, Bill Cullen, Kitty Carlisle, Peggy Cass.

Announcers: Johnny Olsen; Bill Wendell.

Music: Score Productions.

TOUCHE TURTLE

Animated Cartoon. The exploits of Touche Turtle, a fumbling modern-day knight who assists the distressed. A Hanna-Barbera production.

Characters' Voices
Touche Turtle   Bill Thompson
Dum Dum, his
  assistant   Alan Reed

Music: Hoyt Curtin.

TOUCHE TURTLE—05 minutes—Syndicated 1962. 52 episodes.

A TOUCH OF GRACE

Comedy. Background: Oakland, California. The story of Grace Sherwood, a sixty-five-year-old widow struggling to make a life for herself at the home of her married daughter, Myra Bradley, a beautician, and her husband, Walter Bradley, the manager of the produce department of the Penny Mart Supermarket.

One day, while tending her husband's grave, Grace meets and falls in love with the grave digger, a widower, Herbert Morrison.

Believing Herbert is not a gentleman, Myra disapproves of him. A family crisis ensues when Grace, feeling her life is unfulfilled because Myra and Walter are childless, states her intent to continue seeing him.

Serial-type episodes relate Grace and Herbert's courtship, Myra's final acceptance of Herbert when she realizes her mother's feelings, and Herbert's proposal to Grace. Based on the British television series, "For the Love of Ada."

CAST
Grace Sherwood (also known
  as Grace Simpson)   Shirley Booth
Herbert Morrison   J. Pat O'Malley
Myra Bradley   Marian Mercer
Walter Bradley   Warren Berlinger

Music: Pete Rugolo.

A TOUCH OF GRACE—30 minutes—ABC—January 20, 1973 - June 16, 1973.

TOYLAND EXPRESS

See title: "Paul Winchell and Jerry Mahoney."

THE TOY THAT GREW UP

Documentary. The history of the silent era of motion pictures.

Host: Don Ferris.

THE TOY THAT GREW UP—60 minutes. NET—1965 - 1970; PBS—1970 - 1972.

TRACER

Mystery. The investigations of Police Inspector Regan as he attempts to solve baffling acts of criminal injustice.

Starring: James Chandler as Inspector Regan.

TRACER—30 minutes—Syndicated 1957.

TRACKDOWN

Western. Background: The Frontier during the 1870s. The cases of Hoby Gilman, Texas Ranger, as he attempts to apprehend wanted offenders.

Starring: Robert Culp as Hoby Gilman.

TRACKDOWN—30 minutes—CBS—October 4, 1957 - September 23, 1959. 71 episodes. Syndicated.

TRAFFIC COURT

Courtroom Drama. Dramatizations based on official traffic-court files.
Judge: Edgar Allan Jones, Jr.

Defendants and Lawyers: Guest actors.

TRAFFIC COURT—30 minutes—ABC—June 18, 1958 - September 24, 1958.

TRAILS TO ADVENTURE

Travel. Historical landmarks are explored and, through dramatizations, incidents in its past are re-created.

Host-Narrator: Jack Smith.

Performers: Guest actors.

TRAILS TO ADVENTURE—30 minutes—Syndicated 1968.

TRAILS WEST

Anthology. Retitled episodes of western dramas that were originally aired via "Death Valley Days."

Host: Ray Milland.

Music: Marlen Skiles.

Included:

The Little Dressmaker Of Bodie. The story of Tiger Lil, dancehall queen of Virginia City, as she struggles to begin a new life.

CAST
Tracey Roberts, Arthur Space, Myron Healy.

The Diamond Babe. The story of a dancehall queen who is scorned by the townspeople.

CAST
Ann Savage.

Solomon In All His Glory. An ex-newspaperman, who has become the town drunk, struggles to reform in time for the arrival of his younger sister.

CAST
James Griffith, Gloria Winters.

A Woman's Rights. The story of the first woman judge and her fight against corruption.

CAST
Bethel Leslie, Dean Harens.

TRAILS WEST—30 minutes—Syndicated 1958. 104 episodes.

THE TRAP

Anthology. Dramatizations depicting the plight of people suddenly confronted with uncertain situations.

Host: John Bentley.

Producer: Franklin Heller.

Director: Byron Paul.

Included:

Lonely Boy. The story of a chance meeting between two lonely people.

Starring: Cara Williams, Dorothy Sands, Larry Fletcher, Howard Wierum, John Hudson.

The Secret Place. The story of a rich but neglected wife and her attempts to make her husband jealous by letting him believe that she has a secret love.

Starring: Margaret Rawlings.

THE TRAP—30 minutes—CBS 1950.

TRAVEL WITH DON AND BETTINA

See title: "Faces and Places."

THE TRAVELS OF JAIMIE McPHEETERS

Western. Era: 1849. The hardships

The Travels of Jaimie McPheeters. Dan O'Herlihy and Kurt Russell.

encountered by the Beaver Patrol, a wagon train of settlers destined for California. Stories depict their experiences as seen through the eyes of twelve-year-old Jaimie McPheeters.

CAST

Doc Sardius McPheeters, Jaimie's father	Dan O'Herlihy
Jaimie McPheeters	Kurt Russell
Buck Coulter, the wagonmaster	Michael Witney

Settlers:

Dick McBride	John Chandler
Matt Kissel	Mark Allen
Mrs. Kissel	Meg Wyllie
The Kissel Children	The Osmond Brothers
Othello	Vernett Allen III
Murdock	Charles Bronson
Jenny	Jean Engstrom
	Donna Anderson
Shep Bogott	Sandy Kenyon
Hard Luck Slater	Robert Carriort

John Munlett   James Westerfield

Producer: Robert Thompson, Robert Sparks, Don Ingalls.

THE TRAVELS OF JAIMIE McPHEETERS—60 minutes—ABC—September 17, 1963 - March 15, 1964. 26 episodes.

TREASURE

Documentary. Films relating the search for fabled treasures. Legends, strange facts, and histories concerning the particular treasures are also related.

Host-Narrator: Bill Burrud.

TREASURE—30 minutes—Syndicated 1960.

TREASURE HUNT

Game. Two competing players, a male and female. A question, which is based on a specific topic, is related by the host. The player who first identifies himself through a buzzer signal receives a chance to answer. If correct, he receives one point. The winner, the highest point scorer, receives the opportunity to win up to $25,000 in cash.

He or she is escorted to a wall that contains thirty treasure chests. The player chooses one, and its contents—from a head of cabbage to valuable merchandise prizes to large sums of cash—are his or her prize.

Host: Jan Murray.

Pirate Girl (his assistant): Marian Stafford.

TREASURE HUNT—30 minutes. ABC—September 17, 1956 - August 23, 1957; NBC—August 12, 1957 - December 4, 1959.

TREASURE ISLE

Game. Background: A specially constructed island in Florida. Three married couples compete. Object: To seek buried treasure.

Round One: A large pile of styrofoam puzzle pieces are placed opposite the players. In fifteen second intervals, individual players run up to the pile, take one piece at a time, and place it in its appropriate place on a large board. Each piece that is properly fitted awards that team one point. When the puzzle is completed it relates a rhyming clue. The team who correctly decifers it receives additional points.

Round Two: Various stunt contests that award the best performers points.

Round Three: Players, situated on one island, have to cross to another island (about twenty-five yards distant). Each team receives an inflatable raft. The husbands lie face down so as to use their hands as oars; the wives are seated at the opposite side of the raft and direct their husband's rowing. The team that is first to reach the island receives points.

The team with the highest point score is the winner and receives the opportunity to hunt for buried treasure chests. Time limit: three minutes. The host reads clues, one at a time, to the location of buried chests. The couple has to unscramble the clue and dig in the sand until a chest is found. They then return to the position of the host and receive another clue. Players receive what prizes, usually merchandise, that the chests contain (written on cards).

Host: John Bartholemew Tucker.

Models (Pirate Girls): Bonnie Maudsley, Renee Hampton.

TREASURE ISLE—30 minutes—ABC —December 18, 1967 - March 28, 1968.

TREASURE QUEST

See title: "Bon Voyage."

TREASURY MEN IN ACTION

Crime Drama. Dramatizations based on the files of the United States Customs and Treasury departments.

Starring: Walter Greaza as The Chief (introducing stories).

Announcer: Durwood Kirby.

Music: Murray Golden.

Producer: Everett Rosenthal, Robert Sloane, Bernard Prockter.

Director: David Pressman.

Sponsor: Borden; Chevrolet.

TREASURY MEN IN ACTION—30 minutes. ABC—September 11, 1950 - December 4, 1950; NBC—April 5, 1951 - September 30, 1955. Syndicated title: "Federal Men." 39 episodes available for syndication.

THE TRIALS OF O'BRIEN

Drama. Background: New York City. The cases and courtroom defenses of Daniel J. O'Brien, an untidy and disorganized criminal attorney. Spiced with light humor.

CAST
Daniel J. O'Brien	Peter Falk
Katie O'Brien, his ex-wife, whom he seeks to remarry	Joanna Barnes
The Great McGonigle, a conartist, a friend of O'Brien's	David Burns
Margaret, Katie's mother	Ilka Chase
Mrs. G., O'Brien's secretary	Elaine Stritch
Lieutenant Garrison, N.Y.P.D.	Dolph Sweet

Music: Sid Ramin.

THE TRIALS OF O'BRIEN—60 minutes—CBS—September 18, 1965 - May 27, 1966. 20 episodes.

TROPIC HOLIDAY

Musical Variety. Set against a South of the Border motif, a merchant sailor reminisces about his experiences in various South American countries. Through the performances of guest personalities, the music, song, and dance of foreign lands are seen.

Host-Narrator: Sandy Buckert (as the merchant sailor).

Orchestra: Esy Morales.

TROPIC HOLIDAY—30 minutes— NBC 1949.

THE TROUBLESHOOTERS

Adventure. The experiences of Kodiak and Dugan, construction supervisors who intervene in construction-site difficulties and attempt to return the job to normality.

CAST
Kodiak	Keenan Wynn
Dugan	Bob Mathias

Troubleshooter Team:

Loft	Eddie Firestone
Scotty	Bob Fortier
Skinner	Cary Loftin

Producer: Frank Rosenberg, John Gibbs, Richard Steenberg.

THE TROUBLESHOOTERS–30 minutes–NBC–September 11, 1959 - June 17, 1960. 26 episodes.

TROUBLE WITH FATHER

Comedy. Background: The town of Hamilton. The trials and tribulations of the Erwin family: Stu, the principal of Hamilton High School; his wife, June; and their daughters, Joyce and Jackie.

CAST

Stu Erwin	Himself
June Erwin	June Collyer
Joyce Erwin	Ann Todd
	Merry Anders
Jackie Erwin	Sheila James
Marty Clark, Joyce's boyfriend	Martin Milner
Willie, the handyman	Willie Best

Producer: Roland Reed, Hal Roach, Jr.

Sponsor: General Mills.

TROUBLE WITH FATHER–30 minutes–ABC–October 21, 1950 - April 13, 1955. 130 episodes. Syndicated. Original title: "Life With the Erwins" also known as "The Stu Erwin Show" and "The New Stu Erwin Show."

THE TROUBLE WITH TRACY

Comedy. Background: Toronto, Canada. The trials and tribulations of the Youngs: Douglas, an executive with the advertising firm of Hutton, Dutton, Sutton, and Norris; and his well-meaning but scatterbrained wife, Tracy. Produced in Canada.

CAST

Tracy Young	Diane Nyland
Douglas Young	Steve Weston
Sally Anderson, Doug's secretary	Bonnie Brooks
Paul Sherwood, Tracy's unemployed brother	Franz Russell
Jonathan Norris, Doug's employer	Ben Lennick
Margaret Norris, his wife	Sandra Scott

THE TROUBLE WITH TRACY–30 minutes–Syndicated 1971.

TRUE

See title: "General Electric True."

TRUE ADVENTURE

Travel. Films relating the journeys of various explorers.

Host: Bill Burrud.

TRUE ADVENTURE–30 minutes–Syndicated 1960. 78 episodes.

TRUE STORY

Anthology. Dramatic presentations.

Hostess: Kathi Norris.

Included:

The Imperfect Secretary. The trials and tribulations of a trouble-prone male secretary.

Starring: Dick Van Dyke.

Say A Few Words. The complications that ensue when a college coed impersonates a Polish immigrant to attend a handsome English teacher's lectures.

Starring: Phyllis Newman.

Aunt Eppy. An advertising executive's efforts to cope with the antics of his eccentric aunt.

Starring: Barney Martin, Nancy Pollock.

The Accused. A lawyer's efforts to prove his wife is innocent of a murder charge.

Starring: Lorne Greene, Jim Boles, Fred J. Scollay.

TRUE STORY—30 minutes—NBC—March 16, 1957 - December 20, 1958.

TRUTH OR CONSEQUENCES

Game. Selected contestants (numbers vary) are first briefly interviewed, then asked to answer a nonsense riddle. If they are unable to answer it before Beulah the Buzzer sounds, they have to pay the consequences and perform stunts. Prizes are awarded in accord with the success of their performances. Based on the radio program.

Versions:

Truth Or Consequences—30 minutes—NBC—July 5, 1950 - September 25, 1965.

Hosts: Ralph Edwards; Jack Bailey; Bob Barker.

Announcer: Ken Carpenter.

Music: Buddy Cole; Jack Fascinato.

Truth Or Consequences—30 minutes—Syndicated 1967.

Host: Bob Barker.

Announcer: Charles Lyon.

Music: Dave Bacoll.

The New Truth Or Consequences—30 minutes—Syndicated 1977.

Host: Bob Hilton.

Announcer: John Harlan.

Music: Bruce Belland, Gary Edwards.

Executive Producer: Jon Ross.

Producer: Ralph Edwards, Bruce Belland.

Director: Richard Gottlieb.

TRY AND DO IT

Game. Background: A picnic grounds. Object: For contestants to perform stunts. Prizes are awarded to players in accord with the success of their performances.

Host: Jack Bright.

Orchestra: Thomas Lender.

TRY AND DO IT—30 minutes—NBC 1948.

TUESDAY MYSTERY OF THE WEEK

Anthology. Mystery and suspense presentations.

Included:

Nick and Nora. Though technically retired, former private detective Nick Charles and his wealthy wife, Nora, attempt to solve the case of a corpse they find floating in a swimming pool.

CAST

Nick Charles: Craig Stevens; Nora Charles: Jo Ann Pflug; Sgt. Steinmetz: Jack Kruschen.

Mr. and Ms. and the Magic Studio Mystery. The story of a young lawyer and his wife and their attempts to solve the puzzling mystery of a woman who was murdered when she stepped into a magician's trick iron maiden.

CAST

David Robbins: John Rubinstein; Mandy Robbins: Lee Kroeger; Lt. Ben Robbins: Milton Selzer; Barbara: Udana Power.

Mr. and Ms. and the Bandstand Mystery. Lawyer David Robbins and his wife Mandy (Mr. and Ms.) attempt to solve the baffling murder of a British Rock star.

CAST

David Robbins: John Rubinstein; Mandy Robbins: Lee Kroeger; Lt. Ben Robbins: Milton Selzer; Dottie: Lezlie Dalton.

TUESDAY MYSTERY OF THE WEEK—90 minutes—ABC—Premiered: January 13, 1976. Broadcast from 11:30 p.m. to 1:00 a.m., E.T.

TUESDAY NIGHT PILOT FILM

Pilot Films. Proposed comedy series for the 1976 - 1977 season.

Included:

Three Times Daley. The misadventures of Bob Daley, a newspaper columnist.

CAST

Bob Daley: Don Adams; Mr. Daley: Liam Dunn; Wes Daley: Jerry Houser.

Maureen. The life of Maureen Langaree, a middle-aged department store saleswoman.

CAST

Maureen: Joyce Van Patten; Ruth: Sylvia Sidney; Alice: Karen Morrow; Trudy: Leigh French.

This Better Be It. The episode focuses on incidents in the lives of two newlyweds—each of whom has a grown child from a previous marriage that ended in divorce.

CAST

Annie: Anne Meara; Harry: Alex Rocco; Diana: Ballie Gerstein; Paul: David Pollock.

TUESDAY NIGHT PILOT FILM—30 minutes—CBS—July 27, 1976 - September 7, 1976.

TUGBOAT ANNIE

Comedy. Background: The Pacific Northwest. The misadventures of Annie Brennan, the middle-aged, sympathetic, often troubled skipper of the tugboat *Narcissus.* Based on the stories by Norman Reilly Raine.

CAST

"Tugboat" Annie Brennan	Minerva Urecal
Horatio Bullwinkle, Annie's employer	Walter Sande
Murdoch McArdle, the owner of the *Narcissus*	Stan Francis

TUGBOAT ANNIE—30 minutes—Syndicated 1957. 39 episodes. Also known as "The Adventures of Tugboat Annie."

THE TURNING POINT

Anthology. Dramatizations depicting the plight of people suddenly faced with unexpected situations.

Included:

Saddle Tramp. A drifter's search for the murderer of a friend.
Starring: William Joyce.

Borrow My Car. A young man's efforts to prove he is not guilty of stealing a car that he borrowed for a date.
Starring: Lola Albright, Allan Dexter.

The Little Pig Cried. A woman's second thoughts about divorcing her husband.
Starring: Frances Rafferty, Robert Rockwell.

THE TURNING POINT—30 minutes —ABC 1953.

TURNING POINT

Anthology. Dramatic presentations.

Included:

Once Upon a Crime. The story revolves around a thief who steals a money box from an amusement park then attaches himself to a group of children to avoid capture.
Starring: Peter Lawford, Rudy Lee,

Roy Farrell, Wendy Winkelman.

This Land Is Mine. A western drama depicting the plight of homesteaders vs. gunmen for control of land.
Starring: John Ireland, Joy Page.

Heroes Never Grow Up. The story of an acclaimed hero whose heroism is put to the test in a second emergency.
Starring: Dane Clark, Alex Nicol, Barbara Turner.

TURNING POINT—30 minutes— NBC—April 12, 1958 - September 20, 1958.

TURN OF FATE

Anthology. Dramatizations depicting the plight of people who are suddenly involved in unexpected and perilous situations.

Regular performers: Robert Ryan, Jane Powell, Jack Lemmon, David Niven, Charles Boyer.

Included:

Voices In The Fog. Background: London, England. Waiting for a train, an American doctor overhears a plot to murder a man. Boarding the train, he discovers that he is the victim. Previously unable to see the murderers' faces because of a thick fog, and pretending to be unaware of their plans, he attempts to discover who they are and the reason why.

CAST
Dr. Cameron: Jack Lemmon; Cynthia: Joan Banks; Conductor: John Rogers.

Circumstantial. Getting himself arrested, an attorney attempts to prove, through his own defense, that circumstantial evidence can lead to a conviction.

CAST

Mark Garron: David Niven; Mrs. Garim: Angie Dickinson.

Silhouette Of A Killer. An amnesiac, mistaken for a killer, struggles to prove his innocence.

CAST

Man: Robert Ryan; Ellen: Beverly Garland.

TURN OF FATE—30 minutes—NBC —1957-1958. 38 episodes.

TURN ON

Variety. Visual, fast-paced comedy combined with electronic distortion and stop-action photography.

Because gags were said to contain underlying factors* and pictures were said to represent ideas other than presented, the program was cancelled the same night it premiered.

Host (Guest): Tim Conway.

Regulars: Chuck McCann, Bonnie Boland, Hamilton Camp, Teresa Graves, Maura McGiveney, Debbie Macomber, Carlos Manteca, Bob Staats, Mel Stuart, Cecil Ozorio, Ken Greenwald, Alma Murphy, Maxine Green, Alice MaVega.

Announcer: Chuck McCann.

Music: Computerized.

*For example: A scene from the opening. A beautiful woman is standing before a firing squad. The squad leader, instead of saying the customary, "Do you have any last requests?" remarks: "I know this may seem a little unusual miss, but in this case the firing squad has one last request."

TURN ON—30 minutes—ABC—Premiered/Ended: February 5, 1969.

TURN TO A FRIEND

Game. Contestants appear and bear their souls, stating their single most needed possession. The studio audience then selects the person with the saddest story. The player receives her plea, and additional help from the program in terms of prizes.

Host: Dennis James.

TURN TO A FRIEND—30 minutes— ABC—1953 - 1954.

TV AUCTION

Game. Various merchandise items are displayed on stage. The limit price of each item is stated. Via wire or mail, and on a first-come-first-served basis, the items are sold to the home viewers whose bids are found acceptable.

Host (Auctioneer): Sid Stone.

TV AUCTION—30 minutes—ABC— June 1954 - September 1954.

TV GENERAL STORE

Game. Various merchandise items are displayed on stage. The limit price of each item is stated. Via wire or mail home viewers participate. The viewer whose bid is the highest on a particular item is able to purchase it. Arrangements for the actual purchase are made after buyers are selected and off the air.

Host: Dave Clark.

Hostess: Judy Clark.

TV GENERAL STORE—60 minutes —ABC—June 23, 1953 - September 6, 1953.

TV READERS DIGEST

Anthology. Dramatizations based on stories appearing in *Readers Digest* magazine.

Host: Hugh Riley.

Included:

The Last Of The Old Time Shooting Sheriffs. Background: Arizona. A retired sheriff attempts to aid the citizens of a town plagued by a series of bank robberies.
Starring: Russ Simpson.

Master Counterfeiters. Master detective William J. Burns attempts to crack a counterfeiting case.
Starring: Roy Roberts.

The Trigger-Finger Clue. The police search for a criminal who, after robbing a bank president, killed him and his two sons.
Starring: Elisha Cook.

The Manufactured Clue. Police efforts to track a criminal who leaves a trail of false clues.
Starring: Paul Stewart.

TV READERS DIGEST—30 minutes —ABC—January 17, 1955 - July 9, 1956. 65 episodes. Syndicated.

TV SHOPPER

Women. Shopping hints, fashion tips, marketing advice, and consumer values.

Hostess: Kathi Norris.

TV SHOPPER—15 minutes—DuMont 1949.

TV SOUND STAGE

Anthology. Dramatic presentations.

Included:

Innocent Til Proved Guilty. A husband's efforts to end his wife's constant habit of jumping to conclusions.
Starring: Leora Dana, Paul McGrath.

One Small Guy. The story of a man who misuses his talent to make people like him.
Starring: Jack Lemmon, Georgiann Johnson, Doro Merande, Bruce Gordon.

Deception. Returning to his home town, a young man seeks revenge for the wrongs done to him.
Starring: Martin Brookes, Howard Freeman.

TV SOUND STAGE—30 minutes— NBC—July 10, 1953 - September 1953.

TV'S TOP TUNES

Musical Variety. Renditions of popular songs.

Versions:

TV's Top Tunes—15 minutes—CBS— July 4, 1951 - August 26, 1951.
Hosts: Peggy Lee, Mel Tormé.
Vocalists: The Skylarks.
Orchestra: Mitchell Ayres.

TV's Top Tunes—30 minutes—CBS— June 28, 1954 - September 3, 1955.
Host: Julius La Rosa.
Regulars: Helen O'Connell, Bob Eberly, Tommy Mercer, Marcie Miller, Lee Roy, The Ray

Anthony Chorus.

Announcer: Tony Marvin.

Orchestra: Ray Anthony.

TWELVE O'CLOCK HIGH

Drama. Background: England during World War II. The experiences of the men and officers of the American 918th B-17 Bomber Squadron.

CAST
Brigadier General Frank Savage	Robert Lansing
Major General Wiley Crowe	John Larkin
Major Harvey Stovall	Frank Overton
Major Joseph Cobb	Lew Gallo
Major Doc Kaiser	Barney Philips
Colonel Joe Gallagher	Paul Burke
T/Sgt. Sandy Komansky	Chris Robinson
Brigadier General Edward Britt	Andrew Duggan

Music: Dominic Frontiere.

TWELVE O'CLOCK HIGH—60 minutes—ABC—September 18, 1964 - January 13, 1967. 78 episodes. Syndicated.

THE 20th CENTURY

Documentary. Historical films recounting the events of the twentieth century.

Host-Narrator: Walter Cronkite.

Music: Kenyon Hopkins; Laurence Rosenthal.

Producer: Burton Benjamin, Albert Wasserman, Isaac Kleinerman, Peter Poor, Marshall Flaum.

THE 20th CENTURY—30 minutes—CBS—October 20, 1957 - August 28, 1966. Syndicated. Spin-off series: "The 21st Century" (see title).

THE 20th CENTURY FOX HOUR

Anthology. Dramatic presentations.

Host: Joseph Cotten, Robert Sterling.

Director: Lewis Allen, John Brahm, Gerd Oswald, Robert Stevenson, Ted Post, Peter Godfrey, William Seiter, James V. Kern, Jules Bricken, Jerry Thorpe, Albert S. Rogell, Devery Freeman, William Russell.

Included:

Miracle On 34th Street. The heartwarming story of a man who believes he is the real Santa Claus.

Starring: Thomas Mitchell, Teresa Wright, Macdonald Carey.

Child Of The Regiment. The story of an army captain and his wife and their attempts to adopt a Japanese war orphan.

Starring: Teresa Wright.

Men Against Speed. A female photographer struggles to reunite her two feuding brothers in time for an important Italian car race.

Starring: Farley Granger, Mona Freeman.

Men In Her Life. When she discovers that a former student of her's is now running for governor, a teacher recalls the past and the trouble caused by the former problem student.

Starring: Phyllis Kirk, Kendell Scott,

Beverly Washburn, Ann Doran.

THE 20th CENTURY FOX HOUR—
60 minutes—CBS—October 5, 1955 -
September 18, 1957.

TWENTIETH CENTURY TALES

Anthology. Rebroadcasts of dramas
that were originally aired via other
filmed anthology programs.

Included:

Rock Against The Sea. A girl who is
afraid of the sea falls in love with a
handsome sea captain.
Starring: Marjorie Bennett.

My Rival Is A Fiddle. A woman
struggles to snatch the attentions of a
man whose love is his fiddle.
Starring: Hans Conried, Maria Palmer.

TWENTIETH CENTURY TALES—30
minutes—ABC—June 1953 - September 1953.

THE 21st CENTURY

Documentary. Films relating the
scientific and medical advances that
will mark the twenty-first century.
Host: Walter Cronkite.

THE 21st CENTURY—30 minutes—
CBS—January 20, 1967 - September
28, 1969.

THE $25,000 PYRAMID

Game. Two competing teams, each
composed of two members: one celebrity and one noncelebrity contestant.

One team chooses one subject from
six categories that are displayed on a
board (e.g., "Sleepy Head"). A question is then read that relates its
purpose ("Describe things that are
associated with sleep"). One player
has a small monitor before him in
which the key words appear, one at a
time. Through one-word clues, he has
to relate the meaning to his partner.
One point is scored for each correct
identification. Rounds are limited to
thirty seconds and each team competes in three games. The highest
scoring team is the winner and the
contestant receives the opportunity to
win ten thousand dollars.

Appearing in the winner's circle,
one player sits with his back to a large
pyramid that contains six categories,
worth from one hundred to three
hundred dollars each. The player who
is facing the pyramid relates clues to
their identification. If the player identifies all six within one minute, he
wins ten thousand dollars, and the
opportunity to compete in another
game. Should he win again, he returns
to the winner's circle and competes
for twenty-five thousand dollars by
identifying six subjects in one minute.
Should he fail, he receives what
money he has accumulated by identifying individual subjects. A spin-off
from "The $10,000 Pyramid."

Host: Bill Cullen.
Announcer: Bob Clayton.
Executive Producer: Bob Stewart.
Producer: Anne Marie Schmitt.
Director: Mike Gargiulo.

THE $25,000 PYRAMID—30 min-
utes—Syndicated 1974.

TWENTY-ONE

Game. Two competing players.
Object: To score twenty-one points

by answering questions. Players are situated in separate isolation booths. Questions, which are selected from categories over which players have no control, are numbered from one to eleven. The number represents the point value of questions, the higher it is, the more difficult it is. Questions are asked of players as they are chosen, one per time. The first player to score twenty-one is the winner and receives five hundred dollars per point difference between his score and his opponent's score. Players compete until defeated.

Host: Jack Barry.

Announcer: Bill McCord.

Orchestra: Paul Taubman.

TWENTY-ONE—30 minutes—NBC—September 12, 1956 - October 16, 1958.

21 BEACON STREET

Mystery. Background: Boston, Mass. The cases of David Chase, a private detective who incorporates scientific deduction and electronic wizardry as he and his associates attempt to solve baffling crimes. (21 Beacon Street: The address of the David Chase Detective Agency).

CAST

David Chase	Dennis Morgan
Lola, his Girl Friday	Joanna Barnes
Brian, their assistant, a law student	Brian Kelly
Jim, their assistant, a master of disguise	James Maloney

21 BEACON STREET—30 minutes—NBC—July 2, 1959 - September 24, 1959.

TWENTY QUESTIONS

Game. Four players: three regular panelists and one studio-audience contestant. A subject, which is either animal, vegetable, or mineral, is revealed. Players have to identify it by asking questions, twenty being the maximum. If the contestant can identify the subject before the panel he receives a prize.

Hosts: Bill Slater; Jay Jackson.

Announcers: John Gregson; Frank Woldecker.

Panelists: Fred Von Deventer, Florence Rinard, Bobby McGuire, Herb Palesie, Johnny McFee.

Producer: George Elbes, Gary Stevens.

Director: Roger Bower, Dick Sondwick.

Sponsor: Ronson Lighters; Mennen; Luden's; Florida Citrus Growers.

TWENTY QUESTIONS—30 minutes—ABC—March 31, 1950 - June 22, 1951; July 6, 1954 - May 3, 1955.

26 MEN

Western. Background: The Arizona Territory, 1903. Dramatizations based on the files of the Arizona Rangers—men, limited by law to twenty-six, dispensing justice in the final days of the Old West.

CAST

Captain Tom Rynning	Tris Coffin
Ranger Clint Travis	Kelo Henderson

Music: Hal Hopper.

26 MEN—30 minutes—Syndicated 1958. 78 episodes.

THE $20,000 PYRAMID

See title: "The $10, 000 Pyramid."

TWILIGHT THEATRE

Anthology. Retitled episodes of dramas that were originally aired via other filmed anthology programs.

Included:

The Roustabaut. The story of a drifter who is forced into the middle of a fight between ranchers and store-keepers.

Starring: Scott Brady.

That Time In Boston. The story of a married couple and a sophisticated woman who spend a not very tranquil New Year's Eve together.

Starring: Hillary Brooke.

The Black Sleep's Daughter. The story of a wealthy playboy and his attempts to persuade his wife to grant him a divorce.

Starring: Carolyn Jones, Philip Ober, Marcia Patrick.

TWILIGHT THEATRE—30 minutes—ABC—July 1958 - October 8, 1958.

THE TWILIGHT ZONE

Anthology. Tales of people confronted with the mysterious unexplored regions of the fifth dimension—the area that is everywhere, yet nowhere; the ground between all that is known and what is beyond understanding—an area called "The Twilight Zone."

Host-Narrator: Rod Serling.

Music: Leith Stevens; Bernard Herrmann; Jerry Goldsmith; William Lava.

Additional Music: Fred Steiner, Nathan Scott, Van Cleave, Leonard Rosenman, Tommy Morgan.

Executive Producer-Creator: Rod Serling.

Producer: Buck Houghton, William Froug, Herbert Hirschman.

Director: Robert Stevens, Justis Addiss, Douglas Heyes, John Brahm, Ronald Winston, William Claxton, Montgomery Pittman, James Sheldon, Mitchell Leisen, Jack Smight, Robert Sparr, Ida Lupino, Don Medford, Buzz Kulik, Richard L. Bare, John Rich, Elliott Silverstein, Boris Sagal, Anton Leader, Lamont Johnson, Christian Nyby, Robert Enrico (for the French film "An Occurance At Owl Creek Bridge" which was telecast on 2-28-64 and 9-11-64).

Included:

Jess-Belle. The story of a backwoods girl who uses a love potion on her old beau.

CAST

Jess-Belle: Anne Francis; Granny Hart: Jeanette Nolan.

A Most Unusual Camera. The story of a couple who, after their latest heist, acquire a camera that takes pictures of the future.

CAST

Chester: Fred Clark; Paula: Jean Carson; Woodward: Adam Williams.

The Night of the Meek. A heartwarming Christmas story about a department store santa who, after being fired for drinking, discovers that he is the real Santa Claus.

CAST
Henry Corwin: Art Carney; Mr. Dundee: John Fiedler; Officer Flaherty: Robert P. Lieb; Burt: Burt Mustin.

Queen of the Nile. The story of a beautiful movie queen who seems never to age.

CAST
Pamela: Ann Blyth; Jordon: Lee Philips; Mrs. Draper: Ceila Lousky.

Program opening (one of several):

Host: "There is a fifth dimension beyond that which is known to man. It is a dimension as vast as space and as timeless as infinity. It is the middle ground between light and shadow, between science and superstition and it lies between the pit of man's fears and the summit of his knowledge. It is an area which we call The Twilight Zone."

THE TWILIGHT ZONE—30 minutes —CBS—October 2, 1959 - September 14, 1962. Syndicated. 60 minutes— CBS—January 3, 1963 - September 27, 1963. Rebroadcasts (CBS): June 1964 - September 18, 1964; May 1965 - September 1965. Syndicated. 134 half-hour episodes; 17 one-hour episodes.

TWIN TIME

Variety. Performances by undiscovered professional talent.

Host: Jack Lemmon.

Regulars: Arlene and Ardell Terry (the singing teenage twins), Jim Kirkwood, Lee Goodwin, Jack Kriza, Ann Koesun.

Producer: Sherman Marks.

Sponsor: Toni.

TWIN TIME—30 minutes—CBS 1950.

TWO FACES WEST

Western. Background: The town of Gunnison during the 1860s. The efforts of twin brothers Ben January, the marshall, and Rick January, a doctor, to maintain law and order.

CAST
Rick January	Charles Bateman
Ben January	Charles Bateman
Deputy Johnny Evans	Paul Comi

Music: Joe Weiss; Irving Friedman.

TWO FACES WEST—30 minutes— Syndicated 1961. 39 episodes.

TWO FOR THE MONEY

Game. Three competing contestants.

Round One: A general-knowledge type of question is read. The player who is first to identify himself through a buzzer signal receives a chance to answer. If correct, he receives money. The game continues until one player, the highest cash scorer, is declared the winner.

Round Two: The champion competes. Within a fifteen-second time limit, a rapid-fire question-and-answer session is conducted. For each correct answer the player gives, he receives the amount of money he won in the first round.

Round Three: Follows the format of round two. For each correct response the player gives, he receives the total earnings of rounds one and two.

Hosts: Herb Shriner; Sam Levenson.

Announcer: Dennis James.

Orchestra: Milton DeLugg.

Answer Judge: Dr. Mason Gross.

TWO FOR THE MONEY—30 minutes—CBS—August 15, 1953 - June 17, 1956.

TWO GIRLS NAMED SMITH

Comedy. Background: New York City. The misadventures of two small-town girls, aspiring models, sisters Babs and Peggy Smith, as they attempt to further their careers.

CAST
Babs Smith	Peggy Ann Garner
	Marcia Henderson
Peggy Smith	Peggy French
Babs' boyfriend	Richard Hayes
Peggy's boyfriend	Joseph Buloff
The girl's landlady	Aledardi Klein

Also: Jane Dulo, Scott Tennysa, Arthur Walsh.

Producer: Richard Lewis.

Director: Charles S. Dubin.

TWO GIRLS NAMED SMITH—30 minutes—ABC—January 20, 1951 - October 31, 1951.

TWO IN LOVE

Game. Newly married or engaged couples compete. Object: To build a nest egg. Friends and family of the individual couples appear on stage. Each time a personal question is answered by a friend or relative, that couple receives money. After a nest egg has been built for each couple, the couples then compete in a quiz. Before a question is asked, players have to state the amount of time, in seconds, it will require them to answer it. The question is asked and the couple who comes closest to their prediction wins the nest egg.

Host: Bert Parks.

TWO IN LOVE—30 minutes—NBC 1954.

THE TYCOON

Comedy. Background: Thunder Holding Corporation in Los Angeles, California. The story of Walter Andrews, industrialist, millionaire, and board chairman, a sixty-five-year-old widower who, facing objections from younger corporate executives, struggles to operate his company in accord with his established standards.

CAST
Walter Andrews	Walter Brennan
Herbert Wilson; the corporation president	Jerome Cowan
Pat Burns, Walter's aide	Van Williams
Betty Franklin, Walter's secretary	Janet Lake
Martha Keane, Walter's granddaughter	Patricia McNulty
Una Fields, Walter's housekeeper	Monty Margetts
Louise Wilson, Herbert's wife	Grace Albertson
Tom Keane, Martha's husband	George Lindsay

THE TYCOON—30 minutes—ABC—

September 15, 1964 - September 6, 1965. 32 episodes.

U

U.F.O.

Science Fiction Adventure. Background: London, England, 1980. As Unidentified Flying Objects (U.F.O.s) become established and believed to be a threat to the safety of Earth, world governments unite and sponsor the construction of S.H.A.D.O. (Supreme Headquarters, Alien Defense Organization), which is closely guarded under a veil of deep secrecy and housed beneath the Harlington-Straker film studios.

Establishing bases on both the Earth and the Moon, and incorporating highly complex defense equipment, S.H.A.D.O.'s battle of secrecy* against alien invaders is dramatized as it attempts to discover who they are, where they come from and what they want. An I.T.C. presentation.

CAST

Edward Straker, the commander of S.H.A.D.O.	Ed Bishop
Colonel Alec Freeman, his assistant	George Sewell
Lt. Gay Ellis, the commander of Moon Base	Gabrielle Drake

*Public awareness of U.F.O.s is feared to cause worldwide panic.

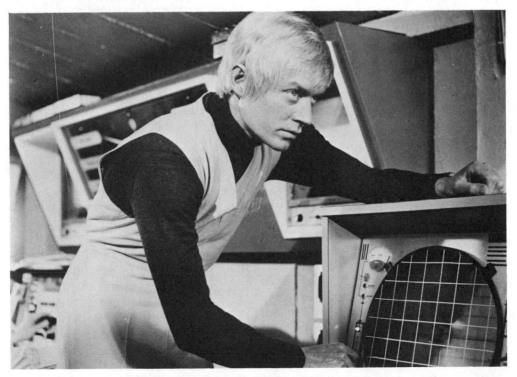

U.F.O. Ed Bishop. *Courtesy Independent Television Corp.; an ATV Company.*

Colonel Paul Foster, Straker's
  assistant   Michael Billington
Lt. Nina Barry, a
  space tracker   Dolores Mantez
Lt. Joan Harrington, a
  space tracker   Antoni Ellis
Colonel Virginia Lake Wanda Ventham
Captain Peter Karlin   Peter Gordeno
Miss Eland, Straker's
  secretary   Norma Roland
Douglas Jackson, the
  psychiatrist   Valdek Sheybol
Lt. Keith Ford   Keith Alexander
Skydiver operator   Georganna Moon
Skydiver navigator   Jeremy Wilkin
Skydiver engineer   Jon Kelly
Skydiver captain   David Warbeck
Moon Base operator   Andrea Allan
Third Mobile officer Hugh Armstrong
General James Henderson, Straker's
  superior   Grant Taylor
S.H.A.D.O. operative   Penny Spencer
S.H.A.D.O. operative   Ayshea
Tunner, the radio
  operator   Patrick Allen
Lew Waterman, an
  Interceptor pilot   Garry Myers
Mark Bradley, an
  Interceptor pilot   Harry Baird
Miss Scott, Henderson's
  secretary   Louise Pajd
Interceptor pilot   Mark Hawkins
Miss Holland, Straker's
  secretary (later
  episodes)   Lois Maxwell
The radar technician Michael Ferrand

Music: Barry Gray.

Producer: Reg Hill, Gerry Anderson.

Director: Ken Turner, David Bell,
  Alan Perry, David Lane, Jeremy
  Summers, Gerry Anderson,
  David Tomblin, Cyril Frankel.

U.F.O.—60 minutes—Syndicated
1972. 26 episodes.

The Ugliest Girl in Town. Peter Kastner as
Timmie Blair. © *Screen Gems.*

THE UGLIEST GIRL
IN TOWN

Comedy. Heartbroken after actress
Julie Renfield returns to London
following her completion of a movie,
Hollywood talent scout Tim Blair is
approached by his photographer-
brother, Gene, who, requiring hippie
pictures, persuades him to pose as a
girl. The photographs, which manage
to find their way to a London ad
agency, impress its head, Mr.
Courtney, who commissions Gene to
shoot a layout using the girl who,
unknown to him, is a man.

Discovering a way to be with Julie,
Tim retains his disguise and adopts the
secret alias of Timmie Blair. Sharing
each other's company, Tim finds himself deeply in love with Julie and
unable to leave London. As the ad
campaign nears completion, Gene
loses eleven thousand pounds in a
gambling casino—money that has to
be paid "or else." Discovering Gene's

plight, Tim voluntarily agrees to continue with the masquerade to assist in paying the debt.

Girlish, modeling by day; and boyish, dating his starlet, Julie, by night, Tim Blair struggles to conceal the fact of, and maintain, two separate existances.

CAST

Tim Blair	Peter Kastner
Timmie Blair	Peter Kastner
Julie Renfield	Patricia Brake
Gene Blair	Gary Marshall
Mr. Courtney	Nicholas Parsons

Music: Howard Greenfield.

THE UGLIEST GIRL IN TOWN—30 minutes—ABC—September 26, 1968 - January 30, 1969. 20 episodes.

UKULELE IKE

Variety. Music, songs, and comedy sketches.

Host: Cliff Edwards, Ukulele Ike.

Vocalist: Beverly Fite.

Music: The Slim Jackson Quartet.

UKULELE IKE—15 minutes—CBS 1950.

ULTRAMAN

Science Fiction Adventure. Background: Twenty-first-century Japan. As two Unidentified Flying Objects approach Earth they collide; one veers off course and crashes in a lake; the other strikes a Scientific Patrol Headquarters exploratory ship and kills its pilot, Iota. Emerging from the grounded alien craft, a mysterious being, from the Nebula M-78 in the fortieth galaxy, appears and to repay Iota for the wrong done to him, gives him his life and a special capsule: "...you and I will become one and we will fight as one for the peace of Earth for all time to come. You will remain in your present form, Iota. Whenever you are in trouble use the Beta Capsule and you, Iota, will become Ultraman."

Stories depict the exploits of Iota, a member of the Scientific Patrol, as he, in his secret alias as Ultraman, battles dangerous and monstrous alien phenomena. Produced in Japan; dubbed in English. Characters are not given screen credit. Created by Eiji Tsuburaya.

ULTRAMAN—30 minutes—Syndicated 1967. 39 episodes.

THE UNCLE AL SHOW

Children. Music, songs, stories, and puppet acts.

CAST

Uncle Al (Host)	Al Lewis
Cinderella	Janet Green
Captain Windy	Wanda Lewis

Also: Larry Smith and his puppets.

THE UNCLE AL SHOW—60 minutes —ABC—October 18, 1958 - September 19, 1959.

UNCLE CROC'S BLOCK

Children. A spoof of children's television programs. The series itself, set in a television studio, focuses on the misadventures that befall Uncle Croc, the costumed (as a crocodile) host of "Croc's Block" a kids show he detests doing. Live action segments are coupled with short cartoons.

CAST

Uncle Croc	Charles Nelson Reilly
Basil Bitterbottom, the director	Jonathan Harris
Rabbit Ears, Croc's assistant	Johnny Silver
	Alfie Wise
The $6.95 Man	Bob Ridgley

Voices (for the cartoon segments): Allan Melvin, Kenneth Mars, Alan Oppenheimer, Bob Ridgley, Lennie Weinrib.

Music: Yvette Blais, Jeff Michael.

Cartoon Segments:

The Uncle Floyd Show. Floyd Vivino and his puppet Oogie.

Fraidy Cat. The misadventures of a cat who, having lost eight of his nine lives, struggles to protect his last remaining life.

The Mush Puppies. The hectic exploits of MUSH (Mangy Unwanted Shabby Heroes), Northwest Mounted Canadian Police dogs.

Wacky and Packy. The story concerns the misadventures of a caveman named Packy and his pet elephant, Wacky, who were caught in an earthquake and transported to modern times.

UNCLE CROC'S BLOCK—55 minutes—ABC—September 6, 1975 - October 18, 1975; 30 minutes—October 25, 1975 - February 14, 1976.

THE UNCLE FLOYD SHOW

Children. Set against the background of a boarding house, the program features music, songs, and comedy sketches that revolve around the antics of the strange characters who inhabit the mythical premises. Ingen-ious puppets (also roomers), coupled with fan club news, birthday announcements, visual displays of viewer drawings, and contests for prizes heightens the program's mystique.

Host-Producer-Creator: Floyd Vivino (as Uncle Floyd).

Regulars: Pat Cupo, Scott Gordon, Marc Nathan, Tony Petrillo.

Announcer: John Pichitino.

Director: Ralph Van Kuiken, Marc Nathan.

Among the characters portrayed by Floyd Vivino:

Rocky Rock 'N' Roll; Briscoe T. Fardell, a con-artist; Don Ho-Hum, the Hawaiian Singer; Don Goomba, a Godfather type character; Flojo, the TV clown; Strongzini; Cowboy Charlie, the off-key singer; Vinnie, the carpenter; The Storyman; Fatso Popasso, the glutton; Senor La Basura, the entrepreneur.

Main Puppets: Oogie, the mischievous boy; Poogie the dog; Donkey Oatie, Senor's cohort; Mr. Jones, the intoxicated singer; Old Hutch the sea captain; Mr. Bones, the dancing skeleton.

THE UNCLE FLOYD SHOW–30 minutes–Premiered: September 30, 1975. Though aired basically in New York and New Jersey (over WBTB-TV, Ch. 68), the program is known in many areas of the country and as faraway as Greece.

UNCLE JOHNNY COONS

Children. Stories, silent films, and sketches that relate good habits to children.

Host: Johnny Coons, ventriloquist.

His dummy: George.

Announcer: Bruce Roberts.

Producer: James Green.

Sponsor: Lever Brothers.

UNCLE JOHNNY COONS–30 minutes–CBS 1954.

UNCLE MISTELTOE AND HIS ADVENTURES

Children. Background: Wonderland. The series focuses on the lives of the magic little people (puppets) who live on Candy Cane Lane, a magic street where dreams come true.

Puppets: Uncle Misteltoe, the jovial story teller; Olio, Molio, and Rolio; Aunt Judy; Skippy Monkey; Obediah Pig; Tony Pony; Humphrey Mouse.

Voices-Puppeteers: The Marshall Field Marionette Company.

UNCLE MISTELTOE AND HIS ADVENTURES–15 minutes–ABC 1950.

UNCOVERED

See title: "Mark Saber."

UNDERCURRENT

Anthology. Retitled episodes of dramas that were originally aired via "The Web."

Included:

Trapmates. The story of a near victim who turns the tables on a would-be burglar by blackmailing him as a partner in an attempted holdup.
Starring: Hugh Beaumont.

The Old Lady's Tears. The story of a private detective, assigned to find the missing grandson of a wealthy old woman, who suddenly finds himself involved in two murders.
Starring: Lex Barker, Jean Byron, Lurene Tuttle.

Integrity. The story of a police informer who poses as a gambler to track down thieves in North Africa.
Starring: Jean Pierre Aumont, Jay Novello, Leon Asken.

UNDERCURRENT–30 minutes–CBS–June 1955 - September 1955.

UNDERDOG

Animated Cartoon. Background: Washington, D.C. The exploits of a lovable, humble dog, Shoeshine Boy, alias Underdog, a dauntless and fearless crusader for justice.

Additional Characters: Sweet Polly Purebred, ace television reporter; Sinister Bar Sinister, an evil scientist; and Cad, his aide.

Characters' Voices
Underdog   Wally Cox
Sweet Polly Purebred Norma McMillan
Additional Voices: Sandy Becker,

Allen Swift, Dello Stokes, Mort Marshall, Kenny Delmar, George S. Irving, Ben Stone.

UNDERDOG—30 minutes. NBC—October 3, 1964 - September 3, 1966; CBS—September 10, 1966 - September 2, 1967; NBC—September 7, 1968 - September 1, 1973. 125 episodes.

THE UNDERSEA WORLD OF JACQUES COUSTEAU

Documentary. Films relating the undersea explorations of Jacques Cousteau and the men of his ship, *Calypso*.
Narrators: Jacques Cousteau; Rod Serling; Joseph Campanella.
Music: Lyn Murray.

THE UNDERSEA WORLD OF JACQUES COUSTEAU—60 minutes —ABC—Premiered: January 8, 1968. Broadcast as a series of specials.

THE UNEXPECTED

Anthology. Dramatizations depicting the plight of people trapped in sudden, unexpected situations.
Host: Herbert Marshall.

THE UNEXPECTED—30 minutes— NBC 1952.

UNICORN TALES

Children. Twentieth-century adaptations of classic fairy tales.
Music: Jack Feldman.
Executive Producer: Nick DeNoia.

Producer: William P. Milling.

UNICORN TALES—30 minutes—Syndicated 1977.

UNION PACIFIC

Western. Background: Dale, Wyoming, 1880s. The saga of the final linking between East and West (Omaha to Cheyenne) of the Union Pacific Railroad.

CAST

Bart McClelland, the operations head	Jeff Morrow
Bill Kinkaid, the chief surveyor	Judd Pratt
Georgia, the owner of the local dancehall	Susan Cummings

UNION PACIFIC—30 minutes—Syndicated 1958. 39 episodes.

UNIVERSAL STAR TIME

Anthology. Retitled episodes of dramas originally aired via "The Bob Hope Chrysler Theatre."

Included:

A Small Rebellion. A playwright attempts to persuade a famous actress to star in a play that he has written and believes will be a success.

CAST
Sara Lescaut: Simone Signoret; Michael Kolinos: George Maharis; Noel Greb: Sam Leven.

Escape Into Jeopardy. Working with authorities, a convicted counterfeiter escapes from prison to assist in exposing a counterfeiting ring.

CAST

Larry Martin: James Franciscus.

Two Is The Number. Police efforts to prove that a woman is responsible for the death of a hoodlum.

CAST

Jenny Dworak: Shelley Winters; Dave Breslau: Martin Balsam.

The Fifth Passenger. A British Intelligence officer attempts to discover if a naval hero is leaking top-secret information to the Soviets.

CAST

Peter Carrington: Mel Ferrer; Jane Day: Dana Wynter.

UNIVERSAL STAR TIME—60 minutes—Syndicated 1971. 30 episodes.

UNK AND ANDY

Children. Amied at preschoolers, the program attempts to relate facts about nature's wildlife through the use of alphabet animals (i.e., letters of the alphabet are drawn to resemble animals—from Andy Auk to Zachary Zebra).

Host-Cartoonist: Jack Kenaston as Uncle Jack.

Assistant: Andy Auk, an animated character voiced by Jack Kenaston.

Producer-Director: Jack Kenaston.

UNK AND ANDY—15 minutes—Syndicated 1950. 25 episodes.

THE UNTAMED WORLD

Documentary. Films exploring the people and animals of the remote regions of the world.

Narrator: Philip Carey.

Music: Mort Garson.

THE UNTAMED WORLD—30 minutes—NBC—January 11, 1969 - August 30, 1969. Syndicated.

THE UNTOUCHABLES

Crime Drama. Background: Chicago during the 1930s, the era of Prohibition and gangland rule. The exploits of the Federal Special Squad, an elite team of U.S. Treasury Department agents known as the Untouchables, as they, under the leadership of Eliot Ness, battle the forces of underworld corruption. A realistic and penetrating look at the violence and corruption that shook America's past.

CAST

Eliot Ness	Robert Stack
Agent Martin Flaherty	Jerry Paris
Agent William Longfellow	Abel Fernandez
Agent Jack Rossman	Steve London
Agent Enrico Rossi	Nicholas Georgiade
Agent Cam Allison	Anthony George
Agent Lee Hobson	Paul Picerni
Mobster Frank Nitti	Bruce Gordon
Mobster Al Capone	Neville Brand

Narrator: Walter Winchell.

Music: Wilbur Hatch; Nelson Riddle.

Executive Producer: Jerry Thorpe, Leonard Freeman.

Producer: Howard Hoffman, Alan A. Armer, Alvin Cooperman, Lloyd Richards, Fred Freiberger, Charles Russell.

Director: John Peyser, Stewart Rosenberg, Robert Butler, Walter Grauman, Ida Lupino.

THE UNTOUCHABLES–60 minutes –ABC–October 15, 1959 - September 10, 1963. 114 episodes. Syndicated.

UPBEAT

Musical Variety. The top songs, dances, and recording personalities of the day.

Versions:
Upbeat–15 minutes–CBS–July 15, 1955 - September 2, 1955.
Hosts: Guests of the week including: Mindy Carson, Teresa Brewer, Georgia Gibbs, The Four Lads, Don Cornell.
Dancers: The Tommy Morton Troupe.
Orchestra: Russ Case.

Upbeat–60 minutes–Syndicated 1966.
Host: Don Webster.
Featured: The Upbeat Dancers.
Music: Provided by guests.

UPSTAIRS, DOWNSTAIRS

See title: "Masterpiece Theatre."

UP TO PAAR

See title: "Jack Paar."

UPTOWN JUBILEE

Variety. Performances by black entertainers.
Host: Willie Bryant.

Producer: Barry Wood.
Director: John Wray.

UPTOWN JUBILEE–60 minutes– CBS 1949.

U.S. BORDER PATROL

Drama. The work of federal agents in conjunction with the U.S. Border Patrol.
Starring: Richard Webb as Don Jagger, deputy chief of the U.S. Border Patrol.

U.S. BORDER PATROL–30 minutes –Syndicated 1958. 39 episodes.

U.S. MARSHAL

See title: "The Sheriff of Cochise."

THE U.S. STEEL HOUR

Anthology. Dramatic and comedic productions.
Producer: Norman Felton, David Alexander, George Kondolf.
Sponsor: U.S. Steel.
Included:

The Bogey Man. Fearing to lose his mother's love, a young boy attempts to thwart her plans to remarry.

CAST
Madge Collins: Celeste Holm; Jack Roberts: Robert Preston; Tony Collins: Darryl Richard.

No Time For Sergeants. The misadventures of Will Stockdale, a naive Georgia farmboy who is drafted into the Air Force. Later made into a feature film.

CAST
Will Stockdale: Andy Griffith; Sgt. King: Harry Clark; Ben Whitledge: Eddie LeRoy; Captain: Alexander Clark.

Freighter. After twenty-five years as the skipper of the freighter *Singapore,* a captain discovers it is to end its operation. The story relates his attempts to adjust to the prospect of losing his beloved job.

CAST
Captain: Henry Hull; Scotty: Thomas Mitchell; Clay: James Daly.

Wish On The Moon. The story of two girls: Frances Barclay, who is determined to become an actress; and Olivia Beech, a carefree art student.

CAST
First version 1953: Frances Barclay: Eva Marie Saint; Olivia Beech: Phyllis Kirk.
Second version 1959: Frances Barclay: Peggy Ann Garner; Olivia Beech: Erin O'Brien.

THE U.S. STEEL HOUR—60 minutes —CBS—October 27, 1953 - June 11, 1963.

U

VAGABOND

Travel. Visits to interesting and unusual places.
Host-Narrator: Don Hobart.

Music: George Wasch.

VAGABOND—30 minutes—Syndicated 1959. 39 episodes.

VACATION PLAYHOUSE

Pilot Films. Proposed comedy series.

Included:

The Hoofer. The misadventures of two small-town vaudevillians in Chicago as they struggle to make the big time.

CAST
Donald Dugan: Donald O'Connor; Freddy Brady: Soupy Sales; Brainsley Gordon: Jerome Cowan.

Ivy League. The misadventures of Bull Mitchell, a retired marine who enrolls as a college freshman.

CAST
Bull: William Bendix; Timmy: Tim Hovey.

The Two Of Us. The story of a young boy who prefers the world of fantasy he has created from his mother's book illustrations to that of making real friends.

CAST
Elizabeth: Patricia Crowley; Chris: Bill Mumy; Captain Gibson: Barry Livingston; Helen: Mary Jane Croft.

Off We Go. The misadventures of a sixteen-year-old boy who enlists with the U.S. Army air corps.

CAST

Rod Ryan: Michael Burns; Jefferson Dale: Dick Foran; Lt. Sue Chamberlain: Nancy Kovack; Debbie Trowbridge: Anne Jilliann.

Mickey And The Contessa. The complications that arise when a football coach applies for a housekeeper and acquires a beautiful Hungarian contessa.

CAST

Mickey Brennan: Mickey Shaughnessey; Contessa Czigonia: Eva Gabor; Argey Tanner: John Fiedler; Sissy Brennan: Ann Marshall.

VACATION PLAYHOUSE—30 minutes—CBS—June 1963 - September 1963; June 1964 - September 1964; June 1965 - September 1965; June 1966 - September 1966. 27 episodes.

THE VAL DOONICAN SHOW

Musical Variety.

Host: Val Doonican.

Regulars: Bob Todd, Bernard Cribbins, The Norman Maen Dancers, The Mike Sammes Singers.

Announcer: Paul Griffith.

Orchestra: Jack Parnell; Kenny Woods.

THE VAL DOONICAN SHOW—60 minutes—ABC—June 5, 1971 - August 14, 1971.

British Version (upon which the above British produced American telecast version is based):

The Val Doonican Show—60 minutes—B.B.C.-1 from London—1967.

Host: Val Doonican.

Regulars: Nana Mouskouri, Daniel Remey, The Pattersons, The Gayos, The Adam Singers.

Orchestra: Peter Knight.

VALENTINE'S DAY

Comedy. Background: New York City. The life and times of playboy Valentine Farrow, the nonfiction editor for a Park Avenue publishing house.

CAST

Valentine Farrow	Tony Franciosa
Rocky Sin, his valet, a Chinese-American con merchant	Jack Soo
Libby, his secretary	Janet Waldo
Mr. Dunstall, his employer	Jerry Hausner
Fipple, the neighborhood handyman	Eddie Quillan

Music: Jeff Alexander.

VALENTINE'S DAY—30 minutes—ABC—September 18, 1964 - September 10, 1965. 34 episodes.

VALIANT LADY

Serial. The dramatic story of Helen Emerson, a woman who, despite financial strain, struggles to raise her three children.

CAST

Helen Emerson	Nancy Coleman
	Flora Campbell
Her husband	Jerome Cowan
Her son, nineteen years of age	James Kirkwood

Her daughter,
seventeen years of
age   Anne Pearson
Her daughter,
nine years of
age   Lydia Reed
Margo, a
friend   Dolores Sutton
Also: Betty Oakes, Marc Cramer,
Abby Lewis, Earl Hammon.

Organist: John Gart.

Producer: Carl Green, Leonard Blair.

Sponsor: Toni; General Mills.

Program Open:

Announcer: "Valiant Lady, the story
of a brave woman and her brilliant but unstable husband; the
story of her struggle to keep his
feet planted firmly on the path-
way to success."

VALIANT LADY—15 minutes—CBS
—October 9, 1953 - August 16, 1957.

Valley of the Dinosaurs. Left to right: Greg,
Kim, Katie, and John (offering a hand to)
Gorak. Behind Gorak: Gera (left) and Tana.
Bottom right: Lock (holding Glomb's tail)
and Digger the dog.© *Hanna-Barbera Produc-
tions.*

VALLEY OF THE DINOSAURS

Animated Cartoon. Exploring an
uncharted river canyon in the
Amazon, a twentieth-century family,
the Butlers, are engulfed by a whirlpool, propelled through an underground cavern and transported to a
time past, the prehistoric era, where
they befriend a cave family parallel to
them. Stories depict their struggles for
survival. Scientific principles are illustrated as both families assist and learn
from one another.

Characters:

The Modern Family:

John Butler, the father, a science
instructor; Kim Butler, his wife; Katie
Butler, their daughter; Greg Butler,
their son; and Digger, their pet dog.

The Cave Family:

Gorak, the father; Gera, his wife;
Tana, their daughter; Lock, their son;
and Glomb, their pet stegasaurus.

Characters' Voices

John Butler	Mike Road
Kim Butler	Shannon Farnon
Katie Butler	Margene Fudenna
Greg Butler	Jackie Haley
Gorak	Alan Oppenheimer
Gera	Joan Gardner
Lock	Steacy Bertheau
Tana	Melanie Baker

Music: Hoyt Curtin.

Executive Producer: William Hanna,
Joseph Barbera.

Director: Charles A. Nichols.

VALLEY OF THE DINOSAURS—25
minutes—CBS—September 7, 1974 -
September 4, 1976. 16 episodes.
Syndicated.

VAN DYKE AND COMPANY

Variety. Music, songs, and comedy sketches.

Host: Dick Van Dyke.

Regulars: Lois January, Marilyn Soko, Mickey Rose, Pat Proft, Andy Kaufman, Al Bloomfield, Bob Einstein, Chuck McCann, The Los Angeles Mime Company.

Ochestra: Lex De Avezedo.

Musical Coordinator: D'Vaughn Pershing.

Choreography: Lester Wilson.

Executive Producer: Byron Paul.

Producer: Allan Blye, Bob Einstein.

Director: John Moffitt.

VAN DYKE AND COMPANY–60 minutes–NBC–September 20, 1976 - December 30, 1976.

VANITY FAIR

Women. Interviews, guests, beauty tips, and advice.

Hostess: Robin Chandler.

Co-hostess: Dorothy Doan.

Announcer: Tony Marvin.

Orchestra: Johnny Green.

Producer: John Cazabon, Gil Fates, Frances Buss.

Director: Frances Buss.

Sponsor: Maiden Form Bras; Airwick Air Freshner.

VANITY FAIR–30 and 45 minute versions–CBS–1948 - 1951.

VAUDEVILLE

Variety. Performances by Vaudeville comedians and re-creations of its associated comedy by new talent discoveries.

Guest Hosts: Milton Berle, Steve Allen and Jayne Meadows, Edgar Bergen, Eddie Foy, Jr., Rudy Vallee, Jack Carter, Red Buttons.

The Card Girl: Donna Jean Young.

Orchestra: George Wyle.

Executive Producer: Burt Rosen.

Producer: Mort Green.

Director: Jack Scott.

VAUDEVILLE–60 minutes–Syndicated 1975.

VAUGHN MONROE

Listed: The television programs of singer-bandleader Vaughn Monroe.

The Vaughn Monroe Show–Musical Variety–30 minutes–CBS–October 10, 1950 - July 3, 1951.

Host: Vaughn Monroe.

Regulars: Shayne Cogan, Ada Lynne, Ziggy Latent, Henry Davis, Olga Suarey, The Moon Maidens.

Orchestra: Vaughn Monroe.

The Vaughn Monroe Show–Musical Variety–15 minutes–NBC–August 31, 1954 - September 28, 1954.

Host: Vaughn Monroe.

Regulars: McCaffrey and Susan; The Satisfiers.

Orchestra: Richard Hayman.

The Vaughn Monroe Show–Musical Variety–15 minutes–NBC–August 31, 1954 - September 28, 1954.

Host: Vaughn Monroe.

Vocalists: The Tunestones.

Orchestra: Richard Maltby.

THE VEIL

Anthology. Dramatizations based on incredible but true phenomena.

Host-Performer: Boris Karloff.

THE VEIL—30 minutes—Syndicated 1958.

THE VERDICT IS YOURS

Courtroom Drama. Dramatizations based on actual court records. The studio audience comprises the jury, which relates the verdict at the end of the trial.

Judges, Witness, Plaintiffs: Guest actors.

Defense Council: Practicing attorneys.

Court Reporters: Jim McKay; Bill Stout.

THE VERDICT IS YOURS—30 minutes—CBS—July 3, 1958 - September 28, 1962.

British Version:

The Verdict Is Yours—30 minutes—Granada TV from Manchester—1958.

CAST
Martin Benson, Simon Kester, David Ensor, John McGregor.

VERSATILE VARIETIES

A variety series, broadcast on NBC in 1949 with host George Givat, and Jerry Terune and his Orchestra.

VERSATILE VARIETIES

Variety. Performances by undiscovered professional talent.

Hosts: Bob Russell; Harold Barry.

Regulars: Janis Paige, Leonardo & Zola, The Delmars, The Youman Brothers & Frances.

Orchestra: Jerry Jerome.

VERSATILE VARIETIES—30 minutes—NBC 1950.

VERSATILE VARIETIES

Musical Variety.

Hostess: Lady Iris Mountbatten.

Orchestra: Mark Towers; Bernie Sands.

Commercial Spokeswoman: Anne Francis.

Producer: Charles Basch, Frances Scott.

Director: Mark Hawley.

Sponsor: Bonafide Mills.

VERSATILE VARIETIES—30 minutes—CBS 1951. Also known as "The Bonny Maid Versatile Varieties Program."

VIC DAMONE

Listed: The television programs of singer-actor Vic Damone.

The Vic Damone Show—Musical Variety—CBS—30 minutes—July 2, 1956 - September 1956.

Host: Vic Damone.

Announcer: Rex Marshall.

Orchestra: Tutti Carmarata.

The Vic Damone Show—Musical Variety—30 minutes—CBS—July 3, 1957 - September 1957.

Host: Vic Damone.

Regulars: Peggy King, The Spellbinders.

Announcer: Johnny Olsen.

Orchestra: Bert Farber.

The Lively Ones—Musical Variety—30 minutes—NBC—1962; 1963. See title.

Dean Martin Presents The Vic Damone Show—Musical Variety—60 minutes—NBC—July 1967 - September 1967. Rebroadcasts: NBC—60 minutes—July 8, 1971 - August 19, 1971.
August 19, 1971.

Host: Vic Damone.

Regulars: Carol Lawrence, Gail Martin.

Orchestra: Les Brown.

THE VICTOR BORGE SHOW

Variety.

Host: Victor Borge.

Orchestra: Phil Ingallis.

THE VICTOR BORGE SHOW—30 minutes—NBC 1951.

VICTORY AT SEA

Documentary. Films detailing the United States Naval operations during World War II.

Narrator: Leonard Graves.

Music: The NBC Symphony Orchestra, conducted by Robert Russell Bennett.

Symphonic Score (13 hours): Richard Rodgers.

VICTORY AT SEA—30 minutes—NBC—October 16, 1952 - April 19, 1953. 26 episodes. Syndicated.

VIDEO CHEF

Cooking. The preparation and making of foreign and American meals.

Host: Jean Holt.

VIDEO CHEF—15 minutes—ABC 1952.

VIDEO VILLAGE

Game. Background: Video Village, a huge game board composed of three lanes of squares, each of which are marked as in a game (e.g., "Lose one turn"; "Move ahead two spaces"; "Go to jail"). Two competing players. Players move up and down the lanes via the roll of two dice (chuck-a-luck). The player who is first to reach the finish line is the winner and receives merchandise prizes.

Host (The Mayor): Jack Narz; Monty Hall.

Assistants: Eileen Barton; Joanna Copeland.

Announcer (The Town Crier): Kenny Williams.

Versions:
VIDEO VILLAGE—30 minutes—CBS —July 11, 1960 - June 11, 1962.

VIDEO VILLAGE JUNIOR (a children's version of the adult game)—30 minutes—September 1960 - June 16, 1962.

THE VIM TALENT SEARCH

Variety. Performances by aspiring entertainers. Highlight of the program was its search to find "Miss U.S. Television." Being new, the medium prompted many local stations to sponsor a "Miss Television Contest," wherein local beauties competed for titles such as "Miss Chicago TV," "Miss New York TV," etc. Girls, at least eighteen years of age, married or single, attractive, and possessing several talents, were eligible. Most notable of the winners was Edythe Adams, the local New York winner who was crowned "Miss U.S. Television of 1950." Today known as Edie Adams, she received prizes and awards valued at $10,000 plus a contract for TV performances.

Host: Dick Kollmar (1949); Skitch Henderson (1950).

Sponsor: Vim.

THE VIM TALENT SEARCH—30 minutes—NBC—1949-1950.

THE VIN SCULLY SHOW

Variety. Guests, music, and celebrity interviews.

Host: Vin Scully.

Announcer: Harry Blackstone Jr.

Orchestra: H.B. Barnum.

THE VIN SCULLY SHOW—30 minutes—CBS—January 15, 1973 - March 23, 1973.

THE VINCENT LOPEZ SHOW

Musical Variety.

Host: Vincent Lopez.

Regulars: Judy Lynn, Teddy Norman, Eddie O'Connor, Johnny Messner, Johnny Amorosa, Danny Davis.

THE VINCENT LOPEZ SHOW—30 minutes—CBS—October 13, 1956 - April 27, 1957.

V.I.P.

Biography. Through films, photographs, and interviews, the lives of Very Important People are recalled.

V.I.P.—15 minutes—Syndicated 1963.

THE VIRGINIA GRAHAM SHOW

Talk-Variety.

Hostess: Virginia Graham.

Music: The Ellie Frankel Quintet; The Jimmy Rowles Quartet.

THE VIRGINIA GRAHAM SHOW —60 and 30 minute versions (depending on the local station)—Syndicated 1970.

THE VIRGINIAN

Western. Background: The Shiloh Ranch in Medicine Bow, Wyoming, 1880s. Events in the shaping of Wyoming as seen through the experiences of a mysterious drifter, the man everybody respects, but nobody really knows, The Virginian, foreman of the Shiloh Ranch.

CAST

The Virginian
(referred to as
Jim in several
episodes)   James Drury

Judge Henry Garth,
the first owner
of the Shiloh
Ranch   Lee J. Cobb
Trampas, the assistant
foreman   Doug McClure
Molly Wood, the newspaper
publisher   Pippa Scott
Betsy Garth, the judge's
daughter   Roberta Shore
Steve Hill, a ranch
hand   Gary Clarke
Emmett Ryker, the deputy
sheriff   Clu Gulager
Randy Garth, the judge's
son   Randy Boone
Belden, a ranch
hand   L. Q. Jones
Jennifer Garth,
the judge's orphaned
niece   Diane Roter
Morgan Starr, the
temporary owner
of the Shiloh
Ranch   John Dehner
Sheriff Mark Abbott   Ross Elliot
John Grainger, the
second owner of
the Shiloh
Ranch   Charles Bickford
Elizabeth Grainger, his
niece   Sara Lane
Stacy Grainger, his
grandson   Don Quine
Clay Grainger, the
third owner of
the Shiloh
Ranch   John McIntire
Holly Grainger, his
wife   Jeanette Nolan
David Sutton, a ranch
hand   David Hartman
Jim Horn, a ranch
hand   Tim Matheson
Sheriff Brannon   Harlan Warde
Gene, a ranch
hand   Jean Peloquin
The town bartenders The Irish Rovers

Music: Leonard Rosenman; Percy

Faith; Hans Salter; Leo Shuken.
Producer: Roy Huggins, Jules Schermer, Richard Irving, Winston Miller, Frank Price.

THE VIRGINIAN—90 minutes—NBC —September 19, 1962 - September 9, 1970. 225 episodes. Syndicated.

Revised format: "The Men From Shiloh."

Background: The Shiloh Ranch in Medicine Bow, Wyoming, 1890s. The exploits of four men: Colonel Alan MacKenzie, Englishman, the owner of the ranch; The Virginian, the foreman; and hired hands Trampas and Roy Tate, as they attempt to maintain law and order.

CAST
The Virginian   James Drury
Colonel Alan
MacKenzie   Stewart Granger
Trampas   Doug McClure
Roy Tate   Lee Majors

Music: Leonard Rosenman.

THE MEN FROM SHILOH—90 minutes—NBC—September 16, 1970 - September 8, 1971. 24 episodes.

THE VISE

Anthology. Dramatizations depicting the plight of people who are caught in a web of their own misdeeds.

Host: Ron Rondell.

Included:

Set Of Murder. Facing financial ruin, a wealthy businessman plots to save himself by murdering an inventor and cashing in on his invention.

CAST
Clifford Evans, Honor Blackman, Martin Baddley.

The Secret Place. Finding some old love letters, a neglected wife plots to test her husband's jealousy.

CAST
Margaret Rawlings, John Stewart.

The Eavsdropper. The story of an older woman's romance with a younger man.

CAST
Milda Parley, Frederick Leister.

Let Murder Be Done. Seeking to marry a younger woman, a man plots to murder his rich but older wife.

CAST
Dennis Price, Avis Scott.

THE VISE—30 minutes—ABC—October 1, 1954 - June 27, 1957. Produced in England.

VISION ON

Educational. Through total visual entertainment (cartoons, sketches, and songs) aspects of the adult world are related to children with impaired hearing. Produced in England.

Host: Tony Hart.

Hostess: Patricia Keysell.

Regulars: Wilfred Lunn, Ben Benison, David Cleveland, Humphrey Umbrage.

Music: Recorded.

VISION ON—30 minutes—Syndicated 1973.

VISIONS

Anthology. Dramatizations of American plays written especially for television.

Music: Mark Snow.

Music Theme: Joe Raposo.

Producer: Barbara Schultz.

Director: Paul Bogart.

Included:

The War Widow. The story centers on the love between two young women: Amy, a lonely girl living with her mother while her husband is serving overseas during W.W. I; and Jenny, an independent woman struggling to succeed as a photographer.

CAST
Amy: Pamela Bellwood; Jenny: Frances Lee McCain; Sarah: Katherine Bard; Emily: Maxine Stuart; Kate: Barbara Cason; Annie: Nan Martin.

Liza's Pioneer Diary. A drama that chronicles the journeys of a young pioneer woman through Oregon in 1848.

CAST
Liza Stedman: Ayn Ruymen; Eben Stedman: Dennis Redfield; Aunt Sara: Katherine Helmond.

VISIONS—60 minutes—PBS—October 21, 1976 - February 10, 1977.

VISUAL GIRL

Advice. Geared to teenage girls. Background: The Visual Workshop. Ideas and suggestions concerning exercise, makeup, and skin care are presented.

Host: Ron Russell.

Model Expert: Lois Rose.

Music: Recorded.

VISUAL GIRL—30 minutes—Syndicated 1971.

VIVA VALDEZ

Comedy. Background: East Los Angeles, California. The trials and tribulations of the Valdezes, a Mexican-American family, as they strive to maintain their traditional values in a rapidly changing world.

CAST

Sophie Valdez, the mother	Carmen Zapata
Luis Valdez, the father, a plumber	Rodolfo Hoyos
Victor Valdez, their son	James Victor
Connie Valdez, their daughter	Lisa Mordente
Ernesto Valdez, their son	Nelson D. Cuevas
Pepe Valdez, their son	Claudio Martinez
Jerry Ramerez, their cousin	Jorge Cervera, Jr.

Music: Shorty Rogers.

Executive Producer: Stan Jacobson, Bernard Rothman, Jack Wohl.

Director: Alan Rafkin.

The Valdez Address: 3632½ La Hamber Street.

VIVA VALDEZ—30 minutes—ABC—May 31, 1976 - September 6, 1976.

VOICE OF FIRESTONE

Music. Classical and semiclassical concerts.

Host-Narrator: John Daly.

Vocalists: The Howard Barlow Chorus.

Announcer: Hugh James.

Orchestra: Howard Barlow.

Producer: Charles Polachek, Herbert Swope, Jr., Frederick Heider.

Director: Clark Jones.

Sponsor: Firestone.

VOICE OF FIRESTONE—60 minutes—NBC—September 5, 1949 - June 1, 1959. Premiered as a special: NBC: March 22, 1948.

VOYAGE TO THE BOTTOM OF THE SEA

Adventure. Era: 1983. The experiences of the men and officers of the atomic-powered submarine *Seaview,* as they explore and battle the sinister elements of the ocean floor on behalf the U.S. government's attempts to further scientific research.

CAST

Admiral Harriman Nelson	Richard Basehart
Cdr. Lee Crane	David Hedison
Chief Petty Officer Curley Jones	Henry Kulky
Chief Francis Sharkey	Terry Becker
Commander Chip Morton	Bob Dowdell
Crewman Kowalski ("Ski")	Del Moore
Crewman Sparks, the radar technician	Arch Whiting
Doc, the medical officer	Richard Bull
	Wright King
	Wayne Heffley

Crewman Patterson   Paul Trinka
Crewman Stu Riley   Allan Hunt
Crewman Malone   Mark Slade

Music: Paul Sawtell, Harry Geller, Lionel Newman, Leith Stevens, Jerry Goldsmith, Nelson Riddle.

Producer: Irwin Allen.

Director: Harry Harris, Charles R. Rondeau, Alan Crosland, Jr., Sobey Martin, Sutton Roley, Gerald Mayer, Josef Leytes, Felix Feist, James Goldstone, Alex March, Tom Gries, Justis Addiss, Robert Sparr, Jerry Hopper, Harmon Jones, James Clark, Nathan Juran, Irwin Allen.

The Wackiest Ship in the Army. The *Kiwi.* © *Screen Gems.*

VOYAGE TO THE BOTTOM OF THE SEA–60 minutes–ABC–September 14, 1964 - September 15, 1968. 110 episodes. Syndicated.

w

THE WACKIEST SHIP IN THE ARMY

Adventure. Background: The South Pacific during World War II. The story of the *USS Kiwi,* a leaky, two-masted 1871 schooner incorporated by U.S. Army Intelligence to assist in winning the war. Posing as neutral Swedish sailors, its crew attempts to observe Japanese movements, assist allies, and inform officials of enemy strategy. Spiced with light comedy. Based on the motion picture.

CAST
Major Simon Butcher   Jack Warden

Lt. Richard "Rip"
    Riddle   Gary Collins
Chief Miller   Mike Kellin
Trivers   Fred Smoot
Tyler   Don Penny
Finch   Duke Hobbie
Nagurski   Rudy Solari
Hollis   Mark Slade
General Cross   Bill Zuckert
Admiral Beckett   Charles Irving

THE WACKIEST SHIP IN THE ARMY–60 minutes–NBC–September 19, 1965 - September 4, 1966. 29 episodes. Syndicated.

WACKO

Children's Variety. Background: The Wacko Clubhouse. A series of unrelated, outlandish comedy and musical skits geared to children.

Starring: Julie McWhirter, Bo Kaprall, Charles Fleischer.

Regulars: Millicent Crisp, Doug Cox,

Bob Comfort, Rick Kellard.

Music: Stu Gardner.

Executive Producer: Chris Bearde, Bob Wood.

Producer: Coslough Johnson, Richard Adamson.

Director: Stanley Dorfman.

Animation: John Wilson.

WACKO—25 minutes—CBS—Premiered: September 17, 1977.

THE WACKY RACES

Animated Cartoon. The saga of a cross-country automobile race. Episodes depict the endless and devious efforts of the evil Dick Dastardly to secure the winning prize, the title "The World's Wackiest Racer."

Competitors: Pat Pending, the ingenious inventor, who drives the Convert-A-Car; Rufus Ruftut and Sawtooth, drivers of the Buzz Wagon; Penelope Pitstop, "the glamour gal of the gas pedal," who drives the Compact Pussycat; The Slag Brothers, Rock and Gravel, drivers of the Boulder Mobile; The Ant Hill Mob, drivers of the Bulletproof Bomb; The Red Max, pilot of the Crimson Haybailer; The Gruesome Twosome, drivers of the Creepy Coupe; Luke and Blubber Bear, drivers of the Arkansas Chugabug; and Dick Dastardly and his aide Mutley (a snickering dog), who command the Mean Machine.

Voices: Paul Winchell, Janet Waldo, Mel Blanc, Don Messick.

Narrator: Dave Willock.

Music: Hoyt Curtin.

THE WACKY RACES—30 minutes—CBS—September 14, 1968 - September 5, 1970.

THE WACKY WORLD OF JONATHAN WINTERS

See title: "Jonathan Winters."

WAGON TRAIN

Western. Era: The 1880s. The saga of a wagon train's journey from the midwest to California. Episodes focus on the lives of individuals who have booked passage—people, both the troubled and carefree, who are alive in the dream of promise that awaits them at their journey's end.

CAST

Seth Adams, the wagonmaster (1957-1961)	Ward Bond
Chris Hale, the wagonmaster (1961-1965)	John McIntire
Flint McCullough, the trail scout	Robert Horton
Charlie Wooster, the cook	Frank McGrath
Bill Hawks, a trail scout	Terry Wilson
Cooper Smith, a trail scout	Robert Fuller
Duke Shannon, a trail scout	Denny Miller
Barnaby West, a teenager who, under Hale's care, is riding with the train	Michael Burns
Kate Crowley, Hale's romantic interest (semiregular role)	Barbara Stanwyck

Wagon Train. Left to right: Frank McGrath, John McIntire, Terry Wilson, Robert Fuller.

Music: Melvyn Lenard; Jerome Moross; Hans Salter; Richard Sendry.

WAGON TRAIN—60 minutes—NBC—September 18, 1957 - September 12, 1962; ABC—60 and 90 minute versions—September 19, 1962 - September 5, 1965. Syndicated. Rebroadcasts, under the title, "Major Adams, Trailmaster"—60 minutes—ABC—January 6, 1963 - September 18, 1963. 442 episodes. Also known as: "Trailmaster."

WAIT TIL YOUR FATHER GETS HOME

Animated Cartoon. Background: Los Angeles, California. The trials and tribulations that befall Harry Boyle, president of the Boyle Restaurant Supply Company, as he, an old-fashioned father, struggles to bridge the generation gap that exists between him and his progressive children.

Characters' Voices
Harry Boyle   Tom Bosley
Irma Boyle, his

wife	Joan Gerber
Alice Boyle, their daughter	Kristina Holland
Chet Boyle, their son	David Hayward
Jaimie Boyle, their son	Jackie Haley
Ralph, their neighbor	Jack Burns

Additional voices: Pat Harrington, Jr., Gil Herman.

Boyle family dog: Julius.

Music: Richard Bowden.

WAIT TIL YOUR FATHER GETS HOME—30 minutes—Syndicated 1972.

WALLY GATOR

Animated Cartoon. The misadventures of Wally Gator, a bon vivant man-about-town. A Hanna-Barbera production.

Characters' Voices

Wally Gator	Daws Butler
Twiddles, his friend	Don Messick

Music: Hoyt Curtin.

WALLY GATOR—05 minutes—Syndicated 1962. 52 episodes.

WALLY WESTERN

Children. Re-edited western feature films presented in cliff-hanger installments.

Hosts: Wally Western and his pal Skeets (animated cartoon characters).

Featuring: Ken Maynard, Hoot Gibson, Tex Ritter, Bob Steele.

WALLY WESTERN—15 minutes—Syndicated 1960.

WALLY'S WORKSHOP

Advice. Home repair instruction, tips, and advice.

Host: Wally Bruner.

Assistant: Natalie Bruner (Mrs.)

Announcer: Johnny Olsen.

Music: Recorded.

WALLY'S WORKSHOP—30 minutes —Syndicated 1972.

WALT DISNEY PRESENTS

Anthology. Various presentations.

Included Miniseries:

Daniel Boone. The exploits of Frontiersman-scout Daniel Boone.

CAST

Daniel Boone	Dewey Martin
Rebecca Boone	Mala Powers
Squire Boone	Richard Banke
John Finley	Eddy Waller

The Nine Lives of Elfego Baca. Western. Background: Socorro County, New Mexico, late 1800s. The true story of Elfego Baca, "the man who couldn't be killed."

CAST

Elfego Baca	Robert Loggia
Sheriff Morgan	Robert Simon
Zangano, Baca's friend	Leonard Strong

Music: William Lava.

Swamp Fox. Adventure. Era: The American Revolutionary War. The exploits of Francis Marion, the Swamp Fox, an American general who

Walt Disney Presents. *The Nine Lives of Elfego Baca.* Left to right: Leonard Strong, Robert Simon, Robert Loggia. © *Walt Disney Productions.*

CAST

John Slaughter	Tom Tryon
Ranger Ben Jenkins	Harry Carey, Jr.
Norma Moore	Adeline Harris
Viola	Betty Lynn
Willie	Brian Corcoran
Addie	Annette Gorman

WALT DISNEY PRESENTS—60 minutes—ABC—September 12, 1958 - June 17, 1959.

WALT DISNEY'S WONDERFUL WORLD OF COLOR

Anthology. Excursions into the realm of reality and fantasy. Various types of presentations, including: cartoon, drama, mystery, action-adventure, educational, comedy, and nature and science studies.

attempts to thwart British advances in the South by attacking silently from the glen.

CAST

General Francis Marion, The Swamp Fox	Leslie Nielsen
Captain Richardson	James Seay
Sergeant O'Reilly	J. Pat O'Malley
Mary, Marion's romantic interest	Barbara Eiler
Ezra	Arthur Hunnicutt

Music: Buddy Baker.

Texas John Slaughter. Western. Background: Friotorian, Texas, 1880s. The exploits of John Slaughter, Texas Ranger, as he attempts to maintain law and order. Stories are based on actual incidents in the life of John Slaughter, Civil War officer, trailblazer, cattleman, and law enforcer.

Walt Disney Presents. *Swamp Fox.* Leslie Nielsen (right) and Barbara Eiler (standing beside him). © *Walt Disney Productions.*

Walt Disney Presents. *Texas John Slaughter.* Tom Tryon as John Slaughter. © *Walt Disney Productions.*

Host: Walt Disney.

Included:

Summer Magic. The heartwarming story of a penniless Boston family and their struggles to survive during the pre-World War I era.

CAST
Hayley Mills, Burl Ives, Dorothy McGuire, Deborah Walley.

The Monkey's Uncle. By perfecting man-powered flight, a college genius struggles to acquire a ten-million-dollar grant for his school.

CAST
Merlin Jones: Tommy Kirk; Jennifer:

Annette Funicello; Judge Holmsby: Leon Ames; Dearborn: Frank Faylen.

Inside Outer Space. A discussion on the problems to be faced by man as he begins his exploration of space.

Host-Narrator: Professor Ludwig Von Drake (an animated cartoon character).

Those Calloways. Background: New England. The story of a backwoodsman and his son, and their attempts to provide a sanctuary for migrating wild geese.

CAST
Cam Calloway: Brian Keith; Liddy Calloway: Vera Miles; Bucky

Calloway: Brandon de Wilde; Alf Simes: Walter Brennan; Ed Parker: Ed Wynn; Bridie Mellott: Linda Evans.

WALT DISNEY'S WONDERFUL WORLD OF COLOR—60 minutes—NBC—Premiered: September 17, 1961.

ABC titles and running dates (all 60 minutes):

DISNEYLAND—October 27, 1954 - September 3, 1958.

WALT DISNEY PRESENTS—September 12, 1958 - June 17, 1959.

WALT DISNEY'S ADVENTURE TIME—September 30, 1958 - September 24, 1959.

WALT DISNEY'S WORLD—October 1, 1959 - September 10, 1961. Moved to NBC the following week, which is stated above.

WALTER WINCHELL

Listed: The television programs of newspaper columnist-reporter Walter Winchell.

The Walter Winchell Show—News Commentary—15 minutes—ABC—October 5, 1952 - June 26, 1955.

Host: Walter Winchell. "Good evening Mr. and Mrs. North America and all the ships at sea..." (his opening).

The Walter Winchell Show—Variety—30 minutes—NBC—October 5, 1956 - December 28, 1956.

Format: Performances by undiscovered professional talent.

Host: Walter Winchell.
Orchestra: Carl Hoff.

The Walter Winchell File—Crime Drama—30 minutes—ABC—October 2, 1957 - March 28, 1958. Syndicated.
   Background: New York City. Dramatizations based on official newspaper files. Appearing as himself, Walter Winchell, newspaper reporter for the *Daily Mirror,* recounts stories and interviews the people involved.

The Walter Winchell Show—Variety—30 minutes—ABC—October 2, 1960 - November 6, 1960.

Host: Walter Winchell.

THE WALTER WOLFE KING SHOW

Variety.
Host: Walter Wolfe King.

THE WALTER WOLFE KING SHOW—15 minutes—DuMont 1954.

THE WALTONS

Drama. Background: Jefferson County, Virginia, 1930s. Events in the lives of a poor, rural family, the Waltons, the operators of a sawmill, as seen through the sentimental eyes of the eldest son, John Boy, a high school (later college) student who hopes to become a writer. John Boy's fond recollections of his youth and his family's struggles to survive during the Depression extol the simple virtues of chastity, honesty, thrift, family unity, and love.

CAST
John Walton, the
   father   Ralph Waite

The Waltons. Left: Jon Walmsley (with guitar), Judy Norton (standing); center: Richard Thomas (on piano bench) and Kami Cotler (on Richard's knee). Right side, from bottom to top: David Harper, Mary McDonough, and Eric Scott (behind Thomas).

Olivia Walton, his
wife   Miss Michael Learned
Zeb (Grandpa) Walton,
John's father   Will Geer
Esther (Grandma) Walton,
John's mother   Ellen Corby

The seven Walton children:

John Boy Walton   Richard Thomas
Mary Ellen Walton   Judy Norton
Jim-Bob Walton   David S. Harper
Elizabeth Walton   Kami Cotler
Jason Walton   Jon Walmsley
Erin Walton
            Mary Elizabeth McDonough
Ben Walton   Eric Scott
Ike Godsey,
the owner of
the general
store   Joe Conley
Corabeth Godsey, Ike's
wife   Ronnie Claire Edwards

Aimee Godsey,
their adopted
daughter   Rachel Longaker
Dr. Curtis Willard,
married Mary
Ellen Walton on
11-14-76   Tom Bower
Mamie Baldwin, a
friend of the
Waltons   Helen Kleeb
Emily Baldwin, Mamie's
sister   Mary Jackson
Reverend Matthew
Fordwick   John Ritter
Rosemary Fordwick, Matthew's
wife*   Mariclare Costello
Sheriff Ep Bridges   John Crawford
Yancy Tucker, a
friend of the
Waltons   Robert Donner
Flossie Brimmer, the
owner of the rooming
house   Norma Marlowe
Maude Gromley, a
friend of
Esther's   Merie Earle
Patsy Brimmer, Flossie's
niece   Eileen McDonough
Professor Parks, John Boy's
English Instructor
at Boatright
University   Paul Jenkins
Nora, the county
nurse   Kaiulani Lee
Clarence Johnson, publisher
of the *Jefferson
County Times*   Walter Brooke
Fannie Tatum, Erin's
employer at
the phone
company   Sheila Allen
Thelma, the owner
of the Dew Drop
Inn, the cafe-bar
where Jason
works   Dorothy Shay

*Originally Rosemary Hunter, the schoolteacher. In 1975 she married Reverend Fordwick.

Walton family dog: Reckless.

Narrator: Earl Hamner, Jr. (the series' creator, upon whose childhood the series is based).

Music: Jerry Goldsmith; Arthur Morton, Alexander Courage.

Executive Producer: Lee Rich, Earl Hamner, Jr.

Producer: Robert Jacks, Andy White.

Director: Harry Harris, Ralph Senesky, Harvey Laidman, Ralph Waite, Lawrence Dobkin, Richard Bennett, Ivan Dixon, Philip Leacock, Lee Philips, Vincent Sherman, Robert Butler.

THE WALTONS—60 minutes—CBS—Premiered: September 14, 1972.

WANDERLUST

Travel. Visits to interesting and unusual places.

Host-Narrator: Bill Burrud.

WANDERLUST—30 minutes—Syndicated 1957. 113 episodes.

WANTED

Documentary. Dramatizations based on incidents in the lives of criminals wanted by the F.B.I. Programs recap their lives and update viewers as to their offenses. Interviews are conducted with friends and family of those involved, and viewers who possess information regarding the subject are urged, under confidential protection, to inform police or F.B.I. officials.

Host-Narrator-Reporter: Walter McGraw.

WANTED—30 minutes—CBS—October 20, 1955 - January 12, 1956.

WANTED: DEAD OR ALIVE

Western. Background: The Frontier during the 1870s. The exploits of Josh Randall, bounty hunter, a man who, though tracking wanted men and women for their offered rewards, often finds himself in the position as protector, struggling to safeguard his prisoners from the less scrupulous bounty hunters.

CAST
Josh Randall	Steve McQueen
Jason Nichols, his partner	Wright King

Also, various parts: Gloria Talbot, Warren Oates.

Randall's gun: His "Mare's Laig," a .30-40 caliber sawed-off carbine rifle.

Jason's dog: an unnamed mutt referred to as "Hey, dog!"

Music: Harry King; Rudy Schrager; Herschel Burke Gilbert.

Producer: John Robinson, Ed Adamson, Harry Harris.

Director: Richard Donner, Thomas Carr, Murray Golden, Ed Adamson, Gene Reynolds, George Blair.

WANTED: DEAD OR ALIVE—30 minutes—CBS—September 6, 1958 - September 1961. 94 episodes. Syndicated.

WAR AND PEACE

Historical Serial. An adaptation of the Leo Tolstoy classic. Background: Moscow. A tableau of Russian society during the turbulent era of the Napoleonic Wars (1805-1820). Produced by the B.B.C.

CAST

Natasha	Morag Hood
Prince Andre Balkonsky	Alan Dobie
Prince Nikolai Bolkonsky	Anthony Jacobs
Maria Bolkonsky	Angela Down
Anatole Kuragin	Colin Baker
Napoleon Bonaparte	David Swift
Prince Vasili Kuragin	Basil Henson
Helene Kuragin	Fiona Gaunt
Pierre Bezuhov	Anthony Hopkins
Dolohov	Donald Burton
Count Ilya Rostov	Rupert Davies
Countess Natalia Rostov	Faith Brook
Sonya	Joanna David
Nicolai Rostov	Sylvester Morand
Denisov	Gary Watson
Boris Drubetskoy	Neil Stacy
Tzar Alexander I	Donald Douglas
Kutuzov	Frank Middleman

Producer: David Conroy.

Director: John Davies.

WAR AND PEACE—PBS—November 20, 1973 - January 15, 1974. Broadcast in seven ninety-minute and two two-hour installments. Originally broadcast in England in twenty forty-five-minute episodes (seventeen hours).

WAR IN THE AIR

Documentary. Films recounting the history of the Royal Air Force during World War II. Produced by the B.B.C.

Host-Narrator: Robert Harris.

Music: The London Philharmonic Orchestra, conducted by Muir Mathieson.

WAR IN THE AIR—30 minutes—Syndicated 1956.

WARNER BROTHERS PRESENTS

Drama. The overall title for four rotating series: "Casablanca"; "Cheyenne"; "Conflict"; and "King's Row."

Host: Gig Young.

Music: David Buttolph.

Producer: Roy Huggins, Richard L. Bare, John Peyser, Jerome Robinson, E. St. Joseph, Paul Stewart.

Casablanca. Mystery. Background: The Café American in Casablanca. The story of Rick Jason, its owner, an American who assists people in distress by offering his establishment as a place of refuge.

CAST

Rick Jason	Charles McGraw
Sam, the piano player	Clarence Muse

Cheyenne. Western. Background: The Frontier, 1870s. The exploits of wanderers Cheyenne Bodie and his friend Smitty, a mapmaker, as they assist people in distress.

CAST

Cheyenne Bodie	Clint Walker
Smitty	L. Q. Jones

Conflict. Anthology. Dramatizations depicting the plight of people whose lives are suddenly changed by unexpected and unfavorable circumstances.

Included(three examples listed):

Capital Punishment. The story of a man, tried and sentenced to death for a murder he did not commit, who struggles to prove his innocence.

CAST
Will Hutchins, Rex Reason, Barbara Eiler.

Anything For Money. The story of a private detective who is secretly hired as a bodyguard to a yachtsman on a pleasure cruise to Havana.

CAST
Efrem Zimbalist, Jr., Barton MacLane, Margaret Hayes.

Shock Wave. The story of a test pilot who takes a plane up before a safety device is perfected.

CAST
Scott Brady, Ted de Corsia, Kenneth Tobey.

King's Row. Drama. Background: The town of King's Row. The work of psychiatrist Parris Mitchell as he attempts to aid people caught in the turmoil of human emotion.

CAST

Dr. Parris Mitchell	Jack Kelly
Randy	Nan Leslie
Drake	Robert Horton
Eloise	Peggy Webber
Dr. Tower	Victor Jory

WARNER BROTHERS PRESENTS— 60 minutes—ABC—September 13, 1955 - September 11, 1956 (for "Casablanca," "Cheyenne," and "King's Row"); September 18, 1956 - September 10, 1957 (for "Cheyenne" and "Conflict").

WASHINGTON: BEHIND CLOSED DOORS

Drama. A six part miniseries loosely based on John Ehrlichman's political novel, *The Company.* Background: Washington, D.C. The complex story, which centers on the rise to power and life of Richard Monckton from senator to President of the United States, exposes the public and intimate lives of the people who control our nation—lives filled with greed, lust, and corruption.

CAST

Richard Monckton	Jason Robards
William Martin, the C.I.A. director	Cliff Robertson
Linda Martin, William's wife	Lois Nettleton
Sally Whalen, the spy	Stefanie Powers
Frank Flaherty, the Chief of Staff	Robert Vaughn
Esker Anderson, the retiring President	Andy Griffith
Bob Bailey, the Press Secretary	Barry Nelson
Carl Tessler, the Foreign Affairs Advisor	Harold Gould
Adam Gardiner, the young idealist	Tony Bill

Also: David Selby (as Roger Castle), Nicholas Pryor (Hank Ferris), Diana Ewing (Kathy Ferris), Meg Foster (Jennie Jameson), Thayer David (Elmer Morse), John Randolph (Bennett Lowman), John Lehne (Tucker Tallford), Lara Parker (Wanda Elliott), John Houseman (Myron Dunn), Frances Lee McCain (Paula Gardiner), Alan Oppenheimer (Simon Cappell), Linden Chiles (Jack Atherton), Frank Marth (Lawrence Allison), June Dayton (Mrs. Monckton), Skip Homeier (Lars Haglund), Mary La Roche (Anne Lowman).

Music: Dominic Frontiere.

Executive Producer: Stanley Kallis.

Producer: Norman S. Powell.

Director: Gary Nelson.

WASHINGTON: BEHIND CLOSED DOORS – 12 hours (total)–ABC–September 6, 1977 - September 11, 1977.

WASHINGTON SQUARE

Variety. Music, songs, dances, and comedy sketches set against the background of New York's Greenwich Village.

Host: Ray Bolger.

Regulars (the people of the square): Elaine Stritch, Rusty Draper, Kay Armen, Arnold Stang, Daniza Ilistsch, Threa Flames, The Bil and Cora Baird Puppets, The Danny Daniels Singers.

Orchestra: Charles Sanford.

WASHINGTON SQUARE–60 minutes–NBC–October 2, 1956 - June 13, 1957.

WATERFRONT

Adventure. Background: The San Pedro Harbor in Los Angeles, California. The experiences of John Herrick, captain of the tugboat *Cheryl Ann.*

CAST

Captain John Herrick	Preston Foster
May Herrick, his wife	Lois Moran
Carl Herrick, their son	Douglas Dick
Tip Hubbard, the captain's friend	Pinky Tomlin
Dan Cord, the captain of the tugboat *Isabel*	Ramon Vallo

Also: Willie Best, Eddie Waller.

Music: Alexander Laszlo.

WATERFRONT–30 minutes–Syndicated. 1954. 78 episodes.

WAY OF THE WORLD

Serial. Adaptations of stories appearing in leading women's magazines. Vignettes are allotted the time needed, in days, to run without any interference to the original content.

Hostess: Gloria Louis, appearing as Linda Porter.

WAY OF THE WORLD–15 minutes –NBC 1955.

WAY OUT

Anthology. Tales of the supernatural.

Host: Roald Dahl.

Included:

Dissolve To Black. The story of a television actress trapped in a deserted studio by a killer.

CAST
Bonnie Draco: Kathleen Widdoes.

Death Wish. Annoyed by his wife's constant habit of relentlessly talking about the television programs she watches, a husband plots her murder

—as she describes a crime show she saw.

CAST

The wife: Charlotte Rae.

Hush Hush. Experimenting with sound waves, a professor attempts to develop a state of perfect tranquility.

CAST

Professor Ernest Lydecker: Philip Coolidge; Bernice Lydecker: Rosemary Murphy; William Rogers: Woodrow Parfrey.

WAY OUT—30 minutes—CBS—June 1961 - July 14, 1961.

WAY OUT GAMES

Game. Two three-member teams of junior high school students compete in various contests of skill with the object being to complete stunts in the least amount of time. Points are awarded after each of the three rounds and the team scoring the highest receives the opportunity to compete in the quarter finals—a tournament for prizes.

Host: Sonny Fox.

Assistant: Mark Smith.

Executive Producer: Jack Barry, Dan Enright.

Director: Richard S. Kline.

WAY OUT GAMES—25 minutes—CBS—Premiered: September 11, 1976.

WAYNE AND SHUSTER TAKE AN AFFECTIONATE LOOK AT . . .

Documentary. Through film and commentary, the comic movie trends of the past and the lives of individual comedians are recalled.

Hosts: Johnny Wayne and Frank Shuster.

WAYNE AND SHUSTER TAKE AN AFFECTIONATE LOOK AT . . .—60 minutes—CBS—June 17, 1966 - July 29, 1966. 13 episodes.

THE WAYNE KING SHOW

Musical Variety.

Host: Wayne King.

Regulars: Jackie Jones, Harry Hull, Barbara Becker, The Don Large Chorus.

Orchestra: Gloria Van.

Producer: Ken Craig, Andy Christian.

Director: Bill Hobin, Dave Brown.

THE WAYNE KING SHOW—30 minutes. NBC 1950; DuMont 1951.

THE WEAKER (?) SEX

Discussion. Women from various fields of business appear and discuss the controversial issues that affect women in their daily lives.

Hostess: Pamela Mason.

Music: Recorded.

THE WEAKER (?) SEX—30 minutes—Syndicated 1968. 260 tapes.

THE WEB

Anthology. Dramatizations depicting the plight of people trapped in sudden, perilous situations.

Host-Narrator: Jonathan Drake.

Producer: Franklin Heller, Mark Goodson, Bill Todman.

Director: Franklin Heller.

Sponsor: Embassy Cigarettes.

Included:

End Of The Line. A mobster's wife attempts to double-cross her husband.

Starring: Jayne Meadows.

Last Chance. A thief attempts to save the life of a young girl who is contemplating suicide.

Starring: John Larch, Rebecca Wells.

Hurricane Coming. Planning to run away with another man, a woman attempts to dispose of her husband by leaving him stranded on an island due to be hit by a hurricane.

Starring: Beverly Garland, Mark Roberts.

Kill And Run. Having borrowed his employer's car without permission, a young man attempts to prove that he is innocent of a hit-and-run killing.

Starring: James Darren.

THE WEB—30 minutes—CBS—July 4, 1950 - September 26, 1954.

WEDDING DAY

Wedding Performances. Actual ceremonies performed on TV.

Hostess: Patricia Vance.

Assistant: Vin Gottschalk.

WEDDING DAY—60 minutes—ABC 1950.

THE WEDDING GAME

Game. Three married couples play. The wives are isolated back-stage; the husbands appear before camera. The husbands each select three similar prizes from a group of merchandise items displayed on the stage. The husbands are then isolated offstage, and the wives, before camera, are permitted to choose three items also. The couples are then reunited. If the husband and wife have both independently chosen the same item or items, they receive it as their gift.

Host: Al Hamel.

THE WEDDING GAME—30 minutes —ABC—April 1, 1968 - July 12, 1968. Also known as "Wedding Party."

WEEKEND WORKSHOP

Advice. Home-repair instruction, tips, and advice.

Host: Bob Hamilton.

Assistant: Kay Westerfield.

WEEKEND WORKSHOP—30 minutes—NBC—1954 - 1955.

WELCOME ABOARD

See title: "Phil Silvers.."

WELCOME BACK, KOTTER

Comedy. Background: James Buchanan High School in Bensonhurst, Brooklyn, New York. The trials and tribulations of Gabe Kotter, a former graduate who returns to his school ten years later to teach Special Guidance Remedial Academics to a

Welcome Back, Kotter. Left to right: Marcia Strassman, Gabriel Kaplan, and Lawrence-Hilton Jacobs. Center, left to right: John Travolta, Ron Palillo, Robert Hegyes. (The actress with Travolta is not credited).

class of incorrigible students known as Sweat Hogs, teenagers who are much like the way he was when he was attending the same school.

CAST

Gabe Kotter	Gabriel Kaplan
Julie Kotter, his wife	Marcia Strassman
Michael Woodman, the vice-principal	John Sylvester White
Voice of the principal	James Komack
Judy Borden, a student	Helaine Lembeck

The Sweat Hogs:

Vinnie Barbarino	John Travolta
Juan Epstein	Robert Hegyes
Fredrick "Boom Boom" Washington	Lawrence-Hilton Jacobs
Arnold Horshack	Ron Palillo
Rosalie "Hotsie" Totzi	Debralee Scott
Vernajean Williams	Vernee Watson

Music: John B. Sebastian.

Executive Producer: James Komack.

Producer: Eric Cohen, Alan Sacs.

Director: James Komack, Bob LaHendro.

WELCOME BACK, KOTTER–30 minutes–ABC–Premiered: September 9, 1975.

WELCOME TRAVELERS

Interview. Travelers, met at bus, railroad, and plane terminals, are invited to a studio where, in exchange for gifts, they relate their experiences and impressions of Chicago.

Host: Tom Bartlett; Bob Cunningham.

Announcer: William T. Lazar.

Producer: Tom Hicks, Charles Powers, Tom O'Connor.

Director: Don Meier, Charles Powers.

Sponsor: Procter and Gamble.

WELCOME TRAVELERS–30 minutes–NBC–September 8, 1952 - October 10, 1955. Based on the radio program.

WE'LL GET BY

Comedy. Background: Suburban New Jersey. Events in the lives of the Platt family: George, a lawyer, his wife, Liz, and their three bright and saucy children, Muff, Andrea, and Kenny. Created by Alan Alda.

CAST

George Platt	Paul Sorvino
Liz Platt	Mitzi Hoag
Michael "Muff" Platt	Jerry Houser
Andrea Platt	Devon Scott
Kenny Platt	Willie Aames

Music: Joe Raposo, Sheldon Harnick.

Producer-Creator: Alan Alda.

Director: Jack Shea, Jay Sandrich.

WE'LL GET BY—30 minutes—CBS—
March 6, 1975 - May 30, 1975.

WENDY AND ME

Comedy. Background: Los Angeles,
California. The marital misadventures
of the Conways: Jeff, an airline pilot;
and his beautiful but scatterbrained
wife, Wendy.

The program has the imprint of
"The George Burns and Gracie Allen
Show." Appearing as the Conway's
landlord, George Burns speaks directly
to the audience, establishes scenes,
relates monologues, and, as in the
past, further complicates what Wendy,
as Gracie, has already complicated.

CAST

George Burns	Himself
Wendy Conway	Connie Stevens
Jeff Conway	Ron Harper
Danny Adams, their neighbor, Jeff's co-pilot	James Callahan
Mr. Bundy, the janitor	J. Pat O'Malley

Wendy and Me. George Burns and Connie
Stevens.

Mr. Norton, Jeff's employer	Bartlett Robinson
Mrs. Norton, his wife	Jane Morgan
Catherine, Wendy's friend	Robyn Grace

Music: Ervin Drake.

WENDY AND ME—30 minutes—ABC
—September 14, 1964 - September 6,
1965. 34 episodes. Syndicated.

THE WENDY BARRIE SHOW

See title: "Through Wendy's
Window."

WESLEY

Comedy. The misadventures of
Wesley, a mischievous twelve-year-old
boy.

CAST

Wesley	Donald Devlin
His father	Frankie Thomas, Sr.
His mother	Mona Thomas
His teenage sister	Joy Reese
Her suitor	Jack Ayres
Wesley's friend	Billy Nevard
Wesley's grandfather	Joe Sweeney

Producer: Worthington Miner.

Director: Franklin Schaffner.

WESLEY—30 minutes CBS 1949.

THE WESTERNER

Western. Background: Various areas
along the Mexican Border during the
1890s. The exploits of Dave Blasingame, a wandering cowboy who aids
people in distress.

CAST

Dave Blasingame	Brian Keith
Burgundy Smith, his friend	John Dehner

Dave's dog: Brown.

Music: Herschel Burke Gilbert.

THE WESTERNER—30 minutes—NBC—September 30, 1960 - December 30, 1960. 13 episodes.

THE WESTERNERS

Anthology. Rebroadcasts of western dramas that were originally aired via: "Black Saddle"; "Dick Powell's Zane Grey Theatre' ; "Johnny Ringo"; and "The Law of the Plainsman." See individual titles for program information.

Host: Keenan Wynn.

THE WESTERNERS—30 minutes—Syndicated 1965. 125 episodes.

WESTERN HOUR

Anthology. Rebroadcasts of western dramas that were originally aired via: "The Rifleman" and "Dick Powell's Zane Grey Theatre." See individual titles for program information.

Host: Chuck Connors.

WESTERN HOUR—60 minutes—Syndicated 1963. 312 episodes.

WESTERN STAR THEATRE

Anthology. Rebroadcasts of western dramas that were originally aired via "Death Valley Days." See either of the following titles for program information: "Death Valley Days"; "The Pioneers"; or "Trails West."

Host: Rory Calhoun.

WESTERN STAR THEATRE—30 minutes—Syndicated 1963. 67 episodes.

WESTERN THEATRE

Anthology. Rebroadcasts of western dramas that were originally aired via "Dick Powell's Zane Grey Theatre."

Included:

The Thousand Dollar Gun. Background: The town of Broken Lance. The story of a gunfighter and his attempts to end the reign of a gang of outlaws.

CAST

George Montgomery, John Agar, Chuck Connors, Jean Allison.

The Castaway. The story of a wagonmaster and his attempts to avert an Indian attack on the train.

CAST

Ronald Reagan, Jeanette Nolan, Dick Crockett.

The Easygoing Man. An easygoing rancher attempts to control a rebellious teenage boy.

CAST

Lee Marvin, Virginia Grey, Danny Richards, Robert Rockwell, Alan Lee.

WESTERN THEATRE—30 minutes—NBC—July 3, 1959 - September 4, 1959.

WESTINGHOUSE SUMMER THEATRE

A series of thirty-minute anthology dramas broadcast on CBS during the summer of 1951. Produced by Montgomery Ford and sponsored by Westinghouse.

WEST POINT

Anthology. Dramatizations based on incidents in the training periods of West Point Academy cadets.

Host: Donald May, appearing as Cadet Charles C. Thompson.

Semiregular: Clint Eastwood.

Producer: James Sheldon, Leon Benson, Henry Kessler, Maurice Unger.

Included:

Contact. Though lacking physical ability, a cadet attempts to compete with his classmates.

CAST

George Nelson: Steve Terrell; Tim Tobin: Del Erickson.

Flareup. The story of a cadet's struggles to control his explosive temper.

CAST

Peter Baldwin, Jerry Charlebous, Rad Fulton.

Cold Peril. When the Hudson River freezes over, a young cadet decides to walk across it to the village to meet his girlfriend. Discovering that an ice breaker is touring the river, three of his friends desperately struggle to get to him before he is stranded.

CAST

Bob Matson: Larry Pennell; Steve Pauley: Brett Halsey; Tom Kennedy: Leonard Nimoy.

WEST POINT—30 minutes—ABC—October 8, 1957 - July 1, 1958. Syndicated.

WEST SIDE COMEDY

See title: "East Side Comedy."

WESTSIDE MEDICAL

Medical Drama. Background: California. The personal and professional lives of Doctors Sam Lanagan, Janet Cottrell, and Phil Parker, staff physicians at Westside Memorial Hospital.

CAST

Dr. Sam Lanagan	James Sloyan
Dr. Janet Cottrell	Linda Carlson
Dr. Phil Parker	Ernest Thompson
Carrie, the woman who assists them in the clinic	Alice Nunn

Music: Billy Goldenberg.

Executive Producer: Martin Starger.

Producer: Alan A. Armer.

Director: Ralph Senesky, Gerald Mayer, Larry Elikann, Vincent Sherman, Paul Stanley.

Creator: Barry Oringer.

WESTSIDE MEDICAL—60 minutes—ABC—March 15, 1977 - April 14, 1977.

THE WESTWIND

Adventure. Background: Hawaii. The

adventures of the Andrews family—Steve, an underwater photographer, his wife Kate, a marine biologist, and their teenage children Robin and Tom—as they travel through the various islands seeking to further man's knowledge of the sea.

CAST

Steve Andrews	Van Williams
Kate Andrews	Niki Dantine
Robin Andrews	Kimberly Beck
Tom Andrews	Steve Burns

Their yacht: The *Westwind.*

Music: Richard La Salle.

THE WESTWIND—30 minutes—NBC—September 6, 1975 - September 4, 1976.

WE TAKE YOUR WORD

Game. Object: For a celebrity panel to relate definitions and derivations of words submitted by home viewers. Words that stump the panel award the senders cash prizes.

Hosts: John Daly; John K. M. McCaffrey.

Panelists: Al Capp, Cornelia Otis Skinner, Abe Burrows.

WE TAKE YOUR WORD—30 minutes—CBS—1950 - 1951.

WE, THE PEOPLE

Celebrity Interview.

Host: Dan Seymour.

Orchestra: Oscar Bradley.

Producer: Dan Seymour, James Sheldon, Rod Erickson.

Sponsor: Gulf Oil.

WE, THE PEOPLE—30 minutes—CBS 1948.

WE'VE GOT EACH OTHER

Comedy. Background: California. The story centers on the chaotic misadventures of the Hibbards: Judy, a not-so-attractive, lanky photographer's assistant, and her husband, Stuart, who works at home as a copywriter for bizarre devices advertised in the Herman Gutman Mail Order Catalogue.

CAST

Judy Hibbard	Beverly Archer
Stuart Hibbard	Oliver Clark
Damon Jerome, Judy's employer	Tom Poston
Dee Dee, Damon's top model	Joan Van Ark
Donna, Damon's secretary	Ren Woods
Ken Redford, the Hibbard's neighbor	Martin Kove

Music and Theme Vocal: Nino Candido.

Executive Producer: Tom Patchett, Jay Tarses.

Producer: Jack Burns.

WE'VE GOT EACH OTHER—30 minutes—CBS—Premiered: October 1, 1977.

WHAT DO YOU HAVE IN COMMON?

Game. Three specially selected contestants, who each possess something in common, but are unknown to each other, compete. Within a three-minute time limit, and through a cross-examination session, each has to discover what the common denominator is. Clues are provided by an unseen fourth party (e.g., the same doctor; the same real estate salesman). The player who is first to identify the common bond is the winner and receives merchandise prizes.

Host: Ralph Story.

WHAT DO YOU HAVE IN COMMON?—30 minutes—CBS 1954.

WHAT EVERY WOMAN WANTS TO KNOW

Discussion. Informative discussions on topics of current concern.

Hostess: Bess Myerson.

Music: Recorded.

WHAT EVERY WOMAN WANTS TO KNOW—30 minutes—Syndicated 1972.

WHAT HAPPENED?

Game. An individual, who performed some unique act for which he received newspaper coverage, appears on the program. A panel of four celebrities then question him with the object being to determine what he did. If they fail, the contestant receives a prize.

Host: Ben Grauer.

Panel: Roger Price, Lisa Ferraday, Maureen Stapleton, Frank Gallop.

Announcer: Frank Gallop.

WHAT HAPPENED?—30 minutes—NBC 1952.

WHAT HAVE YOU GOT TO LOSE?

Game. Four competing contestants. Through question-and-andwer probe rounds with the host, players have to identify white-elephant objects that have been submitted by home viewers. If one of the panelists identifies the mystery article, he receives a prize; if not, the sender receives a prize.

Host: John Reed King.

WHAT HAVE YOU GOT TO LOSE? —30 minutes—ABC—May 25, 1953 - August 7, 1953.

WHAT REALLY HAPPENED TO THE CLASS OF '65?

Anthology. Dramatizations that update the lives of the 1965 graduating class of the fictional Bret Hart High School in Los Angeles. Stories open with the commentary of Sam Ashley, a '65 grad and now a teacher at Bret Hart High, as he recalls his fellow classmates; the program then chronicles the life of a particular grad from 1965 to 1977. Based on the book by Michael Medved and David Wallechinsky.

Starring: Tony Bill as Sam Ashley.

Music: Don Costa.

Executive Producer-Producer: Richard Irving.

WHAT REALLY HAPPENED TO THE CLASS OF '65?—60 minutes— NBC—Premiered: December 8, 1977.

WHAT'S GOING ON?

Game. Two three-member teams compete: The Insiders and The Outsiders. The Outsiders are brought to a remote location and asked to perform certain activities. Through remote pickup, their activities are displayed on a large screen behind each of The Insiders. Through a series of question and answer probe rounds with the host,

The Insiders have to discover where The Outsiders are and what they are doing. Prizes are awarded accordingly: to The Insiders if they correctly identify the situation and activities; to The Outsiders if The Insiders fail.

Host: Lee Bowman.

Players (rotating team assignments): Kitty Carlisle, Hy Gardner, Jayne Meadows, Cliff Norton, Susan Oakland, Gene Raymond.

Announcer: Jimmy Blaine.

WHAT'S GOING ON?—30 minutes— CBS—July 22, 1954 - September 1954.

WHAT'S HAPPENING!!

Comedy. Background: Southern California. An inane series that follows the antics of three black teenagers: Roger Thomas, Dwayne Clemens, and Freddie Stubbs, nicknamed "Rerun" for his constant habit of repeating in summer school what he should have learned in the fall.

CAST
Roger Thomas   Ernest Thomas
Dwayne Clemens   Haywood Nelson
Rerun   Fred Berry
Mabel Thomas, Roger's
    mother   Mabel King
Dee Thomas, Roger's
    sister   Danielle Spencer
Shirley, the waitress
    at the local soda
    shop, Robert's
    Place   Shirley Hemphill
Bill Thomas, Roger's
    father   Thalmus Rasulala

Music: Henry Mancini.

Executive Producer: Saul Turteltaub, Bernie Orenstein, Bud Yorkin.

Director: Dennis Steinmetz, Bud Yorkin, Jack Shea, Mark Warren, Dick Harwood, Alan Rafkin, Hal Alexander.

WHAT'S HAPPENING!!—30 minutes—ABC—August 5, 1976 - August 26, 1976; Returned: Premiered: November 13, 1976.

WHAT'S IN A WORD?

Game. A contestant, selected from the studio audience, presents a single rhyme to the host (e.g., "Pink Mink."). Through one word clues provided by the host, a celebrity panel has to identify the rhyme. For each clue used before the panel identifies it, the contestant receives five dollars.

Hosts: Mike Wallace; Clifton Fadiman.

Panelists: Faye Emerson, Audrey Meadows, Carl Reiner, Jim Moran.

WHAT'S IN A WORD?—30 minutes— ABC—1954 - 1955.

WHAT'S IT ALL ABOUT WORLD?

Variety. An attempt, through the satirization of everyday life, to explain our troubled world—a world that finds it difficult to make light of its faults.

Host: Dean Jones.

Regulars: Dick Clair, Jenna McMahon, Alex Dreier, Geri Granger, Scoey Mitchlll, Dennis Allen, Ron Price, Maureen Arthur, Byan Johnson (Happy Hollywood), The Kevin Carlisle Three.

Orchestra: Denny Vaughn.

Announcer: Roger Carroll.

WHAT'S IT ALL ABOUT WORLD?— 60 minutes—ABC—February 6, 1969 - May 1, 1969. 13 episodes.

WHAT'S IT FOR?

Game. Inventors or their descendants appear with actual working models of thingamajigs patented by the U.S. Patent Office since 1800. Through a series of question-and-answer probe rounds, a panel of four have to identify it and its purpose. Guests receive cash for each question asked by the panel before it is identified.

Host: Hal March.

Panelists: Hans Conried, Betsy Palmer, Abe Burrows, Cornelia Otis Skinner.

WHAT'S IT FOR?—30 minutes—NBC —October 12, 1957 - January 4, 1958.

WHAT'S IT WORTH?

Human Interest. Owners of paintings and objets d'art are the subjects of the program. Each person appears with and tells how he acquired his treasure. A panel of experts then appraise the object and quote its actual value. As the experts give their opinion, cameras reveal the human emotions of the owner.

Host: Gil Fates.

Permanent Panelist: Sigmund Rothschild.

Producer-Director: Frances Buss.

WHAT'S IT WORTH?—30 minutes— CBS 1948.

WHAT'S MY LINE?

Game. Through a series of question-and-answer probe rounds with a guest, a celebrity panel of four has to uncover his or her occupation. Three such rounds are played per broadcast, one involving a mystery guest celebrity (panelists are blindfolded during the questioning). Guests receive merchandise prizes.

Versions:

What's My Line?—30 minutes—CBS— February 2, 1950 - September 3, 1967.

Host: John Daly.

Panelists: Arlene Francis, Dorothy Kilgallen, Bennett Cerf, Fred Allen, Steve Allen, Hal Block, Louis Untermeyer, Harold Hoffman.

Announcers: John Briggs; Johnny Olsen.

Music: Milton DeLugg.

What's My Line?—30 minutes—Syndicated 1968.

Hosts: Wally Bruner; Larry Blyden.

Panelists: Arlene Francis, Soupy Sales, Jack Cassidy, Kaye Ballard, Anita Gillette, Gene Rayburn, Alan Alda, Nancy Dussault, Joanna Barnes, Bennett Cerf, Bert Convy.

Announcers: Johnny Olsen; Chet Gould.

Music: Score Productions.

WHAT'S MY LINE? (British)—30 minutes—B.B.C.-TV—1951.

Host: Eamonn Andrews.

Panelists: Chislaine Alexander, Elizabeth Allen, Jerry Desmonde, Gilbert Harding.

WHAT'S NEW MR. MAGOO

Animated Cartoon. Newly animated adventures of the nearsighted Quincy

Magoo and his equally nearsighted dog, McBarker. See also: "The Famous Adventures of Mr. Magoo," and "Mr. Magoo."

Characters' Voices

Quincy Magoo	Jim Backus
McBarker	Frank Welker

Additional Voices: Hal Smith.

Music: Doug Goodwin, Eric Rodgers, Dean Elliott.

Producer: David DePatie, Friz Freleng.

Director: Sid Marcus, Bob McKimson, Spencer Peel.

WHAT'S NEW MR. MAGOO—30 minutes—NBC—Premiered: September 10, 1977.

WHAT'S THIS SONG?

Game. Two competing teams, each composed of two members: one celebrity captain and one noncelebrity contestant. A song is played. The team who is first to identify itself through a buzzer signal receives a chance to answer. If the team identifies the song title it receives points and the opportunity to score additional points by singing the four opening bars. If the opposing team believes the lyrics are incorrect it is permitted to challenge. If correct, it wins the points if one member can sing the correct lyrics; if incorrect in assuming the lyrics are wrong, the points are deducted from the team's score and awarded to the other team. Winners are the highest-scoring teams. The contestant receives merchandise prizes.

Host: Wink Martindale.

Premiere Guests: Beverly Garland, Lorne Greene.

WHAT'S THIS SONG?—25 minutes—

NBC—October 26, 1964 - September 24, 1965.

WHAT'S THE STORY?

Game. Through dramatizations performed on stage, a panel of four contestants have to identify news events. Prizes are awarded to the individual player who scores the most correct identifications.

Host: Walter Raney.

Producer: David Lowe, Gil Fates.

Sponsor: DuMont Labs.

WHAT'S THE STORY?—30 minutes —DuMont 1951.

WHAT WILL THEY THINK OF NEXT?

Humor. Inventors of clever gadgets (e.g., a music writing typewriter) appear and demonstrate their invention to a panel of three comedians who, in turn, appraise it. A gift is awarded to the inventor who appears with the hope of interesting a manufacturer in his product.

Host: Ed Herlihy.

Panel: Arthur Q. Bryan, Janet Graham, Harry Hirsh.

Producer-Director: Lawrence Schwab.

WHAT WILL THEY THINK OF NEXT?—30 minutes—NBC 1948.

WHAT'S YOUR BID?

Game. A merchandise item is offered for bid. With their own money, studio-audience members bid for it. The highest bidder receives it and donates it to charity. For his generosity, the program awards him a duplicate item plus additional gifts for his kindness.

Hosts: Robert Alda; Leonard Rosen.

Announcers: John Reed King; Dick Shepard.

WHAT'S YOUR BID?—30 minutes—ABC 1953.

WHEELIE AND THE CHOPPER BUNCH

Animated Cartoon. The adventures of Wheelie, and almost human Volkswagon, the world's greatest stunt-racing car, as he, and his girlfriend, Rota Ree, also a V.W., struggle to overcome the evils of the Chopper Bunch, diabolical motorcycles led by Chopper, who seeks and plots to acquire Rota's affections.

Characters' Voices

Wheelie	Frank Welker
Rota	Judy Strangis
Chopper	Frank Welker

Wheelie and the Chopper Bunch. Left to right: Rota, Wheelie, and the Chopper Bunch. © *Hanna-Barbera Productions.*

Revs	Paul Winchell
Hi Riser	Lennie Weinrib

Music: Hoyt Curtin.

Executive Producer: William Hanna, Joseph Barbera.

Director: Charles A. Nichols.

WHEELIE AND THE CHOPPER BUNCH—30 minutes—NBC—September 7, 1974 - August 30, 1975.

WHEEL OF FORTUNE

Testimonial. Good samaritans are honored and awarded prizes for their unselfish acts of kindness to other people. Both individuals appear and relate the circumstances surrounding the good deed.

Host: Todd Russell.

WHEEL OF FORTUNE—30 minutes—CBS—October 3, 1952 - December 25, 1953.

WHEEL OF FORTUNE

Game. Three competing contestants. Involved: a large spinning wheel that contains varying amounts of cash and several columns that assist or hinder players: "Lose one turn"; "One free spin"; and "Bankruptcy." The final category, bankruptcy, erases all a player's earnings if the wheel pinpoints it when it stops.

A line of spaces, which represents the number of letters in a famous name, place, or event is displayed.

One player spins the wheel. If it stops on a cash amount, the player suggests a letter. If it is contained in the name, it appears in its appropriate place on the board. The player then receives that amount of money. He continues to spin the wheel until he suggests an incorrect letter or lands on "Bank-ruptcy" or "Lose one turn." The next player then receives his turn. The player who is first to identify the mystery name is the winner, receives what money he has accumulated, and is permitted to shop for merchandise items—which are offered at their retail selling prices. Any money that the player has that remains is put into an account wherein it can only be spent if he wins another game. The player with the highest cash score (merchan-dise purchases included) is the winner and returns to compete again.

Host: Chuck Woolery.

Hostess: Susan Stafford.

Announcer: Charlie O'Donnell.

First Champion: Ginny Hubert.

WHEEL OF FORTUNE—30 minutes —NBC—Premiered: January 6, 1975.

WHEN TELEVISION WAS LIVE

Nostalgia. Through the use of kine-scopes, the television careers of Peter Lind Hayes and Mary Healy are re-called.

Hosts: Peter Lind Hayes and Mary Healy.

Producer: Peter Lind Hayes.

Director: Debra Gangnebin.

WHEN TELEVISION WAS LIVE—30 minutes—PBS—August 6, 1975 - Sep-tember 17, 1975. 7 episodes.

WHEN THINGS WERE ROTTEN

Comedy. A satire based on the legend of Robin Hood. Background: Twelfth -century England. The series depicts Robin Hood, the man who stole from the rich to give to the poor, as a birdbrain; his Merry Men, free-born Englishmen loyal to the king, as bum-bling klutzes; and Maid Marian, Robin's romantic interest, as a sexy dingbat. The story: When Prince John usurps the throne from his brother, Richard the Lionhearted, he provokes hatred between Normans and Saxons by imposing a tax on the Saxons. When Sir Robin of Locksley, a Saxon, opposes this, he is declared the wanted criminal Robin Hood. Retreat-ing to Sherwood Forest, he establishes a base near the Gallows Oak with his Merry Men (Alan-A-Dale, Friar Tuck, Renaldo, and Little John). Episodes depict Robin's efforts to return the throne to its rightful king, protect the weak, avenge the oppressed, and foil the evils of the Sheriff of Nottingham, who acts on behalf of Prince John. Created by Mel Brooks.

CAST

Robin Hood	Dick Gautier
Maid Marian	Misty Rowe
Alan-A-Dale	Bernie Kopell
Friar Tuck	Dick Van Patten
Renaldo	Richard Dimitri
Little John	David Sabin
Lord Hubert, the Sheriff of Nottingham	Henry Polic II
Bertram, the sheriff's aide	Richard Dimitri
Prince John	Ron Rifkin
Sylvester, a peasant	Jimmy Martinez

Music: Artie Butler

Executive Producer-Creator: Mel Brooks.

Producer: Norman Steinberg.

Director: Jerry Paris, Joshua Shelley, Marty Feldman, Peter H. Hunt, Bruce Bilson.

WHEN THINGS WERE ROTTEN—30 minutes—ABC—September 10, 1975 - December 24, 1975.

WHERE'S HUDDLES

Animated Cartoon. The misadventures of Ed Huddles and Bubba McCoy, quarterback and team center for the Rhinos, a disorganized professional football team. A Hanna-Barbera production.

Characters' Voices

Ed Huddles	Cliff Norton
Bubba McCoy	Mel Blanc
Marge Huddles, Ed's wife	Jean VanderPyl
Penny McCoy, Bubba's wife	Marie Wilson
Claude Pertwee, their perfectionist neighbor	Paul Lynde
The Coach	Alan Reed
Freight Train, a team member	Herb Jeffries

Additional characters: Fumbles, the Huddles's dog; and Beverly, Claude's cat.

Announcer: Dick Enberg.

Music: Hoyt Curtin.

WHERE'S HUDDLES—30 minutes—CBS—July 1, 1970 - September 10, 1971. Rebroadcasts: CBS—July 11, 1971 - September 5, 1971. 17 episodes.

WHERE'S RAYMOND

Musical Comedy. Background: The community of Pelham, New York. The misadventures of Raymond Wallace, a professional song-and-dance man.

CAST

Raymond Wallace	Ray Bolger
Susan, his girlfriend	Margie Millar
Peter Morrisey, his partner	Richard Erdman
Farley, his understudy	Charles Smith
Ruth Farley, his wife	Gloria Winters
Ruth's mother	Verna Felton
Katie, a friend	Chris Nelson

Also: Sylvia Lewis, Allyn Joslyn, Betty Lynn, Rise Stevens, Betty Kean.

Orchestra: Al Goodwin; Herbert Spencer, Earle Hagen.

WHERE'S RAYMOND—30 minutes—ABC—October 8, 1953 - June 10, 1955. 59 episodes. Also titled: "The Ray Bolger Show."

WHERE THE ACTION IS

Variety. Performances by Rock personalities.

Host: Dick Clark.

Regulars: Linda Scott, Steve Alaimo, Paul Revere and the Raiders.

Music: Provided by guests.

WHERE THE ACTION IS—30 minutes—ABC—July 5, 1965 - April 14, 1967.

WHERE THE HEART IS

Serial. Background: Nothcross, Connecticut. The conflicts, tensions, and drives of the close-knit Hathaway family.

CAST

Julian Hathaway	James Mitchell

Mary Hathaway	Diana Walker
Michael Hathaway	Greg Abels
Vicky Hathaway	Lisa Richards
Kate Prescott	Diana Van der Vlis
Alison Jessup	Louise Shaffer
Dr. Hugh Jessup	David Cryer
Dr. Joe Prescott	Bill Post, Jr.
Nancy Prescott	Katherine Meshill
Ed Lucas	Joe Mascolo
Stella O'Brien	Bibi Osterwald
Christine Cameron	Delphi Harrington
Loretta Jorden	Alice Drummond
Peter Jorden	Mike Bersell
Carol Gault	Janet League
Elizabeth Harris Rainey	Tracy Brooks Swope
John Rainey	Peter MacLean
Dr. Adrienne Harris	Priscilla Pointer
Lt. Hayward	Philip Sterling
Amy Snowden	Clarice Blackburn
Dr. Jim Hudson	Ruben Greene
Terry Stevens	Ted La Platt
Will Watts	Robert Symonds
Detective Munford	Gil Rogers
Lt. Fenelli	Ted Beniodes
Dr. Homes Rayburn	Alan Manson
Margaret Jordas	Rue McClanahan
	Barbara Baxley
Daniel Hathaway	Joseph Dolen
Ellie Jordas	Zohra Lampert
Mrs. Harrison	Caroline Coates
Lois Snowden	Jeanne Ruskin
The judge	William Prince
Ben Jessup	Daniel Keyes
Steve Prescott	Laurence Luckinbill
	Ron Harper
Terry Prescott	Ted Leplat
Mrs. Pangborn	Paula Truman
Bill Conway	Barton Hayman
Dave, the bartender	Charles Dobson
Judge Halstad	Mason Adams
Baby Katina	Kara Fleming

Music: Eddie Layton.

WHERE THE HEART IS—30 minutes—CBS—September 8, 1969 - March 23, 1973.

WHERE WAS I?

Game. Through a series of question-and-answer probe rounds with the host, a panel of four celebrities have to locate objects depicted in photographs.

Host: Dan Seymour.

Panelists: Peter Donald, Nancy Guild, David Ross, Bill Cullen.

Announcer: Bob Williams.

WHERE WAS I?—30 minutes—NBC 1952.

WHIPLASH

Adventure. Background: Australia during the 1850s. The story of Chris Cobb, the American owner of the Cobb and Company Stage Coach Lines, as he struggles to maintain the country's first stage route.

CAST
Chris Cobb	Peter Graves
Dan, his partner	Anthony Wickert

WHIPLASH—30 minutes—Syndicated 1961. 39 episodes. Filmed in Australia.

WHIRLPOOL

Anthology. Rebroadcasts of dramas that were originally aired via other filmed anthology programs.

Included:

Beneath The Surface. The struggles that face a woman as she attempts to escape her past.

Starring: Ida Lupino.

The Contest. A detective attempts to clear his brother and his fiancée of a murder charge.

Starring: Dick Powell.

The Stranger. The story of a young woman who finds aid from a stranger just after her husband escapes from prison.

Starring: Charles Boyer, Beverly Garland.

WHIRLPOOL—30 minutes—Syndicated 1959.

THE WHIRLYBIRDS

Adventure. Background: California. The experiences of Chuck Miller and P. T. Moore, pilots for Whirlybirds, Incorporated, a helicopter charter service.

CAST

Chuck Miller	Ken Tobey
P. T. Moore	Craig Hill
Chuck's girlfriend	Nancy Hale
P. T.'s girlfriend	Sandra Spence

Copter pilot (stand-in for Ken Tobey): Robert Gilbreath.

Stuntman (stand-in for Craig Hill): Earl Parker.

THE WHIRLYBIRDS—30 minutes—Syndicated 1957. 39 episodes. Also known as "Copter Patrol."

WHISPERING SMITH

Crime Drama. Background: The Denver Police Department during the 1870s. The investigations of Detectives Tom "Whispering" Smith and his partner, George Romack.

CAST

Tom "Whispering" Smith	Audie Murphy
George Romack	Guy Mitchell
John Richards, the police chief	Sam Buffington

Music: Richard Shores; Leo Shuken.

WHISPERING SMITH—30 minutes—NBC—May 18, 1961 - September 18, 1961. 25 episodes.

THE WHISTLER

Anthology. Mystery presentations. Stories of people who are suddenly caught in a destructive web of their own misdeeds. The Whistler, who is identified by the mournful whistling of the theme music, is never seen. His observations concerning the actions of the individuals prevail throughout each drama.

The Whistler (Narrator): Bill Forman.

Orchestra: Wilbur Hatch.

Theme: "The Whistler," whistled by Dorothy Roberts. Wilbur Hatch is the composer.

Included:

Dark Hour. The story of a man who believes he's committed a murder during a mental blackout.

Starring: Robert Hutton, Nancy Gates.

Windfall. The story of a man who stumbles upon a corpse with a one-hundred-thousand-dollar bank account and the ensuing difficulties when he tries to claim the money.

Starring: Charles McGraw, Dorothy Green.

Fatal Fraud. The story of a larcenous blonde who uses her feminine wiles to convince a clever impersonator to master the voice of a wealthy importer. Her intent: to divert a valuable shipment.

Starring: Marie Windsor.

Backfire. Suspicious of his wife's actions, a man follows her to a nightclub. When he discovers that she is planning to double cross him, he decides to put his own plan into effect.

Starring: Lon Chaney, Jr., Dorothy Green.

Program Opening:

The Whistler: "I am The Whistler. And I know many things, for I walk by night. I know many strange tales hidden in the hearts of men and women who have stepped into the shadows. Yes, I know the nameless terrors of which they dare not speak."

THE WHISTLER—30 minutes—Syndicated 1954. 39 episodes. Based on the radio program.

THE WHISTLING WIZARD

Puppet Adventure. Looking into an enchanted well, J. P., an inquisitive child, loses his balance, falls in, and reappears in the fantasy kingdom of the Land of Beyond. Stories relate his adventures in the bewitched kingdom.

Characters:

J. P., distinguished by four toes on each foot.

Dooley, the Whistling Wizard, an Irish elf who rules the Land of Beyond.

Heathcliff, J.P.'s horse.

Thimble, assistant ruler of the kingdom.

Davey Jones, the guardian of treasures at the bottom of the sea.

King Rutabaga, the ruler of the neighboring kingdom, Nagard.

Spider Lady, a villainess who seeks control of the Land of Beyond.

Character movement and voices: Bil and Cora Baird.

THE WHISTLING WIZARD—15 minutes—CBS 1952.

WHITE HUNTER

Adventure. Background: Africa. Dramatizations based on the experiences of John A. Hunter, game hunter and trapper.

CAST

John Hunter	Rhodes Reason
The Game Commissioner	Tim Turner

WHITE HUNTER—30 minutes—Syndicated 1958. 39 episodes.

WHO DO YOU TRUST?

See title: "Do You Trust Your Wife?"

WHO PAYS?

Game. Through the cross-examination of two of his or her employees, a celebrity panel of three have to identify mystery-guest personalities. The star's employees receive one hundred dollars each if the panel fails to uncover their employer's identity.

Host: Mike Wallace.

Panelists: Sir Cedric Hardwicke, Celeste Holm, Gene Klavan.

Premiere Guests: Carol Channing, Red Buttons.

WHO PAYS?—30 minutes—CBS—July 2, 1959 - September 1959.

WHO SAID THAT?

Game. Quotations taken from news stories are related to a celebrity panel. The panel must then identify the news story from which the quotation was taken. Failure to do so adds, each time, five dollars to a jackpot. At the program's end, a question, submitted by a home viewer, is read to the panel. If they fail to answer it, the viewer receives a $50 savings bond plus the money that has been accumulated in the jackpot.

Host: Robert Trout.

Regular Panelist: John Cameron Swayze.

Announcer: Peter Roberts.

Producer: Fred W. Friendly, Anne Gillis, Herb Leder.

Director: Mark Hawley, Garry Simpson.

WHO SAID THAT?—30 minutes—NBC—December 9, 1948 - July 19, 1954; ABC—30 minutes—February 2, 1955 - July 26, 1955.

WHO'S TALKING?

A game show, hosted by Frann Weigle, in which contestants have to identify celebrities from masked photos and recordings of their voice. Broadcast on CBS for fifteen minutes in 1951.

WHO'S THE BOSS?

Game. Through question-and-answer probe rounds with their secretaries, a celebrity panel of four have to identify their prominent employers. Secretaries receive one hundred dollars each if the panel fails to uncover their employer's identity.

Host: Walter Kiernan.

Panelists: Polly Rowles, Dick Kollman, Sylvia Lyons, Horace Sutton.

WHO'S THE BOSS?—30 minutes—ABC 1954.

WHO'S THERE?

Game. Through props, personal items, and apparel clues, a celebrity panel of three has to identify mystery-guest personalities.

Hostess: Arlene Francis.

Panelists: Bill Cullen, Paula Stone, Robert Coote.

Announcer: Rex Marshall.

WHO'S THERE?—30 minutes—CBS—July 14, 1952 - September 1952.

THE WHO, WHAT OR WHERE GAME

Game. Three competing contestants who each receive one hundred and twenty-five dollars bidding cash. A category topic is revealed, followed by three questions—each characterized by three parts: The Who (even money), the What (two to one), and the Where (three to one). Players then press a button and secretly lock in a "W" of their choice and a cash wager (fifty dollars minimum). Choices are then revealed. If all three have chosen differently, the highest wagerer receives the "W" question. Correct answers award the player his bet amount of money; incorrect responses deduct the amount. If two players have chosen the same "W" a verbal auction is held. The highest cash wagerer receives the question. If all three have bid on the same "W" it is an automatic cancellation and a new category is introduced. Winners, the highest cash scorers, receive the money as their prize.

Host: Art James.

Announcer: Mike Darrow.

Music: George David Weiss.

THE WHO, WHAT OR WHERE GAME–25 minutes–NBC–December 29, 1969 - January 4, 1974.

WHO'S WHO

Documentary. A magazine-type program that reveals the human side of public figures through in-depth interviews.

Host: Dan Rather.

Co-Hosts: Charles Kuralt, Barbara Howar.

Producer: Don Hewitt.

WHO'S WHO–60 minutes–CBS–January 4, 1977 - May 10, 1977; June 5, 1977 - June 26, 1977.

WHO'S WHOSE?

Game. One woman and three men, who each claim to be her husband, appear opposite a panel of four celebrities (three regulars and one guest). Through a series of question-and-answer probe rounds, first with the woman, then with the men, the panel has to identify her spouse. Players receive money for participating.

Host: Phil Barker.

Panelists: Basil Rathbone, Robin Chandler, Art Ford.

Announcer (as identified): "Gunga."

WHO'S WHOSE?–30 minutes–CBS–June 25, 1951 - September 1951.

WHY?

Game. Involved: The five W's–Who, What, When, Where, and Why. The host states the first four W's of a situation; through a series of question and answer probe rounds, a contestant panel has to determine the Why. Prizes are awarded to the panelist with the most correct answers.

Host: John Reed King.

Question Man: Bill Cullen.

WHY?–30 minutes–ABC–July 29, 1952 - September 1952.

WICHITA TOWN

Western. Background: Wichita Town, Kansas, 1870s. The story of Marshall Mike Dunbar and his efforts to maintain law and order.

CAST

Marshall Mike Dunbar	Joel McCrea
Deputy Ben Matheson	Jody McCrea

Music: Hans Salter.

WICHITA TOWN–30 minutes–NBC–September 30, 1959 - April 4, 1960.

WIDE COUNTRY

Adventure. Background: The rodeo circuit between Texas and California. The experiences of Mitch Guthrie, a champion rodeo rider, as he travels from rodeo to rodeo seeking to secure the Gold Buckle, the trophy that is awarded to the world's best bronco buster.

CAST

Mitch Guthrie   Earl Holliman
Andy Guthrie, his
    brother   Andrew Prine

Music: Stanley Wilson.

WIDE COUNTRY—60 minutes—NBC —September 20, 1962 - September 12, 1963. 28 episodes. Syndicated.

Wild Bill Hickok. Guy Madison.

WIDE WIDE WORLD

See title: "Dave Garroway."

THE WILBURN BROTHERS SHOW

Musical Variety. Performances by Country and Western entertainers.

Hosts: Ted and Doyle Wilburn.

Vocalist: Loretta Lynn.

Music: The Nashville Tennessians.

THE WILBURN BROTHERS SHOW—30 minutes—Syndicated 1963. 52 tapes.

WILD BILL HICKOK

Western. Background: The Frontier, 1870s. The exploits of James Butler (Wild Bill) Hickok, U.S. Marshall, and his partner, Jingles, as they battle injustice throughout the West.

CAST

Wild Bill Hickok   Guy Madison
Jingles   Andy Devine

Announcer: John Cannon.

Producer: William F. Brady, Wesley Barry.

Sponsor: Kellogg's.

Wild Bill's Horse: Buckshot.

Jingles P. Jones's Horse: Joker.

WILD BILL HICKOK—30 minutes— Syndicated 1952. Also appeared on ABC—30 minutes—October 2, 1957 - September 24, 1958. 113 episodes.

WILD CARGO

Documentary. Films depicting the capture of wild animals for zoos.

Host-Narrator: Arthur Jones.

WILD CARGO—30 minutes—Syndicated 1963.

WILD KINGDOM

Documentary. Films detailing the life and struggles of animals.

Hosts: Marlin Perkins, Jim Fowler, Stan Brock, Tom Allen.

Narrator: Joe Slattery.

Music: James Bourgeois.

WILD KINGDOM—30 minutes—NBC —January 6, 1963 - September 5, 1973. Syndicated.

THE WILD, WILD WEST

Western. Background: The Frontier, 1870s. The investigations of James T. West and Artemus Gordon, United States government underground intelligence agents, as they incorporate ingenious scientific weapons to battle diabolical villains.

CAST

James T. West	Robert Conrad
Artemus Gordon	Ross Martin
President Ulysses S. Grant, their superior	James Gregory
	Roy Engle
Dr. Miguelito Lovelace, an enemy agent	Michael Dunn
Jeremy Pike, West's assistant for a short period	Charles Aidman
Count Manzeppi, the evil magician	Victor Buono

Music: Richard Shores; Richard Markowitz; Morton Stevens.

Executive Producer: Philip Leacock, Michael Garrison.

Producer: Richard Landau, Leonard Katzman, Fred Freiberger, Collier Young, John Mantley, Gene L. Coon, Bruce Lansbury.

Director: Bill Witney, Richard Sarafian, Bernard Kowalsky, Don Taylor, Irving Moore, Harvey Hart, Alvin Ganzer, Justis Addiss, Alan Crosland, Paul Wendkos, Richard Whorf, Lee H. Katzin, Mark Rydell, Ed Dein, Ralph Senesky, Richard Donner, Robert Sparr, Sherman Marks, Jesse Hibbs, Charles R. Rondeau, Leon Benson, Gunnar Hellstrom, James B. Clark, Marvin Chomsky, Alex Nichol, Mike Moder, Lawrence Dobkin, Michael Caffrey, Vincent McEveety, Paul Stanley, Bernard McEveety, Herb Wallerstein.

Creator: Michael Garrison.

THE WILD, WILD WEST—60 minutes—CBS—September 17, 1965 - September 19, 1969. Rebroadcasts: CBS—June 1970 - September 1970. 104 episodes. Syndicated.

WILD, WILD WORLD OF ANIMALS

Documentary. Films depicting the animal struggle for survival.

Narrator: William Conrad.

Additional Narrative: Hugh Faulk, Mary Batten.

Music: Gerherd Trede, Beatrice Witkin.

WILD, WILD WORLD OF ANIMALS —30 minutes—Syndicated 1973.

WILLIE WONDERFUL

A puppet series for children dealing with the adventures of Willie Wonderful, a young boy who travels with a circus. Voices for the thirty-eight puppet characters are provided by Stan Freberg and Eddie Bracken. The series, composed of 195 thirty-minute episodes, was first broadcast over ABC in 1959.

WILL THE REAL JERRY LEWIS PLEASE SIT DOWN

Animated Cartoon. The misadventures of Jerry Lewis, a fumbling janitor with the Odd Job Employment Agency. The series incorporates the celluloid creations of Jerry Lewis (e.g., The Playboy, The Nutty Professor, The Errand Boy) as it depicts his fruitless attempts to successfully complete his assigned tasks. Created by Jerry Lewis.

Additional characters: Geraldine, Jerry's sister; Mr. Blunderpuss, Jerry's employer; Rhonda, Jerry's girlfriend; and Spot, Geraldine's pet frog.

WILL THE REAL JERRY LEWIS PLEASE SIT DOWN—30 minutes—ABC—September 12, 1970 - September 2, 1972.

WILLY

Comedy. Distinguished by two formats.

Format One: September 18, 1954 - March 31, 1955.
Background: Renfrew, New Hampshire. The misadventures of Willy Dodger, an attorney, as she struggles to practice law in a town where people are distrustful of female barristers.

CAST
Willy Dodger   June Havoc

Mr. Dodger, her
   father   Wheaton Chambers
                             Lloyd Corrigan
Charlie Bush,
   her boyfriend,
   the town
   veterinarian   Whitfield Connar
Emily, her widowed
   sister   Mary Treen
Franklin Sanders, her
   nephew   Danny Richards, Jr.

Willy's dog: Rags.

Format Two: April 7, 1955 - July 7, 1955.
Background: New York City. The cases of Willy Dodger, legal council for the Bannister Vaudeville Company.

CAST
Willy Dodger   June Havoc
Perry Bannister, her
   employer   Hal Peary
Harvey Evelyn,
   her friend,
   the owner of
   a stock
   company   Sterling Holloway

WILLY—30 minutes—CBS—September 18, 1954 - July 7, 1955. Syndicated; withdrawn.

WIN WITH A WINNER

Game. Five competing players, each of whom stands before a numbered post (as in a horse race). Object: For players to reach the finish line by answering questions. Players each select their own questions by point values—the higher the point value, the more difficult the question. If the player correctly answers the question he moves forward in accord with its value. Incorrect answers halt a player until his next turn. The winner receives merchandise prizes.

Host: Sandy Becker.

Assistant: Marilyn Toomey.

Announcer: Bill Wendell.

WIN WITH A WINNER—30 minutes —NBC—June 24, 1958 - September 9, 1958.

WIN WITH THE STARS

Game. Involved: Two celebrity guests and four noncelebrity contestants. Object: the identification of song titles.

Round One: Two of the four contestants compete, each paired with one of the celebrities to form two teams of two. One team at a time competes. A musical selection is played. As soon as the title is recognized, the player presses a button to stop a ticking clock (set for forty-five seconds). If a correct title is given, the team scores two points and receives the opportunity to earn additional points by singing the first two lines of the song. Each correct lyric awards one point. The game continues until the forty-five-second time limit has elapsed. Team two then competes in the same manner with the object being to beat their opponents' score. The winner is the highest scoring team.

Round Two: The remaining two contestants compete in the same manner.

Round Three: The two highest scorers of rounds one and two compete in a final segment, which is played in the same manner. The winner, the highest scorer, receives his points transferred into dollars.

Host: Allen Ludden.

Announcer: Jay Stewart.

Orchestra: Bobby Hammock.

Appearing: Judy Carne, Jaye P. Morgan, Steve Allen, Jayne Meadows, Ruta Lee, Barbara McNair, Paul Lynde, Abby Dalton, Betty White, Bill Dana, Mel Tormé, Rose Marie, Roddy McDowall, Bob Crane.

WIN WITH THE STARS—30 minutes —Syndicated 1968. 26 tapes.

WINDOW ON MAIN STREET

Comedy-Drama. Background: The town of Millsburg. Life in a small American town as seen through the eyes of Cameron Garrett Brooks, a novelist who, after the death of his wife and son, returns to his home town to write about its people.

CAST

Cameron Brooks	Robert Young
Lloyd Ramsey, the newspaper editor	Ford Rainey
Chris Logan, a widow, his assistant	Constance Moore
Wally Evans, the owner of the Majestic Hotel	James Byron
Peggy Evans, his wife	Carol Byron
Henry McGill, the hotel desk clerk	Warner Jones
Arnie Logan, Chris's young son	Brad Berwick

WINDOW ON MAIN STREET—30

minutes—CBS—October 2, 1961 - September 12, 1962. 36 episodes.

WINDOWS

Anthology. Dramatic presentations.

Included:

The World Out There. Through the efforts of her educated younger cousin, an illiterate woman attempts to learn how to read and write.

CAST
Cora: Mary Perry; Benji: Anthony Perkins; Tom: Joseph Perkins.

Rose's Boy. A one-character play. A woman's struggles to face the difficult task of telling a young boy the circumstances surrounding his mother's death.

CAST
The woman: Judith Evelyn.

The Calliope Tree. Through the worship of a young boy, an ex-circus clown attempts to relive the glories of his past.

CAST
The Clown: Henry Hull; The boy: Van Dyke Parks.

Domestic Dilemma. The effect of a woman alcoholic on her family.

CAST
The woman: Geraldine Page.

WINDOWS—30 minutes—CBS—July 8, 1955 - August 26, 1955.

WINDOW SHOPPING

Game. Three competing contestants. A photograph is briefly flashed on a screen. Each player then relates the items that he believes were depicted in the photograph. For each correct identification he receives one point. Several such rounds are played. The player with the highest point total is the winner and receives the opportunity to window shop. His point total is transferred into seconds and for that amount of time, a stage window, which contains numerous merchandise items, is displayed. The items he is then able to describe become his gifts.

Host: Bob Kennedy.

Judge: Professor William Wood, Columbia School of Journalism.

WINDOW SHOPPING—30 minutes—ABC—April 2, 1962 - June 29, 1962.

WINDY CITY JAMBOREE

Musical Variety. Background: Chicago.

Host: Danny O'Neal.

Orchestra: Gloria Van.

WINDY CITY JAMBOREE—30 minutes—DuMont 1950.

WINGO

Game. Two competing players, a champion and a challenger. Basis: Very difficult question-and-answer rounds. The host reads a question. The player who is first to identify himself through a buzzer signal receives a chance to answer. If correct he receives one point; if incorrect the point is deducted from his score. The winner, the highest scorer, receives one thousand dollars. Players compete until defeated vying for the top prize of $250,000.

Host: Bob Kennedy.

WINGO—30 minutes—NBC—April 1, 1958 - May 13, 1958.

WINKY DINK AND YOU

Children. Children participate at home via inexpensive Winky Dink kits. A magic transparent screen is placed over the television screen. The host relates the adventures of Winky Dink, an animated cartoon boy, and his friend Woofer, the animated dog. The events unfold through a series of cartoon drawings that enable children to assist the characters when they are in trouble by drawing the life-saving essentials on their screen with a wax crayon. For example: As Woofer faces a life and death situation, Winky Dink speaks: "Oh boys and girls, we've got to save our pal Woofer. Please draw that special part of the machine...Oh thanks, just in time, Woofer is saved. Quick gang, erase your drawing with your magic cloth while we figure out what to do next." Incidents are also related by the host.

Host: Jack Barry.

Assistant: Mike McBean.

Orchestra: John Gart.

WINKY DINK AND YOU—30 minutes—CBS—October 10, 1953 - April 27, 1957. A five-minute animated version appeared via syndication in 1969.

WINNER TAKE ALL

Game. Two competing contestants, a challenger and the previous champion. Object: To answer questions based on sketches that are performed on stage. The player with the most correct answers is the winner and receives merchandise prizes.

Host: Bill Cullen.

Assistant: Sheila Connolly.

Performers: Barry Gray, Betty Jones Watson, Jerry Austen, Howard Malone.

Orchestra: Bernard Leighton.

Producer: Mark Goodson, Bill Todman, Gil Fates.

Director: Frances Buss, Roland Gillette.

Sponsor: Chevrolet; Gillette.

WINNER TAKE ALL—45 minutes—CBS—July 1, 1948 - April 20, 1951.

WINNING STREAK

Game. Two competing contestants. Sixteen letters of the alphabet, each representing a different point value, are displayed on a large board. One player chooses a letter, which reveals its point value. If the player seeks to earn the points, he is asked a question that corresponds to that letter (e.g., If letter I is chosen, the answer will begin with the letter I). If the player answers correctly he receives the points. The opponent then receives his selection. Should the player pass the question, the opponent automatically has to answer it, and the next selection reverts back to the original player. The first player to reach the goal (varies from 250-350 points) is the winner.

The present champion is placed opposite the previous winner. A board that contains eighteen numbers, numbered as such from one to eighteen, is displayed. The present champion then chooses one number from one to six. A cash amount of money is then revealed, which becomes the cash value of each number from seven to eighteen. The champion then selects one number. A letter of the alphabet is revealed and the player has to give a word using that letter. When he does, the money is placed in a jackpot. The opponent then selects a number and has to give a word using the two letters that are now displayed. The money is again added to the jackpot. The game continues in this manner; for each additional number that is selected the player has to give a word using all the exposed letters. When a player is stumped or gives an incorrect word he is defeated. The other player becomes the champion and receives whatever money has been accumulated in the jackpot. The player remains to face the winner of the qualifying round.

Host: Bill Cullen.

Announcer: Don Pardo.

Music: Recorded.

First champion: Jean Sheridan.

WINNING STREAK—30 minutes—NBC—July 1, 1974 - January 3, 1975.

WINSTON CHURCHILL

Documentary. Through films, interviews, and stills, the life of Sir Winston Churchill is recalled. The series focuses on his career as a statesman during World War II.

Narrator: Gary Merrill.
Reading Churchill's works: Richard Burton.
Music: Richard Rodgers.

WINSTON CHURCHILL—30 minutes —ABC—September 30, 1962 - April 5, 1963. Broadcast under the title "The Valiant Years"—ABC—November 27, 1960 - June 11, 1961.

WIRE SERVICE

Adventure. The global investigations of Dean Evans, Katherine Wells, and Dan Miller, wire-service reporters for *Trans Globe News.* Stories depict their experiences on a rotational basis.

CAST

Dean Evans	George Brent
Katherine Wells	Mercedes McCambridge
Dan Miller	Dane Clark

Program Open (related by the star of the particular episode):

"Nothing travels faster than news. An electronic impulse splinters distance at one hundred and eighty-six thousand miles per second. From Tokyo, from London, from Rio, from New York. An age of speed and curiosity, the news probes and the probe is truth."

WIRE SERVICE—60 minutes—ABC—September 1956 - September 1957. 39 episodes. Syndicated.

WISDOM OF THE AGES

Discussion. Children and adults, from ten to eighty years of age, discuss and suggest possible solutions to problems that have been submitted by home viewers.

Host: Jack Barry.

WISDOM OF THE AGES—30 minutes—DuMont 1953.

WITH THIS RING

Discussion. Two engaged couples, selected from the lists of applicants for marriage licenses, appear. A marital problem, which has been submitted by a home viewer, is read then discussed by the couples who relate their thoughts concerning possible solutions.

Host: Bill Slater.

WITH THIS RING—30 minutes—DuMont 1951.

WITNESS

Crime Drama. People who have witnessed or become innocently involved in crimes appear and through the questioning of a panel of defense attorneys relate their experiences. The program attempts to expose rackets and criminals by making people aware of confidence games.

Panel: William Geoghan, Richard Steele, Benedict Ginsberg, Charles Hayden.

WITNESS—30 minutes—CBS—September 29, 1960 - February 2, 1961.

THE WIZARD OF ODDS

Game. Selected studio-audience members compete in greatly varying contests designed to test their knowledge of national odds and averages and bring forth a "Wizard's Champion."

Regular segments:

"The Elimination Round." Three contestants appear on stage. The host reveals clues to the identity of a mystery celebrity one at a time to a limit of five clues. The player who is first to correctly identify the personality is the winner and receives a valuable merchandise prize.

"The Odds and Averages Board." Two players compete. Three items are displayed on a board, one of which is the odd item. The player who is first to shout the odd item receives one point. Should he give the wrong item his opponent receives the point. The first player to score three points receives a valuable merchandise item.

Before the final round is played the names of all the players who have competed are placed on a large spinning wheel. The player whose name is selected by the wheel when it stops receives the opportunity to play "Wizard's Wheel of Fortune."

One figure is displayed on the top of a large board. Below it are seven questions, each of which is answerable by a number, but only four of which will total just below the established figure. If the player can select the four correct questions (or items as they are also referred to), he receives a new car. If he fails he receives merchandise prizes according to his correct number of selections.

Host: Alex Trebek.

Assistant: Mary Pom.

Announcers: Owen Spam; Charlie O'Donnell.

Music: Stan Worth.

THE WIZARD OF ODDS—30 minutes—NBC—June 17, 1973 - June 28, 1974.

WODEHOUSE PLAYHOUSE

Comedy. A series of humorous stories based on the prolific pen of P.G. Wodehouse.

Introduced By: P.G. Wodehouse.

Regular Performers: John Alderton, Pauline Collins.

Music: Raymond Jones.

Producer: Michael Mills.

WODEHOUSE PLAYHOUSE—30 minutes—Syndicated 1977.

THE WOLFMAN JACK SHOW

Variety. A mixture of music, songs, and comedy sketches.

Host: Wolfman Jack.

Regulars: Peter Cullen, Murray Langston, John Harris, The Incredible Puppets, and Vivian, the talking mule.

Executive Producer: Don Kelley.

Producer: Rif Markowitz.

Director: Mark Warren.

THE WOLFMAN JACK SHOW—30 minutes—Syndicated 1977.

WOMAN

Discussion. Discussions on topics of interest that concern women in their daily lives.

Hostess: Sherrye Henry.

Music: Recorded.

WOMAN—30 minutes—Syndicated 1971.

A WOMAN TO REMEMBER

Serial. Background: An AM radio station in New York City where a daily serial originates. An unknown woman, hired to replace the lead on the program, is disliked by the other members of the cast. Through rehearsal proceedings, the program dramatizes her attempts to overcome existing hostilities and tensions.

Though considered by many to be television's first serial, extensive research disproved this, revealing "Faraway Hill" (1946) the medium's inaugural serialized endeavor.

CAST
The Serial Star	Patricia Wheel
The Replacement	Joan Castle
The Director	John Raby
The Sound Man	Frankie Thomas

A WOMAN TO REMEMBER—15 minutes—DuMont—1947-1949.

WOMAN WITH A PAST

Serial. The dramatic story of Lynn Sherwood, fashion designer.

CAST
Lynn Sherwood	Constance Ford
Her daughter	Barbara Myers
Peggy Sherwood, her sister	Ann Hegira
Gwen	Jean Stapleton

WOMAN WITH A PAST—15 minutes—CBS—February 1, 1954 - July 2, 1954.

WONDERAMA

Children. Cartoons, game contests for prizes, and performances by top-name guests.

Hosts: Sandy Becker; Herb Sheldon; Sonny Fox; Bob McAllister.

Music: Recorded.

WONDERAMA—3 hours—1955

Present. Broadcast on Metromedia stations around the country. Original title: "Let's Have Fun."

WONDERBUG

See title: "The Krofft Supershow," *Wonderbug* segment.

WONDERFUL JOHN ACTION

Comedy. Background: The Ohio River Valley, 1919. Events in the lives of the Actions, an Irish-American family.

CAST

John Action, the father, a court clerk and the owner of the general store	Harry Holcombe
Julia Action, his wife	Virginia Dwyer
Kevin Action, their son	Ronnie Walker
Terrence Action, John's brother, the manager of the general store	Ian Martain
Peter Bodkin, Jr., John's employer at the court	Pat Harrington
Bessie Action, John's sister	Jane Rose

Also: Lou Gilbert, Robert Sullivan.

Orchestra: John Gart.

WONDERFUL JOHN ACTION—30 minutes—ABC—July 13, 1953 - September 1953.

Wonder Woman. Lynda Carter.

WONDER WOMAN

Adventure. In the year circa 200 B.C., when the rival gods Mars and Aphrodite ruled the Earth, Aphrodite, who was unable to defeat Mars, organized a group of superwomen called Amazons and retreated to Paradise Island, an uncharted land mass within the Bermuda Triangle. There, she selected Hippolyte as her queen and presented her with the magic girdle, a gold belt that produces superhuman strength. However, still determined to defeat his adversary, Mars retreated to skullduggery and used love, Hippolyte's own weapon against her, to snatch the magic girdle. Though displeased, Hippolyte received forgiveness from Aphrodite but had to, as all Amazons, wear special wrist bracelets made of feminum to remind them always of the dangers of submitting to men's domination. To further show her sorrow, Hippolyte fashioned a small statue that, when offered to Aphrodite, was brought to life as the baby Diana.

The time: now that of World War II. Crash landing on Paradise Island when his plane is hit by enemy gun fire, U.S. Fighter Pilot Steve Trevor is found by Diana and nursed back to health. An olympic games competition is held and Diana, who proves herself superior, is chosen to escort Steve back to civilization and to assist America in the war effort.

From the Queen Mother, Diana receives the gold belt (to maintain her cunning and strength away from Paradise Island) and the magic lariat, which compels people to tell the truth. Diana then chooses a revealing red, white, and blue costume to signify her allegiance to freedom and democracy. With the final words of her mother, "In the words of ordinary mortals you are a Wonder Woman," Diana incorporates her invisible plane to fly Steve back to Washington, D.C. (Prior to their departure, Steve had been given a special drug from the Hybernia Tree to erase all memory of Paradise Island.)

In order to be at Steve's side, Diana adopts the guise of Diana Prince and, after achieving remarkably high scores on army aptitude tests, she is made Yeoman First Class and assigned to the U.S. War Department as Major Trevor's secretary. Stories depict Diana's crusade, as Wonder Woman, against Nazi activities in America. (By doing a twirling striptease, the plain-looking Diana emerges into the beautiful Wonder Woman.)

CAST

Diana Prince/Wonder Woman	Lynda Carter
Major Steve Trevor	Lyle Waggoner
General Phillip Blankenship	Richard Eastham
Yeoman Etta Candy, the general's secretary	Beatrice Colen
Drusilla/Wonder Girl, Diana's sister	Debra Winger
The Queen Mother	Cloris Leachman Carolyn Jones
Magda, an Amazon	Pamela Shoop
Dalma, an Amazon	Erica Hagen

Music: Artie Kane, Charles Fox.

Theme: "Wonder Woman" by Norman Gimbel, Charles Fox.

Executive Producer: Douglas S. Cramer.

Producer: Wilfred Baumes.

Director: Stuart Margolin, Bruce Bilson, Herb Wallerstein, Charles R. Rondeau, Richard Kinon, Leonard Horn, Alan Crosland, Barry Crane.

WONDER WOMAN—60 minutes—ABC—Premiered: March 31, 1976.

Original title: "The New, Original Wonder Woman."

The character of "Wonder Woman," created by Charles Moulton, was first seen in 1973 as part of the animated series "Super Friends" (which see). On March 12, 1974, ABC presented an unsold pilot film entitled "Wonder Woman," with Cathy Lee Crosby as Diana and Kaz Garas as Steve, in an updated, modern version of the 1940s character that failed to become a series.

THE WOODY WOODBURY SHOW

Talk-Variety.

Host: Woody Woodbury.

Music: The Michael Melvoin Combo.

THE WOODY WOODBURY SHOW—90 minutes—Syndicated 1967.

THE WOODY WOODPECKER SHOW

Animated Cartoon. The misadventures

of Woody Woodpecker, the world's most beloved bird.

Additional segments: "Andy Panda"; "Space Mouse"; "Charley Beary"; "Gabby Gator."

Host: Walter Lantz, Woody's creator.

Woody's voice: Grace Lantz (Mrs.).

Additional Voices: Paul Frees, June Foray, Walter Tetley, Daws Butler.

Music: Charles Wheeler, Walter Greene.

Producer: Walter Lantz.

Director: Paul Smith, Alex Lovey, Sid Marcus.

THE WOODY WOODPECKER SHOW—30 minutes—ABC—1957 - 1958. Syndicated. NBC—30 minutes —September 12, 1970 - September 2, 1972. 52 episodes.

WORD FOR WORD

Game. Two competing players. Object: To form as many three- and four-letter words from larger words (e.g., "Make as many words as you can from aspidistra"). Players receive one point for each acceptable word. The player with the highest score is the winner and receives that score transferred into seconds, which he uses against the Electronic Word-O-Meter. Object: To unscramble a jumbled word before the machine. His cash prize depends on the number of words he successfully unscrambles before the machine and before his time runs out.

Host: Merv Griffin.

Announcer: Frank Sims.

WORD FOR WORD—30 minutes— NBC—September 30, 1963 - October 23, 1964.

WORDS AND MUSIC

Musical Variety.

Hostess: Barbara Marshall.

Music: The Jerry Jerome Trio.

Producer-Director: Duane McKinney.

WORDS AND MUSIC—15 minutes— NBC 1949.

WORDS AND MUSIC

Game. Three contestants compete. A large board that contains sixteen squares (numbered from one to sixteen) is displayed on stage. Each square contains a clue that is associated with a particular word in a particular song. One player (through a flip of coin decision) chooses one number. The host reads the clue (e.g., "The very yeast"), and a song is sung ("The Sound of Music."). The player who is first to associate the clue with the word in the song presses a button to identify himself. If he gives a correct answer ("Rise"—"Of the wings of the birds that rise"), he receives cash. The person with the last correct response selects the next clue. The player with the highest cash score is the winner. The player vies to win three straight games and a new car.

Cash at stake: Round one: twenty dollars; round two: forty dollars; round three: sixty dollars; and round four: eighty dollars for each correct association. Four clues are played per round.

Host: Wink Martindale.

Announcer: Johnny Gilbert.

Vocalists: Peggy Connelly, Bob Marlo, Katie Grant, Don Minter, Pat Henderson.

WORDS AND MUSIC—30 minutes—NBC—September 28, 1970 - February 12, 1971.

WORLD ADVENTURES

Travel. Films depicting the people, music, and life styles of countries throughout the world.

Host: Gunther Less.

Music: Recorded.

WORLD ADVENTURES—30 minutes—Syndicated 1965. Also aired under the title: "Journey to Adventure."

A WORLD APART

Serial. The dramatic story of Betty Kahlam, a serial writer and the unwed mother of two children, Patrice and Chris. Against a plaguing generation gap, she struggles to achieve their love and foster a sense of family unity and togetherness.

CAST
Patrice Kahlam	Susan Sarandon
Betty Kahlam	Augusta Dabney
Chris Kahlam	Matthew Cowles
Dr. John Karr	Robert Gentry
T.D. Drinkard	Tom Logan
Matilda	Rosetta La Noire
Nancy Condon	Susan Sullivan
	Judith Barcroft
Linda Peters	Heather MacRae
Russell Barry	William Prince
Sara Sims	Kathy Parker
Dr. Edward Sims	James Noble
Thomas Walsh	Roy Shuman

Also: M'el Dowd, Elizabeth Lawrence.

A WORLD APART—30 minutes—ABC—March 30, 1970 - June 25, 1971.

THE WORLD AT WAR

Documentary. The history of World War II is traced through film—from the rise of Hitler to Allied victory.

Narrator: Sir Laurence Olivier.

Music: Carl Davis.

THE WORLD AT WAR—60 minutes—Syndicated 1973. Produced in England.

WORLD CRIME HUNT

See title: "Paris Precinct."

THE WORLD OF GIANTS

Adventure. The investigations of Mel Hunter· and Bill Winters, American counterespionage agents reduced, through scientific experimentation, to six inches in height. Stories relate their attempts to infiltrate and expose criminal organizations.

CAST
Mel Hunter	Marshall Thompson
Bill Winters	Arthur Franz

THE WORLD OF GIANTS—30 minutes—Syndicated 1961. 13 episodes.

THE WORLD OF LOWELL THOMAS

Travel. Films exploring remote regions of the world.

Host-Narrator: Lowell Thomas.

THE WORLD OF LOWELL THOMAS—30 minutes—Syndicated 1966.

THE WORLD OF MISTER SWEENY

Comedy. Background: The town of Mapleton. The lighthearted misadventures of Cicero P. Sweeny, a general-store owner who involves himself in and attempts to solve the problems of others.

CAST

Cicero P. Sweeny	Charlie Ruggles
Kippie Sweeny, his grandson	Gene Walker
Marge Sweeny, his daughter	Helen Wagner
Tom Millikan, a friend	Harry Gresham
Abigail Millikan, his wife	Betty Garde
Henrietta, Marge's friend	Janet Fox
Molly, the town spinster	Jane Cleveland
Little Eva, the refugee girl	Lydia Reed

THE WORLD OF MISTER SWEENY —15 minutes (Daily)—NBC—June 30, 1954 - December 30, 1955.

THE WORLD OF SURVIVAL

Documentary. Films depicting the animal struggle for survival.

Host-Narrator: John Forsythe.

Music: Howard Blake.

THE WORLD OF SURVIVAL—30 minutes—Syndicated 1972.

WORLD WAR I

Documentary. Films recalling the events leading up to and the key battles and campaigns of World War I.

Narrator: Robert Ryan.

Music: Morton Gould.

WORLD WAR I—30 minutes—CBS—September 22, 1964 - January 1965. 26 episodes.

WRANGLER

Western. Background: The Frontier during the 1880s. The exploits of Pitcarin, a wandering, two-fisted cowboy who aids people in distress.

Starring: Jason Evers as Pitcarin.

WRANGLER—30 minutes—NBC—August 4, 1960 - September 15, 1960.

WREN'S NEST

Comedy. Background: Suburban New York. The trials and tribulations of marrieds Sam and Virginia Wren.

CAST

Sam Wren	Himself
Virginia Wren	Herself

Producer: Sherling Oliver.

Director: Tom DeHuff.

WREN'S NEST—15 minutes—ABC 1949.

WYATT EARP

See title: "The Life and Legend of Wyatt Earp."

X

THE XAVIER CUGAT SHOW

Musical Variety. The Continental sound.

Host: Xavier Cugat.

Vocalist: Abbe Lane.

Orchestra: Xavier Cugat.

THE XAVIER CUGAT SHOW—15 minutes—NBC—February 27, 1957 - May 24, 1957.

Y

YADAMAN

An animated series about a lovable, slightly mischievous monster. 30 minutes—Syndicated 1966. 26 films.

YANCY DERRINGER

Adventure. Background: New Orleans, Louisiana, 1880s. The exploits of Yancy Derringer, a roguish riverboat gambler, as he and his Indian friend, Pahoo, under city administrator John Colton, struggle to institute a system of law and order in a city overrun with corruption.

CAST

Yancy Derringer	Jock Mahoney
Pahoo-Ka-Ta-Wha	X Brands
John Colton	Kevin Hagen
Mme. Francine, Yancy's romantic interest	Frances Bergen

Music: Don Quinn, Henry Russell.

YANCY DERRINGER—30 minutes—CBS—October 2, 1958 - September 24, 1959. 34 episodes. Syndicated.

A YEAR AT THE TOP

Comedy. Background: Hollywood, California. The story of Greg and Paul, two unknown songwriters offered musical stardom by prominent backer Frederick J. Hanover (of Paragon Records)—the Devil's son—who, on behalf of his father, grants them one year at the top in return for their souls.

CAST

Mickey Durbin, Greg and Paul's uncle	Mickey Rooney
Greg	Greg Evigan
Paul	Paul Shaffer
Frederick J. Hanover	Gabriel Dell
Linda, Greg's girlfriend	Priscilla Lopez
Miss Worley, Hanover's secretary	Priscilla Morrill
Grandma Bell Durbin, Mickey's mother	Nedra Volz
Trish, a friend of Greg and Paul	Julie Cobb

Music Supervision: Don Kirshner.

Executive Producer: Norman Lear.

Producer: Darryl Hickman, Patricia Fass Palmer.

Director: Alan Rafkin, Marlena Laird.

Creator: Woody Kling.

A YEAR AT THE TOP—30 minutes—CBS—August 5, 1977 - September 4, 1977. 5 episodes.

Originally, the series was scheduled

to air beginning January 19, 1977, but was cancelled at the last moment, then revised, supposedly to improve it. Following are the cast and credits to the original version, dealing with the Rock group top (Cliff, Studly, and Lillian), which never aired.

CAST

Mickey: Mickey Rooney; Lillian: Vivian Blaine; Cliff: Robert Alda; Studly: Phil Leeds; Young Cliff: Greg Evigan; Young Studly: Paul Shaffer; Young Lillian: Judith Cohen; Dee Dee: Kelly Bishop; Stage Manager: Kay Dingle.

Credits:

Music Supervision: Don Kirshner.

Musical Coordinator: Jay Siegel.

Special Musical Material: Earl Brown.

Musical Staging: Kevin Carlisle.

Executive Producer: Norman Lear.

Producer: Darryl Hickman.

Director: Jim Drake, Alan Myerson.

Creator: Woody Kling, Don Kirshner.

YES, YES NANETTE

Comedy. Background: Los Angeles, California. Events in the lives of the McGovern family: Dan, a Hollywood writer; Nanette, his wife, a former Broadway actress; and their children: Nancy and Buddy. Stories are based on real-life incidents drawn from the lives of Nanette Fabray and her husband, writer Ranald MacDougall.

CAST

Nanette McGovern	Nanette Fabray
Dan McGovern	Wendell Corey
Nancy McGovern	Jacklyn O'Donnell
Buddy McGovern	Bobby Diamond
Mrs. Harper, their housekeeper	Doris Kemper

YES, YES NANETTE—30 minutes—NBC—January 6, 1961 - July 7, 1961. 26 episodes. Also known as "The Nanette Fabray Show."

YOGA FOR HEALTH

Health. The principal and practical applications of yoga exercises.

Host: Richard Hittleman.

Assistant: Diane Hittleman (Mrs.)

Music: Richard Hittleman, Mike Batt.

YOGA FOR HEALTH—30 minutes—Syndicated 1968.

YOGI BEAR

Animated Cartoon. Background: Jellystone National Park. The misadventures of Yogi Bear, who, despite warnings from the park ranger, ingeniously schemes to acquire picnickers' lunch baskets. A Hanna-Barbera production.

Additional segments: "Snagglepuss" and "Yakky Doodle Duck."

Characters' Voices

Yogi Bear	Daws Butler
Boo Boo Bear, his innocent accomplice	Don Messick
John Smith, the ranger	Don Messick
Snagglepuss	Daws Butler
Yakky Doodle	Jimmy Weldon
Chopper	Vance Colvig

Music Supervision: Hoyt Curtin.

YOGI BEAR—30 minutes—Syndicated 1958. 123 episodes.

Yogi Bear. Yogi Bear. *Courtesy Hanna-Barbera Productions.*

YOGI'S GANG

Animated Cartoon. As living conditions become intolerable, Yogi Bear and his friends decide to do something about it and commission inventor Noah Smith to construct a flying ark. Beginning a crusade to protect the environment, they travel throughout the country and attempt to battle the enemies of man and nature.

Characters' Voices

Yogi Bear	Daws Butler
Boo Boo Bear	Don Messick
Paw Ruggs	Henry Corden
Doggie Daddy	John Stephenson
Huckleberry Hound	Daws Butler
Snagglepuss	Daws Butler
Quick Draw McGraw	Daws Butler
Peter Potomus	Daws Butler
Augie Doggie	Daws Butler
Wally Gator	Daws Butler
Touche Turtle	Don Messick
Squiddly Diddly	Don Messick
Ranger Smith	Don Messick
Magilla Gorilla	Allan Melvin
Atom Ant	Don Messick

Music: Hoyt Curtin.

Executive Producer: William Hanna, Joseph Barbera.

Director: Charles A. Nichols.

Yogi's Gang. Left to right: Yakky Doodle Duck (on top of piano), Snagglepuss, Boo Boo Bear, and Yogi Bear. © *Hanna-Barbera Productions.*

YOGI'S GANG—30 minutes—ABC—September 8, 1973 - August 30, 1975.

YOU ARE THERE

Anthology. Historical dramatizations. Through reenactments and present-day interviews, America's past is brought to life. The people and events that contributed to its founding and growth are seen through eyewitness accounts.

Host: Walter Cronkite.

Reporters-Interviewers: CBS news correspondents.

Music: Glenn Paxton.

Included:

The Mystery Of Amelia Earhart. The mysterious disappearance of the aviatrix on a 1937 flight across the Pacific is chronicled.

CAST
Amelia Earhart: Geraldine Brooks;

Fred Noonan: Thomas Connelly.

The Record Ride For The Pony Express. Bob Haslam's thirty-six-hour ride through three hundred and eighty miles of hostile Indian territory is recalled.

CAST
Bob Haslam: John Glover; Baumer: Gerald Matthews; McCool: John Coe; Tolliman: Ronny Cox.

Ordeal Of A President. The events that caused President Wilson's decision to involve America in World War I are recounted.

CAST
Wilson: G. Wood; Senator Lodge: William Prince.

Paul Revere's Ride. The famed ride of April 18, 1775, is re-created.

CAST
Paul Revere: Richard Branda; Sam Adams: E. G. Marshall.

The Siege Of The Alamo. Santa Anna's final assault and defeat of the Alamo, (March 5, 1836) the Texas stronghold for independence, is dramatized.

CAST
Davy Crockett: Fred Gwynne; Sam Houston: Philip Bosco; Jim Bowie: Bernard Kates; Santa Anna: Manuel Sebastian.

Program open:

Announcer: "The time...; the place... All things are as they were then except YOU ARE THERE."

Program close:

Host: "What kind of day was it? A

day like all days, filled with those unexpected events which alter our lives—and you were there."

Versions:

YOU ARE THERE—30 minutes—CBS—November 4, 1953 - October 13, 1957. 65 episodes.

YOU ARE THERE—30 minutes—CBS—September 11, 1971 - September 2, 1972.

YOU ASKED FOR IT

Variety. Through films, viewers requests—unusual sights or entertainment acts—are presented.

Program Open:

Announcer: "Whatever it is, wherever it is, at home or around the world, you see it here, You Asked For It."

Versions:

You Asked For It—30 minutes—ABC—December 10, 1951 - September 2, 1959.

Hosts: Art Baker; Jack Smith.

You Asked For It—30 minutes—Syndicated 1972.

Host: Jack Smith.

YOU BET YOUR LIFE

Game. Before the proceedings begin, a stuffed duck is lowered to reveal a secret word that, if said during the course of the program, awards players an extra hundred dollars. Two players who work jointly as a team are first

introduced, then comically interviewed by the host. Following the interview they compete in a game segment that is distinguished by two formats.

Format One:

The couple, having previously selected one category from a list of twenty subjects, receives one hundred dollars betting money. Players then select a question by cash value—from ten to one hundred dollars. If it is correctly answered the money is added to their total; if not, they lose half of their one hundred dollars. Four questions are played; each correct answer adds money; each incorrect answer cuts the previous total in half. Of the two, sometimes three couples, the highest cash winners receive a chance to answer the bonus question, which starts at $500 and increases by this amount each time one couple fails to answer it. The question is read and players receive fifteen seconds with which to answer. A correct answer awards the money; an incorrect answer allows them to keep their original earnings, which are divided between them.

Format Two:

Players are asked questions based on the categories they have chosen. Four correct answers in a row awards players one thousand dollars; two misses in a row disqualifies them. The couples who have won a thousand dollars are permitted to risk it in an attempt to win ten thousand dollars. A large spinning wheel with numbers ranging from one to ten is displayed. Couples select two numbers: one for ten thousand dollars and one for five thousand dollars. The wheel is spun. If it stops on one of the two numbers that have been selected, the question is worth that amount of money; if it doesn't, the question is worth two thousand dollars. The question is asked and players receive fifteen seconds with which to answer. If an incorrect answer is given they lose half of their thousand dollars; the five hundred dollars is then divided between them.

Host: Groucho Marx.

Announcer: George Fenneman.

The Secret Word Girl (appearing at times in place of the duck): Marilyn Burtis.

Orchestra: Jack Meakin.

Producer: John Guedel.

Director: Robert Dawn, Bernie Smith.

Sponsor: De Soto Plymouth Dealers.

YOU BET YOUR LIFE—30 minutes —NBC—October 5, 1950 - September 21, 1961. Syndicated title: "The Best of Groucho."

YOU CAN'T SEE
AROUND CORNERS

Drama. Background: Australia. The stresses of today's youth as seen through the eyes of Frankie McCoy, a young, proud, distrustful, and independent Australian adult.

CAST
Frankie McCoy	Ken Shorter
His girlfriend	Rowena Wallace

YOU CAN'T SEE AROUND CORNERS—30 minutes—Syndicated 1967.

YOU DON'T SAY

Game. Two teams, each composed of one celebrity captain and one non-celebrity contestant, compete. One player on each team receives the name of a famous person or place. The player then makes up and relates a sentence to his partner wherein he leaves the last word, which sounds like a part of the name, blank (what you don't say). His partner then receives five seconds to identify the name. If he is able, the team scores one point; if he is unable, his opponent receives a turn. The round continues until the name is identified or five clues have been used. A two-out-of-three match competition is played. The team that is first to score three points is the winner and the contestant receives one hundred dollars and the opportunity to play the bonus round, wherein he can win three hundred dollars by identifying a famous name in one clue. Players compete until they are defeated by losing two games.

Host: Tom Kennedy.

Announcer: John Harlan.

Music: Recorded.

Producer: Bill Yagemann, Ralph Andrews

YOU DON'T SAY—30 minutes—NBC —April 1, 1963 - September 26, 1969.

Revised Version: YOU DON'T SAY.

Four guest celebrities and two contestants are involved. The celebrities are each given the name of a famous person or place. One contestant chooses a celebrity who must then give him a clue by making up a sentence and leaving the last word, which sounds like a part of the name, blank. If the player identifies the name within five seconds he scores two hundred dollars. If not, his opponent receives a chance and a correct identification is worth one hundred and fifty dollars. Two additional clues are played, worth one hundred and finally fifty dollars. If the name is not identified on the fourth clue, it is disqualified and a new round begins. The first player to score six hundred dollars is the winner and receives the opportunity to play the bonus round. The object is for the player to relate clues to the celebrities. If the celebrities identify four names in five clues he wins five thousand dollars. Players compete until defeated by two losses.

Host: Tom Kennedy.

Announcer: John Harlan.

Music: Stan Worth.

Executive Producer: Bill Carruthers.

Producer: John Harlan, Mike Henry.

Director: Tom Cole.

YOU DON'T SAY—30 minutes—ABC —July 7, 1975 - November 26, 1975.

YOU'LL NEVER GET RICH

Comedy. Background: The Camp Freemont army base at Fort Baxter in Roseville, Kansas. The life of Master Sergeant Ernest Bilko, Company B, 24th Division, a master conartist in charge of the motor pool. Totally dedicated to acquiring money, he ingeniously schemes to bamboozle the system and manipulate the U.S. Army for his own personal benefit. A classic television series satirizing army life. Created by Nat Hiken.

CAST

Sgt. Ernie Bilko	Phil Silvers
Colonel John T. Hall, Commanding Officer (also refered to as Jack Hall)	Paul Ford
Master Sgt. Joan Hogan, WAC, Bilko's girlfriend	Elizabeth Fraser
Private Duane Doberman	Maurice Gosfield
Corporal Henshaw	Allan Melvin
Private Dino Paparelli	Billy Sands
Private Fender	Herbie Faye
Private Zimmerman	Mickey Freeman
Corporal Rocco Barbella	Harvey Lembeck
Mess Sgt. Rupbert Ritzik	Joe E. Ross
Sgt. Francis Grover	Jimmy Little
Private Mullin	Jack Healy
Private Lester Mendelsohn	Gerald Hiken
Private Greg Chickeriny	Bruce Kirby
Captain Hodges	Nelson Olmsted
The Chaplin	John Gilson
Nell Hall, the Colonel's wife	Hope Sansberry
Edna, a nurse	Barbara Barry
Emma Ritzik, Rupbert's wife	Beatrice Pons
Major Lewken	Edward Andrews

Also: Tige Andrews, Walter Cartier, Skippy Colby, Bill Hickey, Jack Davis.

Announcer: Bern Bennett.

Music: John Strauss.

Executive Producer: Edward J. Montagne.

Producer: Aaron Ruben.

Director: Al De Caprio.

YOU'LL NEVER GET RICH—30 minutes—CBS—September 20, 1955 - September 1959. 138 episodes. Syndicated title: "Sgt. Bilko." Also known as "The Phil Silvers Show."

YOUNG AND GAY

Comedy. Background: Greenwich Village, New York during the 1920s. The misadventures of Beth Skinner and Mary Kimbrough, young women struggling to make their way in the business world.

CAST

Beth Skinner	Bethel Leslie
Mary Kimbrough	Mary Malone

Also: Kenneth Forbes, Harry Bannister, Agnes Young, Alexander Ivo, John Campbell.

Producer: Carol Irwin.

Director: David Rich.

YOUNG AND GAY—30 minutes—CBS 1950.

THE YOUNG AND THE RESTLESS

Serial. Background: Genoa City. The story of the new morality as seen through the lives of several young, upper-middle-class adults, people seeking to find themselves and love in a contemporary world.

CAST

Brad Eliot	Tom Hallick
Stuart Brooks	Robert Colbert
Jennifer Brooks	Dorothy Green
Leslie Brooks	Janice Lynde
Chris Brooks	Trish Stewart
Peggy Brooks	Pamela Peters
	Pamela Solow
Liz Foster	Julianna McCarthy
Bill "Snapper" Foster	William Gray Espy
	David Hasselhoff
Greg Foster	James Houghton
	Brian Kerwin
Jill Foster	Brenda Dickson
Pierre Rolland	Robert Clary
Sally McGuire	Lee Crawford
Barbara Anderson	Deidre Hall
Marianne	Lilyan Chauvan
Gwen Sherman	Jennifer Leak
Philip Chancelor	Donnelly Rhodes
Kaye Chancelor	Jeanne Cooper
Jed Andrews	Tom Sellick
Laurlee Brooks	Jaime Lyn Bauer
Brock Reynolds	Beau Kayzer
Sam Powers	Barry Cahill
Bruce Henderson	Paul Stevens
Mark Henderson	Steve Carlson
Jed Andrews	Tom Sellick
Lance Prentiss	John McCook
Vanessa Prentiss	K.T. Stevens
Cynthia Harris	Lori Saunders

Music: David McGinnis, J. Wood, B. Todd.

THE YOUNG AND THE RESTLESS —30 minutes—CBS—Premiered: March 26, 1973.

YOUNG DAN'L BOONE

Adventure. Background: Kentucky during the 19th century. The story concerns itself with the exploits of Dan'l Boone, the frontiersman-pioneer, as a young man (aged 25), before he became a legend. See also: "Daniel Boone," and "Walt Disney Presents," *Daniel Boone* segment.

CAST

Dan'l Boone	Rick Moses
Rebecca Bryan, his girlfriend	Devon Ericson
Peter Dawes, the young boy who tags along with Dan'l	John Joseph Thomas
Hawk, the ex-slave	Ji-Tu Cumbuka

Music: Earle Hagen.

Music Supervision: Lionel Newman.

Theme Vocal: The Mike Curb Congregation.

Executive Producer: Ernie Frankel.

Producer: Jimmy Sangster.

Creator: Ernie Frankel.

YOUNG DAN'L BOONE—60 minutes—CBS—Premiered: September 12, 1977.

YOUNG DOCTOR KILDARE

Medical Drama. A spin-off from "Dr. Kildare." Background: Blair General Hospital. The experiences, defeats, and victories of James Kildare, a young resident intern.

CAST
Dr. James Kildare	Mark Jenkins
Dr. Leonard Gillespie, his mentor	Gary Merrill
Nurse Marsha Lord	Marsha Mason
Nurse Ferris	Dixie Marquis
Nurse Newell	Olga James
The orderly	Dennis Robinson

Music: Harry W. Lojewski; Score Productions.

YOUNG DOCTOR KILDARE—30 minutes—Syndicated 1972.

YOUNG DOCTOR MALONE

Serial. Background: Valley Hospital. The dramatic story of the Malone family: Jerry, a doctor, the head of the hospital; his wife, Tracy; and their children, Jill and David, also a doctor.

CAST
Dr. Jerry Malone	William Prince
Tracy Malone	Augusta Dabney
Dr. David Malone	John Donnell
Jill Malone	Freda Holloway
	Sarah Hardy
Emory Bannister	Judson Laire
Lisa Steele	Michele Tuttle
Claire Bannister	Lesley Woods
Miss Fisher	Betty Sinclair
Lionel Steele	Martin Blaine
Stefan	Michael Ingram
Ted Powell	Peter Brandon
Faye Bannister	Lenka Patterson
Natalie	Joan Wetmore
Fran Merrill	Patricia Bosworth
Paul Brown	David Stewart
	Edmond Ryan
Eileen Seaton	Emily McLaughlin
Phyllis Brooks	Barbara O'Neill
Ernest Cooper	Bob Drivas
	Nicholas Pryor
Peter Brooks	Robert Lansing
Carla	Joyce Van Patten
Claire Bannister	Leslie Woods
Dierdre Bannister	Margot Anders
Opal	Ruth Hammond
Gail Prentiss	Joan Hackett
Dorothy Ferris	Liz Gardner
	Florence Mitchell
Cranston	William Post
Miss Fisher	Betty Sinclair
Peter Ferris	Luke Halpin
Lisha	Zina Bethune
	Michelle Tuttle
	Susan Hallaran
Amanda	Ruth McDevitt
Larry Renfrew	Dick Van Patten
Lester	Scott McKay
Marge Wagner	Terri Keane

Creator-Producer: Carol Irwin.

Producer: Doris Quinlan.

Director: Jim Young.

YOUNG DOCTOR MALONE—30 minutes—NBC—December 29, 1958 - December 29, 1961.

THE YOUNG MARRIEDS

Serial. Background: Suburban New York. The dramatic story of three couples: Dan and Peggy Garrett; Ann and Walter Reynolds; and Roy and Lena Gilroy. Episodes depict their relationships within the family and with their friends.

CAST

Susan Garrett	Peggy McCay
Dan Garrett	Paul Picerni
Ann Reynolds	Susan Brown
	Lee Meriwether
Walter Reynolds	Michael Mikler
Lena Gilroy	Norma Connolly
Roy Gilroy	Barry Russo
Paul	Michael Stefani
Jerry	Pat Rossen
Jimmy	Ken Metcalf
Carol	Susan Seaforth
King	Dort Clark
Jill McComb	Betty Conner
	Brenda Benet
Matt Crane	Scott Graham
	Charles Grodin
Liz Forsythe	Floy Dean
Buzz	Les Brown, Jr.
Aunt Alice	Irene Tedrow
Mr. Coleman	Frank Marvel
Mandy	Maria Palmer
Theo	Don Randolph
Mr. Korman	Frank Maxwell
Mrs. Korman	Maxine Stuart

THE YOUNG MARRIEDS—30 minutes—ABC—October 5, 1964 - March 25, 1966.

YOUNG MR. BOBBIN

Comedy. The misadventures of Alexander Bobbin, a determined but trouble-prone young businessman.

CAST

Alexander Bobbin	Jackie Kelk
Nancy, his girlfriend	Pat Holsey
Susie Bobbin, his sister	Laura Webber
Aunt Bridie	Jane Seymour
His other aunt	Nydia Westman

Also: Cameron Prud'Homme.

Announcer: Tex Antoine.

Producer: Jack Scibetta.

Director: Norman Tokar.

Sponsor: General Foods.

YOUNG MR. BOBBIN—30 minutes—NBC—August 26, 1951 - May 18, 1952.

THE YOUNG LAWYERS

Drama. Background: The Neighborhood Law Office (N.L.O.), a legal-aid service in Boston, Massachusetts. The cases and courtroom defenses of its three staff members: David Barrett, Aaron Silverman, and Pat Walters, Bercol University law students.

CAST

David Barrett	Lee J. Cobb
Aaron Silverman	Zalman King
Pat Walters	Judy Pace

Music: Lalo Schifrin; Leith Stevens.

THE YOUNG LAWYERS—60 minutes—ABC—September 21, 1970 - May 5, 1971. 26 episodes.

YOUNG PEOPLE'S CONCERTS

Music. Explanations and demonstrations of various musical categories.

Hosts: Leonard Bernstein; Michael Tilson Thomas.

Narrators: Leonard Bernstein; Peter Ustinov; Michael Tilson Thomas.

Music: The New York Philharmonic Orchestra.

Conductors: Leonard Bernstein; Michael Tilson Thomas.

The Young Rebels. Left to right: Alex Henteloff, Lou Gossett, Rick Ely. © *Screen Gems.*

YOUNG PEOPLE'S CONCERTS—60 minutes—CBS—Premiered: 1958. Broadcast as a series of specials.

THE YOUNG REBELS

Adventure. Background: Chester, Pennsylvania, 1777. The story of the Yankee Doodle Society, a secret organization composed of four people: Jeremy Larken, a man who is regarded as the town fool; Henry Abington, a chemist and explosives expert; Isak Poole, a blacksmith; and Elizabeth Coates, their one-woman auxiliary. Pretending to be indifferent to the American cause, and achieving a front thought of as worthless, they struggle to foil British advances on the Colonies.

CAST

Jeremy Larken	Rick Ely
Isak Poole	Lou Gossett
Henry Abington	Alex Henteloff
Elizabeth Coates	Hilarie Thompson
General Lafayette, their ally	Philippe Forquet

Music Supervision: Lionel Newman.

THE YOUNG REBELS—60 minutes —ABC—September 20, 1970 - January 15, 1971. 13 episodes.

THE YOUNG SENTINELS

Animated Science Fiction Adventure. At a time when the Earth was young, Sentinel One, an intelligent life force from another galaxy, carefully selected three young people for training on his planet. Granting them astounding powers and eternal youth, the three Earthlings—Hercules, with the strength of one hundred men; Astria, the beautiful woman capable of assuming any life form; and Mercury, able to move with the speed of light—were returned to their native planet to watch over the human race and help the good survive and flourish. Now, with the guiding influence of Sentinel One and his maintenance robot, Mo, the series details the exploits of the Young Sentinels as they battle evil on Earth.

Characters' Voices

Hercules	George DiCenzo
Astria	Dee Timberlake
Mercury	Evan Kim
Sentinel One	George DiCenzo
Mo	Evan Kim

Music: Yvette Blais, Jeff Michael.

Executive Producer: Norm Prescott, Lou Scheimer.

Producer: Don Christensen.

Director: Hal Sutherland.

THE YOUNG SENTINELS—30 minutes—NBC—Premiered: September 10, 1977.

THE YOUNG SET

Discussion. Celebrity guests discuss topical issues.

Hostess: Phyllis Kirk.

Premiere Guest: Peter Lawford.

Music (recorded open and close):

"The Young Set," composed by Ray Martin.

THE YOUNG SET—60 minutes—ABC—September 6, 1965 - December 17, 1965.

YOUR ALL AMERICAN COLLEGE SHOW

Variety. Performances by college entertainment acts (four per telecast). Winners, determined by three celebrity guest judges, receive one thousand dollars.

Hosts: Dennis James; Rich Little; Arthur Godfrey.

YOUR ALL AMERICAN COLLEGE SHOW—30 minutes—Syndicated 1968.

YOUR BIG MOMENT

A human-interest type of program wherein host Melvyn Douglas arranges blind dates for people who have written letters requesting a certain type of companion. First broadcast on DuMont in 1953.

YOU'RE IN THE PICTURE

Game. Four competing contestants. Players are situated behind large picture scenes (such as those found in amusement parks) with their heads through appropriate cut outs. Through clues that are related by the host, players have to identify their particular situation. Winners receive merchandise prizes.

Host: Jackie Gleason.

YOU'RE IN THE PICTURE—30 minutes—CBS—January 20, 1961 - March 24, 1961.

YOU'RE INVITED

A thirty minute variety series hosted by Ralph Vincent. Broadcast on ABC in 1949.

YOU'RE ON YOUR OWN

Game. Three competing contestants. The host reads a general-knowledge type of question. The player who is first to identify himself through a buzzer signal receives a chance to answer. If he gives a correct response he scores one point. If he is incorrect he has to pay a penalty by performing a humiliating stunt. Players receive prizes in accord with the number of questions they answer.

Host: Steve Dunne.

Orchestra: Paul Taubman.

YOU'RE ON YOUR OWN—30 minutes—CBS—December 22, 1956 - March 16, 1957.

YOU'RE PUTTING ME ON

Game. Three two-member celebrity teams compete. One member of each team reveals a different name plate and assumes his or her identity. The host states a category (e.g., "The pool room") and a question ("As the person you are now pretending to be, if you were anything or anybody in a pool room, who or what would you be?"). The pretender then relates the person or object that fits the description of the personality he is pretending to be to his partner. The host then reveals four name possibilities. Each team partner has to select the one he believes is being put on by his partner. If correct, one point is scored. Three such rounds are played. Rounds two and three consist of two category questions and a choice of five personalities. Winners are the highest point scorers. Selected studio audience members, who are represented by the celebrities, receive merchandise prizes.

Hosts: Bill Cullen; Larry Blyden.

Announcer: Jack Clark.

Regular Panelists: Larry Blyden (before hosting), Peggy Cass, Bill Cullen, Anne Meara.

YOU'RE PUTTING ME ON—30 minutes—NBC—July 1969 - December 26, 1969.

YOUR FIRST IMPRESSION

Game. Through a series of question-and-answer probe rounds with the host, a panel of three celebrities have to identify a mystery guest celebrity from a list of five possibilities.

Host: Bill Leyden.

Panel: Dennis James, George Kirby, plus one guest celebrity.

YOUR FIRST IMPRESSION—30 minutes—NBC—January 2, 1962 - April 27, 1964.

YOUR FUNNY FUNNY FILMS

Comedy. Amateur-made home movies are showcased. The photographer appears and narrates his films, which have been professionaly reedited for laughs.

Host: George Fenneman.

YOUR FUNNY FUNNY FILMS–30 minutes–ABC–July 8, 1963 - September 9, 1963.

YOUR HIT PARADE

Variety. America's taste in popular music is dramatized. The top songs of the day, which are played from number twelve to "the song that's number one all over America," are determined by surveys of the best sellers, sheet music, phonograph-record sales, jukebox selections, and songs played over the radio.

Version One:

Your Hit Parade–60 and 30 minute productions–NBC–July 10, 1950 - June 17, 1958.

Your Hit Parade. Clockwise from upper right: Tommy Leonetti, Jill Corey, Alan Copeland, Virginia Gibson (CBS 1958).

CAST
Eileen Wilson, June Valli, Dorothy Collins, Snooky Lanson, Russell Arms, Giselle MacKenzie, Tommy Leonetti, Jill Corey, Alan Copeland, Virginia Gibson, Niles & Fosse (dancers), The Hit Paraders (singers), The Hit Parade Dancers.

Choreography: Tony Charmoli; Ernest Flatt; Peter Gennaro.

Announcers: Andre Baruch; John Laing.

Orchestra: Raymond Scott; Peter Van Steeden; Dick Jacobs; Harry Sosnick.

Verstion Two:

Your Hit Parade–30 minutes–CBS–October 10, 1958 - April 14, 1959.

CAST
Dorothy Collins, Johnny Desmond, The Hit Parade Singers and Dancers.

Orchestra: Harry Sosnick.

Version Three:

Your Hit Parade–30 minutes–CBS–August 2, 1974 - August 30, 1974.

CAST
Kelly Garrett, Sheralee, Chuck Woolery, The Tom Hanson Dancers (who are referred to as The Hit Parade Dancers).

Announcer: Art Gilmore.

Orchestra: Milton DeLugg.

YOUR LUNCHEON DATE

Musical Variety.

Host: Hugh Downs.

Vocalist: Nancy Wright.

Music: The Art Van Damme Quintet.

YOUR LUNCHEON DATE—30 minutes—DuMont—1951 - 1952.

YOUR LUCKY CLUE

Game. Two competing two-member teams. A dramatic sketch, which outlines the facts of a criminal case, is enacted on stage. The teams then receive time with which to discuss the facts between them. The team that correctly solves the case is the winner and receives prizes.

Host: Basil Rathbone.

Announcer: Andre Baruch.

YOUR LUCKY CLUE—30 minutes—CBS—July 13, 1952 - September 1952.

YOUR PLAY TIME

Anthology. Dramatic presentations.

Included:

The Loner. The story of a young boy who, neglected by his parents, retreats to a world of fantasy to find happiness.

CAST
Peter Votrian, Ann Lee, Hayden Rorke.

The House Nobody Wanted. The fears that grip a young couple as they move into a house that is believed to be haunted.

CAST
Marilyn Erskine, Craig Stevens, Sheila Bromley, Jack Paine.

Wait For Me Downstairs. A young man's efforts to find his fiancée, who disappeared on the eve of their wedding.

CAST
John Hudson, Allene Roberts.

YOUR PLAY TIME—30 minutes—CBS—June 13, 1954 - September 3, 1955.

YOURS FOR A SONG

Game. Two competing players. The lyrics to a popular song, which contain certain word omissions, are flashed on a screen. The player who is first to identify himself through a buzzer signal receives a chance to answer. For each correct word that he is able to fill in he receives twenty dollars. Winners, who receive their earnings, are the highest cash scorers. Broad clues are provided by the host, and the studio audience is led in sing-a-longs of chorus segments.

Host: Bert Parks.

Orchestra: Ted Raph.

Announcer: Johnny Gilbert.

Model: Michaelina Martel.

Producer: Harry Salter.

YOURS FOR A SONG—30 minutes—ABC. Daytime: December 4, 1961 - March 29, 1963; Evening: November 14, 1961 - September 18, 1963.

YOUR SHOW OF SHOWS

See title: "Sid Caesar."

YOUR STAR SHOWCASE

Anthology. Retitled episodes of "The General Electric Theatre."

Host: Edward Arnold.

YOUR STAR SHOWCASE—30 minutes—Syndicated 1953.

YOUR SURPRISE PACKAGE

Game. Three competing contestants. A large box, which contains merchandise items, is displayed on stage. The host reveals their value but not their identity. A general-knowledge type of question is then read. The player who is first to identify himself through a buzzer signal receives a chance to answer. If correct, he receives cash. After each question, the player with the last correct response is permitted to purchase buying time with which to question the host concerning the contents of the surprise package. The game continues until one player wins it by identifying its contents.

Host: George Fenneman.

YOUR SURPRISE PACKAGE—30 minutes—CBS—March 13, 1961 - February 23, 1962.

YOUR SURPRISE STORE

Game. Selected studio-audience members compete in a series of question-and-answer rounds or by performing various stunts. The person with the highest quiz score, the most correct answers, or the player who is the most successful at completing stunts, receives the opportunity to select valuable merchandise items from a surprise store constructed on stage.

Host: Lew Parker.

Assistant: Jacqueline Susann.

Announcer: Bern Bennett.

YOUR SURPRISE STORE—30 minutes—CBS—May 11, 1952 - June 27, 1952.

YOUTH TAKES A STAND

Discussion. Four high-school and/or junior-college students discuss world affairs with guest newsmen.

Host: Marc Cramer.

YOUTH TAKES A STAND—30 minutes—CBS 1953.

3

ZERO ONE

Adventure. Background: London, England. The cases of an international-airline crime-detection team.

CAST

Alan Garrett, the head of Airline Security International	Nigel Patrick
Jimmy Delaney, his assistant	Bill Smith
Maya, their secretary-assistant	Katya Douglas

ZERO ONE—30 minutes—Syndicated 1964. 39 episodes.

THE ZOO GANG

Crime Drama. Background: Europe. The story of four World War II resistance fighters known as The Zoo Gang who reunite twenty-eight years later to battle crime in Europe.

CAST

Steven Halliday, an antique dealer; code name: The Fox	Brian Keith
Manouche Roget, the owner of the Les Pecheurs Bar in France; code name: The Leopard	Lilli Palmer
Tom Devon, a jeweler; code name: The Elephant	John Mills
Alec Marlowe, a mechanic; code name: The Tiger	Barry Morse
Police Lt. Georges Roget, Manouche's son	Michael Petrovitch
Jill Barton, Tom's niece	Seretta Wilson

Music Theme: Paul and Linda McCartney.

Music Score: Ken Thorne.

Producer: Herbert Hirschman.

Director: Sidney Hayers, John Hough.

THE ZOO GANG—60 minutes—NBC —July 16, 1975 - August 6, 1975.

ZOO PARADE

Educational. Background: The Chicago Zoo. Visits to specific areas of interest.

Host: Marlin Perkins.

Assistant: Jim Hurlbut.

Producer: Don Meier, Reinald Warrenrath.

Sponsor: Quaker Oats.

ZOO PARADE—30 minutes—NBC —1950 - September 1, 1957. Originally broadcast as a local program in Chicago from 1946-1950.

ZOOM

Educational. Nonprofessional preteen children relate stories, songs, dances, games, and jokes either written by themselves or submitted by home viewers. The program represents a television framework for the creative efforts of children.

Hosts (seven per telecast; identified by a first name only): Nancy, Maura, David, Ann, Kenny, Tracy, Jay, Bernadette, Luiz, Edith, Tommy, Jon, Lori, Danny, Neil, Nina, Donna, Mike, Leon, Timmy.

Orchestra: Newton Wayland.

ZOOM—30 minutes—PBS—Premiered: January 9, 1972.

ZOORAMA

Educational. Background: The San Diego Zoo. Visits to specific areas of interest.

Host: Bob Dale.

ZOORAMA—30 minutes—Syndicated 1968.

ZORAN, SPACE BOY

A ninety-six episode series that focuses on the exploits of Zoran, a space boy who, with his pet space squirrel, journeys to Earth to find his lost sister. 30 minutes—Syndicated 1966.

Zorro. Guy Williams, as Zorro, atop his stallion Phantom. © *Walt Disney Productions.*

ZORRO

Adventure. Background: Monterey, California, 1820. Arriving in Monterey at the request of his late father to assist in ending the reign of Monastano, an evil Spanish commandant who has established himself as ruler, Don Diego de la Vega adopts the guise of the mysterious masked rider, Zorro, a defender of the weak and oppressed.

Revealing his dual identity only to Bernardo, his father's deaf mute servant, he poses as a wealthy but lazy man-about-town to protect his secret alias. Appearing whenever the need arises, Don Diego, as the mysterious Spanish nobleman, Zorro, crusades against injustice and attempts to end Monastano's reign.

CAST

Don Diego de la Vega	Guy Williams
Zorro	Guy Williams
Bernardo	Gene Sheldon
Captain Monastano	Britt Lomond
Sergeant Garcia, his bumbling aide	Henry Calvin
Torres, an escaped political prisoner	Jan Arvan
Elena Torres, his daughter	Eugenia Paul
Anita Cabrillo, a friend of Don Diego's	Annette Funicello
Ricardo Del Amo, a friend of Don Diego's	Richard Anderson
Anna Maria, a friend of Don Diego's	Jolene Brand

Zorro's white stallion: Phantom.

Zorro's black stallion: Tornado.

Music: George Bruns.

Producer: Walt Disney, William H. Anderson.

Theme: "Zorro."
Words: Norman Foster.
Music: George Bruns.
© Copyright 1957 by Walt Disney Music Company. Reprinted by permission.

Out of the night when the full moon is bright
Comes the horseman known as Zorro.
This bold renegade carves a Z with his blade,
A Z that stands for Zorro.
Zorro, the fox of cunning and free,
Zorro, who makes the sign of the Z.
Zorro, Zorro, Zorro, Zorro.

ZORRO—30 minutes—ABC—September 19, 1957 - September 24, 1959. Syndicated.

Program Addendum

Network and syndicated series broadcast from January 28, 1978 through January 1, 1979.

A. E. S. HUDSON STREET

Comedy. Spoofing medical series, the program focuses on the hectic goings-on in a poorly-equipped adult emergency service (A. E. S.) hospital on Hudson Street on the lower East Side of Manhattan in New York City.

CAST

Dr. Tony Menzies	Gregory Sierra
Nurse Rose Santiago	Rosana Soto
Nurse Rhonda Todd	Julienne Wells
Foshko, the ambulance driver	Susan Peretz
Stawky, her assistant	Ralph Manza
Nurse Newton	Ray Stewart
Carbow, the administrator	Stefan Gierasch
Dr. Jerry Meckler	Bill Cort
Dr. Glick	Allan Miller

Music: Jack Elliott, Allyn Ferguson.

Executive Producer: Danny Arnold.

Producer: Roland Kibbee.

Director: Noam Pitlik.

Creator: Danny Arnold, Tony Sheenan, Chris Hayward.

A. E. S. HUDSON STREET—30 minutes—ABC—March 16, 1978 - April 20, 1978. 5 episodes.

THE AMAZING SPIDER-MAN

Adventure. Following a demonstration on radioactivity, Peter Parker, a graduate student at Empire State University, is bitten by a spider that had been exposed to the deadly effects of the demonstration. Shortly after, Peter realizes that the spider's venom has become a part of his bloodstream and he has absorbed the proportionate power and ability of a living spider. Developing a special costume to conceal his true identity, and to be able to learn of crimes immediately, Parker acquires a position as a part-time photographer for the *New York Daily Bugle*. The series depicts Parker's battle against crime as the mysterious Spider-Man.

CAST

Peter Parker/ Spider-Man	Nicholas Hammond
Spider-Man (stunt sequences)	Fred Waugh
J. Jonah Jameson, editor of the *Bugle*	Robert F. Simon
Police Captain Barbera	Michael Pataki
Rita Conway, Jonah's secretary	Chip Fields
Julie Masters, a rival freelance	

photographer　　　Ellen Bry

Music: Stu Phillips, Dana Kaproff.

Executive Producer: Charles Fries, Daniel R. Goodman.

Producer: Robert Janes, Ron Satlof, Lionel E. Siegel.

Director: Ron Satlof, Fernando Lamas, Dennis Donnelly, Cliff Bole, Larry Stewart, Tom Blank.

THE AMAZING SPIDER-MAN—60 minutes—CBS—April 5, 1978 - May 3, 1978; September 5, 1978 - September 12, 1978. 7 episodes.

AMERICA ALIVE!

Variety. A daily series of interviews, music, and news events.

Host: Jack Linkletter.

Co-hosts: Janet Langhart, Bruce Jenner, Pat Mitchell.

Regulars: David Horowitz, Virginia Graham, David Sheehan.

Music Theme: Don Costa.

Music: Elliott Lawrence.

Executive Producer: Woody Fraser.

Producer: Susan Winston, Kenny Price.

Senior Director: Don King.

AMERICA ALIVE!—60 minutes—NBC—July 24, 1978 - January 5, 1979. 104 episodes.

THE AMERICAN GIRLS

Drama. The story of Rebecca Tomkins and Amy Waddell, two beautiful, roving, female reporter-researchers for "The American Report," a TV newsmagazine series.

CAST

Rebecca Tomkins	Priscilla Barnes
Amy Waddell	Debra Clinger
Francis X. Casey, their producer	David Spielberg
Jason Cook, the host of "The American Report"	William Prince

Music: Jerrold Immel.

Executive Producer: Harve Bennett, Harris Katleman.

Producer: Simon Muntner, George Lehr.

Director: Rod Holcomb, Alvin Ganzer, James D. Parriott, John Peyser, Lee Philips.

Creator: Lane Slate, Mike Lloyd Ross, Lee Philips.

THE AMERICAN GIRLS—60 minutes—CBS—September 23, 1978 - November 10, 1978. 6 episodes.

AMERICA 2-NIGHT

Satire. A spin-off from "Fernwood 2-Night." Unable to raise the necessary funds to continue his local talk show in Ohio, Barth Gimble relocates to fictional Alta Coma, California, "the unfinished furniture capitol of the world," where he becomes the host of "America 2-Night" over the U.B.S. (United Broadcasting System) Network ("The network that puts U before the B.S."). The series, which spoofs talk-variety programs, presents interviews with well-known celebrities as well as the most grotesque people imaginable.

Host: Martin Mull as the conceited Barth Gimble.

Announcer: Fred Willard as the dim-witted Jerry Hubbard.

Music: Frank DeVol (as Happy Kyne) and his Orchestra (the Mirth Makers).

Regulars: Michelle and Tanya Della Fave, Kenneth Mars (as William W.B. "Bud" Prize, the talent scout), Jim Varney (as Virgil Simms, a mobile home daredevil), Bill Kirchenbauer (as Tony Roletti, the lounge singer).

Producer: Alan Thicke.

Director: Jim Drake, Jerry Leshay, Marvin Kupfer, Randy Winburn, James Field, Dick Weinberg.

Creator: Norman Lear.

AMERICA 2-NIGHT—30 minutes—Syndicated 1978. 65 episodes.

ANOTHER DAY

Comedy. Background: Los Angeles, California. Events in the lives of Don and Ginny Gardner, a married couple whose lives are complicated by their jobs, their children, and Don's outspoken mother.

CAST

Don Gardner	David Groh
Ginny Gardner	Joan Hackett
Kelly Gardner, their daughter	Lisa Lindgren
Mark Gardner, their son	Al Eisenmann
Olive Gardner, Don's mother	Hope Summers

Music: Paul Williams.

Executive Producer: James Komack.

Producer: Paul Mason, George Kirgo.

Director: James Komack, Gary Shimokawa, Nick Havinga, Burt Brinckerhoff.

Creator: James Komack.

ANOTHER DAY—30 minutes—CBS—April 8, 1978 - April 29, 1978. 4 episodes.

APPLE PIE

Comedy. Background: Kansas City, Missouri, 1933. The series depicts the antics of the Hollyhocks, a group of strangers who became a family through the efforts of Ginger-Nell Hollyhock, a lonely woman who acquired them by placing ads in the local newspaper.

CAST

Ginger-Nell Hollyhock, the mother	Rue McClanahan
"Fast" Eddie Barnes, the father	Dabney Coleman
Grandpa	Jack Gilford
Anna Marie, the daughter	Caitlin O'Heaney
Junior, the son	Derrel Maury

Producer: Charlie Hauck.

Associate Producer: Rita Dillon.

Director: Peter Bonerz.

APPLE PIE—30 minutes—ABC—September 23, 1978 - October 7, 1978. 7 episodes produced; 3 aired.

THE AWAKENING LAND

Western Drama. A three part miniseries based on the novels by Conrad Richter. Background: The Ohio Territory from 1790 - 1817. The series follows the life of Sayward Luckett and her triumphant struggles over the hardships of pioneer life.

CAST

Sayward Luckett
    Elizabeth Montgomery

Genny Luckett, her
    sister   Jane Seymour
Achsa Luckett, her
    sister   Derin Altay
Sulie Luckett, her
    sister (as a young
    girl)   Michelle Stacy
Sulie Luckett
    (older)   Theresa Landreth
Worth Luckett, Sayward's
    father   Tony Mockus
Jary Luckett, Worth's
    wife   Louise Latham
Portius Wheeler, the
    lawyer; later Sayward's
    husband   Hal Holbrook
Resolve Wheeler, their
    son   Sean Frye
Resolve (as an
    adult)   Martin Scanlan
Huldah Wheeler, their
    daughter   Pia Romans
Huldah (as an
    adult)   Devon Ericson
Kinzie Wheeler, their
    son   Johnny Timko
Kinzie (as an
    adult)   Paul Swanson

Narrator: Elizabeth Montgomery.

Music: Fred Karlin.

Executive Producer: Harry Bernsen, Tom Kuhn.

Producer: Robert E. Relyea.

Director: Boris Sagal.

THE AWAKENING LAND—7 hours (total)—NBC—February 19, 1978 - February 21, 1978.

BABY, I'M BACK!

Comedy. Background: Washington, D.C. Unable to cope with the responsibilities of raising a family, Ray Ellis departs, leaving his wife Olivia and children Angie and Jordan to fend for themselves. The series follows Ray's misadventures when, returning seven years later, he tries to win back Olivia's affections and prove that he can be a good husband.

CAST

Ray Ellis   Demond Wilson
Olivia Ellis   Denise Nicholas
Luzelle Carter, Olivia's
    mother   Helen Martin
Angie Ellis   Kim Fields
Jordan Ellis   Tony Holmes
Col. Wallace Dickey,
    Olivia's employer at
    the Pentagon   Ed Hall

Music: Jeff Berry.

Executive Producer: Charles Fries, Sandy Krinski.

Producer: Lila Garrett.

Director: Dick Harwood, Nick Havinga, Asaad Keleda, Mark Warren.

Creator: Lila Garrett, Mort Lachman.

BABY, I'M BACK!—30 minutes—CBS—January 30, 1978 - August 12, 1978. 12 episodes.

BATTLE OF THE PLANETS

Animated Cartoon. Era: Earth in the year 2020. The series depicts the exploits of G-Force, five fearless young orphans, members of Center Neptune (an Earth-based defense organization established beneath the sea. They oppose evil beings from other planets, such as Zoltar, the leader of the planet Spectre, with his power-mad attempts to destroy our world.

Characters' Voices

7-Zark-7, the
    head of Center

Neptune	Alan Young
Zoltar	Keye Luke

G-Force:

Mark	Casey Kaseem
Princess	Janet Waldo
Keop	Ronnie Schell
Jason	Ronnie Schell
Tiny	Alan Dinehart

Music: Hoyt Curtin.

Executive Producer: Jameson Brewer.

Producer-Director: David Hanson.

BATTLE OF THE PLANETS—30 minutes—Syndicated 1978. 85 episodes.

BATTLESTAR GALACTICA

Science Fiction Adventure. In the seventh millenium of time, in a galaxy far beyond that of our own, a thousand-year-old war rages: that of mankind versus the Cylons, a mechanical race of beings bent on destroying the human race because they pose a threat to their existence. When a last-ditch effort on the part of mankind to effect peace fails, and their twelve-colony planets are destroyed, the surviving members, representing every known colony in the galaxy, band together (in spaceships) and follow the *Galactica,* a gigantic battlestar spaceship, in an attempt to rebuild their lives on their thirteenth colony—a distant and unknown planet called Earth. The series follows their perilous journey—warding off alien creatures and battling the Cylon robots who are now determined to thwart their plans—as they seek the planet Earth.

CAST

Commander Adama	Lorne Greene
Captain Apollo, his son	Richard Hatch
Athena, his daughter	Maren Jensen
Lieutenant Starbuck	Dirk Benedict
Colonel Tigh	Terry Carter
Boomer, a member of Galactica	Herb Jefferson, Jr.
Boxey, Apollo's son	Noah Hathaway
Cassiopea, a member of Galactica	Laurette Spang
Jolly, a member of Galactica	Tony Swartz
Baltar, the Cylon leader	John Colicos
Regal, a member of Galactica	Sarah Rush
Girl Warrior, a member of Galactica	Jennifer Joseph
Cylon	Bruce Wright
Cylon	Paul Coufos

Music: Stu Phillips.

Music Played By: The Los Angeles Symphonic Orchestra.

Executive Producer: Glen A. Larson.

Supervising Producer: Leslie Stevens.

Producer: John Dykstra, Don Belisario, Paul Playdon, David J. O'Connell.

Director: Richard Colla, Christian Nyby, Rod Holcomb, Vince Edwards.

BATTLESTAR GALACTICA—60 minutes—ABC—Premiered: September 17, 1978.

BONKERS!

Variety. A series of music, songs, and outlandish comedy.

Hosts: Bill, Mark, and Brett Hudson.

Regulars: Bob Monkhouse, Jack Burns, Linda Cunningham, The Bonkettes Chorus.

Music: Jack Parnell.

Executive Producer: Thomas M. Battista.

Producer: Jack Burns.

Director: Peter Harris.

BONKERS!–30 minutes–Syndicated 1978. 26 episodes.

CELEBRITY CHALLENGE OF THE SEXES

Game. The series pits male and female TV personalities against one another in various athletic contests.

Host: Tom Brookshire.

Male Team Coach: McLean Stevenson.

Female Team Coach: Barbara Rhoades.

Judge: Jim Tunney.

Music: Peter Matz.

Executive Producer: Howard Katz.

Producer: Mel Ferber.

Director: Bernie Hoffman.

CELEBRITY CHALLENGE OF THE SEXES–30 minutes–CBS–January 31, 1978 - February 28, 1978. 5 programs.

THE CHEAP SHOW

Game. A spoof of game and quiz shows. Two contestants appear with a friend or relative. One member of each team is placed in the punishment pit. A question based on a ridiculous category (e.g. "Underwater Nostalgia"), is read to two guest celebrities—each of whom gives a response, but only one of which is correct. By a flip-of-the-coin decision, one of the two outside-the-pit players chooses the celebrity he feels has the correct answer. If he chooses the right one, he wins a cheap prize (nothing over $16.00) and his opponent's loved one gets "punished" (hit with foods that are harmless). If the player is wrong, the prize is awarded to the opponent and his loved one is punished. Two such rounds are played, each worth one point. Round two consists of one twenty-point question that determines the winner.

The winning team now plays "The Super Collossal Prize Sweepstakes Finale." A large spinning-wheel board with twelve holes is displayed. Oscar the Wonder Rodent (a white rat) is placed on the board. Oscar runs briefly about the board and into one of the holes. The contestants win a prize corresponding to the number of the hole Oscar chooses to enter. A decent and expensive merchandise prize is awarded to the team.

Host: Dick Martin.

Wanda, the Hostess: Janelle Price.

Polly, the Prize Lady: Shirl Bernheim.

Oscar, the Wonder Rodent: Himself..

Roger, Oscar's Security Guard: Roger Chapline.

The Perveyors of Punishment: Joe Baker, Billy Beck.

Announcer: Charlie O'Donnell.

Music: John "J.C." Phillips.

Executive Producer: Chris Bearde, Bob Wood.

Producer: Terry Kyne, Kathy Connolly.

Director: Terry Kyne.

THE CHEAP SHOW–30 minutes–Syndicated 1978.

THE CHUCK BARRIS
RAH-RAH SHOW

Variety. Performances by professional and amateur talent.

Host: Chuck Barris.

Regulars: Jaye P. Morgan, The Unknown Comic, Gene Gene, The Dancing Machine.

Announcer: Johnny Jacobs.

Orchestra: Milton DeLugg.

Executive Producer: Chuck Barris.

Producer: Gene Banks.

Director: John Dorsey.

THE CHUCK BARRIS RAH-RAH SHOW—60 minutes—NBC—February 28, 1978 - April 11, 1978. 6 tapes.

THE COMEDY SHOP

Comedy. Performances by guest comedians: name celebrities and new and upcoming performers.

Host: Norm Crosby.

Music: Jack Elliott, Allyn Ferguson.

Executive Producer: Paul Roth.

Producer: Joe Siegman, Perry Rosemond.

Director: Perry Rosemond.

THE COMEDY SHOP—30 minutes—Syndicated 1978.

DALLAS

Drama. Background: Dallas, Texas. The story concerns itself with a feud that exists between two families: the Ewings and the Barnes; a feud started when Jock Ewing, an oil-and-cattle baron, supposedly cheated his neighbor, Digger Barnes in earlier days when they were partners drilling for oil. The feud intensified when Jock's youngest son, Bobby, married Digger's beautiful daughter, Pamela. (The Ewings own the Southfork Ranch.)

CAST

Jock Ewing, the oil-and-cattle baron	Jim Davis
Eleanor Ewing, his wife	Barbara BelGeddes
J.R. Ewing, their eldest son	Larry Hagman
Bobby Ewing, their younger son	Patrick Duffy
Sue Ellen Ewing, J.R.'s wife	Linda Gray
Lucy Ewing, Jock's granddaughter	Charlene Tilton
Willard "Digger" Barnes, Jock's neighbor	David Wayne
Pamela Barnes Ewing, Digger's daughter; Bobby's wife	Victoria Principal
Cliff Barnes, Digger's son	Ken Kercheval
Ray Krebbs, the Ewing ranch foreman	Steve Kanaly
Julie, J.R.'s secretary	Tina Louise

Music: Jerrold Immel, John Parker.

Executive Producer: Lee Rich, Philip Capice.

Producer: Leonard Katzman.

Director: Robert Day, Irving J. Moore, Alexander March, Barry Crane, Vincent McEveety.

Creator: David Jacobs.

DALLAS—60 minutes—CBS—April 2, 1978 - April 30, 1978. 5 episodes. Returned: CBS—60 minutes—Premiered: September 23, 1978.

DAVID CASSIDY—
MAN UNDERCOVER

Crime Drama. Background: Los Angeles, California. The cases of Officer Dan Shay, an undercover man for the L.A.P.D.

CAST

Officer Dan Shay	David Cassidy
Joanne Shay, his wife	Wendy Rastatter
Cindy Shay, their daughter	Elizabeth Reddin
Sgt. Walt Abrams, Shay's superior	Simon Oakland

Music: Harold Bettes.

Theme Vocal: David Cassidy.

Executive Producer: David Gerber.

Producer: Mark Rodgers, Mel Swope.

Director: Bernard McEveety, Vincent Edwards, Sam Wanamaker, Alvin Ganzer.

Creator: Richard Fielder.

DAVID CASSIDY—MAN UNDER-COVER—60 minutes—NBC—Premiered: November 2, 1978.

DICK CLARK'S
LIVE WEDNESDAY

Variety. A live Wednesday-evening variety hour (8 p.m., E.T.) that features top show business performers as well as reunions and tributes to screen idols (a prerecorded segment).

Host: Dick Clark.

Orchestra: Lenny Stack.

Executive Producer: Dick Clark.

Producer: Bill Lee.

Director: John Moffitt.

Location Producer-Director: Perry Rosemond.

DICK CLARK'S LIVE WEDNES-DAY—60 minutes—NBC—Premiered: September 20, 1978.

DIFF'RENT STROKES

Comedy. Background: New York City. The story of Phillip Drummond, a Park Avenue millionaire who adopts two Harlem orphans, Arnold and Willis Jackson, the sons of his late housekeeper.

CAST

Phillip Drummond	Conrad Bain
Arnold Jackson	Gary Coleman
Willis Jackson	Todd Bridges
Kimberly Drummond, Phillip's daughter	Dana Plato
Mrs. Garrett, Phillip's housekeeper	Charlotte Rae

Music: Alan Thicke, Al Burton, Gloria Loring.

Executive Producer: Budd Grossman.

Producer: Howard Leeds, Herbert Kenwith.

Director: Herbert Kenwith.

DIFF'RENT STROKES—30 minutes—NBC—Premiered: November 3, 1978.

THE $1.98 BEAUTY SHOW

Contest. A spoof of beauty pageants wherein six females compete in contests of beauty, poise, talent, and swimwear for the title "The Dollar Ninety-eight Beauty of the Week" and the top prize—$1.98—in cash. It is a mythical search to find the most beautiful girl in the world.

Host: Rip Taylor.

Announcer: Johnny Jacobs.

Music: Milton DeLugg.

Executive Producer-Creator: Chuck

Barris.

Producer: Gene Banks.

Director: John Dorsey.

THE $1.98 BEAUTY SHOW—30 minutes—Syndicated 1978.

THE DONNA FARGO SHOW

Variety. Comedy skits coupled with performances by Country and Western entertainers.

Hostess: Donna Fargo.

Regular: Tom Biener.

Announcer: Harrison Henderson.

Music: Bob Rozario.

Executive Producer: The Osmond Brothers.

Producer: Tom Biener.

Director: Rick Bennewitz.

THE DONNA FARGO SHOW—30 minutes—Syndicated 1978.

THE EDDIE CAPRA MYSTERIES

Mystery. Background: Los Angeles, California. The story of Eddie Capra, an attorney with the firm of Devlin, Linkman, and O'Brien, who has an uncanny knack for solving complex crimes. The series gimmick is to challenge viewers to guess the identity of the culprit before Capra does. As in the 1975 version of "Ellery Queen," nothing is withheld from the viewer, and nothing extra is given to Capra.

CAST

Eddie Capra	Vincent Baggetta
Lacey Brown, his secretary	Wendy Phillips
J.J. Devlin, senior partner of the law firm	Ken Swofford
Harvey Mitchell, Capra's legman	Michael Horton
Jennie Brown, Lacey's daughter	Seven Ann McDonald
Devlin's secretary	Lynn Topping

Music: John Addison, John Cacavas.

Executive Producer: Peter S. Fischer.

Producer: James McAdams.

Director: James Frawley, Ronald Satlof, James Benson, Nicholas Sgarro, Edward Abroms, Sigmund Neufeld, Jr.

Creator: Peter S. Fischer.

THE EDDIE CAPRA MYSTERIES—60 minutes—NBC—Premiered: September 22, 1978.

EVERYDAY

Comedy-Variety. A daily series of music, songs, interviews, and comedy.

Hosts: Stephanie Edwards, John Bennett Perry.

Regulars: Tom Chapin, Murray Langston, Anne Bloom, Judy Gibson, Robert Corff, Emily Levine.

Executive Producer: David Salzman.

Producer: Viva Knight.

Director: Louis J. Horvitz.

EVERYDAY—60 minutes—Syndicated 1978.

FANTASY ISLAND

Anthology. A series of interwoven vignettes set against the background of Fantasy Island, a mysterious tropical resort where, for an unspecified price, dreams are granted. Stories open with guests arriving on the island, followed by their meeting with Mr. Roarke, the man who arranges for people to act out their wildest fantasies. The individual's fantasy is then dramatized with the program showing how that person's life changes as a result of the experience.

CAST

Mr. Roarke	Ricardo Montalban
Tattoo, his assistant	Herve Villechaize

Music Theme: Laurence Rosenthal.

Music: Elliot Kaplan, Laurence Rosenthal, Charles Albertine.

Executive Producer: Aaron Spelling, Leonard Goldberg.

Producer: Michael Fisher.

Director: Cliff Bole, John Newland, Phil Bondelli, Earl Bellamy, George McCowan.

Creator: Gene Levitt.

FANTASY ISLAND—60 minutes—ABC—Premiered: January 28, 1978.

FLYING HIGH

Comedy-Drama. The story of Pam Bellagio, Marcy Bower, and Lisa Benton, three beautiful stewardesses for Sun West Airlines.

CAST

Pam Bellagio	Kathryn Witt
Marcy Bower	Pat Klous
Lisa Benton	Connie Sellecca
Capt. Douglas Robert March, a pilot for Sun West	Howard Platt

Music Theme: David Shire.

Music: Robert Prince.

Executive Producer: Mark Carliner.

Producer: Robert Van Scoyk, Marty Cohan.

Director: Peter Hunt, Nicholas Sgarro, Alan Myerson, William Jurgenson, James Sheldon.

FLYING HIGH—60 minutes—CBS—Premiered: September 29, 1978.

FREE COUNTRY

Comedy. Background: Manhattan (New York City). The series focuses on the lives of Joseph and Anna Bresner, Lithuanian immigrants, from 1909 to 1978. The program opens with Joseph at 89 years of age, as he talks about his life. Flashback sequences are used to highlight the events of both his and Anna's arrival and struggles in a new land.

CAST

Joseph Bresner	Rob Reiner
Anna Bresner	Judy Kahan
Ida Gevertsman, their friend	Renee Lippin
Sidney Gevertsman, Ida's husband	Fred McCarren
Leo, their friend	Larry Gelman

Music: Jack Elliott, Allyn Ferguson.

Executive Producer-Creator: Rob Reiner, Phil Mishkin.

Producer: Gareth Davies.

Director: Hal Cooper, James Burrows.

FREE COUNTRY—30 minutes—ABC—June 24, 1978 - July 22, 1978. 5 episodes.

GRANDPA GOES TO WASHINGTON

Comedy-Drama. Forced to retire at age sixty-six, Joe Kelley, an honest and outspoken professor of political science in California, is persuaded to run for the U.S. Senate following a political scandal. Winning the election,

Kelley, now a senator, moves to Washington, D.C., where his adventures, as he tries to practice what he taught—honest government—are dramatized.

CAST

Joe Kelley	Jack Albertson
Gen. Kevin Kelley, his son	Larry Linville
Rosie Kelley, Kevin's wife	Sue Ane Langdon
Cathleen Kelley, their daughter	Michele Tobin
Kevin Kelley, Jr., their son	Sparky Marcus
Madge, Joe's secretary	Madge Sinclair
The President	Richard Eastham
Tony DuVall, Joe's friend and advisor	Tom Mason

Music: Artie Butler.

Executive Producer: Richard P. Rosetti.

Producer: Robert Stambler.

Director: Richard Crenna, Herbert Kenwith, Larry Elikann, Paul Stanley, George Tyne.

GRANDPA GOES TO WASHINGTON—60 minutes—NBC—Premiered: September 20, 1978.

THE HANNA-BARBERA HAPPY HOUR

Variety.

Hosts: Honey and Sis (two life-sized puppets).

Honey and Sis Voices: Udana Power, Wendy McKenzie.

Musical Material: Mitzie Welch, Ken Welch.

Musical Director: Billy Byers.

Executive Producer: Joseph Barbera.

Producer: Ken Welch, Joe Layton, Mitzie Welch.

Director: Jim Washburn, Joe Layton.

Puppeteers: Jerry Vogel, J. Paul Higgins, Greg Dendler.

Honey and Sis Segment Director: Bob Mackie.

THE HANNA-BARBERA HAPPY HOUR—60 minutes—NBC—April 13, 1978 - May 4, 1978. 4 programs.

THE HARVEY KORMAN SHOW

Comedy. Background: Hollywood, California. The misadventures of Harvey A. Kavanaugh, an actor with a small career, as he attempts to find work in a world that he feels is passing him by.

CAST

Harvey A. Kavanaugh	Harvey Korman
Maggie Kavanaugh, his daughter	Christine Lahti
Jake, his agent	Milton Selzer
Stuart Stafford, Maggie's boyfriend	Barry Van Dyke

Music: Peter Matz.

Executive Producer: Hal Dresner.

Producer: Don Van Atta.

Director: Alan Myerson, Jeff Bleckner.

THE HARVEY KORMAN SHOW—30 minutes—ABC—March 4, 1978 - April 18, 1978; July 15, 1978 - August 4, 1978. 6 episodes.

HEADLINERS WITH DAVID FROST

Interview. Live and taped segments are used to interview headliners.

Host: David Frost.

Regulars: Liz Smith, Kelly Garrett.

Music: Elliott Lawrence.

Executive Producer: David Frost.

Producer: John Gilroy.

Director: Bruce Gowers.

HEADLINERS WITH DAVID FROST—60 minutes—NBC—May 31, 1978 - July 5, 1978. 6 programs.

THE HEE HAW HONEYS

Comedy. The story of the Honey family, the owner-operators of a country music night club in Nashville, Tennessee (the home of the TV series "Hee Haw," of which the series is an extension and presents songs by guests).

CAST
Kenny Honey, the father	Kenny Price
Lulu Honey, his wife	Lulu Roman
Kathy Lee Honey, their daughter	Kathy Lee Johnson
Misty Honey, their daughter	Misty Rowe
Willy Billy Honey, their son	Gailard Sartain

Music: Charlie McCoy.

Executive Producer: Sam Louvello.

Producer: Barry Adelman.

Director: Bob Boatman.

THE HEE HAW HONEYS—30 minutes—Syndicated 1978.

The original concept of the series, which was dropped in favor of the above format, was to have been as follows:

The Hee Haw Honeys—The series fol-

lows the misadventures of Chrissy, Lee Anne, and Toby, three former bit-players from the "Hee Haw" TV series, struggling to achieve success as the singing trio, The Hee Haw Honeys.

Starring: Kathy Lee Johnson as Chrissy, Catherine Hickland as Toby, Muffy Durham as Lee Anne, and Kenny Price as Kenny, their mobile home driver.

Music: Charlie McCoy.

Director: Ron Kantor.

HIGH HOPES

Serial. Background: The fictional town of Cambridge. The dramatic story of Dr. Neal Chapman, a family counselor.

CAST
Dr. Neal Chapman	Bruce Gray
Jessie Chapman	Miranne McIsaac
Paula Myles	Nuala Fitzgerald
Trudy Bowen	Barbara Kyle
Walter Telford	Colin Fox
Meg Chapman	Doris Petrie
Amy Sperry	Gena Dick
Louise Bates	Jayne Eastwood
Michael Stewart, Sr.	Michael Tait
Michael Stewart, Jr.	Gordon Thompson
Georgia Morgan	Gerry Salsberg
Carol Tauss	Dorothy Malone
Victor Tauss	Nehemiah Persoff
Dr. Dan Gerard	Jan Muszynski

Music: Aeolus Productions.

Music Supervision: Teri Smith.

Executive Producer: Dick Cox.

Director: Bruce Minnix, Patrick Corbett, Barry Cranston.

HIGH HOPES—30 minutes—Syndicated 1978.

HOT CITY

Disco Music.

Host: Shadoe Stevens; David Jones.

Regulars: The Jeff Kutect Dancers.

Music Theme: Vernee White, Robert Wright, Gary Goetzman.

Executive Producer: Marc Robertson, Ed Warren.

Producer-Director: Kip Walton.

HOT CITY—60 minutes—Syndicated 1978.

HUSBANDS, WIVES, AND LOVERS

Comedy. Background: The San Fernando Valley in California. The series focuses on the hassles, foibles, and frivolities of five suburban couples, each with diverse backgrounds.

CAST

Ron Willis, a dentist	Ron Rifkin
Helene Willis, his wife	Jesse Welles
Harry Bellini, a garbage tycoon	Eddie Barth
Joy Bellini, his wife	Lynne Marie Stewart
Lennie Bellini, Harry's brother, the part owner of a boutique shop	Mark Lonow
Rita DeLatorre, Lennie's partner; the girl with whom he lives	Randee Heller
Dixon Fielding, a lawyer	Charles Siebert
Courtney Fielding, Dixon's wife	Claudette Nevins
Murray Zuckerman, a salesman	Stephen Pearlman
Paula Zuckerman, Murray's wife	Cynthia Harris

Music: Jack Elliott, Allyn Ferguson.

Theme: Ken Welch, Mitzie Welch.

Executive Producer: Hal Dresner.

Producer: Don Van Atta.

Director: Marc Daniels, Alan Myerson, James Burrows.

Creator: Joan Rivers, Hal Dresner.

HUSBANDS, WIVES, AND LOVERS—60 minutes—CBS—March 10, 1978 - June 30, 1978. 9 episodes.

IN THE BEGINNING

Comedy. The story of Father Dan Cleary, an uptight, conservative priest, and Sister Agnes, a free-spirited, street-wise nun, and the bickering that ensues when the two join forces to open · a mission amid the hookers, drunks, runaways, and teenage gangs in the neighborhood. Their inability to agree on issues concerning the welfare of the mission or its people is the focal point of the series.

CAST

Father Dan Cleary	McLean Stevenson
Sister Agnes	Priscilla Lopez
Monsignor Frank Barlow, Dan's superior	Jack Dodson
Sister Lillian, Agnes's superior	Priscilla Morrill
Willie, one of the street-wise kids of the mission	Olivia Barash
Jerome Rockefeller, same as Willie	Bobby Ellerbee
Tony, same as Willie	Cosie Costa
Bad Lincoln, same as Willie	Michael Anthony
Frank, same as Willie	Fred Lehne

Music: Barry DeVorzon.

Executive Producer: Mort Lachman, Norman Steinberg.

Producer: Jim Mulligan, Rita Dillon.

Director: Jack Shea, Doug Rogers, Randy Winburn.

Creator: Jack Shea, Jim Mulligan; developed by Norman Lear.

IN THE BEGINNING—30 minutes—CBS—September 20, 1978 - November 1, 1978. 6 episodes.

THE INCREDIBLE HULK

Science Fiction Adventure. Scientist Dr. David Bruce Banner and his assistant, Elaina Marks, undertake a research program in an attempt to determine how certain people can tap hidden resources of strength under stress situations. During one such experiment, Banner is exposed to an extreme overdose of gamma radiation, which causes a change in his body's DNA chemistry. Whenever he becomes angry or enraged, a startling metamorphosis takes place: the mild Banner is transformed into the green Hulk, a creature of incredible strength. During one such fit of rage, the Hulk destroy's Banner's car. Intrigued by the enormous footprints found at the scene, *National Register* reporter Jack McGee traces the creature to the lab where Banner and Elaina (who previously witnessed the transformation and has agreed to help David find a cure) are planning an experiment. While speaking with Banner outside, a leaking chemical solution triggers an explosion in the lab. McGee and Banner are thrown by its force. Banner, still conscious, becomes

enraged when the flames prevent him from entering the building to help Elaina. Banner, now transformed into the Hulk, rescues Elaina, who dies shortly after. Regaining his senses, McGee sees the Hulk with Elaina and assumes that he killed her. Unable to find Banner, McGee theorizes that he perished in the flames, in a fire he mistakenly believes was caused by the Hulk.

Now, believed to be dead, Banner wanders across the country, seeking a way to control the creature and hopefully find a means by which to reverse the process. His efforts are hindered, however, by McGee, who has vowed to bring the creature to justice. (Though the creature is innocent, David can't prove it—he has little or no recollection when he transforms back to Banner—so he keeps moving until he can stop the occurences.)

CAST

Dr. David Banner	Bill Bixby
The Hulk	Lou Ferrigno
Jack McGee	Jack Colvin
Elaina Marks (pilot episode)	Susan Sullivan

Music: Joseph Harnell.

Executive Producer: Kenneth Johnson.

Producer: James D. Parriott, Chuck Bowman, Nicholas Corea, James G. Hirsch.

Director: Alan J. Levi, Kenneth Gilbert, Larry Stewart, Sigmund Neufeld, Jr., Jeffrey Hayden, Harvey Laidman, Reza S. Badiyi, Frank Orsatti, Joseph Pevney, Ray Danton.

THE INCREDIBLE HULK—60 minutes—CBS—March 10, 1978 - June 30, 1978. 12 episodes. Returned: CBS—60 minutes—Premiered: August 11, 1978.

THE JIM NABORS SHOW

Discussion-Variety.

Host: Jim Nabors.

Regulars: Susan Ford, Ronnie Schell.

Orchestra: Fred Werner.

Executive Producer: Carol Raskin.

Producer: Ken Harris.

Director: Barry Glazer.

THE JIM NABORS SHOW—60 minutes—Syndicated 1978.

JOE AND VALERIE

Comedy. Background: Brooklyn, New York. The romantic misadventures of Joe Pizo, an apprentice plumber, and Valerie Sweetzer, a cosmetics salesgirl. The series, which is partly a takeoff of the film, *Saturday Night Fever,* has its stories centered around a disco.

CAST
Joe Pizo	Paul Regina
Valerie Sweetzer	Char Fontane
Frank Boganski, Joe's friend	Bill Beyers
Paulie Veroni, Joe's friend	David Elliott
Stella Sweetzer, Valerie's mother	Pat Benson
Thelma, Valerie's friend	Donna Ponterotto
Vincent Pizo, Joe's father	Robert Costanzo

Music: Jack Elliott, Allyn Ferguson.

Theme Vocal: Char Fontane, Randy Winburn.

Executive Producer: Linda Hope.

Producer: Bernie Kahn.

Director: Bill Persky.

Creator: Bernie Kahn, Ronald Rubin.

Choreography: Anita Mann.

JOE AND VALERIE—30 minutes—NBC—April 24, 1978 - May 10, 1978. 4 episodes.

JULIE FARR, M.D.

Medical Drama. The story of Julie Farr, an obstetrician in a large Los Angeles hospital. Several stories, not only those dealing with pregnancy, are interwoven into each episode. Originally titled "Having Babies," the series lent itself to dealing with the joys and traumas of childbirth.

CAST
Julie Farr	Susan Sullivan
Dr. Blake Simmons	Mitchell Ryan
Kelly, Julie's receptionist	Beverly Todd
Intern Ron Daniels	Dennis Todd

Music: Lee Holdridge.

Theme Vocal: Marilyn McCoo.

Executive Producer: B. W. Sandefur, Gerald I. Isenberg.

Producer: James Heinz.

Director: Mel Damski, Edward Parone, Bob Kelljan.

Creator: Peggy Elliott, Ann Marcus.

JULIE FARR, M.D.—60 minutes—ABC—March 28, 1978 - April 18, 1978. 2 episodes. As "Having Babies"—60 minutes—ABC—March 7, 1978 - March 21, 1978. 3 episodes.

KAZ

Drama. Background: Los Angeles, California. The story of Martin "Kaz" Kazinski, an ex-con turned attorney who studied for the bar while serving a six-year prison term. Now working with a prestigious law firm, Kaz's cases are dramatized as he attempts to help people in deep trouble.

CAST

Martin Kazinski	Ron Leibman
Samuel Bennett, senior partner in the law firm	Patrick O'Neal
Mary Parnell, the owner of the Starting Gate Nightclub, above which Kaz lives	Gloria LeRoy
Malloy, the bartender	Dick O'Neill
Katie McKenna, the court reporter; Kaz's girlfriend	Linda Carlson
Peter Colcourt, Bennett's partner	Mark Withers
Mrs. Fogel, Bennett's secretary	Edith Atwater
Frank Revko, the D.A.	George Wyner

Music: Fred Karlin.

Executive Producer: Lee Rich, Marc Merson.

Producer: Peter Katz, Sam Rolfe.

Director: Russ Mayberry, Bob Kelljan, Bernard McEveety, David Moessinger.

KAZ—60 minutes—CBS—Premiered: September 24, 1978.

LIFELINE

Profile. An unusual television series that, using no actors or scripts, follows the day-to-day lives of various doctors on and off the job.

Narrator: Jackson Beck.

Music: Theo Mocero.

Executive Producer: Thomas W. Moore.

Producer: Nancy Smith, E. Fuisz,

M.D.

Director: Alfred Kelman, Robert Elfstrom.

LIFELINE—60 minutes—NBC—Premiered: October 8, 1978.

THE LOVE EXPERTS

Advice. A panel of four celebrities offer advice to real people with problems of living and loving in today's world.

Host: Bill Cullen.

Regular Panelist: Geoff Edwards.

Announcer: Jack Clark.

Executive Producer: Bob Stewart.

Producer: Anne Marie Schmitt.

Director: Bruce Burmester.

THE LOVE EXPERTS—30 minutes—Syndicated 1978.

THE MADHOUSE BRIGADE

Comedy. A series of blackouts and sketches that satirize politics and culture.

Starring: J.J. Lewis, Karen Rushmore, Alexander Marshall, Frank Nastasi, Joe Piscopo, Dan Resin, Carlos Carrasco, Rocket Ryan, Nola Fairbanks.

Music: Tony Monte.

Executive Producer: Jim Larkin.

Producer: Dale Keidel, Alexander Marshall.

Director: Dale Keidel.

THE MADHOUSE BRIGADE—30 minutes—Syndicated 1978.

MARY

Variety. A comedy-accented series that spotlights the many talents of Mary Tyler Moore.

Hostess: Mary Tyler Moore.

Regulars: Dick Shawn, Judy Kahan, James Hampton, Swoosie Kurtz, Michael Keaton, David Letterman, Leonard Barr, Jack O'Leary.

Orchestra: Alf Clausen.

Executive Producer: Tom Patchett, Jay Tarses.

Director: Rob Iscove.

Choreographer: Tony Stevens.

MARY—60 minutes—CBS—September 24, 1978 - October 8, 1978. 11 episodes produced; 3 aired.

MEL AND SUSAN TOGETHER

Musical Variety.

Hosts: Mel Tillis, Susan Anton.

Music: Bob Rozario.

Executive Producers: The Osmond Brothers.

Producer: Jerry McPhie, Toby Martin.

Director: Jack Regas.

MEL AND SUSAN TOGETHER—30 minutes—ABC—April 22, 1978 - May 13, 1978. 4 tapes.

MORK AND MINDY

Comedy. Dispatched from the planet Ork to study life on primitive Earth, Mork, an alien, lands in Boulder, Colorado, where he meets and befriends Mindy McConnell, a pretty twenty-one-year-old girl who becomes taken aback by his peculiar manner. When Mork tells Mindy that he is an alien and has been assigned to study Earthlings, she agrees to help him learn our ways and keep his secret. The series focuses on Mork's attempts to adjust to and learn about life on Earth.

CAST

Mork	Robin Williams
Mindy McConnell	Pam Dawber
Frederick McConnell, Mindy's father	Conrad Janis
Cora Hudson, Mindy's grandmother	Elizabeth Kerr
Eugene, a friend of the above regulars	Jeffrey Jacquet
Exidor, the religious fanatic befriended by Mork (recurring role)	Robert Donner
Orson, Mork's superior on Ork	Ralph James

Music: Perry Botkin, Jr.

Executive Producer: Garry K. Marshall, Tony Marshall.

Producer: Dale McRaven, Bruce Johnson.

Director: Howard Storm, Joel Zwick.

MORK AND MINDY—30 minutes—ABC—Premiered: September 14, 1978.

THE NEW AVENGERS

Adventure. A revised and updated version of "The Avengers," which see for original storyline information. The new version, set in England, continues to depict the exploits of John Steed, a debonair British Government Agent, and his new assistants, Purdy, a beautiful and courageous woman, and the daring Mike Gambit.

CAST

John Steed	Patrick Macnee
Purdy	Joanna Lumley
Mike Gambit	Gareth Hunt

Music: Laurie Johnson.

Producer: Albert Fennell, Brian Clemens.

Director: Desmond Davis, Ernest Day, Graeme Clifford, James Hill, Don Thompson, John Hough, Sidney Hayers.

THE NEW AVENGERS—75 minutes—CBS—Premiered: September 15, 1978.

THE NEW OPERATION PETTICOAT

Comedy. A revised and updated version of "Operation Petticoat," which see for information. After most of the original crew of the *Sea Tiger* transfers due to the anxiety problems caused with being stationed on a pink submarine, the *Sea Tiger* is reassigned to duty as a sea-going ambulance and outfitted with a new crew, including three beautiful nurses. The series follows the misadventures of the crew of the *Sea Tiger* as it roams the South Pacific during the early years of W.W. II (1942).

CAST

Captain Haller	Robert Hogan
Lt. Michael Bender	Randolph Mantooth
Lt. Dolores Crandall	Melinda Naud
Lt. Catherine O'Hara	Jo Ann Pflug
Lt. Betty Wheeler	Hilary Thompson
Chief Mechanic Stanley Dobritch	Warren Berlinger
Yeoman Hunkle	Richard Brestoff
Lt. Travis Kern	Sam Chew, Jr.

Music: Peter Matz.

Executive Producer: Jeff Harris, Ber-

nie Kukoff.

Producer: Michael Rhodes.

Director: Hollingsworth Morse, Gene Nelson.

THE NEW OPERATION PETTICOAT—30 minutes—ABC—September 25, 1978 - October 19, 1978. 4 episodes.

THE NEXT STEP BEYOND

Anthology. A revised and updated version of "One Step Beyond." True stories of psychic happenings.

Host-Narrator: John Newland.

Theme: Mark Snow.

Music: Ron Ramin.

Executive Producer: Collier Young.

Producer: Alan Jay Factor.

Director: John Newland.

Creator: Merwin Gerard.

THE NEXT STEP BEYOND—30 minutes—Syndicated 1978.

OPERATION: RUNAWAY

Drama. Background: Los Angeles, California. The story of David McKay, a former vice squad police officer turned private-practice psychologist, who specializes in tracking down runaways. (McKay also teaches psychology at Westwood University.)

CAST

Dr. David McKay	Robert Reed
Karen Wingate, the dean of women at the college	Karen Machon
Mark Johnson, David's assistant	Michael Biehn

Music: Richard Markowitz.

Executive Producer: William Robert Yates.

Producer: Mark Rodgers.

Director: William Waird, Michael Preece, Walter Grauman.

OPERATION: RUNAWAY—60 minutes—NBC—April 27, 1978 - May 18, 1978. 4 episodes. Rebroadcasts: NBC: August 10, 1978 - August 31, 1978.

THE PAPER CHASE

Drama. Background: A prestigious Northeastern university. The series follows the joys and frustrations of first-year law students; in particular, those of James Hart, an earnest, likeable Minnesota farm boy on a paper chase (seeking a diploma that says he graduated from law school). The program focuses also on the relationship between Hart and Professor Charles Kingsfield, a brilliant contract law instructor feared for his classroom tyranny, who will either make or break him. Based on the movie of the same title.

CAST

Professor Charles Kingsfield	John Houseman

Students:

James T. Hart	James Stephens
Franklin Ford	Tom Fitzsimmons
Elizabeth Logan	Francine Tacker
Linda O'Connor	Katherine Dunfee
Willis Bell	James Keane
Jonathan Brooks	Jonathan Segal
Thomas Anderson	Robert Ginty

Also:

Asheley Brooks, Jonathan's wife	Deka Beaudine

Mrs. Nottingham, Kingsfield's secretary	Betty Harford
Ernie, the owner of the tavern where Hart works	Charles Hallahan

Music: Charles Fox, Stephen Seretan, Richard Shores, Lionel Newman.

Executive Producer: Robert C. Thompson.

Producer: Robert Lewin.

Director: Joseph Hardy, Philip Leacock, Gwen Arner, Harvey Laidman, Alex March, William Hale, Robert C. Thompson, Seymour Robbie.

THE PAPER CHASE—60 minutes—CBS—Premiered: September 19, 1978.

PEOPLE

Variety Magazine. An adaptation of *People* magazine to television: celebrity profiles and interviews.

Hostess: Phyllis George.

Music: Tony Romeo.

Executive Producer: David Susskind.

Producer: Charlotte Schiff Jones.

Segment Producers: Clay Cole, Dolores Danska, Sue Solomon.

Director: Merrill Mazuer.

PEOPLE—30 minutes—CBS—September 18, 1978 - November 6, 1978. 6 episodes.

PLEASE STAND BY

Comedy. Discontent with his job in Los Angeles, Frank Lambert, a business executive, moves to the small town of DeQueen, New Mexico with his wife Carol, and their children Susan, David, and Rocky. He is hired to run KRDA, the world's smallest television station, from the family garage. The series focuses on the problems Frank and Carol face as they attempt to run the station.

CAST

Frank Lambert   Richard Schaal
Carol Lambert   Elinor Donahue
Susan Lambert   Darian Mathias
David Lambert   Stephen M. Schwartz
Rocky Lambert   Bryan Scott
Vicki Janes, works at
    the station   Marcie Barkin
Crash, works at
    the station   Danny Mora

Music: Phil Cody.

Theme Vocal: Stephen M. Schwartz.

Executive Producer: Bob Banner.

Producer: William Bickley, Michael Warren.

Director: Howard Storm, Alan Myerson, Jim Drake.

Creator: William Bickley, Michael Warren.

PLEASE STAND BY—30 minutes—Syndicated 1978.

PROJECT U.F.O.

Science Fiction Drama. Dramatizations of incidents as seen through the investigations of USAF Major Jake Gatlin and his assistant, Sgt. Harry Fitz, of reported sightings of U.F.O.s (Unidentified Flying Objects). Based on the official records of the U.S. Air Force's Project Bluebook, the Federal Government's record of U.F.O. reports and investigations.

CAST

Major Jake Gatlin   William Jordan
Staff Sgt. Harry
    Fitz   Caskey Swaim
Libby, their secretary   Aldine King
Capt. Ben Ryan (replaced
    Gatlin)   Edward Winter

Narrator: Jack Webb.

Music: Nelson Riddle.

Executive Producer: Jack Webb.

Producer: Robert Leeds, Colonel W. Coleman, USAF, ret., Gene Levitt, Robert Blees.

Director: Richard Quine, Robert Leeds, Dennis Donnelly, Sigmund Neufeld, Jr., John Patterson.

PROJECT U.F.O.—60 minutes—NBC—Premiered: February 19, 1978.

QUARK

Science Fiction Comedy. Era: 2226 A.D. The voyages of an interplanetary garbage scow whose mission, on behalf of the U.G.S.P. (United Galaxy Sanitation Patrol) is to clean up the Milky Way.

CAST

Captain Adam
    Quark   Richard Benjamin
Betty I, the
    co-pilot   Tricia Barnstable
Betty II, her clone,
    the co-pilot   Cyb Banstable
Ficus, the Vegeton,
    a plant, the
    emotionless science
    officer   Richard Kelton
Gene/Jean, the
    transmute, the chief
    engineer   Tim Thomerson
Andy, the cowardly
    robot   Bobby Porter
The Head, the head

of U.G.S.P.   Allan Caillou

Otto Palindrome, the
chief architect of
Space Station Perma
One, the base for
U.G.S.P.   Conrad Janis

Music: Perry Botkin, Jr.

Executive Producer: David Gerber.

Producer: Bruce Johnson.

Director: Hy Averback, Bruce Bilson, Peter H. Hunt.

Creator: Buck Henry.

QUARK—30 minutes—NBC—February 24, 1978 - April 14, 1978. 8 episodes.

THE RETURN OF CAPTAIN NEMO

Adventure. During routine war games, Tom Franklin and Jim Porter, U.S. Naval underwater intelligence agents, find trapped in a coral reef beneath the sea the fabled submarine *Nautilus*. Upon boarding the ship, they meet its captain, Nemo, and learn what has happened. On March 16, 1877, while searching for Atlantis, the *Nautilus* wedged itself under a coral reef and stuck. After dispensing the crew, Nemo, in the hope that one day help would come, suspended himself in a crystalline cylinder, from which, due to the depth charges, he has emerged. The constant barrage also sets the *Nautilus* free and brings Nemo in contact with Miller, the Naval Intelligence head, who agrees to repair the damaged sub in return for Nemo's help in performing certain hazardous missions for the government. The series depicts Nemo's adventures as he aids the U.S. Government while seeking the fabled Lost Continent of Atlantis. Based on the story by Jules Verne.

CAST

Captain Nemo	Jose Ferrer
Cmdr. Tom Franklin	Tom Hallick
Lt. Jim Porter	Burr DeBenning
Dr. Kate Melton, Nemo's aide	Lynda Day George
Prof. Waldo Cunningham, the evil, modern-day scientist; Nemo's nemesis	Burgess Meredith
Mr. Miller	Warren Stevens

Music: Richard La Salle.

Producer: Irwin Allen.

Director: Alex March.

THE RETURN OF CAPTAIN NEMO—60 minutes—CBS—March 8, 1978 - May 5, 1978. 3 episodes.

RICHIE BROCKELMAN, PRIVATE EYE

Crime Drama. Background: Los Angeles, California. The story of Richie Brockelman, a twenty-three-year-old young man who, despite scrapes with the law, is determined to make his way as a private detective.

CAST

Richie Brockelman	Dennis Dugan
Sharon, his secretary	Barbara Bosson
Sgt. Coopersmith	Robert Hogan
Richie's father	John Randolph

Music: Mike Post and Pete Carpenter.

Executive Producer: Stephen J. Cannell, Steve Bochco.

Supervising Producer: Alex Beaton.

Producer: Peter S. Fischer.

Director: Arnold Laven.

RICHIE BROCKELMAN, PRIVATE EYE—60 minutes—NBC—March 17, 1978 - April 14, 1978. 5 episodes.

THE ROLLERGIRLS

Comedy. Background: Pittsburgh, Pennsylvania. The on-and-off-the-rink antics of the Pittsburgh Pitts, a five woman roller-derby team.

CAST

Don Mitchell, the team owner	Terry Kiser

The Pittsburgh Pitts:

Mongo Sue Lampert	Rhonda Bates
Books Cassidy	Joanna Cassidy
Honeybee Novak	Marcy Hanson
Shana "Pipeline" Akira	Marilyn Tokuda
J. B. Johnson	Candy Ann Brown

Also:

Howard Divine, the
　　rink announcer   James Murtaugh

Music: Tony Asher, John Bahler, Kevin Clark.

Theme Vocal: Shari Saba.

Executive Producer: James Komack, Stan Cutler, George Tricker.

Producer: Tom Cherones.

Director: Burt Brinckerhoff, James Komack, Gary Shimokawa.

Creator: James Komack.

THE ROLLERGIRLS—30 minutes—NBC—April 24, 1978 - May 10, 1978. 4 episodes.

SAM

Crime Drama. Background: Los Angeles, California. The series follows the cases of Officer Mike Breen and his partner, Sam, a yellow Labrador retriever specially trained for police work.

CAST

Officer Mike Breen	Mark Harmon
Captain Tom Clagett	Len Wayland

Music: Billy May.

Executive Producer: Jack Webb.

Producer: Leonard B. Kaufman.

Director: Robert Leeds, Richard Moder, John Florea, Robert Wynn.

Creator: Jack Webb, Dan Noble.

SAM—30 minutes—CBS—March 14, 1978 - April 18, 1978. 6 episodes.

SWORD OF JUSTICE

Adventure. Jack Cole, a wealthy playboy, is framed and imprisoned for a crime he did not commit (embezzling two and a half million dollars from his father's company). Bitter for the wrong done to him, Cole vows to get even with the crooks who framed him. He begins by learning the tricks of the criminal's trade from his fellow prisoners. Released from prison two years short of his five year sentence for good behavior, Cole teams with his cellmate, Hector Ramirez, and together they reveal the people responsible for the frame. Instilled with a goal to seek justice, Cole continues in his dual capacity—a New York playboy by day and an anonymous crime fighter by night, helping the federal authorities get the goods on white-collar thieves.

CAST

Jack Cole	Dack Rambo
Hector Ramierz	Bert Rosario
Arthur Woods, the federal agent Cole helps	Alex Courtney

Music: John Andrew Tartaglia.

Executive Producer: Glen A. Larson.

Supervising Producer: Michael Sloan.

Producer: Joe Boston, Herman Groves.

SWORD OF JUSTICE—60 minutes—NBC—Premiered: October 7, 1978.

TAXI

Comedy. Background: New York City. The series focuses on the trials and tribulations of the drivers and garage crew of the Sunshine Cab Company.

CAST

Alex Reiger, a cabbie	Judd Hirsch
Elaine Nardo, a cabbie	Marilu Henner
Bobby Wheeler, a cabbie	Jeff Conaway
Tony Banta, a cabbie	Tony Danza
Louie DePalmer, the nasty dispatcher	Danny DeVito
Latka Gravas, the mechanic	Andy Kaufman
John Burns, a cabbie	Randall Carver

Music: Bob James.

Executive Producer-Creator: James L. Brooks, Stan Daniels, Ed Weinberger, David Davis.

Producer: Glen Charles, Les Charles.

Director: James Burrows.

TAXI—30 minutes—ABC—Premiered: September 12, 1978.

THE TED KNIGHT SHOW

Comedy. Background: New York City. The misadventures of Roger Dennis, the owner of the Mr. Dennis Escort Service.

CAST

Roger Dennis	Ted Knight
Dottie, his obnoxious secretary	Iris Adrian
Bert Dennis, his brother	Norman Burton
Winston Dennis, Roger's son	Thomas Leopold

The Escort Service Girls:

Graziella	Cissy Colpitts
Honey	Fawne Harriman
Irma	Ellen Regan
Cheryl	Janice Kent
Phil	Tanya Boyd
Joy	Debbie Harmon

Music: Michael Leonard.

Executive Producer: Mark Rothman, Lowell Ganz.

Producer: Martin Cohan.

Director: Joel Zwick, Howard Storm, Martin Cohan.

THE TED KNIGHT SHOW—30 minutes—CBS—April 8, 1978 - May 13, 1978.

TWIGGY'S JUKE BOX

Music. Performances by Rock musicians.

Hostess: Twiggy (the model turned singer).

Music: Recorded and/or provided by guests.

Executive Producer: Malcolm Gold.

Producer-Director: Mike Mansfield.

TWIGGY'S JUKE BOX—30 minutes—Syndicated 1978.

VEGA$

Crime Drama. Background: Las Vegas, Nevada. The cases of Dan Tana, a macho private detective with an eye for finding and helping beautiful women in trouble.

CAST

Dan Tana	Robert Urich
Angie, his secretary	Judy Landers
Beatrice, a showgirl, Dan's friend	Phyllis Elizabeth Davis
Binzer, Dan's inept legman	Bart Braverman
Philip "Slick" Roth, the casino owner	Tony Curtis
Sgt. Bella Archer, the policewoman who supplies Dan with info	Naomi Stevens
Eli Two Leaf, an Indian, Dan's legman	Will Sampson
Beverly, work's in Roth's casino	Barbara McNair

Music: Dominic Frontiere.

Executive Producer: Aaron Spelling, Douglas S. Cramer.

Supervising Producer: E. Duke Vincent.

Producer: Alan Godfrey.

Director: Harry Falk, Sutton Roley, Bernard McEveety, Don Chaffey, Marc Daniels, Lawrence Doheny, Lawrence Dobkin, Paul Stanley.

Creator: Michael Mann.

VEGA$–60 minutes– ABC–Premiered: September 20, 1978.

THE WAVERLY WONDERS

Comedy. The series concerns itself with the misadventures of Joe Casey, a washed-up professional basketball player who now coaches basketball, as well as teaching history, at Waverly High School.

CAST

Joe Casey (originally Harry Casey)	Joe Namath
Linda Harris, the principal	Gwynne Gilford
George Benton, a teacher	Ben Piazza

Students comprising the Waverly Wonders Basketball Team:

Connie Rafkin	Kim Lankford
Tony Faguzzi	Joshua Grentock
Hasty	Tierre Turner
John Pate	Charles Bloom

Music: Fred Karlin.

Executive Producer: Lee Rich, Marc Merson.

Producer: Bruce Kane, Steve Zacharias.

Director: Bill Persky, Dick Martin.

THE WAVERLY WONDERS–30 minutes–NBC–September 22, 1978 - October 6, 1978. 4 episodes.

W.E.B.

Drama. Background: New York City. A behind-the-scenes look at the world of television as seen through the experiences of Ellen Cunningham, an up-and-coming programming executive with the Trans-Atlantic Broadcasting Company (TAB).

CAST

Ellen Cunningham	Pamela Bellwood
Jack Kiley, the programming chief	Alex Cord
Dan Costello, the	

sales executive	Andrew Prine
Gus Dunlap, the news director	Richard Basehart
Walter Matthews, the director of operations	Howard Witt
Harvey Pearlstein, the head of research	Lee Wilkof
Harry Brooks, the board chairman	Stephen McNally
Christine Nichols, Ellen's secretary	Tish Raye
Kevin, Ellen's assistant	Peter Coffield

Music: Jerry Fielding, David Rose, Morton Stevens.

Music Supervision: Lionel Newman.

Executive Producer: Lin Bolen.

Producer: Christopher Morgan.

Director: Harvey Hart, Alex March.

Creator: David Karp.

W.E.B.—60 minutes—NBC—September 13, 1978 - October 5, 1978. 5 episodes.

THE WHITE SHADOW

Drama. Background: Carver High School in Los Angeles, California. The story of Ken Reeves, a former pro-basketball player (washed up when he injured his knee) turned coach for a losing and unruly ghetto high school basketball team. (The title is derived from Reeves remark after his team's first win—he'll be behind them like a White Shadow.)

CAST

Ken Reeves	Ken Howard
Jim Willis, the principal	Jason Bernard
Sybil Buchanan, the vice principal	Joan Pringle
Katie, Ken's sister	Robin Rose
Bill, Katie's husband	Jerry Fogel

Music: Mike Post, Pete Carpenter.

Executive Producer: Bruce Paltrow.

Producer: Mark C. Tinker.

THE WHITE SHADOW—60 minutes—CBS—Premiered: November 27, 1978.

WHO'S WATCHING THE KIDS?

Comedy. Background: Las Vegas, Nevada. The story focuses on the misadventures of Stacy Turner and Angie Vitola, two luscious showgirls at the seedy Club Sand Pile. The girls share an apartment with Frankie, Angie's mischievous sixteen-year-old brother, and Melissa, Stacy's know-it-all nine-year-old sister. The series title is derived from the problem the girls have: who can watch their kids when they're working? Their solution: Larry Parnell, a KVGS TV Newscaster, and Burt Gunkel, his cameraman, neighbors who, to impress Angie and Stacy, babysit when they are able.

CAST

Stacy Turner	Caren Kaye
Angie Vitola	Lynda Goodfriend
Frankie Vitola	Scott Baio
Melissa Turner	Tammy Lauren
Larry Parnell	Larry Breeding
Burt Gunkel	James Belushi
Mitzi Logan, the apartment-house manager	Marcia Lewis
Memphis, a showgirl	Lorrie Mahaffey
Cochise, a showgirl	Shirley Kirkes
Bridget, a showgirl	Elaine Bolton

Music: Charles Bernstein.

Executive Producer: Garry Marshall, Tony Marshall, Don Silverman.

Producer: Martin Nadler, Gary Menteer.

Director: John Thomas Lenox, Ray DeVally, Jr., David Ketchum.

WHO'S WATCHING THE KIDS?—30 minutes—NBC—Premiered: September 22, 1978.

WKRP IN CINCINATTI

Comedy. The series focuses on the antics of the management and staff of WKRP, a 50,000 watt, hard-rock format radio station in Cincinatti, Ohio.

CAST

Andy Travis, the program
    director   Gary Sandy
Arthur Carlson, the
    station manager   Gordon Jump
Jennifer Marlowe, Carlson's
    secretary   Loni Anderson
Herb Tarlek, the
    sales manager   Frank Bonner
Johnny Caravella, the
    d.j. who works
    as Dr. Johnny
    Fever   Howard Hessemen
Bailey Quarters, Andy's
    assistant   Jan Smithers
Les Nesman, the news
    director   Richard Sanders
Venus Flytrap, the
    night man   Tim Reid

Music: Tom Wells.

Producer: Hugh Wilson.

Director: Jay Sandrich, Michael Zinberg, Asaad Keleda.

WKRP IN CINCINATTI—30 minutes—CBS—September 17, 1978 - November 6, 1978. 13 episodes produced; 8 aired.

THE YOUNG PIONEERS

Western Drama. Background: The Dakota Territory during the 1870s. The series follows the enduring hardships of Molly and David Beaton, young newlyweds struggling to establish a life for themselves on the hostile frontier.

CAST

Molly Beaton   Linda Purl
David Beaton   Roger Kern
Dan Gray, their
    neighbor   Robert Hays
Mr. Peters, their
    neighbor, a
    widower   Robert Donner
Nettie Peters, his
    daughter   Shelly Juttner
          Mare Winningham
Flora Peters, his
    daughter   Michelle Stacy
Charlie Peters, his
    son   Jeff Cotler

Narrator: Linda Purl.

Music: Dominic Frontiere.

Executive Producer: Earl Hamner, Lee Rich.

Producer: Robert L. Jacks.

Director: Harry Harris, Alf Kjellin, Irving J. Moore.

THE YOUNG PIONEERS—60 minutes—ABC—April 2, 1978 - April 16, 1978. 3 episodes. Pilot aired January 9, 1977 and January 16, 1977 (a 2-part story).

Index

All personalities are credited as they were known at the time of their appearance on a particular series; changes are noted in parenthesis next to the name. Page numbers appearing in *italics* indicate a photograph appearance.

Bull, Peter, 956
Bull, Richard, 569, 722, 1040
Buller, Neil, 520
Bullock, Harvey, 43, 113, 582, 598, 666, 824
Buloff, Joseph, 196, 1022
Bunce, Alan, 290, 298, 522, 523, 766
Bundy, Brooke, 130, 233, 703, 704
Buneta, Bill, 174
Bunetta, Frank, 171, 442
Bunin, Hope, 335, 592
Bunin, Mory, 335, 592
Buntrock, Bobby, 243, 417, 418
Buono, Victor, 94, 226, 1073
Burdick, Hal, 723
Burford, Ivan, 227
Burge, Greg, 289
Burgess, Bobby, 554, 647
Burgess, Dennis, 969
Burgess, Patricia, 358
Burgess, Vivienne, 841
Burghoff, Gary, 265, 627
Burgundy Street Singers, The, 497, 825
Buriner, Jennifer, 384
Burke, Alan, 38
Burke, Albert E., 809
Burke, Billie, 284
Burke, Caroline, 985
Burke, Cecily, 27
Burke, Consuela, 631
Burke, Frankie, 281
Burke, Georgia, 797
Burke, James, 621
Burke, Jerry, 554
Burke, Melville, 196
Burke, Paul, 410, 696, 725, *988,* 988, 1017
Burke, Soloman, 590
Burke, Sonny, 334, 421, 663
Burkhardt, Bob, 814
Burkley, Dennis, 339, 624
Burmester, Bruce, 487, 888
Burn, Jonathan, 340
Burnell, Peter, 259
Burnet, Donald, 837
Burnett, Carol, 167, 294, 360, 757, 922
Burnett, Don, 726
Burnett, Sadi, 685
Burnett, Sheila, 159
Burnett, Smiley, 785
Burnier, Jennie, 524
Burns, Allan, 582, 627, 831
Burns, Bob, 374
Burns, Bonnie, 487
Burns, Catherine, 640
Burns, David, 464, 1010
Burns, Frank, 623, 683, 736
Burns, George, 201, 337, *367,* 367, 368, 1056, *1056*
Burns, Jack, 57, 152, 294, 372,

751, 940, 1044, 1059
Burns, Marilyn, 173
Burns, Michael, 479, 1032, 1042
Burns, Mona, 62, 143, 985
Burns, Phil, 485, 628
Burns, Ronnie, 367, 368, 408
Burns, Sandra, 368
Burns, Seymour, 683
Burns, Steve, 1059
Burr, Anne, 74, 394
Burr, Eugene, 279
Burr, Lonnie, 647
Burr, Raymond, 473, 532, 535, 778, 881
Burr, Robert, 585, 905
Burris, Neal, 774
Burrows, Abe, 21, 697, 735, 980, 1059, 1062
Burrows, Bill, 44
Burrows, James, 15, 152, 319, 553, 627, 790, 1001
Burrud, Bill, 59, 60, 430, 475, 856, 986, 1009, 1011, 1049
Bursky, Alan, 760
Burston, Janet, 571
Burt Buhram Trio, The, 114
Burtis, Ernie, 821
Burtis, Marilyn, 1091
Burton, Donald, 837, 1050
Burton, Eileen, 906
Burton, Jeff, 845
Burton, LeVar, 849
Burton, Norman (Normann), 669, 714
Burton, Richard, 16, 406, 859, 1078
Burton, Robert, 237
Burton, Sarah, 286, 348
Burton, Shelly, 165
Burton, Skip, 550
Burton, Tod, 568
Busey, Gary, *970,* 970
Bush, Owen, 895
Bushkin, Joe, 284, 333, 508
Buss, Frances, 1034, 1062, 1077
Buswall, Neville, 207
Butch, Danny, 409
Butcher, Joseph, 539
Butler, Artie, 127, 230, 570, 747, 1065
Butler, Blake, 837
Butler, Daws, 83, 97, 170, 354, 395, 420, 448, 454, 496, 469, 783, 816, 846, 853, 869, 911, 997, 1044, 1083, 1087, 1088
Butler, Ed, 919
Butler, Francis, 134
Butler, Lou, 239
Butler, Robert, 94, 251, 433, 731, 1030, 1049
Buttegnat, Val, 196
Butterfield, Billy, 284, 333
Butterfield, Herb, 370, 406

Butterworth, Donna, 941
Butterworth, Peter, 222
Buttolph, David, 636, 1050
Buttons, Red, 14, 271, 795, 824, 1034, 1070
Buttram, Pat, 362, 396, 672
Butts, K. C., 750
Bux, Kuda, 539
Buxton, Frank, 253, 371, 409, 582, 732
Buzzi, Ruth, 83, 235, 551, 581, 971
Byan, Paul, 144
Byington, Spring, 237, 547, 1004
Byner, John, 360, 504, 790, 804, 905
Byner, Tom, 500
Byran, George, 933
Byrd, David, 624
Byrd, Joseph, 496
Byrd, Ralph, 249
Byrd, Richard, 983
Byrd-Nethery, Miriam, 680
Byrds, The, 652
Byrne, Bobby, 929, 1000
Byrnes, Edward (Edd), 880
Byron, Carol, 734, 1075
Byron, Edward, 676
Byron, James, 1075
Byron, Jean, 68, 93, 292, 353, 422, 617, 638, 764, 766, 994, 1027
Byron, Paul, 980
Byron, Ward, 75, 343, 768

Cabal, Robert, 820
Cabot, Bruce, 846
Cabot, Sebastian, 95, 182, *307,* 307, 374, 488, 939, 947, 984
Cacavas, John, 534, 705
Cady, Frank, 31, 396, 785, 977
Caesar, Jimmy, 524
Caesar, Sid, 223, 864, 890, 891
Caffrey, Michael, 90, 101, 291, 361, 482, 532, 661, 699, 879, 1073
Cagney, Jeanne, 815
Cahan, George M., 377, 638, 853
Cahill, Barry, 1093
Cahill, Kathy, 127, 507
Cahn, Sammy, 577, 810
Caillou, Allan, 695, 961
Cain, Jeff, 620
Caine, Howard, 27, 433, 752
Calabrese, Peter, 101
Calder, Bob, 488
Calder, King, 623
Calenbeck, John, 347
Calhoun, Rory, 188, 526, 970, 1057
Californians, The, 173
Calise, Ugo, 876

Ernest Flatt Dancers, The, 167, 294

Ernie Lee's Hillbilly Band, 936

Erskine, Marilyn, 40, 68, 867, 999, 110

Erwin, John, 86, 398, 715, 856, 945

Erwin, Judy, 417

Erwin, Stu, 394, 650, 823, 1011

Erwin, Stu, Jr., 287

Escorts, The, 336

Eskander, Bert, 271

Eskew, Jack, 182, 578, 974

Eskrew, Jack, 85

Espinosa, Mary, 647

Espy, William Gray, 1093

Esquivel, 958

Esser, Carl, 332

Estrada, Erik, 187

Estrin, Patricia, 587

Ettlinger, Norman, 866

Eubanks, Bob, 246, 719, 722, 831

Eure, Wesley, 232, 546

Eustic, Rich, 591

Eustis, Rick, 500, 833

Evan, Jessie, 207, 988

Evanko, Ed, 855

Evans, Barry, 257

Evans, Bill, 186

Evans, Bobby, 649

Evans, Bruce, 950

Evans, Charlie, 633

Evans, Clifford, 808, 937, 1039

Evans, Dale, 396, 535-36, 852

Evans, Damon, 493

Evans, Denny, 783, 865

Evans, Dr. Bergen, 273, 373, 477, 550, 897, 1003

Evans, Gene, 117, 219, 633, 687, 795, 914

Evans, Jeanne, 589

Evans, Linda, 117, 457, 1047

Evans, Madge, 629

Evans, Maurice, 94, 109, 405

Evans, Michael, 363

Evans, Mike, 45, 493, 804

Evans, Monica, 732

Evans, Nancy, 240

Evans, Orrin B., 775

Evans, Osmond, 50

Evans, Ray, 677, 881, 959

Evans, Richard, 786

Everhart, Rex, 321

Evelyn, Judith, 146, 593, 1076

Even Dozen, The, 685

Everett, Chad, 219, 639

Everett, Ethel, 75, 401

Everly, Don, 299

Everly, Phil, 299

Evers, Jason, 178, 402, 1085

Evigan, Greg, 1086, 1087

Ewell, Tom, 89, 873, 999

Ewing, Bill, 535

Ewing, Diana, 1051

Ewing, Roger, 403

Eyer, Richard, 317, 689, 920

Eythe, Bill, 693

Eythe, William, 567

Fabares, Shelley, 265, 339, 570, 649, 804, 941

Fabian. *See* Forte, Fabian

Fabian, Olga, 383

Fabiani, Joel, 241, *242*

Fabray, Nanette, 196, 222, 431, 483, 571, 626, 981, 1087

Fadden, Tom, 35, 147, 786

Fadiman, Clifton, 49, 465, 817, 980, 1061

Fafara, Stanley (Tiger), 555, 556

Fagas, James, 52

Fahey, Myrna, 94, 318, 787

Faichney, James, 38

Fairbanks, Douglas, Jr., 272, 280, 830

Fairbanks, Jerry, 111, 349

Fairbanks, Peggy, 465

Fairbairn, Bruce, 847

Fairchild, Iris, 365

Fairchild, Margaret, 881

Fairchild, Morgan, 873

Faire, Sandra, 513

Fairfax, James, 357, 527

Fairman, Michael, 585, 855

Faith, Percy, 394, 1038

Falan, Tanya, 554

Falana, Avie, 252

Falana, Lola, 715

Falcon, Errol, 718

Falis, Terri, 877

Falk, Harry, 56, 101, 112, 212, 497, 707, 847, 397, 948, 972

Falk, Peter, 704, 705, 1010

Falkenberg, Jinx, 629, 805, 949

Fallien, Nicole, 469

Falloner, Scott, 953

Fann, Al, 453

Fanning, Bill, 497

Fanning, Gene, 905

Fant, Lou, 978

Faracy, Stephanie, 15

Farber, Bert, 782, 783, 855, 1036

Farentino, James, 132, 438, 708, 799

Fargé, Annie, 59

Fargas, Antonio, 925

Fargo, Donna, 234

Faris, Alexander, 631

Farleigh, Lynn, 936

Farley, Duke, 165, 749

Farley, Elizabeth, 286

Farmer, Frances, 823

Farmer, Lillian, 525

Farnon, Shannon, 720, 944, 1033

Farnum, Brian, 841

Farr, Derek, 924

Farr, Felicia, 133, 438, 918

Farr, Gordon, 584

Farr, Hugh, 852

Farr, Jamie, 185, 235, 386, 465, 627, 831

Farr, Judi, 691

Farr, Karl, 852

Farr, Lee, 244

Farr, Lynne, 584

Farrah, Catherine, 896

Farrand, Jan, 285

Farrar, Vivian, 878

Farrell, Brian, 585

Farrell, Brioni, 1005

Farrell, Charlie (Charles), 180, *689*, 690

Farrell, Dick, 407

Farrell, Gail, 554

Farrell, Glenda, 290

Farrell, Judy, 628

Farrell, Mike, 232, 469, *470*, 610, 628

Farrell, Roy, 1014

Farrell, Sharon, 804

Farrell, Skip, 898, 967

Farrell, Tim, 22

Farrell, Tommy, 32, 618, 980

Farrell, Wes, 892

Farrington, Kenneth, 207

Farrow, Mia, 112, 786

Fascinato, Jack, 448, 540, 899, 967, 1012

Fashko, Robert, 948

Faso, Laurie, 622

Fates, Gil, 280, 433, 1034, 1062, 1063, 1077

Faulds, Andrew, 536, 837

Faulk, Hugh, 1073

Faulk, John Henry, 420, 480

Faulkner, Ed, 271

Fauntelle, Dian, 843

Faussett, Hudson, 990

Favor, Rinky, 953

Fawcett, William, 356, 534

Fawcett-Majors, Farrah, 180, *180*, 412

Fax, Jesslyn, 616, 751

Faye, Herbie (Herbert), 254, 590, 789, 1092

Faye, Janina, 308

Faye, Joey, 158, 218, 324, 399, 600, 721, 733

Faylen, Carol, 120

Faylen, Frank, 172, 617, *618*, 971, 1046

Faylen, Kay, 256

Fayni, Charlotte, 196

Fedderson, Don, 226, 307, 695

Fedderson, Gregg, 307

Fee, Melinda, 401, 473

Feeney, Joe, 555

Fegan, John, 440

Feigel, Sylvia, 935

314, 439, 809, 904, 929, 972, 1000, 1062, 1070
Francis, Bob, 531
Francis, Cedric, 198
Francis, Connie, 497
Francis, Ivor, 280
Francis, Joan, 488
Francis, Nick, 943
Francis, Raymond, 725
Francis, Stan, 1013
Franciscus, James, 255, 375, 457, 471, 578, 678, 696, 1029
Francs, Don, 494, 851
Fangblau, Rose, 439
Frangione, Nancy, 46
Frank, Allan, 179
Frank, Bob, 90, 174
Frank, Carl, 285, 472
Frank, Charles, 46
Frank, Gary, 306, 907
Frankboner, Sarah, 127
Franke, Tony, 233
Frankel, Cyril, 79, 241, 692, 1024
Frankel, Ernie, 674, 701, 1094
Franken, Steve, 199, 563, 617, 725, 1001
Frankham, David, 363
Frank Hunter Band, The, 654
Franklen, Maurice, 739
Frank Lewis Dancers, The, 1001
Franklin, Bonnie, *737,* 737
Franklin, Carl, 166, 312
Franklin, Cass, 350
Franklin, Hugh, 46
Franklin, Jim, 388
Franklin, Joe, 502, *502*
Franklin, Milt, 150, 802, 951
Franklin, Nancy, 741, 992
Franklin, Pamela, 589
Franklin, Susan, 260
Franklyn, William, 1004
Franks, Gordon, 316
Frann, Mary, 233
Franz, Arthur, 327, 730, 975, 1084
Franz, Eduard, 141, 920
Fraser, Elizabeth, 216, 324, 600, 738, 1092
Fraser, Jeri Lynn, 733
Fraser, Liz, 78
Fraser, Sonia, 630
Frawley, Bob, 310
Frawley, Barbara, 310
Frawley, James, 664, 972
Frawley, William, 462, *694,* 694
Fray, Jacques, 488
Frazee, June, 107
Frazer, Dan, 534
Freberg, Stan, 97, 1074
Frederic, Norman, 518
Frederick, Hal, 135, 469, *470*
Frederick, Rita, 328

Fredericks, Carlton, 166
Fredericks, Pauline, 913
Fredericks, Dean, 930
Freed, Bert, 183, 882
Freedly, Vinton, 890
Freedman, Louis, 110, 279
Freeling, Fritz, 951
Freeman, Al, Jr., 447, 740
Freeman, Arny, 394
Freeman, Everett, 81
Freeman, Devery, 781, 1017
Freeman, Fred, 15
Freeman, Harvey, 1092
Freeman, Howard, 987, 1016
Freeman, Joan, 152, 195
Freeman, Kathleen, 355, 433, 477, 581, 638, 1003
Freeman, Leonard, 415, 851, 1029
Freeman, Melanie, 520
Freeman, Mona, 449, 508, 1017
Freeman, Morgan, 289
Freeman, Pamela, 812
Freeman, Ray, 872
Freeman, Stan, 404, 642, 985
Freer, Randall, 354
Frees, Paul, 76, 85, 156, 250, 277, 309, 311, 344, 419, 445, 487, 530, 654, 713, 749, 790, 842, 1002, 1083
Frees, Randall, 246
Freiberger, Fred, 912, 927, 1029, 1073
Freleng, Friz, 83, 1063
French, Arthur, 751
French, Jack, 369
French, Leigh, 247, 910, 1013
French, Peggy, 1022
French, Valerie, 285, 740
French, Victor, 167, 372, 426, 569, 570
Fresco, David, 251
Frey, Nathaniel, 165
Friberg, Richard, 564
Frid, Jonathan, *224,* 224, 225
Fridell, Squire, 850
Friebus, Florida, 131, 346, 617, 787
Fried, Gerald, 301, 307, 377, 477, 613, 658, 680, 849, 927, 969
Friedkin, David E., 101, 522, 534
Friedlander, Sylvia, 336
Friedman, Ada, 659
Friedman, Charles, 196, 336
Friedman, Dr. Sonia, 50
Friedman, Gary William, 289
Friedman, Hal, 880
Friedman, Harlene Kim, 625
Friedman, Irving, 240, 317, 958, 1021
Friedman, Peter, 683
Friendly, Fred W., 82, 564, 878,

1070
Friesen, Paul, 894
Frim, Claire, 522
Frisch, Frank, 67
Fritter, Stan, 533
Frizzell, Lou, 133, 187
Frye, Margaret, 14
Frye, William, 363, 406, 948, 987
Froman, Jane, 489
Froman, Joan, 48
Frome, Milton, 108, 160, 201, 552
Fromkess, Leon, 356, 399, 712
Frommer, Ben, 351
Frontiere, Dominic, 140, 187, 320, 334, 464, 470, 752, 820, 871, 931, 1017, 1052
Frost, Alice, 314, 472
Frost, David, 229, 974
Froug, William, 110, 377, 1020
Frumkin, Paul, 946
Fuccello, Tom, 584
Fuchs, Matthias, 969
Fudenna, Margene, 1033
Fudge, Alan, 612
Fuest, Robert, 78
Fujikawa, Jerry Hatsuo, 680
Fuller, Ann, 62
Fuller, Lorenzo, 495
Fuller, Penny, 520
Fuller, Robert, 291, 547, 710, 1042, *1043*
Fuller, Sam, 196
Fullerton, Melanie, 1005
Fullerton, Scott, 546
Fullilove, Donald, 291
Fulmore, Ray, 418
Fulton, Eileen, 74, 751
Fulton, Rad, 1058
Funai, Helen, 232, 235, 825, 905, 940
Funicello, Annette, 110, 283, 607, 647, *648,* 648, 649, *651,* 651, 672, 1046, 1103
Funt, Allen, 158, 159, 965
Furia, John, 376
Furlan, Alan, 984
Furlong, Kirby, 499
Furness, Betty, 153, 436, 640, 774, 939
Furness, James, 77
Furth, George, 144, 278, 387, 959

Gable, June, 91, 551
Gable, Munia, 313
Gabor, Eva, 113, 298, 396, 786, 1032
Gabor, Zsa Zsa, 94, 196, 902
Gabriel, Bob, 905
Gabriel, John, 585, 626, 855
Gae, Nadine, 345
Gaetano, Hal, 696